TWO-LEVEL FUNCTIONAL LANGUAGES

Cambridge Tracts in Theoretical Computer Science

Titles in the series

1. G. Chaitin *Algorithmic Information Theory*
2. L.C. Paulson *Logic and Computation*
3. M. Spivey *Understanding Z*
4. G. Revesz *Lambda Calculus, Combinators and Functional Programming*
5. A. Ramsay *Formal Methods in Artificial Intelligence*
6. S. Vickers *Topology via Logic*
7. J-Y. Girard, Y. Lafont & P. Taylor *Proofs and Types*
8. J. Clifford *Formal Semantics & Pragmatics for Natural Language Processing*
9. M. Winslett *Updating Logical Databases*
10. K. McEvoy & J.V. Tucker (eds) *Theoretical Foundations of VLSI Design*
11. T.H. Tse *A Unifying Framework for Structured Analysis and Design Models*
12. G. Brewka *Nonmonotonic Reasoning*
15. S. Dasgupta *Design Theory and Computer Science*
17. J.C.M. Baeten (ed) *Applications of Process Algebra*
18. J.C.M. Baeten & W.P. Weijland *Process Algebra*
23. E.-R. Olderog *Nets, Terms and Formulas*
27. W.H. Hesselink *Programs, Recursion and Unbounded Choice*
29. P. Gärdenfors (ed) *Belief Revision*
30. M. Anthony & N. Biggs *Computational Learning Theory*
34. F. Nielson & H.R. Nielson *Two Level Functional Languages*

TWO-LEVEL FUNCTIONAL LANGUAGES

FLEMMING NIELSON & HANNE RIIS NIELSON
Department of Computer Science
Aarhus University, Denmark

CAMBRIDGE
UNIVERSITY PRESS

CAMBRIDGE
UNIVERSITY PRESS

University Printing House, Cambridge CB2 8BS, United Kingdom

Cambridge University Press is part of the University of Cambridge.

It furthers the University's mission by disseminating knowledge in the pursuit of education, learning and research at the highest international levels of excellence.

www.cambridge.org
Information on this title: www.cambridge.org/9780521403849

First published 1992

A catalogue record for this publication is available from the British Library

ISBN 978-0-521-40384-9 Hardback
ISBN 978-0-521-01847-0 Paperback

Contents

List of Figures

List of Tables

Preface

The subject area of this book concerns the implementation of functional languages. The main perspective is that part of the implementation process amounts to

making computer science concepts explicit

in order to facilitate the application, and the development, of general frameworks for program analysis and code generation.

This is illustrated on a specimen functional language patterned after the λ-calculus:

- *Types* are made explicit in Chapter 2 by means of a Hindley/Milner/Damas type analysis.

- *Binding times* are made explicit in Chapter 3 using an approach inspired by the one for type analysis. The binding times of chief interest are *compile-time* and *run-time*.

- *Combinators* are made explicit in Chapter 4 but only for run-time computations whereas the compile-time computations retain their λ-calculus syntax.

The advantages of this approach are illustrated in the remainder of the book where the emphasis also shifts from a 'syntactic perspective' to a more 'semantic perspective':

- A notion of *parameterized semantics* is defined in Chapter 5 and this allows a wide variety of semantics to be given.

- It is illustrated for *code generation* in Chapter 6. Code is generated for a structured abstract machine and the correctness proof exploits Kripke-logical relations and layered predicates.

- It is illustrated for *abstract interpretation* in Chapter 7. We generalize Wadler's strictness analysis to general lists, show the correctness using logical relations, and illustrate the similarity between tensor products and Wadler's case analysis.

Finally, Chapter 8 discusses possible ways of extending the development. This includes the use of abstract interpretation to obtain an improved code generation that may still be proved correct. We also illustrate the role of the mixed λ-calculus and combinatory logic as a metalanguage for denotational semantics; this allows a systematic approach to compiler generation from semantic specifications.

Notes for the Reader

This book is intended for researchers and for students who already have some formal training. Much of the work reported here has been documented elsewhere in the scientific literature and we have therefore aimed at a style of exposition where we concentrate on the main insights and methods, including proofs and proof techniques, but where we feel free to refer to the literature for technically complex generalizations and details of tedious proofs. To facilitate this, we provide bibliographic notes covering variations of the technical development. Our notation is mostly standard but we find '$\hookrightarrow$' a more readable notation for 'partial functions' than '$\rightharpoonup$'.

Acknowledgements

The research reported here has been supported by The Danish Natural Sciences Research Council. The presentation has benefited from comments from our students and colleagues, in particular Torben Amtoft, Poul Christiansen, Fritz Henglein, Torben Lange, Jens Mikkelsen, Thorleif Nielson, Jens Palsberg, Hans J. Pedersen, Anders Pilegaard, Kirsten L. Solberg, Bettina B. Sørensen and Phil Wadler. Finally, David Tranah made a number of suggestions concerning how to improve the presentation.

Aarhus, January 1992

Flemming Nielson

Hanne Riis Nielson

Chapter 1

Introduction

The *functional programming style* is closely related to the use of higher-order functions. In particular, it suggests that many function definitions are instances of the same general computational pattern and that this pattern is defined by a higher-order function. The various instances of the pattern are then obtained by supplying the higher-order function with some of its arguments.

One of the benefits of this programming style is the reuse of function definitions and, more importantly, the reuse of properties proved to hold for them: usually a property of a higher-order function carries over to an instance by verifying that the arguments satisfy some simple properties.

One of the disadvantages is that the efficiency is often rather poor. The reason is that when generating code for a higher-order function it is impossible to make any assumptions about its arguments and to optimize the code accordingly. Furthermore, conventional machine architectures make it rather costly to use functions as data.

We shall therefore be interested in *transforming* instances of higher-order functions into functions that can be implemented more efficiently. The key observation in the approach to be presented here is that an instance of a higher-order function is a function where some of the arguments are known and others are not. To be able to exploit this we shall introduce an *explicit* distinction between *known* and *unknown* values or, using traditional compiler terminology, between *compile-time* entities and *run-time* entities.

The functional paradigm

To motivate the notation to be used we begin by reviewing the `reduce` function. In Miranda[1] it may be written as

```
reduce f u = g
```

[1]Miranda is a trademark of Research Software Limited.

```
where g [] = u
      g (x:xs) = f x (g xs)
```

Here the left hand side of an equation specifies the name of the function and a list of patterns for its parameters. The right hand side is an expression being the body of the function. If more than one equation is given for the same function (as is the case for g) there is an *implicit* conditional matching the argument with the patterns in the parameter list. Recursion is left *implicit* because a function name on the right hand side of an equation that defines that function name indicates recursion (as is the case for g). Finally, function application is left *implicit* as the function is just juxtaposed with its argument(s).

By supplying `reduce` with some of its arguments we can define a number of well-known functions. Some examples are

```
sum = reduce (+) 0
append xs ys = reduce (:) ys xs
reverse = reduce h []
          where h x xs = append xs [x]
map f = reduce h []
        where h x ys = (f x) : ys
```

A similar equational definition of functions is allowed in Standard ML. Slightly rewriting the definition of `reduce` above we obtain the Standard ML program

```
fun reduce f u = let fun g [] = u
                       |   g (x::xs) = f x (g xs)
                 in g end;
```

An alternative formulation is

```
val reduce = fn f => fn u =>
             let val rec g = fn xs =>
                             if xs = [] then u
                             else f (hd xs) (g (tl xs))
             in g end;
```

Here function abstraction is expressed explicitly by `fn` ··· `=>` ··· and the recursive structure of `g` is expressed by the occurrence of `rec`. Also the test on the form of the list argument is expressed directly whereas function application is still implicit. In short, we have obtained a somewhat more explicit, but perhaps less readable, definition of `reduce`.

The enriched λ-calculus

The development to be performed in this book will require *all* the operations to be expressed explicitly. We shall define a small language, an *enriched λ-calculus*, that captures a few of the more important constructs present in modern functional languages. The formal development will then be performed for that language and in many cases it will be straightforward to extend it to richer languages.

The enriched λ-calculus will only have explicit operations and, in particular, there will be an explicit function application ···(···). Additionally we shall use parentheses of the form (···) to indicate parsing of the concrete syntax. In the enriched λ-calculus the program `sum` may be written

```
DEF reduce = λf.λu.fix (λg.λxs.
                          if isnil xs then u
                          else f (hd xs) (g (tl xs)))
VAL reduce (λx.λy.+(⟨x,y⟩)) (0)
HAS Int list → Int
```

A *program* in the enriched λ-calculus is a sequence of definitions together with an expression and a type:

DEF d_1 ··· DEF d_n VAL e HAS t

Each *definition* d_i has the form $x_i = e_i$ where x_i is the name of the entity and e_i is its defining expression. The name x_i can be used in the expressions of the definitions given after its definition and in e. The type of e is supposed to be t.

The *basic types* in the enriched λ-calculus include amongst others `Int`, denoting the type of integers, and `Bool`, denoting the type of truth values. A *function type* is written as $t \to t'$, a *product type* as $t \times t'$ and a *list type* as t `list`. We follow the convention that the function type constructor binds less tightly than the product type constructor which in turn binds less tightly than the list type constructor. Furthermore, the function type constructor associates to the right and the product type constructor to the left. As an example `Int` → `Int` × `Int` × `Int list` → `Int` should be read as `Int` → (((`Int` × `Int`) × (`Int list`)) → `Int`).

We shall assume that we have a number of *constants*. For example, constants representing values of the basic types such as

`true` and `false` of type `Bool` and

`0`, `1`, `-1`, ··· of type `Int`

In addition there are constants for the primitive operations such as

`+` and $*$ of type `Int` × `Int` → `Int`,

`=` of type `Int` × `Int` → `Bool`,

∧ and ∨ of type `Bool` × `Bool` → `Bool` and

¬ of type `Bool` → `Bool`.

Functions are constructed using λ-abstraction as in $\lambda x.e$, where x is the bound variable and e is the body of the abstraction. Function application is denoted by the explicit operation $e(e')$ where e is the operator and e' the operand. *Pairs* are constructed using angle brackets as in $\langle e,e' \rangle$ and the components of a pair are selected by **fst** e and **snd** e. *Lists* are built using the two constructs **nil** and e:e' where the first gives the empty list and the second prefixes the list e' with the element e. The head and the tail of a (non-empty) list can be selected by **hd** e and **tl** e and the construct **isnil** e tests whether a list is empty. The *conditional* of the language is written as **if** e **then** e' **else** e'' and *recursion* is expressed by the fixed point operator **fix** e.

Overview

The next three chapters follow the approach sketched above: underlying notions and ideas which are *implicit* (in some language) are made *explicit* in order to construct a stable platform from which to study the implementation of functional languages.

- In Chapter 2 the *types are made explicit*: We show how an untyped program plus an overall type for that program may be transformed into a typed program. Even if the original program was typed it would most likely not have all the type information in an explicit form at every place where it might be useful in the implementation, and so some variant of this development would still be needed.

- In Chapter 3 the *binding times are made explicit*. This is done by introducing a notation that allows an explicit distinction between the compile-time and run-time binding times. It is then shown how to propagate partial binding time annotations throughout the program.

- In Chapter 4 the *combinators are made explicit* but only for the run-time computations. The key observation is that run-time computations should give rise to code but that compile-time computations should not. To facilitate code generation, and program analyses intended to aid in this, we need the dependency on free variables to be made explicit and this is achieved by an algorithm for introducing the combinators.

This approach is summarized in Figure 1.1.

The remainder of the book exploits the, by now fully explicit, notation to develop and illustrate a flexible notion of semantics.

- In Chapter 5 the framework of *parameterized semantics* is developed. Here run-time types and combinators may be interpreted in virtually any way desired and this interpretation is then extended to all well-formed programs. Example interpretations include lazy and eager 'standard interpretations'.

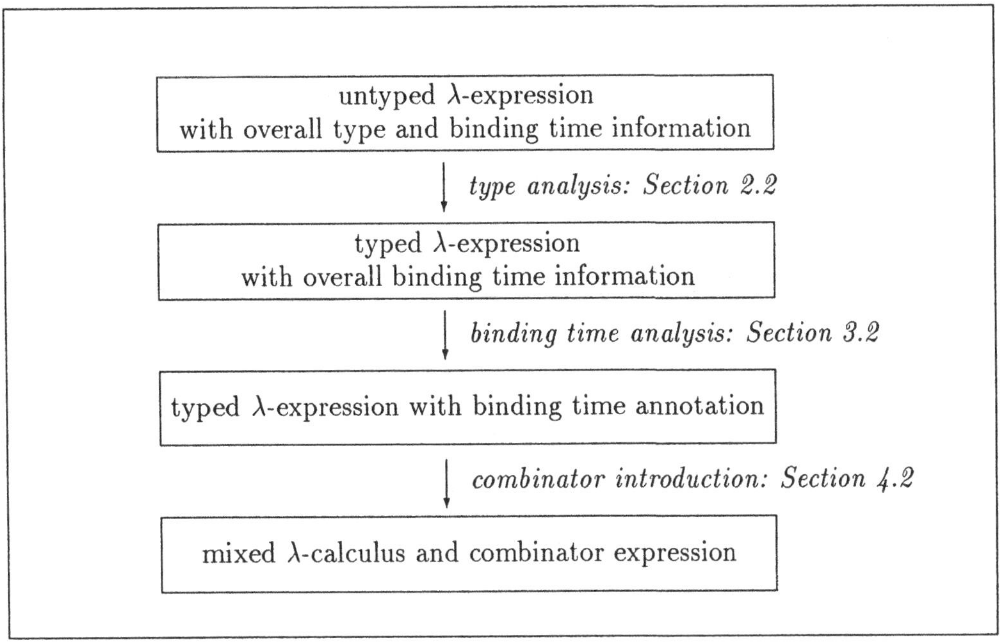

Figure 1.1: Overview of Chapters 2, 3 and 4

- In Chapter 6 the more interesting example of *code generation* is studied, again through the definition of an interpretation. This involves the definition of a structured abstract machine. A subset of the translation is proved correct using Kripke-logical relations and layered predicates.

- In Chapter 7 it is shown how to formulate *abstract interpretation* (a compile-time program analysis technique) by means of an interpretation. We formulate a generalized version of Wadler's strictness analysis for lists and prove its correctness using logical relations. Tensor products are introduced as a companion to Wadler's notion of case analysis.

Throughout this development we shall concentrate on *non-strict*, i.e. *lazy*, semantics although most of the development could be modified to apply to a language with a *strict*, i.e. *eager*, semantics. Finally, in Chapter 8 we conclude with a discussion about how to extend this development by incorporating the results of abstract interpretation in order to perform improved code generation. We also show how the development may be used to generate compilers, or compiling specifications, from language specifications written in the style of denotational semantics.

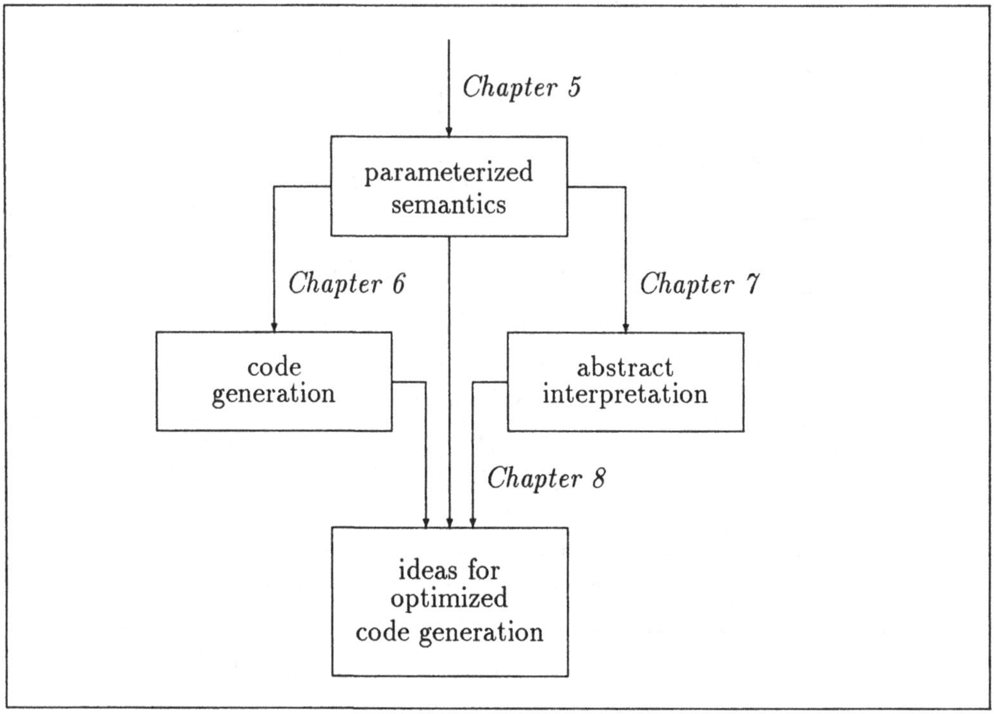

Figure 1.2: Overview of Chapters 5, 6, 7 and 8

Bibliographical Notes

The programming language Standard ML is defined in [56] and Miranda is described in [102, 103]. Introductions to functional programming may be found in [107] and [11].

Chapter 2

Types Made Explicit

Both Miranda and Standard ML enjoy the property that a programmer need not specify the types of all the entities defined in the program. This is because the implementations are able to infer the remaining types assuming that the program is well-formed. The benefit for the functional programming style is that higher-order functions can be defined in a rather straightforward manner.

As an example, implementations of Miranda and Standard ML will infer that the type of the `reduce` function considered in Chapter 1 is

$$(\alpha\to\beta\to\beta)\to\beta\to\alpha\ \texttt{list}\to\beta$$

Here α and β are so-called type variables that may be instantiated (or replaced) with arbitrary types. The occurrence of `reduce` in the definition of `sum` (in Chapter 1) has the type

$$(\texttt{Int}\to\texttt{Int}\to\texttt{Int})\to\texttt{Int}\to\texttt{Int list}\to\texttt{Int}$$

because it is applied to arguments of type $\texttt{Int}\to\texttt{Int}\to\texttt{Int}$ and `Int`. On the other hand, the occurrence of `reduce` in the definition of `append` (in Chapter 1) is applied to arguments of type $\gamma\to\gamma\ \texttt{list}\to\gamma\ \texttt{list}$ and $\gamma\ \texttt{list}$ so its type will be

$$(\gamma\to\gamma\ \texttt{list}\to\gamma\ \texttt{list})\to\gamma\ \texttt{list}\to\gamma\ \texttt{list}\to\gamma\ \texttt{list}$$

In this chapter the enriched λ-calculus is equipped with a type inference system closely related to that found in Miranda and Standard ML. The type inference is based upon a few rules for how to build well-formed expressions. As an example, the function application $e(e')$ is only well-formed if the type of e has the form $t\to t'$ and if the type of e' is t and then the type of the application is t'. Similar rules exist for the other composite constructs of the language. For the constants we have axioms stating, for example, that `+` has type $\texttt{Int}\times\texttt{Int}\to\texttt{Int}$ and that `0` has type `Int`. Based upon such axioms and rules we can infer that the program `sum` is well-formed and we can determine the types of the various subexpressions.

Of course the results obtained are the same as those mentioned above for Miranda and Standard ML. The details are provided in Section 2.1.

The next step is to *annotate* the program with the inferred type information: we shall add the actual types to the constants and the bound variables of λ-abstractions. This means that the `sum` program will be transformed into the following program, to be called $\texttt{sum}_t$:

```
DEF reduce = λf[Int→Int→Int].λu[Int].
                fix (λg[Int list → Int]. λxs[Int list].
                    if isnil xs then u
                    else f(hd xs)(g(tl xs)))
VAL reduce (λx[Int].λy[Int].+[Int×Int→Int](⟨x,y⟩)) (0[Int])
HAS Int list → Int
```

Here the type of `reduce` has been fixed and this is possible because there is only *one* application of `reduce` in the program. (In general we may have to duplicate the definition of some of the functions, see Exercise 2.) The details are presented in Section 2.2 where the Hindley/Milner/Damas type inference algorithm for the λ-calculus is reviewed. As we shall see, it frees the user from having to worry too much about types.

2.1 The Typed λ-Calculus

The base language underlying our development is the typed λ-calculus. It has types, $t \in T$, and expressions, $e \in E$, and its syntax is displayed in Table 2.1. The A_i are base types where i ranges over an unspecified index set I and we shall write `Bool` for the type $\mathsf{A}_{\mathsf{bool}}$ of booleans, `Int` for the type $\mathsf{A}_{\mathsf{int}}$ of integers and `Void` for the type $\mathsf{A}_{\mathsf{void}}$ that intuitively only has a dummy element. Product types, function types and list types are constructed using the type constructors ×, → and `list`, respectively. The $\mathtt{f}_i[t]$ are primitives of type t as indicated and we shall write eq[Int×Int→Bool] for $\mathtt{f}_{\mathsf{eq}}$[Int×Int→Bool] etc. Related to products we have notation for forming pairs and for selecting their components. Associated with function space we have notation for λ-abstraction, application and variables. As for constants we shall write `env` for $\mathtt{x}_{\mathsf{env}}$ etc.[1] Related to lists we have notation for constructing lists, for selecting their components and for testing for emptiness of lists. Finally, we have the truth values, conditional and notation for recursive definitions.

We shall consider typed λ-expressions together with their overall types and to smooth the explanation we shall use the term *programs* for such specifications. To obtain readable examples it is desirable that a program allows the definition

[1] A less desirable consequence of this choice is that it depends on the context whether an identifier like `ide` means $\mathtt{f}_{\mathsf{ide}}$ or $\mathtt{x}_{\mathsf{ide}}$; however, in practice no confusion is likely to arise.

$t \in T$

$t ::= \mathtt{A_i} \mid t \times t \mid t \rightarrow t \mid t\ \mathtt{list}$

$e \in E$

$e ::= \mathtt{f_i}[t] \mid \langle e,e \rangle \mid \mathtt{fst}\ e \mid \mathtt{snd}\ e \mid \lambda \mathtt{x_i}[t].e \mid e(e) \mid \mathtt{x_i} \mid$
$\quad e{:}e \mid \mathtt{nil}[t] \mid \mathtt{hd}\ e \mid \mathtt{tl}\ e \mid \mathtt{isnil}\ e \mid$
$\quad \mathtt{true} \mid \mathtt{false} \mid \mathtt{if}\ e\ \mathtt{then}\ e\ \mathtt{else}\ e \mid \mathtt{fix}\ e$

Table 2.1: The typed λ-calculus

$ue \in UE$

$ue ::= \mathtt{f_i} \mid \langle ue,ue \rangle \mid \mathtt{fst}\ ue \mid \mathtt{snd}\ ue \mid \lambda \mathtt{x_i}.ue \mid ue(ue) \mid \mathtt{x_i} \mid$
$\quad ue{:}ue \mid \mathtt{nil} \mid \mathtt{hd}\ ue \mid \mathtt{tl}\ ue \mid \mathtt{isnil}\ ue \mid$
$\quad \mathtt{true} \mid \mathtt{false} \mid \mathtt{if}\ ue\ \mathtt{then}\ ue\ \mathtt{else}\ ue \mid \mathtt{fix}\ ue$

Table 2.2: The untyped λ-calculus

of 'global' functions in much the same way that the functional programming languages considered in Chapter 1 do. This motivates the definition of the syntactic category $P(E,T)$ of programs. Actually, it is more convenient to give a general definition of a syntactic category $P(E^*,T^*)$ of programs over expressions E^* and types T^*. It is given by:

$e \in E^*$

$t \in T^*$

$p \in P(E^*,T^*)$

$p ::= \mathtt{DEF}\ \mathtt{x_i}{=}e\ p \mid \mathtt{VAL}\ e\ \mathtt{HAS}\ t$

So $P(E,T)$ is the syntactic category of programs where the expressions are typed λ-expressions and the types are as above. If UE is the syntactic category of expressions in the untyped λ-calculus, as given in Table 2.2, the programs in $P(UE,T)$ have expressions that are untyped and types as above.

Example 2.1.1 The program `sum` in Chapter 1 is in $P(UE,T)$ whereas the program $\mathtt{sum_t}$ above is in $P(E,T)$. □

When we allow the user to specify a typed λ-expression and its corresponding type, by giving an untyped expression and its intended type, we pretend that we have a function of functionality

$$P(UE,T) \rightarrow P(E,T)$$

that can automatically introduce the required type information into the untyped expression. This transformation will be studied in Section 2.2.

Example 2.1.2 Consider the program `double` given by

$$\begin{array}{l}\texttt{DEF + = +[Int}\rightarrow\texttt{Int}\rightarrow\texttt{Int]}\\ \texttt{VAL }\lambda\texttt{v[Int].(+(v))(v)}\\ \texttt{HAS Int}\rightarrow\texttt{Int}\end{array}$$

Here we have abbreviated the constant f_+ to + and the variables x_+ and x_v to + and v so that the unabbreviated program is

$$\begin{array}{l}\texttt{DEF } x_+ = f_+[A_{int}\rightarrow A_{int}\rightarrow A_{int}]\\ \texttt{VAL } \lambda x_v [A_{int}].(x_+(x_v))\ (x_v)\\ \texttt{HAS } A_{int}\rightarrow A_{int}\end{array}$$

In practice it might increase the readability to abbreviate x_+ to `plus` rather than +. Also note that we have used the parentheses (and) to indicate grouping whereas (and) are used for function application. □

Well-formedness

We need to be precise about when an expression in the typed λ-calculus has a given type. The details are given in Table 2.3 where we define a relation

$$tenv \vdash e : t$$

for when the expression e has type t. Here $tenv$ is a *type environment*, i.e. a map from a finite set dom($tenv$) of variables to types, so it gives information about the type of any (free) variable in e. We use the notation $tenv[t/x_i]$ for an environment that is like $tenv$ except that it maps the variable x_i to the type t. We shall sometimes write graph($tenv$) for the set $\{(x_i, tenv(x_i)) | x_i \in \text{dom}(tenv)\}$ and we shall write $\emptyset$ for the environment whose domain is empty. Well-formedness of a program is then given by

$$\frac{\begin{array}{c}\emptyset \vdash e_1 : t_1\\ \vdots\\ \emptyset[t_1/x_1]\cdots[t_{n-1}/x_{n-1}] \vdash e_n : t_n\\ \emptyset[t_1/x_1]\cdots[t_n/x_n] \vdash e : t\end{array}}{\vdash \texttt{DEF } x_1 = e_1 \cdots \texttt{DEF } x_n = e_n \texttt{ VAL } e \texttt{ HAS } t}$$

where we have extended the relation ⊢ to work on programs as well as on expressions. To be completely precise we should have written x_{i_j} instead of x_j as we really intend that x_1, ..., x_n are n (distinct) variables rather than any particular ones, but it is commonplace to misuse notation as we have done here. Note that there is no mutual or implicit recursion between the x_j's as each e_j may only refer to $x_1, \cdots, x_{j-1}$.

[f]	$tenv \vdash \mathtt{f}_i[t] : t$
[⟨⟩]	$\dfrac{tenv \vdash e_1 : t_1 \quad tenv \vdash e_2 : t_2}{tenv \vdash \langle e_1,e_2\rangle : t_1\times t_2}$
[fst]	$\dfrac{tenv \vdash e : t_1\times t_2}{tenv \vdash \mathtt{fst}\ e : t_1}$
[snd]	$\dfrac{tenv \vdash e : t_1\times t_2}{tenv \vdash \mathtt{snd}\ e : t_2}$
[λ]	$\dfrac{tenv[t'/\mathtt{x}_i] \vdash e : t}{tenv \vdash \lambda\mathtt{x}_i[t'].e : t'\rightarrow t}$
[()]	$\dfrac{tenv \vdash e_1 : t'\rightarrow t \quad tenv \vdash e_2 : t'}{tenv \vdash e_1(e_2) : t}$
[x]	$tenv \vdash \mathtt{x}_i : t \quad \text{if } (\mathtt{x}_i,t)\in\text{graph}(tenv)$
[:]	$\dfrac{tenv \vdash e_1 : t \quad tenv \vdash e_2 : t\ \mathtt{list}}{tenv \vdash e_1{:}e_2 : t\ \mathtt{list}}$
[nil]	$tenv \vdash \mathtt{nil}[t] : t\ \mathtt{list}$
[hd]	$\dfrac{tenv \vdash e : t\ \mathtt{list}}{tenv \vdash \mathtt{hd}\ e : t}$
[tl]	$\dfrac{tenv \vdash e : t\ \mathtt{list}}{tenv \vdash \mathtt{tl}\ e : t\ \mathtt{list}}$
[isnil]	$\dfrac{tenv \vdash e : t\ \mathtt{list}}{tenv \vdash \mathtt{isnil}\ e : \mathtt{Bool}}$
[true]	$tenv \vdash \mathtt{true} : \mathtt{Bool}$
[false]	$tenv \vdash \mathtt{false} : \mathtt{Bool}$
[if]	$\dfrac{tenv \vdash e_1 : \mathtt{Bool} \quad tenv \vdash e_2 : t \quad tenv \vdash e_3 : t}{tenv \vdash \mathtt{if}\ e_1\ \mathtt{then}\ e_2\ \mathtt{else}\ e_3 : t}$
[fix]	$\dfrac{tenv \vdash e : t\rightarrow t}{tenv \vdash \mathtt{fix}\ e : t}$

Table 2.3: Well-formedness of the typed λ-calculus

Example 2.1.3 The well-formedness of `double` (of Example 2.1.2) amounts to ⊢`double` and to prove this it suffices to show that

$$\emptyset \vdash \mathtt{f}_+[\mathtt{Int}\rightarrow\mathtt{Int}\rightarrow\mathtt{Int}] : \mathtt{Int}\rightarrow\mathtt{Int}\rightarrow\mathtt{Int}$$

$$\emptyset[\mathtt{Int}\rightarrow\mathtt{Int}\rightarrow\mathtt{Int}/\mathtt{x}_+] \vdash \lambda\mathtt{v}[\mathtt{Int}].(\mathtt{x}_+(\mathtt{v}))(\mathtt{v}) : \mathtt{Int}\rightarrow\mathtt{Int}$$

where we have used a mixture of abbreviated and unabbreviated notation. The first result amounts to a single application of the axiom [f]. To prove the second result it is sufficient to show that

$$\emptyset[\mathtt{Int}\rightarrow\mathtt{Int}\rightarrow\mathtt{Int}/\mathtt{x}_+][\mathtt{Int}/\mathtt{v}] \vdash (\mathtt{x}_+(\mathtt{v}))(\mathtt{v}) : \mathtt{Int} \qquad (\star)$$

since then the result can be obtained by a single application of the rule [λ]. To show (⋆) we note that two applications of the axiom [x] give

$$\emptyset[\texttt{Int}\rightarrow\texttt{Int}\rightarrow\texttt{Int}/\texttt{x}_+][\texttt{Int}/\texttt{v}] \vdash \texttt{x}_+ : \texttt{Int}\rightarrow\texttt{Int}\rightarrow\texttt{Int}$$

$$\emptyset[\texttt{Int}\rightarrow\texttt{Int}\rightarrow\texttt{Int}/\texttt{x}_+][\texttt{Int}/\texttt{v}] \vdash \texttt{v} : \texttt{Int}$$

Using the rule [()] we then have

$$\emptyset[\texttt{Int}\rightarrow\texttt{Int}\rightarrow\texttt{Int}/\texttt{x}_+][\texttt{Int}/\texttt{v}] \vdash \texttt{x}_+\texttt{(v)} : \texttt{Int}\rightarrow\texttt{Int}$$

and one more application of the rule [()] gives

$$\emptyset[\texttt{Int}\rightarrow\texttt{Int}\rightarrow\texttt{Int}/\texttt{x}_+][\texttt{Int}/\texttt{v}] \vdash \texttt{(x}_+\texttt{(v))(v)} : \texttt{Int}$$

as desired. □

In the syntax of the typed λ-calculus we have included sufficient type information in the expressions for the type of an expression to be determined by the types of its free variables:

Fact 2.1.4 The relation $tenv \vdash e{:}t$ is functional in $tenv$ and e; this means that $tenv \vdash e{:}t_1$ and $tenv \vdash e{:}t_2$ imply $t_1{=}t_2$. □

Proof: This is a straightforward structural induction on e and is left to Exercise 4. □

We could thus define a (partial) function *type-of* such that *type-of*($tenv$,e) = t if and only if $tenv \vdash e : t$. However, we shall prefer a phrase like 'let t be given by $tenv \vdash e : t$' or 'let $tenv \vdash e : t$ determine t'.

2.2 Type Analysis

Let us now consider how to propagate type information from a type into an untyped λ-expression so as to obtain an expression in the typed λ-calculus. In other words we consider the transformation

$$\mathcal{P}_{\mathrm{TA}}\text{: } P(UE,T) \rightarrow P(E,T)$$

However, we have to realize that so far we have made too few assumptions about the number of, and nature of, primitives of form $\texttt{f}_\mathrm{i}[t]$. To remedy this we shall define a constraint C as a partial map from $\{\texttt{f}_\mathrm{i}|\mathrm{i}{\in}I\}$ to information about the permissible types. Taking an equality predicate $\texttt{f}_{\mathrm{eq}}$ as an example we intend that it may be used as $\texttt{f}_{\mathrm{eq}}[t]$ whenever the type t has the form $t'{\rightarrow}t'{\rightarrow}\texttt{Bool}$[2]. We model this by setting

[2]It might be argued that t' should not be allowed to contain function spaces as the extensional equality on function types is not computable in general and the intentional equality is of limited use. To express this we should modify $C(\texttt{f}_{\mathrm{eq}})$ to use a form of bounded quantification rather than the general quantification indicated by ∀. However, this goes beyond the standard Hindley/Milner/Damas type inference and we shall abstain from this.

$$C(\mathtt{f}_{\mathrm{eq}}) = \forall \mathrm{X}_1.\ \mathrm{X}_1 \rightarrow \mathrm{X}_1 \rightarrow \mathtt{Bool}$$

and to explain this notation we need some concepts from the literature on 'polymorphic type inference'; this will also serve as a useful preparation for constructing the translation $\mathcal{P}_{\mathrm{TA}}$.

2.2.1 Polytypes

A syntactic category of *type variables* may be introduced by

$$tv \in TV$$

$$tv ::= \mathrm{X}_1 \mid \mathrm{X}_2 \mid \ldots \qquad \text{(infinite)}$$

Often in the literature type variables are denoted by Greek letters α, α_1, β etc. or `'a`, `'b` etc. but this is entirely a matter of taste. A *polytype* is then like a type except that it may contain type variables and this motivates defining

$$pt \in PT$$

$$pt ::= \mathsf{A}_\mathrm{i} \mid pt \times pt \mid pt \rightarrow pt \mid pt\ \mathtt{list} \mid tv$$

An example polytype is $\mathrm{X}_1 \rightarrow \mathrm{X}_1 \rightarrow \mathtt{Bool}$. We shall write $\mathrm{FTV}(pt)$ for the set of (free) type variables in pt. If $\mathrm{FTV}(pt)=\emptyset$ we shall say that pt is a *monotype* and we shall not distinguish between monotypes in PT and types in T. A *type scheme* then is a polytype where some of the type variables may be universally bound. More precisely

$$ts \in TS$$

$$ts ::= pt \mid \forall tv.ts$$

Thus $\forall \mathrm{X}_1.\mathrm{X}_1 \rightarrow \mathrm{X}_1 \rightarrow \mathtt{Bool}$ is a type scheme as is $\forall \mathrm{X}_1.\mathrm{X}_1 \rightarrow \mathrm{X}_2 \rightarrow \mathtt{Bool}$. The free type variables $\mathrm{FTV}(ts)$ of a type scheme $ts = \forall tv_1.\cdots\forall tv_\mathrm{n}.pt$ are $\mathrm{FTV}(pt) \setminus \{tv_1,\cdots,tv_\mathrm{n}\}$. A type scheme with an empty set of free type variables is said to be *closed*, for example the type scheme displayed for $C(\mathtt{f}_{\mathrm{eq}})$ above. From now on we shall assume that the constraint C maps constants to *closed* type schemes.

Closely related to polytypes is the notion of a *substitution*. There are several ways to explain substitutions and we prefer to model them as total functions from TV to PT. However, for a total function $S: TV \rightarrow PT$ to qualify as a substitution we require that the set

$$\mathrm{Dom}(S) = \{\ tv \in TV \mid S(tv) \neq tv\ \}$$

is *finite*. Hence one could represent a substitution S as $[pt_1/\mathrm{X}_1,\ldots,pt_\mathrm{n}/\mathrm{X}_\mathrm{n}]$ where $\mathrm{Dom}(S) = \{\mathrm{X}_1,\ldots,\mathrm{X}_\mathrm{n}\}$ and $S(\mathrm{X}_\mathrm{i}) = pt_\mathrm{i}$. We may extend a substitution to work on polytypes by an obvious structural induction and we shall feel free to write simply

$S(pt)$ for the result of applying the substitution S to the polytype pt. We may thus regard a substitution S as a total function $S{:}PT{\rightarrow}PT$ and this allows us to define composition of substitutions as merely functional composition. We shall write

$$\mathrm{FTV}(S) = \bigcup \{\ \mathrm{FTV}(S(tv)) \mid tv{\in}\mathrm{Dom}(S)\ \}$$

for the free type variables that S 'uses'. If this set is empty we shall say that S is a *ground substitution.*

An *instance* of a polytype pt is a polytype of the form $S(pt)$ for a substitution S. As an example $\texttt{Int}{\rightarrow}\texttt{Int}{\rightarrow}\texttt{Bool}$ is an instance of $\mathrm{X}_1{\rightarrow}\mathrm{X}_1{\rightarrow}\texttt{Bool}$ (using a substitution $S = [\texttt{Int}/\mathrm{X}_1]$). We shall say that S *covers* pt if $\mathrm{Dom}(S){\supseteq}\mathrm{FTV}(pt)$. When S covers pt and is a ground substitution the polytype $S(pt)$ will be a monotype because all type variables in pt will be replaced by monotypes. Turning to a closed type scheme $ts = \forall tv_1.\cdots\forall tv_n.pt$, an instance of ts is simply an instance of pt. A *generic instance* of the closed type scheme ts is an instance pt' of pt such that pt is also an instance of pt'. So $\mathrm{X}_2{\rightarrow}\mathrm{X}_2{\rightarrow}\texttt{Bool}$ is a generic instance of $C(\texttt{f}_{\mathrm{eq}})$ whereas $\texttt{Int}{\rightarrow}\texttt{Int}{\rightarrow}\texttt{Bool}$ is only an instance.

Example 2.2.1 In this notation the general type scheme for the `reduce` function is

$$ts = \forall \mathrm{X}_1.\ \forall \mathrm{X}_2.\ (\mathrm{X}_1 \rightarrow \mathrm{X}_2 \rightarrow \mathrm{X}_2) \rightarrow \mathrm{X}_2 \rightarrow \mathrm{X}_1\ \texttt{list} \rightarrow \mathrm{X}_2$$

and the type of the `reduce` function in the `sum` program is

$$t = (\texttt{Int} \rightarrow \texttt{Int} \rightarrow \texttt{Int}) \rightarrow \texttt{Int} \rightarrow \texttt{Int list} \rightarrow \texttt{Int}$$

To see that the concrete type t is an instance of the general type scheme ts we define the polytype

$$pt = (\mathrm{X}_1 \rightarrow \mathrm{X}_2 \rightarrow \mathrm{X}_2) \rightarrow \mathrm{X}_2 \rightarrow \mathrm{X}_1\ \texttt{list} \rightarrow \mathrm{X}_2$$

and the substitution S by

$$S(\mathrm{X}_i) = \begin{cases} \texttt{Int} & \text{if } \mathrm{X}_i \text{ is } \mathrm{X}_1 \text{ or } \mathrm{X}_2 \\ \mathrm{X}_i & \text{otherwise} \end{cases}$$

We may note that $\mathrm{Dom}(S) = \{\mathrm{X}_1,\mathrm{X}_2\}$ and that $\mathrm{FTV}(S) = \emptyset$ so that S is a ground substitution. Then $t = S(pt)$ so that t is an instance of pt and ts. However, t is not a generic instance of ts because pt is not an instance of t. □

We can then define a modified typing relation

$$tenv \vdash_{\mathrm{C}} e : t$$

which is like $tenv \vdash e : t$ except that

$tenv \vdash_C \mathtt{f}_i[t] : t$

if $\mathtt{f}_i \in \mathrm{dom}(C)$ and t is an instance of $C(\mathtt{f}_i)$

Similarly, we shall write

$\vdash_C p$

if a program p is well-formed under this assumption. So if $C(\mathtt{f}_{eq})$ is as displayed above we are sure that $\mathtt{f}_{eq}[t]$ is allowed if and only if t is of the form $t' \to t' \to \mathtt{Bool}$.

Example 2.2.2 Returning to Examples 2.1.2 and 2.1.3 we still have $\vdash_C$ `double` provided that $C(\mathtt{f}_+)$ is as usual, i.e.

$$C(\mathtt{f}_+) = \mathtt{Int} \to \mathtt{Int} \to \mathtt{Int}$$

Note that `Int` → `Int` → `Int` is indeed a closed type scheme, albeit not a very interesting one. □

The main purpose of substitutions is to make distinct polytypes equal. So if pt_1 and pt_2 are distinct polytypes we want a unifying substitution S such that $S(pt_1) = S(pt_2)$. Such a substitution need not exist, e.g. if pt_1=`Bool` and pt_2=`Int`, and if it exists it need not be unique, e.g. if $pt_1=\mathrm{X}_1$ and $pt_2=\mathrm{X}_2$. When a unifying substitution S exists we want it to be as 'small' as possible, i.e. whenever S' is a substitution such that $S'(pt_1)=S'(pt_2)$ there should exist a substitution S'' such that $S'=S''\circ S$. That this is possible in general follows from:

Lemma 2.2.3 (Robinson [90]) There exists an algorithm $\mathcal{U}$ which when supplied with a set $\{pt_1,...,pt_n\}$ of polytypes, either fails or produces a substitution S:

- It fails if and only if there exists no substitution S such that $S(pt_1) = ... = S(pt_n)$.
- If it produces a substitution S then
  - S unifies $\{pt_1,...,pt_n\}$, i.e. $S(pt_1) = ... = S(pt_n)$,
  - S is a most general unifier for $\{pt_1,...,pt_n\}$, i.e. whenever $S'(pt_1) = ... = S'(pt_n)$ for a substitution S' there exists a substitution S'' such that $S'=S''\circ S$,
  - S only involves type variables in the pt_i; a bit more formally this may be expressed as $\mathrm{Dom}(S)\cup\mathrm{FTV}(S) \subseteq \bigcup_{i=1}^{n} \mathrm{FTV}(pt_i)$. □

We shall sketch a construction of an algorithm $\mathcal{U}$ in Exercise 5. Note, however, that the lemma does not guarantee the existence of a unique substitution but merely a most general unifier (if any unifier exists). So writing I for the identity substitution one is free to let $\mathcal{U}(\{\mathrm{X}_1,\mathrm{X}_2\})$ be either $\mathrm{I}[\mathrm{X}_2/\mathrm{X}_1]$ or $\mathrm{I}[\mathrm{X}_1/\mathrm{X}_2]$.

2.2.2 The algorithm

We now have sufficient background information for approaching the central ingredient in the transformation from 'untyped programs' in $P(UE,T)$ to 'typed programs' in $P(E,T)$. This amounts to inferring a typed λ-expression e given an untyped λ-expression ue. For this we shall allow the types in the λ-expression e to be polytypes. For technical reasons we shall further request that variables be annotated with their types in the same way constants are. In other words, rather than producing an expression $e \in E$ we shall produce a polytyped expression $pe \in PE$ where the syntactic category of polytyped expressions is given by

$$pe \in PE$$

$$pe ::= \mathtt{f_i[}pt\mathtt{]} \;|\ldots|\; \lambda\mathtt{x_i[}pt\mathtt{]}.pe \;|\ldots|\; \mathtt{x_i[}pt\mathtt{]} \;|\ldots|\; \mathtt{nil[}pt\mathtt{]} \;|\ldots$$

Clearly, if we remove the polytypes in pe we must obtain the untyped λ-expression ue that we started with. We may formalise this by the condition

$$ue = \varepsilon_{\mathrm{TA}}(pe)$$

for an obvious type erasing function $\varepsilon_{\mathrm{TA}}:PE \rightarrow UE$.

Example 2.2.4 One may calculate that

$$\varepsilon_{\mathrm{TA}}(\lambda\mathtt{x_1[X_1\ list \rightarrow Int].\ x_1[X_1\ list \rightarrow Int]\ (nil[X_1])})$$

amounts to $\lambda\mathtt{x_1.x_1(nil)}$. □

The functionality of the type analysis algorithm thus is

$$\mathcal{E}^C_{\mathrm{TA}}\colon\ UE \hookrightarrow PE \times PT$$

because it is helpful to obtain also the overall polytype of the polytyped expression. This function is partial, i.e. is allowed to *fail*, because it will need to use the algorithm $\mathcal{U}$ that is also allowed to fail.

The functionality of $\mathcal{E}^C_{\mathrm{TA}}$ is slightly simpler here than in some other presentations in the literature. This is because the explicit typing of the polytyped variables obviates the need for producing a set of assumptions $A \in \mathcal{P}_{\mathrm{fin}}(\{\mathtt{x_i}|\mathrm{i}\in I\}\times PT)$, that is a finite subset A of $\{\mathtt{x_i}|\mathrm{i}\in I\} \times PT$. Instead we must define a function

$$\mathcal{A}_{\mathrm{TA}}\colon\ PE \rightarrow \mathcal{P}_{\mathrm{fin}}(\{\mathtt{x_i}|\mathrm{i}\in I\} \times PT)$$

that extracts the required information. The definition of this function is by analogy with the definition of the free (expression) variables $\mathrm{FEV}(e)$ of an expression e and is left to Exercise 7.

Example 2.2.5 Consider the expression

$$e = \lambda \mathtt{x}_1.\langle\langle \mathtt{x}_1,\mathtt{x}_2\rangle,\langle \mathtt{x}_2,\mathtt{x}_1\rangle\rangle$$

The set of free variables in e is $\mathrm{FEV}(e) = \{\mathtt{x}_2\}$. Similarly consider the polytyped expression

$$pe = \lambda \mathtt{x}_1\,\mathtt{[Int]}.\ \langle\langle \mathtt{x}_1\mathtt{[Int]},\mathtt{x}_2\mathtt{[Bool]}\rangle,\ \langle \mathtt{x}_2\mathtt{[Int]},\mathtt{x}_1\mathtt{[Bool]}\rangle\rangle$$

The assumptions that are free in pe are $\mathcal{A}_{\mathrm{TA}}(pe) = \{(\mathtt{x}_2,\mathtt{Bool}),(\mathtt{x}_2,\mathtt{Int})\}$. □

Before presenting the definition of $\mathcal{E}^C_{\mathrm{TA}}$ we need to introduce the following notation. For $A \in \mathcal{P}_{\mathrm{fin}}(\{\mathtt{x}_\mathrm{i} \mid \mathrm{i} \in I\} \times PT)$ we shall write

$$\mathrm{FTV}(A) = \bigcup \{\ \mathrm{FTV}(pt) \mid (\mathtt{x}_\mathrm{i},pt){\in}A\ \}$$

for the type variables that A 'uses',

$$S{\circ}A = \{\ (\mathtt{x}_\mathrm{i},S(pt)) \mid (\mathtt{x}_\mathrm{i},pt){\in}A\ \}$$

for the result of applying a substitution S to an assumption A,

$$A_\mathtt{x} = \{\ (\mathtt{x}_\mathrm{i},pt){\in}A \mid \mathtt{x}_\mathrm{i}{\neq}\mathtt{x}\ \}$$

for the part of A that does not involve the variable $\mathtt{x}$, and

$$A(\mathtt{x}) = \{\ pt \mid (\mathtt{x},pt){\in}A\ \}$$

for the set of polytypes that A associates with $\mathtt{x}$. We shall say that A is *functional* if each $A(\mathtt{x})$ is empty or a singleton. When A is functional we may identify it with the partial function, $\mathrm{fun}(A)$, that maps $\mathtt{x}_\mathrm{i}$ to pt whenever $(\mathtt{x}_\mathrm{i},pt){\in}A$. With respect to the notation $\mathrm{graph}(\cdots)$ introduced earlier, we observe that $A{=}\mathrm{graph}(\mathrm{fun}(A))$ for any functional set and that $tenv{=}\mathrm{fun}(\mathrm{graph}(tenv))$ for any partial function $tenv$.

The type analysis algorithm $\mathcal{E}^C_{\mathrm{TA}}$ is defined in Tables 2.4 and 2.5 by a structural induction in which we ask for 'fresh' type variables, i.e. type variables that have not been used before[3]. Also, we extend substitutions to work on polytyped expressions in much the same way they were extended to work on polytypes. The intention is that $\mathcal{E}^C_{\mathrm{TA}}$ fails if any of the invocations of $\mathcal{U}$ fail or if an $\mathtt{f}_\mathrm{i}$ is encountered that is not in the domain of the constraint C.

Basically $\mathcal{E}^C_{\mathrm{TA}}$ inspects its argument in a bottom-up manner. For each occurrence of a variable it introduces a 'fresh' type variable. These type variables may be replaced by other polytypes as a result of unifying the polytypes of various sub-expressions. However, only when the enclosing λ-abstraction is encountered will the polytypes of the variable occurrences be unified. This is illustrated in the following example.

[3]This could be made more precise by adding the set of 'fresh' type variables as an extra argument to $\mathcal{E}^C_{\mathrm{TA}}$ but following tradition we shall dispense with this.

$$\mathcal{E}^{C}_{\mathrm{TA}}[\![\ \mathtt{f_i}\ ]\!] = \begin{cases} (\mathtt{f_i}[pt], pt) & \text{if } C(\mathtt{f_i}) = ts \\ & \text{and } pt \text{ is a generic instance of } ts \\ & \text{and FTV}(pt) \text{ are all `fresh'} \\ \mathit{fail} & \text{otherwise} \end{cases}$$

$$\begin{aligned} \mathcal{E}^{C}_{\mathrm{TA}}[\![\ \langle ue_1, ue_2\rangle\ ]\!] = {} & \text{let } (pe_1,pt_1) = \mathcal{E}^{C}_{\mathrm{TA}}[\![ue_1]\!] \\ & \text{let } (pe_2,pt_2) = \mathcal{E}^{C}_{\mathrm{TA}}[\![ue_2]\!] \\ & \text{in } (\langle pe_1,pe_2\rangle,\ pt_1\times pt_2) \end{aligned}$$

$$\begin{aligned} \mathcal{E}^{C}_{\mathrm{TA}}[\![\ \mathtt{fst}\ ue\ ]\!] = {} & \text{let } (pe,pt) = \mathcal{E}^{C}_{\mathrm{TA}}[\![ue]\!] \\ & \text{let } tv_1 \text{ and } tv_2 \text{ be `fresh'} \\ & \text{let } S = \mathcal{U}(\{pt,\ tv_1\times tv_2\}) \\ & \text{in } (\mathtt{fst}\ S(pe),\ S(tv_1)) \end{aligned}$$

$$\begin{aligned} \mathcal{E}^{C}_{\mathrm{TA}}[\![\ \mathtt{snd}\ ue\ ]\!] = {} & \text{let } (pe,pt) = \mathcal{E}^{C}_{\mathrm{TA}}[\![ue]\!] \\ & \text{let } tv_1 \text{ and } tv_2 \text{ be `fresh'} \\ & \text{let } S = \mathcal{U}(\{pt,\ tv_1\times tv_2\}) \\ & \text{in } (\mathtt{snd}\ S(pe),\ S(tv_2)) \end{aligned}$$

$$\begin{aligned} \mathcal{E}^{C}_{\mathrm{TA}}[\![\ \lambda \mathtt{x_i}.ue\ ]\!] = {} & \text{let } (pe,pt) = \mathcal{E}^{C}_{\mathrm{TA}}[\![ue]\!] \\ & \text{let } tv \text{ be `fresh'} \\ & \text{let } S = \mathcal{U}(\{tv\}\cup\mathcal{A}_{\mathrm{TA}}(pe)(\mathtt{x_i})) \\ & \text{in } (\lambda\mathtt{x_i}[S(tv)].S(pe),\ S(tv)\rightarrow S(pt)) \end{aligned}$$

$$\begin{aligned} \mathcal{E}^{C}_{\mathrm{TA}}[\![\ ue_1(ue_2)\ ]\!] = {} & \text{let } (pe_1,pt_1) = \mathcal{E}^{C}_{\mathrm{TA}}[\![ue_1]\!] \\ & \text{let } (pe_2,pt_2) = \mathcal{E}^{C}_{\mathrm{TA}}[\![ue_2]\!] \\ & \text{let } tv \text{ be `fresh'} \\ & \text{let } S = \mathcal{U}(\{pt_1,\ pt_2\rightarrow tv\}) \\ & \text{in } (S(pe_1)(S(pe_2)),\ S(tv)) \end{aligned}$$

$$\begin{aligned} \mathcal{E}^{C}_{\mathrm{TA}}[\![\ \mathtt{x_i}\ ]\!] = {} & \text{let } tv \text{ be `fresh'} \\ & \text{in } (\mathtt{x_i}[tv],\ tv) \end{aligned}$$

$$\begin{aligned} \mathcal{E}^{C}_{\mathrm{TA}}[\![\ ue_1{:}ue_2\ ]\!] = {} & \text{let } (pe_1,pt_1) = \mathcal{E}^{C}_{\mathrm{TA}}[\![ue_1]\!] \\ & \text{let } (pe_2,pt_2) = \mathcal{E}^{C}_{\mathrm{TA}}[\![ue_2]\!] \\ & \text{let } S = \mathcal{U}(\{pt_1\ \mathtt{list},\ pt_2\}) \\ & \text{in } (S(pe_1){:}S(pe_2),\ S(pt_2)) \end{aligned}$$

$$\begin{aligned} \mathcal{E}^{C}_{\mathrm{TA}}[\![\ \mathtt{hd}\ ue\ ]\!] = {} & \text{let } (pe,pt) = \mathcal{E}^{C}_{\mathrm{TA}}[\![ue]\!] \\ & \text{let } tv \text{ be `fresh'} \\ & \text{let } S = \mathcal{U}(\{pt,\ tv\ \mathtt{list}\}) \\ & \text{in } (\mathtt{hd}\ S(pe),\ S(tv)) \end{aligned}$$

Table 2.4: $\mathcal{E}^{C}_{\mathrm{TA}}$: Type analysis of expressions (part 1)

$$\mathcal{E}^{C}_{\text{TA}}[\![\ \texttt{tl}\ ue\ ]\!] = \text{let } (pe,pt) = \mathcal{E}^{C}_{\text{TA}}[\![ue]\!]$$
$$\text{let } tv \text{ be `fresh'}$$
$$\text{let } S = \mathcal{U}(\{pt,\ tv\ \texttt{list}\})$$
$$\text{in } (\texttt{tl}\ S(pe),\ S(pt))$$

$$\mathcal{E}^{C}_{\text{TA}}[\![\ \texttt{nil}\ ]\!] = \text{let } tv \text{ be `fresh'}$$
$$\text{in } (\texttt{nil[}tv\texttt{]},\ tv\ \texttt{list})$$

$$\mathcal{E}^{C}_{\text{TA}}[\![\ \texttt{isnil}\ ue\ ]\!] = \text{let } (pe,pt) = \mathcal{E}^{C}_{\text{TA}}[\![ue]\!]$$
$$\text{let } tv \text{ be `fresh'}$$
$$\text{let } S = \mathcal{U}(\{pt,\ tv\ \texttt{list}\})$$
$$\text{in } (\texttt{isnil}\ S(pe),\ \texttt{Bool})$$

$$\mathcal{E}^{C}_{\text{TA}}[\![\ \texttt{true}\ ]\!] = (\texttt{true},\ \texttt{Bool})$$

$$\mathcal{E}^{C}_{\text{TA}}[\![\ \texttt{false}\ ]\!] = (\texttt{false},\ \texttt{Bool})$$

$$\mathcal{E}^{C}_{\text{TA}}[\![\ \texttt{if}\ ue_1\ \texttt{then}\ ue_2\ \texttt{else}\ ue_3\ ]\!] =$$
$$\text{let } (pe_1,pt_1) = \mathcal{E}^{C}_{\text{TA}}[\![ue_1]\!]$$
$$\text{let } (pe_2,pt_2) = \mathcal{E}^{C}_{\text{TA}}[\![ue_2]\!]$$
$$\text{let } (pe_3,pt_3) = \mathcal{E}^{C}_{\text{TA}}[\![ue_3]\!]$$
$$\text{let } S_1 = \mathcal{U}(\{pt_1,\ \texttt{Bool}\})$$
$$\text{let } S_2 = \mathcal{U}(\{pt_2,\ pt_3\})$$
$$\text{in } (\texttt{if}\ S_1(pe_1)\ \texttt{then}\ S_2(pe_2)\ \texttt{else}\ S_2(pe_3), S_2(pt_2))$$

$$\mathcal{E}^{C}_{\text{TA}}[\![\ \texttt{fix}\ ue\ ]\!] = \text{let } (pe,pt) = \mathcal{E}^{C}_{\text{TA}}[\![ue]\!]$$
$$\text{let } tv \text{ be `fresh'}$$
$$\text{let } S = \mathcal{U}(\{pt,\ tv \rightarrow tv\})$$
$$\text{in } (\texttt{fix}\ S(pe),\ S(tv))$$

Table 2.5: $\mathcal{E}^{C}_{\text{TA}}$: Type analysis of expressions (part 2)

Example 2.2.6 Consider the (untyped) expression

$$\lambda \texttt{g}.\lambda \texttt{x}.\texttt{g(g(x))}$$

and the computation of $\mathcal{E}^{C}_{\text{TA}}[\![\lambda\texttt{g}.\lambda\texttt{x}.\texttt{g(g(x))}]\!]$. This initiates a series of calls. In these we obtain

$$\mathcal{E}^{C}_{\text{TA}}[\![\texttt{g}]\!] = (\texttt{g[}X_1\texttt{]},\ X_1)$$
$$\mathcal{E}^{C}_{\text{TA}}[\![\texttt{g}]\!] = (\texttt{g[}X_2\texttt{]},\ X_2)$$
$$\mathcal{E}^{C}_{\text{TA}}[\![\texttt{x}]\!] = (\texttt{x[}X_3\texttt{]},\ X_3)$$

where X_1, X_2 and X_3 are distinct type variables. Using $\mathcal{U}(\{X_2, X_3 \rightarrow X_4\}) = I[X_3 \rightarrow X_4/X_2]$ we get

$$\mathcal{E}^{C}_{\text{TA}}[\![\texttt{g(x)}]\!] = (\texttt{g[}X_3 \rightarrow X_4\texttt{]}\ \texttt{(x[}X_3\texttt{])},\ X_4)$$

Repeating the process we use $\mathcal{U}(\{X_1,X_4\to X_5\}) = I[X_4\to X_5/X_1]$ and we get

$$\mathcal{E}^C_{\mathrm{TA}}[\![\mathtt{g(g(x))}]\!] = (\mathtt{g}[X_4\to X_5]\ (\mathtt{g}[X_3\to X_4]\ (\mathtt{x}[X_3])),\ X_5)$$

To compute $\mathcal{E}^C_{\mathrm{TA}}[\![\lambda\mathtt{x.g(g(x))}]\!]$ we observe that

$$\mathcal{A}_{\mathrm{TA}}(\mathtt{g}[X_4\to X_5]\ (\mathtt{g}[X_3\to X_4]\ (\mathtt{x}[X_3]))) = \{(\mathtt{g},X_4\to X_5),(\mathtt{g},X_3\to X_4),(\mathtt{x},X_3)\}$$

and $\mathcal{U}(\{X_3,X_6\}) = I[X_3/X_6]$ so that

$$\mathcal{E}^C_{\mathrm{TA}}[\![\lambda\mathtt{x.g(g(x))}]\!] = (\lambda\mathtt{x}[X_3].\mathtt{g}[X_4\to X_5]\ (\mathtt{g}[X_3\to X_4]\ (\mathtt{x}[X_3])),\ X_3\to X_5)$$

Note that the two occurrences of g are annotated with different polytypes. It is only when encountering the enclosing λg that the necessary identifications will be made. This is illustrated when computing $\mathcal{E}^C_{\mathrm{TA}}[\![\lambda\mathtt{g}.\lambda\mathtt{x.g(g(x))}]\!]$. Here we observe that

$$\mathcal{A}_{\mathrm{TA}}(\lambda\mathtt{x}[X_3].\mathtt{g}[X_4\to X_5]\ (\mathtt{g}[X_3\to X_4]\ (\mathtt{x}[X_3]))) = \{(\mathtt{g},X_4\to X_5),(\mathtt{g},X_3\to X_4)\}$$

and that $\mathcal{U}(\{X_7,X_4\to X_5,X_3\to X_4\}) = I[X_3/X_4][X_3/X_5][X_3\to X_3/X_7]$ so that

$$\mathcal{E}^C_{\mathrm{TA}}[\![\lambda\mathtt{g}.\lambda\mathtt{x.g(g(x))}]\!] = (\lambda\mathtt{g}[X_3\to X_3].\lambda\mathtt{x}[X_3].\mathtt{g}[X_3\to X_3]\ (\mathtt{g}[X_3\to X_3]\ (\mathtt{x}[X_3])),\ (X_3\to X_3)\to X_3\to X_3)$$

This completes the calculations. □

We can now define the translation function $\mathcal{P}^C_{\mathrm{TA}}$ for programs. It has functionality

$$\mathcal{P}^C_{\mathrm{TA}} : P(UE,T) \hookrightarrow P(E,T)$$

and it is partial because it invokes $\mathcal{E}^C_{\mathrm{TA}}$ and $\mathcal{U}$ and these might fail. The definition is

$$\begin{array}{l}\mathcal{P}^C_{\mathrm{TA}}[\![\ \mathtt{DEF}\ \mathtt{x}_1{=}ue_1\ \cdots\ \mathtt{DEF}\ \mathtt{x}_n{=}ue_n\ \mathtt{VAL}\ ue_0\ \mathtt{HAS}\ t\ ]\!] = \\ \quad \text{let } ((\lambda\mathtt{x}_1[pt_1].\cdots\ (\lambda\mathtt{x}_n[pt_n].pe_0)(pe_n)\ \cdots)(pe_1),\ pt) = \\ \qquad\qquad \mathcal{E}^C_{\mathrm{TA}}[\![\ (\lambda\mathtt{x}_1.\cdots\ (\lambda\mathtt{x}_n.ue_0)(ue_n)\ \cdots)(ue_1)\ ]\!] \\ \quad \text{let } S_1 = \mathcal{U}(\{pt,t\}) \\ \quad \text{let } S_2 = (\lambda tv.\mathtt{Void}) \circ S_1 \\ \quad \text{in } \mathtt{DEF}\ \mathtt{x}_1{=}\varepsilon'_{\mathrm{TA}}(S_2(pe_1))\ \cdots\ \mathtt{DEF}\ \mathtt{x}_n{=}\varepsilon'_{\mathrm{TA}}(S_2(pe_n)) \\ \qquad \mathtt{VAL}\ \varepsilon'_{\mathrm{TA}}(S_2(pe_0))\ \mathtt{HAS}\ t\end{array}$$

The general idea is to use the close relationship between programs, e.g.

DEF $\mathtt{x}_1 = ue_1$ VAL ue_0 HAS t

and expressions containing a λ-abstraction that is immediately applied to an argument, e.g.

$(\lambda\mathtt{x}_1.ue_0)(ue_1)$

To obtain the desired result we need to unify the overall polytype produced by $\mathcal{E}^C_{\mathrm{TA}}$ with the monotype, t, supplied. Also we need to get rid of any remaining type variables and this motivates the substitution[4] $\lambda tv.$Void that replaces type variables with the uninteresting type Void. Finally, the expressions $S_2(pe_\mathrm{i})$ are not yet in E because variables in $S_2(pe_\mathrm{i})$ will be annotated with their types and this is not the case for expressions in E. We therefore need to use the type erasing function $\varepsilon'_{\mathrm{TA}}$ that has

$\varepsilon'_{\mathrm{TA}}(\mathtt{x}_\mathrm{i}[t]) = \mathtt{x}_\mathrm{i}$

but otherwise behaves as the identity.

Example 2.2.7 If we used S_2=S_1 instead of S_2=(λtv.Void)oS_1 we would get

$\mathcal{P}^C_{\mathrm{TA}}[\![$ VAL ($\lambda\mathtt{x}_1$.true) ($\lambda\mathtt{x}_2.\mathtt{x}_2$) HAS Bool $]\!]$

to be

VAL ($\lambda\mathtt{x}_1[\mathrm{X}_1\rightarrow\mathrm{X}_1]$.true) ($\lambda\mathtt{x}_2[\mathrm{X}_1].\mathtt{x}_2$) HAS Bool

but with S_2=(λtv.Void)oS_1 we get

VAL ($\lambda\mathtt{x}_1$[Void→Void].true) ($\lambda\mathtt{x}_2$[Void].$\mathtt{x}_2$) HAS Bool

which is a program in $P(E,T)$. If we had dispensed with $\varepsilon'_{\mathrm{TA}}$ the result would have been

VAL ($\lambda\mathtt{x}_1$[Void→Void].true) ($\lambda\mathtt{x}_2$[Void].$\mathtt{x}_2$[Void]) HAS Bool

which does not conform to the syntax of $P(E,T)$. □

[4]Actually, Dom(λtv.Void) is the infinite set TV so in order to satisfy the conditions on substitutions we should use λtv. **if** $tv \in \bigcup_\mathrm{i}\mathrm{FTV}(S_1(pe_\mathrm{i}))$ **then Void else** tv.

2.2.3 Syntactic soundness and completeness

To express soundness and completeness of $\mathcal{E}^C_{\mathrm{TA}}$ we need two auxiliary sets. The set

$$\mathrm{WFF}_C(ue) = \{\ (tenv,e,t) \mid tenv \vdash_C e{:}t \wedge ue{=}\varepsilon_{\mathrm{TA}}(e) \wedge \mathrm{dom}(tenv){=}\mathrm{FEV}(ue)\ \}$$

contains the set of triples of the form $(tenv,e,t)$ such that e has type t, that is $tenv \vdash_C e : t$, and e equals ue when the types are erased. For technical reasons it is assumed that the domain of the type environment equals the set of free (expression) variables in ue and hence in e. Analogously, the set

$$\begin{aligned}\mathrm{INS}_C(ue) = \{\ (S{\circ}\mathcal{A}_{\mathrm{TA}}(pe),\ \varepsilon'_{\mathrm{TA}}(S(pe)),\ S(pt)) \mid\ & \mathcal{E}^C_{\mathrm{TA}}[\![ue]\!] = (pe,pt)\\ & \wedge \mathrm{Dom}(S) \supseteq \mathrm{FTV}(pe){\cup}\mathrm{FTV}(pt)\\ & \wedge S \text{ is a ground substitution}\\ & \wedge S{\circ}\mathcal{A}_{\mathrm{TA}}(pe) \text{ is functional }\}\end{aligned}$$

contains a set of triples obtained from $\mathcal{E}^C_{\mathrm{TA}}[\![ue]\!] = (pe,pt)$. The type is obtained as $S(pt)$, that is a ground substitution applied to the polytype pt. The expression would similarly be $S(pe)$, except that the polytyped variables are annotated with their types so that we have to use the erasing function $\varepsilon'_{\mathrm{TA}}$. Finally, the analogue of the type environment is $S{\circ}\mathcal{A}_{\mathrm{TA}}(pe)$ where it is required that this set may be regarded as a function. It should be stressed that $\mathrm{INS}_C(ue)$ is the empty set, $\emptyset$, if $\mathcal{E}^C_{\mathrm{TA}}[\![ue]\!]$ fails. Furthermore, it should be noted that for the two sets $\mathrm{WFF}_C(ue)$ and $\mathrm{INS}_C(ue)$ to be comparable we should really have replaced $tenv$ by $\mathrm{graph}(tenv)$, or $S{\circ}\mathcal{A}_{\mathrm{TA}}(pe)$ by $\mathrm{fun}(S{\circ}\mathcal{A}_{\mathrm{TA}}(pe))$, but for readability we shall retain this imprecision.

Proposition 2.2.8 (Soundness and Completeness of $\mathcal{E}^C_{\mathrm{TA}}$)

$$\mathrm{WFF}_C(ue) = \mathrm{INS}_C(ue)$$

for all expressions $ue{\in}UE$ and all constraints C. □

Discussion: This proposition is really a conjunction of two results. One is the *soundness* (or *correctness*) result

$$\mathrm{WFF}_C(ue) \supseteq \mathrm{INS}_C(ue)$$

which says that $\mathcal{E}^C_{\mathrm{TA}}$ only specifies well-formed expressions. The other result is the *completeness* result

$$\mathrm{WFF}_C(ue) \subseteq \mathrm{INS}_C(ue)$$

which says that each and every well-formed expression is obtainable from the result that $\mathcal{E}^C_{\mathrm{TA}}$ specifies.

Proof: We proceed by structural induction on ue using the 'fresh'-ness of the type variables generated in $\mathcal{E}^C_{TA}$ and leaving some of the less interesting cases as an exercise.

The case $ue::=\mathtt{f}_i$. If $\mathtt{f}_i \notin \mathrm{dom}(C)$ both $\mathrm{WFF}_C(ue)$ and $\mathrm{INS}_C(ue)$ are empty so assume that $\mathtt{f}_i \in \mathrm{dom}(C)$. We have

$$\mathrm{WFF}_C(ue) = \{\ (\emptyset,\mathtt{f}_i[t],t) \mid t \text{ is an instance of } C(\mathtt{f}_i)\ \}$$

$$\begin{aligned}\mathrm{INS}_C(ue) = \{\ (\emptyset,\mathtt{f}_i[S(pt)],S(pt)) \mid\ & S \text{ covers } pt,\ S \text{ is ground,}\\ & \text{and } pt \text{ is a generic instance of } C(\mathtt{f}_i)\\ & \text{with FTV}(pt) \text{ all being `fresh'}\ \}\end{aligned}$$

The result then follows because the set of types that are instances of a closed type scheme equals the set of types that are ground instances of a polytype that is a generic instance of the same closed type scheme.

The case $ue::=\lambda\mathtt{x}_i.ue_0$. We assume first that $\mathtt{x}_i \in \mathrm{FEV}(ue_0)$. We then have

$$\begin{aligned}\mathrm{WFF}_C(ue) = \{\ & (tenv,\ \lambda\mathtt{x}_i[t].e_0,\ t\rightarrow t_0)\\ & \mid (tenv[t/\mathtt{x}_i],e_0,t_0) \in \mathrm{WFF}_C(ue_0)\\ & \wedge\ \mathrm{dom}(tenv) = \mathrm{FEV}(ue)\ \}\end{aligned}$$

because the inference system in Table 2.3 is such that $[\lambda]$ must be the last rule used in a proof of well-formedness of $\lambda\mathtt{x}_i.e_0$. Writing $tenv\lceil X$ for the restriction of an environment $tenv$ to a subset X of its domain $\mathrm{dom}(tenv)$ we have

$$\begin{aligned}\mathrm{WFF}_C(ue) = \{\ & (tenv\lceil\mathrm{FEV}(ue),\ \lambda\mathtt{x}_i[tenv(\mathtt{x}_i)].e_0,\ tenv(\mathtt{x}_i)\rightarrow t_0)\\ & \mid (tenv,e_0,t_0) \in \mathrm{WFF}_C(ue_0)\ \}\end{aligned}$$

Turning to the other set we have

$$\begin{aligned}\mathrm{INS}_C(ue) = \{\ & ((S\circ S')\circ\mathcal{A}_{TA}(pe_0)_{\mathtt{x}_i},\ \lambda\mathtt{x}_i[(S\circ S')(tv)].\mathcal{E}'_{TA}((S\circ S')(pe_0)),\\ & \quad (S\circ S')(tv)\rightarrow(S\circ S')(pt_0))\\ & \mid \mathcal{E}^C_{TA}[\![ue_0]\!] = (pe_0,pt_0)\ \wedge\ tv \text{ `fresh'}\\ & \wedge\ \mathcal{U}(\{tv\}\cup\mathcal{A}_{TA}(pe_0)(\mathtt{x}_i))=S'\\ & \wedge\ S \text{ covers all of } S'\circ\mathcal{A}_{TA}(pe_0)_{\mathtt{x}_i},\ S'(tv),\ S'(pe_0)\\ & \quad \text{and } S'(pt_0)\\ & \wedge\ S \text{ is ground } \wedge\ (S\circ S')\circ\mathcal{A}_{TA}(pe_0)_{\mathtt{x}_i} \text{ is functional}\ \}\end{aligned}$$

where we have used

$$(S\circ S')\circ\mathcal{A}_{TA}(pe_0)_{\mathtt{x}_i} = S\circ(S'\circ\mathcal{A}_{TA}(pe_0)_{\mathtt{x}_i}),$$

$$(S\circ S')(pe_0)=S(S'(pe_0)),$$

$$(S\circ S')(pt_0)=S(S'(pt_0)), \text{ and}$$

$$\mathcal{A}_{TA}(\lambda\mathtt{x}_i[tv].pe_0)=\mathcal{A}_{TA}(pe_0)_{\mathtt{x}_i}.$$

Next observe that $((S \circ S') \circ \mathcal{A}_{\mathrm{TA}}(pe_0))(\mathbf{x}_i)$ is a singleton because S' unifies the set $\mathcal{A}_{\mathrm{TA}}(pe_0)(\mathbf{x}_i)$ and hence $(S \circ S')(tv)$ may be replaced by $((S \circ S') \circ \mathcal{A}_{\mathrm{TA}}(pe_0))(\mathbf{x}_i)$ or, to be precise, the single element in that set. Since $\mathrm{FEV}(ue) = \mathrm{FEV}(ue_0) \backslash \{\mathbf{x}_i\}$ we may replace $(S \circ S') \circ \mathcal{A}_{\mathrm{TA}}(pe_0)_{\mathbf{x}_i}$ by $((S \circ S') \circ \mathcal{A}_{\mathrm{TA}}(pe_0)) \lceil \mathrm{FEV}(ue)$. Using this we have

$$
\begin{aligned}
\mathrm{INS}_C(ue) = \{\ & (((S \circ S') \circ \mathcal{A}_{\mathrm{TA}}(pe_0)) \lceil \mathrm{FEV}(ue), \\
& \quad \lambda \mathbf{x}_i[((S \circ S') \circ \mathcal{A}_{\mathrm{TA}}(pe_0))(\mathbf{x}_i)].\ \varepsilon'_{\mathrm{TA}}((S \circ S')(pe_0)), \\
& \quad ((S \circ S') \circ \mathcal{A}_{\mathrm{TA}}(pe_0))(\mathbf{x}_i) \to (S \circ S')(pt_0)) \\
& \mid \mathcal{E}^C_{\mathrm{TA}}[\![ue_0]\!] = (pe_0, pt_0) \\
& \wedge ((S \circ S') \circ \mathcal{A}_{\mathrm{TA}}(pe_0))(\mathbf{x}_i) \text{ is a singleton} \\
& \wedge (S \circ S') \text{ covers all of } \mathcal{A}_{\mathrm{TA}}(pe_0)_{\mathbf{x}_i}, \mathcal{A}_{\mathrm{TA}}(pe_0)(\mathbf{x}_i), \\
& \quad pe_0 \text{ and } pt_0 \\
& \wedge (S \circ S') \text{ is ground} \\
& \wedge ((S \circ S') \circ \mathcal{A}_{\mathrm{TA}}(pe_0)) \lceil \mathrm{FEV}(ue) \text{ is functional } \}
\end{aligned}
$$

because the need for tv has vanished, given that $((S \circ S') \circ \mathcal{A}_{\mathrm{TA}}(pe_0))(\mathbf{x}_i)$ has replaced $(S \circ S')(tv)$, and that it follows from Lemma 2.2.3 that the $(S \circ S')$ ranged over in the previous equation for INS_C equal the $(S \circ S')$ ranged over in the present equation for INS_C. We then have

$$
\begin{aligned}
\mathrm{INS}_C(ue) = \{\ & (tenv \lceil \mathrm{FEV}(ue), \lambda \mathbf{x}_i[tenv(\mathbf{x}_i)].e_0, tenv(\mathbf{x}_i) \to t_0) \\
& \mid (tenv, e_0, t_0) \in \mathrm{INS}_C(ue_0) \ \}
\end{aligned}
$$

The desired result then follows from the induction hypothesis. Finally, we observe that if $\mathbf{x}_i \notin \mathrm{FEV}(ue_0)$ the result may be obtained in much the same manner.

The case $ue ::= ue_1(ue_2)$. We have

$$
\begin{aligned}
\mathrm{WFF}_C(ue) = \{\ & (tenv, e_1(e_2), t) \\
& \mid (tenv \lceil \mathrm{FEV}(ue_1), e_1, t_2 \to t) \in \mathrm{WFF}_C(ue_1) \\
& \wedge (tenv \lceil \mathrm{FEV}(ue_2), e_2, t_2) \in \mathrm{WFF}_C(ue_2) \\
& \wedge \mathrm{dom}(tenv) = \mathrm{FEV}(ue) \ \}
\end{aligned}
$$

because the inference system of Table 2.3 is such that [()] must be the last rule used in a proof of well-formedness of $e_1(e_2)$. Furthermore

$$
\begin{aligned}
\mathrm{WFF}_C(ue) = \{\ & (tenv_1 \cup tenv_2, e_1(e_2), t) \\
& \mid (tenv_1, e_1, t_2 \to t) \in \mathrm{WFF}_C(ue_1) \\
& \wedge (tenv_2, e_2, t_2) \in \mathrm{WFF}_C(ue_2) \\
& \wedge \forall \mathbf{x} \in \mathrm{FEV}(ue_1) \cap \mathrm{FEV}(ue_2) \colon tenv_1(\mathbf{x}) = tenv_2(\mathbf{x}) \ \}
\end{aligned}
$$

Here we write $tenv_1 \cup tenv_2$ for the partial function that maps $\mathbf{x} \in \mathrm{FEV}(ue_1)$ to $tenv_1(\mathbf{x})$ and $\mathbf{x} \in \mathrm{FEV}(ue_2)$ to $tenv_2(\mathbf{x})$; this does not give rise to any confusion as $tenv_1(\mathbf{x}) = tenv_2(\mathbf{x})$ whenever $\mathbf{x} \in \mathrm{FEV}(ue_1) \cap \mathrm{FEV}(ue_2)$. (If we wanted to be more precise about the distinction between a partial function and a functional set we could have written $\mathrm{fun}(\mathrm{graph}(tenv_1) \cup \mathrm{graph}(tenv_2))$ instead of $tenv_1 \cup tenv_2$.)

Turning to the other set we have

$$
\begin{aligned}
\mathrm{INS}_C(ue) = \{\ & ((S \circ S' \circ \mathcal{A}_{\mathrm{TA}}(pe_1)) \cup (S \circ S' \circ \mathcal{A}_{\mathrm{TA}}(pe_2)),\\
&\qquad \varepsilon'_{\mathrm{TA}}((S \circ S')(pe_1)\ ((S \circ S')(pe_2))),\ (S \circ S')(tv))\\
&\mid \mathcal{E}^C_{\mathrm{TA}}[\![ue_1]\!] = (pe_1, pt_1)\\
&\wedge \mathcal{E}^C_{\mathrm{TA}}[\![ue_2]\!] = (pe_2, pt_2)\\
&\wedge tv \text{ `fresh' } \wedge \mathcal{U}(\{pt_1,\ pt_2 \rightarrow tv\}) = S'\\
&\wedge S \text{ covers all of } S' \circ \mathcal{A}_{\mathrm{TA}}(pe_1),\ S' \circ \mathcal{A}_{\mathrm{TA}}(pe_2),\\
&\qquad S'(pe_1),\ S'(pe_2) \text{ and } S'(tv)\\
&\wedge S \text{ is ground}\\
&\wedge (S \circ S' \circ \mathcal{A}_{\mathrm{TA}}(pe_1)) \cup (S \circ S' \circ \mathcal{A}_{\mathrm{TA}}(pe_2)) \text{ is functional } \}
\end{aligned}
$$

where we have used $\mathcal{A}_{\mathrm{TA}}(pe_1(pe_2)) = \mathcal{A}_{\mathrm{TA}}(pe_1) \cup \mathcal{A}_{\mathrm{TA}}(pe_2)$. Furthermore

$$
\begin{aligned}
\mathrm{INS}_C(ue) = \{\ & ((S'' \circ \mathcal{A}_{\mathrm{TA}}(pe_1)) \cup (S'' \circ \mathcal{A}_{\mathrm{TA}}(pe_2)),\\
&\qquad \varepsilon'_{\mathrm{TA}}(S''(pe_1)(S''(pe_2))),\ t)\\
&\mid \mathcal{E}^C_{\mathrm{TA}}[\![ue_1]\!] = (pe_1, pt_1)\\
&\wedge \mathcal{E}^C_{\mathrm{TA}}[\![ue_2]\!] = (pe_2, pt_2)\\
&\wedge S''(pt_1) = S''(pt_2) \rightarrow t\\
&\wedge S'' \text{ covers all of } \mathcal{A}_{\mathrm{TA}}(pe_1),\ \mathcal{A}_{\mathrm{TA}}(pe_2),\ pe_1,\ pe_2,\\
&\qquad pt_1 \text{ and } pt_2\\
&\wedge S'' \text{ is ground}\\
&\wedge S'' \circ (\mathcal{A}_{\mathrm{TA}}(pe_1) \cup \mathcal{A}_{\mathrm{TA}}(pe_2)) \text{ is functional } \}
\end{aligned}
$$

and since the 'fresh' type variables generated by $\mathcal{E}^C_{\mathrm{TA}}[\![ue_1]\!]$ are disjoint from those generated by $\mathcal{E}^C_{\mathrm{TA}}[\![ue_2]\!]$ we have

$$
\begin{aligned}
\mathrm{INS}_C(ue) = \{\ & ((S''_1 \circ \mathcal{A}_{\mathrm{TA}}(pe_1)) \cup (S''_2 \circ \mathcal{A}_{\mathrm{TA}}(pe_2)),\\
&\qquad \varepsilon'_{\mathrm{TA}}(S''_1(pe_1)\ (S''_2(pe_2))),\ t)\\
&\mid \mathcal{E}^C_{\mathrm{TA}}[\![ue_1]\!] = (pe_1, pt_1)\\
&\wedge \mathcal{E}^C_{\mathrm{TA}}[\![ue_2]\!] = (pe_2, pt_2)\\
&\wedge S''_1(pt_1) = S''_2(pt_2) \rightarrow t\\
&\wedge S''_1 \text{ covers all of } \mathcal{A}_{\mathrm{TA}}(pe_1),\ pe_1, \text{ and } pt_1\\
&\wedge S''_2 \text{ covers all of } \mathcal{A}_{\mathrm{TA}}(pe_2),\ pe_2, \text{ and } pt_2\\
&\wedge S''_1 \text{ is ground} \wedge S''_1 \circ \mathcal{A}_{\mathrm{TA}}(pe_1) \text{ is functional}\\
&\wedge S''_2 \text{ is ground} \wedge S''_2 \circ \mathcal{A}_{\mathrm{TA}}(pe_2) \text{ is functional}\\
&\wedge \forall \mathbf{x} \in \mathrm{FEV}(ue_1) \cap \mathrm{FEV}(ue_2):\\
&\qquad (S''_1 \circ \mathcal{A}_{\mathrm{TA}}(pe_1))(\mathbf{x}) = (S''_2 \circ \mathcal{A}_{\mathrm{TA}}(pe_2))(\mathbf{x})\ \}\\
= \{\ & (tenv_1 \cup tenv_2, e_1(e_2), t)\\
&\mid (tenv_1, e_1, t_2 \rightarrow t) \in \mathrm{INS}_C(ue_1)\\
&\wedge (tenv_2, e_2, t_2) \in \mathrm{INS}_C(ue_2)\\
&\wedge \forall \mathbf{x} \in \mathrm{FEV}(ue_1) \cap \mathrm{FEV}(ue_2):\ tenv_1(\mathbf{x}) = tenv_2(\mathbf{x})\ \}
\end{aligned}
$$

and the desired result then follows from the induction hypothesis.

The case $ue ::= \mathbf{x}_i$. We have

$$\mathrm{WFF}_C(ue) = \{\ (\emptyset[t/\mathtt{x}_i],\mathtt{x}_i,t) \mid t{\in}T\ \}$$

$$\begin{aligned}\mathrm{INS}_C(ue) = \{\ &(\{(\mathtt{x}_i,S(tv))\},\mathtt{x}_i,S(tv))\\ &\mid tv \text{ `fresh', } S \text{ is ground, and } \mathrm{Dom}(S){=}\{tv\}\ \}\end{aligned}$$

and clearly these sets are equal.

The remaining cases will be left as an exercise as they follow the general pattern of the previous ones. In fact we may express this similarity in the following strong way. We shall take ue ::= $\texttt{if}\ ue_1\ \texttt{then}\ ue_2\ \texttt{else}\ ue_3$ as our example since this is one of the harder cases. We may assume that

$$C(\mathtt{f}_{\mathrm{if}}) = \forall \mathrm{X}_1.\ \mathtt{Bool}{\rightarrow}\mathrm{X}_1{\rightarrow}\mathrm{X}_1{\rightarrow}\mathrm{X}_1$$

and it then easily follows that

$$\begin{aligned}&(tenv,\ \texttt{if}\ e_1\ \texttt{then}\ e_2\ \texttt{else}\ e_3,\ t) \in\\ &\mathrm{WFF}_C(\texttt{if}\ ue_1\ \texttt{then}\ ue_2\ \texttt{else}\ ue_3)\\ &\Updownarrow\\ &(tenv,\ \mathtt{f}_{\mathrm{if}}[\mathtt{Bool}{\rightarrow}t{\rightarrow}t{\rightarrow}t](e_1)(e_2)(e_3),\ t) \in\\ &\mathrm{WFF}_C(\mathtt{f}_{\mathrm{if}}(ue_1)(ue_2)(ue_3))\end{aligned}$$

We also have

$$\begin{aligned}&(tenv,\ \texttt{if}\ e_1\ \texttt{then}\ e_2\ \texttt{else}\ e_3,\ t) \in\\ &\mathrm{INS}_C(\texttt{if}\ ue_1\ \texttt{then}\ ue_2\ \texttt{else}\ ue_3)\\ &\Updownarrow\\ &(tenv,\ \mathtt{f}_{\mathrm{if}}[\mathtt{Bool}{\rightarrow}t{\rightarrow}t{\rightarrow}t](e_1)(e_2)(e_3),\ t) \in\\ &\mathrm{INS}_C(\mathtt{f}_{\mathrm{if}}(ue_1)(ue_2)(ue_3))\end{aligned}$$

because

$$\begin{aligned}&\mathcal{E}^C_{\mathrm{TA}}[\![\ \texttt{if}\ ue_1\ \texttt{then}\ ue_2\ \texttt{else}\ ue_3\ ]\!] =\\ &(\texttt{if}\ pe_1\ \texttt{then}\ pe_2\ \texttt{else}\ pe_3,\ pt)\end{aligned}$$

if and only if

$$\begin{aligned}&\mathcal{E}^C_{\mathrm{TA}}[\![\ \mathtt{f}_{\mathrm{if}}(ue_1)(ue_2)(ue_3)\ ]\!] =\\ &(\mathtt{f}_{\mathrm{if}}[\mathtt{Bool}{\rightarrow}S(pt){\rightarrow}S(pt){\rightarrow}S(pt)](S(pe_1))(S(pe_2))(S(pe_3)),\ S(pt))\end{aligned}$$

for a bijection $S{:}TV{\rightarrow}TV$ (which is needed because the different invocations of $\mathcal{E}^C_{\mathrm{TA}}$ need not generate the *same* type variables in *corresponding* places). Hence the desired result follows from the cases that we have proved already. □

The correctness of the translation of programs now follows. In the formulation we shall make use of the type erasing function

$$\pi_{\text{TA}}: P(E,T) \rightarrow P(UE,T)$$

defined by

$$\pi_{\text{TA}}[\![\texttt{DEF } \texttt{x}_1 = e_1 \ \ldots \ \texttt{DEF } \texttt{x}_n = e_n \ \texttt{VAL } e \ \texttt{HAS } t]\!] =$$

$$\texttt{DEF } \texttt{x}_1 = \varepsilon_{\text{TA}}[\![e_1]\!] \ \ldots \ \texttt{DEF } \texttt{x}_n = \varepsilon_{\text{TA}}[\![e_n]\!] \ \texttt{VAL } \varepsilon_{\text{TA}}[\![e]\!] \ \texttt{HAS } t$$

Theorem 2.2.9 (Soundness and Completeness of $\mathcal{P}^C_{\text{TA}}$) Consider a program

$$up = \texttt{DEF } \texttt{x}_1 = ue_1 \ \ldots \ \texttt{DEF } \texttt{x}_n = ue_n \ \texttt{VAL } ue \ \texttt{HAS } t$$

and consider the outcome of $\mathcal{P}^C_{\text{TA}}[\![up]\!]$. If it produces the program

$$p = \texttt{DEF } \texttt{x}_1 = e_1 \ \ldots \ \texttt{DEF } \texttt{x}_n = e_n \ \texttt{VAL } e \ \texttt{HAS } t$$

then

- p is well-formed, i.e. $\vdash_C p$,
- the underlying program of p is up, i.e. $up = \pi_{\text{TA}}(p)$.

If $\mathcal{P}^C_{\text{TA}}[\![up]\!]$ fails then

- there is no well-formed program p in $P(E,T)$ that has up as its underlying program. □

Proof: This is a straightforward corollary of Proposition 2.2.8. □

If we compare the theorem with Proposition 2.2.8 we note that the soundness part, that $\mathcal{P}^C_{\text{TA}}[\![up]\!]$ is well-formed, is as we would expect because we have arranged it such that there are no type variables left in $\mathcal{P}^C_{\text{TA}}[\![up]\!]$ and hence there is no need to consider ground substitutions. The completeness part, that $\mathcal{P}^C_{\text{TA}}[\![up]\!]$ only fails if there are no well-formed programs, is slightly weaker than in Proposition 2.2.8 because we do not claim that *every* well-formed program may be obtained from $\mathcal{P}^C_{\text{TA}}[\![up]\!]$. This is the price to pay for having replaced type variables by `Void`; however, many properties of programs will be 'polymorphic invariant' (in the sense of [1]) and for these the 'arbitrariness' does not matter.

Bibliographical Notes

The original type analysis algorithm was developed by Milner in [57] and is related to work by Hindley [37]. The type analysis algorithm presented here is inspired by Chapter 1 in L. Damas' Ph.D.-thesis [23]. The formulation of soundness and completeness has much in common with the treatment in [1].

It is worth observing that the type inference system of Table 2.3 ensures that the expressions are monotyped; the use of polytypes (in the type analysis algorithm) is merely an aid in calculating the desired monotypes. It would be relatively easy to adapt the type inference algorithm so as to allow the DEF construct to introduce polymorphism. However, profound changes would then have to be made in the type inference system (not to speak of the development of the following chapters).

Our treatment of soundness and completeness is purely syntactic in that we did not consider any (denotational) semantics of the untyped or typed λ-calculus. This is contrary to the development of [57] where the untyped λ-calculus is given a denotational semantics and it is proved that 'well-typed programs do not go wrong'. Continuing along these lines, a series of papers have studied how to map types to the sets of semantic values described; this centers around non-empty and Scott-closed sets (called ideals in [53]). However, in this book we have taken the perspective that type analysis, as well as binding time analysis (Chapter 3) and combinator introduction (Chapter 4), is merely a preprocessing stage before developing our notion of parameterized semantics in Chapter 5.

A very brief appraisal of the material of this chapter may be found in [22].

Exercises

1. Use Table 2.3 to infer the type of the `sum` program.

2. Consider the following program computing the length of string lists

```
DEF reduce = λf.λu.fix(λg.λxs.
                         if isnil xs then u
                         else f (hd xs) (g (tl xs))
DEF sum = reduce (λx.λy.+(⟨x,y⟩)) (0)
DEF map = λf.reduce (λx.λxs.f(x):xs) (nil)
VAL λxs.sum (map (λx.1) (xs))
HAS String list → Int
```

- Infer the type of the various subexpressions, in particular determine the type of the two occurrences of `reduce`. Is the program well-formed according to Section 2.1?
- Duplicate the definition of `reduce` so that the program gets the form

```
DEF reduce1 = ···
DEF reduce2 = ···
DEF sum = reduce1 ···
DEF map = λf.reduce2 ···
VAL λxs.··· HAS ···
```

Annotate this program with type information. Is it well-formed?

3. (*) It is undesirable that the original length program from Exercise 2 is not well-formed. As suggested in Exercise 2 one approach might be to duplicate function definitions. Try to *modify* the development in Section 2.2 such that function definitions are duplicated as the need arises. How would you *formulate* soundness and completeness?

4. Prove that $tenv \vdash e{:}t$ is functional in $tenv$ and e, i.e. if $tenv \vdash e{:}t_1$ and $tenv \vdash e{:}t_2$ then $t_1 = t_2$. Observe that this holds for $tenv \vdash_C e{:}t$ as well. (Hint: use structural induction on e.)

5. Consider the algorithm

    INPUT: two polytypes pt_1 and pt_2
    OUTPUT: a substitution S or *fail*ure
    METHOD:
    S:=I; $X1$:=$pt1$; $X2$:=$pt2$;
    WHILE $X1 \neq X2$ DO
    D := the first node in a preorder traversal where $X1$ differs from $X2$;
    $Y1$:= the subtype of $X1$ starting at D;
    $Y2$:= the subtype of $X2$ starting at D;
    IF $Y2 \in TV \wedge Y1 \notin TV$ THEN $(Y1, Y2) := (Y2, Y1)$;
    IF $Y1 \notin TV \vee \mathrm{FTV}(Y2) \cap \mathrm{FTV}(Y1) \neq \emptyset$ THEN *fail*;
    $S := (\mathrm{I}[Y2/Y1]) \circ S$;
    $X1 := (\mathrm{I}[Y2/Y1])(X1)$;
    $X2 := (\mathrm{I}[Y2/Y1])(X2)$;

    Prove that this algorithm behaves as the algorithm $\mathcal{U}$ guaranteed by Lemma 2.2.3 (in the case of two inputs).

    To do so it may be helpful to show that

    $$(\mathcal{U}(\{pt_1,pt_2\}) \text{ exists if and only if } \mathcal{U}(\{X1,X2\}) \text{ exists) and}$$

    $$(\mathcal{U}(\{pt_1,pt_2\}) \text{ exists implies } \mathcal{U}(\{pt_1,pt_2\}) = \mathcal{U}(\{X1,X2\}) \circ S)$$

    is an invariant of the WHILE loop. Deduce that the algorithm behaves as $\mathcal{U}$ provided that it terminates. To show that the algorithm always terminates it suffices to show that $\mathrm{FTV}(X1) \cup \mathrm{FTV}(X2)$ decreases on each iteration.

6. Give an inductive definition of $\varepsilon_{\mathrm{TA}}{:}PE \to UE$ and note that this carries over to $\varepsilon_{\mathrm{TA}}{:}E \to UE$. Similarly define $\varepsilon'_{\mathrm{TA}}$.

7. Give an inductive definition of the free (expression) variables $\mathrm{FEV}(ue)$ in ue. Note that $\mathrm{FEV}(e)$ and $\mathrm{FEV}(pe)$ may be defined in much the same way. Give an inductive definition of $\mathcal{A}_{\mathrm{TA}}(pe)$.

8. Let $tenv\lceil X$ denote the type environment whose domain is $X \subseteq \text{dom}(tenv)$. Prove that if $tenv \vdash e : t$ and $tenv' = tenv\lceil\text{FEV}(e)$ then $tenv' \vdash e : t$.

9. Use the type analysis algorithm $\mathcal{P}_{\text{TA}}^{C}$ to compute the type of the `sum` program.

10. Prove that if $\mathcal{E}_{\text{TA}}^{C}[\![ue]\!] = (pe,pt)$ then $\text{FTV}(pt) \subseteq \text{FTV}(pe)$. (Hint: use structural induction on ue.)

11. Consider the clause for $\mathcal{E}_{\text{TA}}^{C}[\![$ `if` ue_1 `then` ue_2 `else` ue_3 $]\!]$ in Table 2.5. A possible modification is to replace the last two lines by:

    let $S_2 = \mathcal{U}(\{S_1(pt_2),\ S_1(pt_3)\})$

    in (`if` $S_2(pe_1)$ `then` $S_2(pe_2)$ `else` $S_2(pe_3)$, $S_2(pt_2)$)

    Discuss whether or not this makes a difference (modulo a bijective renaming of type variables).

12. In this exercise we extend the typed λ-calculus with notation for binary trees. Types are given by

    $t ::= \cdots \mid t$ `tree`

    and expressions are given by

    $e ::= \cdots \mid$ `value` $e \mid$ `left` $e \mid$ `right` $e \mid$ `isatom` $e \mid$ `atom` $e \mid e_1{::}e_2$

    For us a binary tree may be a leaf (or atom) e with some data value `value` e, or it may be an internal node e with a left son `left` e, and a right son `right` e; the expression `isatom` e indicates which of the two cases that applies. A tree with just one node is constructed by `atom` e whereas two trees are grafted together using the notation $e_1{::}e_2$.

    - Extend the well-formedness rules of Table 2.3.
    - Extend the type analysis algorithm of Tables 2.4 and 2.5.

13. In this exercise we extend the typed λ-calculus with a monomorphic `let` expression. The syntax is

    $e ::= \mid$ `let` $\mathtt{x_i}{=}e_1$ `in` e_2

    and the intention is that `let` $\mathtt{x_i}{=}e_1$ `in` e_2 behaves as $(\lambda\mathtt{x_i}[\cdots].e_2)(e_1)$.

    - Extend the well-formedness rules of Table 2.3.
    - Extend the type analysis algorithm of Tables 2.4 and 2.5.

    Note that all occurrences of $\mathtt{x_i}$ in e_2 must have the same monotype; briefly discuss the complications that would arise from lifting this restriction.

14. As a modification of the previous exercise consider the construct `letrec` $\mathtt{x_i}=e_1$ `in` e_2 where any occurrence of $\mathtt{x_i}$ in e_1 recursively refers to the $\mathtt{x_i}$ being defined. Repeat Exercise 13 for this construct.

Chapter 3

Binding Time Made Explicit

Neither Miranda, Standard ML nor the enriched λ-calculus has an explicit distinction between kinds of binding times. However, for higher-order functions we can distinguish between the parameters that are available and those that are not. In standard compiler terminology this corresponds to the distinction between compile-time and run-time. The idea is now to capture this implicit distinction between binding times and then to annotate the operations of the enriched λ-calculus accordingly.

In this chapter we present such a development for the enriched λ-calculus by defining a so-called *2-level λ-calculus*. To be precise, Section 3.1 first presents the syntax of the *2*-level λ-calculus and the accompanying explanations indicate how it may carry over to more than two levels or a base language different from the typed λ-calculus. Next we present well-formedness conditions for *2*-level λ-expressions and again we sketch the more general setting. Of the many well-formedness definitions that are possible we choose one that interacts well with the approach to combinator introduction to be presented in Chapter 4. Section 3.2 then studies how to transform binding time information (in the form of *2*-level types) into an already typed λ-expression. This transformation complements the transformation developed in Section 2.2.

3.1 The *2*-Level λ-Calculus

We shall use the types of functions to record when their parameters will be available and their results produced. For the program $\texttt{sum}_t$ of Chapter 2 it is clear that the list parameter is not available at compile-time and we shall record this by *underlining* the corresponding component of the type:

$$\texttt{Sum}_t = \underline{\texttt{Int}}\ \underline{\texttt{list}} \rightarrow \underline{\texttt{int}}$$

The fact that the argument list is not available at compile-time will have consequences for when the parameters are available for `reduce`. Again we shall record

$t \in T2$

$t ::= \mathtt{A_i} \mid \underline{\mathtt{A_i}} \mid t{\times}t \mid t\,\underline{\times}\,t \mid t{\rightarrow}t \mid t\,\underline{\rightarrow}\,t \mid t\ \mathtt{list} \mid t\ \underline{\mathtt{list}}$

$e \in E2$

$$\begin{aligned} e ::= {} & \mathtt{f_i}[t] \mid \underline{\mathtt{f_i}}[t] \mid \langle e,e\rangle \mid \underline{\langle} e,e\underline{\rangle} \mid \mathtt{fst}\ e \mid \underline{\mathtt{fst}}\ e \mid \mathtt{snd}\ e \mid \underline{\mathtt{snd}}\ e \mid \\ & \lambda\mathtt{x_i}[t].e \mid \underline{\lambda}\mathtt{x_i}[t].e \mid e(e) \mid e\underline{(}e\underline{)} \mid \mathtt{x_i} \mid \\ & e{:}e \mid e\,\underline{:}\,e \mid \mathtt{nil}[t] \mid \underline{\mathtt{nil}}[t] \mid \mathtt{hd}\ e \mid \underline{\mathtt{hd}}\ e \mid \mathtt{tl}\ e \mid \underline{\mathtt{tl}}\ e \mid \\ & \mathtt{isnil}\ e \mid \underline{\mathtt{isnil}}\ e \mid \mathtt{true} \mid \underline{\mathtt{true}} \mid \mathtt{false} \mid \underline{\mathtt{false}} \mid \\ & \mathtt{if}\ e\ \mathtt{then}\ e\ \mathtt{else}\ e \mid \underline{\mathtt{if}}\ e\ \underline{\mathtt{then}}\ e\ \underline{\mathtt{else}}\ e \mid \mathtt{fix}\ e \mid \underline{\mathtt{fix}}\ e \end{aligned}$$

Table 3.1: The *2*-level λ-calculus

this by underlining parts of the type:

$$\mathtt{Reduce_t} = (\mathtt{Int}{\rightarrow}\mathtt{Int}{\rightarrow}\mathtt{Int}){\rightarrow}\mathtt{Int}{\rightarrow}\ \underline{\mathtt{Int}}\ \underline{\mathtt{list}}\ {\rightarrow}\mathtt{Int}$$

Both $\mathtt{Sum_t}$ and $\mathtt{Reduce_t}$ are examples of what we shall call *2-level types.*

This motivates defining the syntax of the *2*-level λ-calculus as indicated in Table 3.1. Here we have two constructs for each construct in the typed λ-calculus of Table 2.1 on which we are based: one underlined construct and one construct that is not underlined[1]. Underlining indicates the non-availability of data, that is run-time entities, and non-underlining indicates availability of data, that is compile-time entities. One exception to this rule is that we have only one kind of variables; this is because a variable merely acts as a placeholder for the enclosing (underlined or non-underlined) λ-abstraction.

To prepare for the well-formedness rules and for the binding time analysis in Section 3.2, it is helpful to expand on the methodology behind the construction of the *2*-level λ-calculus. It should be clear that it is based upon two underlying notions: One is the underlying base language which in our case is the typed λ-calculus as presented in Chapter 2. In general we just imagine a typed language L, that is a language with types and expressions.

The other general notion is the distinction between when values are available. We have used the terminology 'compile-time' versus 'run-time' but other presentations of essentially the same material sometimes use the terminology 'early' versus 'late', 'known' versus 'unknown' or 'static' versus 'dynamic'. Writing $\mathtt{c}$ for compile-time and $\mathtt{r}$ for run-time we have the picture in Figure 3.1. Here $\mathtt{r}$ is below $\mathtt{c}$ because compile-time takes place before run-time and we imagine that this intuition is formalised by a partial order $\preceq$ with $\mathtt{r}{\preceq}\mathtt{c}$[2]. In general, the distinction between when values are available is a distinction between *binding times.* So if we

[1] In some papers overlining is used instead of 'non-underlining'.

[2] One is of course free to use a dual ordering instead; however, in terms of Scott's notion of information content it seems fair to say that 'compile-time' entities yield more information than 'run-time' entities, hence $\mathtt{r}{\preceq}\mathtt{c}$.

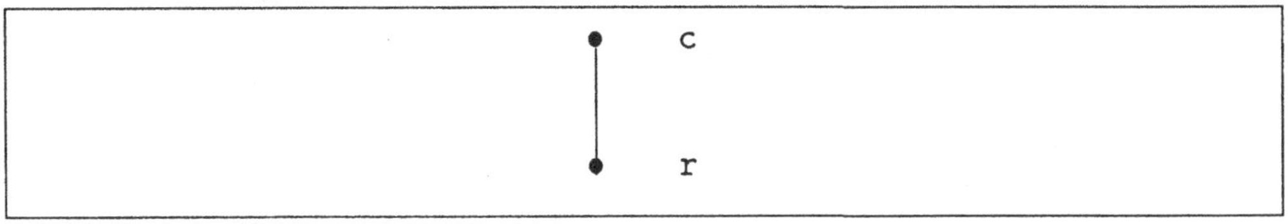

Figure 3.1: The structure of *2* binding times

are to consider a more general setup we will assume that there is a partially ordered set $B=(B,\preceq)$ of binding times $b\in B$ with $b_1\preceq b_2$ whenever b_2 takes place before b_1. Using the common mathematical practice of writing *2* for any two-element set[3] we shall write *2* for the partially ordered set depicted in Figure 3.1, i.e. the elements are r and c and the partial order $\preceq$ is given by r$\preceq$r, r$\preceq$c and c$\preceq$c.

One may then define the following general procedure for constructing the syntax of the B-level language L. The *2*-level λ-calculus is obtained by taking B to be the partial order in Figure 3.1 and by letting L be the typed λ-calculus. For types, the procedure is:

> For each type formation rule $t::=\phi(t_1,...,t_n)$ in L and for each binding time $b\in B$ we add the rule $t::=\phi^b(t_1,...,t_n)$ to the types TB of the B-level language L.

In Table 3.1 we have written ϕ for $\phi^{\mathtt{c}}$ and $\underline{\phi}$ for $\phi^{\mathtt{r}}$ in order to obtain a more readable syntax. For expressions, the procedure is:

> For each expression formation rule $e::=\phi(t_1,...,t_n,e_1,...,e_m)$ in L and for each binding time $b\in B$ we add the rule $e::=\phi^b(t_1,...,t_n,e_1,...,e_m)$ to the expressions TE of the B-level language L.

This would result in two kinds of variables, written $\mathbf{x}_i$ and $\underline{\mathbf{x}}_i$, but in Table 3.1 we have written both as $\mathbf{x}_i$. As we are mostly interested in closed expressions, that is expressions without free variables, each occurrence of a variable $\mathbf{x}_i$ will have a unique defining occurrence of the form $\lambda\mathbf{x}_i[t]$ or $\underline{\lambda}\mathbf{x}_i[t]$. The intention is that $\mathbf{x}_i$ has the same binding time information as the corresponding λ has, just as the intention is that $\mathbf{x}_i$ has the type t listed in connection with the corresponding λ. Thus little or no generality is lost by having only one kind of variables.

As we will also be using programs with the *2*-level λ-calculus we should remark that we view the programs as something built on top of the *2*-level λ-calculus and, in general, on top of the B-level language L. As a consequence, if the language L already has a notion of programs then we are only interested in the programs corresponding to the binding time $b\in B$ given by the requirement that b is the greatest element in B (assuming that such an element exists).

[3] In some approaches to numbers (e.g. [34]) a non-negative number n is built as the set of all the non-negative numbers below it. So *0* is the empty set, i.e. *0*$=\emptyset$, *1* is the set having *0* as its only element, i.e. *1*$=\{\emptyset\}$, *2* is the set having *0* and *1* as elements, i.e. *2*$=\{\emptyset,\{\emptyset\}\}$, etc.

To relate the *2*-level types, *2*-level expressions and *2*-level programs to the types, expressions and programs of the previous chapter, it is helpful to have the transformation functions

$$\tau_{\mathrm{BTA}}\colon T2 \to T$$

$$\varepsilon_{\mathrm{BTA}}\colon E2 \to E$$

$$\pi_{\mathrm{BTA}}\colon P(E2,T2) \to P(E,T)$$

which simply remove the underlinings. Similarly, we shall occasionally need the transformation functions

$$\tau^{b}_{\mathrm{BTA}}\colon T \to T2$$

$$\varepsilon^{b}_{\mathrm{BTA}}\colon E \to E2$$

$$\pi^{b}_{\mathrm{BTA}}\colon P(E,T) \to P(E2,T2)$$

which annotate each (relevant) symbol with the binding time information b. As usual, we may record annotations with `r` by underlinings and annotations with `c` by the absence of underlining.

Well-formedness of *2*-level types

The well-formedness conditions of the *2*-level λ-calculus are based on the well-formedness conditions of the underlying typed λ-calculus (as presented in Chapter 2). In addition to ensuring that the type information agrees, we must now also ensure that the binding time information agrees, and a consequence of this is that well-formedness of the types themselves becomes of interest.

To motivate our definition of a *well-formed* *2*-level type we need to take a closer look at the interplay between the compile-time level and the run-time level. Thinking in terms of a compiler it is quite clear that at compile-time we can manipulate pieces of code (to be executed at run-time) but we cannot manipulate entities computed at run-time. Hence at compile-time we cannot directly manipulate objects of type $\underline{\mathtt{Int}}\ \underline{\mathtt{list}}$ whereas we can manipulate objects of type $\underline{\mathtt{Int}}\ \underline{\mathtt{list}}\ \underline{\to}\ \underline{\mathtt{Int}}$ because the latter type may be regarded as the type of code for functions (to be executed at run-time). So $\mathtt{Int} \to \underline{\mathtt{Int}}\ \underline{\mathtt{list}}\ \underline{\to}\ \underline{\mathtt{Int}}$ will be the type of a function that given an integer at compile-time will produce a piece of code that has to be executed at run-time. Similarly $\underline{\mathtt{Int}}\ \underline{\to}\ \underline{\mathtt{Int}}\ \underline{\mathtt{list}}\ \underline{\to}\ \underline{\mathtt{Int}}$ will be the type of a function to be executed at run-time whereas $\mathtt{Int} \to \mathtt{Int}\ \mathtt{list} \to \mathtt{Int}$ will be the type of a function to be executed at compile-time.

Informally, the idea is that an 'all underlined' function type will always be well-formed; it will be called a *frontier type*. Furthermore, a type with no underlinings whatsoever will also be well-formed; it will be called a *pure type*. The well-formed compile-time types are then built from frontier types and pure types using the

$$
\begin{array}{l}
\mathtt{Reduce}_1 = (\mathtt{Int}\rightarrow\mathtt{Int}\rightarrow\mathtt{Int}) \rightarrow \mathtt{Int} \rightarrow \mathtt{Int\ list} \rightarrow \mathtt{Int}\\
\mathtt{Reduce}_2 = (\mathtt{Int}\rightarrow\underline{\mathtt{Int}\rightarrow\mathtt{Int}}) \rightarrow \mathtt{Int} \rightarrow \mathtt{Int\ list} \rightarrow \mathtt{Int}\\
\mathtt{Reduce}_3 = (\mathtt{Int}\rightarrow\mathtt{Int}\rightarrow\mathtt{Int}) \rightarrow \mathtt{Int} \rightarrow \underline{\mathtt{Int}}\ \underline{\mathtt{list}}\ \underline{\rightarrow}\ \underline{\mathtt{Int}}\\
\mathtt{Reduce}_4 = (\underline{\mathtt{Int}\rightarrow\mathtt{Int}\rightarrow\mathtt{Int}}) \rightarrow \mathtt{Int} \rightarrow \mathtt{Int\ list} \rightarrow \mathtt{Int}\\
\mathtt{Reduce}_5 = (\mathtt{Int}\rightarrow\underline{\mathtt{Int}\rightarrow\mathtt{Int}}) \rightarrow \mathtt{Int} \rightarrow \underline{\mathtt{Int}}\ \underline{\mathtt{list}}\ \underline{\rightarrow}\ \underline{\mathtt{Int}}\\
\mathtt{Reduce}_6 = (\mathtt{Int}\rightarrow\mathtt{Int}\rightarrow\mathtt{Int}) \rightarrow \underline{\mathtt{Int}}\ \underline{\rightarrow}\ \underline{\mathtt{Int}}\ \underline{\mathtt{list}}\ \underline{\rightarrow}\ \underline{\mathtt{Int}}\\
\mathtt{Reduce}_7 = (\underline{\mathtt{Int}\rightarrow\mathtt{Int}\rightarrow\mathtt{Int}}) \rightarrow \mathtt{Int} \rightarrow \underline{\mathtt{Int}}\ \underline{\mathtt{list}}\ \underline{\rightarrow}\ \underline{\mathtt{Int}}\\
\mathtt{Reduce}_8 = (\mathtt{Int}\rightarrow\underline{\mathtt{Int}\rightarrow\mathtt{Int}}) \rightarrow \underline{\mathtt{Int}}\ \underline{\rightarrow}\ \underline{\mathtt{Int}}\ \underline{\mathtt{list}}\ \underline{\rightarrow}\ \underline{\mathtt{Int}}\\
\mathtt{Reduce}_9 = (\underline{\mathtt{Int}\rightarrow\mathtt{Int}\rightarrow\mathtt{Int}}) \rightarrow \underline{\mathtt{Int}}\ \underline{\rightarrow}\ \underline{\mathtt{Int}}\ \underline{\mathtt{list}}\ \underline{\rightarrow}\ \underline{\mathtt{Int}}\\
\mathtt{Reduce}_{10} = (\underline{\mathtt{Int}\rightarrow\mathtt{Int}\rightarrow\mathtt{Int}})\ \underline{\rightarrow}\ \underline{\mathtt{Int}}\ \underline{\rightarrow}\ \underline{\mathtt{Int}}\ \underline{\mathtt{list}}\ \underline{\rightarrow}\ \underline{\mathtt{Int}}
\end{array}
$$

Table 3.2: Well-formed 2-level types for `reduce`

type constructors →, × and `list`. As an example consider the type of $\mathtt{sum}_t$; here we have two well-formed 2-level types

$$
\begin{array}{l}
\mathtt{Sum}_1 = \mathtt{Int\ list} \rightarrow \mathtt{Int}\\
\mathtt{Sum}_2 = \underline{\mathtt{Int}}\ \underline{\mathtt{list}}\ \underline{\rightarrow}\ \underline{\mathtt{Int}}
\end{array}
$$

For the type of `reduce` we have the ten well-formed 2-level types shown in Table 3.2.

Formally, well-formedness of types is given by a well-formedness relation

$$\vdash t : b$$

saying that t is a well-formed type of binding time b. The typed λ-calculus might be regarded as having just a single binding time and so it may seem surprising that it had no well-formedness relation $\vdash t$. The reason is that the natural rules and axioms would be

$$\vdash \mathtt{A}_i \qquad \frac{\vdash t_1 \quad \vdash t_2}{\vdash t_1 \times t_2} \qquad \frac{\vdash t_1 \quad \vdash t_2}{\vdash t_1 \rightarrow t_2} \qquad \frac{\vdash t}{\vdash t\ \mathtt{list}}$$

and so $\vdash t$ is always true. In the case of 2-level types, well-formedness is more discriminating as we shall see and thus there is a real need for a well-formedness relation.

The first eight rules and axioms in Table 3.3 simply follow the structure of the type t. The last rule then allows types of different binding times to be mixed. It simply says that a well-formed run-time function type may be manipulated at compile-time. To motivate the rule we shall mention two potential generalizations that we decided *not* to incorporate. One is

$$\frac{\vdash t : \mathtt{r}}{\vdash t : \mathtt{c}}$$

$[\underline{\mathtt{A}}]$	$\vdash \underline{\mathtt{A}_i} : \mathtt{r}$	$[\mathtt{A}]$	$\vdash \mathtt{A}_i : \mathtt{c}$
$[\underline{\times}]$	$\dfrac{\vdash t_1 : \mathtt{r} \quad \vdash t_2 : \mathtt{r}}{\vdash t_1 \underline{\times} t_2 : \mathtt{r}}$	$[\times]$	$\dfrac{\vdash t_1 : \mathtt{c} \quad \vdash t_2 : \mathtt{c}}{\vdash t_1 \times t_2 : \mathtt{c}}$
$[\underline{\rightarrow}]$	$\dfrac{\vdash t_1 : \mathtt{r} \quad \vdash t_2 : \mathtt{r}}{\vdash t_1 \underline{\rightarrow} t_2 : \mathtt{r}}$	$[\rightarrow]$	$\dfrac{\vdash t_1 : \mathtt{c} \quad \vdash t_2 : \mathtt{c}}{\vdash t_1 \rightarrow t_2 : \mathtt{c}}$
$[\underline{\mathtt{list}}]$	$\dfrac{\vdash t : \mathtt{r}}{\vdash t\ \underline{\mathtt{list}} : \mathtt{r}}$	$[\mathtt{list}]$	$\dfrac{\vdash t : \mathtt{c}}{\vdash t\ \mathtt{list} : \mathtt{c}}$
[up]	$\dfrac{\vdash t_1 \underline{\rightarrow} t_2 : \mathtt{r}}{\vdash t_1 \underline{\rightarrow} t_2 : \mathtt{c}}$		

Table 3.3: Well-formedness of the *2*-level types

where t is not restrained to be of the form $t_1 \underline{\rightarrow} t_2$. We reject this because $t_1 \underline{\rightarrow} t_2$:c, unlike e.g. $t_1 \underline{\times} t_2$:c, may be regarded as *code* for some machine and using the analogies from compiler construction it is clear that a compiler may (indeed should) manipulate code, i.e. entities of type $t_1 \underline{\rightarrow} t_2$:c, but that it may not manipulate other entities 'living' at run-time, e.g. entities of type $t_1 \underline{\times} t_2$:c.

Another rule we decided *not* to incorporate is of the form

$$\dfrac{\vdash \cdots t \cdots : \mathtt{c}}{\vdash \cdots t \cdots : \mathtt{r}}$$

This may be a more debatable choice but we shall see in Chapters 5 and 7 that compile-time types will be interpreted as structures called domains and that it will often be useful to interpret run-time types as enriched structures called algebraic lattices; since not all domains are algebraic lattices it would seem justified not to regard all compile-time types as being run-time types.

Example 3.1.1 Returning to the types considered for the `reduce` function, we shall show that

$$\mathtt{Reduce}_3 = (\mathtt{Int}\rightarrow\mathtt{Int}\rightarrow\mathtt{Int})\rightarrow\mathtt{Int}\rightarrow\underline{\mathtt{Int}}\ \underline{\mathtt{list}\rightarrow\mathtt{Int}}$$

is a well-formed type and that

$$\mathtt{Reduce}_t = (\mathtt{Int}\rightarrow\mathtt{Int}\rightarrow\mathtt{Int})\rightarrow\mathtt{Int}\rightarrow\underline{\mathtt{Int}}\ \underline{\mathtt{list}}\rightarrow\mathtt{Int}$$

is not. The well-formedness of $\mathtt{Reduce}_3$, i.e.

$$\vdash \mathtt{Reduce}_3 : \mathtt{c}$$

is a straightforward application of the rules in Table 3.3 using the rule [up] just once. It is harder to show the non-well-formedness of $\mathtt{Reduce}_t$, i.e.

$$\neg\exists b \in \{\mathtt{r},\mathtt{c}\}\colon \vdash \mathtt{Reduce}_t : b$$

because one has, in principle, to consider an infinite set of deductions using the rules in Table 3.3. However, the only rule that would allow us to prove a statement of the form $\vdash t_1 \rightarrow t_2{:}b$ is $[\rightarrow]$ and we see that then $b{=}\mathtt{c}$. So if $\vdash$**Reduce**$_t$:c then also $\vdash$Int→Int→Int:c and $\vdash$Int→<u>Int list→</u>Int:c. Repeating this argument we see that $\vdash$Int:c and $\vdash$(<u>Int list</u>)→Int:c. Repeating the argument once more we see the need for $\vdash$(<u>Int list</u>):c. However, none of [<u>A</u>], [<u>×</u>], [<u>→</u>] or [<u>list</u>] are applicable because of the c, and none of [A], [×], [→], [list] or [up] are applicable because of the form of <u>Int list</u>. We thus have a contradiction and conclude that **Reduce**$_t$ is not well-formed. □

The more we get into the actual details of the 2-level λ-calculus the harder it is to give a similar development at the level of a B-level language L and in particular the harder it gets to motivate the decisions made. However, we do wish to stress that our definition of the 2-level λ-calculus is a *variation on a theme* and that other variations may be studied in contexts where other intuitions or concepts from computer science need to be taken into account. So to stress this view we shall continue, in this section, to *sketch* the form of the general construction.

For each well-formedness rule or axiom

$$[\mathrm{R}] \quad \frac{\vdash t_1 \quad \cdots \quad \vdash t_n}{\vdash \phi(t_1,\cdots,t_n)}$$

for types in L, and for each binding time $b{\in}B$, we add the rule or axiom

$$[\mathrm{R}^b] \quad \frac{\vdash \underline{t_1}{:}b \quad \cdots \quad \vdash \underline{t_n}{:}b}{\vdash \phi^b(t_1,\cdots,t_n){:}b}$$

(This is harder if side conditions are present.) Finally, we add the rule for relating the binding times

$$[\mathrm{up}] \quad \frac{\vdash \phi^b(t_1,\cdots,t_n){:}b}{\vdash \phi^b(t_1,\cdots,t_n){:}b'} \quad \text{if } \phi{\in}\Phi \wedge b{\neq}b' \wedge b{\preceq}b'$$

where Φ is a fixed set of type constructors.

In our case $\Phi{=}\{\rightarrow\}$ and $b{\neq}b'{\wedge}b{\preceq}b'$ automatically means $b{=}\mathtt{r}$ and $b'{=}\mathtt{c}$. It should thus be clear that an important property of the general construction is that whenever $\vdash t : b$ holds in TB then we expect that $\vdash \tau_{\mathrm{BTA}}(t)$ holds in T.

Well-formedness of 2-level expressions

The well-formedness of expressions is formalised by a well-formedness relation of the form

$$tenv \vdash e : t : b$$

This says that the expression e has type t and that the type t has binding time b. In most cases the binding time b is uniquely determined by the type t but when t is of the form $t_1 \underline{\rightarrow} t_2$ both $b=\mathtt{c}$ and $b=\mathtt{r}$ may be possible and the explicit occurrence of the intended b will then be used to restrict the use of the type t as we shall see below. Intuitively, the idea is to regard $tenv \vdash e : t : b$ as a judgement in a 'b-context', i.e. a 'compile-time context' when $b=\mathtt{c}$ and a 'run-time context' when $b=\mathtt{r}$. To make the technical definitions possible the type environment $tenv$ is a map from a finite set of variables to pairs consisting of a type and a binding time. The definition is given in Tables 3.4 and 3.5 and all but the last two rules in Table 3.5 simply follow the structure of the expression e much as in Table 2.3 for the typed λ-calculus. In other words, except for the last two rules in Table 3.5, we just have two copies of the rules in Table 2.3.

The last two rules are of interest whenever we have a judgement of the form $tenv \vdash e : t_1 \underline{\rightarrow} t_2 : b$ because they allow to change $b=\mathtt{c}$ to $b=\mathtt{r}$ and (under certain conditions) to change $b=\mathtt{r}$ to $b=\mathtt{c}$. Rule [down] thus allows to transfer a judgement in a compile-time context to the same judgement in a run-time context. Intuitively, this may be regarded as allowing a piece of code to be executed at run-time. Rule [up] then allows to transform a judgement in a run-time context back into a compile-time context. Intuitively, this means that a computation at run-time may be encapsulated as a piece of code that the compiler may manipulate. For this to be sensible the piece of code may not contain explicit references to other run-time data and this is expressed by the side-condition to rule [up].

Example 3.1.2 To illustrate the rules [up] and [down] we shall consider the *2*-level λ-expressions

$$\Psi^{-1} = \lambda\mathtt{x}[(\underline{\mathtt{A}\rightarrow\mathtt{A}})\underline{\rightarrow}(\underline{\mathtt{A}\rightarrow\mathtt{A}})].\ \lambda\mathtt{y}[\underline{\mathtt{A}\rightarrow\mathtt{A}}].\ \mathtt{x}\underline{(}\mathtt{y}\underline{)}$$

$$\Psi = \lambda\mathtt{x}[(\underline{\mathtt{A}\rightarrow\mathtt{A}})\rightarrow(\underline{\mathtt{A}\rightarrow\mathtt{A}})].\ \underline{\lambda}\mathtt{y}[\underline{\mathtt{A}\rightarrow\mathtt{A}}].\ \mathtt{x}(\mathtt{y})$$

of intended type

$$t_{\Psi^{-1}} = ((\underline{\mathtt{A}\rightarrow\mathtt{A}})\underline{\rightarrow}(\underline{\mathtt{A}\rightarrow\mathtt{A}})) \rightarrow ((\underline{\mathtt{A}\rightarrow\mathtt{A}})\rightarrow(\underline{\mathtt{A}\rightarrow\mathtt{A}}))$$

$$t_{\Psi} = ((\underline{\mathtt{A}\rightarrow\mathtt{A}})\rightarrow(\underline{\mathtt{A}\rightarrow\mathtt{A}})) \rightarrow ((\underline{\mathtt{A}\rightarrow\mathtt{A}})\underline{\rightarrow}(\underline{\mathtt{A}\rightarrow\mathtt{A}}))$$

First we show that Ψ^{-1} is a well-formed expression of type $t_{\Psi^{-1}}$. To be precise we show that

$$\emptyset \vdash \Psi^{-1} : t_{\Psi^{-1}} : \mathtt{c}$$

By using $[\lambda]$ twice we see that it is sufficient to show that

$$tenv \vdash \mathtt{x}\underline{(}\mathtt{y}\underline{)} : \underline{\mathtt{A}\rightarrow\mathtt{A}} : \mathtt{c}$$

for $tenv = \emptyset[((\underline{\mathtt{A}\rightarrow\mathtt{A}})\underline{\rightarrow}(\underline{\mathtt{A}\rightarrow\mathtt{A}}):\mathtt{c})/\mathtt{x}][(\underline{\mathtt{A}\rightarrow\mathtt{A}}:\mathtt{c})/\mathtt{y}]$. Using [x] and [down] we get

$[\underline{\mathtt{f}}]$	$tenv \vdash \underline{\mathtt{f}}_{\mathrm{i}}[t] : t : \mathtt{r} \quad \text{if} \vdash t : \mathtt{r}$
$[\mathtt{f}]$	$tenv \vdash \mathtt{f}_{\mathrm{i}}[t] : t : \mathtt{c} \quad \text{if} \vdash t : \mathtt{c}$
$[\underline{\langle\rangle}]$	$\dfrac{tenv \vdash e_1 : t_1 : \mathtt{r} \qquad tenv \vdash e_2 : t_2 : \mathtt{r}}{tenv \vdash \underline{\langle} e_1,e_2 \underline{\rangle} : t_1 \underline{\times} t_2 : \mathtt{r}}$
$[\langle\rangle]$	$\dfrac{tenv \vdash e_1 : t_1 : \mathtt{c} \qquad tenv \vdash e_2 : t_2 : \mathtt{c}}{tenv \vdash \langle e_1,e_2 \rangle : t_1 \times t_2 : \mathtt{c}}$
$[\underline{\mathtt{fst}}]$	$\dfrac{tenv \vdash e : t_1 \underline{\times} t_2 : \mathtt{r}}{tenv \vdash \underline{\mathtt{fst}}\ e : t_1 : \mathtt{r}}$
$[\mathtt{fst}]$	$\dfrac{tenv \vdash e : t_1 \times t_2 : \mathtt{c}}{tenv \vdash \mathtt{fst}\ e : t_1 : \mathtt{c}}$
$[\underline{\mathtt{snd}}]$	$\dfrac{tenv \vdash e : t_1 \underline{\times} t_2 : \mathtt{r}}{tenv \vdash \underline{\mathtt{snd}}\ e : t_2 : \mathtt{r}}$
$[\mathtt{snd}]$	$\dfrac{tenv \vdash e : t_1 \times t_2 : \mathtt{c}}{tenv \vdash \mathtt{snd}\ e : t_2 : \mathtt{c}}$
$[\underline{\lambda}]$	$\dfrac{tenv[(t'{:}\mathtt{r})/\mathbf{x}_{\mathrm{i}}] \vdash e : t : \mathtt{r}}{tenv \vdash \underline{\lambda}\mathbf{x}_{\mathrm{i}}[t'].e : t' \underline{\rightarrow} t : \mathtt{r}} \quad \text{if} \vdash t' : \mathtt{r}$
$[\lambda]$	$\dfrac{tenv[(t'{:}\mathtt{c})/\mathbf{x}_{\mathrm{i}}] \vdash e : t : \mathtt{c}}{tenv \vdash \lambda\mathbf{x}_{\mathrm{i}}[t'].e : t' \rightarrow t : \mathtt{c}} \quad \text{if} \vdash t' : \mathtt{c}$
$[\underline{()}]$	$\dfrac{tenv \vdash e_1 : t' \underline{\rightarrow} t : \mathtt{r} \qquad tenv \vdash e_2 : t' : \mathtt{r}}{tenv \vdash e_1 \underline{(} e_2 \underline{)} : t : \mathtt{r}}$
$[()]$	$\dfrac{tenv \vdash e_1 : t' \rightarrow t : \mathtt{c} \qquad tenv \vdash e_2 : t' : \mathtt{c}}{tenv \vdash e_1 (e_2) : t : \mathtt{c}}$
$[\mathbf{x}]$	$tenv \vdash \mathbf{x}_{\mathrm{i}} : t : b \quad \text{if } (\mathbf{x}_{\mathrm{i}},(t{:}b)) \in \mathrm{graph}(tenv) \wedge \vdash t{:}b$
$[\underline{:}]$	$\dfrac{tenv \vdash e_1 : t : \mathtt{r} \qquad tenv \vdash e_2 : t\ \underline{\mathtt{list}} : \mathtt{r}}{tenv \vdash e_1 \underline{:} e_2 : t\ \underline{\mathtt{list}} : \mathtt{r}}$
$[:]$	$\dfrac{tenv \vdash e_1 : t : \mathtt{c} \qquad tenv \vdash e_2 : t\ \mathtt{list} : \mathtt{c}}{tenv \vdash e_1 : e_2 : t\ \mathtt{list} : \mathtt{c}}$
$[\underline{\mathtt{nil}}]$	$tenv \vdash \underline{\mathtt{nil}}[t] : t\ \underline{\mathtt{list}} : \mathtt{r} \quad \text{if} \vdash t : \mathtt{r}$
$[\mathtt{nil}]$	$tenv \vdash \mathtt{nil}[t] : t\ \mathtt{list} : \mathtt{c} \quad \text{if} \vdash t : \mathtt{c}$
$[\underline{\mathtt{hd}}]$	$\dfrac{tenv \vdash e : t\ \underline{\mathtt{list}} : \mathtt{r}}{tenv \vdash \underline{\mathtt{hd}}\ e : t : \mathtt{r}}$
$[\mathtt{hd}]$	$\dfrac{tenv \vdash e : t\ \mathtt{list} : \mathtt{c}}{tenv \vdash \mathtt{hd}\ e : t : \mathtt{c}}$
$[\underline{\mathtt{tl}}]$	$\dfrac{tenv \vdash e : t\ \underline{\mathtt{list}} : \mathtt{r}}{tenv \vdash \underline{\mathtt{tl}}\ e : t\ \underline{\mathtt{list}} : \mathtt{r}}$
$[\mathtt{tl}]$	$\dfrac{tenv \vdash e : t\ \mathtt{list} : \mathtt{c}}{tenv \vdash \mathtt{tl}\ e : t\ \mathtt{list} : \mathtt{c}}$

Table 3.4: Well-formedness of the 2-level λ-calculus (part 1)

$$tenv \vdash \mathbf{x} : (\underline{\mathtt{A}\rightarrow\mathtt{A}})\underline{\rightarrow}(\underline{\mathtt{A}\rightarrow\mathtt{A}}) : \mathtt{r}$$

$[\underline{\texttt{isnil}}]$	$\dfrac{tenv \vdash e : t\ \underline{\texttt{list}} : \texttt{r}}{tenv \vdash \underline{\texttt{isnil}}\ e : \underline{\texttt{Bool}} : \texttt{r}}$
$[\texttt{isnil}]$	$\dfrac{tenv \vdash e : t\ \texttt{list} : \texttt{c}}{tenv \vdash \texttt{isnil}\ e : \texttt{Bool} : \texttt{c}}$
$[\underline{\texttt{true}}]$	$tenv \vdash \underline{\texttt{true}} : \underline{\texttt{Bool}} : \texttt{r}$
$[\texttt{true}]$	$tenv \vdash \texttt{true} : \texttt{Bool} : \texttt{c}$
$[\underline{\texttt{false}}]$	$tenv \vdash \underline{\texttt{false}} : \underline{\texttt{Bool}} : \texttt{r}$
$[\texttt{false}]$	$tenv \vdash \texttt{false} : \texttt{Bool} : \texttt{c}$
$[\underline{\texttt{if}}]$	$\dfrac{tenv \vdash e_1 : \underline{\texttt{Bool}} : \texttt{r} \quad tenv \vdash e_2 : t : \texttt{r} \quad tenv \vdash e_3 : t : \texttt{r}}{tenv \vdash \underline{\texttt{if}}\ e_1\ \underline{\texttt{then}}\ e_2\ \underline{\texttt{else}}\ e_3 : t : \texttt{r}}$
$[\texttt{if}]$	$\dfrac{tenv \vdash e_1 : \texttt{Bool} : \texttt{c} \quad tenv \vdash e_2 : t : \texttt{c} \quad tenv \vdash e_3 : t : \texttt{c}}{tenv \vdash \texttt{if}\ e_1\ \texttt{then}\ e_2\ \texttt{else}\ e_3 : t : \texttt{c}}$
$[\underline{\texttt{fix}}]$	$\dfrac{tenv \vdash e : t \underline{\rightarrow} t : \texttt{r}}{tenv \vdash \underline{\texttt{fix}}\ e : t : \texttt{r}}$
$[\texttt{fix}]$	$\dfrac{tenv \vdash e : t \rightarrow t : \texttt{c}}{tenv \vdash \texttt{fix}\ e : t : \texttt{c}}$
[down]	$\dfrac{tenv \vdash e : t : \texttt{c}}{tenv \vdash e : t : \texttt{r}}$ if $\vdash t : \texttt{r}$
[up]	$\dfrac{tenv' \vdash e : t : \texttt{r}}{tenv \vdash e : t : \texttt{c}}$ if $\vdash t : \texttt{c} \wedge tenv' = tenv\rceil\texttt{r}$

where $\mathrm{graph}(tenv\rceil\texttt{r}) = \{(\texttt{x}_i,(t'{:}b)) \in \mathrm{graph}(tenv) \mid b \neq \texttt{r}\}$

Table 3.5: Well-formedness of the *2*-level λ-calculus (part 2)

and similarly

$$tenv \vdash \texttt{y} : \underline{\texttt{A}\rightarrow\texttt{A}} : \texttt{r}$$

Using $[\underline{()}]$ we get

$$tenv \vdash \texttt{x}\underline{(}\texttt{y}\underline{)} : \underline{\texttt{A}\rightarrow\texttt{A}} : \texttt{r}$$

and the desired result then follows using [up] as *tenv* is already on the required form. (Intuitively this means that there are no $\underline{\lambda}$'s having $\texttt{x}\underline{(}\texttt{y}\underline{)}$ in its scope.)

Next we show that Ψ is not well-formed. Again this is a negative result and so a bit harder to substantiate. However, it should be reasonably clear that to show

$$\exists t,b\colon \emptyset \vdash \Psi\colon t : b$$

we would need to show

$$tenv \vdash \texttt{x(y)} : \underline{\texttt{A}\rightarrow\texttt{A}} : b$$

for $tenv = \emptyset[((\underline{\texttt{A}\rightarrow\texttt{A}})\rightarrow(\underline{\texttt{A}\rightarrow\texttt{A}}){:}\texttt{c})/\texttt{x}][(\underline{\texttt{A}\rightarrow\texttt{A}}{:}\texttt{r})/\texttt{y}]$. As $[()]$ is the only rule that can introduce a $\cdots(\cdots)$ we see that we may take $b{=}\texttt{c}$ above and thus have to show

$tenv \vdash \texttt{y} : \underline{\texttt{A}\rightarrow\texttt{A}} : \texttt{c}$

Clearly [x] allows us to deduce

$tenv \vdash \texttt{y} : \underline{\texttt{A}\rightarrow\texttt{A}} : \texttt{r}$

but the side condition to rule [up] is not fulfilled and no other rule would allow us to show the desired result. We may thus conclude from our informal argument that Ψ is not well-formed.

This ends the technical explanation for why Ψ^{-1} is allowed but Ψ is not. However, there is also a more intuitive explanation. The combinator Ψ^{-1} takes two pieces of code (**x** and **y**) as arguments and then returns a piece of code ($\texttt{x}\underline{(}\texttt{y}\underline{)}$) that views **y** as a closure and runs **x** on it to obtain a new closure. This would seem to be a perfectly sensible thing to do. Turning to the combinator Ψ, it takes a first argument **x** that is a compile-time transformation on code, and a second argument **y** that is a closure. It then applies **x** at compile-time to the closure **y** which is not known until run-time, in order to produce a closure that can further be manipulated at run-time. This violates the idea that *all* compile-time computations take place before any run-time computation. □

As we did for types we shall again *sketch* the ideas underlying the general construction of the well-formedness relation for expressions in the B-level language L. The well-formedness rules for L, e.g. the typed λ-calculus, may have various side conditions so we do not claim that the following explanation captures *all* the considerations needed.

For each well-formedness rule or axiom

$$[\text{R}] \quad \frac{tenv_1 \vdash e_1 : t_1 \quad \cdots \quad tenv_n \vdash e_n : t_n}{tenv \vdash \phi(e_1,\cdots,e_n,t_1,\cdots,t_n) : \psi(t_1,\ldots,t_n)} \quad \text{if } \Psi(tenv_i,t_i)$$

for expressions in L and for each binding time $b \in B$ we add the rule or axiom

$$[\text{R}^b] \quad \frac{tenv_1 \vdash e_1 : t_1 : b \quad \cdots \quad tenv_n \vdash e_n : t_n : b}{tenv \vdash \phi^b(e_1,\cdots,e_n,t_1,\cdots,t_n) : \psi^b(t_1,\ldots,t_n) : b} \quad \text{if } \Psi(tenv_i,t_i)$$

Finally, we add two rules for relating the binding times

$$[\text{down}] \quad \frac{tenv \vdash e : t : b}{tenv \vdash e : t : b'} \quad \text{if } b \neq b' \wedge b' \preceq b \wedge \vdash t : b'$$

$$[\text{up}] \quad \frac{tenv' \vdash e : t : b'}{tenv \vdash e : t : b} \quad \text{if } b \neq b' \wedge b' \preceq b \wedge \vdash t : b \wedge tenv' = tenv\rceil b'$$

where $\text{graph}(tenv\rceil b') = \{(\text{x}_i,(t_i : b_i)) \in \text{graph}(tenv) \mid \neg(b_i \preceq b')\}$

(At this point it is helpful to assume that B is linearly ordered.)

Comparing Tables 3.4 and 3.5 with the above general procedure we note the following features that are not fully accounted for. In the rules [$\underline{\texttt{f}}$], [f], [$\underline{\lambda}$], [λ], [x], [$\underline{\texttt{nil}}$] and [nil] we have added a side condition; no analogue was present in Table

2.2 because there all types were well-formed. In the rules $[\underline{\lambda}]$ and $[\lambda]$ the general procedure does not precisely characterize the dependency of $tenv_i$ on $tenv$. Finally, we have only one rule $[\mathtt{x}]$ for variables in accord with the decision earlier in this section to have only one kind of variable.

For later reference it is helpful to state a few simple properties of the well-formedness relation for the *2*-level λ-calculus. For the statement of the first of these it is helpful to extend τ_{BTA}: $T2 \to T$ to operate on type environments. For this we define

$$\tau_{\mathrm{BTA}}(tenv) = (\lambda(t{:}b).\tau_{\mathrm{BTA}}(t)) \circ tenv$$

so that, for example, $\tau_{\mathrm{BTA}}(\emptyset[(\underline{\mathtt{A}\to\mathtt{A}}{:}\mathtt{c})/\mathtt{x}]) = \emptyset[\mathtt{A}\to\mathtt{A}/\mathtt{x}]$.

Fact 3.1.3 If $tenv \vdash e : t : b$ then $\tau_{\mathrm{BTA}}(tenv) \vdash \varepsilon_{\mathrm{BTA}}(e) : \tau_{\mathrm{BTA}}(t)$. □

Proof: This is a straightforward induction on the deduction $tenv \vdash e : t : b$. □

Fact 3.1.4 If $tenv \vdash e : t : b$ then $\vdash t : b$. □

Proof: This is a straightforward induction on the deduction $tenv \vdash e : t : b$. □

Finally, we have a (weak) analogue of Fact 2.1.4 about the well-formedness relation being functional:

Fact 3.1.5 If $tenv \vdash e : t_1 : b_1$ and $tenv \vdash e : t_2 : b_2$ then $t_1 = t_2$. □

Proof: This is a straightforward structural induction on e. □

Because of the rules [down] and [up] we clearly do not always have $b_1{=}b_2$ in the above fact. However, if t_1 (and hence t_2) is *not* a run-time function type (i.e. is not a frontier type) we will indeed have $b_1{=}b_2$.

Finally, we must define the well-formedness relation $tenv \vdash_C e : t : b$ where C is a *constraint* as in Chapter 2. Again this amounts to supplying new definitions for the axioms $[\underline{\mathtt{f}}]$ and $[\mathtt{f}]$ and these new axioms will be of the form

$[\underline{\mathtt{f}}]$	$tenv \vdash_C \underline{\mathtt{f}_i}[t] : t : \mathtt{r}$	if $\vdash t : \mathtt{r}$, $\mathtt{f}_i{\in}\mathrm{dom}(C)$ and t is a *2*-level instance of $C(\mathtt{f}_i)$
$[\mathtt{f}]$	$tenv \vdash_C \mathtt{f}_i[t] : t : \mathtt{c}$	if $\vdash t : \mathtt{c}$, $\mathtt{f}_i{\in}\mathrm{dom}(C)$ and t is a *2*-level instance of $C(\mathtt{f}_i)$

To explain the notion of *2-level instance* we observe that the notion of polytype generalizes to the notion of *2*-level polytype, i.e.

$$pt2 \in PT2$$

$$pt2 ::= \underline{\mathtt{A}_i} \mid \mathtt{A}_i \mid pt2 \underline{\times} pt2 \mid pt2 \times pt2 \mid pt2 \underline{\to} pt2 \mid pt2 \to pt2 \mid pt2\ \underline{\mathtt{list}} \mid pt2\ \mathtt{list} \mid tv$$

Furthermore, the notion of *substitution* generalizes to both $S : TV \rightarrow PT2$ and $S : PT2 \rightarrow PT2$ and the notion of *instance* therefore generalizes to 2-level polytypes as well. By

a *2-level instance* of a closed type scheme $ts = \forall X_1.\cdots\forall X_n.pt$

we then mean

an instance of a 2-level polytype $pt2$ for which $\tau_{BTA}(pt2)=pt$

Clearly a 2-level instance $t \in T2$ of a closed type scheme ts, as above, will have $\tau_{BTA}(t)$ to be an instance of ts but the condition ensures more than just this. As an example, the 2-level instances of

$$C(\mathtt{f}_{eq}) = \forall X_1.\ X_1 \rightarrow X_1 \rightarrow \mathtt{Bool}$$

include $\mathtt{Int}\rightarrow\mathtt{Int}\rightarrow\mathtt{Bool}$ and $\underline{\mathtt{Int}\rightarrow\mathtt{Int}\rightarrow\mathtt{Bool}}$ but not $\mathtt{Int}\rightarrow\underline{\mathtt{Int}\rightarrow\mathtt{Bool}}$ although $\mathtt{Int}\rightarrow\underline{\mathtt{Int}\rightarrow\mathtt{Bool}}$ is a well-formed 2-level type and $\tau_{BTA}(\mathtt{Int}\rightarrow\underline{\mathtt{Int}\rightarrow\mathtt{Bool}})$ is an instance of $C(\mathtt{f}_{eq})$. In other words we ensure that the type variables must be the same 2-level type.

Well-formedness of 2-level programs

For a program of the form $\mathtt{DEF}\ \mathtt{x}_1 = e_1\ \cdots\ \mathtt{DEF}\ \mathtt{x}_n = e_n\ \mathtt{VAL}\ e_0\ \mathtt{HAS}\ t$ in $P(E2,T2)$ we need to decide the binding times for the types of the e_i. In accordance with the intention, expressed in Section 3.1, that the programs do not participate in the binding time distinction and thus correspond to the greatest binding time (assuming that such a binding time exists), we shall demand that the types of the e_i have binding time c. This motivates the rule

$$\frac{\begin{array}{c}\emptyset \vdash e_1 : t_1 : \mathsf{c} \\ \vdots \\ \emptyset[(t_1{:}\mathsf{c})/\mathtt{x}_1]\cdots[(t_{n-1}{:}\mathsf{c})/\mathtt{x}_{n-1}] \vdash e_n : t_n : \mathsf{c} \\ \emptyset[(t_1{:}\mathsf{c})/\mathtt{x}_1]\cdots[(t_n{:}\mathsf{c})/\mathtt{x}_n] \vdash e_0 : t : \mathsf{c}\end{array}}{\vdash \mathtt{DEF}\ \mathtt{x}_1 = e_1\ \cdots\ \mathtt{DEF}\ \mathtt{x}_n = e_n\ \mathtt{VAL}\ e_0\ \mathtt{HAS}\ t}$$

where again we use $\vdash p$ to express the well-formedness of the program p. Finally, we write $\vdash_C p$ for the well-formedness relation where all occurrences of $\mathtt{f}_i[t]$ or $\underline{\mathtt{f}_i}[t]$ must have t to be a 2-level instance of $C(\mathtt{f}_i)$.

Example 3.1.6 Returning to the $\mathtt{sum}_t$ program of Chapter 2 there are a couple of well-formed 2-level programs that have $\mathtt{sum}_t$ as the underlying program, i.e. that are equal to $\mathtt{sum}_t$ when underlinings have been removed. One of the more interesting programs is $\mathtt{sum}_9$ given by

```
DEF reduce9 = λf[Int→Int→Int]. λu[Int].
                 fix (λg[Int list → Int]. λxs[Int list].
                      if isnil xs then u
                      else f(hd xs)(g(tl xs)))
VAL reduce9 (λx[Int].λy[Int].+[Int×Int→Int](⟨x,y⟩)) (0[Int])
HAS Int list → Int
```

where $\texttt{reduce}_9$ has type $\texttt{Reduce}_9$. Note that we cannot use λu[Int].··· instead of λu[Int].··· as the well-formedness conditions on types only allow us to manipulate run-time *function* types at compile-time and not run-time data types like Int.

The remaining well-formed *2*-level programs are less interesting. Corresponding to the *2*-level type $\texttt{Reduce}_1$ we have a program with no underlinings at all and corresponding to $\texttt{Reduce}_{10}$ we have a program where all operations are underlined. These are the only well-formed *2*-level programs with $\texttt{sum}_t$ as the underlying program. Note that in each of these programs the binding time for `reduce` is fixed and this does not cause problems because there is only *one* application of `reduce` in the program. In general, we may have to duplicate the definition of the function (see Exercise 15). □

3.2 Binding Time Analysis

In Section 2.2 we developed an algorithm

$$\mathcal{P}^{C}_{\mathrm{TA}}\colon P(UE,T) \hookrightarrow P(E,T)$$

for transferring type information into an otherwise untyped λ-expression. We showed that when it succeeded the resulting program would be well-formed and that it *failed* only when it had to. This transformation naturally extends to an algorithm

$$\mathcal{P}^{C}_{\mathrm{TA}}\colon P(UE,T2) \hookrightarrow P(E,T2)$$

for transferring the underlying type of a *2*-level type into an otherwise untyped λ-expression. To be precise the extension is given by

$$\begin{array}{l}\lambda up.\ \text{let DEF } \mathtt{x}_1{=}ue_1 \cdots \text{DEF } \mathtt{x}_n{=}ue_n \text{ VAL } ue \text{ HAS } t2 = up\\ \quad \text{let } t = \tau_{\mathrm{BTA}}(t2)\\ \quad \text{let DEF } \mathtt{x}_1{=}e_1 \cdots \text{DEF } \mathtt{x}_n{=}e_n \text{ VAL } e \text{ HAS } t =\\ \qquad \mathcal{P}^{C}_{\mathrm{TA}}[\![\text{DEF } \mathtt{x}_1{=}ue_1 \cdots \text{DEF } \mathtt{x}_n{=}ue_n \text{ VAL } ue \text{ HAS } t]\!]\\ \quad \text{in DEF } \mathtt{x}_1{=}e_1 \cdots \text{DEF } \mathtt{x}_n{=}e_n \text{ VAL } e \text{ HAS } t2\end{array}$$

and this algorithm fails if and only if the explicit invocation of $\mathcal{P}^{C}_{\mathrm{TA}}$ fails. When the algorithm succeeds we know that the resulting program, or rather the result of applying π_{BTA} to it, will be well-formed when regarded as a program in $P(E,T)$.

In this section we now extend the transformation process by developing an algorithm

$$\mathcal{P}^{C}_{\mathrm{BTA}}\colon P(E,T2) \hookrightarrow P(E2,T2)$$

for transferring binding time information (in the form of *2*-level types) into a typed λ-expression. By combining $\mathcal{P}^{C}_{\mathrm{BTA}}$ and $\mathcal{P}^{C}_{\mathrm{TA}}$ we thus have an algorithm for transferring type and binding time information into an untyped λ-expression. By analogy with $\mathcal{P}^{C}_{\mathrm{TA}}$ we require the program produced by $\mathcal{P}^{C}_{\mathrm{BTA}}$ to be well-formed as a program in $P(E2,T2)$. This is not all, however, as this would be possible if $\mathcal{P}^{C}_{\mathrm{BTA}}$ just underlined every basic construct and thereby transferred all computations to run-time. Rather, we insist that as many computations as possible are performed at compile-time in order to achieve greater run-time efficiency, as then code has to be generated for fewer computations.

To formalise the condition that *as many computations as possible are performed at compile-time* we shall extend the partial order $\preceq$ from binding times to apply also to *2*-level types, *2*-level expressions and *2*-level programs. Taking *2*-level types as an example the idea is that

$$t_1 \preceq t_2$$

if t_1 and t_2 are the same types once we forget about underlining and if every symbol underlined in t_2 is also underlined in t_1. So the intention will be that, for example,

$$\underline{\mathtt{Int}\to\mathtt{Int}\to\mathtt{Bool}} \preceq \mathtt{Int}\to\underline{\mathtt{Int}\to\mathtt{Bool}} \preceq \mathtt{Int}\to\mathtt{Int}\to\mathtt{Bool}$$

This can be expressed more formally by giving a structural definition of $\preceq$ but we shall dispense with the details; it is important to note, however, that $t_1 \preceq t_2$ implies that $\tau_{\mathrm{BTA}}(t_1) = \tau_{\mathrm{BTA}}(t_2)$. In a similar way we can define

$$e_1 \preceq e_2$$

and

$$p_1 \preceq p_2$$

Example 3.2.1 The ordering between the ten well-formed *2*-level types for `reduce` is shown in Figure 3.2. □

A subset Y of a partially ordered set may have a greatest lower bound $\sqcap Y$: a *lower bound* y_0 of Y is an element such that

$$y_0 \preceq y \text{ for all elements } y \text{ of } Y$$

and a *greatest lower bound* $\sqcap Y$ is a lower bound such that

$$y_0 \preceq \sqcap Y \text{ for all lower bounds } y_0 \text{ of } Y$$

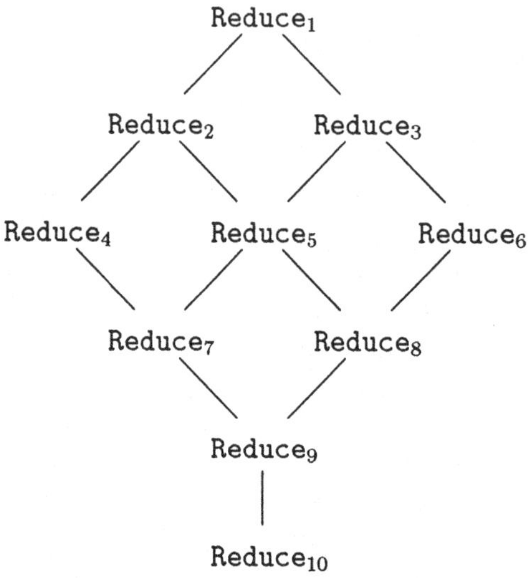

Figure 3.2: Comparison of the *2*-level types for `reduce`

Since a partial order is antisymmetric the greatest lower bound is unique if it exists. We usually write $y_1 \sqcap y_2$ for $\sqcap\{y_1,y_2\}$.

For the partially ordered set *2* any subset has a greatest lower bound: $\sqcap Y =$ c unless $\mathtt{r} \in Y$ in which case $\sqcap Y =$ r. A subset Y of *T2* is said to be *consistent* if $\{\tau_{\mathrm{BTA}}(y) | y \in Y\}$ is a singleton. This notion is of interest because all consistent subsets of *T2* have greatest lower bounds: simply underline a symbol if it is underlined in any of the elements of the (non-empty) set Y. Similar remarks apply to consistent subsets of *E2* and of $P(E2, T2)$.

3.2.1 Binding time analysis of types

We begin with developing a transformation algorithm

$$\mathcal{T}_{\mathrm{BTA}}\colon\ T2 \times 2 \rightarrow T2 \times 2$$

for types. Here, as in Section 3.1, we write *2* for the partially ordered set with elements c and r and partial order given by $\mathtt{r} \preceq \mathtt{r}$, $\mathtt{r} \preceq \mathtt{c}$ and $\mathtt{c} \preceq \mathtt{c}$. We shall write the elements in $T2 \times 2$ in the form $t{:}b$ rather than in the more usual form (t,b) and we shall write $t_1{:}b_1 \preceq t_2{:}b_2$ to mean $(t_1 \preceq t_2) \wedge (b_1 \preceq b_2)$. The intention with $\mathcal{T}_{\mathrm{BTA}}[\![t{:}b]\!]$ then is that it is greatest among the pairs $t'{:}b'$ with the properties $\vdash t'{:}b'$ and $t'{:}b' \preceq t{:}b$; this just says that $\mathcal{T}_{\mathrm{BTA}}[\![t{:}b]\!]$ is greatest among all $t'{:}b'$ that are well-formed and that respect all run-time annotations given in $t{:}b$.

To present the algorithm as concisely as possible it is helpful to use the general notation for the B-level language L. We thus propose the definition of Table 3.6;

$$\mathcal{T}_{\mathrm{BTA}}[\![\ \mathtt{A}_{\mathrm{i}}^{b1}{:}b2\ ]\!] = \text{let } b = b1 \sqcap b2 \text{ in } \mathtt{A}_{\mathrm{i}}^{b}{:}b$$

$$\begin{aligned}\mathcal{T}_{\mathrm{BTA}}[\![\ t_1 \times^{b1} t_2{:}b2\ ]\!] = \ & \text{let } t_1'{:}b1' = \mathcal{T}_{\mathrm{BTA}}[\![\ t_1{:}b1 \sqcap b2\ ]\!] \\ & \text{let } t_2'{:}b2' = \mathcal{T}_{\mathrm{BTA}}[\![\ t_2{:}b1 \sqcap b2\ ]\!] \\ & \text{in if } b1' = b2' \\ & \quad \text{then } t_1' \times^{b1'} t_2'{:}b1' \\ & \quad \text{else } \mathcal{T}_{\mathrm{BTA}}[\![\ t_1' \times^{b} t_2'{:}b\ ]\!] \\ & \qquad \text{where } b = b1' \sqcap b2'\end{aligned}$$

$$\begin{aligned}\mathcal{T}_{\mathrm{BTA}}[\![\ t_1 \rightarrow^{b1} t_2{:}b2\ ]\!] = \ & \text{let } t_1'{:}b1' = \mathcal{T}_{\mathrm{BTA}}[\![\ t_1{:}b1 \sqcap b2\ ]\!] \\ & \text{let } t_2'{:}b2' = \mathcal{T}_{\mathrm{BTA}}[\![\ t_2{:}b1 \sqcap b2\ ]\!] \\ & \text{in if } b1' = b2' \\ & \quad \text{then } t_1' \rightarrow^{b1'} t_2'{:}b2 \\ & \quad \text{else } \mathcal{T}_{\mathrm{BTA}}[\![\ t_1' \rightarrow^{b} t_2'{:}b2\ ]\!] \\ & \qquad \text{where } b = b1' \sqcap b2'\end{aligned}$$

$$\begin{aligned}\mathcal{T}_{\mathrm{BTA}}[\![\ t\ \mathtt{list}^{b1}{:}b2\ ]\!] = \ & \text{let } t'{:}b' = \mathcal{T}_{\mathrm{BTA}}[\![\ t{:}b1 \sqcap b2\ ]\!] \\ & \text{in } t'\ \mathtt{list}^{b'}{:}b'\end{aligned}$$

Table 3.6: $\mathcal{T}_{\mathrm{BTA}}$: Binding time analysis of types

it is by cases on the structure of the underlying type.

Proposition 3.2.2 (Correctness and Optimality of $\mathcal{T}_{\mathrm{BTA}}$) The equations of Table 3.6 define a *total* function

$$\mathcal{T}_{\mathrm{BTA}}\colon\ T2{\times}2 \rightarrow T2{\times}2$$

and it satisfies, for $t{:}b \in T2{\times}2$ arbitrary:

$$\vdash \mathcal{T}_{\mathrm{BTA}}[\![t{:}b]\!]$$

$$\mathcal{T}_{\mathrm{BTA}}[\![t{:}b]\!] \preceq t{:}b$$

and that $\mathcal{T}_{\mathrm{BTA}}[\![t{:}b]\!]$ is greatest with this property, that is

$$t'{:}b' \preceq t{:}b \land \vdash t'{:}b' \Rightarrow t'{:}b' \preceq \mathcal{T}_{\mathrm{BTA}}[\![t{:}b]\!] \qquad \square$$

Note that the last condition expresses that the annotation produced by $\mathcal{T}_{\mathrm{BTA}}$ is *optimal* in the sense that any other well-formed annotation complying with the original annotation must be smaller in the ordering.

The proof of this proposition needs the *principle of complete induction*. First, for a partial order $\leq$ we shall write $<$, or *strictly* $\leq$, for the irreflexive part of it, so $u<v$ means $(u \leq v) \land (u \neq v)$. A partial order $\leq$ is *well-founded* if there is no countably infinite sequence $(v_{\mathrm{i}})_{\mathrm{i}}$ such that $v_{\mathrm{i}+1} < v_{\mathrm{i}}$ for all i. The principle of complete induction (or well-founded induction) then says that if $\forall v$: ($\forall u$: $u<v \Rightarrow P(u)$) $\Rightarrow P(v)$

then $\forall v$: $P(v)$

This means that if $P(v)$ holds whenever $P(u)$ holds for all $u<v$, then $P(v)$ holds for all v.

The proof of this principle is by contradiction. So assume that $\leq$ is a well-founded partial order, that $P(v)$ holds whenever $P(u)$ holds for all $u<v$ but that there is some v_0 such that $P(v_0)$ does not hold. There must be some $v_1<v_0$ such that $P(v_1)$ does not hold because otherwise $P(v_0)$ would follow from our assumptions. Proceeding in this way we get a countably infinite sequence $(v_i)_i$ such that $v_{i+1}<v_i$ and $P(v_{i+1})$ does not hold. This contradicts our assumptions and hence $P(v)$ must hold for all v.

Proof of the Proposition: It is quite clear that the equations for $\mathcal{T}_{\text{BTA}}$ define a *partial* function because the patterns in the different equations are mutually exclusive.

To prove the remaining results we use the principle of complete induction. First, we define the relation $\leq$ to be used here by

$$t_1{:}b_1 \leq t_2{:}b_2$$

if and only if

$$t_1{:}b_1 \preceq t_2{:}b_2 \text{ or } \tau_{\text{BTA}}(t_1) \text{ is a proper subtype of } \tau_{\text{BTA}}(t_2)$$

Examples include <u>Int</u>:r $\leq$ Int:c and Int:c $\leq$ <u>Int→Int</u>:r but not Int:c $\leq$ <u>Int</u>:r. We observe that $\preceq$ is a partial order and that it is well-founded because for a type t of length n there are at most 2^{n+1} pairs $t'{:}b'$ such that $t'{:}b' \preceq t{:}b$. We also observe that the statement *is a subtype of* is a partial order and that it is well-founded; indeed well-foundedness of this relation simply amounts to the validity of structural induction. It then follows that $\leq$ is a partial order because $t_1{:}b_1 \preceq t_2{:}b_2$ implies that $\tau_{\text{BTA}}(t_1) = \tau_{\text{BTA}}(t_2)$ so that $\tau_{\text{BTA}}(t_1)$ is *not* a proper subtype of $\tau_{\text{BTA}}(t_2)$. Furthermore, $\leq$ is well-founded.

Stage 1: We shall now prove that $\mathcal{T}_{\text{BTA}}$ is a total function that produces a result that is less than or equal to its argument. The predicate P to be used is

$$P(t{:}b) \equiv \mathcal{T}_{\text{BTA}}[\![\ t{:}b\ ]\!] \text{ is defined and } \mathcal{T}_{\text{BTA}}[\![\ t{:}b\ ]\!] \preceq t{:}b$$

To prove the desired result we may assume that $P(t'{:}b')$ holds for all $t'{:}b'<t{:}b$ and we must show that $P(t{:}b)$ holds.

The proof is formally by cases on $\tau_{\text{BTA}}(t)$, i.e. by cases on which of the four clauses that applies to $t{:}b$, but the reasoning is much the same in all cases. The general observation is that for an equation

$$\mathcal{T}_{\text{BTA}}[\![\ t{:}b\ ]\!] = \cdots \mathcal{T}_{\text{BTA}}[\![\ t'{:}b'\ ]\!] \cdots$$

any recursive call on the right hand side will have $t':b'<t:b$. It then easily follows that $\mathcal{T}_{\text{BTA}}[\![\ t:b\ ]\!]$ is defined because by assumption each $\mathcal{T}_{\text{BTA}}[\![\ t':b'\ ]\!]$ was, and that $\mathcal{T}_{\text{BTA}}[\![\ t:b\ ]\!] \preceq t:b$, because by assumption $\mathcal{T}_{\text{BTA}}[\![\ t':b'\ ]\!] \preceq t':b'$ for each occurrence of $\mathcal{T}_{\text{BTA}}[\![\ t':b'\ ]\!]$ on the right hand side.

As an example of such a proof consider the case where $t:b$ is of the form $t_1 \to^{b1} t_2:b2$. Clearly

$$t_1:b1 \sqcap b2 < t:b$$

$$t_2:b1 \sqcap b2 < t:b$$

because t_1 and t_2 are actually proper subtypes of t. Furthermore, it follows from the inductive assumption that

$$t'_1:b1' = \mathcal{T}_{\text{BTA}}[\![\ t_1:b1 \sqcap b2\ ]\!]$$

$$t'_2:b2' = \mathcal{T}_{\text{BTA}}[\![\ t_2:b1 \sqcap b2\ ]\!]$$

are both defined and

$$t'_1:b1' \preceq t_1:b1 \sqcap b2$$

$$t'_2:b2' \preceq t_2:b1 \sqcap b2$$

If $b1' = b2'$ we then have

$$t'_1 \to^{b1'} t'_2:b2 \preceq t:b$$

and this shows the result in this case. If $b1' \neq b2'$ we set $b = b1' \sqcap b2'$ and observe that

$$t'_1 \to^{b} t'_2:b2 \prec t:b$$

(because $b \neq b1$ must be the case) and the result then follows from the inductive assumption.

Stage 2: That $\mathcal{T}_{\text{BTA}}$ only produces well-formed pairs amounts to yet another complete induction with respect to the well-founded order $\leq$ but this time using the predicate

$$P(t:b) \equiv\ \vdash \mathcal{T}_{\text{BTA}}[\![\ t:b\ ]\!]$$

Again it is straightforward to inspect the equations one by one and to use Table 3.3 to show the desired result and we shall illustrate this for function space.

Let $t:b$ be of the form $t_1 \to^{b1} t_2:b2$ and write $t'_1:b1'$ for $\mathcal{T}_{\text{BTA}}[\![\ t_1:b1 \sqcap b2\ ]\!]$ and $t'_2:b2'$ for $\mathcal{T}_{\text{BTA}}[\![\ t_2:b1 \sqcap b2\ ]\!]$. As $t_1:b1 \sqcap b2 < t:b$ and $t_2:b1 \sqcap b2 < t:b$ we know from the inductive assumption that $\vdash t'_1:b1'$ and $\vdash t'_2:b2'$. If $b1' = b2'$ it follows from $[\to^{b1'}]$ (in Table 3.3) that $\vdash t'_1 \to^{b1'} t'_2 : b1'$. If $b1' = b2$ this is the desired result; otherwise the desired result follows from rule [up] and the observation that $b1' \preceq$

$b1 \sqcap b2 \preceq b2$ so that $\vdash t_1' \rightarrow^{b1'} t_2'{:}b2$. It remains to consider the case where $b1' \neq b2'$. Here $t_1' \rightarrow^{b} t_2'{:}b2 < t_1 \rightarrow^{b1} t_2{:}b2$ where $b = b1' \sqcap b2'$ and the result follows from the inductive assumption.

Stage 3: Finally we must show that the result of $\mathcal{T}_{\text{BTA}}\llbracket\, t{:}b \,\rrbracket$ is greatest among those pairs $t''{:}b''$ with the properties $\vdash t''{:}b''$ and $t''{:}b'' \preceq t{:}b$. This will also be proved by complete induction with respect to $\leq$ and the predicate will be

$$P(t{:}b) \equiv \forall t''{:}b''{:}\ (\ \vdash t''{:}b'' \wedge t''{:}b'' \preceq t{:}b \Rightarrow t''{:}b'' \preceq \mathcal{T}_{\text{BTA}}\llbracket\, t{:}b \,\rrbracket\ )$$

Again the method of proof is to inspect the equations one by one and to use Table 3.3 to show the desired result. We shall illustrate this for function space.

Let $t{:}b$ be of the form $t_1 \rightarrow^{b1} t_2{:}b2$ and write $t_1'{:}b1'$ for $\mathcal{T}_{\text{BTA}}\llbracket\, t_1{:}b1 \sqcap b2 \,\rrbracket$ and $t_2'{:}b2'$ for $\mathcal{T}_{\text{BTA}}\llbracket\, t_2{:}b1 \sqcap b2 \,\rrbracket$. Next let $\vdash t''{:}b''$ and $t''{:}b'' \preceq t{:}b$. Then $t''{:}b''$ must be of the form $t_1'' \rightarrow^{b1''} t_2''{:}b2''$ and furthermore $b1'' \preceq b2''$ since otherwise inspection of Table 3.3 shows that $t''{:}b''$ could not be well-formed. It follows that $\vdash t_1''{:}b1''$ and that $t_1''{:}b1'' \preceq t_1{:}b1 \sqcap b2$ so that $t_1''{:}b1'' \preceq t_1'{:}b1'$. In a similar way it follows that $t_2''{:}b1'' \preceq t_2'{:}b2'$. Setting $b = b1' \sqcap b2'$ we have $b1'' \preceq b$ because $b1'' \preceq b1'$ and $b1'' \preceq b2'$. We thus have $t_1'' \rightarrow^{b1''} t_2''{:}b2'' \preceq t_1' \rightarrow^{b} t_2'{:}b2$. If $b1' = b2'$ this is the desired result and if $b1' \neq b2'$ the desired result follows from the inductive assumption.

This completes the proof of Proposition 3.2.2. □

Example 3.2.3 Recall the types

$$\texttt{Reduce}_{\text{t}} = (\texttt{Int}\rightarrow\texttt{Int}\rightarrow\texttt{Int})\rightarrow\texttt{Int}\rightarrow\underline{\texttt{Int}}\ \underline{\texttt{list}}\rightarrow\texttt{Int}$$

$$\texttt{Reduce}_3 = (\texttt{Int}\rightarrow\texttt{Int}\rightarrow\texttt{Int})\rightarrow\texttt{Int}\rightarrow\underline{\texttt{Int}}\ \underline{\texttt{list}\rightarrow\texttt{Int}}$$

We shall show that

$$\mathcal{T}_{\text{BTA}}\llbracket\, \texttt{Reduce}_{\text{t}}{:}\texttt{c} \,\rrbracket = \texttt{Reduce}_3{:}\texttt{c}$$

thus validating the claim made earlier that $\texttt{Reduce}_3$ is the greatest well-formed type that obeys all the run-time annotations of $\texttt{Reduce}_{\text{t}}$. We calculate

$$\mathcal{T}_{\text{BTA}}\llbracket\, \underline{\texttt{Int}}\ \underline{\texttt{list}} \rightarrow \texttt{Int} : \texttt{c} \,\rrbracket =$$

(as $\mathcal{T}_{\text{BTA}}\llbracket\, \underline{\texttt{Int}}\ \underline{\texttt{list}} : \texttt{c} \,\rrbracket = \underline{\texttt{Int}}\ \underline{\texttt{list}} : \texttt{r}$ and $\texttt{r}\neq\texttt{c}$)

$$\mathcal{T}_{\text{BTA}}\llbracket\, \underline{\texttt{Int}}\ \underline{\texttt{list}}\ \underline{\rightarrow}\ \texttt{Int} : \texttt{c} \,\rrbracket =$$

(as $\mathcal{T}_{\text{BTA}}\llbracket\, \texttt{Int}{:}\texttt{r} \,\rrbracket = \underline{\texttt{Int}}{:}\texttt{r}$)

$$\underline{\texttt{Int}}\ \underline{\texttt{list}}\ \underline{\rightarrow}\ \underline{\texttt{Int}} : \texttt{c}$$

Next we note that

$$\mathcal{T}_{\text{BTA}}[\![\ \texttt{Int}\rightarrow\underline{\texttt{Int}}\ \underline{\texttt{list}}\rightarrow\texttt{Int} : \texttt{c}\ ]\!] = \texttt{Int} \rightarrow \underline{\texttt{Int}}\ \underline{\texttt{list}}\ \underline{\rightarrow}\ \underline{\texttt{Int}} : \texttt{c}$$

and it follows that the desired result holds. □

Proposition 3.2.2 has a number of consequences that we shall need later on.

Corollary 3.2.4 If $\vdash t : b$ then $\mathcal{T}_{\text{BTA}}[\![\ t{:}b\ ]\!] = t{:}b$. □

Corollary 3.2.5 $\mathcal{T}_{\text{BTA}}$ is monotonic with respect to $\preceq$. □

Next let $Y \subseteq T2 \times 2$ be a non-empty subset that is *consistent* in the sense that $\{\tau_{\text{BTA}}(t) | t{:}b \in Y\}$ is a singleton. Then every consistent subset Y of $T2 \times 2$ has a greatest lower bound. It is given by

$$\sqcap Y = t{:}b$$

where b is $\sqcap\{b_i | t_i{:}b_i \in Y\}$ and $t = \sqcap\{t_i | t_i{:}b_i \in Y\}$.

Corollary 3.2.6 For a non-empty and consistent set Y, as above, the pair

$$\mathcal{T}_{\text{BTA}}[\![\ \sqcap Y\ ]\!]$$

is well-formed, is less than or equal to (wrt. $\preceq$) all the elements $t_i{:}b_i$ of Y, and is the greatest such pair. □

Proof: Clearly $\sqcap Y$ is the greatest lower bound of Y wrt. $\preceq$. Therefore $\mathcal{T}_{\text{BTA}}[\![\ \sqcap Y\ ]\!]$ is well-formed and a lower bound of Y. If some $t'{:}b'$ is well-formed and a lower bound of Y then $t'{:}b' \preceq \sqcap Y$ so that $t'{:}b' \preceq \mathcal{T}_{\text{BTA}}[\![\ \sqcap Y\ ]\!]$ by Proposition 3.2.2. □

The final consequence of Proposition 3.2.2 to be studied here concerns how to transform a *2*-level type to one that is a *2*-level instance of some closed type scheme. (This will be relevant when we consider the $\mathbf{f}_i$ below.) So let *ts* be a closed type scheme of the form $\forall X_1 \cdots \forall X_n.pt$ and where, without loss of generality, we assume that each X_i does occur in *pt* so that the set FTV(*pt*) of free type variables of *pt* is $\{X_1,\cdots,X_n\}$. Next consider the following definition of a function $\mathcal{T}^{ts}_{\text{BTA}}$:

$\mathcal{T}^{ts}_{\text{BTA}}[\![\ t{:}b\ ]\!] =$ if $\tau_{\text{BTA}}(t)$ is not an instance of *pt* then *fail* else
  let $t'{:}b' = \mathcal{T}_{\text{BTA}}[\![\ t{:}b\ ]\!]$
  let $Y_i = \{\ t_i{:}\texttt{c}\ |\ t_i$ occurs in t' where X_i occurs in *pt* $\}$
  let $t_i{:}b_i = \mathcal{T}_{\text{BTA}}[\![\ \sqcap Y_i\ ]\!]$
  let $t'' = t'$ with t_i substituted into those occurrences
    where X_i occur in *pt*
  if $t''{=}t'$ then $t'{:}b'$ else $\mathcal{T}^{ts}_{\text{BTA}}[\![\ t''{:}b'\ ]\!]$

Example 3.2.7 Returning to the equality predicate of the previous chapter we consider the closed type scheme

$$ts = C(\mathtt{f_{eq}}) = \forall \mathrm{X}_1.\ \mathrm{X}_1 \to \mathrm{X}_1 \to \mathtt{Bool}$$

where the polytype

$$pt = \mathrm{X}_1 \to \mathrm{X}_1 \to \mathtt{Bool}$$

has $\mathrm{FTV}(pt) = \{\mathrm{X}_1, \cdots, \mathrm{X}_n\}$ for n=1. Next consider the type

$$t = \mathtt{Int} \to \underline{\mathtt{Int}} \to \mathtt{Bool}$$

and the call $\mathcal{T}^{ts}_{\mathrm{BTA}}[\![\ t{:}\mathsf{c}\ ]\!]$. We note that

$$\tau_{\mathrm{BTA}}(t) = \mathtt{Int} \to \mathtt{Int} \to \mathtt{Bool} \text{ is an instance of } pt = \mathrm{X}_1 \to \mathrm{X}_1 \to \mathtt{Bool}$$

$$t'{:}b' = \mathcal{T}_{\mathrm{BTA}}[\![\ t{:}\mathsf{c}\ ]\!] = \mathtt{Int} \to \underline{\mathtt{Int} \to \mathtt{Bool}}{:}\mathsf{c}$$

$$Y_1 = \{\ \mathtt{Int}{:}\mathsf{c},\ \underline{\mathtt{Int}}{:}\mathsf{c}\ \}$$

$$t_1{:}b_1 = \mathcal{T}_{\mathrm{BTA}}[\![\ \underline{\mathtt{Int}}{:}\mathsf{c}\ ]\!] = \underline{\mathtt{Int}}{:}\mathsf{r}$$

$$t'' = \underline{\mathtt{Int}} \to \underline{\mathtt{Int} \to \mathtt{Bool}}$$

As $t'' \neq t'$ we have $\mathcal{T}^{ts}_{\mathrm{BTA}}[\![\ t{:}\mathsf{c}\ ]\!] = \mathcal{T}^{ts}_{\mathrm{BTA}}[\![\ \underline{\mathtt{Int}} \to \underline{\mathtt{Int} \to \mathtt{Bool}}{:}\mathsf{c}\ ]\!]$ and next consider the call $\mathcal{T}^{ts}_{\mathrm{BTA}}[\![\ \underline{\mathtt{Int}} \to \underline{\mathtt{Int} \to \mathtt{Bool}}{:}\mathsf{c}\ ]\!]$. We note that

$$\tau_{\mathrm{BTA}}(t) \text{ is an instance of } pt$$

$$t'{:}b' = \mathcal{T}_{\mathrm{BTA}}[\![\ \underline{\mathtt{Int}} \to \underline{\mathtt{Int} \to \mathtt{Bool}}{:}\mathsf{c}\ ]\!] = \underline{\mathtt{Int}} \to \underline{\mathtt{Int} \to \mathtt{Bool}}{:}\mathsf{r}$$

$$Y_1 = \{\ \underline{\mathtt{Int}}{:}\mathsf{c}\ \}$$

$$t_1{:}b_1 = \mathcal{T}_{\mathrm{BTA}}[\![\ \underline{\mathtt{Int}}{:}\mathsf{c}\ ]\!] = \underline{\mathtt{Int}}{:}\mathsf{r}$$

$$t'' = \underline{\mathtt{Int}} \to \underline{\mathtt{Int} \to \mathtt{Bool}}$$

Since $t''=t'$ we conclude that

$$\mathcal{T}^{ts}_{\mathrm{BTA}}[\![\ \mathtt{Int} \to \underline{\mathtt{Int}} \to \mathtt{Bool}{:}\mathsf{c}\ ]\!] = \underline{\mathtt{Int}} \to \underline{\mathtt{Int} \to \mathtt{Bool}}{:}\mathsf{r}$$

Note that $\underline{\mathtt{Int}} \to \underline{\mathtt{Int} \to \mathtt{Bool}}$ is a *2*-level instance of pt whereas the *2*-level type $\mathtt{Int} \to \underline{\mathtt{Int} \to \mathtt{Bool}}$ resulting from $\mathcal{T}_{\mathrm{BTA}}[\![\ \mathtt{Int} \to \underline{\mathtt{Int}} \to \mathtt{Bool}{:}\mathsf{c}\ ]\!]$ is not. □

Lemma 3.2.8 Let $ts = \forall \mathrm{X}_1 \cdots \forall \mathrm{X}_n.pt$ be as above. If $\tau_{\mathrm{BTA}}(t)$ is an instance of ts then

$$\mathcal{T}^{ts}_{\mathrm{BTA}}[\![\ t{:}b\ ]\!] \text{ terminates with a result } t'{:}b'$$

The result satisfies

$$\mathcal{T}^{ts}_{\mathrm{BTA}}[\![\ t'{:}b'\ ]\!] = \mathcal{T}_{\mathrm{BTA}}[\![\ t'{:}b'\ ]\!] = t'{:}b'$$

as well as the property

$$\vdash t':b' \wedge t':b' \preceq t:b \wedge t' \text{ is a } 2\text{-level instance of } ts$$

and that it is the greatest pair with the above property. □

Proof: A recursive call of $\mathcal{T}^{ts}_{\mathrm{BTA}}$ is only performed on $t'':b'$ when $t'':b' \prec t':b' \preceq t:b$. Hence complete induction with respect to the well-founded order $\preceq$ (not $\leq$) shows that $\mathcal{T}^{ts}_{\mathrm{BTA}}$ terminates without failure on arguments of the form $t:b$ where t is an instance of pt. (Recall that $t'':b' \prec t:b$ implies $\tau_{\mathrm{BTA}}(t'') = \tau_{\mathrm{BTA}}(t)$.) Clearly the result $t':b'$ is $\mathcal{T}_{\mathrm{BTA}}[\![\, t'':b'' \,]\!]$ for some $t'':b''$ and by Corollary 3.2.4 we have that $\mathcal{T}_{\mathrm{BTA}}[\![\, t':b' \,]\!] = t':b'$ so that also $\mathcal{T}^{ts}_{\mathrm{BTA}}[\![\, t':b' \,]\!] = t':b'$. Much as in the proof of Proposition 3.2.2 we can then show by complete induction on $\preceq$ (not $\leq$) that the result of $\mathcal{T}^{ts}_{\mathrm{BTA}}$ satisfies the property above and by another complete induction that it is greatest with this property. □

3.2.2 Binding time analysis of expressions

The main task in the binding time analysis is to develop a transformation algorithm for expressions. Previous formulations of such a transformation have been rather lengthy and fairly complicated. To overcome this we shall pattern the transformation after the type analysis algorithm presented in Section 2.2. This calls for replacing variables $\mathbf{x}_i$ with variables $\mathbf{x}^b_i[t]$ that are explicitly annotated with their (*2*-level) type and binding time information. Thus variables are treated much like constants.

To be precise about this approach we define a modified class of *2*-level expressions where variables are as indicated above:

$$e \in E2'$$
$$e ::= \mathbf{f}^b_i[t] \mid \ldots \mid \lambda^b \mathbf{x}_i[t].e \mid e\,(^b\; e) \mid \mathbf{x}^b_i[t] \mid \ldots$$

The function

$$\varepsilon'_{\mathrm{BTA}}\colon E2' \to E2$$

then removes the annotation of variables, i.e. replaces $\mathbf{x}^b_i[t]$ by $\mathbf{x}_i$. Then the function $\varepsilon_{\mathrm{BTA}} \circ \varepsilon'_{\mathrm{BTA}}\colon E2' \to E$ removes annotations of variables as well as underlinings; to allow for a more readable notation we shall allow to write it simply as

$$\varepsilon_{\mathrm{BTA}}\colon E2' \to E$$

By analogy with our definition for type analysis we also define

$$\mathcal{A}_{\mathrm{BTA}}\colon E2' \to \mathcal{P}_{\mathrm{fin}}(\{\mathbf{x}_i \mid i \in I\} \times (T2 \times 2))$$

which records the annotations given to free variables in a *2*-level expression. As the definition is much the same as for $\mathcal{A}_{\mathrm{TA}}$ we omit the details.

Example 3.2.9 The definition of $\varepsilon'_{\mathrm{BTA}}$ is such that

$$\varepsilon'_{\mathrm{BTA}}(\lambda^{c}\mathtt{x}_1[\mathtt{Int}^{c}\ \mathtt{list}^{c} \rightarrow^{c} \mathtt{Int}^{c}].\ \mathtt{x}_1^{c}[\mathtt{Int}^{c}\ \mathtt{list}^{c} \rightarrow^{c} \mathtt{Int}^{c}]\ ({}^{c}\mathtt{nil}^{c}[\mathtt{Int}^{c}]))$$

amounts to

$$\lambda^{c}\mathtt{x}_1[\mathtt{Int}^{c}\ \mathtt{list}^{c} \rightarrow^{c} \mathtt{Int}^{c}].\ \mathtt{x}_1\ ({}^{c}\mathtt{nil}^{c}[\mathtt{Int}^{c}])$$

Similarly

$$\varepsilon'_{\mathrm{BTA}}(\lambda^{c}\mathtt{x}_1[\mathtt{Int}^{c}].\ \langle^{c}\langle^{c}\ \mathtt{x}_1^{c}[\mathtt{Int}^{c}],\mathtt{x}_1^{r}[\mathtt{Bool}^{r}]\rangle,\ \langle^{c}\ \mathtt{x}_2^{c}[\mathtt{Int}^{c}],\mathtt{x}_2^{r}[\mathtt{Bool}^{r}]\rangle\rangle)$$

amounts to

$$\lambda^{c}\mathtt{x}_1[\mathtt{Int}^{c}].\ \langle^{c}\langle^{c}\ \mathtt{x}_1,\mathtt{x}_1\rangle,\ \langle^{c}\ \mathtt{x}_2,\mathtt{x}_2\rangle\rangle$$

The definition of $\mathcal{A}_{\mathrm{BTA}}$ is such that

$$\mathcal{A}_{\mathrm{BTA}}(\lambda^{c}\mathtt{x}_1[\mathtt{Int}^{c}].\ \langle^{c}\langle^{c}\ \mathtt{x}_1^{c}[\mathtt{Int}^{c}],\mathtt{x}_1^{r}[\mathtt{Bool}^{r}]\rangle,\ \langle^{c}\ \mathtt{x}_2^{c}[\mathtt{Int}^{c}],\mathtt{x}_2^{r}[\mathtt{Bool}^{r}]\rangle\rangle)$$

amounts to

$$\{(\mathtt{x}_2,(\mathtt{Int}^{c},\mathtt{c})),(\mathtt{x}_2,(\mathtt{Bool}^{r},\mathtt{r}))\}$$

We shall sometimes write this set as $\{(\mathtt{x}_2,\mathtt{Int}^{c}\mathtt{:c}),(\mathtt{x}_2,\mathtt{Bool}^{r}\mathtt{:r})\}$. □

For finite subsets A of $\{\mathtt{x}_i|i\in I\} \times (T2 \times 2)$ we shall use much the same notation that was used in Section 2.2 for finite subsets of $\{\mathtt{x}_i|i\in I\} \times PT$. In particular

$$A(\mathtt{x}_i) = \{(t_i{:}b_i)|(\mathtt{x}_i,t_i{:}b_i)\in A\}$$

and A is *functional* if each $A(\mathtt{x}_i)$ is empty or a singleton. There is an obvious bijective correspondence between finite and functional sets A and type environments *tenv*: if A is finite and functional then fun(A) is a type environment and if *tenv* is a type environment then graph(*tenv*) is finite and functional. Finally, our definition of a partial order upon *2*-level expressions in *E2* carries over to expressions in *E2'* as does the definition of *consistent* sets and the characterization of greatest lower bounds.

The transformation function then has the functionality

$$\mathcal{E}^{C}_{\mathrm{BTA}}\colon\ E2'\times T2\times 2 \hookrightarrow E2'\times T2\times 2$$

We shall take care only to apply $\mathcal{E}^{C}_{\mathrm{BTA}}$ to an argument $e{:}t{:}b$ if the underlying typed expression is well-formed; this means that

$\{(\mathtt{x}_i,\tau_{\mathrm{BTA}}(t_i))|(\mathtt{x}_i,t_i{:}b_i)\in\mathcal{A}_{\mathrm{BTA}}(e)\}$ is functional, and

$$\mathrm{fun}(\{(\mathtt{x}_i,\tau_{\mathrm{BTA}}(t_i))|(\mathtt{x}_i,t_i{:}b_i)\in\mathcal{A}_{\mathrm{BTA}}(e)\}) \vdash_C \varepsilon_{\mathrm{BTA}}(e) : \tau_{\mathrm{BTA}}(t)$$

$$\begin{array}{ll} \mathcal{E}^{C}_{\mathrm{BTA}}[\![\ \mathtt{f}_{\mathrm{i}}^{b1}[t_1] : t_0 : b0\ ]\!] = & \\ \quad \text{let } t_0'{:}b0' = \mathcal{T}_{\mathrm{BTA}}[\![\ t_0{:}b0\ ]\!] & (1) \\ \quad \text{let } t_1'{:}b1' = \mathcal{T}^{C(\mathtt{f}_{\mathrm{i}})}_{\mathrm{BTA}}[\![\ (t_1{:}b1)\sqcap(t_0'{:}\mathtt{c})\ ]\!] & (2) \\ \quad \text{in UD}(\ \mathtt{f}_{\mathrm{i}}^{b1'}[t_1'] : t_1' : b1',\ b0') & (3) \end{array}$$

Table 3.7: $\mathcal{E}^{C}_{\mathrm{BTA}}$: Binding time analysis of expressions (part 1)

and we shall say that $e{:}t{:}b$ is *1*-well-formed when this is the case. We shall make use of this assumption when we encounter constructs where too little type information is explicitly given and where we thus have to rely on Fact 2.1.4 to infer the (*1*-level!) type information that is missing. For brevity we shall write $\tau_{\mathrm{BTA}}(\mathcal{A}_{\mathrm{BTA}}(e))$ for $\{(\mathtt{x}_{\mathrm{i}},\tau_{\mathrm{BTA}}(t_{\mathrm{i}}))|(\mathtt{x}_{\mathrm{i}},t_{\mathrm{i}}{:}b_{\mathrm{i}})\in\mathcal{A}_{\mathrm{BTA}}(e)\}$ in the presentation of the transformation function below. The result of $\mathcal{E}^{C}_{\mathrm{BTA}}[\![\ e{:}t{:}b\ ]\!]$ should then be the greatest among the triples $e'{:}t'{:}b'$ that satisfy the well-formedness conditions:

$$\mathcal{A}_{\mathrm{BTA}}(e') \text{ is functional}$$

$$\text{fun}(\mathcal{A}_{\mathrm{BTA}}(e')) \vdash_{\mathrm{C}} \varepsilon'_{\mathrm{BTA}}(e'){:}t'{:}b'$$

and that satisfy the condition of being less than the argument to $\mathcal{E}^{C}_{\mathrm{BTA}}$:

$$e'{:}t'{:}b' \preceq e{:}t{:}b$$

Here we have once more extended the partial order $\preceq$ in a componentwise manner. A more informal wording of the last inequality is that $e'{:}t'{:}b'$ *respects* the annotations in $e{:}t{:}b$.

Interspersed with the definition of the transformation function we shall motivate and explain the clauses. We begin with the clause for constants as given in Table 3.7. The intention with the first two lines and the first argument to UD in the third line is to obtain the best result corresponding to the well-formedness rules of Tables 3.4 and 3.5 but with rules [up] and [down] excluded. For this reason neither $b0$ nor $b0'$ should be allowed to influence the annotation $b1'$ of $\mathtt{f}_{\mathrm{i}}$. The intention with UD is then to investigate whether rules [up] or [down] may be used to change the overall binding time $b1'$ to the binding time $b0'$.

Ignoring rules [up] and [down] the procedure is thus as follows. In line (1) we ensure that the type t_0 is consistent with the binding time $b0$. This may change the type (to t_0') but may also change the binding time (to $b0'$). In line (2) we ensure that the types supplied for $\mathtt{f}_{\mathrm{i}}$ agree with one another and with the constraints expressed by the type scheme $C(\mathtt{f}_{\mathrm{i}})$. Here we do not use the binding time $b0'$ (or $b0$) for t_0' as the applicability of $b0'$ may depend on rules [up] and [down]. For example even if the argument to $\mathcal{E}^{C}_{\mathrm{BTA}}$ is $\mathtt{f}^{\mathtt{c}}_{\mathrm{eq}}[\underline{\mathtt{Int}\rightarrow\mathtt{Int}\rightarrow\mathtt{Bool}}]{:}\underline{\mathtt{Int}\rightarrow\mathtt{Int}\rightarrow\mathtt{Bool}}{:}\mathtt{r}$ there is no need to change the annotation of $\mathtt{f}_{\mathrm{eq}}$ from $\mathtt{c}$ to $\mathtt{r}$. The best result then is $\mathtt{f}_{\mathrm{i}}^{b1'}[t_1']{:}t_1'{:}b1'$ provided that rules [up] and [down] are ignored.

Taking rules [up] and [down] into account we must investigate whether or not they could be used to change the overall binding time $b1'$ to $b0'$ which is closer to what was originally desired (i.e. $b0$). This is accomplished by the auxiliary function UD whose general definition is

$$
\begin{array}{lr}
\mathrm{UD}(\ e : t : b,\ b') = & \\
\quad \text{if } b{=}\mathtt{c} \wedge b'{=}\mathtt{r} \wedge \vdash t{:}b' & \text{(a)} \\
\quad \text{then } e{:}t{:}b' & \text{(b)} \\
\quad \text{else if } b{=}\mathtt{r} \wedge b'{=}\mathtt{c} \wedge \vdash t{:}b' \wedge & \\
\qquad\qquad \mathcal{A}_{\mathrm{BTA}}(e) \subseteq \{\mathtt{x_i} | \mathtt{i} {\in} I\} {\times} (T2 {\times} \{\mathtt{c}\}) & \text{(c)} \\
\qquad \text{then } e{:}t{:}b' & \text{(d)} \\
\qquad \text{else } e{:}t{:}b & \text{(e)}
\end{array}
$$

Line (a) tests for the applicability of rule [down] and if it is applicable the result is produced in line (b). Line (c) tests for the applicability of rule [up] and if it is applicable the result is produced in line (d). If neither [down] nor [up] is applicable the result must be equal to the first parameter to UD and this is produced in line (e). — There is one snag in this definition, however, because to prove the correctness of $\mathcal{E}^{C}_{\mathrm{BTA}}$ we should like $\mathrm{UD}(e{:}t{:}b, b') \preceq e{:}t{:}b'$ to hold in order to establish $\mathcal{E}^{C}_{\mathrm{BTA}}[\![e{:}t{:}b]\!] \preceq e{:}t{:}b$. This may fail if $b{=}\mathtt{c}$ and $b'{=}\mathtt{r}$ but $\vdash t{:}b'$ does not hold. We shall therefore verify that

$$(b{=}\mathtt{c}) \wedge (b'{=}\mathtt{r}) \Rightarrow \vdash t{:}b'$$

whenever we use $\mathrm{UD}(e{:}t{:}b,b')$. In the clause for constants this amounts to verifying that $\vdash t'_1{:}b0'$ holds when $b1'{=}\mathtt{c}$ and $b0'{=}\mathtt{r}$. But line (1) ensures that t'_0 is all underlined in this case, hence $t'_1{=}t'_0$ and $\vdash t'_1{:}\mathtt{r}$ as required.

Example 3.2.10 The call

$$\mathcal{E}^{C}_{\mathrm{BTA}}[\![\ \underline{\mathtt{eq}}[\mathtt{Int}{\rightarrow}\mathtt{Int}{\rightarrow}\mathtt{Bool}] : \mathtt{Int}{\rightarrow}\underline{\mathtt{Int}}{\rightarrow}\mathtt{Bool} : \mathtt{c}\ ]\!]$$

amounts to

$$\mathcal{E}^{C}_{\mathrm{BTA}}[\![\ \mathtt{f}^{\mathtt{r}}_{\mathrm{eq}}[\mathtt{Int}{\rightarrow}\mathtt{Int}{\rightarrow}\mathtt{Bool}] : \mathtt{Int}{\rightarrow}\underline{\mathtt{Int}}{\rightarrow}\mathtt{Bool} : \mathtt{c}\ ]\!]$$

We get

$$t'_0{:}b0' = \mathtt{Int}{\rightarrow}\underline{\mathtt{Int}{\rightarrow}\mathtt{Bool}} : \mathtt{c}$$

$$t'_1{:}b1' = \underline{\mathtt{Int}{\rightarrow}\mathtt{Int}{\rightarrow}\mathtt{Bool}} : \mathtt{r}$$

so that the result is

$$\mathrm{UD}(\ \mathtt{f}^{\mathtt{r}}_{\mathrm{eq}}[\underline{\mathtt{Int}{\rightarrow}\mathtt{Int}{\rightarrow}\mathtt{Bool}}] : \underline{\mathtt{Int}{\rightarrow}\mathtt{Int}{\rightarrow}\mathtt{Bool}} : \mathtt{r},\ \mathtt{c})$$

Now clearly we may use rule [up] to deduce that

$$\emptyset \vdash_C \mathtt{f}^{\mathtt{r}}_{\mathtt{eq}}[\underline{\mathtt{Int}\rightarrow\mathtt{Int}\rightarrow\mathtt{Bool}}] : \underline{\mathtt{Int}\rightarrow\mathtt{Int}\rightarrow\mathtt{Bool}} : \mathtt{r}$$

implies

$$\emptyset \vdash_C \mathtt{f}^{\mathtt{r}}_{\mathtt{eq}}[\underline{\mathtt{Int}\rightarrow\mathtt{Int}\rightarrow\mathtt{Bool}}] : \underline{\mathtt{Int}\rightarrow\mathtt{Int}\rightarrow\mathtt{Bool}} : \mathtt{c}$$

Thus the result is

$$\mathtt{f}^{\mathtt{r}}_{\mathtt{eq}}[\underline{\mathtt{Int}\rightarrow\mathtt{Int}\rightarrow\mathtt{Bool}}] : \underline{\mathtt{Int}\rightarrow\mathtt{Int}\rightarrow\mathtt{Bool}} : \mathtt{c}$$

which amounts to

$$\underline{\mathtt{eq}}[\underline{\mathtt{Int}\rightarrow\mathtt{Int}\rightarrow\mathtt{Bool}}] : \underline{\mathtt{Int}\rightarrow\mathtt{Int}\rightarrow\mathtt{Bool}} : \mathtt{c}$$

in the 'usual' notation. Note that eq is underlined even though the resulting binding time is c. □

Turning to products the clauses for tupling and projection are given in Table 3.8. The intention with the first two lines of the clause for tupling is to obtain the desired result for each of the components. Here the desired binding time is indicated by all of *b1*, *b2* and *b0* and we therefore use their greatest lower bound. If the resulting binding times agree we then have the desired result. If they do not agree we have to perform yet another recursive call. This is a phenomenon not present in the type analysis in Section 2.2 because there we would have constructed a substitution that would equate all that needed to be equated. We cannot do so here and thus have to introduce the additional recursive call. This also motivates why the domain of $\mathcal{E}^C_{\mathrm{BTA}}$ equals its codomain (rather than e.g. $E\times T2\times 2$). Finally, we observe that the rules [up] and [down] are not applicable so that there is no need to include a call to UD.

Next consider the clause for the projection on first components. In the first line it is ensured that the overall type and binding time agree. This is necessary in order to verify the condition for using UD in the fifth line: $\vdash t''_0{:}b0'$ when b'=c and $b0'$=r. For the verification, note that t'_0 is all underlined in this case so that t''_0 equals t'_0. In the absence of information about the type of the other component of *e* we obtain the (*1*-level!) type in the second line using Fact 2.1.4 and

$$\tau_{\mathrm{BTA}}(A) = \{\ (\mathtt{x}_i,\tau_{\mathrm{BTA}}(t_i)) \mid (\mathtt{x}_i,t_i{:}b_i) \in A\ \}$$

In the third line all symbols are annotated with c so as to produce the most conservative *2*-level type. This then facilitates the recursive call in the fourth line. Here we have taken the liberty of using the binding time b' twice in the pattern on the left hand side because the rules [down] and [up] are not applicable to product types and therefore the two occurrences must always agree (given the correctness of $\mathcal{E}^C_{\mathrm{BTA}}$ to be shown in Proposition 3.2.13). The clause for the projection on the second component of a pair is analogous.

$$
\begin{array}{l}
\mathcal{E}^C_{\mathrm{BTA}}[\![\ \langle^{b1} e_1,e_2\rangle : t_1\times^{b2}t_2 : b0 \ ]\!] = \\
\quad \text{let } e_1'{:}t_1'{:}b1' = \mathcal{E}^C_{\mathrm{BTA}}[\![\ e_1 : t_1 : b1\sqcap b2\sqcap b0 \ ]\!] \\
\quad \text{let } e_2'{:}t_2'{:}b2' = \mathcal{E}^C_{\mathrm{BTA}}[\![\ e_2 : t_2 : b1\sqcap b2\sqcap b0 \ ]\!] \\
\quad \text{if } b1'{=}b2' \\
\quad \text{then } \langle^{b1'} e_1',e_2'\rangle : t_1'\times^{b1'}t_2' : b1' \\
\quad \text{else } \mathcal{E}^C_{\mathrm{BTA}}[\![\ \langle^{b'} e_1',e_2'\rangle : t_1'\times^{b'}t_2' : b' \ ]\!] \\
\qquad \text{where } b' = b1'\sqcap b2'
\end{array}
$$

$$
\begin{array}{l}
\mathcal{E}^C_{\mathrm{BTA}}[\![\ \mathtt{fst}^{b1} \ e : t_0 : b0 \ ]\!] = \\
\quad \text{let } t_0'{:}b0' = \mathcal{T}_{\mathrm{BTA}}[\![\ t_0{:}b0 \ ]\!] \\
\quad \text{let } t_1 \text{ be given by } \mathrm{fun}(\tau_{\mathrm{BTA}}(\mathcal{A}_{\mathrm{BTA}}(e))) \vdash_{\mathrm{C}} \varepsilon_{\mathrm{BTA}}(e){:} \\
\qquad\qquad\qquad \tau_{\mathrm{BTA}}(t_0)\times t_1 \\
\quad \text{let } t_1' = \tau^{\mathrm{c}}_{\mathrm{BTA}}(t_1) \\
\quad \text{let } e'{:}t_0''\times^{b'}t_1''{:}b' = \mathcal{E}^C_{\mathrm{BTA}}[\![\ e{:}t_0'\times^{b1}t_1'{:}b1 \ ]\!] \\
\quad \text{in } \mathrm{UD}(\ \mathtt{fst}^{b'} \ e' : t_0'' : b',\ b0')
\end{array}
$$

$$
\begin{array}{l}
\mathcal{E}^C_{\mathrm{BTA}}[\![\ \mathtt{snd}^{b1} \ e : t_0 : b0 \ ]\!] = \\
\quad \text{let } t_0'{:}b0' = \mathcal{T}_{\mathrm{BTA}}[\![\ t_0{:}b0 \ ]\!] \\
\quad \text{let } t_1 \text{ be given by } \mathrm{fun}(\tau_{\mathrm{BTA}}(\mathcal{A}_{\mathrm{BTA}}(e))) \vdash_{\mathrm{C}} \varepsilon_{\mathrm{BTA}}(e){:} \\
\qquad\qquad\qquad t_1\times\tau_{\mathrm{BTA}}(t_0) \\
\quad \text{let } t_1' = \tau^{\mathrm{c}}_{\mathrm{BTA}}(t_1) \\
\quad \text{let } e'{:}t_1''\times^{b'}t_0''{:}b' = \mathcal{E}^C_{\mathrm{BTA}}[\![\ e{:}t_1'\times^{b1}t_0'{:}b1 \ ]\!] \\
\quad \text{in } \mathrm{UD}(\ \mathtt{snd}^{b'} \ e' : t_0'' : b',\ b0')
\end{array}
$$

Table 3.8: $\mathcal{E}^C_{\mathrm{BTA}}$: Binding time analysis of expressions (part 2)

Example 3.2.11 The call

$$\mathcal{E}^C_{\mathrm{BTA}}[\![\ \mathtt{fst} \ \langle \mathtt{eq[A}\rightarrow\mathtt{A}\rightarrow\mathtt{Bool]},\ \mathtt{eq[A}\rightarrow\mathtt{A}\rightarrow\mathtt{Bool]}\rangle : \mathtt{A}\rightarrow\mathtt{A}\rightarrow\mathtt{Bool} : \mathtt{r} \ ]\!]$$

amounts to

$$\mathcal{E}^C_{\mathrm{BTA}}[\![\ \mathtt{fst}^{\mathtt{c}} \ \langle^{\mathtt{c}} \mathtt{f}^{\mathtt{c}}_{\mathrm{eq}}\mathtt{[A}\rightarrow\mathtt{A}\rightarrow\mathtt{Bool]},\ \mathtt{f}^{\mathtt{c}}_{\mathrm{eq}}\mathtt{[A}\rightarrow\mathtt{A}\rightarrow\mathtt{Bool]}\rangle : \mathtt{A}\rightarrow\mathtt{A}\rightarrow\mathtt{Bool} : \mathtt{r} \ ]\!]$$

Using the equation for `fst` we get, in the notation with underlining,

$$t_0'{:}b0' = \underline{\mathtt{A}\rightarrow\mathtt{A}\rightarrow\mathtt{Bool}} : \mathtt{r}$$

$$t_1' = \mathtt{A}\rightarrow\mathtt{A}\rightarrow\mathtt{Bool}$$

We shall shortly see that

$$
\begin{array}{l}
\mathcal{E}^C_{\mathrm{BTA}}[\![\ \langle^{\mathtt{c}} \mathtt{f}^{\mathtt{c}}_{\mathrm{eq}}\mathtt{[A}\rightarrow\mathtt{A}\rightarrow\mathtt{Bool]},\ \mathtt{f}^{\mathtt{c}}_{\mathrm{eq}}\mathtt{[A}\rightarrow\mathtt{A}\rightarrow\mathtt{Bool]}\rangle : \\
\qquad (\underline{\mathtt{A}\rightarrow\mathtt{A}\rightarrow\mathtt{Bool}})\times(\mathtt{A}\rightarrow\mathtt{A}\rightarrow\mathtt{Bool}) : \mathtt{c} \ ]\!]
\end{array}
$$

equals

$$\begin{aligned}&\langle{}^{c}\mathtt{f}^{c}_{eq}[\underline{\mathtt{A}\to\mathtt{A}\to\mathtt{Bool}}],\ \mathtt{f}^{c}_{eq}[\mathtt{A}\to\mathtt{A}\to\mathtt{Bool}]\rangle :\\ &\qquad(\underline{\mathtt{A}\to\mathtt{A}\to\mathtt{Bool}})\times(\mathtt{A}\to\mathtt{A}\to\mathtt{Bool}) : \mathtt{c}\end{aligned}$$

so that the result is

$$\begin{aligned}&\mathrm{UD}(\ \mathbf{\mathtt{fst}}^{c}\ \langle{}^{c}\mathtt{f}^{c}_{eq}[\underline{\mathtt{A}\to\mathtt{A}\to\mathtt{Bool}}],\ \mathtt{f}^{c}_{eq}[\mathtt{A}\to\mathtt{A}\to\mathtt{Bool}]\rangle :\\ &\qquad(\underline{\mathtt{A}\to\mathtt{A}\to\mathtt{Bool}}) : \mathtt{c},\ \mathtt{r})\end{aligned}$$

and, in the notation with underlining, this amounts to

$$\mathtt{fst}\ \langle\mathtt{eq}[\underline{\mathtt{A}\to\mathtt{A}\to\mathtt{Bool}}],\ \mathtt{eq}[\mathtt{A}\to\mathtt{A}\to\mathtt{Bool}]\rangle : \underline{\mathtt{A}\to\mathtt{A}\to\mathtt{Bool}} : \mathtt{r}$$

Returning to the call

$$\begin{aligned}&\mathcal{E}^{C}_{\mathrm{BTA}}[\![\ \langle{}^{c}\mathtt{f}^{c}_{eq}[\mathtt{A}\to\mathtt{A}\to\mathtt{Bool}],\ \mathtt{f}^{c}_{eq}[\mathtt{A}\to\mathtt{A}\to\mathtt{Bool}]\rangle :\\ &\qquad(\underline{\mathtt{A}\to\mathtt{A}\to\mathtt{Bool}})\times(\mathtt{A}\to\mathtt{A}\to\mathtt{Bool}) : \mathtt{c}\ ]\!]\end{aligned}$$

we get

$$\begin{aligned}e_1':t_1':b1' &= \mathtt{f}^{c}_{eq}[\underline{\mathtt{A}\to\mathtt{A}\to\mathtt{Bool}}] : \underline{\mathtt{A}\to\mathtt{A}\to\mathtt{Bool}} : \mathtt{c}\\ e_2':t_2':b2' &= \mathtt{f}^{c}_{eq}[\mathtt{A}\to\mathtt{A}\to\mathtt{Bool}] : \mathtt{A}\to\mathtt{A}\to\mathtt{Bool} : \mathtt{c}\end{aligned}$$

As $b1' = b2'$ we get the result

$$\begin{aligned}&\langle{}^{c}\mathtt{f}^{c}_{eq}[\underline{\mathtt{A}\to\mathtt{A}\to\mathtt{Bool}}],\ \mathtt{f}^{c}_{eq}[\mathtt{A}\to\mathtt{A}\to\mathtt{Bool}]\rangle :\\ &\qquad(\underline{\mathtt{A}\to\mathtt{A}\to\mathtt{Bool}})\times(\mathtt{A}\to\mathtt{A}\to\mathtt{Bool}) : \mathtt{c}\end{aligned}$$

as was claimed above. □

Turning to function space the clauses are given in Table 3.9. First consider the simplest clause which is the one for variables. As may be seen this is analogous to the clause for constants. The only difference is in the second line where we use $\mathcal{T}_{\mathrm{BTA}}$ instead of $\mathcal{T}^{C(\mathtt{f}_i)}_{\mathrm{BTA}}$. The verification condition for UD is that $\vdash t_1':b0'$ when $b1'$=c and $b0'$=r and we may verify this as we did for constants.

Next consider the clause for λ-abstraction. Intuitively, the first line ensures that the result type and binding time are consistent. The second line is the recursive call and in the third line all assumptions about the type and binding time of $\mathbf{x}_i$ are collected in the set Y. This set is consistent in the sense that $\{\tau_{\mathrm{BTA}}(t) | t{:}b{\in}Y\}$ is a singleton as follows from our assumption that $\mathcal{E}^{C}_{\mathrm{BTA}}$ is only applied to *2*-level expressions that are well-formed regarded as typed expressions in the sense of Chapter 2. It follows that $\sqcap Y$ exists and the fourth line therefore tests whether Y is a singleton, i.e. whether all assumptions about $\mathbf{x}_i$ are consistent. If this is the case we produce the result in the fifth line. The verification condition for UD is that $\vdash t_1 \to^{b1} t' : b0'$ when $b1$=c and $b0'$=r and this follows from the first line

$$\begin{array}{l}
\mathcal{E}^{C}_{\mathrm{BTA}}[\![\ \mathbf{x}_{\mathrm{i}}^{b1}[t_1] : t_0 : b0\ ]\!] = \\
\qquad \text{let } t_0'{:}b0' = \mathcal{T}_{\mathrm{BTA}}[\![\ t_0{:}b0\ ]\!] \\
\qquad \text{let } t_1'{:}b1' = \mathcal{T}_{\mathrm{BTA}}[\![\ (t_1{:}b1)\sqcap(t_0'{:}\mathtt{c})\ ]\!] \\
\qquad \text{in UD}(\ \mathbf{x}_{\mathrm{i}}^{b1'}[t_1'] : t_1' : b1',\ b0')
\end{array}$$

$$\begin{array}{l}
\mathcal{E}^{C}_{\mathrm{BTA}}[\![\ \lambda^{b1}\mathbf{x}_{\mathrm{i}}[t_1].e : t_2 \rightarrow^{b2} t_3 : b0\ ]\!] = \\
\qquad \text{let } t_2' \rightarrow^{b2'} t_3' : b0' = \mathcal{T}_{\mathrm{BTA}}[\![\ t_2 \rightarrow^{b2} t_3 : b0\ ]\!] \\
\qquad \text{let } e'{:}t'{:}b' = \mathcal{E}^{C}_{\mathrm{BTA}}[\![\ e{:}t_3'{:}b2'\ ]\!] \\
\qquad \text{let } Y = \{(t_1{:}b1),(t_2',b')\} \cup \mathcal{A}_{\mathrm{BTA}}(e')(\mathbf{x}_{\mathrm{i}}) \\
\qquad \text{if } Y = \{\sqcap Y\} \\
\qquad \text{then UD}(\ \lambda^{b1}\mathbf{x}_{\mathrm{i}}[t_1].e' : t_1 \rightarrow^{b1} t' : b1,\ b0'\ ) \\
\qquad \text{else } \mathcal{E}^{C}_{\mathrm{BTA}}[\![\ \lambda^{b}\mathbf{x}_{\mathrm{i}}[t].e'[\mathbf{x}_{\mathrm{i}}^{b}[t]/\mathbf{x}_{\mathrm{i}}] : t \rightarrow^{b} t' : b0'\ ]\!] \\
\qquad\qquad \text{where } t{:}b = \sqcap Y
\end{array}$$

$$\begin{array}{l}
\mathcal{E}^{C}_{\mathrm{BTA}}[\![\ e_1\ (^{b1}\ e_2\ ) : t_0 : b0\ ]\!] = \\
\qquad \text{let } t_1 \text{ be given by fun}(\tau_{\mathrm{BTA}}(\mathcal{A}_{\mathrm{BTA}}(e_2))) \vdash_{\mathrm{C}} \varepsilon_{\mathrm{BTA}}(e_2){:}t_1 \\
\qquad \text{let } t_1' = \tau^{\mathtt{c}}_{\mathrm{BTA}}(t_1) \\
\qquad \text{in } \mathcal{E}^{\bullet C}_{\mathrm{BTA}}[\![\ e_1(e_2) : t_1' \rightarrow^{b1} t_0 : b0\ ]\!]
\end{array}$$

$$\begin{array}{l}
\mathcal{E}^{\bullet C}_{\mathrm{BTA}}[\![\ e_1(e_2) : t_1 \rightarrow^{b1} t_2 : b0\ ]\!] = \\
\qquad \text{let } t_2'{:}b0' = \mathcal{T}_{\mathrm{BTA}}[\![\ t_2{:}b0\ ]\!] \\
\qquad \text{let } e_1'{:}t_1' \rightarrow^{b1'} t_2''{:}b1'' = \mathcal{E}^{C}_{\mathrm{BTA}}[\![\ e_1{:}t_1 \rightarrow^{b1} t_2'{:}b1\ ]\!] \\
\qquad \text{let } e_2'{:}t_1''{:}b2' = \mathcal{E}^{C}_{\mathrm{BTA}}[\![\ e_2{:}t_1{:}b1\ ]\!] \\
\qquad \text{if } (t_1'{:}b1') = (t_1''{:}b2') \\
\qquad \text{then UD}(\ e_1'\ (^{b1'} e_2') : t_2'' : b1',\ b0') \\
\qquad \text{else } \mathcal{E}^{\bullet C}_{\mathrm{BTA}}[\![\ e_1'(e_2') : t' \rightarrow^{b'} t_2'' : b0'\ ]\!] \\
\qquad\qquad \text{where } t'{:}b' = (t_1'{:}b1') \sqcap (t_1''{:}b2')
\end{array}$$

Table 3.9: $\mathcal{E}^{C}_{\mathrm{BTA}}$: Binding time analysis of expressions (part 3)

(because $b1$=c and $b0'$=r is in fact impossible). If Y is not a singleton we must perform a new recursive call where we have replaced all assumptions about $\mathbf{x}_{\mathrm{i}}$ with the new assumption $t{:}b = \sqcap Y$. In the body of e' this is expressed by overloading the notation for substitution[4], so that $e'[\mathbf{x}_{\mathrm{i}}^{b}[t]/\mathbf{x}_{\mathrm{i}}]$ equals $\mathbf{x}_{\mathrm{i}}^{b}[t]$ when e' is of the form $\mathbf{x}_{\mathrm{i}}^{b'}[t']$.

The equation for application is somewhat more intricate as it uses an auxiliary function. The problem is that we shall also need the type of the operand part of the application. In the first line of the body for $\mathcal{E}^{C}_{\mathrm{BTA}}$ we use Fact 2.1.4 to compute the missing (*'1*-level'!) type information and in the second line we obtain a *2*-

[4]Without this 'overloading' it might be argued that $e'[\mathbf{x}_{\mathrm{i}}^{b}[t]/\mathbf{x}_{\mathrm{i}}]$ equals $\mathbf{x}_{\mathrm{i}}^{b}[t]^{b'}[t']$ when e' is of the form $\mathbf{x}_{\mathrm{i}}^{b'}[t']$.

level type by annotating each symbol with c. In the third line we obtain the desired result using $\mathcal{E}^{\bullet C}_{\text{BTA}}$ which is supplied with full information about the type of the operator. In the body for $\mathcal{E}^{\bullet C}_{\text{BTA}}$ the first line ensures the consistency between the overall type and binding time. The second and third lines then contain the recursive calls. The fourth line tests whether or not the assumptions about the type and binding time of the operand agree. If this is the case we produce the result in the fifth line. The verification condition for UD is that $\vdash t_2'':b0'$ when $b1'$=c and $b0'$=r and this is enforced by the first line. If the assumptions do not agree we perform a recursive call. Since it might well be the case that t_1' differs from t_1'' this shows the need for the auxiliary function $\mathcal{E}^{\bullet C}_{\text{BTA}}$ that allows also to record the type of the operand as otherwise we would start with $\tau^{\text{c}}_{\text{BTA}}(t_1)$ in $\mathcal{E}^{C}_{\text{BTA}}$ once again and this might lead to a non-terminating computation.

Example 3.2.12 Returning to Example 3.1.2 we write

$$\Psi = \lambda x[(\underline{A{\rightarrow}A}){\rightarrow}(\underline{A{\rightarrow}A})].\ \underline{\lambda} y[\underline{A{\rightarrow}A}].\ x(y)$$
$$t_\Psi = ((\underline{A{\rightarrow}A}){\rightarrow}(\underline{A{\rightarrow}A})) \rightarrow ((\underline{A{\rightarrow}A})\underline{\rightarrow}(\underline{A{\rightarrow}A}))$$

We intend to perform the call

$$\mathcal{E}^{C}_{\text{BTA}}[\![\ \Psi : t_\Psi : \text{c}\ ]\!]$$

in order to obtain the best well-formed expression that is consistent with Ψ, which is not itself well-formed. Before we can do this, however, we must transform the expression Ψ from *E2* to *E2'*, i.e. all variables in Ψ must be annotated with their type and binding time. So the call we do perform is

$$\mathcal{E}^{C}_{\text{BTA}}[\![\ \lambda^{\text{c}}x[t_0 \rightarrow^{\text{c}} t_0].\ \lambda^{\text{r}}y[t_0].\ x^{\text{c}}[t_0 \rightarrow^{\text{c}} t_0]\ (^{\text{c}}\ y^{\text{r}}[t_0]\ ) : t_\Psi : \text{c}\ ]\!]$$

where t_0 abbreviates $\underline{A{\rightarrow}A}$, i.e. $A^{\text{r}} \rightarrow^{\text{r}} A^{\text{r}}$. This call gives rise to the call

$$\mathcal{E}^{C}_{\text{BTA}}[\![\ \lambda^{\text{r}}y[t_0].\ x^{\text{c}}[t_0 \rightarrow^{\text{c}} t_0]\ (^{\text{c}}\ y^{\text{r}}[t_0]\ ) : t_0 \rightarrow^{\text{r}} t_0 : \text{c}\ ]\!]$$

which yields the call

$$\begin{aligned}\mathcal{E}^{C}_{\text{BTA}}[\![\ & x^{\text{c}}[t_0 \rightarrow^{\text{c}} t_0]\ (^{\text{c}}\ y^{\text{r}}[t_0]\ ) : t_0 : \text{r}\ ]\!] = \\ & \mathcal{E}^{\bullet C}_{\text{BTA}}[\![\ x^{\text{c}}[t_0 \rightarrow^{\text{c}} t_0]\ (\ y^{\text{r}}[t_0]\ ) : (A^{\text{c}} \rightarrow^{\text{c}} A^{\text{c}}) \rightarrow^{\text{c}} t_0 : \text{r}\ ]\!]\end{aligned}$$

We have

$$\begin{aligned}\mathcal{E}^{C}_{\text{BTA}}[\![\ & x^{\text{c}}[t_0 \rightarrow^{\text{c}} t_0] : (A^{\text{c}} \rightarrow^{\text{c}} A^{\text{c}}) \rightarrow^{\text{c}} t_0 : \text{c}\ ]\!] = \\ & x^{\text{c}}[t_0 \rightarrow^{\text{c}} t_0] : t_0 \rightarrow^{\text{c}} t_0 : \text{c}\end{aligned}$$
$$\mathcal{E}^{C}_{\text{BTA}}[\![\ y^{\text{r}}[t_0] : A^{\text{c}} \rightarrow^{\text{c}} A^{\text{c}} : \text{c}\ ]\!] = y^{\text{r}}[t_0] : t_0 : \text{r}$$

Note the final r since the clause in UD that corresponds to [up] is not applicable. As t_0:c differs from t_0:r the above call to $\mathcal{E}^{\bullet C}_{\text{BTA}}$ gives rise to the call

$$\mathcal{E}^{\bullet C}_{\mathrm{BTA}}[\![\ \mathtt{x}^{\mathtt{c}}[t_0 \to^{\mathtt{c}} t_0]\ (\ \mathtt{y}^{\mathtt{r}}[t_0]\ ) : t_0 \to^{\mathtt{r}} t_0 : \mathtt{r}\ ]\!]$$

We have

$$\mathcal{E}^{C}_{\mathrm{BTA}}[\![\ \mathtt{x}^{\mathtt{c}}[t_0 \to^{\mathtt{c}} t_0] : t_0 \to^{\mathtt{r}} t_0 : \mathtt{r}\ ]\!] = \mathtt{x}^{\mathtt{c}}[t_0 \to^{\mathtt{r}} t_0] : t_0 \to^{\mathtt{r}} t_0 : \mathtt{r}$$

$$\mathcal{E}^{C}_{\mathrm{BTA}}[\![\ \mathtt{y}^{\mathtt{r}}[t_0] : t_0 : \mathtt{r}\ ]\!] = \mathtt{y}^{\mathtt{r}}[t_0] : t_0 : \mathtt{r}$$

and since t_0:r $=$ t_0:r the call to $\mathcal{E}^{\bullet C}_{\mathrm{BTA}}$ returns

$$\mathtt{x}^{\mathtt{c}}[t_0 \to^{\mathtt{r}} t_0]\ (^{\mathtt{r}}\ \mathtt{y}^{\mathtt{r}}[t_0]\ ) : t_0 : \mathtt{r}$$

where again we note the final r. Hence

$$\mathcal{E}^{C}_{\mathrm{BTA}}[\![\ \lambda^{\mathtt{r}}\mathtt{y}[t_0].\ \mathtt{x}^{\mathtt{c}}[t_0 \to^{\mathtt{c}} t_0]\ (^{\mathtt{c}}\ \mathtt{y}^{\mathtt{r}}[t_0]\ ) : t_0 \to^{\mathtt{r}} t_0 : \mathsf{c}\ ]\!] = \lambda^{\mathtt{r}}\mathtt{y}[t_0].\ \mathtt{x}^{\mathtt{c}}[t_0 \to^{\mathtt{r}} t_0]\ (^{\mathtt{r}}\ \mathtt{y}^{\mathtt{r}}[t_0]\ ) : t_0 \to^{\mathtt{r}} t_0 : \mathsf{c}$$

because the set Y turns out to be a singleton and the clause in UD that corresponds to [up] is applicable. However, the original call to $\mathcal{E}^{C}_{\mathrm{BTA}}$ gives rise to the call

$$\mathcal{E}^{C}_{\mathrm{BTA}}[\![\ \lambda^{\mathtt{c}}\mathtt{x}[t_0 \to^{\mathtt{r}} t_0].\ \lambda^{\mathtt{r}}\mathtt{y}[t_0].\ \mathtt{x}^{\mathtt{c}}[t_0 \to^{\mathtt{r}} t_0]\ (^{\mathtt{r}}\ \mathtt{y}^{\mathtt{r}}[t_0]\ ) : (t_0 \to^{\mathtt{r}} t_0) \to^{\mathtt{c}} (t_0 \to^{\mathtt{r}} t_0) : \mathsf{c}\ ]\!]$$

because the set Y becomes $\{(t_0 \to^{\mathtt{c}} t_0 : \mathsf{c}), (t_0 \to^{\mathtt{r}} t_0 : \mathsf{c})\}$ which is not a singleton. It is fairly straightforward to see that this call returns

$$\lambda^{\mathtt{c}}\mathtt{x}[t_0 \to^{\mathtt{r}} t_0].\ \lambda^{\mathtt{r}}\mathtt{y}[t_0].\ \mathtt{x}^{\mathtt{c}}[t_0 \to^{\mathtt{r}} t_0]\ (^{\mathtt{r}}\ \mathtt{y}^{\mathtt{r}}[t_0]\ ) : (t_0 \to^{\mathtt{r}} t_0) \to^{\mathtt{c}} (t_0 \to^{\mathtt{r}} t_0) : \mathsf{c}$$

(which is equal to the argument of $\mathcal{E}^{C}_{\mathrm{BTA}}$). Thus Ψ gets transformed to

$$\lambda\mathtt{x}[(\underline{\mathtt{A}\to\mathtt{A}})\underline{\to}(\underline{\mathtt{A}\to\mathtt{A}})].\ \underline{\lambda}\mathtt{y}[\underline{\mathtt{A}\to\mathtt{A}}].\ \mathtt{x}\ \underline{(}\mathtt{y}\underline{)}$$

which is well-formed but unfortunately is nothing but the identity. However, given that Ψ was not well-formed one could hardly hope for better. □

We now turn to the equations for the constructs associated with lists. As no new phenomena arise we cut down on the explanations and examples. The clauses are given in Table 3.10. Turning to conditional, the truth values and fixed points we have the clauses of Table 3.11.

It remains to verify that these clauses define a function $\mathcal{E}^{C}_{\mathrm{BTA}}$ with the desired properties. Recall that a triple e:t:b in $E2' \times T2 \times 2$ is *1-well-formed* if the underlying expression is well-formed in the sense of Section 2.1:

$$\tau_{\mathrm{BTA}}(\mathcal{A}_{\mathrm{BTA}}(e)) \text{ is functional}$$

$$\mathrm{fun}(\tau_{\mathrm{BTA}}(\mathcal{A}_{\mathrm{BTA}}(e))) \vdash_{\mathrm{C}} \varepsilon_{\mathrm{BTA}}(e) : \tau_{\mathrm{BTA}}(t)$$

$$
\begin{array}{l}
\mathcal{E}^{C}_{\text{BTA}}[\![\ e_1 :^{b1} e_2 : t\ \texttt{list}^{b2} : b0\ ]\!] = \\
\quad \text{let } e_1' : t_1' : b1' = \mathcal{E}^{C}_{\text{BTA}}[\![\ e_1 : t : b1 \sqcap b2 \sqcap b0\ ]\!] \\
\quad \text{let } e_2' : t_2' : b2' = \mathcal{E}^{C}_{\text{BTA}}[\![\ e_2 : t\ \texttt{list}^{b1 \sqcap b2 \sqcap b0} : b1 \sqcap b2 \sqcap b0\ ]\!] \\
\quad \text{if } t_1'\ \texttt{list}^{b1'} : b1' = t_2' : b2' \\
\quad \text{then } e_1' :^{b1'} e_2' : t_1'\ \texttt{list}^{b1'} : b1' \\
\quad \text{else } \mathcal{E}^{C}_{\text{BTA}}[\![\ e_1' :^{b'} e_2' : t' : b'\ ]\!] \\
\qquad \text{where } t' : b' = (t_1'\ \texttt{list}^{b1'} : b1') \sqcap (t_2' : b2') \\
\\
\mathcal{E}^{C}_{\text{BTA}}[\![\ \texttt{nil}^{b1}[t_1] : t_2\ \texttt{list}^{b2} : b0\ ]\!] = \\
\quad \text{let } t' : b' = \mathcal{T}_{\text{BTA}}[\![\ (t_1 : b1) \sqcap (t_2 : b2 \sqcap b0)\ ]\!] \\
\quad \text{in } \texttt{nil}^{b'}[t'] : t'\ \texttt{list}^{b'} : b' \\
\\
\mathcal{E}^{C}_{\text{BTA}}[\![\ \texttt{hd}^{b1}\ e : t_0 : b0\ ]\!] = \\
\quad \text{let } t_0' : b0' = \mathcal{T}_{\text{BTA}}[\![\ t_0 : b0\ ]\!] \\
\quad \text{let } e' : t_0''\ \texttt{list}^{b1'} : b1' = \mathcal{E}^{C}_{\text{BTA}}[\![\ e : t_0'\ \texttt{list}^{b1} : b1\ ]\!] \\
\quad \text{in UD}(\ \texttt{hd}^{b1'}\ e' : t_0'' : b1', b0') \\
\\
\mathcal{E}^{C}_{\text{BTA}}[\![\ \texttt{tl}^{b1}\ e : t\ \texttt{list}^{b2} : b0\ ]\!] = \\
\quad \text{let } e' : t'\ \texttt{list}^{b0'} : b0' = \\
\qquad \mathcal{E}^{C}_{\text{BTA}}[\![\ e : t\ \texttt{list}^{b1 \sqcap b2 \sqcap b0} : b1 \sqcap b2 \sqcap b0\ ]\!] \\
\quad \text{in } \texttt{tl}^{b0'}\ e' : t'\ \texttt{list}^{b0'} : b0' \\
\\
\mathcal{E}^{C}_{\text{BTA}}[\![\ \texttt{isnil}^{b1}\ e : \texttt{Bool}^{b2} : b0\ ]\!] = \\
\quad \text{let } t_1 \text{ be given by fun}(\tau_{\text{BTA}}(\mathcal{A}_{\text{BTA}}(e))) \vdash_{\text{C}} \varepsilon_{\text{BTA}}(e) : t_1 \\
\quad \text{let } t_1' = \tau^{\text{c}}_{\text{BTA}}(t_1) \\
\quad \text{let } e' : t' : b' = \mathcal{E}^{C}_{\text{BTA}}[\![\ e : t_1' : b1 \sqcap b2 \sqcap b0\ ]\!] \\
\quad \text{in } \texttt{isnil}^{b'}\ e' : \texttt{Bool}^{b'} : b'
\end{array}
$$

Table 3.10: $\mathcal{E}^{C}_{\text{BTA}}$: Binding time analysis of expressions (part 4)

Similarly, we shall say that $e{:}t{:}b$ is *2-well-formed* if the underlying expression is well-formed in the sense of Section 3.1:

$$\mathcal{A}_{\text{BTA}}(e) \text{ is functional}$$

$$\text{fun}(\mathcal{A}_{\text{BTA}}(e)) \vdash_{\text{C}} \varepsilon'_{\text{BTA}}(e) : t : b$$

With this terminology we may rephrase Fact 3.1.3 as saying that every *2*-well-formed triple is *1*-well-formed. We then have

Proposition 3.2.13 (Correctness and Optimality of $\mathcal{E}^{C}_{\text{BTA}}$) If $e{:}t{:}b$ is *1*-well-formed then $\mathcal{E}^{C}_{\text{BTA}}[\![\ e{:}t{:}b\ ]\!]$ defines a result $e'{:}t'{:}b' \preceq e{:}t{:}b$ that is *2*-well-formed if $\mathcal{A}_{\text{BTA}}(e')$

$$\mathcal{E}^C_{\text{BTA}}[\![\ \texttt{true}^{\,b1} : \texttt{Bool}^{\,b2} : b0\ ]\!] = \\ \quad \texttt{true}^{b1\sqcap b2\sqcap b0} : \texttt{Bool}^{b1\sqcap b2\sqcap b0} : b1\sqcap b2\sqcap b0$$

$$\mathcal{E}^C_{\text{BTA}}[\![\ \texttt{false}^{\,b1} : \texttt{Bool}^{\,b2} : b0\ ]\!] = \\ \quad \texttt{false}^{b1\sqcap b2\sqcap b0} : \texttt{Bool}^{b1\sqcap b2\sqcap b0} : b1\sqcap b2\sqcap b0$$

$$\begin{array}{l}
\mathcal{E}^C_{\text{BTA}}[\![\ \texttt{if}^{\,b1}\ e_1\ \texttt{then}\ e_2\ \texttt{else}\ e_3 : t_0 : b0\ ]\!] = \\
\quad \text{let } t_0'{:}b0' = \mathcal{T}_{\text{BTA}}[\![\ t_0{:}b0\ ]\!] \\
\quad \text{let } e_1'{:}\texttt{Bool}^{b1'}{:}b1' = \mathcal{E}^C_{\text{BTA}}[\![\ e_1{:}\texttt{Bool}^{\,b1}{:}b1\ ]\!] \\
\quad \text{let } e_2'{:}t_2'{:}b2' = \mathcal{E}^C_{\text{BTA}}[\![\ e_2{:}t_0'{:}b1\ ]\!] \\
\quad \text{let } e_3'{:}t_3'{:}b3' = \mathcal{E}^C_{\text{BTA}}[\![\ e_3{:}t_0'{:}b1\ ]\!] \\
\quad \text{if } (t_2'{:}b2') = (t_3'{:}b3') \wedge (b1'{=}b2'{=}b3') \\
\quad \text{then UD}(\ \texttt{if}^{\,b1'}\ e_1'\ \texttt{then}\ e_2'\ \texttt{else}\ e_3' : t_2' : b2',\ b0') \\
\quad \text{else } \mathcal{E}^C_{\text{BTA}}[\![\ \texttt{if}^{\,b'}\ e_1'\ \texttt{then}\ e_2'\ \texttt{else}\ e_3' : t' : b0'\ ]\!] \\
\qquad \text{where } t'{:}b' = (t_2'{:}b2')\sqcap(t_3'{:}b3')\sqcap(t_3'{:}b1')
\end{array}$$

$$\begin{array}{l}
\mathcal{E}^C_{\text{BTA}}[\![\ \texttt{fix}^{\,b1}\ e : t_0 : b0\ ]\!] = \\
\quad \text{let } t_0'{:}b0' = \mathcal{T}_{\text{BTA}}[\![\ t_0{:}b0\ ]\!] \\
\quad \text{let } e'{:}t_1'{\rightarrow}^{b1'}t_2'{:}b1'' = \mathcal{E}^C_{\text{BTA}}[\![\ e{:}t_0'{\rightarrow}^{\,b1}t_0'{:}b1\ ]\!] \\
\quad \text{if } (t_1'{:}b1') = (t_2'{:}b1') \\
\quad \text{then UD}(\ \texttt{fix}^{\,b1'}\ e' : t_1' : b1',\ b0') \\
\quad \text{else } \mathcal{E}^C_{\text{BTA}}[\![\ \texttt{fix}^{\,b'}\ e' : t' : b0'\ ]\!] \\
\qquad \text{where } t'{:}b' = (t_1'{:}b1')\sqcap(t_2'{:}b1')
\end{array}$$

Table 3.11: $\mathcal{E}^C_{\text{BTA}}$: Binding time analysis of expressions (part 5)

is functional and that satisfies $\vdash t_i{:}b_i$ for all $(\mathbf{x}_i, t_i, b_i) \in \mathcal{A}_{\text{BTA}}(e')$. Furthermore, if $e''{:}t''{:}b'' \preceq e{:}t{:}b$ is *2*-well-formed then $e''{:}t''{:}b'' \preceq e'{:}t'{:}b'$. □

Proof: As in the proof of Proposition 3.2.2 the overall proof strategy is to use complete induction. The well-founded order $\leq$ to be used is defined by

$$e_1{:}t_1{:}b_1 \leq e_2{:}t_2{:}b_2$$

if and only if

$e_1{:}t_1{:}b_1 \preceq e_2{:}t_2{:}b_2$, or

$\varepsilon_{\text{BTA}}(e_1)$ is a proper subexpression of $\varepsilon_{\text{BTA}}(e_2)$

For the first claim about $\mathcal{E}^C_{\text{BTA}}$ we may use the predicate

$$P_1(e{:}t{:}b) \equiv e{:}t{:}b \text{ is } \textit{1}\text{-well-formed}$$

$$\Downarrow$$

$$\begin{array}{l} \mathcal{E}^{C}_{\mathrm{BTA}}[\![\ e{:}t{:}b\ ]\!] \text{ defines a result } e'{:}t'{:}b' \wedge \\ e'{:}t'{:}b' \preceq e{:}t{:}b \wedge \\ (\mathcal{A}_{\mathrm{BTA}}(e') \text{ is functional} \Rightarrow e'{:}t'{:}b' \text{ is } \mathit{2}\text{-well-formed}) \wedge \\ \forall\ (\mathbf{x}_i, t_i{:}b_i) \in \mathcal{A}_{\mathrm{BTA}}(e') \text{: } \vdash t_i : b_i \end{array}$$

and for the second claim about $\mathcal{E}^{C}_{\mathrm{BTA}}$ we may use the predicate

$$\begin{array}{rl} P_2(e{:}t{:}b) \equiv & e{:}t{:}b \text{ is } \mathit{1}\text{-well-formed} \wedge \\ & e'{:}t'{:}b' \text{ is } \mathit{2}\text{-well-formed} \wedge \\ & e'{:}t'{:}b' \preceq e{:}t{:}b \\ & \Downarrow \\ & e'{:}t'{:}b' \preceq \mathcal{E}^{C}_{\mathrm{BTA}}[\![\ e{:}t{:}b\ ]\!] \end{array}$$

The formal proof that P_1 and P_2 hold on all arguments amounts to formalising the explanations we gave in presenting the equations for $\mathcal{E}^{C}_{\mathrm{BTA}}$. There are no profound problems in this, but as may be guessed from the length of the definition of $\mathcal{E}^{C}_{\mathrm{BTA}}$ there are very many minor points to be made. For this reason we shall *not* present the formal proof but refer to the Bibliographical Notes for a reference to a full proof for a version of the *2*-level λ-calculus where the notion of well-formedness is only slightly different from here.

We should point out however, the complication due to the auxiliary function $\mathcal{E}^{\bullet C}_{\mathrm{BTA}}$. For each of P_1 and P_2 we then have to define properties $P_1^\bullet$ and $P_2^\bullet$ that express the intention of P_1 and P_2 on the arguments of $\mathcal{E}^{\bullet C}_{\mathrm{BTA}}$. Similarly, we must define an analogue, $\leq^\bullet$, of the well-founded order. To allow for a clean presentation of the interaction between $\mathcal{E}^{C}_{\mathrm{BTA}}$ and $\mathcal{E}^{\bullet C}_{\mathrm{BTA}}$ it is helpful to regard them as the same function, $\overline{\mathcal{E}}$, which behaves like $\mathcal{E}^{C}_{\mathrm{BTA}}$ upon arguments of the form $e{:}t{:}b$ and like $\mathcal{E}^{\bullet C}_{\mathrm{BTA}}$ upon arguments of the form $e_1(e_2){:}t{:}b$. Similarly, we may amalgamate each P_i and $P_i^\bullet$ to a predicate $\overline{P}_i$. We then define a well-founded order, $\overline{\leq}$, which behaves like $\leq$ on pairs of arguments that are both of the form $e{:}t{:}b$; which behaves like $\leq^\bullet$ on pairs of arguments that are both of the form $e_1(e_2){:}t{:}b$; and otherwise is given by

$$e_1(e_2) : t_1 \rightarrow^{b1} t_0 : b0 \mathrel{\overline{<}} e_1(^{b1}\ e_2) : t_0 : b0$$

to allow $\mathcal{E}^{C}_{\mathrm{BTA}}$ to call $\mathcal{E}^{\bullet C}_{\mathrm{BTA}}$, and

$$e_i : t : b \mathrel{\overline{<}} e_1(e_2) : t_0 : b0$$

to allow $\mathcal{E}^{\bullet C}_{\mathrm{BTA}}$ to call $\mathcal{E}^{C}_{\mathrm{BTA}}$. □

Corollary 3.2.14 If $e{:}t{:}b$ is *2*-well-formed then $\mathcal{E}^{C}_{\mathrm{BTA}}[\![\ e{:}t{:}b\ ]\!] = e{:}t{:}b$. □

Corollary 3.2.15 $\mathcal{E}^C_{\mathrm{BTA}}$ is monotonic (with respect to $\preceq$) on *1*-well-formed arguments. □

Proof: For a *1*-well-formed argument with no free variables the result of $\mathcal{E}^C_{\mathrm{BTA}}$ will be *2*-well-formed. The corollary therefore follows from Proposition 3.2.13 for *1*-well-formed arguments with no free variables. For the general statement a proof by complete induction is needed. □

3.2.3 Binding time analysis of programs

We now have the tools needed to define the transformation

$$\mathcal{P}^C_{\mathrm{BTA}}\colon P(E,T2) \hookrightarrow P(E2,T2)$$

for programs. We only intend to apply $\mathcal{P}^C_{\mathrm{BTA}}$ to programs $p\in P(E,T2)$ for which the underlying program $\pi_{\mathrm{BTA}}(p)\in P(E,T)$ is well-formed. Using $\mathcal{T}_{\mathrm{BTA}}$ and $\mathcal{E}^C_{\mathrm{BTA}}$ and the general notation from the B-level language L this allows us to define

$$\begin{array}{l}
\mathcal{P}^C_{\mathrm{BTA}}[\![\ \mathtt{DEF}\ \mathtt{x}_1{=}e_1 \cdots \mathtt{DEF}\ \mathtt{x}_n{=}e_n\ \mathtt{VAL}\ e_0\ \mathtt{HAS}\ t\ ]\!] = \\
\quad \text{let } \emptyset \vdash_C e_1 : t_1 \text{ determine } t_1 \\
\quad \vdots \\
\quad \text{let } \emptyset[t_1/\mathtt{x}_1]\cdots[t_{n-1}/\mathtt{x}_{n-1}] \vdash_C e_n : t_n \text{ determine } t_n \\
\quad \text{let } e = (\lambda \mathtt{x}_1[t_1].\cdots(\lambda \mathtt{x}_n[t_n].e_0)(e_n)\cdots)(e_1) \\
\quad \text{let } (\lambda^{b1'}\mathtt{x}_1[t_1'].\cdots(\lambda^{bn'}\mathtt{x}_n[t_n'].e_0')({}^{bn'}e_n')\cdots)({}^{b1'}e_1') : t' : b' \\
\qquad = \mathcal{E}^C_{\mathrm{BTA}}[\![\ \bar{\varepsilon}^{\emptyset}_{\mathrm{BTA}}(\varepsilon^{\mathtt{c}}_{\mathrm{BTA}}(e)) : t : \mathtt{c}\ ]\!] \\
\quad \text{if } b1'{=}\cdots{=}bn'{=}b'{=}\mathtt{c} \\
\quad \text{then } \mathtt{DEF}\ \mathtt{x}_1{=}\varepsilon'_{\mathrm{BTA}}(e_1') \cdots \mathtt{DEF}\ \mathtt{x}_n{=}\varepsilon'_{\mathrm{BTA}}(e_n') \\
\qquad\quad \mathtt{VAL}\ \varepsilon'_{\mathrm{BTA}}(e_0')\ \mathtt{HAS}\ t' \\
\quad \text{else } \mathit{fail}
\end{array}$$

Here we first use Fact 2.1.4 to determine the types $t_1, \cdots, t_n$ of the typed λ-expressions $e_1, \cdots, e_n$. We then construct the typed expression e and note that $\emptyset \vdash_C e : \tau_{\mathrm{BTA}}(t)$ holds if and only if $\pi_{\mathrm{BTA}}(p)$ is well-formed, where p is the argument to $\mathcal{P}^C_{\mathrm{BTA}}$. To apply $\mathcal{E}^C_{\mathrm{BTA}}$ we first use $\varepsilon^{\mathtt{c}}_{\mathrm{BTA}}$ to transform e in E to an expression in $E2$. Next we use a function $\bar{\varepsilon}^{\emptyset}_{\mathrm{BTA}}$ for transforming an expression in $E2$ into one in $E2'$. The argument $\emptyset$ is an empty type environment and the interesting clauses are

$$\bar{\varepsilon}^{tenv}_{\mathrm{BTA}}(\lambda^b \mathtt{x}_i[t].e) = \lambda^b \mathtt{x}_i[t].\ \bar{\varepsilon}^{tenv[t:b/\mathtt{x}_i]}_{\mathrm{BTA}}(e)$$

$$\bar{\varepsilon}^{tenv}_{\mathrm{BTA}}(\mathtt{x}_i) = \mathtt{x}_i{}^b[t] \text{ where } tenv(\mathtt{x}_i) = t : b$$

We leave the remaining clauses as an exercise (Exercise 13) but note that $\overline{\varepsilon}^{\emptyset}_{\mathrm{BTA}}$ was already *implicitly* used in Example 3.2.12. Turning to the result of $\mathcal{E}^{C}_{\mathrm{BTA}}$ it must have the form indicated and if all the binding times equal c we can produce a program in $P(E2,T2)$. If one or more binding times differ from c we have to fail due to the definition of well-formedness of programs in $P(E2,T2)$.

To express the correctness of $\mathcal{P}^{C}_{\mathrm{BTA}}$ we shall first extend $\pi^{\mathsf{c}}_{\mathrm{BTA}}$: $P(E,T) \to P(E2,T2)$ to $\pi^{\mathsf{c}}_{\mathrm{BTA}}$: $P(E,T2) \to P(E2,T2)$ by

$$\begin{array}{l}\pi^{\mathsf{c}}_{\mathrm{BTA}}(\mathtt{DEF}\ \mathtt{x}_1{=}e_1\ \cdots\ \mathtt{x}_n{=}e_n\ \mathtt{VAL}\ e_0\ \mathtt{HAS}\ t) = \\ \qquad \mathtt{DEF}\ \mathtt{x}_1{=}\varepsilon^{\mathsf{c}}_{\mathrm{BTA}}(e_1)\ \cdots\ \mathtt{x}_n{=}\varepsilon^{\mathsf{c}}_{\mathrm{BTA}}(e_n)\ \mathtt{VAL}\ \varepsilon^{\mathsf{c}}_{\mathrm{BTA}}(e_0)\ \mathtt{HAS}\ t\end{array}$$

Theorem 3.2.16 (Correctness and Optimality of $\mathcal{P}^{C}_{\mathrm{BTA}}$) Consider some program $p{\in}P(E,T2)$ of the form DEF $\mathtt{x}_1{=}e_1\ \cdots$ DEF $\mathtt{x}_n{=}e_n$ VAL e_0 HAS t that satisfies

$$\vdash_C \mathtt{DEF}\ \mathtt{x}_1{=}e_1\ \cdots\ \mathtt{DEF}\ \mathtt{x}_n{=}e_n\ \mathtt{VAL}\ e_0\ \mathtt{HAS}\ \tau_{\mathrm{BTA}}(t)$$

in the typed λ-calculus $P(E,T)$. Then $\mathcal{P}^{C}_{\mathrm{BTA}}[\![p]\!]$ *fails* only if there is no well-formed program p'' that respects the run-time annotations in p, i.e. there is no $p''{\in}P(E2,T2)$ such that $(\vdash_C p'') \wedge (p'' {\preceq} \pi^{\mathsf{c}}_{\mathrm{BTA}}(p))$. If $\mathcal{P}^{C}_{\mathrm{BTA}}[\![p]\!]$ does not fail the result satisfies the property

$$\vdash_C \mathcal{P}^{C}_{\mathrm{BTA}}[\![p]\!] \wedge \mathcal{P}^{C}_{\mathrm{BTA}}[\![p]\!] \preceq \pi^{\mathsf{c}}_{\mathrm{BTA}}(p)$$

and it is the greatest program with this property, i.e.

$$\vdash_C p'' \wedge p'' \preceq \pi^{\mathsf{c}}_{\mathrm{BTA}}(p) \Rightarrow p'' \preceq \mathcal{P}^{C}_{\mathrm{BTA}}[\![p]\!] \qquad \square$$

Proof: Let p be as given in the Theorem. From $\vdash_C \pi_{\mathrm{BTA}}(p)$ and the definition of $\vdash_C$ in the typed λ-calculus, i.e. $P(E,T)$, it follows that there are types $t_1, \cdots, t_n$ in T such that

$$\begin{array}{l}\emptyset \vdash_C e_1 : t_1 \\ \vdots \\ \emptyset[t_1/\mathtt{x}_1]\cdots[t_{n-1}/\mathtt{x}_{n-1}] \vdash_C e_n : t_n \\ \emptyset[t_1/\mathtt{x}_1]\cdots[t_n/\mathtt{x}_n] \vdash_C e_0 : \tau_{\mathrm{BTA}}(t)\end{array}$$

From Fact 2.1.4 it follows that $t_1, \cdots, t_n$ are uniquely determined. It follows that

$$\emptyset \vdash_C e : \tau_{\mathrm{BTA}}(t)$$

where e is as in the definition of $\mathcal{P}^{C}_{\mathrm{BTA}}$. Hence

$$\mathcal{E}^{C}_{\mathrm{BTA}}[\![\ \overline{\varepsilon}^{\emptyset}_{\mathrm{BTA}}(\varepsilon^{\mathsf{c}}_{\mathrm{BTA}}(e)) : t : \mathsf{c}\ ]\!]$$

is well-defined and produces a result of the form

$$(\lambda^{b1'}\mathtt{x}_1[t_1'].\cdots(\lambda^{bn'}\mathtt{x}_n[t_n'].e_0')(^{bn'}e_n')\cdots)(^{b1'}e_1') : t' : b'$$

Writing

$$p' = \texttt{DEF } \mathtt{x}_1{=}\varepsilon'_{\mathrm{BTA}}(e'_1) \cdots \texttt{DEF } \mathtt{x}_n{=}\varepsilon'_{\mathrm{BTA}}(e'_n) \texttt{ VAL } \varepsilon'_{\mathrm{BTA}}(e'_0) \texttt{ HAS } t'$$

we have $p' \preceq \pi^{\mathsf{c}}_{\mathrm{BTA}}(p)$ because the result produced by $\mathcal{E}^{C}_{\mathrm{BTA}}$ will be less than its argument. Also the result of $\mathcal{E}^{C}_{\mathrm{BTA}}$ is *2*-well-formed and if $b1'=\cdots=bn'=b'=\mathsf{c}$ this implies that also p' is well-formed, that is $\vdash_C p'$. Next let

$$p'' = \texttt{DEF } \mathtt{x}_1{=}e''_1 \cdots \texttt{DEF } \mathtt{x}_n{=}e''_n \texttt{ VAL } e''_0 \texttt{ HAS } t''$$

be a well-formed program satisfying the run-time annotations in p, i.e. $(\vdash_C p'') \wedge (p'' \preceq \pi^{\mathsf{c}}_{\mathrm{BTA}}(p))$. We then have types $t''_1, \cdots, t''_n$ in *T2* such that

$$\begin{array}{l}
\emptyset \vdash_C e''_1 : t''_1 : \mathsf{c} \\
\vdots \\
\emptyset[(t''_1 : \mathsf{c})/\mathtt{x}_1]\cdots[(t''_{n-1} : \mathsf{c})/\mathtt{x}_{n-1}] \vdash_C e''_n : t''_n : \mathsf{c} \\
\emptyset[(t''_1 : \mathsf{c})/\mathtt{x}_1]\cdots[(t''_n : \mathsf{c})/\mathtt{x}_n] \vdash_C e''_0 : t'' : \mathsf{c}
\end{array}$$

and by Fact 3.1.5 the types $t''_1, \cdots, t''_n$ are uniquely determined. Hence

$$\overline{\varepsilon}^{\emptyset}_{\mathrm{BTA}}((\lambda^{\mathsf{c}}\mathtt{x}_1[t''_1].\cdots(\lambda^{\mathsf{c}}\mathtt{x}_n[t''_n].e''_0)(^{\mathsf{c}}e''_n)\cdots)(^{\mathsf{c}}e''_1)) : t'' : \mathsf{c}$$

is *2*-well-formed and less than or equal to (wrt. $\preceq$) the argument to $\mathcal{E}^{C}_{\mathrm{BTA}}$. From the correctness of $\mathcal{E}^{C}_{\mathrm{BTA}}$ we then have

$$\begin{array}{l}
\overline{\varepsilon}^{\emptyset}_{\mathrm{BTA}}((\lambda^{\mathsf{c}}\mathtt{x}_1[t''_1].\cdots(\lambda^{\mathsf{c}}\mathtt{x}_n[t''_n].e''_0)(^{\mathsf{c}}e''_n)\cdots)(^{\mathsf{c}}e''_1)) : t'' : \mathsf{c} \preceq \\
(\lambda^{b1'}\mathtt{x}_1[t'_1].\cdots(\lambda^{bn'}\mathtt{x}_n[t'_n].e'_0)(^{bn'}e'_n)\cdots)(^{b1'}e'_1) : t' : b'
\end{array}$$

so that

$$(p'' \preceq p') \wedge (b1'=\cdots=bn'=b'=\mathsf{c})$$

It then follows that $\mathcal{P}^{C}_{\mathrm{BTA}}$ only fails when it is allowed to and that when it does not fail it produces the greatest program that is both well-formed and respects the run-time annotations in the argument. □

Example 3.2.17 As a simple example consider the programs

$$\begin{array}{rl}
p_1 = & \texttt{DEF x = fix } \lambda\texttt{y[A].y} \\
& \texttt{VAL } \lambda\texttt{z[A}\rightarrow\texttt{A]. }\langle\texttt{z,x}\rangle \\
& \texttt{HAS } (\underline{\texttt{A}\rightarrow\texttt{A}})\rightarrow((\texttt{A}\rightarrow\texttt{A})\times\texttt{A})
\end{array}$$

$$\begin{array}{rl}
p_2 = & \texttt{DEF x = fix } \lambda\texttt{y[A].y} \\
& \texttt{VAL } \lambda\texttt{z[A}\rightarrow\texttt{A]. }\langle\texttt{z,x}\rangle \\
& \texttt{HAS } (\texttt{A}\rightarrow\texttt{A})\rightarrow((\underline{\texttt{A}\rightarrow\texttt{A}})\underline{\times}\underline{\texttt{A}})
\end{array}$$

Note that $\pi_{\text{BTA}}(p_1)$ equals $\pi_{\text{BTA}}(p_2)$ and that it is a well-formed program in $P(E,T)$. When calculating $\mathcal{P}^C_{\text{BTA}}[\![p_1]\!]$ we perform the call

$$\begin{array}{rl} & \mathcal{E}^C_{\text{BTA}}[\![\ (\lambda^c \mathtt{x}[\mathtt{A}].\lambda^c \mathtt{z}[\mathtt{A}\to\mathtt{A}].\langle \mathtt{z}^c[\mathtt{A}\to\mathtt{A}],\mathtt{x}^c[\mathtt{A}]\rangle)\ (\mathtt{fix}\ \lambda^c \mathtt{y}[\mathtt{A}].\mathtt{y}^c[\mathtt{A}]) : \\ & \quad (\underline{\mathtt{A}\to\mathtt{A}})\to((\mathtt{A}\to\mathtt{A})\times\mathtt{A}) : \mathtt{c}\ ]\!] \\ = & (\lambda^c \mathtt{x}[\mathtt{A}].\lambda^c \mathtt{z}[\underline{\mathtt{A}\to\mathtt{A}}].\langle \mathtt{z}^c[\underline{\mathtt{A}\to\mathtt{A}}],\mathtt{x}^c[\mathtt{A}]\rangle)\ (\mathtt{fix}\ \lambda^c \mathtt{y}[\mathtt{A}].\mathtt{y}^c[\mathtt{A}]) : \\ & (\underline{\mathtt{A}\to\mathtt{A}})\to((\underline{\mathtt{A}\to\mathtt{A}})\times\mathtt{A}) : \mathtt{c} \end{array}$$

and get

$$\begin{array}{rl} \mathcal{P}^C_{\text{BTA}}[\![p_1]\!] = & \mathtt{DEF\ x} = \mathtt{fix}\ \lambda\mathtt{y}[\mathtt{A}].\mathtt{y} \\ & \mathtt{VAL}\ \lambda\mathtt{z}[\underline{\mathtt{A}\to\mathtt{A}}].\ \langle \mathtt{z},\mathtt{x}\rangle \\ & \mathtt{HAS}\ (\underline{\mathtt{A}\to\mathtt{A}})\to((\underline{\mathtt{A}\to\mathtt{A}})\times\mathtt{A}) \end{array}$$

When calculating $\mathcal{P}^C_{\text{BTA}}[\![p_2]\!]$ we perform the call

$$\begin{array}{rl} & \mathcal{E}^C_{\text{BTA}}[\![\ (\lambda^c \mathtt{x}[\mathtt{A}].\lambda^c \mathtt{z}[\mathtt{A}\to\mathtt{A}].\langle \mathtt{z}^c[\mathtt{A}\to\mathtt{A}],\mathtt{x}^c[\mathtt{A}]\rangle)\ (\mathtt{fix}\ \lambda^c \mathtt{y}[\mathtt{A}].\mathtt{y}^c[\mathtt{A}]) : \\ & \quad (\mathtt{A}\to\mathtt{A})\to((\underline{\mathtt{A}\to\mathtt{A}})\underline{\times}\underline{\mathtt{A}}) : \mathtt{c}\ ]\!] \\ = & (\lambda^r \mathtt{x}[\underline{\mathtt{A}}].\lambda^r \mathtt{z}[\underline{\mathtt{A}\to\mathtt{A}}].\ \underline{\langle} \mathtt{z}^r[\underline{\mathtt{A}\to\mathtt{A}}],\mathtt{x}^r[\underline{\mathtt{A}}]\underline{\rangle})\ \underline{(\mathtt{fix}}\ \lambda^r \mathtt{y}[\underline{\mathtt{A}}].\mathtt{y}^r[\underline{\mathtt{A}}]\underline{)} : \\ & (\underline{\mathtt{A}\to\mathtt{A}})\underline{\to}((\underline{\mathtt{A}\to\mathtt{A}})\underline{\times}\underline{\mathtt{A}}) : \mathtt{c} \end{array}$$

However, the condition $b1'=\cdots=bn'=b'=\mathtt{c}$ is not satisfied so rather than getting the program

$$\mathtt{DEF\ x} = \underline{\mathtt{fix}}\ \underline{\lambda}\mathtt{y}[\underline{\mathtt{A}}].\mathtt{y}\ \mathtt{VAL}\ \underline{\lambda}\mathtt{z}[\underline{\mathtt{A}\to\mathtt{A}}].\ \underline{\langle}\mathtt{z},\mathtt{x}\underline{\rangle}\ \mathtt{HAS}\ (\underline{\mathtt{A}\to\mathtt{A}})\underline{\to}((\underline{\mathtt{A}\to\mathtt{A}})\underline{\times}\underline{\mathtt{A}})$$

we let

$$\mathcal{P}^C_{\text{BTA}}[\![p_2]\!] = \mathit{fail}$$

This is due to the definition of the well-formedness predicate for programs in the *2*-level λ-calculus where we insisted on using the binding time c for the type associated with **x**. □

Ideally we would have liked $\mathcal{P}^C_{\text{BTA}} \circ \mathcal{P}^C_{\text{TA}}$: $P(UE,T2) \hookrightarrow P(E2,T2)$ to fail only when $\mathcal{P}^C_{\text{TA}}$ fails. However, in the example above we saw that this cannot be arranged. It is therefore worth pointing out that the call to $\mathcal{E}^C_{\text{BTA}}$ in the body of $\mathcal{P}^C_{\text{BTA}}[\![p]\!]$ will not fail if $\vdash_C \pi_{\text{BTA}}(p)$. Hence, to arrange for $\mathcal{P}^C_{\text{BTA}} \circ \mathcal{P}^C_{\text{TA}}$ to fail only when $\mathcal{P}^C_{\text{TA}}$ does we might consider generalizing the well-formedness condition for programs in $P(E2,T2)$ but we shall not go into this here.

3.3 Improving the Binding Time Analysis

The annotation obtained from the binding time analysis is *optimal* in the sense that as few computations as possible are postponed until run-time. However, it is often the case that a slight rewriting of the program will produce an even better distinction between the binding times. As an example, the order of the parameters of a function may be changed or the representation of data types may be modified. To illustrate this consider the function `lookup` of type

$$(\texttt{Name} \times \underline{\texttt{Int}})\ \texttt{list} \rightarrow \texttt{Name} \rightarrow \texttt{Int}$$

where we assume that the second components of all pairs in the first argument are unknown at compile-time. We then have a situation where known and unknown data are mixed and the binding time analysis will return a function with the annotated type

$$(\underline{\texttt{Name}}\ \underline{\times}\ \underline{\texttt{Int}})\ \underline{\texttt{list}}\ \underline{\rightarrow}\ \underline{\texttt{Name}}\ \underline{\rightarrow}\ \underline{\texttt{Int}}$$

so that all computations will be postponed until run-time. Alternatively, we may split the list of pairs into two lists and rearrange the order of the parameters so that the type becomes

$$\texttt{Name list} \rightarrow \texttt{Name} \rightarrow \underline{\texttt{Int}}\ \texttt{list} \rightarrow \texttt{Int}$$

We then get a much better distinction between the binding times because now only the elements of the *second* list will be unknown at compile-time and the binding time analysis will return a function with the annotated type

$$\texttt{Name list} \rightarrow \texttt{Name} \rightarrow \underline{\texttt{Int}}\ \underline{\texttt{list}}\ \underline{\rightarrow}\ \underline{\texttt{Int}}$$

Hence some of the computations can be performed at compile-time and this idea is further explored in [81].

The above example is rather involved in that it changes the overall type of the function. This is not necessary for a transformation to be useful. Consider the program $\texttt{sum}_9$ from Example 3.1.6. Here the fixed point operation of $\texttt{reduce}_9$ is underlined and intuitively this means that we cannot use the recursive structure of its body at compile-time, for example during abstract interpretation or when generating code. We may therefore want to replace the run-time fixed point by a compile-time fixed point. Since $\texttt{sum}_9$ is the best completion of $\texttt{sum}_t$ we cannot obtain this effect by simply changing the annotation. The idea is therefore first

- to *transform* the underlying program, and then
- to *repeat* the binding time analysis.

In our case we shall apply the transformation

$$\lambda x[t_1].\mathtt{fix}\ (\lambda f[t_2 \rightarrow t_3].e)\ \rhd\ \mathtt{fix}\ (\lambda g[t_1 \rightarrow t_2 \rightarrow t_3].\lambda x[t_1].e[g(x)/f])$$

that replaces the first pattern with the second. Here $e[g(x)/f]$ is e with all occurrences of f replaced by $g(x)$ and g is assumed to be a fresh identifier. Intuitively the transformation moves the fixed point operation to an outer level by passing the first parameter as an additional parameter during the computation of the fixed point. We then repeat the binding time analysis with $\mathtt{Sum_t}$ as the 'goal type' and get the program $\mathtt{sum_{9a}}$:

```
DEF reduce9a = λf[Int→Int→Int].
                  fix (λg'[Int → Int list → Int].
                         λu[Int]. λxs[Int list].
                           if isnil xs then u
                           else f(hd xs)(g'(u)(tl xs)))
VAL reduce9a (λx[Int].λy[Int].+[Int×Int→Int](⟨x,y⟩))
             (0[Int])
HAS Int list → Int
```

where the fixed point now is computed at compile-time and the function g′ is bound at compile-time.

As a side effect the functionality of the fixed point has been changed and, in particular, g′ has become a higher-order function. For some stack-based implementations it is expensive to handle higher-order functions and we may therefore want to transform the program further to change the functionality of g′. To do that we first apply the following transformation to the underlying program of $\mathtt{sum_{9a}}$:

$$\mathtt{fix}\ (\lambda f[t_1 \rightarrow t_2 \rightarrow t_3].\lambda x[t_1].\lambda y[t_2].e)\ \rhd$$

$$\lambda x[t_1].\lambda y[t_2].(\mathtt{fix}(\lambda g[t_1 \times t_2 \rightarrow t_3].\lambda z[t_1 \times t_2].\ e[\lambda x[t_1].\lambda y[t_2].g(\langle x,y\rangle)/f][\mathtt{fst}\ z/x][\mathtt{snd}\ z/y]))\ (\langle x,y\rangle)$$

Here g and z are assumed to be fresh identifiers. Intuitively this transformation will uncurry the parameter of the fixed point operation and in order to keep the overall type unchanged, the fixed point itself will be curried at the outermost level. Next we apply the β-transformation

$$(\lambda x[t].e)(e')\ \rhd\ e[e'/x]$$

(recalling that our semantics is supposed to be non-strict). The binding time analysis is then applied to the resulting program with $\mathtt{Sum_t}$ as the overall annotated type and we get the program $\mathtt{sum_{9b}}$:

```
DEF reduce9b = λf[Int→Int→Int]. λu[Int]. λxs[Int list].
                  (fix (λg[Int × Int list → Int].
                          λz[Int × Int list].
```

```
                        if isnil (snd z) then fst z
                        else f (hd (snd z))
                                (g ((fst z, tl (snd z)))))
             (⟨u,xs⟩)
VAL reduce9b (λx[Int].λy[Int].+[Int×Int→Int](⟨x,y⟩))
             (0[Int])
HAS Int list → Int
```

Bibliographical Notes

The *2*-level formalism as presented in this and the next chapter dates back to [66]. A sketch of the *2*-level λ-calculus of this chapter was given in [66, Chapter 6] and the complete account may be found in [73] (in the context of partial evaluation). Also [74, 75, 76, 80] consider versions of the *2*-level λ-calculus; the notation used in this chapter has incorporated the explicit distinction between $\mathtt{f}_i[t]$ and $\underline{\mathtt{f}}_i[t]$ suggested by Mycroft [64]. Relaxing the need for run-time constructs to be well-formed, or perhaps by assuming a run-time recursive type as in [75], one may develop variations of the *2*-level λ-calculus. One such line of development is illustrated by Gomard and Jones [32] and by Henglein [36].

The notion of well-formed types is much as in [73, 74, 75, 76, 80] and apart from presentational details (see Exercise 6) also as in [66, 69, 72, 78]. We should stress that the rule $\frac{\vdash t{:}\mathtt{r}}{\vdash t{:}\mathtt{c}}$ only holds for t of the form $t{=}t_1\underline{\rightarrow}t_2$ and that there is no rule $\frac{\vdash t{:}\mathtt{c}}{\vdash t{:}\mathtt{r}}$. A slightly more permissive well-formedness notion is considered in [45]. Rules of the form $\frac{\vdash t{:}\mathtt{c}}{\vdash t{:}\mathtt{r}}$ are likely to be needed for serious work on partial evaluation; this observation was made already in [73, Section 5] and is made in a strong way by Gomard and Jones [32]. We do not regard this as a criticism of the well-formedness relation studied here; rather we take the point of view that a well-formedness relation formalises a particular intuition and that different intuitions may be appropriate for different tasks. Despite this potential difference in the formulation of the well-formedness relation we believe that the techniques used to study it (e.g. for binding time analysis, see below) are rather similar.

The notion of well-formed expressions is much as for $\mathbf{TML}_l$ of [76]. Apart from a different representation of type environments the main difference is that in $\mathbf{TML}_l$ there is no condition $\vdash t{:}\mathtt{c}$ in the rule [if]. The well-formedness rules studied here are superficially close to the well-formedness rules of [73, 74, 75, 80] for $\mathbf{TML}_e$. The difference is that for $\mathbf{TML}_e$ there is no overall binding time associated with each type. This corresponds to weakening the side condition of rule [up] to $\vdash t{:}\mathtt{c}$. While being a very local change this has far reaching consequences. As should be expected, the notation of well-formedness of [32, 36] differs in many ways from the notion studied here, not least because the run-time level of [32, 36] needs not be fully typed.

Binding time analysis may be approached in many different ways. The approach of [73] was to take least upper bounds in a structure that was shown to be a complete lattice. The approach of [75, 74] was to develop a binding time analysis based on Milner's original type inference algorithm $\mathcal{W}$ and [32] takes a similar approach. The present approach is based on Damas' type inference algorithm $\mathcal{T}$. A main difference is that we have no counterpart of substitutions and that we therefore need to perform some extra recursive calls to 'unify' the binding time annotations. Other approaches include [47, 48, 59, 58, 92] and several of these are based on abstract interpretation. The approach of [48, 59] performs binding time analysis in conjunction with certain program transformations; in our approach program transformation, for example using fold/unfold [16] or partial evaluation [47], is a separate issue. The approach of [36] breaks new ground by reformulating binding time analysis as a constraint problem and then using more or less standard techniques to obtain an efficient solution.

As in Chapter 2 our treatment of soundness and completeness is purely syntactic and for the same reasons as mentioned in the Bibliographical Notes of Chapter 2. If a semantic characterization is desired there are several ways to go. One is to use the notion of *faithfulness* of [71]. Another is to use the notion of *partial equivalence relations*, PER's, of [44]. A third is to use the notion of *projection analysis* as in [58]. Actually, these approaches are not so dissimilar as one might expect. Recent work has shown the ability of PER's to encapsulate the power of projections and the faithfulness of [71] amounts to a study of PER's restricted to a setting where they turn out to be equivalence relations. Semantic correctness is also studied in [32].

An obvious extension of the work carried out here would be to allow *2*-level polytypes. A problem to be overcome is how to allow the *2*-level polymorphic type of the identity function to include $X_1 \underline{\rightarrow} X_1$ as well as $X_1 \rightarrow X_1$, depending on the kind of *2*-level type that X_1 ranges over.

A brief appraisal of the material of this chapter may be found in [74].

Exercises

1. Discuss the relationship between 'constant expressions' in PASCAL and our expressions of binding time c on the one hand, and between 'expressions' in PASCAL and our expressions of binding time r on the other hand.

2. Consider the programming language Standard ML and try to classify its ingredients with respect to two binding times.

3. Consider designing a *3*-level λ-calculus, e.g. with binding times 'run-time' (r), 'link-time' (l) and 'compile-time' (c) and with $r \preceq l \preceq c$.

4. Discuss whether the partially ordered set $B=(B,\preceq)$ of binding times should always be a totally ordered set or whether it makes sense to have incomparable elements.

5. Use Table 3.1 to prove the well-formedness of the types $\texttt{Reduce}_1$, ..., $\texttt{Reduce}_{10}$. Try to argue that these are *all* the well-formed types with $\tau_{\mathrm{BTA}}(\texttt{Reduce}_1)$ as the underlying type.

6. Consider the following piece of syntax:

$$ct ::= \mathtt{A_i} \mid ct \times ct \mid ct \rightarrow ct \mid ct\ \texttt{list} \mid ft$$

$$ft ::= rt \underline{\rightarrow} rt$$

$$rt ::= \underline{\mathtt{A_i}} \mid rt \underline{\times} rt \mid rt \underline{\rightarrow} rt \mid rt\ \underline{\texttt{list}}$$

Let L_{rt} be the context free language generated by the nonterminal *rt* and let L_{ct} be the context free language generated by the nonterminal *ct*. Similarly, let L_{t} be the context free language generated by the nonterminal *t* of Table 2.3, and let $L_{\mathrm{t}}^{b} = \{\mathrm{w} \in L_{\mathrm{t}} | \vdash \mathrm{w}:b\}$ be the subset of those types in L_{t} that have binding time *b*. Show that $L_{\mathrm{rt}} = L_{\mathrm{t}}^{\mathrm{r}}$ and that $L_{\mathrm{ct}} = L_{\mathrm{t}}^{\mathrm{c}}$.

7. Give an inductive definition of $t_1 \preceq t_2$.

8. Try to sketch a version of $\mathcal{T}_{\mathrm{BTA}}$ where the formulation is independent of the actual choice of binding times B and underlying language L. (Hint: it may be easier if you assume that $B = (B,\preceq)$ is finite and linearly ordered. If you do not adopt this simplification you will probably have to impose other conditions on B, e.g. that B is a $\sqcap$-semilattice with a greatest element.)

9. Calculate $\mathcal{T}_{\mathrm{BTA}}^{ts}[\![t:b]\!]$ when

$$ts = \forall \mathrm{X}_1.\forall \mathrm{X}_2.\ \mathrm{X}_1 \rightarrow \mathrm{X}_2 \rightarrow \mathrm{X}_1 \times \mathrm{X}_2$$

$$t = (\underline{\texttt{Int}} \rightarrow \texttt{Int}) \rightarrow (\texttt{Bool} \rightarrow \texttt{Bool}) \rightarrow (\texttt{Int} \rightarrow \texttt{Int}) \times (\texttt{Bool} \rightarrow \texttt{Bool})$$

and $b = \mathrm{c}$.

10. Verify that $\leq$ in the proof of Proposition 3.2.2, is a partial order, i.e. is reflexive, transitive and antisymmetric. Also verify that $\leq$ is well-founded.

11. Give detailed proofs of the cases $\underline{\times}$ and $\times$ in Proposition 3.2.2.

12. Prove Corollaries 3.2.4 and 3.2.5.

13. Define $\overline{\varepsilon}_{\mathrm{BTA}}^{\emptyset}$: $\{e \in E2 | FEV(e) = \emptyset\} \rightarrow E2'$ using structural induction on the underlying expression.

14. Annotate the program from Exercise 2 of Chapter 2 with the best possible binding time information, assuming that the overall type is $\underline{\texttt{String}}\ \underline{\texttt{list}} \underline{\rightarrow}\ \underline{\texttt{Int}}$.

15. In Exercise 2 of Chapter 2 we saw a program where one of the DEF-clauses needed to be duplicated in order for the type analysis to succeed. Give an example of a program where duplication is needed in order for the binding time analysis to succeed but where the type analysis succeeds without duplication.

16. Extend the types of the typed λ-calculus with sum types, recursive types, type variables and type synonyms. Types are then given by

    $$t ::= \cdots \mid t + t \mid \texttt{rec}\ \mathrm{X_i} = t \mid \mathrm{X_i} \mid \texttt{let}\ \mathrm{X_i} = t\ \texttt{in}\ t$$

    With this notation we could use

    $$\texttt{rec}\ \mathrm{X_1} = \texttt{Unit} + (t_1 \times \mathrm{X_1})$$

    instead of

    $$t_1\ \texttt{list}$$

    Our primary interest will be in closed types, that is types without free type variables.

    - Define the syntax of *2*-level types.
    - Define the well-formedness relation for *2*-level types. (Hint: take care to account for the possibility of free type variables.)
    - Try to define a binding time analysis of types.

17. Extend the expressions of the typed λ-calculus with `let` and `letrec`. Expressions are then given by

    $$e ::= \cdots \mid \texttt{let}\ \mathtt{x_i} = e\ \texttt{in}\ e \mid \texttt{letrec}\ \mathtt{x_i} = e\ \texttt{in}\ e$$

    As usual, our primary interest will be in closed expressions, that is expressions without free variables.

    - Define the syntax of *2*-level expressions.
    - Define the well-formedness relation for *2*-level expressions.
    - Try to define a binding time analysis of expressions.

Chapter 4

Combinators Made Explicit

The binding time information of a *2*-level program clearly indicates which computations should be carried out at compile-time and which should be carried out at run-time. The compile-time computations should be executed by a compiler and it is well-known how to do this. The run-time computations should give rise to code instead. We may also want to perform some data flow analyses in order to validate some program transformations or to improve the efficiency of the code generated. It is important to observe that it is the run-time computations, not the compile-time computations, that should be analysed, just as it is the run-time computations, not the compile-time computations, that should give rise to code. This then calls for the ability to *interpret the run-time constructs* in different ways depending upon the task at hand.

This is not straightforward when the run-time computations are expressed in the form of λ-expressions. As an example, the usual meaning of

$$\underline{\lambda}\mathtt{x}[\underline{\mathtt{Int}}\underline{\times}\underline{\mathtt{Int}}].\ \mathtt{f}\ \underline{(}\mathtt{g}\ \underline{(}\mathtt{x}\underline{)}\underline{)}$$

is $\lambda v.f\,(g\ \ v)$. However, we may be interested in an analysis which determines whether both components of `x` are needed in order to compute the result. This is an example of a backward data flow analysis and the natural interpretation of the expression will then be $\lambda v.g\,(f\ \ v)$. It is not straightforward to interpret function abstraction and function application so as to be able to obtain both meanings. The idea is therefore to focus on functions and functionals (expressed as combinators) rather than values and functions. We then write

$$\mathtt{f}\ \Box\ \mathtt{g}$$

for the expression above and the effect of both $\lambda v.f\,(g\ \ v)$ and $\lambda v.g\,(f\ \ v)$ can be obtained by suitably reinterpreting the functional $\Box$.

This observation calls for transforming the run-time computations into combinator form. Similar considerations have motivated the use of combinators in the implementation of functional languages [101, 19, 41] and the use of categorical combinators when interpreting the typed λ-calculus in an arbitrary cartesian closed category [49]. However, we shall stress once more that we leave the compile-time computations in the form of λ-expressions and only transform the run-time computations into combinator form.

In Section 4.1 we prepare for this transformation by defining the mixed λ-calculus and combinatory logic. The types are as in the *2*-level λ-calculus, and the well-formedness conditions also have much in common with the well-formedness conditions of Section 3.1. The actual transformation is accomplished by the algorithm developed in Section 4.2.

4.1 Mixed λ-Calculus and Combinatory Logic

The syntax of the mixed λ-calculus and combinatory logic is given by Table 4.1. The difference, with respect to the syntax of the *2*-level λ-calculus given by Table 3.1, is that combinators are used to express the computations at the run-time level. The meaning of the combinators is best expressed by sketching a run-time λ-expression with the same meaning:

$$\mathtt{F}_i[t'\underline{\rightarrow}t''] = \underline{\lambda}\mathtt{x}[t'].\ \underline{\mathtt{f}_i}[t'']$$

$$\mathtt{Tuple}(e_1,e_2) = \underline{\lambda}\mathtt{x}[\cdots].\ \underline{\langle} e_1\underline{(}\mathtt{x}\underline{)},\ e_2\underline{(}\mathtt{x}\underline{)}\underline{\rangle}$$

$$\mathtt{Fst}[t'\underline{\times}t''] = \underline{\lambda}\mathtt{x}[t'\underline{\times}t''].\ \underline{\mathtt{fst}}\ \mathtt{x}$$

$$\mathtt{Snd}[t'\underline{\times}t''] = \underline{\lambda}\mathtt{x}[t'\underline{\times}t''].\ \underline{\mathtt{snd}}\ \mathtt{x}$$

$$\mathtt{Curry}\ e = \underline{\lambda}\mathtt{x}[\cdots].\ \underline{\lambda}\mathtt{y}[\cdots].\ e\underline{(}\underline{\langle}\mathtt{x},\ \mathtt{y}\underline{\rangle}\underline{)}$$

$$\mathtt{Apply}[t'\underline{\rightarrow}t''] = \underline{\lambda}\underline{\langle}\mathtt{x},\mathtt{y}\underline{\rangle}[(t'\underline{\rightarrow}t'')\underline{\times}t'].\ \mathtt{x}\underline{(}\mathtt{y}\underline{)}$$

$$e_1 \,\square\, e_2 = \underline{\lambda}\mathtt{x}[\cdots].\ e_1\underline{(}e_2\underline{(}\mathtt{x}\underline{)}\underline{)}$$

$$\mathtt{Id}[t] = \underline{\lambda}\mathtt{x}[t].\ \mathtt{x}$$

$$\mathtt{Cons}(e_1,e_2) = \underline{\lambda}\mathtt{x}[\cdots].\ (e_1\underline{(}\mathtt{x}\underline{)})\underline{:}(e_2\underline{(}\mathtt{x}\underline{)})$$

$$\mathtt{Nil}[t'\underline{\rightarrow}t''\underline{\mathtt{list}}] = \underline{\lambda}\mathtt{x}[t'].\ \underline{\mathtt{nil}}[t'']$$

$$\mathtt{Hd}[t] = \underline{\lambda}\mathtt{x}[t\ \underline{\mathtt{list}}].\ \underline{\mathtt{hd}}\ \mathtt{x}$$

$$\mathtt{Tl}[t] = \underline{\lambda}\mathtt{x}[t\ \underline{\mathtt{list}}].\ \underline{\mathtt{tl}}\ \mathtt{x}$$

$$\mathtt{Isnil}[t] = \underline{\lambda}\mathtt{x}[t\ \underline{\mathtt{list}}].\ \underline{\mathtt{isnil}}\ \mathtt{x}$$

$$\mathtt{True}[t] = \underline{\lambda}\mathtt{x}[t].\ \underline{\mathtt{true}}$$

$$\mathtt{False}[t] = \underline{\lambda}\mathtt{x}[t].\ \underline{\mathtt{false}}$$

$$\mathtt{Cond}(e_1,e_2,e_3) = \underline{\lambda}\mathtt{x}[\cdots].\ \underline{\mathtt{if}}\ e_1\underline{(}\mathtt{x}\underline{)}\ \underline{\mathtt{then}}\ e_2\underline{(}\mathtt{x}\underline{)}\ \underline{\mathtt{else}}\ e_3\underline{(}\mathtt{x}\underline{)}$$

$$\mathtt{Fix}[t] = \underline{\lambda}\mathtt{x}[t\underline{\rightarrow}t].\ \underline{\mathtt{fix}}\ \mathtt{x}$$

$t \in T2$

$t ::= \mathtt{A_i} \mid t{\times}t \mid t{\to}t \mid t\ \mathtt{list} \mid \underline{\mathtt{A_i}} \mid t\underline{\times}t \mid t\underline{\to}t \mid t\ \underline{\mathtt{list}}$

$e \in CE2$

$e ::= \mathtt{f_i}[t] \mid \langle e,e\rangle \mid \mathtt{fst}\ e \mid \mathtt{snd}\ e \mid$
$\quad \lambda\mathtt{x_i}[t].e \mid e(e) \mid \mathtt{x_i} \mid$
$\quad e\mathtt{:}e \mid \mathtt{nil}[t] \mid \mathtt{hd}\ e \mid \mathtt{tl}\ e \mid \mathtt{isnil}\ e \mid$
$\quad \mathtt{true} \mid \mathtt{false} \mid \mathtt{if}\ e\ \mathtt{then}\ e\ \mathtt{else}\ e \mid \mathtt{fix}\ e \mid$
$\quad \mathtt{F_i}[t] \mid \mathtt{Tuple}(e,e) \mid \mathtt{Fst}[t] \mid \mathtt{Snd}[t] \mid$
$\quad \mathtt{Curry}\ e \mid \mathtt{Apply}[t] \mid e \,\square\, e \mid \mathtt{Id}[t] \mid$
$\quad \mathtt{Cons}(e,e) \mid \mathtt{Nil}[t] \mid \mathtt{Hd}[t] \mid \mathtt{Tl}[t] \mid \mathtt{Isnil}[t] \mid$
$\quad \mathtt{True}[t] \mid \mathtt{False}[t] \mid \mathtt{Cond}(e,e,e) \mid \mathtt{Fix}[t]$

Table 4.1: The mixed λ-calculus and combinatory logic

Here we have indicated the general form of the type parameters associated with the combinators and we have used ellipses $(\cdots)$ to indicate missing type information in the run-time λ-expressions. We shall provide a more precise relationship later in this section.

Example 4.1.1 As an example of a program in combinator form consider the program $\mathtt{sum_{9B}} \in P(CE2, T2)$ given by

```
DEF reduce9B = λf[ ]. Curry (fix(λg[ ].
                  Cond(Isnil[ ] □ Snd[ ], Fst[ ],
                       Apply[ ] □ Tuple(f □ Hd[ ] □ Snd[ ],
                         g □ Tuple(Fst[ ], Tl[ ] □ Snd[ ])))))
VAL Apply[ ] □ Tuple((reduce9B (Curry +[ ])) □ (Zero[ ]), Id[ ])
HAS Int list → Int
```

For the sake of readability we have omitted the type information (in square brackets). Note that □ behaves like functional composition in that an expression $e_1 \square e_2$ should be read backwards. □

The methodology behind the construction of the combinators is not entirely arbitrary. Concerning

$\underline{\mathtt{fst}}$, $\underline{\mathtt{snd}}$, $\underline{\mathtt{hd}}$, $\underline{\mathtt{tl}}$, $\underline{\mathtt{isnil}}$ and $\underline{\mathtt{fix}}$

of the *2*-level λ-calculus, we have proceeded as follows: instead of underlining we now use capitals and instead of an expression argument we provide explicit type information. The intention has been to supply as little type information as possible while ensuring that any expression without free variables still has a unique type. (This will become clearer when we present the well-formedness rules below.) A similar procedure has been used for

$\underline{\texttt{nil}}$, $\underline{\texttt{true}}$, $\underline{\texttt{false}}$ and $\underline{\texttt{f}}_i$

except that there was no expression argument to remove. For the constructs

$\underline{:}$, $\underline{\langle}\ \underline{\rangle}$ and $\underline{\texttt{if}}$

which take more than one expression argument, a new combinator name has been introduced. (This is a minor point, due to the fact that in the *2*-level λ-calculus one writes $e_1\underline{:}e_2$ rather than $\underline{\texttt{cons}}(e_1,e_2)$.) However, the 'functionality' of the expression arguments have changed: the combinators now take 'functions' as arguments rather than 'values'. Finally, the constructs

$\underline{\lambda}$, $\underline{(}\ \underline{)}$ and $\mathtt{x}_i$

related to function space, have been replaced by four new combinators: `Curry`, `Apply`, □ and `Id`.

There are some subtleties involved in motivating the combinators for function space and in deciding which combinators should take expression arguments and which should not. To give a detailed motivation requires a somewhat technical study of how to interpret typed λ-calculi in so-called cartesian closed categories [40, 49] and this incorporates a study of *why* the approach to parameterized semantics in Chapter 5 works. We shall not go into these details, however, and in Chapter 5 we merely show *that* the approach to parameterized semantics works. Concerning the more general setting of the B-level language L we therefore do not have much to say in general, except to note that the intention is to eliminate variables associated with some binding time in B. This is done by replacing constructs operating on values of that binding time with combinators operating on functions whose domain contain information about the values of the eliminated variables, e.g. as shown in the equation for `Tuple`.

Remark 4.1.2 The essence of the categorical motivation is as follows. The combinators □ and `Id` express the basic categorical data. The combinators `Fst`, `Snd` and `Tuple` arise in the categorical characterization of cartesian product. In this `Fst` and `Snd` are morphisms, i.e. functions, that depend on no other morphism while `Tuple` depends on two. Hence `Fst` and `Snd` are used without any argument expression and `Tuple` is used with two. The combinators `Hd`, `Tl`, `Isnil`, `Nil` and `Cons` are intended to mimic this although they don't quite tally with a categorical characterization. (An alternative is to use a `Case` construct as discussed in Exercise 9.) Finally, the combinators `Apply` and `Curry` are the key morphisms involved in the characterization of cartesian closedness, i.e. function spaces. We refer to [40] for a quite readable introduction to such explanations. □

4.1.1 Well-formedness

The well-formedness relation for *2*-level types is as in Table 3.3 and will not be repeated here. For expressions in combinator form, i.e. in *CE2*, the details are given by Tables 4.2 and 4.3. The form of the well-formedness relation is

$$tenv \vdash e : t$$

where $e \in CE2$ is a *2*-level expression in combinator form, $t \in T2$ is a *2*-level type and *tenv* is a type environment. Unlike in Chapter 3 the type environment now only maps variables to *2*-level types rather than pairs consisting of a type and a binding time. The reason simply is that we have only two binding times and since we are in the process of eliminating run-time variables, the type environments would have to associate all variables with the binding time c. For much the same reasons we do not explicitly indicate the intended binding time of the type t as this would also always equal c. The appearance of the well-formedness rules thus has much in common with the rules presented in Chapter 2.

The well-formedness rules are presented in two tables. In Table 4.2 we have the fragment of the well-formedness rules from the *2*-level λ-calculus that still apply. In Table 4.3 we have the new rules that relate to the combinators. No rules analogous to [up] or [down] are present because removing one of only two binding times leaves us with just one binding time. However, we still have analogues of Facts 3.1.4 and 3.1.5.

Fact 4.1.3 If $tenv \vdash e : t$ then $\vdash t : \mathtt{c}$. □

Fact 4.1.4 If $tenv \vdash e : t_1$ and $tenv \vdash e : t_2$ then $t_1 = t_2$. □

This also holds for the variation of the well-formedness rules where the types of the primitives are constrained. In this case the well-formedness rules must be changed to

[f] $tenv \vdash_C \mathtt{f}_i[t] : t$ if $\vdash t{:}\mathtt{c}$, $\mathtt{f}_i \in \mathrm{dom}(C)$ and t is a *2*-level instance of $C(\mathtt{f}_i)$

[F] $tenv \vdash_C \mathtt{F}_i[t' \underline{\rightarrow} t] : t' \underline{\rightarrow} t$ if $\vdash t' \underline{\rightarrow} t{:}\mathtt{c}$, $\mathtt{f}_i \in \mathrm{dom}(C)$ and t is a *2*-level instance of $C(\mathtt{f}_i)$

Note in the axiom [F] that it is t, not $t' \underline{\rightarrow} t$, that should be a *2*-level instance of $C(\mathtt{f}_i)$. This has already been motivated by the equation $\mathtt{F}_i[t' \underline{\rightarrow} t] = \underline{\lambda}\mathtt{x}[t'].\ \underline{\mathtt{f}}_i[t]$.

For programs the well-formedness relation is much as in the previous chapters:

$$\frac{\begin{array}{c}\emptyset \vdash e_1 : t_1 \\ \vdots \\ \emptyset[t_1/\mathtt{x}_1]\cdots[t_{n-1}/\mathtt{x}_{n-1}] \vdash e_n : t_n \\ \emptyset[t_1/\mathtt{x}_1]\cdots[t_n/\mathtt{x}_n] \vdash e_0 : t\end{array}}{\vdash \mathtt{DEF}\ \mathtt{x}_1{=}e_1 \cdots \mathtt{DEF}\ \mathtt{x}_n{=}e_n\ \mathtt{VAL}\ e_0\ \mathtt{HAS}\ t}$$

[f]	$tenv \vdash \mathtt{f}_i[t] : t \qquad \text{if} \vdash t : \mathsf{c}$
[⟨⟩]	$\dfrac{tenv \vdash e_1 : t_1 \qquad tenv \vdash e_2 : t_2}{tenv \vdash \langle e_1, e_2 \rangle : t_1 \times t_2}$
[fst]	$\dfrac{tenv \vdash e : t_1 \times t_2}{tenv \vdash \mathtt{fst}\ e : t_1}$
[snd]	$\dfrac{tenv \vdash e : t_1 \times t_2}{tenv \vdash \mathtt{snd}\ e : t_2}$
[λ]	$\dfrac{tenv[t'/\mathbf{x}_i] \vdash e : t}{tenv \vdash \lambda \mathbf{x}_i[t'].e : t' \to t} \quad \text{if} \vdash t' : \mathsf{c}$
[()]	$\dfrac{tenv \vdash e_1 : t' \to t \qquad tenv \vdash e_2 : t'}{tenv \vdash e_1(e_2) : t}$
[x]	$tenv \vdash \mathbf{x}_i : t \qquad \text{if } (\mathbf{x}_i, t) \in \text{graph}(tenv) \wedge \vdash t{:}\mathsf{c}$
[:]	$\dfrac{tenv \vdash e_1 : t \qquad tenv \vdash e_2 : t\ \mathtt{list}}{tenv \vdash e_1{:}e_2 : t\ \mathtt{list}}$
[nil]	$tenv \vdash \mathtt{nil}[t] : t\ \mathtt{list} \qquad \text{if} \vdash t : \mathsf{c}$
[hd]	$\dfrac{tenv \vdash e : t\ \mathtt{list}}{tenv \vdash \mathtt{hd}\ e : t}$
[tl]	$\dfrac{tenv \vdash e : t\ \mathtt{list}}{tenv \vdash \mathtt{tl}\ e : t\ \mathtt{list}}$
[isnil]	$\dfrac{tenv \vdash e : t\ \mathtt{list}}{tenv \vdash \mathtt{isnil}\ e : \mathtt{Bool}}$
[true]	$tenv \vdash \mathtt{true} : \mathtt{Bool}$
[false]	$tenv \vdash \mathtt{false} : \mathtt{Bool}$
[if]	$\dfrac{tenv \vdash e_1 : \mathtt{Bool} \quad tenv \vdash e_2 : t \quad tenv \vdash e_3 : t}{tenv \vdash \mathtt{if}\ e_1\ \mathtt{then}\ e_2\ \mathtt{else}\ e_3 : t}$
[fix]	$\dfrac{tenv \vdash e : t \to t}{tenv \vdash \mathtt{fix}\ e : t}$

Table 4.2: Well-formedness of the mixed λ-calculus and combinatory logic (1)

A similar definition applies when constraints are considered.

Example 4.1.5 The $\mathtt{sum}_{9B}$ program of Example 4.1.1 is well-formed: $\vdash \mathtt{sum}_{9B}$. □

Example 4.1.6 Consider the function

$$\mathtt{twice} = \lambda \mathtt{g}[\mathtt{Int} \to \mathtt{Int}].\ \lambda \mathtt{x}[\mathtt{Int}].\ \mathtt{g}(\mathtt{g}(\mathtt{x}))$$

which applies its first argument twice to its second argument. This is a typed λ-expression, i.e. $\mathtt{twice} \in E$, and it is well-formed, i.e.

$$\emptyset \vdash \mathtt{twice} : (\mathtt{Int} \to \mathtt{Int}) \to (\mathtt{Int} \to \mathtt{Int})$$

[F]	$tenv \vdash \mathtt{F_i}[t'\underline{\rightarrow}t] : t'\underline{\rightarrow}t \quad \text{if} \vdash t'\underline{\rightarrow}t : \mathsf{c}$
[Tuple]	$\dfrac{tenv \vdash e_1 : t\underline{\rightarrow}t_1 \qquad tenv \vdash e_2 : t\underline{\rightarrow}t_2}{tenv \vdash \mathtt{Tuple}(e_1,e_2) : t\underline{\rightarrow}t_1\underline{\times}t_2}$
[Fst]	$tenv \vdash \mathtt{Fst}[t'\underline{\times}t''] : t'\underline{\times}t''\underline{\rightarrow}t' \quad \text{if} \vdash t'\underline{\times}t''\underline{\rightarrow}t' : \mathsf{c}$
[Snd]	$tenv \vdash \mathtt{Snd}[t'\underline{\times}t''] : t'\underline{\times}t''\underline{\rightarrow}t'' \quad \text{if} \vdash t'\underline{\times}t''\underline{\rightarrow}t'' : \mathsf{c}$
[Curry]	$\dfrac{tenv \vdash e : t'\underline{\times}t''\underline{\rightarrow}t}{tenv \vdash \mathtt{Curry}\ e : t'\underline{\rightarrow}(t''\underline{\rightarrow}t)}$
[Apply]	$tenv \vdash \mathtt{Apply}[t'\underline{\rightarrow}t''] : ((t'\underline{\rightarrow}t'')\underline{\times}t')\underline{\rightarrow}t''$ $\quad \text{if} \vdash ((t'\underline{\rightarrow}t'')\underline{\times}t')\underline{\rightarrow}t'' : \mathsf{c}$
[□]	$\dfrac{tenv \vdash e_1 : t'\underline{\rightarrow}\ t'' \qquad tenv \vdash e_2 : t\underline{\rightarrow}t'}{tenv \vdash e_1 \,\Box\, e_2 : t\underline{\rightarrow}t''}$
[Id]	$tenv \vdash \mathtt{Id}[t] : t\underline{\rightarrow}t \quad \text{if} \vdash t\underline{\rightarrow}t{:}\mathsf{c}$
[Cons]	$\dfrac{tenv \vdash e_1 : t\underline{\rightarrow}t' \qquad tenv \vdash e_2 : t\underline{\rightarrow}t'\underline{\mathtt{list}}}{tenv \vdash \mathtt{Cons}(e_1,e_2) : t\underline{\rightarrow}t'\underline{\mathtt{list}}}$
[Nil]	$tenv \vdash \mathtt{Nil}[t'\underline{\rightarrow}t''\underline{\mathtt{list}}] : t'\underline{\rightarrow}t''\underline{\mathtt{list}}$ $\quad \text{if} \vdash t'\underline{\rightarrow}t''\underline{\mathtt{list}} : \mathsf{c}$
[Hd]	$tenv \vdash \mathtt{Hd}[t] : t\underline{\mathtt{list}\rightarrow}t \quad \text{if} \vdash t\underline{\mathtt{list}\rightarrow}t : \mathsf{c}$
[Tl]	$tenv \vdash \mathtt{Tl}[t] : t\underline{\mathtt{list}\rightarrow}t\underline{\mathtt{list}} \quad \text{if} \vdash t\underline{\mathtt{list}\rightarrow}t\underline{\mathtt{list}} : \mathsf{c}$
[Isnil]	$tenv \vdash \mathtt{Isnil}[t] : t\underline{\mathtt{list}\rightarrow\mathtt{Bool}}$ $\quad \text{if} \vdash t\underline{\mathtt{list}\rightarrow\mathtt{Bool}} : \mathsf{c}$
[True]	$tenv \vdash \mathtt{True}[t] : t\underline{\rightarrow\mathtt{Bool}} \quad \text{if} \vdash t\underline{\rightarrow\mathtt{Bool}} : \mathsf{c}$
[False]	$tenv \vdash \mathtt{False}[t] : t\underline{\rightarrow\mathtt{Bool}} \quad \text{if} \vdash t\underline{\rightarrow\mathtt{Bool}} : \mathsf{c}$
[Cond]	$\dfrac{tenv \vdash e_1 : t\underline{\rightarrow\mathtt{Bool}} \quad tenv \vdash e_2 : t\underline{\rightarrow}t' \quad tenv \vdash e_3 : t\underline{\rightarrow}t'}{tenv \vdash \mathtt{Cond}(e_1,e_2,e_3) : t\underline{\rightarrow}t'}$
[Fix]	$tenv \vdash \mathtt{Fix}[t] : (t\underline{\rightarrow}t)\underline{\rightarrow}t \quad \text{if} \vdash (t\underline{\rightarrow}t)\underline{\rightarrow}t : \mathsf{c}$

Table 4.3: Well-formedness of the mixed λ-calculus and combinatory logic (2)

There are five well-formed *2*-level types with $(\mathtt{Int}\rightarrow\mathtt{Int})\rightarrow(\mathtt{Int}\rightarrow\mathtt{Int})$ as their underlying type and three of them are

$$t_1 = (\mathtt{Int}\rightarrow\mathtt{Int})\rightarrow(\mathtt{Int}\rightarrow\mathtt{Int})$$

$$t_2 = (\underline{\mathtt{Int}\rightarrow\mathtt{Int}})\rightarrow(\underline{\mathtt{Int}\rightarrow\mathtt{Int}})$$

$$t_3 = (\underline{\mathtt{Int}\rightarrow\mathtt{Int}})\underline{\rightarrow}(\underline{\mathtt{Int}\rightarrow\mathtt{Int}})$$

Corresponding to these types we have *2*-level expressions in combinator form. For t_1 it is

$$\texttt{twice}_1 = \lambda\texttt{g}[\texttt{Int}\rightarrow\texttt{Int}].\ \lambda\texttt{x}[\texttt{Int}].\ \texttt{g(g(x))}$$

and one may check that $\emptyset\vdash\texttt{twice}_1{:}t_1$. For t_2 it is

$$\texttt{twice}_2 = \lambda\texttt{g}[\underline{\texttt{Int}\rightarrow\texttt{Int}}].\ \texttt{g}\ \square\ \texttt{g}$$

and one may check that $\emptyset\vdash\texttt{twice}_2{:}t_2$. For t_3 it is

$$\begin{aligned}\texttt{twice}_3 = \texttt{Curry}\ (&\\ &\texttt{Apply}[\underline{\texttt{Int}\rightarrow\texttt{Int}}]\ \square\ \texttt{Tuple(Fst}[(\underline{\texttt{Int}\rightarrow\texttt{Int}})\underline{\times}\underline{\texttt{Int}}],\\ &\texttt{Apply}[\underline{\texttt{Int}\rightarrow\texttt{Int}}]\ \square\ \texttt{Tuple(Fst}[(\underline{\texttt{Int}\rightarrow\texttt{Int}})\underline{\times}\underline{\texttt{Int}}],\\ &\texttt{Snd}[(\underline{\texttt{Int}\rightarrow\texttt{Int}})\underline{\times}\underline{\texttt{Int}}])))\end{aligned}$$

In order to understand this formula it may help to write `twice` as

$$\begin{aligned}\texttt{twice} = \ &\lambda\texttt{g}[\texttt{Int}\rightarrow\texttt{Int}].\ \lambda\texttt{x}[\texttt{Int}].\\ &\texttt{g(}\\ &\texttt{g(}\\ &\texttt{x))}\end{aligned}$$

and to check that $\emptyset\vdash\texttt{twice}_3{:}t_3$. □

4.1.2 Combinator expansion

In the previous chapters we showed how the expressions of a newly introduced language could be transformed back into the more well-known language upon which it was based. In Chapter 2 we provided the functions ε_{TA} and π_{TA} for erasing the type information, and in Chapter 3 the functions τ_{BTA}, ε_{BTA} and π_{BTA} for erasing the binding time information. We shall now perform a similar development that expands the combinators into *2*-level expressions. This amounts to reconsidering the equations above that show the intended meaning of the combinators. However, we need to be more precise in order to be able to fill in the type information left implicit above. We therefore define transformation functions $\varepsilon_{\text{CI}}^{tenv} : CE2 \rightarrow E2$ and $\pi_{\text{CI}} : P(CE2,T2) \rightarrow P(E2,T2)$. There is no need for a function τ_{CI} for types as the *2*-level λ-calculus and the mixed λ-calculus and combinatory logic have the same type systems. It is, however, convenient to write $\tau_{\text{CI}}(tenv)$ for the type environment that maps $\texttt{x}_i$ to $t_i{:}\texttt{c}$ whenever $tenv$ maps $\texttt{x}_i$ to t_i.

The superscript parameter to $\varepsilon_{\text{CI}}^{tenv}$ is a type environment in the sense of this chapter and together with Fact 4.1.4, this will suffice for filling in the required type information. The intended functionality of $\varepsilon_{\text{CI}}^{tenv}$ is therefore

$$\varepsilon_{\text{CI}}^{tenv} : \{\ e{\in}CE2 \mid \exists t\text{: } tenv \vdash e : t\ \} \rightarrow E2$$

i.e. $\varepsilon_{\mathrm{CI}}^{tenv}$ only applies to well-formed expressions, unlike $\varepsilon_{\mathrm{BTA}}$ and $\varepsilon_{\mathrm{TA}}$. (One could define a function $\varepsilon : CE2 \rightarrow UE$ that works for all expressions but this would not be what we need in the sequel.) The inductive definition is fairly straightforward, however, so we shall leave most of the cases as an exercise and only illustrate a few of the more interesting ones:

$$\varepsilon_{\mathrm{CI}}^{tenv}[\![\ \mathtt{f}_{\mathrm{i}}[t]\ ]\!] = \mathtt{f}_{\mathrm{i}}[t]$$

$$\varepsilon_{\mathrm{CI}}^{tenv}[\![\ \lambda\mathtt{x}_{\mathrm{i}}[t].e\ ]\!] = \lambda\mathtt{x}_{\mathrm{i}}[t].\ \varepsilon_{\mathrm{CI}}^{tenv[t/\mathtt{x}_{\mathrm{i}}]}[\![e]\!]$$

$$\varepsilon_{\mathrm{CI}}^{tenv}[\![\ e_1(e_2)\ ]\!] = \varepsilon_{\mathrm{CI}}^{tenv}[\![e_1]\!]\ (\ \varepsilon_{\mathrm{CI}}^{tenv}[\![e_2]\!]\ )$$

$$\varepsilon_{\mathrm{CI}}^{tenv}[\![\ \mathtt{x}_{\mathrm{i}}\ ]\!] = \mathtt{x}_{\mathrm{i}}$$

$$\vdots$$

$$\varepsilon_{\mathrm{CI}}^{tenv}[\![\ \mathtt{F}_{\mathrm{i}}[t' \underline{\rightarrow} t]\ ]\!] = \underline{\lambda}\mathtt{x}_{\mathrm{a}}[t'].\ \underline{\mathtt{f}}_{\mathrm{i}}[t]$$

$$\varepsilon_{\mathrm{CI}}^{tenv}[\![\ \mathtt{Curry}\ e\ ]\!] = \text{let } tenv \vdash e : t' \underline{\times} t'' \underline{\rightarrow} t \text{ determine } t' \text{ and } t'' \text{ in } \underline{\lambda}\mathtt{x}_{\mathrm{a}}[t'].\ \underline{\lambda}\mathtt{x}_{\mathrm{b}}[t''].\ \varepsilon_{\mathrm{CI}}^{tenv}[\![e]\!]\ \underline{(\langle}\mathtt{x}_{\mathrm{a}},\mathtt{x}_{\mathrm{b}}\underline{\rangle)}$$

$$\varepsilon_{\mathrm{CI}}^{tenv}[\![\ \mathtt{Apply}[t' \underline{\rightarrow} t'']\ ]\!] = \underline{\lambda}\mathtt{x}_{\mathrm{a}}[(t' \underline{\rightarrow} t'') \underline{\times} t'].\ (\underline{\mathtt{fst}}\ \mathtt{x}_{\mathrm{a}})\underline{(}\underline{\mathtt{snd}}\ \mathtt{x}_{\mathrm{a}}\underline{)}$$

$$\varepsilon_{\mathrm{CI}}^{tenv}[\![\ e_1 \Box e_2\ ]\!] = \text{let } tenv \vdash e_2 : t \underline{\rightarrow} t' \text{ determine } t \text{ in } \underline{\lambda}\mathtt{x}_{\mathrm{a}}[t].\ \varepsilon_{\mathrm{CI}}^{tenv}[\![e_1]\!]\ \underline{(}\ \varepsilon_{\mathrm{CI}}^{tenv}[\![e_2]\!]\ \underline{(}\ \mathtt{x}_{\mathrm{a}}\ \underline{))}$$

$$\varepsilon_{\mathrm{CI}}^{tenv}[\![\ \mathtt{Id}[t]\ ]\!] = \underline{\lambda}\mathtt{x}_{\mathrm{a}}[t].\ \mathtt{x}_{\mathrm{a}}$$

$$\vdots$$

In this definition we have taken the liberty of assuming that $\mathtt{x}_{\mathrm{a}}$ and $\mathtt{x}_{\mathrm{b}}$ are not in dom($tenv$). To be precise we should have used some enumeration of variables, e.g. $\mathtt{x}_1$, $\mathtt{x}_2$, $\cdots$, and then let $\mathtt{x}_{\mathrm{a}}$ and $\mathtt{x}_{\mathrm{b}}$ correspond to the smallest and second-smallest index not in dom($tenv$). By analogy with Fact 3.1.3 we then have:

Fact 4.1.7 If $tenv \vdash e : t$ using the well-formedness rules of Tables 4.2 and 4.3 then

$$\tau_{\mathrm{CI}}(tenv) \vdash \varepsilon_{\mathrm{CI}}^{tenv}[\![e]\!] : t : \mathsf{c}$$

using the well-formedness rules of Tables 3.4 and 3.5. A similar fact holds for the well-formedness relation $\vdash_{\mathrm{C}}$ where the types of constants are constrained. □

Example 4.1.8 Returning to the functions $\mathtt{twice}_1$ and $\mathtt{twice}_2$ from Example 4.1.6 it is straightforward to verify that

$$\varepsilon_{\mathrm{CI}}^{\emptyset}[\![\ \mathtt{twice}_1\ ]\!] = \lambda\mathtt{g}[\mathtt{Int}\rightarrow\mathtt{Int}].\ \lambda\mathtt{x}[\mathtt{Int}].\ \mathtt{g}(\mathtt{g}(\mathtt{x}))$$

$$\varepsilon_{\mathrm{CI}}^{\emptyset}[\![\ \mathtt{twice}_2\ ]\!] = \lambda\mathtt{g}[\underline{\mathtt{Int}\rightarrow\mathtt{Int}}].\ \underline{\lambda}\mathtt{x}_{\mathrm{a}}[\underline{\mathtt{Int}}].\ \mathtt{g}\underline{(}\mathtt{g}\underline{(}\mathtt{x}_{\mathrm{a}}\underline{))}$$

Both of these *2*-level expressions have `twice` as their underlying expression (modulo renaming of variables). For $\texttt{twice}_3$, however, $\varepsilon_{\mathrm{CI}}^{\emptyset}[\![\texttt{twice}_3]\!]$ will be a fairly large expression. We return to this in Exercise 4. □

It remains to define the combinator expansion for programs. We define

$$\pi_{\mathrm{CI}} : \{\ p {\in} P(CE2,T2) \mid \vdash p\ \} \to P(E2,T2)$$

by

$$\begin{array}{l}
\pi_{\mathrm{CI}}[\![\ \texttt{DEF}\ \texttt{x}_1{=}e_1\ \cdots\ \texttt{DEF}\ \texttt{x}_\mathrm{n}{=}e_\mathrm{n}\ \texttt{VAL}\ e_0\ \texttt{HAS}\ t\ ]\!] = \\
\quad \text{let } \emptyset \vdash e_1 : t_1 \text{ determine } t_1 \\
\quad \vdots \\
\quad \text{let } \emptyset[t_1/\texttt{x}_1]\cdots[t_{\mathrm{n}-1}/\texttt{x}_{\mathrm{n}-1}] \vdash e_\mathrm{n} : t_\mathrm{n} \text{ determine } t_\mathrm{n} \\
\quad \text{in } \texttt{DEF}\ \texttt{x}_1\ =\ \varepsilon_{\mathrm{CI}}^{\emptyset}[\![e_1]\!] \\
\qquad \vdots \\
\qquad \texttt{DEF}\ \texttt{x}_\mathrm{n}\ =\ \varepsilon_{\mathrm{CI}}^{\emptyset[t_1/\texttt{x}_1]\cdots[t_{\mathrm{n}-1}/\texttt{x}_{\mathrm{n}-1}]}[\![e_\mathrm{n}]\!] \\
\qquad \texttt{VAL}\ \varepsilon_{\mathrm{CI}}^{\emptyset[t_1/\texttt{x}_1]\cdots[t_\mathrm{n}/\texttt{x}_\mathrm{n}]}[\![e_0]\!]\ \texttt{HAS}\ t
\end{array}$$

It follows from Fact 4.1.7 that $\vdash \pi_{\mathrm{CI}}[\![p]\!]$ whenever $\vdash p$ and similarly that $\vdash_{\mathrm{C}} \pi_{\mathrm{CI}}[\![p]\!]$ whenever $\vdash_{\mathrm{C}} p$.

4.2 Combinator Introduction

The developments of Sections 2.2 and 3.2 constitute a definition of a function

$$\mathcal{P}_{\mathrm{BTA}}^{C} \circ \mathcal{P}_{\mathrm{TA}}^{C} : P(UE,T2) \hookrightarrow P(E2,T2)$$

that transforms programs in the form of untyped λ-expressions together with an overall *2*-level type into programs that are in the form of *2*-level λ-expressions together with a (possibly different) overall type. In other words, the type and binding time information has been propagated into the untyped expressions. In this section we will complement these developments by defining a function

$$\mathcal{P}_{\mathrm{CI}} : P(E2,T2) \hookrightarrow P(CE2,T2)$$

that transforms the run-time λ-constructs into combinators in order to alleviate run-time variables. The definition of $\mathcal{P}_{\mathrm{CI}}$ will be quite straightforward once a similar function has been defined for expressions. (Unlike the development in Section 3.2 we need no function for types as the types are the same in the *2*-level λ-calculus and the mixed λ-calculus and combinatory logic.)

To facilitate the definition of combinator introduction for expressions we shall work with a linearised version of type environments. Intuitively, the reason is that now the run-time parameters will be implicit parameters so rather than referencing them by their name we shall reference them by their position as determined by the position environment. A *position environment*, *penv*, is a finite list of triples consisting of a variable name, a *2*-level type and a binding time:

$$penv \in (\{\mathtt{x}_i | i \in I\} \times T2 \times 2)\ \mathtt{list}$$

To obtain the type environment contained in a position environment we introduce functions ρ_{BTA} and $\rho^{\mathtt{c}}_{\mathrm{CI}}$. The function ρ_{BTA} is defined by

$$\rho_{\mathrm{BTA}}(penv)(\mathtt{x}_i) = \begin{cases} t{:}b & \text{if the rightmost } (\mathtt{x}_j,t_j,b_j) \text{ in } penv \\ & \text{with } \mathtt{x}_i{=}\mathtt{x}_j \text{ has } t{=}t_j \text{ and } b{=}b_j \\ \text{undefined} & \text{if no } (\mathtt{x}_j,t_j,b_j) \text{ in } penv \text{ has } \mathtt{x}_j{=}\mathtt{x}_i \end{cases}$$

and gives the type environment in the sense of the *2*-level λ-calculus of Chapter 3. Similarly, the function $\rho^{\mathtt{c}}_{\mathrm{CI}}$ is defined by

$$\rho^{\mathtt{c}}_{\mathrm{CI}}(penv)(\mathtt{x}_i) = \begin{cases} t & \text{if } \rho_{\mathrm{BTA}}(penv)(\mathtt{x}_i) = t{:}\mathtt{c} \\ \text{undefined} & \text{otherwise} \end{cases}$$

and gives the type environment in the sense of the mixed λ-calculus and combinatory logic studied in this chapter. By analogy we may define a function $\rho^{\mathtt{r}}_{\mathrm{CI}}$ by $\rho^{\mathtt{r}}_{\mathrm{CI}}(penv)(\mathtt{x}_i) = t$ if and only if $\rho_{\mathrm{BTA}}(penv)(\mathtt{x}_i) = t{:}\mathtt{r}$.

Special interest centers around those triples in a position environment that relate to run-time variables. In particular it will frequently be of interest whether there are any such triples and we may define the function β by

$$\beta(penv) = \begin{cases} \mathtt{c} & \text{if all triples } (\mathtt{x}_i,t_i,b_i) \text{ in } penv \text{ have } b_i{=}\mathtt{c} \\ \mathtt{r} & \text{otherwise} \end{cases}$$

in order to express this succinctly. Note that $\beta(penv){=}\mathtt{c}$ implies $\mathrm{dom}(\rho^{\mathtt{r}}_{\mathrm{CI}}(penv)){=}\emptyset$ but that the converse implication need not hold since a variable may occur in more than one triple. Assuming that $\beta(penv){=}\mathtt{r}$ we may define the product $\Pi(penv)$ of the types of the run-time variables as follows:

$$\Pi(penv) = \begin{cases} \text{undefined} & \text{if } \beta(penv){=}\mathtt{c} \\ \Pi(penv_0) & \text{if } penv{=}penv_0{:}(\mathtt{x}_i,t_i,\mathtt{c}) \\ & \quad \wedge\ \beta(penv_0){=}\mathtt{r} \\ t_i & \text{if } penv{=}penv_0{:}(\mathtt{x}_i,t_i,\mathtt{r}) \\ & \quad \wedge\ \beta(penv_0){=}\mathtt{c} \\ \Pi(penv_0)\underline{\times}t_i & \text{if } penv{=}penv_0{:}(\mathtt{x}_i,t_i,\mathtt{r}) \\ & \quad \wedge\ \beta(penv_0){=}\mathtt{r} \end{cases}$$

To obtain the element of $\Pi(penv)$ that corresponds to some $\mathtt{x}_j$ in the domain of $\rho^{\mathtt{r}}_{\mathrm{CI}}(penv)$ we may define the projection function π_j^{penv} by

$$\pi_j^{penv} = \begin{cases} \text{undefined} & \text{if } \mathtt{x}_j \notin \text{dom}(\rho_{\text{CI}}^{\underline{\mathtt{r}}}(penv)) \\ \pi_j^{penv_0} & \text{if } penv{=}penv_0{:}(\mathtt{x}_i,t,\mathtt{c}) \\ & \quad \wedge\ \mathtt{x}_i{\neq}\mathtt{x}_j \wedge \mathtt{x}_j{\in}\text{dom}(\rho_{\text{CI}}^{\underline{\mathtt{r}}}(penv_0)) \\ \pi_j^{penv_0} \Box \mathtt{Fst}[\Pi(penv)] & \text{if } penv{=}penv_0{:}(\mathtt{x}_i,t,\mathtt{r}) \\ & \quad \wedge\ \mathtt{x}_i{\neq}\mathtt{x}_j \wedge \mathtt{x}_j{\in}\text{dom}(\rho_{\text{CI}}^{\underline{\mathtt{r}}}(penv_0)) \\ \mathtt{Snd}[\Pi(penv)] & \text{if } penv{=}penv_0{:}(\mathtt{x}_j,t,\mathtt{r}) \\ & \quad \wedge\ \beta(penv_0){=}\mathtt{r} \\ \mathtt{Id}[\Pi(penv)] & \text{if } penv{=}penv_0{:}(\mathtt{x}_j,t,\mathtt{r}) \\ & \quad \wedge\ \beta(penv_0){=}\mathtt{c} \end{cases}$$

When π_j^{penv} is defined it will be of functionality $\Pi(penv)\underline{\rightarrow}t_j$ where t_j is given by $\rho_{\text{CI}}^{\underline{\mathtt{r}}}(penv)(\mathtt{x}_j)$.

Example 4.2.1 Consider the position environment *penv* given by

$$((\mathtt{x}_1,\underline{\mathtt{Bool}},\mathtt{r}),\ (\mathtt{x}_2,\underline{\mathtt{Int}},\mathtt{r}),\ (\mathtt{x}_2,\mathtt{Bool},\mathtt{c}),\ (\mathtt{x}_3,\underline{\mathtt{Bool}},\mathtt{r}),\ (\mathtt{x}_3,\underline{\mathtt{Bool}{\rightarrow}\mathtt{Int}},\mathtt{r}))$$

The type environment $\rho_{\text{BTA}}(penv)$ is defined on $\mathtt{x}_1$, $\mathtt{x}_2$ and $\mathtt{x}_3$ and maps $\mathtt{x}_1$ to $\underline{\mathtt{Bool}}$:r, $\mathtt{x}_2$ to Bool:c and $\mathtt{x}_3$ to $\underline{\mathtt{Bool}{\rightarrow}\mathtt{Int}}$:r. The type environment $\rho_{\text{CI}}^{\mathtt{c}}(penv)$ is defined on $\mathtt{x}_2$, and it maps $\mathtt{x}_2$ to Bool. By analogy we may note that $\rho_{\text{CI}}^{\underline{\mathtt{r}}}(penv)$ is defined on $\mathtt{x}_1$ and $\mathtt{x}_3$, and it maps $\mathtt{x}_1$ to $\underline{\mathtt{Bool}}$ and $\mathtt{x}_3$ to $\underline{\mathtt{Bool}{\rightarrow}\mathtt{Int}}$. Clearly $\beta(penv)$ equals r so that $\Pi(penv)$ is defined and we have

$$\Pi(penv) = ((\underline{\mathtt{Bool}}\underline{\times}\underline{\mathtt{Int}})\underline{\times}\underline{\mathtt{Bool}})\underline{\times}(\underline{\mathtt{Bool}{\rightarrow}\mathtt{Int}})$$

The only projection functions that are defined are π_1^{penv} and π_3^{penv} and one may calculate

$$\begin{aligned} \pi_3^{penv} &= \mathtt{Snd}[((\underline{\mathtt{Bool}}\underline{\times}\underline{\mathtt{Int}})\underline{\times}\underline{\mathtt{Bool}})\underline{\times}(\underline{\mathtt{Bool}{\rightarrow}\mathtt{Int}})] \\ \pi_1^{penv} &= \mathtt{Id}[\underline{\mathtt{Bool}}] \\ &\quad \Box\ \mathtt{Fst}[\underline{\mathtt{Bool}}\underline{\times}\underline{\mathtt{Int}}] \\ &\quad \Box\ \mathtt{Fst}[(\underline{\mathtt{Bool}}\underline{\times}\underline{\mathtt{Int}})\underline{\times}\underline{\mathtt{Bool}}] \\ &\quad \Box\ \mathtt{Fst}[((\underline{\mathtt{Bool}}\underline{\times}\underline{\mathtt{Int}})\underline{\times}\underline{\mathtt{Bool}})\underline{\times}(\underline{\mathtt{Bool}{\rightarrow}\mathtt{Int}})] \end{aligned}$$

□

We now have sufficient apparatus that we may state our intentions with the function $\mathcal{E}_{\text{CI}}^{penv}$ that performs combinator introduction for expressions. It has functionality

$$\mathcal{E}_{\text{CI}}^{penv} : \mathit{E2} \hookrightarrow \mathit{CE2}$$

and we shall take care only to apply it to a *2*-level expression *e* that is well-formed. More precisely we shall assume that

$$\rho_{\text{BTA}}(penv) \vdash e : t : \beta(penv)$$

for some *2*-level type t. Thus if *penv* contains run-time triples we shall insist that $\vdash t$:$\mathtt{r}$ and otherwise that $\vdash t$:$\mathtt{c}$. Further we shall assume that the position environment *penv* is *well-formed*: that $\vdash t_i$:b_i holds whenever $(\mathtt{x}_i,t_i,b_i)$ is some triple in *penv*. It is our intention that

$$\rho^{\mathtt{c}}_{\mathrm{CI}}(penv) \vdash \mathcal{E}^{penv}_{\mathrm{CI}}[\![e]\!] : t \qquad \text{if } \beta(penv){=}\mathtt{c}$$

$$\rho^{\mathtt{c}}_{\mathrm{CI}}(penv) \vdash \mathcal{E}^{penv}_{\mathrm{CI}}[\![e]\!] : \Pi(penv)\underline{\rightarrow}t \qquad \text{if } \beta(penv){=}\mathtt{r}$$

This means that all run-time variables have been eliminated and that the eliminated 'values' are instead supplied explicitly to the combinator expression. We shall find it helpful here, and in similar situations later, to write this more succinctly. To do so we define

$$\Delta(penv)\ t = \begin{cases} t & \text{if } \beta(penv){=}\mathtt{c} \\ \Pi(penv)\underline{\rightarrow}t & \text{if } \beta(penv){=}\mathtt{r} \end{cases}$$

and thus merely write

$$\rho^{\mathtt{c}}_{\mathrm{CI}}(penv) \vdash \mathcal{E}^{penv}_{\mathrm{CI}}[\![e]\!] : \Delta(penv)\ t$$

A problem to be encountered in the definition of $\mathcal{E}^{penv}_{\mathrm{CI}}[\![e]\!]$ is the fact that the rules [up] and [down] may have been used to show the well-formedness of e, that is to show that

$$\exists t,b\text{: } \rho_{\mathrm{BTA}}(penv) \vdash e : t : b \wedge b = \beta(penv)$$

It is to handle this problem that we only consider the possibility that b equals $\beta(penv)$. We therefore need operations for shortening and enlarging position environments. A position environment *penv* may be *shortened* by removing all triples whose binding time is $\mathtt{r}$:

$$\delta\bullet\ penv = \begin{cases} penv & \text{if } penv = () \\ \delta\bullet(penv_0)\text{:}(\mathtt{x}_i,t_i,\mathtt{c}) & \text{if } penv{=}penv_0\text{:}(\mathtt{x}_i,t_i,\mathtt{c}) \\ \delta\bullet(penv_0) & \text{if } penv{=}penv_0\text{:}(\mathtt{x}_i,t_i,\mathtt{r}) \end{cases}$$

One may note that $\beta(\delta\bullet\ penv)$ always equals $\mathtt{c}$. To overcome the effect of shortening we need

$$\delta(penv,t)\ e = \begin{cases} e & \text{if } \beta(penv){=}\mathtt{c} \\ \mathtt{Curry}(e\square\mathtt{Snd}[\Pi(penv)\underline{\times}t']) & \text{if } \beta(penv){=}\mathtt{r}\wedge t{=}t'\underline{\rightarrow}t'' \end{cases}$$

For this to be well-defined we need to ensure that

$$\beta(penv){=}\mathtt{r} \Rightarrow \exists t',t''\text{: } t{=}t'\underline{\rightarrow}t''$$

holds for all invocations of $\delta(penv,t)\ e$.

Example 4.2.2 To illustrate the combined effect of $\delta\bullet$ and δ we shall assume that

$$\rho_{\text{BTA}}(penv) \vdash e{:}t{:}\beta(penv), \qquad \beta(penv)=\mathtt{r}, \qquad \text{and } t=t'\underline{\rightarrow}t''.$$

Provided that

$$\rho^{\mathtt{c}}_{\text{CI}}(penv) \vdash \mathcal{E}^{\delta\bullet penv}_{\text{CI}}[\![e]\!] : t$$

we then have

$$\rho^{\mathtt{c}}_{\text{CI}}(penv) \vdash \delta(penv,t)\ \mathcal{E}^{\delta\bullet penv}_{\text{CI}}[\![e]\!] : \Delta(penv)\ t$$

so that $\mathcal{E}^{penv}_{\text{CI}}[\![e]\!] = \delta(penv,t)\ \mathcal{E}^{\delta\bullet penv}_{\text{CI}}[\![e]\!]$ seems feasible. This will become clearer in the definition of $\mathcal{E}^{penv}_{\text{CI}}$ below. □

Turning to *enlarging* a position environment, we may add a dummy variable of the binding time $\mathtt{r}$:

$$\omega\bullet(t)\ penv = \begin{cases} penv & \text{if } \beta(penv)=\mathtt{r} \\ penv{:}(\mathtt{x_a},t',\mathtt{r}) & \text{if } \beta(penv)=\mathtt{c} \wedge t=t'\underline{\rightarrow}t'' \end{cases}$$

Note that $\beta(\omega\bullet(t)\ penv)$ always equals $\mathtt{r}$ provided that $\omega\bullet(t)\ penv$ is indeed defined. For this to be the case we need to ensure that

$$\beta(penv)=\mathtt{c} \Rightarrow \exists t',t''{:}\ t=t'\underline{\rightarrow}t''$$

holds for all invocations of $\omega\bullet(t)\ penv$. Furthermore, we assume that $\mathbf{x_a}$ does not occur already in *penv*. (This can be made more precise in the way indicated earlier.) Finally, to overcome the effect of enlargement we need

$$\omega(penv,t)\ e = \begin{cases} e & \text{if } \beta(penv)=\mathtt{r} \\ \mathtt{Apply}[t]\square\mathtt{Tuple}(e,\mathtt{Id}[t']) & \text{if } \beta(penv)=\mathtt{c} \wedge t=t'\underline{\rightarrow}t'' \end{cases}$$

where again the condition

$$\beta(penv)=\mathtt{c} \Rightarrow \exists t',t''{:}\ t=t'\underline{\rightarrow}t''$$

needs to be verified for each invocation of $\omega(penv,t)\ e$.

Example 4.2.3 To illustrate the combined effect of $\omega\bullet$ and ω we shall assume that

$$\rho_{\text{BTA}}(penv) \vdash e{:}t{:}\beta(penv), \qquad \beta(penv)=\mathtt{c}, \qquad \text{and } t=t'\underline{\rightarrow}t''.$$

Provided that

$$\rho^{\mathtt{c}}_{\text{CI}}(penv) \vdash \mathcal{E}^{\omega\bullet(t)penv}_{\text{CI}}[\![e]\!] : t'\underline{\rightarrow}t$$

we then have

$$\rho^{\mathtt{c}}_{\text{CI}}(penv) \vdash \omega(penv,t)\ \mathcal{E}^{\omega\bullet(t)penv}_{\text{CI}}[\![e]\!] : t$$

$$\mathcal{E}_{\mathrm{CI}}^{penv}[\![\ \mathtt{f}_i[t]\ ]\!] = \delta(penv,t)\ \mathtt{f}_i[t]$$
$$\mathcal{E}_{\mathrm{CI}}^{penv}[\![\ \underline{\mathtt{f}}_i[t]\ ]\!] = \omega(penv,t)\ \mathtt{F}_i[\Delta(\omega\bullet(t)\ penv)\ t]$$

Table 4.4: $\mathcal{E}_{\mathrm{CI}}^{penv}$: Combinator introduction for expressions (part 1)

so that $\mathcal{E}_{\mathrm{CI}}^{penv}[\![e]\!] = \omega(penv,t)\ \mathcal{E}_{\mathrm{CI}}^{\omega\bullet(t)penv}[\![e]\!]$ seems feasible. This will become clearer in the definition of $\mathcal{E}_{\mathrm{CI}}^{penv}$ below. □

The definition of $\mathcal{E}_{\mathrm{CI}}^{penv}$ is by induction on the structure of its argument. When defining $\mathcal{E}_{\mathrm{CI}}^{penv}[\![e]\!]$ we shall assume that *penv* is well-formed and that

$$\rho_{\mathrm{BTA}}(penv) \vdash e : t : \beta(penv)$$

For primitives we then have the clauses of Table 4.4 and these will be explained below. We should stress that δ, ω, Δ etc. are all intended to be expanded according to the value of *penv*.

A good reading guide to Table 4.4 (as well as subsequent tables) is first to read the equations in the case where no expansion of δ or ω is necessary. Thus if $\beta(penv)$=c we have $\mathcal{E}_{\mathrm{CI}}^{penv}[\![\mathtt{f}_i[t]]\!] = \mathtt{f}_i[t]$ and if $\beta(penv)$=r we have $\mathcal{E}_{\mathrm{CI}}^{penv}[\![\underline{\mathtt{f}}_i[t]]\!] = \mathtt{F}_i[t_0 \underline{\rightarrow} t]$ where t_0 equals $\Pi(penv)$. For the latter clause recall that $\mathtt{F}_i[t_0 \underline{\rightarrow} t]$ is to correspond to $\underline{\lambda}\mathtt{x}_a[t_0].\ \underline{\mathtt{f}}_i[t]$.

Next consider the case where expansion is needed. When $\beta(penv)$=r the idea will be to define $\mathcal{E}_{\mathrm{CI}}^{penv}[\![\mathtt{f}_i[t]]\!]$ as $\delta(penv,t)\ \mathcal{E}_{\mathrm{CI}}^{\delta\bullet penv}[\![\mathtt{f}_i[t]]\!]$ and this is already accomplished by the definition given. We also note that t must have the form $t' \underline{\rightarrow} t''$ in this case so that our use of δ is valid. Similarly, when $\beta(penv)$=c the idea will be to define $\mathcal{E}_{\mathrm{CI}}^{penv}[\![\underline{\mathtt{f}}_i[t]]\!]$ as $\omega(penv,t)\ \mathcal{E}_{\mathrm{CI}}^{\omega\bullet(t)penv}[\![\underline{\mathtt{f}}_i[t]]\!]$ and this is also accomplished by the definition given. We also note that t must have the form $t' \underline{\rightarrow} t''$ in this case so that our use of ω and $\omega\bullet$ is valid. The reasoning of Examples 4.2.2 and 4.2.3 shows that $\mathcal{E}_{\mathrm{CI}}^{penv}[\![\mathtt{f}_i[t]]\!]$ and $\mathcal{E}_{\mathrm{CI}}^{penv}[\![\underline{\mathtt{f}}_i[t]]\!]$ have the functionality $\Delta(penv)\ t$ in all cases.

Turning to compile-time and run-time products the clauses are given in Table 4.5. In the clause for compile-time tupling we know by the well-formedness assumptions that $\beta(penv)$=c and in the clause for run-time tupling we know that $\beta(penv)$=r. This obviates the need for any use of δ, $\delta\bullet$, ω, or $\omega\bullet$. Turning to the projection functions we need to use Fact 3.1.5 to obtain the types of the argument expression. As we do not know the value of $\beta(penv)$, i.e. whether or not the rules [up] or [down] have been used in inferring that the argument to $\mathcal{E}_{\mathrm{CI}}^{penv}$ is well-formed, we have to be prepared for all possibilities and thus have to use δ, $\delta\bullet$, ω and $\omega\bullet$. In all cases our use of δ, $\delta\bullet$, ω and $\omega\bullet$ is valid.

Example 4.2.4 Consider the expressions

$$e_1 = \mathtt{fst}\ \langle\ \mathtt{f}_1[\underline{\mathtt{A}\rightarrow\mathtt{A}}],\ \mathtt{f}_2[\underline{\mathtt{A}\rightarrow\mathtt{A}}]\ \rangle$$
$$e_2 = \underline{\mathtt{fst}}\ \underline{\langle}\ \underline{\mathtt{f}}_1[\underline{\mathtt{A}\rightarrow\mathtt{A}}],\ \underline{\mathtt{f}}_2[\underline{\mathtt{A}\rightarrow\mathtt{A}}]\ \underline{\rangle}$$

$$
\begin{aligned}
\mathcal{E}_{\mathrm{CI}}^{penv}[\![\ \langle e_1,e_2\rangle\ ]\!] &= \langle\ \mathcal{E}_{\mathrm{CI}}^{penv}[\![e_1]\!],\ \mathcal{E}_{\mathrm{CI}}^{penv}[\![e_2]\!]\ \rangle\\
\mathcal{E}_{\mathrm{CI}}^{penv}[\![\ \underline{\langle} e_1,e_2\underline{\rangle}\ ]\!] &= \mathtt{Tuple}(\mathcal{E}_{\mathrm{CI}}^{penv}[\![e_1]\!],\ \mathcal{E}_{\mathrm{CI}}^{penv}[\![e_2]\!])\\
\mathcal{E}_{\mathrm{CI}}^{penv}[\![\ \mathtt{fst}\ e\ ]\!] &= \text{let } \rho_{\mathrm{BTA}}(penv) \vdash e : t_1 \times t_2 : \mathtt{c} \text{ determine } t_1\\
&\quad\ \text{in } \delta(penv,t_1)\ \mathtt{fst}\ \mathcal{E}_{\mathrm{CI}}^{\delta\bullet penv}[\![e]\!]\\
\mathcal{E}_{\mathrm{CI}}^{penv}[\![\ \underline{\mathtt{fst}}\ e\ ]\!] &= \text{let } \rho_{\mathrm{BTA}}(penv) \vdash e : t_1 \underline{\times} t_2 : \mathtt{r} \text{ determine } t_1,\ t_2\\
&\quad\ \text{in } \omega(penv,t_1)\ \mathtt{Fst}[t_1\underline{\times}t_2] \ \square\ \mathcal{E}_{\mathrm{CI}}^{\omega\bullet(t_1)penv}[\![e]\!]\\
\mathcal{E}_{\mathrm{CI}}^{penv}[\![\ \mathtt{snd}\ e\ ]\!] &= \text{let } \rho_{\mathrm{BTA}}(penv) \vdash e : t_1 \times t_2 : \mathtt{c} \text{ determine } t_2\\
&\quad\ \text{in } \delta(penv,t_2)\ \mathtt{snd}\ \mathcal{E}_{\mathrm{CI}}^{\delta\bullet penv}[\![e]\!]\\
\mathcal{E}_{\mathrm{CI}}^{penv}[\![\ \underline{\mathtt{snd}}\ e\ ]\!] &= \text{let } \rho_{\mathrm{BTA}}(penv) \vdash e : t_1 \underline{\times} t_2 : \mathtt{r} \text{ determine } t_1,\ t_2\\
&\quad\ \text{in } \omega(penv,t_2)\ \mathtt{Snd}[t_1\underline{\times}t_2] \ \square\ \mathcal{E}_{\mathrm{CI}}^{\omega\bullet(t_2)penv}[\![e]\!]
\end{aligned}
$$

Table 4.5: $\mathcal{E}_{\mathrm{CI}}^{penv}$: Combinator introduction for expressions (part 2)

and the well-formed position environments

$$
\begin{aligned}
penv_1 &= ()\\
penv_2 &= (\mathtt{x_a},\underline{\mathtt{A}},\mathtt{r})
\end{aligned}
$$

Clearly we have

$$\rho_{\mathrm{BTA}}(penv_{\mathrm{i}}) \vdash e_{\mathrm{j}} : \underline{\mathtt{A}\rightarrow\mathtt{A}} : \beta(penv_{\mathrm{i}})$$

for all choices of $\mathrm{i}\in\{1,2\}$ and $\mathrm{j}\in\{1,2\}$. It is straightforward to calculate that

$$
\begin{aligned}
\mathcal{E}_{\mathrm{CI}}^{penv_1}[\![e_1]\!] &= \mathtt{fst}\ \mathcal{E}_{\mathrm{CI}}^{penv_1}[\![\ \langle\ \mathtt{f}_1[\underline{\mathtt{A}\rightarrow\mathtt{A}}],\ \mathtt{f}_2[\underline{\mathtt{A}\rightarrow\mathtt{A}}]\ \rangle\ ]\!]\\
&= \mathtt{fst}\ \langle\ \mathtt{f}_1[\underline{\mathtt{A}\rightarrow\mathtt{A}}],\ \mathtt{f}_2[\underline{\mathtt{A}\rightarrow\mathtt{A}}]\ \rangle
\end{aligned}
$$

and that

$$
\begin{aligned}
\mathcal{E}_{\mathrm{CI}}^{penv_2}[\![e_2]\!] &= \mathtt{Fst}[(\underline{\mathtt{A}\rightarrow\mathtt{A}})\underline{\times}(\underline{\mathtt{A}\rightarrow\mathtt{A}})]\ \square\ \mathcal{E}_{\mathrm{CI}}^{penv_2}[\![\ \underline{\langle}\ \underline{\mathtt{f}}_1[\underline{\mathtt{A}\rightarrow\mathtt{A}}],\ \underline{\mathtt{f}}_2[\underline{\mathtt{A}\rightarrow\mathtt{A}}]\ \underline{\rangle}\ ]\!]\\
&= \mathtt{Fst}[(\underline{\mathtt{A}\rightarrow\mathtt{A}})\underline{\times}(\underline{\mathtt{A}\rightarrow\mathtt{A}})]\ \square\\
&\quad\ \mathtt{Tuple}(\mathtt{F}_1[\underline{\mathtt{A}\rightarrow}(\underline{\mathtt{A}\rightarrow\mathtt{A}})],\mathtt{F}_2[\underline{\mathtt{A}\rightarrow}(\underline{\mathtt{A}\rightarrow\mathtt{A}})])
\end{aligned}
$$

since there is no need for δ, $\delta\bullet$, ω or $\omega\bullet$ in these cases. Turning to the harder cases we have

$$
\begin{aligned}
\mathcal{E}_{\mathrm{CI}}^{penv_2}[\![e_1]\!] &= \delta(penv_2,\underline{\mathtt{A}\rightarrow\mathtt{A}})\ \mathtt{fst}\ \mathcal{E}_{\mathrm{CI}}^{penv_1}[\![\ \langle\ \mathtt{f}_1[\underline{\mathtt{A}\rightarrow\mathtt{A}}],\ \mathtt{f}_2[\underline{\mathtt{A}\rightarrow\mathtt{A}}]\ \rangle\ ]\!]\\
&= \mathtt{Curry}(\mathcal{E}_{\mathrm{CI}}^{penv_1}[\![e_1]\!]\square\mathtt{Snd}[\underline{\mathtt{A}}\underline{\times}\underline{\mathtt{A}}])
\end{aligned}
$$

where `Curry` and `Snd` are needed to get rid of the value for $\mathtt{x_a}$. Similarly,

$$
\begin{aligned}
\mathcal{E}_{\mathrm{CI}}^{penv_1}[\![e_2]\!] &= \omega(penv_1,\underline{\mathtt{A}\rightarrow\mathtt{A}})\ \mathtt{Fst}[(\underline{\mathtt{A}\rightarrow\mathtt{A}})\underline{\times}(\underline{\mathtt{A}\rightarrow\mathtt{A}})]\ \square\\
&\qquad\qquad \mathcal{E}_{\mathrm{CI}}^{penv_2}[\![\ \underline{\langle}\ \underline{\mathtt{f}}_1[\underline{\mathtt{A}\rightarrow\mathtt{A}}],\ \underline{\mathtt{f}}_2[\underline{\mathtt{A}\rightarrow\mathtt{A}}]\ \underline{\rangle}\ ]\!]\\
&= \mathtt{Apply}[\underline{\mathtt{A}\rightarrow\mathtt{A}}]\square\mathtt{Tuple}(\mathcal{E}_{\mathrm{CI}}^{penv_2}[\![e_2]\!],\mathtt{Id}[\underline{\mathtt{A}}])
\end{aligned}
$$

$$\mathcal{E}_{\text{CI}}^{penv}[\![\ \lambda \mathtt{x}_{\text{i}}[t'].\ e\ ]\!] = \lambda \mathtt{x}_{\text{i}}[t'].\ \mathcal{E}_{\text{CI}}^{penv:(\mathtt{x}_{\text{i}},t',\mathtt{c})}[\![e]\!]$$

$$\begin{aligned}\mathcal{E}_{\text{CI}}^{penv}[\![\ \underline{\lambda} \mathtt{x}_{\text{i}}[t'].\ e\ ]\!] = {} & \text{if } \beta(penv)=\mathtt{r} \\ & \text{then } \mathtt{Curry}\ \mathcal{E}_{\text{CI}}^{penv:(\mathtt{x}_{\text{i}},t',\mathtt{r})}[\![e]\!] \\ & \text{else } \mathcal{E}_{\text{CI}}^{penv:(\mathtt{x}_{\text{i}},t',\mathtt{r})}[\![e]\!]\end{aligned}$$

$$\begin{aligned}\mathcal{E}_{\text{CI}}^{penv}[\![\ e_1\mathtt{(}e_2\mathtt{)}\ ]\!] = {} & \text{let } \rho_{\text{BTA}}(penv) \vdash e_1 : t' \rightarrow t : \mathtt{c} \text{ determine } t \\ & \text{in } \delta(penv,t)\ (\mathcal{E}_{\text{CI}}^{\delta\bullet penv}[\![e_1]\!]\ (\ \mathcal{E}_{\text{CI}}^{\delta\bullet penv}[\![e_2]\!]\ ))\end{aligned}$$

$$\begin{aligned}\mathcal{E}_{\text{CI}}^{penv}[\![\ e_1\underline{\mathtt{(}}e_2\underline{\mathtt{)}}\ ]\!] = {} & \text{let } \rho_{\text{BTA}}(penv) \vdash e_1 : t' \underline{\rightarrow} t : \mathtt{r} \text{ determine } t \text{ and } t' \\ & \text{in } \omega(penv,t)\ (\mathtt{Apply}[t' \underline{\rightarrow} t]\ \square \\ & \qquad \mathtt{Tuple}(\ \mathcal{E}_{\text{CI}}^{\omega\bullet(t)penv}[\![e_1]\!],\ \mathcal{E}_{\text{CI}}^{\omega\bullet(t)penv}[\![e_2]\!]))\end{aligned}$$

$$\mathcal{E}_{\text{CI}}^{penv}[\![\ \mathtt{x}_{\text{i}}\ ]\!] = \begin{cases} \delta(penv,t_{\text{i}})\ \mathtt{x}_{\text{i}} & \text{if } \rho_{\text{BTA}}(penv)(\mathtt{x}_{\text{i}}) = t_{\text{i}}\mathtt{:c} \\ \pi_{\text{i}}^{penv} & \text{if } \rho_{\text{BTA}}(penv)(\mathtt{x}_{\text{i}}) = t_{\text{i}}\mathtt{:r} \end{cases}$$

Table 4.6: $\mathcal{E}_{\text{CI}}^{penv}$: Combinator introduction for expressions (part 3)

where `Apply`, `Tuple` and `Id` are needed to construct the artificial parameter for $\mathtt{x}_{\text{a}}$.

It is vital for the operation of δ, $\delta\bullet$, ω and $\omega\bullet$ that $\vdash t{:}b$ holds for b=`r` as well as b=`c` if and only if t is of the form $t' \underline{\rightarrow} t''$. □

Turning to compile-time and run-time function spaces the clauses are given in Table 4.6. In the clause for compile-time λ-abstraction we know by the well-formedness assumptions that $\beta(penv)$=`c` and so can perform a rather straightforward translation. In the clause for run-time λ-abstraction we do not know the value of $\beta(penv)$. If it is `r` then we have a straightforward expression involving `Curry`. If it is `c` we simply use $\mathcal{E}_{\text{CI}}^{penv:(\mathtt{x}_{\text{i}},t',\mathtt{r})}[\![e]\!]$ as $\mathtt{x}_{\text{i}}$ will be the only run-time variable in $penv$:($\mathtt{x}_{\text{i}}$,t',`r`). This explains why ω and $\omega\bullet$ were not used. For the applications we again need to use Fact 3.1.5 to infer type information about the type of the argument and we do not know the value of $\beta(penv)$ and so have to use δ, $\delta\bullet$, ω and $\omega\bullet$. These uses are valid as may easily be checked. For variables we have two cases depending on whether the variable is retained or eliminated.

Example 4.2.5 It is straightforward to calculate

$$\mathcal{E}_{\text{CI}}^{()}[\![\ \lambda\mathtt{g[Int}\rightarrow\mathtt{Int]}.\ \lambda\mathtt{x[Int]}.\ \mathtt{g(g(x))}\ ]\!] =$$

$$\lambda\mathtt{g[Int}\rightarrow\mathtt{Int]}.\ \lambda\mathtt{x[Int]}.\ \mathtt{g(g(x))}$$

which equals the function $\mathtt{twice}_1$ from Example 4.1.6. Next

$$\mathcal{E}_{\mathrm{CI}}^{penv}\llbracket\ e_1{:}e_2\ \rrbracket = \mathcal{E}_{\mathrm{CI}}^{penv}\llbracket e_1\rrbracket : \mathcal{E}_{\mathrm{CI}}^{penv}\llbracket e_2\rrbracket$$

$$\mathcal{E}_{\mathrm{CI}}^{penv}\llbracket\ e_1\underline{:}e_2\ \rrbracket = \texttt{Cons}(\mathcal{E}_{\mathrm{CI}}^{penv}\llbracket e_1\rrbracket, \mathcal{E}_{\mathrm{CI}}^{penv}\llbracket e_2\rrbracket)$$

$$\mathcal{E}_{\mathrm{CI}}^{penv}\llbracket\ \texttt{nil}[t]\ \rrbracket = \texttt{nil}[t]$$

$$\mathcal{E}_{\mathrm{CI}}^{penv}\llbracket\ \underline{\texttt{nil}}[t]\ \rrbracket = \texttt{Nil}[\Delta(penv)\ (t\ \underline{\texttt{list}})]$$

$$\begin{aligned}\mathcal{E}_{\mathrm{CI}}^{penv}\llbracket\ \texttt{hd}\ e\ \rrbracket = {} & \text{let } \rho_{\mathrm{BTA}}(penv) \vdash e : t\ \texttt{list} : \mathrm{c} \text{ determine } t \\ & \text{in } \delta(penv,t)\ \texttt{hd}\ \mathcal{E}_{\mathrm{CI}}^{\delta\bullet penv}\llbracket e\rrbracket\end{aligned}$$

$$\begin{aligned}\mathcal{E}_{\mathrm{CI}}^{penv}\llbracket\ \underline{\texttt{hd}}\ e\ \rrbracket = {} & \text{let } \rho_{\mathrm{BTA}}(penv) \vdash e : t\ \underline{\texttt{list}} : \mathrm{r} \text{ determine } t \\ & \text{in } \omega(penv,t)\ (\texttt{Hd}[t]\ \Box\ \mathcal{E}_{\mathrm{CI}}^{\omega\bullet(t)penv}\llbracket e\rrbracket)\end{aligned}$$

$$\mathcal{E}_{\mathrm{CI}}^{penv}\llbracket\ \texttt{tl}\ e\ \rrbracket = \texttt{tl}\ \mathcal{E}_{\mathrm{CI}}^{penv}\llbracket e\rrbracket$$

$$\begin{aligned}\mathcal{E}_{\mathrm{CI}}^{penv}\llbracket\ \underline{\texttt{tl}}\ e\ \rrbracket = {} & \text{let } \rho_{\mathrm{BTA}}(penv) \vdash e : t\ \underline{\texttt{list}} : \mathrm{r} \text{ determine } t \\ & \text{in } \texttt{Tl}[t]\ \Box\ \mathcal{E}_{\mathrm{CI}}^{penv}\llbracket e\rrbracket\end{aligned}$$

$$\mathcal{E}_{\mathrm{CI}}^{penv}\llbracket\ \texttt{isnil}\ e\ \rrbracket = \texttt{isnil}\ \mathcal{E}_{\mathrm{CI}}^{penv}\llbracket e\rrbracket$$

$$\begin{aligned}\mathcal{E}_{\mathrm{CI}}^{penv}\llbracket\ \underline{\texttt{isnil}}\ e\ \rrbracket = {} & \text{let } \rho_{\mathrm{BTA}}(penv) \vdash e : t\ \underline{\texttt{list}} : \mathrm{r} \text{ determine } t \\ & \text{in } \texttt{Isnil}[t]\ \Box\ \mathcal{E}_{\mathrm{CI}}^{penv}\llbracket e\rrbracket\end{aligned}$$

Table 4.7: $\mathcal{E}_{\mathrm{CI}}^{penv}$: Combinator introduction for expressions (part 4)

$$\begin{aligned}&\mathcal{E}_{\mathrm{CI}}^{()}\llbracket\ \lambda\texttt{g}[\underline{\texttt{Int}\to\texttt{Int}}].\ \underline{\lambda}\texttt{x}[\underline{\texttt{Int}}].\ \texttt{g}\underline{(}\texttt{g}\underline{(}\texttt{x}\underline{))}\ \rrbracket = \\ &\lambda\texttt{g}[\underline{\texttt{Int}\to\texttt{Int}}].\ \texttt{Apply}[\underline{\texttt{Int}\to\texttt{Int}}]\ \Box\ \texttt{Tuple}(\texttt{Curry}(\texttt{g}\Box\texttt{Snd}[\underline{\texttt{Int}}\underline{\times}\underline{\texttt{Int}}]), \\ &\qquad\qquad\texttt{Apply}[\underline{\texttt{Int}\to\texttt{Int}}]\ \Box\ \texttt{Tuple}(\texttt{Curry}(\texttt{g}\Box\texttt{Snd}[\underline{\texttt{Int}}\underline{\times}\underline{\texttt{Int}}]), \\ &\qquad\qquad\texttt{Id}[\underline{\texttt{Int}}]))\end{aligned}$$

which is somewhat more complicated than the function $\texttt{twice}_2$ from Example 4.1.6. Finally,

$$\begin{aligned}&\mathcal{E}_{\mathrm{CI}}^{()}\llbracket\ \underline{\lambda}\texttt{g}[\underline{\texttt{Int}\to\texttt{Int}}].\ \underline{\lambda}\texttt{x}[\underline{\texttt{Int}}].\ \texttt{g}\underline{(}\texttt{g}\underline{(}\texttt{x}\underline{))}\ \rrbracket = \texttt{Curry}\ (\\ &\quad\texttt{Apply}[\underline{\texttt{Int}\to\texttt{Int}}]\ \Box\ \texttt{Tuple}(\texttt{Id}[\underline{\texttt{Int}\to\texttt{Int}}]\Box\texttt{Fst}[(\underline{\texttt{Int}\to\texttt{Int}})\underline{\times}\underline{\texttt{Int}}], \\ &\quad\texttt{Apply}[\underline{\texttt{Int}\to\texttt{Int}}]\ \Box\ \texttt{Tuple}(\texttt{Id}[\underline{\texttt{Int}\to\texttt{Int}}]\Box\texttt{Fst}[(\underline{\texttt{Int}\to\texttt{Int}})\underline{\times}\underline{\texttt{Int}}], \\ &\quad\texttt{Snd}[(\underline{\texttt{Int}\to\texttt{Int}})\underline{\times}\underline{\texttt{Int}}])))\end{aligned}$$

which is almost equal to the function $\texttt{twice}_3$ from Example 4.1.6. □

The clauses for compile-time and run-time lists are mostly straightforward because it is only when taking the head (hd or $\underline{\texttt{hd}}$) of a list that we cannot determine the value of $\beta(penv)$. The clauses are given in Table 4.7. The clauses for the remaining constructs are given in Table 4.8 and exhibit no new features.

$$\mathcal{E}_{\rm CI}^{penv}[\![\ \texttt{true}\ ]\!] = \texttt{true}$$

$$\mathcal{E}_{\rm CI}^{penv}[\![\ \underline{\texttt{true}}\ ]\!] = \texttt{True}[\Pi(penv)]$$

$$\mathcal{E}_{\rm CI}^{penv}[\![\ \texttt{false}\ ]\!] = \texttt{false}$$

$$\mathcal{E}_{\rm CI}^{penv}[\![\ \underline{\texttt{false}}\ ]\!] = \texttt{False}[\Pi(penv)]$$

$$\begin{array}{l} \mathcal{E}_{\rm CI}^{penv}[\![\ \texttt{if}\ e_1\ \texttt{then}\ e_2\ \texttt{else}\ e_3\ ]\!] = \\ \quad \text{let } \rho_{\rm BTA}(penv) \vdash e_2 : t : \beta(penv) \text{ determine } t \\ \quad \text{in } \delta(penv,t)\ \texttt{if}\ \mathcal{E}_{\rm CI}^{\delta\bullet penv}[\![e_1]\!]\ \texttt{then}\ \mathcal{E}_{\rm CI}^{\delta\bullet penv}[\![e_2]\!]\ \texttt{else}\ \mathcal{E}_{\rm CI}^{\delta\bullet penv}[\![e_3]\!] \end{array}$$

$$\begin{array}{l} \mathcal{E}_{\rm CI}^{penv}[\![\ \underline{\texttt{if}}\ e_1\ \underline{\texttt{then}}\ e_2\ \underline{\texttt{else}}\ e_3\ ]\!] = \\ \quad \text{let } \rho_{\rm BTA}(penv) \vdash e_2 : t : \beta(penv) \text{ determine } t \\ \quad \text{in } \omega(penv,t)\ \texttt{Cond}(\mathcal{E}_{\rm CI}^{\omega\bullet(t)penv}[\![e_1]\!], \mathcal{E}_{\rm CI}^{\omega\bullet(t)penv}[\![e_2]\!], \mathcal{E}_{\rm CI}^{\omega\bullet(t)penv}[\![e_3]\!]) \end{array}$$

$$\begin{array}{l} \mathcal{E}_{\rm CI}^{penv}[\![\ \texttt{fix}\ e\ ]\!] = \text{let } \rho_{\rm BTA}(penv) \vdash e : t \rightarrow t : \texttt{c} \text{ determine } t \\ \qquad\qquad\qquad\quad \text{in } \delta(penv,t)\ \texttt{fix}\ \mathcal{E}_{\rm CI}^{\delta\bullet penv}[\![e]\!] \end{array}$$

$$\begin{array}{l} \mathcal{E}_{\rm CI}^{penv}[\![\ \underline{\texttt{fix}}\ e\ ]\!] = \text{let } \rho_{\rm BTA}(penv) \vdash e : t \underline{\rightarrow} t : \texttt{r} \text{ determine } t \\ \qquad\qquad\qquad\quad \text{in } \omega(penv,t)\ (\texttt{Fix}[t] \,\square\, \mathcal{E}_{\rm CI}^{\omega\bullet(t)penv}[\![e]\!]) \end{array}$$

Table 4.8: $\mathcal{E}_{\rm CI}^{penv}$: Combinator introduction for expressions (part 5)

Proposition 4.2.6 (Correctness of $\mathcal{E}_{\rm CI}^{penv}$) If the position environment *penv* is well-formed and the *2*-level expression e satisfies

$$\rho_{\rm BTA}(penv) \vdash e : t : \beta(penv)$$

then $\mathcal{E}_{\rm CI}^{penv}[\![e]\!]$ is defined and

$$\rho_{\rm CI}^{\texttt{c}}(penv) \vdash \mathcal{E}_{\rm CI}^{penv}[\![e]\!] : \Delta(penv)\ t$$

A similar result holds for $\vdash_{\rm C}$. □

Proof: The proof is by structural induction on the argument expression e. In each case the general strategy will be as follows:

(i) First consider the subcase where the value of $\beta(penv)$ is such that the potential occurrences of δ, $\delta\bullet$, ω and $\omega\bullet$ have no effect. For compile-time constructs this is when $\beta(penv)$=c and for run-time constructs this is when $\beta(penv)$=r.

(ii) Next consider the subcase where $\beta(penv)$ has the opposite value. In some cases this conflicts with the assumption

$$\rho_{\mathrm{BTA}}(penv) \vdash e : t : \beta(penv)$$

and then the proposition holds vacuously. When there is no conflict we proceed as follows:

(a) Verify that the type arguments to δ, ω and $\omega\bullet$ satisfy the conditions.

(b) Show that the equation for $\mathcal{E}_{\mathrm{CI}}^{penv}[\![e]\!]$ amounts to $\delta(penv,\cdots)\ \mathcal{E}_{\mathrm{CI}}^{\delta\bullet penv}[\![e]\!]$ when $\beta(penv)$=$\mathtt{r}$ and $\omega(penv,\cdots)\ \mathcal{E}_{\mathrm{CI}}^{\omega\bullet(\cdots)penv}[\![e]\!]$ when $\beta(penv)$=$\mathtt{c}$.

(c) Combine (i) and (iib) using the insights about the combined effects of $\delta\bullet$ and δ and of $\omega\bullet$ and ω that were presented in Examples 4.2.2 and 4.2.3.

This proof is mostly straightforward as it only amounts to formalising the explanations given when motivating the definition of $\mathcal{E}_{\mathrm{CI}}^{penv}$. We shall therefore only consider the cases corresponding to those also considered in the proof of Proposition 2.2.8.

The case e::=$\mathtt{f}_{\mathrm{i}}[t]$. If $\beta(penv)$=$\mathtt{c}$ we have

$$\mathcal{E}_{\mathrm{CI}}^{penv}[\![\mathtt{f}_{\mathrm{i}}[t]]\!] = \mathtt{f}_{\mathrm{i}}[t]$$

and clearly

$$\rho_{\mathrm{CI}}^{\mathtt{c}}(penv) \vdash \mathtt{f}_{\mathrm{i}}[t] : \Delta(penv)\ t$$

If $\beta(penv)$=$\mathtt{r}$ we have

$$\mathcal{E}_{\mathrm{CI}}^{penv}[\![\mathtt{f}_{\mathrm{i}}[t]]\!] = \mathtt{Curry}(\mathtt{f}_{\mathrm{i}}[t]\Box\mathtt{Snd}[t_0\underline{\times}t_1])$$

where t_0 is $\Pi(penv)$ and t is of the form $t_1\underline{\rightarrow}t_2$. To see that t is indeed of the form $t_1\underline{\rightarrow}t_2$ note first that $\vdash t$:$\mathtt{r}$ follows from $\beta(penv)$=$\mathtt{r}$ and

$$\rho_{\mathrm{BTA}}(penv) \vdash \mathtt{f}_{\mathrm{i}}[t] : t : \beta(penv)$$

and second that $\vdash t$:$\mathtt{c}$ follows because rule [f] must have been used in order to obtain this. We then clearly have

$$\rho_{\mathrm{CI}}^{\mathtt{c}}(penv) \vdash \mathtt{Curry}(\mathtt{f}_{\mathrm{i}}[t]\Box\mathtt{Snd}[t_0\underline{\times}t_1]) : \Delta(penv)\ t$$

as was desired.

The case e::=$\underline{\mathtt{f}}_{\mathrm{i}}[t]$. If $\beta(penv)$=$\mathtt{r}$ we have

$$\mathcal{E}_{\mathrm{CI}}^{penv}[\![\underline{\mathtt{f}}_{\mathrm{i}}[t]]\!] = \mathtt{F}_{\mathrm{i}}[t_0\underline{\rightarrow}t]$$

where t_0=$\Pi(penv)$ and clearly

$$\rho_{\mathrm{CI}}^{\mathtt{c}}(penv) \vdash \mathtt{F}_{\mathrm{i}}[t_0\underline{\rightarrow}t] : \Delta(penv)\ t$$

If $\beta(penv)$=c we have

$$\mathcal{E}_{\text{CI}}^{penv}[\![\underline{\mathtt{f}}_{\mathtt{i}}[t]]\!] = \mathtt{Apply}[t] \;\square\; \mathtt{Tuple}(\mathtt{F}_{\mathtt{i}}[t_1\underline{\rightarrow}t],\mathtt{Id}[t_1])$$

where t is of the form $t_1\underline{\rightarrow}t_2$. To see that t is indeed of the form $t_1\underline{\rightarrow}t_2$ note first that $\vdash t$:c follows from $\beta(penv)$=c and $\rho_{\text{BTA}}(penv)\vdash\underline{\mathtt{f}}_{\mathtt{i}}[t]:t:\beta(penv)$ and second that $\vdash t$:r follows because rule [$\underline{\mathtt{f}}$] must have been used in order to obtain this. We then clearly have

$$\rho_{\text{CI}}^{\mathtt{c}}(penv) \vdash \mathtt{Apply}[t] \;\square\; \mathtt{Tuple}(\mathtt{F}_{\mathtt{i}}[t_1\underline{\rightarrow}t],\mathtt{Id}[t_1]) : \Delta(penv)\ t$$

(By way of digression, it might be tempting to use $\mathtt{F}_{\mathtt{i}}[t]$ for $\mathcal{E}_{\text{CI}}^{penv}[\![\underline{\mathtt{f}}_{\mathtt{i}}[t]]\!]$ in this case; however, then $\mathtt{F}_{\mathtt{i}}[\cdots]$ would no longer correspond to $\underline{\lambda}\mathtt{x}[\cdots].\ \underline{\mathtt{f}}_{\mathtt{i}}[\cdots]$.)

The case e::=$\lambda\mathtt{x}_{\mathtt{i}}[t'].e_0$. If $\beta(penv)$=c we have

$$\mathcal{E}_{\text{CI}}^{penv}[\![\lambda\mathtt{x}_{\mathtt{i}}[t'].e_0]\!] = \lambda\mathtt{x}_{\mathtt{i}}[t'].\ \mathcal{E}_{\text{CI}}^{penv:(\mathtt{x}_{\mathtt{i}},t',\mathtt{c})}[\![e_0]\!]$$

and it follows from the well-formedness of e that t must be of the form $t'\rightarrow t''$. Using the induction hypothesis we then have

$$\rho_{\text{CI}}^{\mathtt{c}}(penv:(\mathtt{x}_{\mathtt{i}},t',\mathtt{c})) \vdash \mathcal{E}_{\text{CI}}^{penv:(\mathtt{x}_{\mathtt{i}},t',\mathtt{c})}[\![e_0]\!] : \Delta(penv:(\mathtt{x}_{\mathtt{i}},t',\mathtt{c}))\ t''$$

since we know from the well-formedness assumptions about e and $penv$ that

$penv:(\mathtt{x}_{\mathtt{i}},t',\mathtt{c})$ is well-formed

$$\rho_{\text{BTA}}(penv:(\mathtt{x}_{\mathtt{i}},t',\mathtt{c})) \vdash e_0 : t'' : \beta(penv:(\mathtt{x}_{\mathtt{i}},t',\mathtt{c}))$$

We then have

$$\rho_{\text{CI}}^{\mathtt{c}}(penv) \vdash \lambda\mathtt{x}_{\mathtt{i}}[t'].\ \mathcal{E}_{\text{CI}}^{penv:(\mathtt{x}_{\mathtt{i}},t',\mathtt{c})}[\![e_0]\!] : \Delta(penv)\ t$$

Since $\beta(penv)$ must equal c this completes the present case.

The case e::=$\underline{\lambda}\mathtt{x}_{\mathtt{i}}[t'].e_0$. If $\beta(penv)$=r we have

$$\mathcal{E}_{\text{CI}}^{penv}[\![\underline{\lambda}\mathtt{x}_{\mathtt{i}}[t'].e_0]\!] = \mathtt{Curry}\ \mathcal{E}_{\text{CI}}^{penv:(\mathtt{x}_{\mathtt{i}},t',\mathtt{r})}[\![e_0]\!]$$

Much as above, it follows from the induction hypothesis that

$$\rho_{\text{CI}}^{\mathtt{c}}(penv:(\mathtt{x}_{\mathtt{i}},t',\mathtt{r})) \vdash \mathcal{E}_{\text{CI}}^{penv:(\mathtt{x}_{\mathtt{i}},t',\mathtt{r})}[\![e_0]\!] : \Delta(penv:(\mathtt{x}_{\mathtt{i}},t',\mathtt{r}))\ t''$$

where t is of the form $t'\underline{\rightarrow}t''$. We then have

$$\rho_{\text{CI}}^{\mathtt{c}}(penv) \vdash \mathtt{Curry}\ \mathcal{E}_{\text{CI}}^{penv:(\mathtt{x}_{\mathtt{i}},t',\mathtt{r})}[\![e_0]\!] : \Delta(penv)\ t$$

If $\beta(penv)$=c we have

$$\mathcal{E}_{\text{CI}}^{penv}[\![\underline{\lambda}\mathtt{x}_{\mathtt{i}}[t'].e_0]\!] = \mathcal{E}_{\text{CI}}^{penv:(\mathtt{x}_{\mathtt{i}},t',\mathtt{r})}[\![e_0]\!]$$

and the result follows immediately from the induction hypothesis.

The case e::=$e_1(e_2)$. If $\beta(penv)$=c we have

$$\mathcal{E}_{\mathrm{CI}}^{penv}[\![e_1(e_2)]\!] = \mathcal{E}_{\mathrm{CI}}^{penv}[\![e_1]\!]\ (\ \mathcal{E}_{\mathrm{CI}}^{penv}[\![e_2]\!]\ )$$

It follows from the induction hypothesis that

$$\rho_{\mathrm{CI}}^{\mathtt{c}}(penv) \vdash \mathcal{E}_{\mathrm{CI}}^{penv}[\![e_1]\!] : t' \rightarrow t$$
$$\rho_{\mathrm{CI}}^{\mathtt{c}}(penv) \vdash \mathcal{E}_{\mathrm{CI}}^{penv}[\![e_2]\!] : t'$$

for a suitable type t' and it is then immediate that

$$\rho_{\mathrm{CI}}^{\mathtt{c}}(penv) \vdash \mathcal{E}_{\mathrm{CI}}^{penv}[\![e_1(e_2)]\!] : \Delta(penv)\ t$$

If $\beta(penv)$=r we have

$$\mathcal{E}_{\mathrm{CI}}^{penv}[\![e_1(e_2)]\!] = \mathtt{Curry}(\mathcal{E}_{\mathrm{CI}}^{\delta\bullet penv}[\![e_1(e_2)]\!] \square \mathtt{Snd}[\Pi(penv)\underline{\times}t_1])$$

where t is of the form $t_1\underline{\rightarrow}t_2$. This is because $\vdash t$:r comes from the well-formedness assumption about e, and $\vdash t$:c follows because rule [()] must have been used to obtain this. We saw above that the induction hypothesis guarantees

$$\rho_{\mathrm{CI}}^{\mathtt{c}}(\delta\bullet penv) \vdash \mathcal{E}_{\mathrm{CI}}^{\delta\bullet penv}[\![e_1(e_2)]\!] : \Delta(\delta\bullet penv)\ t$$

and we then have

$$\rho_{\mathrm{CI}}^{\mathtt{c}}(penv) \vdash \mathtt{Curry}(\mathcal{E}_{\mathrm{CI}}^{\delta\bullet penv}[\![e_1(e_2)]\!] \square \mathtt{Snd}[\Pi(penv)\underline{\times}t_1]) : \Delta(penv)\ t$$

as desired.

The case e::=$e_1\underline{(}e_2\underline{)}$. If $\beta(penv)$=r we have

$$\mathcal{E}_{\mathrm{CI}}^{penv}[\![e_1\underline{(}e_2\underline{)}]\!] = \mathtt{Apply}[t'\underline{\rightarrow}t] \square \mathtt{Tuple}(\mathcal{E}_{\mathrm{CI}}^{penv}[\![e_1]\!],\mathcal{E}_{\mathrm{CI}}^{penv}[\![e_2]\!])$$

where $t'\underline{\rightarrow}t$ is the type of e_1. It follows from the induction hypothesis that

$$\rho_{\mathrm{CI}}^{\mathtt{c}}(penv) \vdash \mathcal{E}_{\mathrm{CI}}^{penv}[\![e_1]\!] : \Pi(penv)\underline{\rightarrow}t'\underline{\rightarrow}t$$
$$\rho_{\mathrm{CI}}^{\mathtt{c}}(penv) \vdash \mathcal{E}_{\mathrm{CI}}^{penv}[\![e_2]\!] : \Pi(penv)\underline{\rightarrow}t'$$

and it is then immediate that

$$\rho_{\mathrm{CI}}^{\mathtt{c}}(penv) \vdash \mathtt{Apply}[t'\underline{\rightarrow}t] \square \mathtt{Tuple}(\mathcal{E}_{\mathrm{CI}}^{penv}[\![e_1]\!],\mathcal{E}_{\mathrm{CI}}^{penv}[\![e_2]\!]) : \Delta(penv)\ t$$

If $\beta(penv)$=c we have

$$\mathcal{E}_{\mathrm{CI}}^{penv}[\![e_1\underline{(}e_2\underline{)}]\!] = \mathtt{Apply}[t] \square \mathtt{Tuple}(\mathcal{E}_{\mathrm{CI}}^{\omega\bullet(t)penv}[\![e_1\underline{(}e_2\underline{)}]\!],\mathtt{Id}[t_1])$$

where t is of the form $t_1\underline{\rightarrow}t_2$. That t must be of this form follows much as in the previous case. We saw above that the induction hypothesis guarantees

$$\rho^{\mathtt{c}}_{\mathrm{CI}}(\omega\bullet(t)\ penv) \vdash \mathcal{E}^{\omega\bullet(t)penv}_{\mathrm{CI}}[\![e_1\underline{(}e_2\underline{)}]\!] : \Delta(\omega\bullet(t)\ penv)\ t$$

and we then have

$$\rho^{\mathtt{c}}_{\mathrm{CI}}(penv) \vdash \mathtt{Apply}[t]\Box\mathtt{Tuple}(\mathcal{E}^{\omega\bullet(t)penv}_{\mathrm{CI}}[\![e_1\underline{(}e_2\underline{)}]\!],\mathtt{Id}[t_1]) : \Delta(penv)\ t$$

as desired.

The case e::=$\mathbf{x}_i$. If $\rho_{\mathrm{BTA}}(penv)(\mathbf{x}_i)$=$t$:c and $\beta(penv)$=c we have

$$\mathcal{E}^{penv}_{\mathrm{CI}}[\![\mathbf{x}_i]\!] = \mathbf{x}_i$$

and clearly

$$\rho^{\mathtt{c}}_{\mathrm{CI}}(penv) \vdash \mathbf{x}_i : \Delta(penv)\ t$$

If $\rho_{\mathrm{BTA}}(penv)(\mathbf{x}_i)$=$t$:c and $\beta(penv)$=r we have

$$\mathcal{E}^{penv}_{\mathrm{CI}}[\![\mathbf{x}_i]\!] = \mathtt{Curry}(\mathbf{x}_i\Box\mathtt{Snd}[t_0\underline{\times}t_1])$$

where t_0 is $\Pi(penv)$ and t is of the form $t_1\underline{\rightarrow}t_2$. That t must be of this form follows much as in the previous cases. It is then immediate that

$$\rho^{\mathtt{c}}_{\mathrm{CI}}(penv) \vdash \mathtt{Curry}(\mathbf{x}_i\Box\mathtt{Snd}[t_0\underline{\times}t_1]) : \Delta(penv)\ t$$

If $\rho_{\mathrm{BTA}}(penv)(\mathbf{x}_i)$=$t$:r then $\beta(penv)$=r and we have

$$\mathcal{E}^{penv}_{\mathrm{CI}}[\![\mathbf{x}_i]\!] = \pi^{penv}_i$$

When defining π^{penv}_i we argued that it would have type $\Pi(penv)\underline{\rightarrow}t$ and hence

$$\rho^{\mathtt{c}}_{\mathrm{CI}}(penv) \vdash \pi^{penv}_i : \Delta(penv)\ t$$

as desired. □

We can now define the function $\mathcal{P}_{\mathrm{CI}}$ that performs combinator introduction for programs. It has functionality

$$\mathcal{P}_{\mathrm{CI}} : P(E2,T2) \hookrightarrow P(CE2,T2)$$

and we shall take care only to apply it to well-formed programs. The definition is

$$\begin{array}{l}
\mathcal{P}_{\mathrm{CI}}[\![\ \mathtt{DEF}\ \mathbf{x}_1 = e_1\ \cdots\ \mathtt{DEF}\ \mathbf{x}_n = e_n\ \mathtt{VAL}\ e_0\ \mathtt{HAS}\ t\ ]\!] = \\
\quad \text{let } \emptyset \vdash e_1 : t_1 : \mathtt{c} \text{ determine } t_1 \\
\quad \vdots \\
\quad \text{let } \emptyset[t_1{:}\mathtt{c}/\mathbf{x}_1]\cdots[t_{n-1}{:}\mathtt{c}/\mathbf{x}_{n-1}] \vdash e_n : t_n \text{ determine } t_n \\
\quad \text{let } e = (\lambda\mathbf{x}_1[t_1].\cdots(\lambda\mathbf{x}_n[t_n].e_0)(e_n)\cdots)(e_1) \\
\quad \text{let } (\lambda\mathbf{x}_1[t_1].\cdots(\lambda\mathbf{x}_n[t_n].e'_0)(e'_n)\cdots)(e'_1) \\
\qquad = \mathcal{E}^{()}_{\mathrm{CI}}[\![\ e\ ]\!] \\
\quad \text{in } \mathtt{DEF}\ \mathbf{x}_1 = e'_1\ \cdots\ \mathtt{DEF}\ \mathbf{x}_n = e'_n\ \mathtt{VAL}\ e'_0\ \mathtt{HAS}\ t
\end{array}$$

Here we have used Fact 3.1.5 to determine the types of the expressions in the well-formed program. The correctness is given by

Theorem 4.2.7 (Correctness of $\mathcal{P}_{\mathrm{CI}}$) If $p \in P(E2, T2)$ is well-formed, i.e. $\vdash p$, then $\mathcal{P}_{\mathrm{CI}}[\![p]\!] \in P(CE2, T2)$ is defined and is well-formed, i.e. $\vdash \mathcal{P}_{\mathrm{CI}}[\![p]\!]$. A similar result holds for $\vdash_{\mathrm{C}}$. □

Proof: This is a straightforward consequence of Proposition 4.2.6. □

4.3 Improving the Combinator Introduction

The transformations presented for combinator expansion ($\varepsilon_{\mathrm{CI}}^{tenv}$) and combinator introduction ($\mathcal{E}_{\mathrm{CI}}^{penv}$) have the disadvantage that they often produce rather large expressions that no human would have produced. One way to explain this difference is that the algorithms do not take account of certain identities, or simplifications, that humans expect to hold. In this section we shall present two classes of such simplifications and suggest that they could be used to develop improved versions of combinator introduction and combinator expansion.

One class is often called *partial evaluation* [27, 47, 73] and amounts to performing simplifications like

$$\texttt{DEF x} = e \ \texttt{VAL}\ e' \ \texttt{HAS}\ t \ \triangleright \ \texttt{VAL}\ e'[e/\texttt{x}] \ \texttt{HAS}\ t$$

$$(\lambda \texttt{x}.e')(e) \ \triangleright \ e'[e/\texttt{x}]$$

Applied to the $\texttt{sum}_{9\mathrm{B}}$ program of Example 4.1.1 we may obtain

```
VAL Apply[ ] □ Tuple((Curry (fix(λg[ ].
    Cond(Isnil[ ] □ Snd[ ], Fst[ ],
         Apply[ ]□Tuple((Curry +[ ])□Hd[ ]□Snd[ ],
           g □ Tuple(Fst[ ], Tl[ ] □ Snd[ ])))))
      □ Zero[ ], Id[ ])
HAS Int list → Int
```

Here partial evaluation supplies $\texttt{reduce}_{9\mathrm{B}}$ with its first parameter, that is (`Curry +[ ]`), which is already known at compile-time. Since these simplifications only change the compile-time structure, they could equally well be performed on the program $\texttt{sum}_9$ from Example 3.1.6.

The run-time counterpart of partial evaluation is called *algebraic transformation* [7]. An example is the transformation

$$\texttt{Apply[ ]} \,\square\, \texttt{Tuple((Curry}\ e) \,\square\, e', e'') \ \triangleright \ e \,\square\, \texttt{Tuple}(e', e'')$$

If we apply this transformation twice to the above program we get the program $\texttt{sum}'_{9\mathrm{B}}$ defined by

```
VAL fix(λg[ ].Cond(Isnil[ ] □ Snd[ ], Fst[ ],
                   +[ ] □ Tuple(Hd[ ] □ Snd[ ],
                   g □ Tuple(Fst[ ], Tl[ ] □ Snd[ ]))))
    □ Tuple(Zero[ ], Id[ ])
HAS Int list → Int
```

Note that by now all higher-order run-time functions have disappeared.

Algebraic transformations play an important role in simplifying programs. The algorithm for combinator introduction proceeds by structural induction and algebraic transformations can be used to reduce certain unnecessarily complicated expressions that arise in this process. This is illustrated in the exercises.

Bibliographical Notes

The mixed λ-calculus and combinatory logic of this chapter dates back to [66]. In its present form it is closely related to the combinator language $\mathbf{TML_m}$ of [76] (with close cousins in [72] and [78]). The major difference is that we have no general `Const`$[t]$ e construct that transforms an expression e of type t' to one of type $t \underline{\rightarrow} t'$. Instead we have used a formula with `Curry`, as is demonstrated in δ, and we have translated a constant of the form $\underline{\mathtt{f}}_i[t']$ to one of the form $\mathtt{F}_i[t \underline{\rightarrow} t']$.

The algorithm $\mathcal{E}_{\mathrm{CI}}^{()}$ for combinator introduction is much as in [76] where a language called $\mathbf{TML_l}$ is translated into $\mathbf{TML_m}$. In short, $\mathcal{E}_{\mathrm{CI}}^{()}$ is an extension of the usual algorithm for translating the typed λ-calculus into categorical combinators (as in [21]). A more general algorithm is presented in [80] where a language called $\mathbf{TML_e}$ is translated into a version of $\mathbf{TML_m}$. In this algorithm the type of λ-bound variables may change during the translation. A brief comparison of $\mathbf{TML_l}$ and $\mathbf{TML_e}$ was given in the Bibliographical Notes of Chapter 3. Concerning the present version of $\mathcal{E}_{\mathrm{CI}}^{()}$ it is worth observing that $\delta(\cdots)\ e$ roughly corresponds to $e^{>}$ in [21] and that similarly $\omega(\cdots)\ e$ roughly corresponds to $e^{<}$.

The use of combinators (for part of the notation) is best motivated by the development of the following chapters. In essence, it amounts to providing a flexible framework that allows interpreting the constructs for different purposes (including code generation and abstract interpretation). Given the use of categorical combinators for the interpretation of typed λ-calculi in cartesian closed categories it should not be surprising that they crop up here as well. Intuitively it is important that free variables are handled in an explicit way. Formally the combinator notation must be functionally complete in the sense that the expressive power is equivalent to that of the typed λ-calculus.

It is not unlikely that the development of this and the following chapters can be performed for another fixed set of sufficiently well-behaved (i.e. functionally complete) combinators. However, it is important for the development of the following chapters that there is only a fixed selection of combinators. This means that supercombinators [41, 86], a very popular tool for the implementation of lazy functional languages, would not be immediately usable; the reason is that the number of and form of supercombinators depend on the actual program at hand. Despite the problems of using supercombinators for the development of the following chapters it might still be worth investigating whether the development of the present chapter could be modified so as to produce supercombinators for the run-time level; we leave this as an open problem.

As in the previous chapters we have not considered any semantic implications of the transformation function. One possibility would be to define an operational semantics of the *2*-level λ-calculus, to define an operational semantics of the mixed λ-calculus and combinatory logic, and to show that the transformation functions preserve 'reducibility'; we refer to [21] for an approach based on these ideas (but in the *1*-level case). For our purposes it might be more natural to define a denotational semantics of each of the two languages and to show that the transformation functions preserve semantics; the problem with this approach is that our ultimate semantics for the mixed λ-calculus and combinatory logic is the notion of parameterized semantics of Chapter 5 and that this notion of semantics is not definable for the *2*-level λ-calculus *except* by using considerations that boil down to the transformation functions of the present chapter.

A brief appraisal of the material of this chapter may be found in [76].

Exercises

1. List the five well-formed *2*-level types that have (Int→Int)→(Int→Int) as their underlying type. Use the development of Chapter 3 to show that only three of these correspond to *2*-level λ-expressions that have the function `twice` of Example 4.1.6 as their underlying expression. Deduce from this and the development in this chapter that Example 4.1.6 lists all *2*-level expressions in combinator form that 'correspond' to `twice`.

2. One might consider adding a combinator `Uncurry` that is to be the 'inverse' of `Curry`. Its well-formedness rule would be

$$\frac{tenv \vdash e : t' \underline{\rightarrow} (t'' \underline{\rightarrow} t)}{tenv \vdash \texttt{Uncurry}\ e : t' \underline{\times} t'' \underline{\rightarrow} t}$$

   Show that this is not necessary by defining `Uncurry` e in terms of the combinators of Table 4.1.

3. Complete the definition of $\varepsilon_{\text{CI}}^{tenv}$.

4. Evaluate $\varepsilon_{\text{CI}}^{\emptyset}[\![\texttt{twice}_3]\!]$ where $\texttt{twice}_3$ is as in Example 4.1.6. Use the rule

$$(\underline{\lambda}\mathtt{x}_i[t].e)\underline{(}e'\underline{)} \rhd e[e'/\mathtt{x}_i]$$

to simplify the expression. Can you achieve $\underline{\lambda}\mathtt{g}[\underline{\mathtt{Int}\rightarrow\mathtt{Int}}].\underline{\lambda}\mathtt{x}[\underline{\mathtt{Int}}].\mathtt{g}\underline{(}\mathtt{g}\underline{(}\mathtt{x}\underline{)}\underline{)}$? If not, suggest additional simplification rules.

5. Consider the $\mathtt{twice}_2$ functions of Example 4.1.6 and the $\mathtt{twice}'$ function resulting from

$$\mathcal{E}_{\mathrm{CI}}^{()}[\![\lambda\mathtt{g}[\underline{\mathtt{Int}\rightarrow\mathtt{Int}}].\ \underline{\lambda}\mathtt{x}[\underline{\mathtt{Int}}].\ \mathtt{g}\underline{(}\mathtt{g}\underline{(}\mathtt{x}\underline{)}\underline{)}]\!]$$

in Example 4.2.5. Suggest rewriting rules on combinator forms that may be used to simplify $\mathtt{twice}'$ to $\mathtt{twice}_2$ and perform these simplifications.

6. (*) Try to use the insights of Exercises 4 and 5 to define improved versions of $\varepsilon_{\mathrm{CI}}^{\emptyset}$ and $\mathcal{E}_{\mathrm{CI}}^{()}$.

7. Evaluate $\mathcal{P}_{\mathrm{CI}}[\![\mathtt{sum}_9]\!]$ where the program $\mathtt{sum}_9$ is defined in Example 3.1.6. Try to simplify the program using rewriting rules of the kind considered in Exercise 5.

8. (*) Consider a version of the *2*-level λ-calculus of Chapter 3 where the side condition to rule [up] is strengthened to include also the condition that e is of the form $\underline{\lambda}\mathtt{x}_i[t].e_0$. Does $\mathtt{sum}_9$ belong to this version? Develop a simplified translation function $\mathcal{E}_{\mathrm{CI}}^{penv}$ for this version of the *2*-level λ-calculus. Modify $\mathcal{E}_{\mathrm{BTA}}^{C}$ so as to produce *2*-level λ-expressions in this version of the *2*-level λ-calculus.

9. (*) For the type t $\underline{\mathtt{list}}$ we have used the combinators

$$\mathtt{Cons}(e,e),\ \mathtt{Nil}[t],\ \mathtt{Hd}[t],\ \mathtt{Tl}[t],\ \mathtt{Isnil}[t]$$

Instead of this it is possible to use

$$\mathtt{Cons}(e,e),\ \mathtt{Nil}[t],\ \mathtt{Case}(e,e)$$

where the idea is that

$$\begin{aligned}\mathtt{Case}(e_1,e_2) = {} & \underline{\lambda}\mathtt{x}[t\ \underline{\mathtt{list}}].\\ & \underline{\mathtt{if}}\ \underline{\mathtt{isnil}}\ \mathtt{x}\ \underline{\mathtt{then}}\ e_1\underline{(\mathtt{void})}\\ & \underline{\mathtt{else}}\ e_2\underline{(}\underline{\langle}\underline{\mathtt{hd}}\ \mathtt{x},\ \underline{\mathtt{tl}}\ \mathtt{x}\underline{\rangle}\underline{)}\end{aligned}$$

where $\underline{\mathtt{void}}$ is the only element of the type $\underline{\mathtt{Void}}$ (one of the $\underline{\mathtt{A}}_i$). Try to *modify* Chapter 4 so as to change to this new set of combinators.

Chapter 5

Parameterized Semantics

We want to interpret the run-time constructs of our language in different ways depending on the task at hand and at the same time we want the meaning of the compile-time constructs to be fixed. To make this possible we shall *parameterize* the semantics on an *interpretation* that specifies the meaning of the run-time level. The interpretation will define

- the meaning of the run-time function types, and
- the meaning of the combinators.

Relative to an interpretation one can then define the semantics of all well-formed *2*-level types, of all well-formed *2*-level expressions in combinator form and of all well-formed *2*-level programs in combinator form. In this chapter we shall provide the detailed development of this framework and illustrate it by definitions of various forms of eager and lazy semantics. In the following chapters we shall use the framework to specify various forms of code generation and abstract interpretation; this will substantiate the claim that the development of parameterized semantics gives the desired flexibility.

In Section 5.1 we concentrate on the *2*-level types. This begins with covering the required domain theory, defining the semantics of *2*-level types relative to an interpretation and then providing examples of eager and lazy interpretations. In Section 5.2 we perform an analogous development for *2*-level expressions in combinator form. We conclude with a treatment of *2*-level programs and a discussion of our approach to semantics.

5.1 Types

The syntax of *2*-level types was introduced in Chapter 3 and is given by

$$t \in T2$$

$$t ::= \mathtt{A_i} \mid \underline{\mathtt{A_i}} \mid t \times t \mid t \,\underline{\times}\, t \mid t \rightarrow t \mid t \,\underline{\rightarrow}\, t \mid t\ \mathtt{list} \mid t\ \underline{\mathtt{list}}$$

Our task is to associate a set of values with each of these types. More precisely, the sets of values will be equipped with a partial order so that they become *domains*. We therefore begin by expounding the domain theory that we need in order to account for the types A_i and the type constructors $\times$, $\rightarrow$ and `list`.

5.1.1 Domain theory

We already encountered partially ordered sets in Section 3.1, that is structures $(D,\sqsubseteq)$ where D is a set and $\sqsubseteq$ is a partial order on D. In this section we shall consider certain partially ordered sets where, intuitively, $d_1 \sqsubseteq d_2$ means that d_2 is at least as informative as d_1. We shall provide examples to justify this later but it is worth pointing out that we shall not feel constrained to only considering partially ordered sets that can meaningfully be understood in this way.

To prepare for the definition of domains we need the concept of a least upper bound. A subset Y of a partially ordered set $(D,\sqsubseteq)$ is said to be *consistent* if there is an element $d \in D$ such that $y \sqsubseteq d$ for all $y \in Y$ and if this is the case we say that d is an *upper bound* of Y. An element $d \in D$ is the *least upper bound* of the subset Y if it is an upper bound and if $d \sqsubseteq d'$ holds for all upper bounds d' of Y. Since a partial order is antisymmetric, the least upper bound of Y is unique if it exists and is written $\bigsqcup Y$. Intuitively, the idea is that $\bigsqcup Y$ combines all the information expressed by the elements of Y but without adding additional information. A partially ordered set $(D,\sqsubseteq)$ is said to be a *complete lattice* if every subset Y of D has a least upper bound $\bigsqcup Y$. When the partial order $\sqsubseteq$ associated with $(D,\sqsubseteq)$ is obvious from the context we sometimes write D rather than $(D,\sqsubseteq)$.

Example 5.1.1 Let $\mathbf{P}\omega$ be the set of subsets of natural numbers:

$$\mathbf{P}\omega = \{\ K \mid K \subseteq \{0,1,2,\cdots\}\ \}$$

Then $(\mathbf{P}\omega,\subseteq)$ and $(\mathbf{P}\omega,\supseteq)$ are partially ordered sets where $\subseteq$ is subset inclusion and $\supseteq$ is superset inclusion, i.e. $K \supseteq K'$ means $K' \subseteq K$. In $(\mathbf{P}\omega,\subseteq)$ every subset Y has a least upper bound $\bigsqcup Y$ given by $\bigcup Y$ where

$$\bigcup Y = \{\ n \in \{0,1,2,\cdots\} \mid \exists K \in Y\colon n \in K\ \}$$

Thus $(\mathbf{P}\omega,\subseteq)$ is a complete lattice.

In $(\mathbf{P}\omega,\supseteq)$ every subset Y has a least upper bound $\bigsqcup Y$ given by $\bigcap Y$ where

$$\bigcap Y = \{\ n \in \{0,1,2,\cdots\} \mid \forall K \in Y\colon n \in K\ \}$$

In particular, $\bigcup\emptyset = \emptyset$ and $\bigcap\emptyset = \{0,1,2,\cdots\}$. Thus also $(\mathbf{P}\omega,\supseteq)$ is a complete lattice.

In Chapter 3 we defined the notion of a greatest lower bound of a subset Y. In $(\mathbf{P}\omega,\subseteq)$ every subset Y has a greatest lower bound given by $\bigcap Y$. In $(\mathbf{P}\omega,\supseteq)$ every subset Y has a greatest lower bound given by $\bigcup Y$. Thus least upper bounds in $(\mathbf{P}\omega,\subseteq)$ correspond to greatest lower bounds in $(\mathbf{P}\omega,\supseteq)$ and vice versa. For this reason $(\mathbf{P}\omega,\subseteq)$ and $(\mathbf{P}\omega,\supseteq)$ are often said to be *dual* of one another. □

Example 5.1.2 Given a set S we note that $(S,=)$ is a partially ordered set, where $s_1=s_2$ means that s_1 is equal to s_2. We shall say that $(S,=)$ is a *discrete* partial order. □

For the purpose of semantics it is too demanding to require all subsets to have least upper bounds. Rather we restrict our attention to least upper bounds of two classes of subsets. One class is very trivial since it contains only the empty set; it is of interest because the least upper bound of the empty set (if it exists) will be less than or equal to (i.e. $\sqsubseteq$) any other element. It is said to be the *least element* and is denoted $\perp$. The other class of subsets are the chains: a subset Y of $(D,\sqsubseteq)$ is a *chain* if it is of the form

$$Y = \{ d_{\mathrm{n}} \mid \mathrm{n}\geq 0 \}$$

where the elements $d_{\mathrm{n}}\in D$ satisfy the condition

$$\mathrm{n}\leq\mathrm{m} \Rightarrow d_{\mathrm{n}}\sqsubseteq d_{\mathrm{m}}$$

It is commonplace to write $(d_{\mathrm{n}})_{\mathrm{n}}$ for $\{d_{\mathrm{n}}|\mathrm{n}\geq 0\}$ and $\bigsqcup_{\mathrm{n}} d_{\mathrm{n}}$ for $\bigsqcup\{d_{\mathrm{n}}|\mathrm{n}\geq 0\}$. We then define a *cpo* (complete partially ordered set) to be a partially ordered set that has a least element and that has least upper bounds of all chains. Clearly any complete lattice is a cpo. If all chains are finite the cpo is said to have *finite height* and if all chains have at most two elements the cpo is said to be *flat*.

Example 5.1.3 Given a set S and an element $\star$ not in S we may define a *flat* cpo $(S_\perp,\sqsubseteq)$ by

$$S_\perp = S\cup\{\star\}$$

$$d\sqsubseteq d' \text{ if and only if } d=\star \vee d=d'$$

If we take care of the possibility that $\star$ was already in S we would take $S_\perp=\{(1,s)|s\in S\}\cup\{(0,\star)\}$ and define $\sqsubseteq$ accordingly but this gives rise to a rather cumbersome notation. Since $\star$ is the least element it is common to write $\perp$ instead of $\star$ in the above definition. Examples of flat cpo's include the truth values

$$\mathbf{B} = \{\mathbf{true},\mathbf{false}\}_\perp$$

which may be depicted as

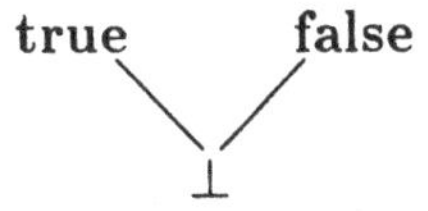

and the integers

$$\mathbf{Z} = \{\cdots,\mathbf{-1},\mathbf{0},\mathbf{1},\cdots\}_\perp$$

which may be depicted as

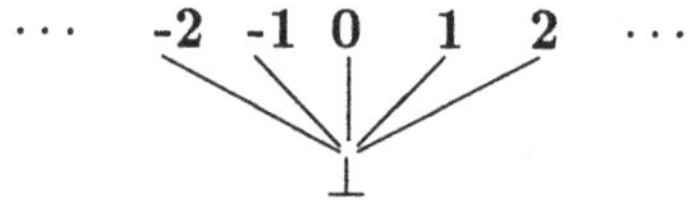

In these examples one may explain $\perp$ as modelling an evaluation of a truth value or an integer that never succeeds in producing a value. Thus $d_1 \sqsubseteq d_2$ means that d_2 is at least as informative as d_1. □

An element $d \in D$ is *compact* if the condition

$$d \sqsubseteq \bigsqcup_{\mathrm{n}} d_{\mathrm{n}} \Rightarrow \exists \mathrm{n}\colon\ d \sqsubseteq d_{\mathrm{n}}$$

holds for all chains $(d_{\mathrm{n}})_{\mathrm{n}}$. The set of compact elements is usually denoted

$$B_D = \{\ b \in D \mid b \text{ is compact }\}$$

It equals D when D is of finite height (or finite) but is, in general, a proper subset of D. The cpo $(D,\sqsubseteq)$ is *algebraic* if B_D is countable and each element $d \in D$ is the least upper bound of a chain of compact elements:

$$d = \bigsqcup_{\mathrm{n}} b_{\mathrm{n}} \text{ where } (b_{\mathrm{n}})_{\mathrm{n}} \subseteq B_D \text{ is a chain}$$

The cpo $(D,\sqsubseteq)$ is *consistently complete* if each consistent subset (i.e. subset with an upper bound) has a least upper bound. We then define a *Scott-domain* to be a consistently complete and algebraic cpo.

Example 5.1.4 The partially ordered set $(\mathbf{P}\omega,\subseteq)$ is a Scott-domain and the compact elements are the finite sets. The partially ordered set $(\mathbf{P}\omega,\supseteq)$ is a Scott-domain and the compact elements are the cofinite sets, that is, those sets that equal $\{0,1,2,\cdots\}$ once a finite number of elements have been added. The cpo's $\mathbf{B}$ and $\mathbf{Z}$ are Scott-domains and in general $(S_\perp,\sqsubseteq)$ is a Scott-domain if and only if S is countable and in that case every element is compact. □

A *domain* is usually taken to be a Scott-domain and this will also be the reading in this book. However, large parts of domain theory may be developed by simply taking the domains to be the cpo's; this includes virtually all of the domain theory developed in this book since we do not have recursive types. This means that little is lost if the remainder of this book is read with domain meaning cpo and ignoring all mention of compact elements, algebraicity and consistent completeness.

Construction 5.1.5 Given partially ordered sets $(D,\sqsubseteq)$ and $(E,\sqsubseteq)$ we may define their *cartesian product* $(D \times E,\sqsubseteq)$ by

$$D{\times}E = \{ (d,e) \mid d{\in}D \wedge e{\in}E \}$$

$$(d,e) \sqsubseteq (d',e') \text{ if and only if } ((d{\sqsubseteq}d') \wedge (e{\sqsubseteq}e'))$$

This is a partially ordered set. It is a cpo if D and E are; the least element is $(\bot,\bot)$ and the formula for least upper bounds of chains is

$$\bigsqcup_n (d_n,e_n) = (\bigsqcup_n d_n, \bigsqcup_n e_n)$$

It is a domain if D and E are, and the compact elements are the pairs of compact elements:

$$B_{D\times E} = B_D \times B_E$$

Finally, it is a complete lattice if D and E are, and the formula for least upper bounds is

$$\bigsqcup Y = (\bigsqcup\{d|\exists e{:}(d,e){\in}Y\}, \bigsqcup\{e|\exists d{:}(d,e){\in}Y\})$$

(much like the formula for chains above). □

Example 5.1.6 The cartesian product of the domain **B** of booleans and the domain **Z** of integers may partially be depicted as

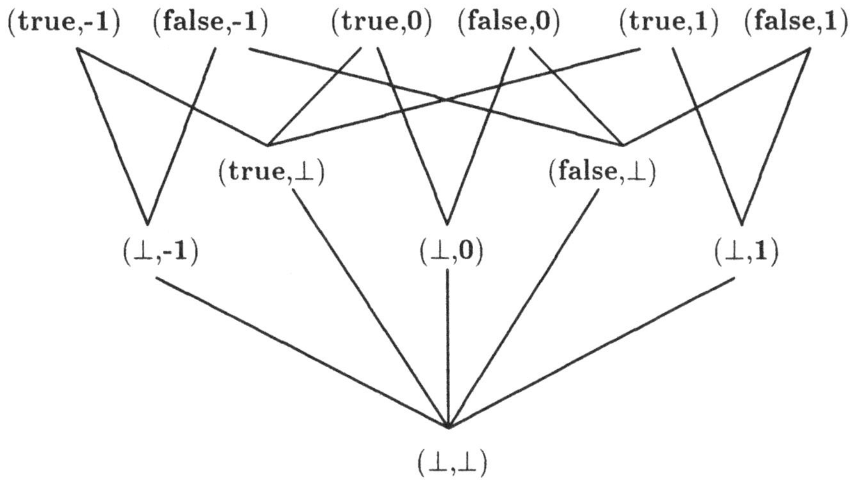

Intuitively, $d_1{\sqsubseteq}d_2$ means that d_2 is at least as informative as d_1. This holds for the partial orders of **B**, **Z** and **B**×**Z** and we note that $(b,z){\sqsubseteq}(b',z')$ indicates that (b',z') is at least as informative as (b,z) because z' and b' are at least as informative as z and b, respectively. If (b',z') is strictly more informative than (b,z) it may be because b' and/or z' is strictly more informative than b and/or z. □

A function $f{:}(D,\sqsubseteq){\rightarrow}(E,\sqsubseteq)$ from a partially ordered set $(D,\sqsubseteq)$ to a partially ordered set $(E,\sqsubseteq)$ is a total function $f{:}D{\rightarrow}E$ from D to E. It is *monotonic* if

$$d \sqsubseteq d' \Rightarrow f(d) \sqsubseteq f(d')$$

(for all d and d' in D); it is *strict* if

$$d \text{ is least in } D \Rightarrow f(d) \text{ is least in } E$$

(for all $d \in D$); and it is *continuous* if

$$(d_n)_n \text{ is a chain in } D \text{ with least upper bound } d$$
$$\Downarrow$$
$$(f(d_n))_n \text{ is a chain in } E \text{ with least upper bound } f(d)$$

(for all chains $(d_n)_n$ of D). Every continuous function is monotonic. If f is monotonic and $(d_n)_n$ is a chain then $(f(d_n))_n$ is a chain in E; if d is the least upper bound of $(d_n)_n$ then $f(d)$ is an upper bound of $(f(d_n))_n$ but not necessarily the least upper bound.

Lemma 5.1.7 If $f:(D,\sqsubseteq)\to(D,\sqsubseteq)$ is a continuous function from the cpo $(D,\sqsubseteq)$ to itself the formula

$$\text{FIX}(f) = \bigsqcup_n f^n(\bot)$$

defines the least (pre-) fixed point of f, that is

$$f(\text{FIX}(f)) = \text{FIX}(f)$$
$$f(d) \sqsubseteq d \Rightarrow \text{FIX}(f) \sqsubseteq d$$

Proof: Since $\bot \sqsubseteq f(\bot)$ induction gives $f^n(\bot) \sqsubseteq f^{n+1}(\bot)$ and it follows that $(f^n(\bot))_n$ is a chain. Hence FIX(f) is well-defined and furthermore $\text{FIX}(f) = \bigsqcup_n f^{n+1}(\bot)$ since $(f^n(\bot))_n$ and $(f^{n+1}(\bot))_n$ have the same upper bounds. By continuity of f we then have

$$f(\text{FIX}(f)) = f(\bigsqcup_n f^n(\bot)) = \bigsqcup_n f^{n+1}(\bot) = \text{FIX}(f)$$

Next let $f(d) \sqsubseteq d$. Since $\bot \sqsubseteq d$ it follows by induction that $f^n(\bot) \sqsubseteq d$ so that also $\text{FIX}(f) \sqsubseteq d$. □

Corollary 5.1.8 Under the assumptions of Lemma 5.1.7 we have $\text{FIX}(f) \sqsubseteq d$ for every fixed point d of f, that is for every d such that $f(d)=d$. □

Construction 5.1.9 Given partially ordered sets $(D,\sqsubseteq)$ and $(E,\sqsubseteq)$ we may define their *function space* $(D\to E,\sqsubseteq)$ by

$$D\to E = \{\, f \mid f \text{ is a continuous function from } (D,\sqsubseteq) \text{ to } (E,\sqsubseteq) \,\}$$
$$f \sqsubseteq f' \Leftrightarrow (\forall d \in D\colon f(d) \sqsubseteq f'(d))$$

Since we have already used the notation $f{:}D{\rightarrow}E$ to indicate that f is a total function from the set D to the set E we must be careful about the newly defined notation in order to avoid confusion. Sometimes this leads to writing $[D{\rightarrow}E]$, $D{\rightarrow_c}E$ or $(D,\sqsubseteq){\rightarrow}(E,\sqsubseteq)$ for what we defined as $D{\rightarrow}E$ above. However, the risk of confusion is only slight. To see this recall that the discrete partial order $(D,=)$ only has constant chains, so if $(d_n)_n$ is a chain in $(D,=)$ then $\exists d{\in}D$: $\forall$n: $d_n{=}d$. Therefore any total function from D to E will be a continuous function from $(D,=)$ to $(E,\sqsubseteq)$. Thus $f{:}D{\rightarrow}E$ amounts to nothing but $f{\in}(D,=){\rightarrow}(E,\sqsubseteq)$.

When D and E are partial orders then so is $D{\rightarrow}E$ as defined above. When D and E are cpo's then so is $D{\rightarrow}E$. The least element $\bot_{D\rightarrow E}$ in $D{\rightarrow}E$ is $\lambda d.\bot_E$ where $\bot_E$ is the least element in E and the formula for least upper bounds of chains is

$$\bigsqcup_n f_n = \lambda d.\ \bigsqcup_n (f_n(d))$$

(that is, $\bigsqcup_n f_n$ is a continuous function and is the point-wise least upper bound of the chain $(f_n)_n$). When D and E are complete lattices so is $D{\rightarrow}E$ and

$$\bigsqcup Y = \lambda d.\ \bigsqcup\{f(d) | f{\in}Y\}$$

is the formula for least upper bounds.

Recall that $d_1{\sqsubseteq}d_2$ is supposed to express that d_2 is at least as informative as d_1 and similarly for $e_1{\sqsubseteq}e_2$. Monotonicity of functions in $D{\rightarrow}E$ then says that a function cannot retract information already given for less informative arguments. The partial ordering of functions reflects the fact that a function is more informative the more informative the results it produces. — That functions should not only be monotonic but also continuous may be motivated in a similar sort of way and we refer to [93] and [94] for this. □

Remark 5.1.10 It is slightly more complicated to describe the compact elements in $D{\rightarrow}E$. For $d{\in}D$ and $e{\in}E$ the *step-function* $(d{\mapsto}e) : D{\rightarrow}E$ is defined by

$$d{\mapsto}e = \lambda d'. \begin{cases} e & \text{if } d'{\sqsupseteq}d \\ \bot & \text{otherwise} \end{cases}$$

and it is continuous if d is compact. It is a compact element of $D{\rightarrow}E$ if e is also compact. The general form of a compact element in $D{\rightarrow}E$ is a least upper bound of a finite subset of such step functions; this means that

$$\begin{aligned} B_{D\rightarrow E} = \{ & \textstyle\bigsqcup\{(d_1{\mapsto}e_1),\cdots,(d_n{\mapsto}e_n)\} \\ & | \ n{\geq}0 \wedge \forall i{\in}\{1,\cdots,n\}\text{: } d_i{\in}B_D \wedge e_i{\in}B_E \wedge \\ & \{(d_1{\mapsto}e_1),\cdots,(d_n{\mapsto}e_n)\} \text{ is consistent } \} \end{aligned}$$

It makes no harm to take n>0 above as $\bigsqcup\emptyset$ equals $(\bot{\mapsto}\bot)$ and the least element of a cpo is always compact. One can show that if D and E are domains (not merely algebraic cpo's!) then $D{\rightarrow}E$ is an algebraic cpo as well as a domain. □

A *predicate* on a cpo D is a total function $P : D \rightarrow$ {true,false}. It is an *admissible* predicate if

- $P(\bot)$ = true, and
- for every chain $(d_n)_n$, if $P(d_n)$ = true holds for n≥0 then $P(\bigsqcup d_n)$ = true

Then we have the following *fixed point principle*:

Lemma 5.1.11 Let $f \in D \rightarrow D$ be a continuous function on the cpo D and let P be an admissible predicate on D. If for all $d \in D$

$$P(d) = \text{true} \Rightarrow P(f(d)) = \text{true}$$

then $P(\text{FIX } f)$ = true. □

Proof: Since P is admissible we have $P(\bot)$ = true. Induction on n shows that $P(f^n(\bot))$ = true and hence $P(\text{FIX } f)$ = true follows from the admissibility of the predicate P. □

Construction 5.1.12 Given a partially ordered set $(D,\sqsubseteq)$ we next define the partially ordered set $(D^\infty,\sqsubseteq)$ of *potentially infinite lists.* To prepare for this we shall say that a set of positive numbers is *convex* if it equals {1,2,···} or if it is of the form {1,2,···,n} for some n≥0. We shall say that the set has supremum n exactly when it equals {1,2,···,n}.

Assuming that $\star$ is an element not in D we define

$$D^\infty = \{\ l{:}K \rightarrow D \cup \{\star\} \mid (K \text{ is a } \textit{convex} \text{ set of positive integers}) \land$$
$$(\forall n \in K{:}\ l(n) = \star \Rightarrow n \text{ is the supremum of } K)\ \}$$

We shall feel free to write dom(l) = K when $l{:}K \rightarrow D \cup \{\star\}$ and we shall also write $\text{dom}^\star(l) = \{i \in \text{dom}(l) \mid l(i) \neq \star\}$. To allow for a more convenient notation for the elements of D^∞ we shall write

$[d_1,d_2,\cdots]$	for $l{:}\{1,2,3,\cdots\} \rightarrow D \cup \{\star\}$ given by $l(i) = d_i \in D$
$[d_1,d_2,\cdots,d_n]$	for $l{:}\{1,2,3,\cdots,n+1\} \rightarrow D \cup \{\star\}$ given by $l(i) = d_i \in D$ when $i \leq n$ and $l(n+1) = \star$
$[d_1,d_2,\cdots,d_n\partial$	for $l{:}\{1,2,\cdots,n\} \rightarrow D \cup \{\star\}$ given by $l(i) = d_i \in D$ when $i \leq n$

For a concrete example consider the potentially infinite lists of booleans, $\mathbf{B}^\infty$. Here l_1=[**true**,**true**,···] denotes the infinite list of **true**'s, and l_2=[**true**,**true**,**true**] denotes a finite list of length 3, and finally l_3=[**true**,**true**,**true**∂ denotes the list where the first 3 elements are **true** but where the remainder of the list is undefined. In Miranda one may define

```
l1 = True:l1
l2 = True:True:True:[]
l3 = True:True:True:l4 where l4=l4
```

and then `l1` evaluates to l_1 etc. Next define

$$l \sqsubseteq l' \text{ if and only if } ((\mathrm{dom}(l) \subseteq \mathrm{dom}(l')) \wedge (\forall \mathrm{n} \in \mathrm{dom}(l): l(\mathrm{n}) \sqsubseteq l'(\mathrm{n})))$$

where $l(\mathrm{n}) \sqsubseteq l'(\mathrm{n})$ implies that if one of $l(\mathrm{n})$ or $l'(\mathrm{n})$ is $\star$ then so is the other.

Intuitively, the partial order on $\mathbf{B}$ means that $d_1 \sqsubseteq d_2$ amounts to d_2 being at least as informative as d_1 and this carries over to the partial order $\mathbf{B}^\infty$. In particular, $[d_1,\cdots,d_\mathrm{n}] \sqsubseteq [d'_1,\cdots,d'_\mathrm{m}]$ holds if and only if n=m and each $d_\mathrm{i} \sqsubseteq d'_\mathrm{i}$ so that a finite list is at least as informative as another when they have the same length and each element in one list is at least as informative as the corresponding element in the other. Similarly, $[d_1,\cdots,d_\mathrm{n}\partial \sqsubseteq [d'_1,\cdots,d'_\mathrm{m}\partial$ holds if n≤m and each $d_\mathrm{i} \sqsubseteq d'_\mathrm{i}$ for i≤n, so that a partial list is at least as informative as another when an element is at least as informative as the corresponding element in the other list (if this element exists).

When D is a cpo also D^∞ is: clearly $[\partial$ is the least element of D^∞ and the formula for least upper bounds of chains is

$$(\bigsqcup_\mathrm{n} l_\mathrm{n}) : \bigcup_\mathrm{n} \mathrm{dom}(l_\mathrm{n}) \rightarrow D \cup \{\star\}$$
$$(\bigsqcup_\mathrm{n} l_\mathrm{n})(\mathrm{i}) = \bigsqcup\{l_\mathrm{j}(\mathrm{i}) | \mathrm{dom}(l_\mathrm{j}) \ni \mathrm{i}\}$$

When D is a domain also D^∞ is and

$$B_{D^\infty} = \{\ l \in D^\infty \mid (\mathrm{dom}(l) \text{ is finite}) \wedge (\forall \mathrm{i} \in \mathrm{dom}(l): l(\mathrm{i}) \text{ is compact (or } \star)) \ \}$$

This means that the compact elements in D^∞ are the finite lists $[d_1,\cdots,d_\mathrm{n}]$ and the partial lists $[d_1,\cdots,d_\mathrm{n}\partial$ where each d_i is compact in D. □

Construction 5.1.13 To prepare for the semantics of expressions we need some auxiliary notation for lists in D^∞. For prepending an element d to a list l we need the function $\mathrm{CONS}_{\mathrm{PS}}$ defined by

$$\mathrm{CONS}_{\mathrm{PS}}(d,l) = l' \text{ where}$$

$$l'(\mathrm{i}) = \begin{cases} d & \text{if i=1} \\ l(\mathrm{i}-1) & \text{if i}-1 \in \mathrm{dom}(l) \\ \text{undefined} & \text{otherwise} \end{cases}$$

Here we have identified $l':K \rightarrow D \cup \{\star\}$ with a partial function $l':\{1,2,\cdots\} \hookrightarrow D \cup \{\star\}$ that is defined on the convex subset K of the positive integers. The empty list is denoted by $\mathrm{NIL}_{\mathrm{PS}}$ and is given by

$$\text{NIL}_{\text{PS}} = l' \text{ where}$$

$$l'(\text{i}) = \begin{cases} \star & \text{if i=1} \\ \text{undefined} & \text{otherwise} \end{cases}$$

The first element of the list l is denoted by $\text{HD}_{\text{PS}}(l)$ and is given by

$$\text{HD}_{\text{PS}}(l) = \begin{cases} l(1) & \text{if } (1 \in \text{dom}(l)) \wedge (l(1) \neq \star) \\ \bot & \text{otherwise} \end{cases}$$

and the remainder of the list l is denoted by $\text{TL}_{\text{PS}}(l)$ and is given by

$$\text{TL}_{\text{PS}}(l) = l' \text{ where}$$

$$l'(\text{i}) = \begin{cases} l(\text{i}+1) & \text{if i+1} \in \text{dom}(l) \\ \text{undefined} & \text{otherwise} \end{cases}$$

Thus NIL_{PS}=[], $\text{HD}_{\text{PS}}([\,])=\bot_D$ and $\text{TL}_{\text{PS}}([\,])=[\partial$. Finally, $\text{ISNIL}_{\text{PS}}(l)$ tests whether or not the list l is empty and is given by

$$\text{ISNIL}_{\text{PS}}(l) = \begin{cases} \textbf{true} & \text{if } l = \text{NIL}_{\text{PS}} \\ \textbf{false} & \text{if } l \neq \text{NIL}_{\text{PS}} \wedge 1 \in \text{dom}(l) \\ \bot & \text{if } l \neq \text{NIL}_{\text{PS}} \wedge 1 \notin \text{dom}(l) \end{cases}$$

5.1.2 Interpretation of types

We now return to the task of associating domains with well-formed *2*-level types of compile-time kind. Our goal will be to define a function

$$[\![\cdots]\!](\mathcal{I}) : \{\ t \mid \vdash t\text{:c}\ \} \to \{\ D \mid D \text{ is a domain}\ \}$$

where $\mathcal{I}$ provides the interpretation of the run-time function types. The definition of $[\![t]\!](\mathcal{I})$ is by induction on the structure of t and will be explained below:

$$[\![\mathsf{A_i}]\!](\mathcal{I}) = \mathbf{A}_{\text{i}}$$

$$[\![t_1 \times t_2]\!](\mathcal{I}) = [\![t_1]\!](\mathcal{I}) \times [\![t_2]\!](\mathcal{I})$$

$$[\![t_1 \rightarrow t_2]\!](\mathcal{I}) = [\![t_1]\!](\mathcal{I}) \rightarrow [\![t_2]\!](\mathcal{I})$$

$$[\![t \ \texttt{list}]\!](\mathcal{I}) = [\![t]\!](\mathcal{I})^{\infty}$$

$$[\![t_1 \underline{\rightarrow} t_2]\!](\mathcal{I}) = \mathcal{I}(t_1 \underline{\rightarrow} t_2)$$

The domains $\mathbf{A}_{\text{i}}$ are assumed to be fixed once and for all for each index 'i' in the unspecified index set I introduced in Chapter 2. We shall assume that

$$\mathbf{A}_{\text{bool}} = \mathbf{B}$$

$$\mathbf{A}_{\text{int}} = \mathbf{Z}$$

$$\mathbf{A}_{\text{void}} = \mathbf{Void} = \{\mathbf{void}\}_{\bot}$$

but otherwise we shall not further enunciate the choices of the $\mathbf{A}_i$. For the product type constructor we use the cartesian product introduced in Construction 5.1.5; for the function space type constructor we use the continuous function space introduced in Construction 5.1.9; and for the list type constructor we use the potentially infinite lists introduced in Construction 5.1.12. Finally, the meaning of the run-time functions is left to the parameter $\mathcal{I}$.

To ensure the well-definedness of $[\![\cdots]\!](\mathcal{I})$ we must clarify our assumptions about $\mathcal{I}$. We shall say that t is a *frontier type* if and only if $\vdash t{:}\mathtt{r} \land \vdash t{:}\mathtt{c}$; this just means that t is a well-formed run-time function type (and hence of form $t_1 \underline{\rightarrow} t_2$).

Definition 5.1.14 An *interpretation $\mathcal{I}$ of types* is a mapping from frontier types to domains:

$$\mathcal{I} : \{\ t \mid \vdash t{:}\mathtt{r} \land \vdash t{:}\mathtt{c}\ \} \rightarrow \{\ D \mid D \text{ is a domain }\}$$

Proposition 5.1.15 If $\mathcal{I}$ is an interpretation of types then

$$[\![\cdots]\!](\mathcal{I}) : \{\ t \mid \vdash t{:}\mathtt{c}\ \} \rightarrow \{\ D \mid D \text{ is a domain }\}$$

is well-defined; this means that $[\![t]\!](\mathcal{I})$ is a domain whenever $\vdash t{:}\mathtt{c}$. □

Proof: We prove by structural induction on a type t that *if* $\vdash t{:}\mathtt{c}$ *then* $[\![t]\!](\mathcal{I})$ *defines a domain.*

The case t::=$\mathtt{A}_i$. This is a consequence of the assumptions about the $\mathbf{A}_i$.

The case t::=$\underline{\mathtt{A}_i}$. This is immediate as $\vdash t{:}\mathtt{c}$ does not hold.

The case t::=$t_1 \times t_2$. This is a consequence of the induction hypothesis and Construction 5.1.5.

The case t::=$t_1 \underline{\times} t_2$. This is immediate as $\vdash t{:}\mathtt{c}$ does not hold.

The case t::=$t_1 \rightarrow t_2$. This is a consequence of the induction hypothesis and Construction 5.1.9.

The case t::=$t_1 \underline{\rightarrow} t_2$. This is a consequence of the assumption that $\mathcal{I}$ is an interpretation of types.

The case t::=t_0 `list`. This is a consequence of the induction hypothesis and Construction 5.1.12.

The case t::= t_0 $\underline{\mathtt{list}}$. This is immediate as $\vdash t{:}\mathtt{c}$ does not hold. □

Example interpretations

In the remainder of this section we now provide some example interpretations of types.

Example 5.1.16 The interpretation $\mathbf{S}_{\mathrm{lll}}$ is defined structurally by

$$\mathbf{S}_{\mathrm{lll}}(\underline{\mathtt{A}_{\mathrm{i}}}) = \mathbf{A}_{\mathrm{i}}$$

$$\mathbf{S}_{\mathrm{lll}}(t_1 \underline{\times} t_2) = \mathbf{S}_{\mathrm{lll}}(t_1) \times \mathbf{S}_{\mathrm{lll}}(t_2)$$

$$\mathbf{S}_{\mathrm{lll}}(t_1 \underline{\rightarrow} t_2) = \mathbf{S}_{\mathrm{lll}}(t_1) \rightarrow \mathbf{S}_{\mathrm{lll}}(t_2)$$

$$\mathbf{S}_{\mathrm{lll}}(t_0\ \underline{\mathtt{list}}) = \mathbf{S}_{\mathrm{lll}}(t_0)^{\infty}$$

This is all very natural given the interpretation of the compile-time types above. (The use of the subscript 'lll' is to indicate that all of $\underline{\times}$, $\underline{\rightarrow}$ and $\underline{\mathtt{list}}$ are interpreted in a lazy manner.) That this defines a function

$$\mathbf{S}_{\mathrm{lll}} : \{\ t \mid \vdash t{:}\mathtt{r} \wedge \vdash t{:}\mathtt{c}\ \} \rightarrow \{\ D \mid D \text{ is a domain }\}$$

follows much as in the proof of Proposition 5.1.15. □

To illustrate additional interpretations of types we need to introduce new ways of constructing domains.

Construction 5.1.17 Given cpo's $(D,\sqsubseteq)$ and $(E,\sqsubseteq)$ we may define their *smash product* $(D{*}E,\sqsubseteq)$ by

$$D{*}E = \{\ (d,e) \mid (d{\in}D) \wedge (e{\in}E) \wedge ((d{=}\bot) \Leftrightarrow (e{=}\bot))\ \}$$

$$(d,e) \sqsubseteq (d',e') \text{ if and only if } ((d{\sqsubseteq}d') \wedge (e{\sqsubseteq}e'))$$

This is a cpo with least element $(\bot,\bot)$ and least upper bounds of chains given by

$$\bigsqcup_{\mathrm{n}} (d_{\mathrm{n}},e_{\mathrm{n}}) = (\bigsqcup_{\mathrm{n}} d_{\mathrm{n}}, \bigsqcup_{\mathrm{n}} e_{\mathrm{n}})$$

The compact elements are

$$B_{D*E} = \{\ (d,e){\in}D{*}E \mid (d{\in}B_D) \wedge (e{\in}B_E)\ \}$$

and $D{*}E$ is a domain if D and E are. □

Example 5.1.18 The smash product of the domain **B** of booleans and the domain **Z** of integers may partially be depicted as follows (where **t** abbreviates **true** and **f** abbreviates **false**):

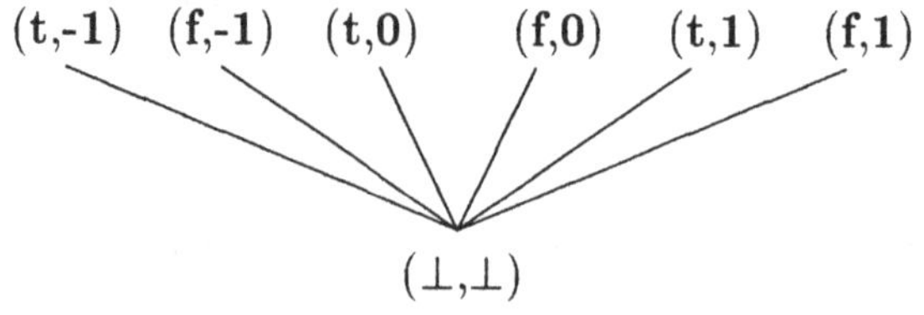

In **B** and **Z** one may read $d_1 \sqsubseteq d_2$ as saying that d_2 is at least as informative as d_1; this also holds for **B**$*$**Z**. Compared with **B**$\times$**Z** one notes the absence of partly evaluated tuples like (**true**,$\bot$) or ($\bot$,**0**). This suggests that $*$ models the notion of product in an eager language like Standard ML whereas $\times$ models the notion of product in a lazy language like Miranda. □

Construction 5.1.19 Given cpo's $(D,\sqsubseteq)$ and $(E,\sqsubseteq)$ we may define their *strict function space* $(D\rightarrow_s E,\sqsubseteq)$ by

$$D\rightarrow_s E = \{\ f \mid f \text{ is a strict and continuous function from } D \text{ to } E\ \}$$

$$f\sqsubseteq f' \text{ if and only if } (\forall d\in D\text{: } f(d)\sqsubseteq f'(d))$$

This is a cpo: the least element is $\lambda d.\bot$ and the formula for least upper bounds of chains is as for $D\rightarrow E$. If $(D,\sqsubseteq)$ and $(E,\sqsubseteq)$ are domains then so is $D\rightarrow_s E$ and the compact elements are the strict compact elements of $D\rightarrow E$. (A step function $(d\mapsto e)$ turns out to be strict if $e=\bot$ whenever $d=\bot$.)

Assume next that $d_1\sqsubseteq d_2$ means that d_2 is at least as informative as d_1 and similarly for $e_1\sqsubseteq e_2$. As with the continuous function space this way of reading the partial order also carries over to $D\rightarrow_s E$: a function is more informative than another if it produces more informative results than the other. The requirement that functions in $D\rightarrow_s E$ must be strict may be read as saying that the function cannot produce any information (or value) before it has been supplied with some. Thus the strict function space would seem to model 'functions' that exploit the call-by-value parameter mechanism whereas the continuous function space would seem to model 'functions' that exploit the call-by-name parameter mechanism. This motivates the use of continuous function space for a language like Miranda and strict function space for a language like Standard ML. □

Construction 5.1.20 Given a cpo $(D,\sqsubseteq)$ we shall next define the partially ordered set $(D^*,\sqsubseteq)$ of *finite lists*. We adapt the definition of D^∞ and thus assume that $\star$ is an element not in D. We define

$$\begin{aligned} D^* = \{\ l\text{:}\{1,\cdots,\mathrm{n}\}\rightarrow D\cup\{\star\} \mid (\mathrm{n}\geq 0) \land (\forall \mathrm{m}\in\{1,\cdots,\mathrm{n}\}\text{: } l(\mathrm{m})\neq\bot) \land \\ (\forall \mathrm{m}\in\{1,\cdots,\mathrm{n}\}\text{: } l(\mathrm{m})=\star\Leftrightarrow \mathrm{m}=\mathrm{n})\ \} \end{aligned}$$

$$l\sqsubseteq l' \text{ if and only if } (\ (\mathrm{dom}(l)\subseteq\mathrm{dom}(l')) \land (\forall \mathrm{n}\in\mathrm{dom}(l)\text{: } l(\mathrm{n})\sqsubseteq l'(\mathrm{n}))\ )$$

To allow for a convenient notation we shall write

$[d_1,\cdots,d_{\mathrm{n}}]$ for $l\text{:}\{1,\cdots,\mathrm{n},\mathrm{n}+1\}\rightarrow D\cup\{\star\}$
given by $l(\mathrm{i})=d_{\mathrm{i}}\in D\setminus\{\star\}$ when $\mathrm{i}\leq\mathrm{n}$
and $l(\mathrm{n}+1)=\star$

$\bot$ for the unique function $l\text{:}\emptyset\rightarrow D\cup\{\star\}$

This defines $(D^*,\sqsubseteq)$ as a cpo: the least element is $\perp$ as indicated above and the formula for least upper bounds of chains is as for D^∞. Furthermore, $(D^*,\sqsubseteq)$ is a domain if $(D,\sqsubseteq)$ is, and the compact elements are $\perp$ as well as the finite lists $[d_1,\cdots,d_n]$ where each d_i is compact. □

Example 5.1.21 For a concrete example consider the finite lists $\mathbf{B}^*$ of truth values. This domain may be depicted as

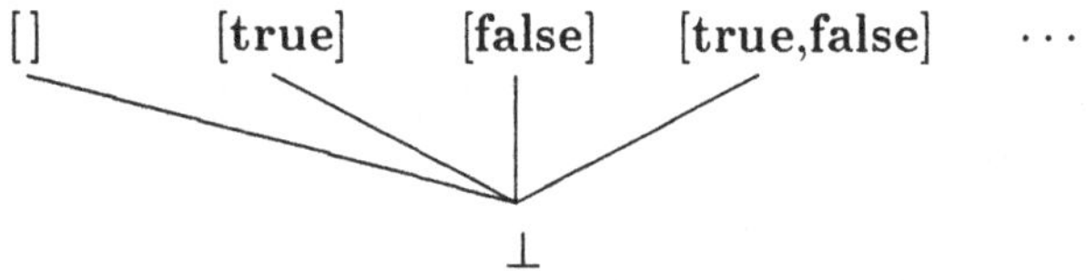

Recall that in $\mathbf{B}$ we have $d_1 \sqsubseteq d_2$ when d_2 is at least as informative as d_1. This also applies to $\mathbf{B}^*$ and compared with $\mathbf{B}^\infty$ we note that all lists now have finite length (or are $\perp$). This suggests that $(\cdots)^*$ models the notion of lists in an eager language like Standard ML whereas $(\cdots)^\infty$ models the notion of lists in a lazy language like Miranda. □

Construction 5.1.22 By analogy with the definition of $S_\perp$ in Example 5.1.3 we may define the *lifted* partially ordered set $(D_\perp,\sqsubseteq)$ whenever $(D,\sqsubseteq)$ is a partially ordered set. For this we assume that there is an element $\star$ not in D and define

$$D_\perp = D \cup \{\star\}$$

$$d \sqsubseteq d' \text{ if and only if } ((d{=}\star) \vee ((d{\neq}\star) \wedge (d'{\neq}\star) \wedge (d \sqsubseteq d')))$$

Writing $(D,\sqsubseteq)_\perp$ for $(D_\perp,\sqsubseteq)$ as defined above we note that $(S_\perp,\sqsubseteq)$, as defined in Example 5.1.3, amounts to $(S,=)_\perp$, where $(S,=)$ is the discrete partial order of Example 5.1.2. It is straightforward to verify that $D_\perp$ is a cpo if D is, that $D_\perp$ is a domain if D is, and that the compact elements are those of D together with $\star$.

If $d_1 \sqsubseteq d_2$ in D means that d_2 is at least as informative as d_1 then the same holds for $d_1 \sqsubseteq d_2$ in $D_\perp$. The difference is that the least element $\perp_D$ of D is now regarded as providing some useful information whereas $\star$, the least element of $D_\perp$, is the element regarded as providing no useful information whatsoever. □

Example 5.1.23 The interpretation $\mathbf{S}_{\text{eee}}$ is defined structurally by

$$\mathbf{S}_{\text{eee}}(\underline{\mathbf{A}}_i) = \mathbf{A}_i$$

$$\mathbf{S}_{\text{eee}}(t_1 \underline{\times} t_2) = \mathbf{S}_{\text{eee}}(t_1) * \mathbf{S}_{\text{eee}}(t_2)$$

$$\mathbf{S}_{\text{eee}}(t_1 \underline{\rightarrow} t_2) = (\mathbf{S}_{\text{eee}}(t_1) \rightarrow_s \mathbf{S}_{\text{eee}}(t_2))_\perp$$

$$\mathbf{S}_{\text{eee}}(t_0\ \underline{\texttt{list}}) = \mathbf{S}_{\text{eee}}(t_0)^*$$

That this defines a function

$$\mathbf{S}_{\text{eee}} : \{\ t \mid \vdash t{:}\mathrm{r} \wedge \vdash t{:}\mathrm{c}\ \} \rightarrow \{\ D \mid D \text{ is a domain }\}$$

follows much as in the proof of Proposition 5.1.15.

The use of the subscript 'eee' is to indicate that all of $\underline{\times}$, $\underline{\rightarrow}$ and $\underline{\texttt{list}}$ are interpreted in an eager manner. We already argued that the use of $*$ for $\underline{\times}$ and $(\cdots)^*$ for $\underline{\texttt{list}}$ models the behaviour of products and lists in an eager language like Standard ML. We also argued that $\mathbf{S}_{\text{eee}}(t_1) {\rightarrow_{\mathrm{s}}} \mathbf{S}_{\text{eee}}(t_2)$ corresponds to 'functions' from $\mathbf{S}_{\text{eee}}(t_1)$ to $\mathbf{S}_{\text{eee}}(t_2)$ that exploit the call-by-value parameter mechanism. But the totally undefined function, that is $\lambda d.\bot$, is still to be regarded as a bona fide data element, and this motivates adding a new least element, that is to use $\mathbf{S}_{\text{eee}}(t_1 \underline{\rightarrow} t_2) = (\mathbf{S}_{\text{eee}}(t_1) {\rightarrow_{\mathrm{s}}} \mathbf{S}_{\text{eee}}(t_2))_\bot$. In this way the function $\lambda d.\bot$ may be an element in tuples or lists, in accord with what is possible in an eager language like Standard ML. □

Example 5.1.24 To illustrate that eager and lazy components may be mixed rather freely consider the interpretation $\mathbf{S}_{\text{lel}}$ defined by

$$\mathbf{S}_{\text{lel}}(\underline{\mathrm{A}}_{\mathrm{i}}) = \mathbf{A}_{\mathrm{i}}$$

$$\mathbf{S}_{\text{lel}}(t_1 \underline{\times} t_2) = (\mathbf{S}_{\text{lel}}(t_1) \times \mathbf{S}_{\text{lel}}(t_2))_\bot$$

$$\mathbf{S}_{\text{lel}}(t_1 \underline{\rightarrow} t_2) = (\mathbf{S}_{\text{lel}}(t_1) {\rightarrow_{\mathrm{s}}} \mathbf{S}_{\text{lel}}(t_2))_\bot$$

$$\mathbf{S}_{\text{lel}}(t_0\ \underline{\texttt{list}}) = \mathbf{S}_{\text{lel}}(t_0)^\infty$$

Here functions are assumed to be strict corresponding to the parameter mechanism call-by-value as used in an eager language. We have used lifting as well for much the same reasons put forward in Example 5.1.23, for example to allow the totally undefined function to be passed as a bona fide data element to a strict function. Products and lists are modelled by the 'lazy operators' also used in $\mathbf{S}_{\text{lll}}$. One difference is that we also use lifting for products; in the presence of strict function spaces this is needed to allow $(\bot,\bot)$ as a bona fide data element. — We believe that this interpretation of types comes pretty close in modelling Hope [30], which employs eager evaluation but has lazy data constructors. □

In the remainder of this book we will mostly be concerned with an interpretation called $\mathbf{S}$. Its effect on types is given by

$$\mathbf{S}(\underline{\mathrm{A}}_{\mathrm{i}}) = \mathbf{A}_{\mathrm{i}}$$

$$\mathbf{S}(t_1 \underline{\times} t_2) = (\mathbf{S}(t_1) \times \mathbf{S}(t_2))_\bot$$

$$\mathbf{S}(t_1 \underline{\rightarrow} t_2) = (\mathbf{S}(t_1) \rightarrow \mathbf{S}(t_2))_\bot$$

$$\mathbf{S}(t_0\ \underline{\texttt{list}}) = \mathbf{S}(t_0)^\infty$$

We shall motivate this shortly. But first we note that well-definedness of

$$\mathbf{S} : \{\ t \mid \vdash t{:}\mathsf{r} \wedge \vdash t{:}\mathsf{c}\ \} \rightarrow \{\ D \mid D \text{ is a domain }\}$$

may be proved much as in the proof of Proposition 5.1.15.

There is little to be said about the use of $\mathbf{A}_i$ for A_i. The use of $\cdots\times\cdots$, $\cdots\rightarrow\cdots$ and $\cdots^{\infty}$ all suggest that we are modelling a lazy language rather than an eager language. In this respect $\mathbf{S}$ is close to $\mathbf{S}_{lll}$ of Example 5.1.16 and distinctly different from $\mathbf{S}_{eee}$ of Example 5.1.23 and $\mathbf{S}_{lel}$ of Example 5.1.24. However, $\mathbf{S}$ differs from $\mathbf{S}_{lll}$ in the use of lifting, $\cdots_{\perp}$, for products and functions much as in $\mathbf{S}_{lel}$ and to some extent as in $\mathbf{S}_{eee}$. This means that we may model the difference between $\perp$ and $(\perp,\perp)$ and between $\perp$ and $\lambda d.\perp$. This is going to be vital for our simple-minded code generation of Chapter 6. However, there is some debate as to whether the use of 'lifting' should be present when modelling a lazy functional language.

One may read the Miranda manual [103] as saying that there should be no difference between $\perp$ and $(\perp,\perp)$ and between $\perp$ and $\lambda d.\perp$. However, when experimenting with Miranda it is possible to construct examples where a difference seems to arise. Turning to Haskell [39] it would seem that one should distinguish between $\perp$ and $(\perp,\perp)$ but that there is no need to distinguish between $\perp$ and $\lambda d.\perp$. Finally, the lazy λ-calculus [3] has a clear distinction between $\perp$ and $(\perp,\perp)$ and between $\perp$ and $\lambda d.\perp$.

Given the decision to use lifting for run-time products and run-time functions it may very well be asked whether we should also use lifting for compile-time products and compile-time functions. This is a feasible suggestion but in the absence of a clear solution to the above debate we shall stick to the 'more traditional' use of cartesian products and continuous functions *without* using lifting.

5.2 Expressions

In general an expression e of the mixed λ-calculus and combinatory logic will have a type of compile-time kind and may have some free variables whose types are also of compile-time kind.

To express this succinctly we write

$$tenv \vdash_{\mathsf{C}} e : t$$

where *tenv* is a type environment as in Section 4.1 and t is a *2*-level type of compile-time kind. From Fact 4.1.4 we see that the type t is uniquely determined by the expression e and the type environment *tenv*. Much as in Section 4.2 we shall find it convenient to work with a linearised form of type environment. This motivates defining a *position environment*, *penv*, to be a list of pairs of variable names and *2*-level types. (Compared with Section 4.2 we have dispensed with the binding time component as it is always going to be c.) The type environment, $\rho_{PS}(penv)$, corresponding to a position environment, *penv*, may be defined as follows:

$$\rho_{PS}(penv)(\mathtt{x}_i) = \begin{cases} t & \text{if the rightmost } (\mathtt{x}_j,t_j) \text{ in } penv \\ & \text{with } \mathtt{x}_i\text{=}\mathtt{x}_j \text{ has } t\text{=}t_j \\ \text{undefined} & \text{if no } (\mathtt{x}_j,t_j) \text{ in } penv \text{ has } \mathtt{x}_i\text{=}\mathtt{x}_j \end{cases}$$

Much as in Section 4.2 we shall say that a position environment is *well-formed* when all *2*-level types contained in it are, in fact, well-formed *2*-level types of compile-time kind. When *penv* is well-formed all $\rho_{PS}(penv)(\mathtt{x}_i)$ will be well-formed *2*-level types of compile-time kind, and by Fact 4.1.3 the type t will also be a well-formed *2*-level type of compile-time kind.

Semantics of expressions then amounts to defining a function

$$[\![e]\!](\mathcal{I})_{penv} : [\![penv]\!](\mathcal{I}) \rightarrow [\![t]\!](\mathcal{I})$$

whenever *penv* is a well-formed position environment and t is the unique type such that $\rho_{PS}(penv)\vdash_C e{:}t$. The domain $[\![penv]\!](\mathcal{I})$ is defined by

$$[\![penv]\!](\mathcal{I}) = \begin{cases} \textbf{Void} & \text{if } penv\text{=}() \\ [\![penv']\!](\mathcal{I})\times[\![t']\!](\mathcal{I}) & \text{if } penv\text{=}penv'{:}(\mathtt{x}',t') \end{cases}$$

It follows from Proposition 5.1.15, Construction 5.1.9, Fact 4.1.3 and the well-definedness of the position environment, that $[\![penv]\!](\mathcal{I}) \rightarrow [\![t]\!](\mathcal{I})$ is indeed a domain. By stretching our notation a little bit we may summarize the functionality of each $[\![e]\!](\mathcal{I})_{penv}$ as the definition of a function

$$[\![\cdots]\!](\mathcal{I})_{penv} : \{\ e \mid \rho_{PS}(penv) \vdash e : t\ \} \rightarrow ([\![penv]\!](\mathcal{I})\rightarrow[\![t]\!](\mathcal{I}))$$

In the definition of $[\![e]\!](\mathcal{I})_{penv}$ below we shall be rather precise about the position environment, *penv*, but later we shall allow ourselves to dispense with it. Also we shall need to impose stronger demands on the parameter $\mathcal{I}$ than merely being an interpretation of types; we shall return to this afterwards. Finally, we shall use the type t below to denote the overall type of the expression between the semantic brackets '[[' and ']]'.

$$[\![\ \mathtt{f}_i[t]\ ]\!](\mathcal{I})_{penv} = \lambda\textbf{env}.\ \mathcal{I}(\mathtt{f}_i[t])$$

$$[\![\ \langle e_1,e_2\rangle\ ]\!](\mathcal{I})_{penv} = \lambda\textbf{env}.\ ([\![e_1]\!](\mathcal{I})_{penv}(\textbf{env}),\ [\![e_2]\!](\mathcal{I})_{penv}(\textbf{env}))$$

$$[\![\ \mathtt{fst}\ e\ ]\!](\mathcal{I})_{penv} = \lambda\textbf{env}.\ \mathrm{v}_1 \text{ where } (\mathrm{v}_1,\mathrm{v}_2) = [\![e]\!](\mathcal{I})_{penv}(\textbf{env})$$

$$[\![\ \mathtt{snd}\ e\ ]\!](\mathcal{I})_{penv} = \lambda\textbf{env}.\ \mathrm{v}_2 \text{ where } (\mathrm{v}_1,\mathrm{v}_2) = [\![e]\!](\mathcal{I})_{penv}(\textbf{env})$$

$$[\![\ \lambda\mathtt{x}_i[t'].e\ ]\!](\mathcal{I})_{penv} = \lambda\textbf{env}.\ \lambda\mathrm{v}.\ [\![e]\!](\mathcal{I})_{penv:(\mathtt{x}_i,t')}(\textbf{env},\mathrm{v})$$

$$[\![\ e_1\mathtt{(}e_2\mathtt{)}\ ]\!](\mathcal{I})_{penv} = \lambda\textbf{env}.\ [\![e_1]\!](\mathcal{I})_{penv}(\textbf{env})\ ([\![e_2]\!](\mathcal{I})_{penv}(\textbf{env}))$$

$$[\![\ \mathtt{x}_i\ ]\!](\mathcal{I})_{penv} = \lambda\textbf{env}.\ \pi_{PS}(\mathtt{x}_i,penv)(\textbf{env})$$

$$\text{where } \pi_{PS}(\mathtt{x}_i,penv'{:}(\mathtt{x}_j,t_j))((\textbf{env}',\mathrm{v})) =$$

$$\begin{cases} \mathrm{v} & \text{if } \mathtt{x}_i\text{=}\mathtt{x}_j \\ \pi_{PS}(\mathtt{x}_i,penv')(\textbf{env}') & \text{otherwise} \end{cases}$$

$$[\![\ e_1\texttt{:}e_2\ ]\!](\mathcal{I})_{penv} = \lambda\text{env. } \text{CONS}_{\text{PS}}([\![e_1]\!](\mathcal{I})_{penv}(\text{env}), [\![e_2]\!](\mathcal{I})_{penv}(\text{env}))$$

$$[\![\ \texttt{nil}[t]\ ]\!](\mathcal{I})_{penv} = \lambda\text{env. } \text{NIL}_{\text{PS}}$$

$$[\![\ \texttt{hd}\ e\ ]\!](\mathcal{I})_{penv} = \lambda\text{env. } \text{HD}_{\text{PS}}([\![e]\!](\mathcal{I})_{penv}(\text{env}))$$

$$[\![\ \texttt{tl}\ e\ ]\!](\mathcal{I})_{penv} = \lambda\text{env. } \text{TL}_{\text{PS}}([\![e]\!](\mathcal{I})_{penv}(\text{env}))$$

$$[\![\ \texttt{isnil}\ e\ ]\!](\mathcal{I})_{penv} = \lambda\text{env. } \text{ISNIL}_{\text{PS}}([\![e]\!](\mathcal{I})_{penv}(\text{env}))$$

$$[\![\ \texttt{true}\ ]\!](\mathcal{I})_{penv} = \lambda\text{env. } \mathbf{true}$$

$$[\![\ \texttt{false}\ ]\!](\mathcal{I})_{penv} = \lambda\text{env. } \mathbf{false}$$

$$[\![\ \texttt{if}\ e_1\ \texttt{then}\ e_2\ \texttt{else}\ e_3\ ]\!](\mathcal{I})_{penv} =$$

$$\lambda\text{env. } \begin{cases} [\![e_2]\!](\mathcal{I})_{penv}(\text{env}) & \text{if v=}\mathbf{true} \\ [\![e_3]\!](\mathcal{I})_{penv}(\text{env}) & \text{if v=}\mathbf{false} \\ \bot & \text{if v=}\bot \end{cases}$$

$$\text{where v} = [\![e_1]\!](\mathcal{I})_{penv}(\text{env})$$

$$[\![\ \texttt{fix}\ e\ ]\!](\mathcal{I})_{penv} = \lambda\text{env. } \mathcal{I}(\texttt{fix}[t])([\![e]\!](\mathcal{I})_{penv}(\text{env}))$$

$$[\![\ \texttt{F}_i[t]\ ]\!](\mathcal{I})_{penv} = \lambda\text{env. } \mathcal{I}(\texttt{F}_i[t])$$

$$[\![\ \texttt{Tuple}(e_1,e_2)\ ]\!](\mathcal{I})_{penv} = \lambda\text{env. } \mathcal{I}(\texttt{Tuple}[t])\ ([\![e_1]\!](\mathcal{I})_{penv}(\text{env}))\ ([\![e_2]\!](\mathcal{I})_{penv}(\text{env}))$$

$$[\![\ \texttt{Fst}[t']\ ]\!](\mathcal{I})_{penv} = \lambda\text{env. } \mathcal{I}(\texttt{Fst}[t'])$$

$$[\![\ \texttt{Snd}[t']\ ]\!](\mathcal{I})_{penv} = \lambda\text{env. } \mathcal{I}(\texttt{Snd}[t'])$$

$$[\![\ \texttt{Curry}\ e\ ]\!](\mathcal{I})_{penv} = \lambda\text{env. } \mathcal{I}(\texttt{Curry}[t])\ ([\![e]\!](\mathcal{I})_{penv}(\text{env}))$$

$$[\![\ \texttt{Apply}[t']\ ]\!](\mathcal{I})_{penv} = \lambda\text{env. } \mathcal{I}(\texttt{Apply}[t'])$$

$$[\![\ e_1\square e_2\ ]\!](\mathcal{I})_{penv} = \lambda\text{env. } \mathcal{I}(\square[t_1\times t_2])\ ([\![e_1]\!](\mathcal{I})_{penv}(\text{env}))\ ([\![e_2]\!](\mathcal{I})_{penv}(\text{env}))$$

$$\text{where } \rho_{\text{PS}}(penv) \vdash e_i : t_i$$

$$[\![\ \texttt{Id}[t']\ ]\!](\mathcal{I})_{penv} = \lambda\text{env. } \mathcal{I}(\texttt{Id}[t'])$$

$$[\![\ \texttt{Cons}(e_1,e_2)\ ]\!](\mathcal{I})_{penv} = \lambda\text{env. } \mathcal{I}(\texttt{Cons}[t])\ ([\![e_1]\!](\mathcal{I})_{penv}(\text{env}))\ ([\![e_2]\!](\mathcal{I})_{penv}(\text{env}))$$

$$[\![\ \texttt{Nil}[t']\ ]\!](\mathcal{I})_{penv} = \lambda\text{env. } \mathcal{I}(\texttt{Nil}[t'])$$

$$[\![\ \texttt{Hd}[t']\ ]\!](\mathcal{I})_{penv} = \lambda\text{env. } \mathcal{I}(\texttt{Hd}[t'])$$

$$[\![\ \texttt{Tl}[t']\ ]\!](\mathcal{I})_{penv} = \lambda\text{env. } \mathcal{I}(\texttt{Tl}[t'])$$

$$[\![\ \texttt{Isnil}[t']\ ]\!](\mathcal{I})_{penv} = \lambda\text{env. } \mathcal{I}(\texttt{Isnil}[t'])$$

ϕ	TYPE(ϕ)
$\mathtt{Tuple}[t_0\underline{\rightarrow}t_1\underline{\times}t_2]$	$(t_0\underline{\rightarrow}t_1)\rightarrow(t_0\underline{\rightarrow}t_2)\rightarrow(t_0\underline{\rightarrow}t_1\underline{\times}t_2)$
$\mathtt{Fst}[t_1\underline{\times}t_2]$	$(t_1\underline{\times}t_2)\underline{\rightarrow}t_1$
$\mathtt{Snd}[t_1\underline{\times}t_2]$	$(t_1\underline{\times}t_2)\underline{\rightarrow}t_2$
$\mathtt{Cons}[t_0\underline{\rightarrow}(t_1\ \underline{\mathtt{list}})]$	$(t_0\underline{\rightarrow}t_1)\rightarrow(t_0\underline{\rightarrow}(t_1\ \underline{\mathtt{list}}))\rightarrow(t_0\underline{\rightarrow}(t_1\ \underline{\mathtt{list}}))$
$\mathtt{Nil}[t_0\underline{\rightarrow}(t_1\ \underline{\mathtt{list}})]$	$t_0\underline{\rightarrow}(t_1\ \underline{\mathtt{list}})$
$\mathtt{Hd}[t]$	$(t\ \underline{\mathtt{list}})\underline{\rightarrow}t$
$\mathtt{Tl}[t]$	$(t\ \underline{\mathtt{list}})\underline{\rightarrow}(t\ \underline{\mathtt{list}})$
$\mathtt{Isnil}[t]$	$(t\ \underline{\mathtt{list}})\underline{\rightarrow}\underline{\mathtt{Bool}}$
$\mathtt{f}_\mathrm{i}[t]$	t
$\mathrm{F}_\mathrm{i}[t_0\underline{\rightarrow}t_1]$	$t_0\underline{\rightarrow}t_1$
$\square[(t_1\underline{\rightarrow}t_2)\times(t_0\underline{\rightarrow}t_1)]$	$(t_1\underline{\rightarrow}t_2)\rightarrow(t_0\underline{\rightarrow}t_1)\rightarrow(t_0\underline{\rightarrow}t_2)$
$\mathtt{Id}[t]$	$t\underline{\rightarrow}t$
$\mathtt{True}[t]$	$t\underline{\rightarrow}\underline{\mathtt{Bool}}$
$\mathtt{False}[t]$	$t\underline{\rightarrow}\underline{\mathtt{Bool}}$
$\mathtt{Cond}[t_0\underline{\rightarrow}t_1]$	$(t_0\underline{\rightarrow}\underline{\mathtt{Bool}})\rightarrow(t_0\underline{\rightarrow}t_1)\rightarrow(t_0\underline{\rightarrow}t_1)\rightarrow(t_0\underline{\rightarrow}t_1)$
$\mathtt{fix}[t]$	$(t\rightarrow t)\rightarrow t$
$\mathtt{Curry}[t_0\underline{\rightarrow}(t_1\underline{\rightarrow}t_2)]$	$((t_0\underline{\times}t_1)\underline{\rightarrow}t_2)\rightarrow(t_0\underline{\rightarrow}(t_1\underline{\rightarrow}t_2))$
$\mathtt{Apply}[t_0\underline{\rightarrow}t_1]$	$((t_0\underline{\rightarrow}t_1)\underline{\times}t_0)\underline{\rightarrow}t_1$
$\mathtt{Fix}[t]$	$(t\underline{\rightarrow}t)\underline{\rightarrow}t$

Table 5.1: Operators and their actual types

$$[\![\ \mathtt{True}[t']\ ]\!](\mathcal{I})_{penv} = \lambda\mathbf{env}.\ \mathcal{I}(\mathtt{True}[t'])$$

$$[\![\ \mathtt{False}[t']\ ]\!](\mathcal{I})_{penv} = \lambda\mathbf{env}.\ \mathcal{I}(\mathtt{False}[t'])$$

$$\begin{aligned}[\![\ \mathtt{Cond}(e_1,e_2,e_3)\ ]\!](\mathcal{I})_{penv} = \lambda\mathbf{env}.\ \mathcal{I}(\mathtt{Cond}[t])\ &([\![e_1]\!](\mathcal{I})_{penv}(\mathbf{env}))\\ &([\![e_2]\!](\mathcal{I})_{penv}(\mathbf{env}))\\ &([\![e_3]\!](\mathcal{I})_{penv}(\mathbf{env}))\end{aligned}$$

$$[\![\ \mathtt{Fix}[t']\ ]\!](\mathcal{I})_{penv} = \lambda\mathbf{env}.\ \mathcal{I}(\mathtt{Fix}[t'])$$

The definition of $[\![\cdots]\!](\mathcal{I})_{penv}$ is mostly straightforward. Several of the clauses demand that $\mathcal{I}$ interprets certain 'operators' (like $\mathtt{f}_\mathrm{i}$ or Cond). We shall therefore define a notion of 'an interpretation of operators' and demand that $\mathcal{I}$ is an interpretation of operators (as well as of types). The 'operators' of concern are those candidate ϕ's that are listed in Table 5.1. Each operator ϕ includes a type component in square brackets and generally this is the minimal amount of information needed to define the 'type', TYPE(ϕ), of the operator. One may note from the definition of TYPE and $[\![\cdots]\!](\mathcal{I})_{penv}$ that operators are regarded as being curried (e.g. Cond). In the examples we shall often dispense with the type component of operators as an aid to readability. Finally, the semantic clause for variables makes use of an auxiliary function π_{PS} for locating a value in an environment.

Example 5.2.1 Consider the expression

$$\texttt{fix}(\lambda\texttt{f}[\underline{\texttt{Int}}\underline{\rightarrow}(\underline{\texttt{Int}}\ \underline{\texttt{list}})].\texttt{Cons}(\texttt{Id}[\underline{\texttt{Int}}],\texttt{f}))$$

Given an interpretation $\mathcal{I}$ and an empty position environment () the meaning

$$[\![\texttt{fix}(\lambda\texttt{f}[\underline{\texttt{Int}}\underline{\rightarrow}(\underline{\texttt{Int}}\ \underline{\texttt{list}})].\texttt{Cons}(\texttt{Id}[\underline{\texttt{Int}}],\texttt{f}))]\!](\mathcal{I})_{()}$$

will be an element of the domain

$$\mathbf{Void} \rightarrow \mathcal{I}(\underline{\texttt{Int}}\underline{\rightarrow}(\underline{\texttt{Int}}\ \underline{\texttt{list}}))$$

It is given by

$$\lambda\text{v}.\mathcal{I}(\texttt{fix}[\ ])(\lambda\mathbf{f}.\mathcal{I}(\texttt{Cons})(\mathcal{I}(\texttt{Id}[\ ]))(\mathbf{f}))$$

where we have omitted the type information from the square brackets. □

Definition 5.2.2 An *interpretation* $\mathcal{I}$ of *operators* (or just *interpretation*) is an *interpretation* $\mathcal{I}$ of *types* together with a designated element

$$\mathcal{I}(\phi) \in [\![\text{TYPE}(\phi)]\!](\mathcal{I})$$

for every operator ϕ, such that TYPE(ϕ) is defined according to the definitions given in Table 5.1 and such that TYPE(ϕ) is a well-formed *2*-level type of compile-time kind, i.e. $\vdash$TYPE(ϕ):c. A *C-restricted* interpretation of operators is defined analogously except that $\mathcal{I}(\texttt{f}_i[t])$ and $\mathcal{I}(\texttt{F}_i[t'\underline{\rightarrow}t])$ only need to be defined if t is a *2*-level instance of $C(\texttt{f}_i)$. □

Proposition 5.2.3 If $\mathcal{I}$ is an interpretation, *penv* is a well-formed position environment and

$$\rho_{\text{PS}}(penv) \vdash e : t$$

then the clauses for $[\![e]\!](\mathcal{I})_{penv}$ define a continuous function from $[\![penv]\!](\mathcal{I})$ to $[\![t]\!](\mathcal{I})$:

$$[\![e]\!](\mathcal{I})_{penv} \in [\![penv]\!](\mathcal{I})\rightarrow[\![t]\!](\mathcal{I})$$

If $\rho_{\text{PS}}(penv)\vdash_C e{:}t$ we need only assume that $\mathcal{I}$ is a C-restricted interpretation rather than a general interpretation. □

Proof: The proof is by structural induction on expressions and makes use of Proposition 5.1.15. It amounts to showing that:

(i) each clause for $[\![\cdots]\!](\mathcal{I})_{penv}$ defines an element $[\![e]\!](\mathcal{I})_{penv}(\mathbf{env})$ of $[\![t]\!](\mathcal{I})$ when **env** is an element of $[\![penv]\!](\mathcal{I})$;

(ii) the interpretation $\mathcal{I}$ is never applied to an operator ϕ such that Table 5.1 contains no definition of TYPE(ϕ) or such that TYPE(ϕ) is not a well-formed *2*-level type of compile-time kind;

(iii) $[\![e]\!](\mathcal{I})_{penv}(\mathbf{env})$ depends continuously on **env**.

The latter involves showing the continuity of the functions CONS_{PS}, HD_{PS}, TL_{PS} and ISNIL_{PS} introduced in Construction 5.1.13. As the proof is largely routine we shall dispense with the details. □

Example interpretations

We next illustrate this set-up by defining some example interpretations. These all have the flavour of so-called 'standard interpretations' in that they prescribe the input-output semantics. This is quite unlike the 'non-standard interpretations' to be encountered in Chapters 6, 7 and 8 where we will study code generation and abstract interpretation.

Example 5.2.4 We begin by extending the interpretation $\mathbf{S}_{\text{lll}}$ of types (Example 5.1.16) to an interpretation of operators. When considering an operator ϕ with type component $[t]$ we shall assume that t is such that TYPE(ϕ) is defined and is a well-formed *2*-level type of compile-time kind.

$$\mathbf{S}_{\text{lll}}(\texttt{Tuple}[t_0 \underline{\rightarrow} t_1 \underline{\times} t_2]) = \lambda f_1.\lambda f_2.\lambda \mathbf{v}.\ (f_1(\mathbf{v}), f_2(\mathbf{v}))$$

$$\mathbf{S}_{\text{lll}}(\texttt{Fst}[t_1 \underline{\times} t_2]) = \lambda \mathbf{v}.\ \mathbf{v}_1 \text{ where } (\mathbf{v}_1,\mathbf{v}_2) = \mathbf{v}$$

$$\mathbf{S}_{\text{lll}}(\texttt{Snd}[t_1 \underline{\times} t_2]) = \lambda \mathbf{v}.\ \mathbf{v}_2 \text{ where } (\mathbf{v}_1,\mathbf{v}_2) = \mathbf{v}$$

$$\mathbf{S}_{\text{lll}}(\texttt{Cons}[t_0 \underline{\rightarrow} (t_1\ \underline{\texttt{list}})]) = \lambda f_1.\lambda f_2.\lambda \mathbf{v}.\ \text{CONS}_{\text{PS}}(f_1(\mathbf{v}), f_2(\mathbf{v}))$$

$$\mathbf{S}_{\text{lll}}(\texttt{Nil}[t_0 \underline{\rightarrow} t_1\ \underline{\texttt{list}}]) = \lambda \mathbf{v}.\ \text{NIL}_{\text{PS}}$$

$$\mathbf{S}_{\text{lll}}(\texttt{Hd}[t]) = \lambda \mathbf{v}.\ \text{HD}_{\text{PS}}(\mathbf{v})$$

$$\mathbf{S}_{\text{lll}}(\texttt{Tl}[t]) = \lambda \mathbf{v}.\ \text{TL}_{\text{PS}}(\mathbf{v})$$

$$\mathbf{S}_{\text{lll}}(\texttt{Isnil}[t]) = \lambda \mathbf{v}.\ \text{ISNIL}_{\text{PS}}(\mathbf{v})$$

$$\mathbf{S}_{\text{lll}}(\texttt{f}_{\text{i}}[t]) = \mathbf{f}_{\text{i}}^{t}$$

where $\mathbf{f}_{\text{i}}^{t}$ are unspecified elements in $[\![t]\!](\mathbf{S}_{\text{lll}})$

$$\mathbf{S}_{\text{lll}}(\texttt{F}_{\text{i}}[t_0 \underline{\rightarrow} t_1]) = \mathbf{F}_{\text{i}}^{t_0 \underline{\rightarrow} t_1}$$

where $\mathbf{F}_{\text{i}}^{t_0 \underline{\rightarrow} t_1}$ are unspecified elements in $[\![t_0 \underline{\rightarrow} t_1]\!](\mathbf{S}_{\text{lll}})$

$$\mathbf{S}_{\text{lll}}(\square[(t_1 \underline{\rightarrow} t_2) \times (t_0 \underline{\rightarrow} t_1)]) = \lambda f_1.\lambda f_2.\lambda \mathbf{v}.\ f_1(f_2(\mathbf{v}))$$

$$\mathbf{S}_{\text{lll}}(\texttt{Id}[t]) = \lambda \mathbf{v}.\mathbf{v}$$

$$\mathbf{S}_{\text{lll}}(\texttt{True}[t]) = \lambda \mathbf{v}.\ \mathbf{true}$$

$$\mathbf{S}_{\text{III}}(\texttt{False}[t]) = \lambda \mathrm{v}.\ \mathbf{false}$$

$$\mathbf{S}_{\text{III}}(\texttt{Cond}[t_0\underline{\rightarrow}t_1]) = \lambda f_1.\lambda f_2.\lambda f_3.\lambda \mathrm{v}.\ \begin{cases} f_2(\mathrm{v}) & \text{if } f_1(\mathrm{v})=\mathbf{true} \\ f_3(\mathrm{v}) & \text{if } f_1(\mathrm{v})=\mathbf{false} \\ \bot & \text{if } f_1(\mathrm{v})=\bot \end{cases}$$

$$\mathbf{S}_{\text{III}}(\texttt{fix}[t]) = \text{FIX}$$

$$\text{where } \text{FIX}(F) = \bigsqcup_n F^n(\bot)$$

$$\mathbf{S}_{\text{III}}(\texttt{Curry}[t_0\underline{\rightarrow}(t_1\underline{\rightarrow}t_2)]) = \lambda f.\lambda \mathrm{v}_1.\lambda \mathrm{v}_2.\ f(\mathrm{v}) \text{ where } \mathrm{v} = (\mathrm{v}_1,\mathrm{v}_2)$$

$$\mathbf{S}_{\text{III}}(\texttt{Apply}[t_0\underline{\rightarrow}t_1]) = \lambda \mathrm{w}.\ f(\mathrm{v}) \text{ where } (f,\mathrm{v}) = \mathrm{w}$$

$$\mathbf{S}_{\text{III}}(\texttt{Fix}[t]) = \lambda f.\ \text{FIX}(f)$$

It is straightforward, but tedious, to verify that this defines an interpretation of operators. If we intend to define $\mathbf{S}_{\text{III}}$ as a C-restricted interpretation, $\mathcal{I}(\mathtt{f}_i[t])$ need only be defined when t is a *2*-level instance of $C(\mathtt{f}_i)$ and $\mathcal{I}(\mathtt{F}_i[t_0\underline{\rightarrow}t_1])$ need only be defined when t_1 is a *2*-level instance of $C(\mathtt{f}_i)$.

Using the interpretation $\mathbf{S}_{\text{III}}$ the meaning of the expression

$$\texttt{fix}(\lambda\texttt{f}[\underline{\texttt{Int}}\underline{\rightarrow}(\underline{\texttt{Int}}\ \underline{\texttt{list}})].\texttt{Cons}(\texttt{Id}[\underline{\texttt{Int}}],\texttt{f}))$$

of Example 5.2.1 is an element of

$$\mathbf{Void} \rightarrow (\mathbf{Z} \rightarrow \mathbf{Z}^\infty)$$

and it is given by

$$\lambda \mathrm{v}.\text{FIX}(\lambda \mathbf{f}.\lambda \mathbf{u}.\textsc{cons}_{\text{PS}}(\mathbf{u},\mathbf{f}(\mathbf{u})))$$

which is equivalent to

$$\lambda \mathrm{v}.\lambda \mathbf{u}.[\mathbf{u},\mathbf{u},\cdots]$$

Applying this function to a dummy argument and the integer **1** will thus produce an infinite list of **1**'s. □

To complete the definition of the interpretation **S** of Section 5.1 we need the auxiliary functions $up{:}D\rightarrow D_\bot$ and $dn{:}D_\bot\rightarrow D$ defined by

$$up(d) = d$$

$$dn(d) = \begin{cases} d & \text{if } d\neq\star \\ \bot & \text{if } d=\star \end{cases}$$

Here we have used the definition $D_\bot = D\cup\{\star\}$ from Construction 5.1.22; had we used the definition $D_\bot = (\{1\}\times D)\cup(\{0\}\times\{\star\})$ we would have had $up(d) = (1,d)$, $dn((1,d)) = d$ and $dn((0,\star)) = \bot$ instead.

We then have the following definitions (leaving an explanation of $\mathbf{S}(\texttt{fix}[t])$ until afterwards):

$\mathbf{S}(\texttt{Tuple}[t_0\underline{\rightarrow}t_1\underline{\times}t_2]) = \lambda f_1.\lambda f_2.$

$$\begin{cases} up(\lambda\mathbf{v}.up(dn(f_1)(\mathbf{v}),dn(f_2)(\mathbf{v}))) & \text{if } f_1 \neq \bot \text{ and } f_2 \neq \bot \\ \bot & \text{otherwise} \end{cases}$$

$\mathbf{S}(\texttt{Fst}[t_1\underline{\times}t_2]) = up(\lambda\mathbf{v}.\ \mathbf{v}_1 \text{ where } (\mathbf{v}_1,\mathbf{v}_2) = dn(\mathbf{v}))$

$\mathbf{S}(\texttt{Snd}[t_1\underline{\times}t_2]) = up(\lambda\mathbf{v}.\ \mathbf{v}_2 \text{ where } (\mathbf{v}_1,\mathbf{v}_2) = dn(\mathbf{v}))$

$\mathbf{S}(\texttt{Cons}[t_0\underline{\rightarrow}(t_1\ \underline{\texttt{list}})]) = \lambda f_1.\lambda f_2.$

$$\begin{cases} up(\lambda\mathbf{v}.\text{CONS}_{\text{PS}}(dn(f_1)(\mathbf{v}),\ dn(f_2)(\mathbf{v}))) & \text{if } f_1 \neq \bot \text{ and } f_2 \neq \bot \\ \bot & \text{otherwise} \end{cases}$$

$\mathbf{S}(\texttt{Nil}[t_0\underline{\rightarrow}(t_1\ \underline{\texttt{list}})]) = up(\lambda\mathbf{v}.\ \text{NIL}_{\text{PS}})$

$\mathbf{S}(\texttt{Hd}[t]) = up(\lambda\mathbf{v}.\ \text{HD}_{\text{PS}}(\mathbf{v}))$

$\mathbf{S}(\texttt{Tl}[t]) = up(\lambda\mathbf{v}.\ \text{TL}_{\text{PS}}(\mathbf{v}))$

$\mathbf{S}(\texttt{Isnil}[t]) = up(\lambda\mathbf{v}.\ \text{ISNIL}_{\text{PS}}(\mathbf{v}))$

$\mathbf{S}(\texttt{f}_{\text{i}}[t]) = \mathbf{f}_{\text{i}}^{t}$

where $\mathbf{f}_{\text{i}}^{t}$ are unspecified elements in $[\![t]\!](\mathbf{S})$

$\mathbf{S}(\texttt{F}_{\text{i}}[t_0\underline{\rightarrow}t_1]) = \mathbf{F}_{\text{i}}^{t_0\underline{\rightarrow}t_1}$

where $\mathbf{F}_{\text{i}}^{t_0\underline{\rightarrow}t_1}$ are unspecified elements in $[\![t_0\underline{\rightarrow}t_1]\!](\mathbf{S})$

$\mathbf{S}(\square[(t_1\underline{\rightarrow}t_2)\times(t_0\underline{\rightarrow}t_1)]) = \lambda f_1.\lambda f_2.$

$$\begin{cases} up(\lambda\mathbf{v}.dn(f_1)(dn(f_2)(\mathbf{v}))) & \text{if } f_1 \neq \bot \text{ and } f_2 \neq \bot \\ \bot & \text{otherwise} \end{cases}$$

$\mathbf{S}(\texttt{Id}[t]) = up(\lambda\mathbf{v}.\mathbf{v})$

$\mathbf{S}(\texttt{True}[t]) = up(\lambda\mathbf{v}.\ \mathbf{true})$

$\mathbf{S}(\texttt{False}[t]) = up(\lambda\mathbf{v}.\ \mathbf{false})$

$\mathbf{S}(\texttt{Cond}[t_0\underline{\rightarrow}t_1]) = \lambda f_1.\lambda f_2.\lambda f_3.$

$$\begin{cases} up(\lambda\mathbf{v}. \begin{cases} dn(f_2)(\mathbf{v}) & \text{if } dn(f_1)(\mathbf{v})=\mathbf{true} \\ dn(f_3)(\mathbf{v}) & \text{if } dn(f_1)(\mathbf{v})=\mathbf{false} \\ \bot & \text{if } dn(f_1)(\mathbf{v})=\bot \end{cases}) & \text{if } f_1 \neq \bot, f_2 \neq \bot, f_3 \neq \bot \\ \bot & \text{otherwise} \end{cases}$$

$\mathbf{S}(\texttt{fix}[t]) = \text{FIX where FIX}(F) = \bigsqcup_{\text{n}} F^{\text{n}}(\bot)$

if t is pure (see below)

$$\mathbf{S}(\mathtt{fix}[t_1 \underline{\rightarrow} t_2]) = \lambda F.\ \bigsqcup_{n\geq 1} F^n(up(\bot))$$

$$\mathbf{S}(\mathtt{fix}[t_1 \times t_2]) = \lambda F.(F_1, F_2(F_1)) \text{ where}$$

$$F_1 = \mathbf{S}(\mathtt{fix}[t_1])(\lambda \mathbf{v}_1.\mathbf{w}_1 \text{ where } (\mathbf{w}_1,\mathbf{w}_2) = F((\mathbf{v}_1, F_2(\mathbf{v}_1))))$$

$$F_2 = \lambda \mathbf{v}_1.\mathbf{S}(\mathtt{fix}[t_2])(\lambda \mathbf{v}_2.\mathbf{w}_2 \text{ where } (\mathbf{w}_1,\mathbf{w}_2) = F((\mathbf{v}_1,\mathbf{v}_2)))$$

and $t_1 \times t_2$ is composite but not pure (see below)

$$\mathbf{S}(\mathtt{Curry}[t_0 \underline{\rightarrow} (t_1 \underline{\rightarrow} t_2)]) = \lambda f.$$

$$\begin{cases} up(\lambda \mathbf{v}_1.\ up(\lambda \mathbf{v}_2.\ dn(f)(\mathbf{v}) \text{ where } \mathbf{v} = up(\mathbf{v}_1,\mathbf{v}_2))) \\ \quad \text{if } f \neq \bot \\ \bot \quad \text{otherwise} \end{cases}$$

$$\mathbf{S}(\mathtt{Apply}[t_0 \underline{\rightarrow} t_1]) = up(\lambda \mathbf{w}.\ dn(f)(\mathbf{v}) \text{ where } (f,\mathbf{v}) = dn(\mathbf{w}))$$

$$\mathbf{S}(\mathtt{Fix}[t]) = up(\lambda f.\ \mathrm{FIX}(dn(f)))$$

$$\text{where } \mathrm{FIX}(F) = \bigsqcup_n F^n(\bot)$$

Apart from the definition of $\mathbf{S}(\mathtt{fix}[t])$ it is straightforward but tedious to verify that this is indeed an interpretation. We shall return to the well-definedness of $\mathbf{S}(\mathtt{fix}[t])$ shortly.

Example 5.2.5 To illustrate the difference between $\mathbf{S}_{\mathrm{lll}}$ and $\mathbf{S}$ consider the expression

$$\mathtt{Tuple}(\mathtt{Fst}[\underline{\mathtt{Int}} \underline{\times} \underline{\mathtt{Int}}], \mathtt{Snd}[\underline{\mathtt{Int}} \underline{\times} \underline{\mathtt{Int}}])$$

It has type $\underline{\mathtt{Int}} \underline{\times} \underline{\mathtt{Int}} \underline{\rightarrow} \underline{\mathtt{Int}} \underline{\times} \underline{\mathtt{Int}}$ and thus $\mathbf{S}_{\mathrm{lll}}$ will produce an element of the domain $\mathbf{Void} \rightarrow (\mathbf{Z}\times\mathbf{Z} \rightarrow \mathbf{Z}\times\mathbf{Z})$ and $\mathbf{S}$ one of $\mathbf{Void} \rightarrow ((\mathbf{Z}\times\mathbf{Z})_\bot \rightarrow (\mathbf{Z}\times\mathbf{Z})_\bot)_\bot$. In the case of $\mathbf{S}_{\mathrm{lll}}$ it is

$$\lambda \mathbf{v}.\lambda \mathbf{u}.\mathbf{u}$$

so whenever the void environment is supplied this is the identity function. In the case of $\mathbf{S}$ we get

$$\lambda \mathbf{v}.up(\lambda \mathbf{u}.up(dn\ \mathbf{u}))$$

Note that this does *not* correspond to the identity function once the void environment is supplied.

Experiments with Miranda show that Tuple(Fst[ ],Snd[ ]) does indeed behave differently from the identity function. To be explicit consider the Miranda definitions

```
id1 v = v

id2 v = (fst v, snd v)

bot = bot
```

Then the behaviours of `id1 bot` and `id2 bot` are slightly different. Since similar phenomena arise in Chapter 6 we decide to concentrate on interpretation **S** rather than interpretation $\mathbf{S}_{\text{lll}}$, but as discussed in Section 5.1 this decision may be subject to debate as far as Miranda is concerned.

Finally we note that a similar example can be constructed using `Curry` and `Apply` to show that **S** and $\mathbf{S}_{\text{lll}}$ differ here as well, and again **S** is close to the way the Miranda implementation behaves. □

The definition of $\mathbf{S}(\texttt{fix}[t])$ requires some clarification. The most natural thing would be to set

$$\mathbf{S}(\texttt{fix}[t])(F) = \text{FIX}(F) \qquad (\star)$$

for all types t. However, we have arranged that operators are in fact strict in their arguments, e.g. $\mathbf{S}(\texttt{Tuple})(\bot)(f){=}\bot$. So when t is a frontier type it is very likely that $F\ \bot = \bot$ which means that FIX(F) would always be $\bot$. This relates to the decision to use

$$\mathbf{S}(t_1\underline{\rightarrow}t_2) = (\mathbf{S}(t_1)\rightarrow\mathbf{S}(t_2))_\bot \qquad (\sharp)$$

and to distinguish between the least element, $\bot$, and the second least element, $up(\bot)$, where the latter corresponds to the 'undefined' function that may freely be passed around but that never terminates when called. Similar distinctions will be made in Chapter 6 when specifying code generation. This motivates retaining $(\sharp)$ but to be more careful about $(\star)$. In particular,

$$\mathbf{S}(\texttt{fix}[t_1\underline{\rightarrow}t_2])(F) = \textstyle\bigsqcup_{n\geq 1} F^n(up(\bot))$$

would seem to give the required effect. If $F(up(\bot)) = \bot$ then $F(\bot) = \bot$ by monotonicity so $\mathbf{S}(\texttt{fix}[t_1\underline{\rightarrow}t_2])(F)$ is defined and equals $\bot$. If $F(up(\bot)) \neq \bot$ then $F(up(\bot)) \sqsupseteq up(\bot)$ so $(F^n(up(\bot)))_{n\geq 1}$ is a chain and therefore $\mathbf{S}(\texttt{fix}[t_1\underline{\rightarrow}t_2])(F)$ is well-defined.

This leaves us with the remaining types. If no frontier types are involved we should still be able to make do with $(\star)$. To make this precise we define the predicate *pure* by

pure($\mathtt{A}_i$) holds for all $\mathtt{A}_i$
if pure(t_1) and pure(t_2) then pure($t_1 \times t_2$)
if pure(t_1) and pure(t_2) then pure($t_1 \rightarrow t_2$)
if pure(t) then pure(t **list**)

and note that pure(t) would seem to formalise the notion of t not involving any frontier types. We thus define

$$\mathbf{S}(\texttt{fix}[t]) = \text{FIX if pure}(t)$$

and clearly this is well-defined.

We are left with the more complex combinations of pure and frontier types. As a simple example, consider $t = (t_1 \underline{\rightarrow} t_2) \times (t_1 \underline{\rightarrow} t_2)$. Here it would be natural to define $\mathbf{S}(\mathtt{fix}[t])(F)$ to be $\bigsqcup_n F^n(up(\bot), up(\bot))$. However, well-definedness is a problem. To see this let d be such that $d \sqsupseteq up(\bot)$ and $d \neq up(\bot)$. Then it is conceivable that $F(up(\bot), up(\bot)) = (d,\bot)$, $F(d,\bot) = (\bot,d)$, $F(\bot,d) = (d,\bot)$ and $F(d,d) \neq (d,d)$. This means that no fixed point arises[1].

We will thus have to take a different route and for this we shall be content with only considering cartesian products; the reason is that lists and function spaces pose some problems when we come to code generation (as discussed in [72]). We then say that a type t is *composite* if

- it is pure, or
- it has the form $t_1 \underline{\rightarrow} t_2$, or
- it is a product of composite types.

In this case we define

$$\mathbf{S}(\mathtt{fix}[t_1 \times t_2]) = \lambda F.(F_1, F_2(F_1))$$

where

$$F_1 = \mathbf{S}(\mathtt{fix}[t_1])(\lambda \mathbf{v}_1.\mathbf{w}_1 \text{ where } (\mathbf{w}_1,\mathbf{w}_2) = F((\mathbf{v}_1, F_2(\mathbf{v}_1))))$$

$$F_2 = \lambda \mathbf{v}_1.\mathbf{S}(\mathtt{fix}[t_2])(\lambda \mathbf{v}_2.\mathbf{w}_2 \text{ where } (\mathbf{w}_1,\mathbf{w}_2) = F((\mathbf{v}_1,\mathbf{v}_2)))$$

Clearly we have a well-defined definition. To show that it is sensible we note

Lemma 5.2.6 If $F : D \times E \rightarrow D \times E$ and

- F_1 is a fixed point of $(\lambda \mathbf{v}_1.\mathbf{w}_1 \text{ where } (\mathbf{w}_1,\mathbf{w}_2) = F((\mathbf{v}_1, F_2(\mathbf{v}_1))))$
- $F_2(\mathbf{v}_1)$ is a fixed point of $(\lambda \mathbf{v}_2.\mathbf{w}_2 \text{ where } (\mathbf{w}_1,\mathbf{w}_2) = F((\mathbf{v}_1,\mathbf{v}_2)))$
  for all values of $\mathbf{v}_1 \in D$

then

- $(F_1, F_2(\mathrm{F}_1))$ is a fixed point of F □

Proof: It is convenient to write

$\cdots\downarrow\mathrm{i}$

[1] Alternatively one might reconsider the use of cartesian product for × and use smash product instead. (In a similar vein one might use lifted strict and bottom-reflecting functions for →.) However, the use of smash product is not to be recommended for pure components so this approach would lead to a rather complex mixture of smash and cartesian product.

for

$$\mathbf{w}_i \text{ where } (\mathbf{w}_1,\mathbf{w}_2)=\cdots$$

The assumptions then yield that

$$F_1 = F(F_1,F_2(F_1))\downarrow 1$$
$$F_2(F_1) = F(F_1,F_2(F_1))\downarrow 2$$

from which the desired result

$$(F_1,F_2(F_1)) = F(F_1,F_2(F_1))$$

easily follows. □

This result is adapted after the following much more well-known result.

Lemma 5.2.7 ('Bekić's Theorem') If $F : D\times E \to D\times E$ then

$$\mathrm{FIX}(F) = (F_1,F_2(\mathrm{F}_1))$$

where

$$F_1=\mathrm{FIX}(\lambda\mathbf{v}_1.\mathbf{w}_1 \text{ where } (\mathbf{w}_1,\mathbf{w}_2)=F((\mathbf{v}_1,F_2(\mathbf{v}_1))))$$

$$F_2=\lambda\mathbf{v}_1.\mathrm{FIX}(\lambda\mathbf{v}_2.\mathbf{w}_2 \text{ where } (\mathbf{w}_1,\mathbf{w}_2)=F((\mathbf{v}_1,\mathbf{v}_2)))$$ □

Proof: We shall leave the proof to Exercise 17. □

The restriction to composite types t when interpreting $\mathbf{S}(\mathtt{fix}[t])$ means that technically we have not provided an interpretation of operators. To amend this we modify rule [fix] of Table 4.2 and use

$$[\mathtt{fix}^{\mathrm{K}}] \qquad \frac{tenv \vdash e : t\to t}{tenv \vdash \mathtt{fix}\ e : t} \quad \text{if } t \text{ is composite}$$

We shall write $\overset{\mathrm{K}}{\vdash}$ for the well-formedness relation $\vdash$ when $[\mathtt{fix}^{\mathrm{K}}]$ is used instead of [fix]. We shall thus be content with only defining an interpretation of operators for the designated subset of the mixed λ-calculus and combinatory logic.

5.3 Programs

To define the semantics of programs we shall once more use the relationship between a program

$$\mathtt{DEF}\ \mathtt{x}_1=e_1 \cdots \mathtt{DEF}\ \mathtt{x}_n=e_n\ \mathtt{VAL}\ e_0\ \mathtt{HAS}\ t$$

and a nested λ-expression

$$(\lambda \mathtt{x}_1[t_1].\cdots(\lambda \mathtt{x}_n[t_n].e_0)(e_n)\cdots)(e_1)$$

that has been used in the definitions of $\mathcal{P}^C_{\mathrm{TA}}$, $\mathcal{P}^C_{\mathrm{BTA}}$ and $\mathcal{P}_{\mathrm{CI}}$. We thus define

$$[\![\ \mathtt{DEF}\ \mathtt{x}_1{=}e_1 \cdots \mathtt{DEF}\ \mathtt{x}_n{=}e_n\ \mathtt{VAL}\ e_0\ \mathtt{HAS}\ t\ ]\!](\mathcal{I}) \in [\![t]\!](\mathcal{I})$$

whenever $\vdash \mathtt{DEF}\ \mathtt{x}_1{=}e_1 \cdots \mathtt{DEF}\ \mathtt{x}_n{=}e_n\ \mathtt{VAL}\ e_0\ \mathtt{HAS}\ t$

by

$$
\begin{array}{l}
[\![\ \mathtt{DEF}\ \mathtt{x}_1{=}e_1 \cdots \mathtt{DEF}\ \mathtt{x}_n{=}e_n\ \mathtt{VAL}\ e_0\ \mathtt{HAS}\ t\ ]\!](\mathcal{I}) = \\
\qquad \text{let } \emptyset \vdash e_1{:}t_1 \text{ determine } t_1 \\
\qquad \vdots \\
\qquad \text{let } \emptyset[t_1/\mathtt{x}_1]\cdots[t_{n-1}/\mathtt{x}_{n-1}] \vdash e_n{:}t_n \text{ determine } t_n \\
\qquad \text{in } [\![\ (\lambda \mathtt{x}_1[t_1].\cdots(\lambda \mathtt{x}_n[t_n].e_0)(e_n)\cdots)(e_1)\ ]\!](\mathcal{I})_{()}(\mathbf{void})
\end{array}
$$

where **void** is the unique element of **Void** that is not $\perp$.

Theorem 5.3.1 If $\mathcal{I}$ is an interpretation and $p \in P(\mathit{CE2},\mathit{T2})$ is a well-formed program (that is $\vdash p$) of the form

$$\mathtt{DEF}\ \mathtt{x}_1{=}e_1 \cdots \mathtt{DEF}\ \mathtt{x}_n{=}e_n\ \mathtt{VAL}\ e_0\ \mathtt{HAS}\ t$$

the above equation defines

$$[\![p]\!](\mathcal{I}) \in [\![t]\!](\mathcal{I})$$

If $\vdash_C p$ we need only assume that $\mathcal{I}$ is a C-restricted interpretation. □

Proof: The result is straightforward from Propositions 5.2.3 and 5.1.15. □

Example 5.3.2 Consider the program $\mathtt{sum}'_{\mathrm{9B}}$ defined in Section 4.3:

```
VAL fix(λg[ ].Cond(Isnil[ ] □ Snd[ ], Fst[ ],
                    +[ ] □ Tuple(Hd[ ] □ Snd[ ],
                    g □ Tuple(Fst[ ], Tl[ ] □ Snd[ ]))))
     □ Tuple(Zero[ ], Id[ ])
HAS Int list → Int
```

(In the printed type, Int, list and → are underlined.)

The semantics in the lazy interpretation $\mathbf{S}_{\mathrm{lll}}$ amounts to

$$
\begin{array}{l}
[\![\ \mathtt{sum}'_{\mathrm{9B}}\ ]\!](\mathbf{S}_{\mathrm{lll}}) \\
\quad = \lambda l.\ \mathrm{FIX}(G)(0,l) \\
\qquad\qquad \text{where } G(g)(v,l) = \left\{ \begin{array}{ll} v & \text{if } l{=}[\,] \\ v' & \text{if } (l{\neq}[\,]) \wedge (l{\neq}\perp) \\ \perp & \text{if } l{=}\perp \end{array} \right.
\end{array}
$$

and v' abbreviates $\text{PLUS}(\text{HD}_{\text{PS}}(l),g(v,\text{TL}_{\text{PS}}(l)))$

$$= \lambda l. \begin{cases} v_1+\cdots+v_n & \text{if } (l=[v_1,\cdots,v_n]) \wedge (\forall i\colon\ v_i\neq\bot) \\ \bot & \text{if } (l=[v_1,\cdots,v_n]) \wedge (\exists i\colon\ v_i=\bot) \\ \bot & \text{if } l=[v_1,\cdots,v_n\partial \\ \bot & \text{if } l=[v_1,\cdots] \end{cases}$$

assuming that $\mathbf{S}_{\text{III}}(+) = \lambda v.\text{PLUS}$ and

$$\text{PLUS}(v_1,v_2) = \begin{cases} v_1+v_2 & \text{if } (v_1\neq\bot)\wedge(v_2\neq\bot) \\ \bot & \text{otherwise} \end{cases}$$ □

On the role of semantics

In the previous chapters we have presented type inference, binding time analysis and combinator introduction as purely syntactic manipulations of programs. We have only referred to a vague and unspecified notion of semantics when considering program transformations and the extent to which they are correctness-preserving. Having introduced parameterized semantics and the 'standard interpretation' **S**, we can now take at least two approaches.

One approach is to view the parameterized semantics as the ultimate semantics for the original enriched λ-calculus of Chapter 2. Taking `sum` as an example we thus have to

- transform it into an explicitly typed program,
- then into a program that is annotated with explicit binding time information, and
- finally into combinator form.

Calling the resulting program $\texttt{sum}_\text{C}$ we thus define the semantics of `sum` to be the parameterized semantics of $\texttt{sum}_\text{C}$. We can then express the correctness of the program transformations, partial evaluations and algebraic transformations as the condition that they do not change the final semantics regardless of the 'standard interpretation' used.

Another approach is to give a direct definition of the semantics of the enriched λ-calculus. Then one must ensure that the semantics of an untyped program (like `sum`) corresponds to the parameterized semantics of the transformed program (that is $\texttt{sum}_\text{C}$) with respect to some 'standard interpretation'. We mentioned some possibilities in the Bibliographical Notes of Chapters 2, 3 and 4. However, we shall not pursue this approach since our ultimate interest is in non-standard interpretations which cannot be defined directly in terms of the untyped λ-calculus.

Bibliographical Notes

Standard references to domain theory include [93], [94] and [98] and text books on the subject include [96] and [91]. A less detailed account may be found in [83] but it should suffice for understanding the material of this chapter. The notion of parameterized semantics used here is based on [72] and [78].

A brief appraisal of the material of this chapter, with a view towards Chapter 7, may be found in [70].

Exercises

1. Prove the claims made about ($\mathbf{P}\omega$,$\subseteq$) and ($\mathbf{P}\omega$,$\supseteq$) in Examples 5.1.1 and 5.1.4.

2. Prove that the cartesian product $\times$ of Construction 5.1.5 preserves the following properties: is a cpo; is a complete lattice; is a cpo of finite height; is a domain. (That is prove that if D and E are cpo's then so is $D\times E$; that if D and E are complete lattices then so is $D\times E$, etc.)

3. Prove that every continuous function is monotonic. (Hint: if $d\sqsubseteq d'$ then $\{d,d'\}$ is a chain.)

4. Prove that if f:(D,$\sqsubseteq$)$\rightarrow$(E,$\sqsubseteq$) is a monotonic function, and (D,$\sqsubseteq$) and (E,$\sqsubseteq$) are cpo's, then f is continuous provided that

   $$f(\bigsqcup_{\mathrm{n}} d_{\mathrm{n}}) \sqsubseteq \bigsqcup_{\mathrm{n}} f(d_{\mathrm{n}})$$

   holds for all chains $(d_{\mathrm{n}})_{\mathrm{n}}$ of D.

5. Show that a chain in a partially ordered set D amounts to a monotonic function from (ω,$\leq$) to D, where ω=$\{0,1,\cdots\}$ is the set of natural numbers and $\leq$ is the usual order relation for natural numbers.

6. Prove that the continuous function space $\rightarrow$ of Construction 5.1.9 preserves the following properties: is a cpo; is a complete lattice; is a finite cpo.

7. (*) Prove that $D\rightarrow E$ is a domain if D and E are.

8. (*) Prove that D^∞ is a cpo when D is, and that D^∞ is a domain when D is.

9. Prove that the smash product $*$ of Construction 5.1.17 preserves the following properties: is a cpo; is a complete lattice; is a flat cpo; is a cpo of finite height; is a domain.

10. Prove that the strict function space $\rightarrow_{\mathrm{s}}$ of Construction 5.1.19 preserves the following properties: is a cpo; is a complete lattice; is a finite cpo.

11. (*) Prove that $D \rightarrow_s E$ is a domain if D and E are.

12. Prove that the finite lists $(\cdots)^*$ of Construction 5.1.20 preserves the following properties: is a cpo; is a flat cpo; is a cpo of finite height; is a domain.

13. Prove that the lifting $(\cdots)_\perp$ of Construction 5.1.22 preserves the following properties: is a cpo; is a complete lattice; is a cpo of finite height; is a domain.

14. Define (at least partially) $\mathbf{S}_{\text{eee}}$ as an interpretation of operators.

15. Define (at least partially) $\mathbf{S}_{\text{lel}}$ as an interpretation of operators.

16. Repeat the development of Chapter 5 so as to interpret compile-time constructs in the manner of interpretation $\mathbf{S}$ (rather than in the manner of interpretation $\mathbf{S}_{\text{lll}}$).

17. Prove 'Bekić's Theorem' (Lemma 5.2.7). (Hint: consult [72] or [9].)

18. (*) When changing [`fix`] of Table 4.2 to [$\texttt{fix}^{\text{K}}$] we may want also to change [`fix`] of Table 3.5 in a similar way. Investigate whether or not this influences the algorithm for combinator introduction as developed in Chapter 4.

    When changing [`fix`] of Table 3.5 we might consider changing [`fix`] of Table 2.3. Try to show that this is not necessary by modifying the binding time analysis as developed in Chapter 3.

Chapter 6

Code Generation

The previous chapter developed the notion of parameterized semantics for the mixed λ-calculus and combinatory logic. This was applied to showing that the run-time part of the language could be equipped with various mixtures of lazy and eager features. In this chapter we shall stick to one of these: the lazy semantics **S**. The power of parameterized semantics will then be used to specify code that describes how to compute the results specified by the lazy semantics.

The abstract machine and the code generation are both developed in Section 6.1 as it is hard to understand the details of the instructions in the abstract machine without some knowledge of how they are used for code generation and vice versa. The abstract machine is a variant of the categorical abstract machine and its semantics is formulated as a transition system on configurations consisting of a code component and a stack of values. The code generation is specified as an interpretation **K** in the sense of Chapter 5.

The remainder of the chapter is devoted to demonstrating the correctness of the code generation, **K**, with respect to the lazy semantics, **S**. To cut down on the overall length of the proof we shall exclude lists from our consideration. Section 6.2 then begins by showing that the code generation function behaves in a way that admits substitution. Next, Section 6.3 shows that the code generated is 'well-behaved' in that it operates in a stack-like manner. This is a useful preparation for Section 6.4 where it is shown that the results produced by the code agree with the semantics.

6.1 The Coding Interpretation

The *configurations* of the abstract machine have the form (C,ST) where C is the sequence of instructions to be executed and ST is the stack of intermediate results. The instructions, values and configurations of the machine are summarized in Table 6.1 and will be explained in the remainder of this section. We shall write $i{:}C$ for the code sequence with i as its first instruction and C as the remaining code

$l \in Labels = N$
$i \in Ins$
$i ::= \text{CONST } \mathbf{b}_i \mid \text{PRIM } o_i \mid \text{ENTER} \mid \text{SWITCH} \mid \text{BRANCH}(C,C) \mid$
$\quad \text{TUPLE} \mid \text{FST} \mid \text{SND} \mid \text{CONS} \mid \text{NIL} \mid \text{HD} \mid \text{TL} \mid \text{ISNIL} \mid$
$\quad \text{CURRY}(C) \mid \text{APPLY} \mid \text{DELAY}(C) \mid \text{RESUME} \mid$
$\quad \text{CALLREC}(l,C) \mid \text{CALL } l \mid \text{REC}$
$C \in Code = \{ i_1{:}i_2{:}\cdots{:}i_k{:}\varepsilon \mid 0 \le k,\ i_j \in Ins \text{ for } 1 \le j \le k \}$
$v \in Val$
$v ::= \mathbf{b}_i \mid \langle v,v \rangle \mid [\,] \mid [v{:}v] \mid \{C;v\} \mid \{C,v\}$
$ST \in Stack = \{ [v_1,\cdots,v_n] \mid 0 \le n,\ v_j \in Val \text{ for } 1 \le j \le n \}$
$Config = \{ (C,ST) \mid C \in Code,\ ST \in Stack \}$

Table 6.1: Configurations of the abstract machine

sequence and similarly, we write $v{:}ST$ for the stack with v as its top element and ST as the remaining stack. The concatenation of two code fragments C_1 and C_2 is written $C_1\hat{\ }C_2$ and similarly for stacks. Finally, the code sequence $i_1{:}i_2{:}\cdots{:}i_k{:}\varepsilon$ is written $i_1{:}i_2{:}\cdots{:}i_k$ if $k>0$.

The *transition relation* is a binary relation $\to$ on configurations. The intuition is that

$$(C,ST) \to (C',ST')$$

means that the first instruction of C is executed and changes the configuration from (C,ST) to (C',ST'). The definition of the relation is summarized in Table 6.2 and will be explained in the remainder of this section.

We shall mostly be interested in *finite execution sequences* which are sequences, Δ, of the form

$$((C_0,ST_0), (C_1,ST_1), \cdots, (C_m,ST_m))$$

where

- $(C_i,ST_i) \to (C_{i+1},ST_{i+1})$ for all $i<m$, and
- there is no configuration (C,ST) such that $(C_m,ST_m) \to (C,ST)$.

To aid readability we often write Δ in the form

$$(C_0,ST_0) \to (C_1,ST_1) \to \cdots \to (C_m,ST_m)$$

and we shall write $\Delta(i)$ for (C_i,ST_i), and if $0 \le i \le j \le m$ we write $\Delta(i..j)$ for the subsequence $(\Delta(i),\cdots,\Delta(j))$ and $\Delta(i..)$ for the subsequence $\Delta(i..m)$. We shall feel

$$(\textsc{const}\ \mathbf{b}_i{:}C,\ v{:}ST) \rightarrow (C,\ \mathbf{b}_i{:}ST)$$

$$(\textsc{prim}\ o_i{:}C,\ v{:}ST) \rightarrow (C,\ \tilde{o}_i(v){:}ST)\ \text{if}\ \tilde{o}_i(v)\ \text{is defined}$$

$$(\textsc{prim}\ o_i{:}C,\ v{:}ST) \rightarrow (\textsc{prim}\ o_i{:}C,\ v{:}ST)\ \text{if}\ \tilde{o}_i(v)\ \text{is not defined}$$

$$(\textsc{enter}{:}C,\ v{:}ST) \rightarrow (C,\ v{:}v{:}ST)$$

$$(\textsc{switch}{:}C,\ v_1{:}v_2{:}ST) \rightarrow (C,\ v_2{:}v_1{:}ST)$$

$$(\textsc{branch}(C_1,C_2){:}C,\ \mathbf{true}{:}ST) \rightarrow (C_1\hat{}C,\ ST)$$

$$(\textsc{branch}(C_1,C_2){:}C,\ \mathbf{false}{:}ST) \rightarrow (C_2\hat{}C,\ ST)$$

$$(\textsc{tuple}{:}C,\ v_1{:}v_2{:}ST) \rightarrow (C,\ \langle v_1,v_2\rangle{:}ST)$$

$$(\textsc{fst}{:}C,\ \langle v_1,v_2\rangle{:}ST) \rightarrow (C,\ v_1{:}ST)$$

$$(\textsc{snd}{:}C,\ \langle v_1,v_2\rangle{:}ST) \rightarrow (C,\ v_2{:}ST)$$

$$(\textsc{cons}{:}C,\ v_1{:}v_2{:}ST) \rightarrow (C,\ [v_1{:}v_2]{:}ST)$$

$$(\textsc{nil}{:}C,\ v{:}ST) \rightarrow (C,\ []{:}ST)$$

$$(\textsc{hd}{:}C,\ [v_1{:}v_2]{:}ST) \rightarrow (C,\ v_1{:}ST)$$

$$(\textsc{hd}{:}C,\ []{:}ST) \rightarrow (\textsc{hd}{:}C,\ []{:}ST)$$

$$(\textsc{tl}{:}C,\ [v_1{:}v_2]{:}ST) \rightarrow (C,v_2{:}ST)$$

$$(\textsc{tl}{:}C,\ []{:}ST) \rightarrow (\textsc{tl}{:}C,\ []{:}ST)$$

$$(\textsc{isnil}{:}C,\ [v_1{:}v_2]{:}ST) \rightarrow (C,\ \mathbf{false}{:}ST)$$

$$(\textsc{isnil}{:}C,\ []{:}ST) \rightarrow (C,\ \mathbf{true}{:}ST)$$

$$(\textsc{curry}(C'){:}C,\ v{:}ST) \rightarrow (C,\ \{C';v\}{:}ST)$$

$$(\textsc{apply}{:}C,\ \{C';v_1\}{:}v_2{:}ST) \rightarrow (C,\ \{C',\langle v_1,v_2\rangle\}{:}ST)$$

$$(\textsc{delay}(C'){:}C,\ v{:}ST) \rightarrow (C,\ \{C',v\}{:}ST)$$

$$(\textsc{resume}{:}C,\ \{C',v\}{:}ST) \rightarrow (C'\hat{}\textsc{resume}\hat{}C,\ v{:}ST)$$

$$(\textsc{resume}{:}C,\ v{:}ST) \rightarrow (C,\ v{:}ST) \quad \text{otherwise}$$

$$(\textsc{callrec}(l,C'){:}C,\ ST) \rightarrow (C'[\textsc{callrec}(l,C')/l]\hat{}C,\ ST)$$

$$(\textsc{rec}{:}C,\ \{C';v\}{:}ST) \rightarrow (C,\ \{C',\langle v,v'\rangle\}{:}ST)$$

$$\text{where } v' = \{\textsc{rec}{:}\textsc{resume},\{C';v\}\}$$

Table 6.2: Transition relation for the abstract machine

free to write $\#\Delta$ for m and to call this the length of Δ even though there are in fact m+1 configurations in the sequence Δ.

Later we shall be interested in *infinite execution sequences* which are sequences,

Δ, of the form

$$((C_0,ST_0), (C_1,ST_1), \cdots, (C_m,ST_m), \cdots)$$

where

- $(C_i,ST_i) \rightarrow (C_{i+1},ST_{i+1})$ for all i.

To aid readability we often write Δ in the form

$$(C_0,ST_0) \rightarrow (C_1,ST_1) \rightarrow \cdots \rightarrow (C_m,ST_m) \rightarrow \cdots$$

and we shall write Δ(i) for (C_i,ST_i), and if $0 \leq i \leq j$ we write Δ(i..j) for the subsequence (Δ(i),$\cdots$,Δ(j)) and Δ(i..) for the subsequence (Δ(i),$\cdots$). We shall feel free to write $\#\Delta=\omega$ and to call ω the length of Δ.

It is convenient with notation for the execution sequences of various lengths. To this end we define

$$\begin{aligned}
\text{ExSeq}(*) &= \{\ \Delta \mid \Delta \text{ is a finite execution sequence }\} \\
\text{ExSeq}(m) &= \{\ \Delta \in \text{ExSeq}(*) \mid \#\Delta = m\ \} \\
\text{ExSeq}(\omega) &= \{\ \Delta \mid \Delta \text{ is an infinite execution sequence }\} \\
\text{ExSeq}(\infty) &= \text{ExSeq}(*) \cup \text{ExSeq}(\omega)
\end{aligned}$$

Often it is convenient with notation for the execution sequences that start with a specific code component or stack component. To this end we define

$$\begin{aligned}
\text{ExSeq}(\ell,C) &= \{\ \Delta \in \text{ExSeq}(\ell) \mid \exists ST\text{: } \Delta(0) = (C,ST)\ \} \\
\text{ExSeq}(\ell,C,v) &= \{\ \Delta \in \text{ExSeq}(\ell,C) \mid \Delta(0) = (C,[v])\ \}
\end{aligned}$$

where ℓ is any one of $*$, m, ω or ∞.

In later developments we shall exploit that the machine defined by Table 6.2 is in fact deterministic:

Fact 6.1.1 For all code sequences $C \in \mathit{Code}$ and values $v \in \mathit{Val}$, the set

$$\text{ExSeq}(\infty,C,v)$$

is a singleton; this means that there is precisely one (finite or infinite) execution sequence Δ with $\Delta(0) = (C,[v])$. □

6.1.1 First order aspects of the abstract machine

The machine has an unspecified set of *base values* $\mathbf{b}_i$ ($i \in I$). We shall assume that we have base values $\mathbf{b}_{\text{true}}$ and $\mathbf{b}_{\text{false}}$, written **true** and **false**, for the booleans and $\mathbf{b}_0$, $\mathbf{b}_1$, $\mathbf{b}_{-1}$, $\cdots$, written $\mathbf{0}$, $\mathbf{1}$, $-\mathbf{1}$, $\cdots$, for the integers. The base values are used to build composite values like

- *pairs* of the form $\langle v_1, v_2 \rangle$,
- *lists* which may be empty, written $[\,]$, or non-empty, written $[v_1{:}v_2]$ where v_1 is the head and v_2 the tail of the list,
- *closures* of the form $\{C;v\}$ where C is a code sequence — these values represent functions and will be discussed in Subsection 6.1.4, and
- *thunks* of the form $\{C,v\}$ where C is a code sequence — these values represent the eventual outcome of executing C on a stack with v on top; however, the actual execution has been postponed.

We shall assume that the representation of the various values in the machine allow to determine whether a value is a base value, a pair, a list, a closure or a thunk. In particular, if $\mathbf{b}_i = \mathbf{b}_j$ then i=j and no $\mathbf{b}_i$ has the form $\langle \cdots, \cdots \rangle$, $[\,]$, $[\cdots{:}\cdots]$, $\{\cdots;\cdots\}$ or $\{\cdots,\cdots\}$.

For each base value $\mathbf{b}_i$ the machine has an instruction CONST $\mathbf{b}_i$ that pops the stack and pushes the value $\mathbf{b}_i$ on top of it. Furthermore, there is an unspecified set of primitive operations o_i ($i \in I$). An example is o_+, written $+$, and its semantics is given by

$$\tilde{+}(v) = n_1 + n_2 \text{ if } v = \langle n_1, n_2 \rangle \text{ and } n_1 \text{ and } n_2 \text{ are integers.}$$

Note that if the top of the stack does not have the expected form then PRIM o_i will cause the machine to *enter a loop* (rather than simply stop).

The machine has instructions for building composite values on the stack and for taking them apart. As an example TUPLE builds a pair from two values on the stack and FST and SND extract components from a pair. Similar remarks hold for CONS, HD and TL with the addition that if the stack top is the special value $[\,]$ then the machine will loop rather than simply stop. The instruction NIL replaces the stack top with $[\,]$ and ISNIL tests the form of the stack top. In addition to this there are a few general instructions: ENTER and SWITCH rearrange the stack and BRANCH(C_1,C_2) is a conditional whose outcome depends on the value on top of the stack.

The instructions CALLREC(l,C), CALL l and REC handle recursion and will be discussed in Subsections 6.1.3 and 6.1.4. The instructions CURRY(C) and APPLY cope with closures and will be discussed in Subsection 6.1.4.

The thunks are central for achieving laziness in that they represent computations that are postponed. The instruction DELAY(C) will construct a thunk from the code C and the value on top of the stack. The postponed computation may be initiated by the RESUME instruction and it will repeat itself until the postponed computation eventually terminates with a 'non-thunk' value. This is illustrated in the following example.

Example 6.1.2 The instruction PRIM + will add the two components of a pair of integers on top of the stack. However, the addition may appear in a context where the top of the stack is a thunk, for example

$$\{\text{ENTER:CONST } \mathbf{1}\text{:TUPLE,}\mathbf{7}\},$$

and the machine will enter a loop when started in the configuration

$$(\text{PRIM } +,\ [\{\text{ENTER:CONST } \mathbf{1}\text{:TUPLE,}\mathbf{7}\}]).$$

To overcome this we will have to use the RESUME instruction to evaluate the thunk and we obtain the finite execution sequence

$$\begin{array}{l}
(\text{RESUME:PRIM } +,\ [\{\text{ENTER:CONST } \mathbf{1}\text{:TUPLE,}\mathbf{7}\}]) \to \\
(\text{ENTER:CONST } \mathbf{1}\text{:TUPLE:RESUME:PRIM } +,\ [\mathbf{7}]) \to \\
(\text{CONST } \mathbf{1}\text{:TUPLE:RESUME:PRIM } +,\ [\mathbf{7},\mathbf{7}]) \to \\
(\text{TUPLE:RESUME:PRIM } +,\ [\mathbf{1},\mathbf{7}]) \to \\
(\text{RESUME:PRIM } +,\ [\langle\mathbf{1},\mathbf{7}\rangle]) \to \\
(\text{PRIM } +,\ [\langle\mathbf{1},\mathbf{7}\rangle]) \to \\
(\varepsilon,\ [\mathbf{8}])
\end{array}$$

In general, the top of the stack may be a thunk that evaluates to a pair of thunks and each component must then be evaluated before the addition can take place. So the general code for addition will be

RESUME:ENTER:SND:RESUME:SWITCH:FST:RESUME:TUPLE:PRIM +

6.1.2 First order aspects of the coding interpretation

We shall follow the approach of Chapter 5 and specify the code generation as an interpretation **K**. At first sight one may expect the type part of **K** to have $\mathbf{K}(t_1 \underline{\rightarrow} t_2) = \mathit{Code}_\perp$ for all frontier types $t_1 \underline{\rightarrow} t_2$ because this reflects the generation of code for the computations to be performed at run-time. However, when coming to recursion we have to generate *relocatable code* in order to get fresh labels. Instead of $\mathit{Code}_\perp$ we shall therefore use the domain

$$\mathbf{RelCode} = N \to (\mathit{Code}_\perp)$$

where N is the set of natural numbers or the discrete partial order $(N,=)$, and where the ordering $\sqsubseteq$ is defined by

$$\mathbf{K}(\texttt{Tuple}[t_0 \underline{\rightarrow} t_1 \underline{\times} t_2]) = \lambda RC_1.\lambda RC_2.\lambda d.
\begin{cases} \text{ENTER:DELAY}(RC_2(d))\text{:SWITCH:DELAY}(RC_1(d))\text{:TUPLE} \\ \qquad \text{if } RC_1(d) \neq \bot \text{ and } RC_2(d) \neq \bot \\ \bot \qquad \text{otherwise} \end{cases}$$

$$\mathbf{K}(\texttt{Fst}[t_1 \underline{\times} t_2]) = \lambda d.\text{RESUME:FST:RESUME}$$

$$\mathbf{K}(\texttt{Snd}[t_1 \underline{\times} t_2]) = \lambda d.\text{RESUME:SND:RESUME}$$

$$\mathbf{K}(\texttt{Cons}[t_0 \underline{\rightarrow} t_1 \underline{\texttt{list}}]) = \lambda RC_1.\lambda RC_2.\lambda d.
\begin{cases} \text{ENTER:DELAY}(RC_2(d))\text{:SWITCH:DELAY}(RC_1(d))\text{:CONS} \\ \qquad \text{if } RC_1(d) \neq \bot \text{ and } RC_2(d) \neq \bot \\ \bot \qquad \text{otherwise} \end{cases}$$

$$\mathbf{K}(\texttt{Nil}[t_0 \underline{\rightarrow} t_1 \underline{\texttt{list}}]) = \lambda d.\text{NIL}$$

$$\mathbf{K}(\texttt{Hd}[t]) = \lambda d.\text{RESUME:HD:RESUME}$$

$$\mathbf{K}(\texttt{Tl}[t]) = \lambda d.\text{RESUME:TL:RESUME}$$

$$\mathbf{K}(\texttt{Isnil}[t]) = \lambda d.\text{RESUME:ISNIL}$$

Table 6.3: The coding interpretation **K** (part 1)

$$RC_1 \sqsubseteq RC_2 \text{ if and only if } \forall d \in N\text{: } RC_1(d) = \bot \vee RC_1(d) = RC_2(d)$$

To see that **RelCode** is indeed a domain it suffices to observe that it is isomorphic to $(N_\bot) \rightarrow_s (\mathit{Code}_\bot)$ which is a domain (Construction 5.1.19). We shall then define

$$\mathbf{K}(t_1 \underline{\rightarrow} t_2) = \mathbf{RelCode}$$

for all frontier types $t_1 \underline{\rightarrow} t_2$.

The interpretation of the operators is specified in Tables 6.3, 6.4 and 6.5 and will be explained in the remainder of this section. The code generation will obey the following rules:

A: The code makes no assumptions about whether the initial value on top of the stack is a thunk or not.

B: If the execution of the code terminates then the top of the stack will never be a thunk, and except for the top value, the stacks in the initial and final configurations will be the same.

In Section 6.3 we shall formally prove that this is indeed the case. But for now we turn towards explaining the code generation.

First consider the clause for $\texttt{Fst}[t_1 \underline{\times} t_2]$:

$$\mathbf{K}(\texttt{Fst}[t_1 \underline{\times} t_2]) = \lambda d.\text{RESUME:FST:RESUME}$$

$$\mathbf{K}(\mathtt{f_i}[t]) = \mathbf{f}_i^t$$

where $\mathbf{f}_i^t$ are unspecified elements in $[\![t]\!](\mathbf{K})$

$$\mathbf{K}(\mathtt{F_i}[t_0\underline{\rightarrow}t_1]) = \lambda d.\ \mathbf{F}_i^{t_0\underline{\rightarrow}t_1}$$

where $\mathbf{F}_i^{t_0\underline{\rightarrow}t_1}$ are unspecified elements in $Code_\bot$

$$\mathbf{K}(\Box[(t_1\underline{\rightarrow}t_2)\times(t_0\underline{\rightarrow}t_1)]) = \lambda RC_1.\lambda RC_2.\lambda d.$$
$$\begin{cases} \text{DELAY}(RC_2(d)):(RC_1(d)) \\ \qquad \text{if } RC_1(d) \neq \bot \text{ and } RC_2(d) \neq \bot \\ \bot \quad \text{otherwise} \end{cases}$$

$$\mathbf{K}(\mathtt{Id}[t]) = \lambda d.\text{RESUME}$$

$$\mathbf{K}(\mathtt{True}[t]) = \lambda d.\text{CONST } \mathbf{true}$$

$$\mathbf{K}(\mathtt{False}[t]) = \lambda d.\text{CONST } \mathbf{false}$$

$$\mathbf{K}(\mathtt{Cond}[t_0\underline{\rightarrow}t_1]) = \lambda RC_1.\lambda RC_2.\lambda RC_3.\lambda d.$$
$$\begin{cases} \text{ENTER}:(RC_1(d)):\text{BRANCH}(RC_2(d),RC_3(d)) \\ \qquad \text{if } RC_1(d) \neq \bot,\ RC_2(d) \neq \bot \text{ and } RC_3(d) \neq \bot \\ \bot \quad \text{otherwise} \end{cases}$$

Table 6.4: The coding interpretation **K** (part 2)

To fulfill condition **A** we first execute a RESUME instruction. If necessary this will replace the top of the stack with a value that is not a thunk. If it is a pair we can execute FST to select its first component. This may or may not be a thunk and in order to fulfill condition **B** we execute yet another RESUME instruction. The code generated for `Snd`, `Hd` and `Tl` is similar. In the case of `Isnil` we can dispense with the last RESUME instruction because the instruction ISNIL never produces a thunk as result. In the case of `True`, `False` and `Nil` we must dispense with the initial RESUME instruction in order to behave in a lazy way and we can dispense with the last RESUME instruction because CONST **true**, CONST **false** and NIL never leave a thunk on top of the stack. Also note that the code generated for `Id` is a single RESUME instruction so that condition **B** will be fulfilled.

The interpretation of `Tuple`, □, `Cons` and `Cond` shows how code fragments supplied as parameters may be composed to produce new code fragments. Consider the clause for `Tuple`:

$$\mathbf{K}(\mathtt{Tuple}[t_0\underline{\rightarrow}t_1\underline{\times}t_2]) = \lambda RC_1.\lambda RC_2.\lambda d.$$
$$\begin{cases} \text{ENTER:DELAY}(RC_2(d)):\text{SWITCH:DELAY}(RC_1(d)):\text{TUPLE} \\ \qquad \text{if } RC_1(d) \neq \bot \text{ and } RC_2(d) \neq \bot \\ \bot \quad \text{otherwise} \end{cases}$$

First note that we only generate 'proper' code if $RC_1(d)$ and $RC_2(d)$ are indeed code fragments. The DELAY instructions are used because $RC_1(d)$ and $RC_2(d)$

$$\mathbf{K}(\texttt{fix}[t]) = \text{FIX where FIX}(H) = \bigsqcup_n H^n(\bot)$$
$$\text{if } t \text{ is pure}$$

$$\mathbf{K}(\texttt{fix}[t_1 \underline{\rightarrow} t_2]) = \lambda H.\lambda d. \begin{cases} \text{CALLREC}(d, H(\lambda d'.\text{CALL } d)(d+1)) \\ \qquad \text{if } H(\lambda d'.\text{CALL } d)(d+1) \neq \bot \\ \bot \quad \text{otherwise} \end{cases}$$

$$\mathbf{K}(\texttt{fix}[t_1 \times t_2]) = \lambda H.(H_1, H_2(H_1)) \text{ where}$$
$$H_1 = \mathbf{K}(\texttt{fix}[t_1])(\lambda \mathrm{v}_1.\mathrm{w}_1 \text{ where } (\mathrm{w}_1,\mathrm{w}_2) = H((\mathrm{v}_1, H_2(\mathrm{v}_1)))),$$
$$H_2 = \lambda \mathrm{v}_1.\mathbf{K}(\texttt{fix}[t_2])(\lambda \mathrm{v}_2.\mathrm{w}_2 \text{ where } (\mathrm{w}_1,\mathrm{w}_2) = H((\mathrm{v}_1,\mathrm{v}_2)))$$
$$\text{and } t_1 \times t_2 \text{ is composite but not pure}$$

$$\mathbf{K}(\texttt{Curry}[t_0 \underline{\rightarrow} (t_1 \underline{\rightarrow} t_2)]) = \lambda RC.\lambda d. \begin{cases} \text{CURRY}(RC(d)) & \text{if } RC(d) \neq \bot \\ \bot & \text{otherwise} \end{cases}$$

$$\mathbf{K}(\texttt{Apply}[t_0 \underline{\rightarrow} t_1]) = \lambda d.\ \text{RESUME:ENTER:SND:SWITCH:FST:RESUME:APPLY:RESUME}$$

$$\mathbf{K}(\texttt{Fix}[t]) = \lambda d.\ \text{RESUME:REC:RESUME}$$

Table 6.5: The coding interpretation **K** (part 3)

are supposed to fulfill condition **B** so that they will execute to produce non-thunk values. However, in a lazy setting this is not permissible and we postpone the computations using the DELAY instruction. The ENTER, SWITCH and TUPLE instructions ensure that the postponed computations are given the same argument and that the pair is constructed on top of the stack. Note that it is not necessary to start with a RESUME instruction in order to fulfill condition **A** nor is it necessary to end with a RESUME instruction in order to fulfill condition **B**. The interpretation of `Cons` is similar to that for `Tuple`.

Next consider the clause for $\Box$:

$$\mathbf{K}(\Box[(t_1 \underline{\rightarrow} t_2) \times (t_0 \underline{\rightarrow} t_1)]) = \lambda RC_1.\lambda RC_2.\lambda d. \begin{cases} \text{DELAY}(RC_2(d)) \text{:} (RC_1(d)) \\ \qquad \text{if } RC_1(d) \neq \bot \text{ and } RC_2(d) \neq \bot \\ \bot \quad \text{otherwise} \end{cases}$$

At first sight one might expect that the correct code is $RC_2(d)$:$RC_1(d)$ but in a lazy setting we must avoid executing $RC_2(d)$ if the result is not used by $RC_1(d)$. Since $RC_2(d)$ is assumed to fulfill condition **B** we therefore postpone the execution of the code fragment using the DELAY instruction. Because $RC_1(d)$ fulfills condition **A** it will initiate the postponed computation if necessary. The combined code will fulfill condition **A** as well as **B**.

The interpretation of `Cond` is straightforward as there is no need to postpone parts of the computations of a conditional.

The interpretation **K** will specify how to generate code for the various constants of type $t_0 \underline{\rightarrow} t_1$. An example is `+`[$\underline{\texttt{Int}}\underline{\times}\underline{\texttt{Int}}\underline{\rightarrow}\underline{\texttt{Int}}$] where we use

$$\mathbf{K}(\texttt{+}[\underline{\texttt{Int}}\underline{\times}\underline{\texttt{Int}}\underline{\rightarrow}\underline{\texttt{Int}}]) = \lambda d.\text{RESUME:ENTER:SND:RESUME:} \\ \text{SWITCH:FST:RESUME:TUPLE:PRIM } +$$

as explained in Example 6.1.2. The code will fulfill conditions **A** and **B**. Another example is `Zero`[$\underline{\texttt{Int}}\underline{\rightarrow}\underline{\texttt{Int}}$] where we use

$$\mathbf{K}(\texttt{Zero}[\underline{\texttt{Int}}\underline{\rightarrow}\underline{\texttt{Int}}]) = \lambda d.\text{CONST } \mathbf{0}$$

Example 6.1.3 Consider the expression

$$\texttt{Tuple}(\texttt{Fst}[\underline{\texttt{Int}}\underline{\times}\underline{\texttt{Int}}],\texttt{Snd}[\underline{\texttt{Int}}\underline{\times}\underline{\texttt{Int}}])$$

The interpretation **K** gives the element

$$\lambda \mathbf{env}.\lambda d.\text{ENTER:DELAY(RESUME:SND:RESUME):} \\ \text{SWITCH:DELAY(RESUME:FST:RESUME):} \\ \text{TUPLE}$$

of the domain **Void** → **RelCode**. Given a void environment and a relocation parameter we see that the code generated will *always* terminate when executed. This is contrary to the code generated for `Id` which in certain cases may loop. Thus the code generated by **K** behaves in much the same way as the interpretation **S** of Chapter 5. □

6.1.3 Recursion

The interpretation of `fix`[t] depends on the actual form of t. We already saw this happening in Chapter 5 when specifying **S** but the reasons here will be even more compelling. In the case of pure types, that is types that do not contain any run-time constituents, we simply have

$$\mathbf{K}(\texttt{fix}[t]) = \text{FIX where FIX}(H) = \bigsqcup_n H^n(\bot)$$

as in the standard interpretations of Chapter 5.

The case where $t = t_1 \underline{\rightarrow} t_2$ is more interesting because we are to generate code. The idea is that the instruction CALLREC(l,C') defines a label l and its associated piece of code C'. Whenever the instruction CALL l appears in C' it is interpreted as a recursive call to the label l. This is reflected in the operational semantics of the machine where we have

$$(\text{CALLREC}(l,C'){:}C,\ ST) \rightarrow (C'[\text{CALLREC}(l,C')/l]\hat{\ }C,\ ST)$$

In general the effect of the substitution $\Sigma = [C_1,\cdots,C_n/l_1,\cdots,l_n]$ (where the l_i's are all distinct) is defined by

$$(C\hat{\ }C')[\Sigma] = (C[\Sigma])\hat{\ }(C'[\Sigma])$$

$$(\textsc{const}\ \mathbf{b}_i)[\Sigma] = \textsc{const}\ \mathbf{b}_i$$

$$\vdots$$

$$(\textsc{branch}(C,C'))[\Sigma] = \textsc{branch}(C[\Sigma],C'[\Sigma])$$

$$\vdots$$

$$(\textsc{callrec}(l,C))[\Sigma] =$$

$$\begin{cases} \textsc{callrec}(l,C[\Sigma']) \text{ if } l = l_i \text{ and where} \\ \qquad \Sigma' = [C_1,\cdots,C_{i-1},C_{i+1},\cdots,C_n/l_1,\cdots,l_{i-1},l_{i+1},\cdots,l_n] \\ \textsc{callrec}(l,C[\Sigma]) \text{ if } l \neq l_i \text{ for all i, } 1 \leq i \leq n \end{cases}$$

$$(\textsc{call}\ l)[\Sigma] = \begin{cases} C_i & \text{if } l = l_i \\ \textsc{call}\ l & \text{if } l \neq l_i \text{ for all i, } 1 \leq i \leq n \end{cases}$$

Note that the effect of the substitution is very similar to that of the λ-calculus except that $\textsc{callrec}(l,C)[\Sigma]$ does not consider the situation where some C_i contains the instruction CALL l. The reason is that this situation will never arise in the code generation.

The actual code generated for $\mathbf{K}(\mathtt{fix}[t_1 \underline{\rightarrow} t_2])$ is given by

$$\mathbf{K}(\mathtt{fix}[t_1 \underline{\rightarrow} t_2]) = \lambda H.\lambda d.$$

$$\begin{cases} \textsc{callrec}(d,H(\lambda d'.\textsc{call}\ d)(d+1)) \\ \qquad \text{if } H(\lambda d'.\textsc{call}\ d)(d+1) \neq \bot \\ \bot \quad \text{otherwise} \end{cases}$$

The idea is that H is the relocatable code for the body of the recursive definition but with holes for where the recursive calls are to be inserted. This means that $H(\lambda d'.\textsc{call}\ d)(d+1)$ will insert the instruction CALL d in the holes and the code itself will be relocated from $d+1$ rather than d. When executing the CALLREC instruction the intended effect of the substitution is to insert the CALLREC instruction itself into the holes in the code for the body, so that the resulting code is $H(\lambda d'.\textsc{callrec}(d,H(\lambda d'.\textsc{call}\ d)(d+1)))(d+1)$.

We may note, in passing, that a more realistic scheme would have configurations to be triples (C,ST,ENV) where ENV maps labels to their code. Then CALL d would simply expand into $ENV(d)$, we would have no CALLREC instruction, and rather than generate $\textsc{callrec}(d,C)$ one would generate CALL d and update ENV to map d to C.

Example 6.1.4 To illustrate the relocatability of the code consider an expression of the form

$$\mathtt{fix}(\lambda f[t \underline{\rightarrow} t].\cdots f \cdots \mathtt{fix}(\lambda g[t \underline{\rightarrow} t].\cdots g \cdots f \cdots)\cdots)$$

The overall code will have the form

$$\text{CALLREC}(d,\mathbf{F}(\lambda d'.\text{CALL } d)(d+1))$$

The idea is that the function **F** corresponds to the argument of the outermost fixed point and has the form

$$\lambda RC_f.\lambda d'.\cdots:(RC_f(d')):\cdots:\widetilde{\mathbf{G}}(d'):\cdots$$

where $\widetilde{\mathbf{G}}(d')$ is the code for the inner fixed point but relocated from d'. Thus the idea is that $\widetilde{\mathbf{G}}(d')$ has the form

$$\text{CALLREC}(d',\mathbf{G}(\lambda d''.\text{CALL } d')(d'+1))$$

where **G** has the form

$$\lambda RC_g.\lambda d''.\cdots:(RC_g(d'')):\cdots:(RC_f(d'')):\cdots$$

Rewriting the earlier clause for $\widetilde{\mathbf{G}}(d')$ we see that is has the form

$$\text{CALLREC}(d',\cdots:\text{CALL } d':\cdots:(RC_f(d'+1)):\cdots)$$

Returning to **F** we see that it has the form

$$\lambda RC_f.\lambda d'.\cdots:(RC_f(d')):\cdots:$$
$$\text{CALLREC}(d',\cdots:\text{CALL } d':\cdots:(RC_f(d'+1)):\cdots):\cdots$$

and thereby the overall code generated for the outermost fixed point will have the form

$$\text{CALLREC}(d,\cdots:\text{CALL } d:\cdots:$$
$$\text{CALLREC}(d+1,\cdots:\text{CALL } d+1:\cdots:$$
$$\text{CALL } d:\cdots):\cdots)$$

Example 6.1.5 Consider the expression of the $\mathbf{sum}'_{9B}$ program of Section 4.3. The semantics under the interpretation **K** is the function

```
λenv.λd.
DELAY(ENTER:DELAY(RESUME):
    SWITCH:DELAY(CONST 0):
    TUPLE):
CALLREC(d,
ENTER:DELAY(RESUME:SND:RESUME):RESUME:ISNIL:
BRANCH(RESUME:FST:RESUME,
    DELAY(ENTER:
          DELAY(DELAY(ENTER:
```

```
                              DELAY(DELAY(RESUME:SND:RESUME):
                                    RESUME:TL:RESUME):
                              SWITCH:
                              DELAY(RESUME:FST:RESUME):
                              TUPLE):CALL d):
                SWITCH:
                DELAY(DELAY(RESUME:SND:RESUME):
                      RESUME:HD:RESUME):
                TUPLE):
          RESUME:ENTER:SND:RESUME:
                SWITCH:FST:RESUME:TUPLE:PRIM +))
```

where we have used the definition of **K**(+) given in Subsection 6.1.2. □

Example 6.1.6 A somewhat simpler `sum` program would be the following:

```
VAL fix(λg[Int list → Int].
        Cond(Isnil[Int],
             Zero[Int list → Int],
             +[Int×Int→Int] □ Tuple(Hd[Int], g □ Tl[Int])))
HAS Int list → list
```

Here our code generation **K** is able to generate better code than in Example 6.1.5:

```
λenv.λd.
CALLREC(d, ENTER:RESUME:ISNIL:
           BRANCH(CONST 0,
                  DELAY(ENTER:
                        DELAY(DELAY(RESUME:TL:RESUME):
                              CALL d):
                        SWITCH:
                        DELAY(RESUME:HD:RESUME):
                        TUPLE):
                  RESUME:ENTER:SND:RESUME:
                  SWITCH:FST:RESUME:TUPLE:PRIM +))
```

We shall return to this particular example in Chapters 7 and 8 and show how an even more substantial improvement can be obtained. □

Consider now the case where the type t of $\texttt{fix}[t]$ has the form $t_1 \times t_2$ but is not pure. Assuming that $\mathbf{K}(\texttt{fix}[t_1])$ and $\mathbf{K}(\texttt{fix}[t_2])$ are well-defined we define

$$\mathbf{K}(\texttt{fix}[t_1 \times t_2]) = \lambda H.(H_1, H_2(H_1))$$

where

$$H_1 = \mathbf{K}(\texttt{fix}[t_1])(\lambda \mathbf{v}_1.\mathbf{w}_1 \text{ where } (\mathbf{w}_1,\mathbf{w}_2){=}H((\mathbf{v}_1,H_2(\mathbf{v}_1))))$$
$$H_2 = \lambda \mathbf{v}_1.\mathbf{K}(\texttt{fix}[t_2])(\lambda \mathbf{v}_2.\mathbf{w}_2 \text{ where } (\mathbf{w}_1,\mathbf{w}_2){=}H((\mathbf{v}_1,\mathbf{v}_2)))$$

As in Chapter 5 we may remark that this is motivated by Lemma 5.2.6 (an 'analogue' of Bekic's Theorem). To appreciate the definition consider the case where both t_1 and t_2 have the form $t\underline{\rightarrow}t$. Then the expression would typically have the form

$$\texttt{fix}(\lambda \texttt{f}[t_1{\times}t_2].(\cdots\ \texttt{fst f}\ \cdots\ \texttt{snd f}\ \cdots\ ,\ \cdots\ \texttt{fst f}\ \cdots\ \texttt{snd f}\ \cdots))$$

and the function H is

$$\lambda(RC_1,RC_2).(\lambda d.\cdots RC_1(d)\cdots RC_2(d)\cdots,\ \lambda d.\cdots RC_1(d)\cdots RC_2(d)\cdots)$$

Thus

$$H_1 = \lambda d.\text{CALLREC}(d,\cdots{:}\text{CALL } d{:}\cdots{:}H_2(\lambda d'.\text{CALL } d)(d{+}1){:}\cdots)$$
$$H_2 = \lambda RC_1.\lambda d.\text{CALLREC}(d,\cdots{:}(RC_1(d{+}1)){:}\cdots{:}\text{CALL } d{:}\cdots)$$

and thereby

$$\begin{aligned} H_1 = \lambda d.\text{CALLREC}(d,&\cdots{:}\text{CALL } d{:}\cdots{:}\\ &\text{CALLREC}(d{+}1,\cdots{:}\text{CALL } d{:}\cdots{:}\\ &\qquad \text{CALL } d{+}1{:}\cdots){:}\cdots) \end{aligned}$$

$$\begin{aligned} H_2(H_1) = \lambda d.\text{CALLREC}(d,&\cdots{:}\\ &\text{CALLREC}(d{+}1,\cdots{:}\text{CALL } d{+}1{:}\cdots{:}\\ &\qquad \text{CALLREC}(d{+}2,\cdots{:}\text{CALL } d{+}1{:}\cdots{:}\\ &\qquad\qquad \text{CALL } d{+}2{:}\cdots){:}\\ &\qquad \cdots){:}\\ &\cdots{:}\text{CALL } d{:}\cdots) \end{aligned}$$

6.1.4 Higher-order aspects

Closures of the form $\{C;v\}$ are used to represent functions as data objects. The closures differ from the thunks in that they must be supplied with an additional argument in order to be ready for execution. One builds closures using the CURRY instruction; the APPLY instruction then incorporates the additional argument and thereby transforms the closure into a thunk.

The CURRY instruction corresponds directly to the `Curry` construct of the language and this is reflected in

$$\mathbf{K}(\texttt{Curry}[t_0\underline{\rightarrow}(t_1\underline{\rightarrow}t_2)]) = \lambda RC.\lambda d.$$
$$\begin{cases} \text{CURRY}(RC(d)) & \text{if } RC(d) \neq \bot \\ \bot & \text{otherwise} \end{cases}$$

The clause for $\texttt{Apply}[t_1\underline{\rightarrow}t_2]$ is slightly more complicated for much the same reason that $\mathbf{K}(\texttt{+})$ is not simply $\lambda d.\text{PRIM} +$. In the standard semantics `Apply` is given a pair as argument where the first component must be a function. Thus the code generated for `Apply` must manipulate the top of the stack such that its first component is a closure and not a thunk (that would evaluate to a closure, once RESUME'd). This motivates defining:

$$\mathbf{K}(\texttt{Apply}[t_0\underline{\rightarrow}t_1]) = \text{RESUME:ENTER:SND:SWITCH:}$$
$$\text{FST:RESUME:APPLY:RESUME}$$

where the final RESUME instruction ensures that condition **B** is fulfilled.

Example 6.1.7 Consider the expression $\texttt{twice}_3$ of Example 4.1.6:

$$\begin{aligned}\texttt{twice}_3 = \texttt{Curry}\ (&\\ &\texttt{Apply}[\underline{\texttt{Int}\rightarrow\texttt{Int}}] \square \texttt{Tuple(Fst}[(\underline{\texttt{Int}\rightarrow\texttt{Int}})\underline{\times}\underline{\texttt{Int}}],\\ &\texttt{Apply}[\underline{\texttt{Int}\rightarrow\texttt{Int}}] \square \texttt{Tuple(Fst}[(\underline{\texttt{Int}\rightarrow\texttt{Int}})\underline{\times}\underline{\texttt{Int}}],\\ &\texttt{Snd}[(\underline{\texttt{Int}\rightarrow\texttt{Int}})\underline{\times}\underline{\texttt{Int}}])))\end{aligned}$$

We then get

$$[\![\texttt{twice}_3]\!](\mathbf{K}) = \lambda\text{env}.\lambda d.$$

```
CURRY(DELAY(ENTER:
            DELAY(DELAY(ENTER:
                        DELAY(RESUME:SND:RESUME):
                        SWITCH:
                        DELAY(RESUME:FST:RESUME):
                        TUPLE):
                  RESUME:ENTER:SND:SWITCH:
                     FST:RESUME:APPLY:RESUME):
            SWITCH:
            DELAY(RESUME:FST:RESUME):
            TUPLE):
      RESUME:ENTER:SND:SWITCH:
         FST:RESUME:APPLY:RESUME)
```

as the code of $\texttt{twice}_3$ under the interpretation **K**. □

Finally, we consider the code generated for the construct $\texttt{Fix}[t]$. The idea is that the top of the stack contains a closure and we must compute the fixed point of the corresponding function. We define

$$\mathbf{K}(\texttt{Fix}[t]) = \lambda d.\ \text{RESUME:REC:RESUME}$$

where the first RESUME instruction ensures that the top of the stack is a closure (and not a thunk that may evaluate to a closure) and the second RESUME instruction ensures that condition **B** is fulfilled. To explain the use of the REC instruction we first recall that its operational semantics is

$$(\text{REC}{:}C,\ \{C';v\}{:}ST) \rightarrow (C,\ \{C',\langle v,v'\rangle\}{:}ST)$$
$$\text{where } v' = \{\text{REC:RESUME},\{C';v\}\}$$

The idea is then that C' must be supplied with a pair $\langle v,v'\rangle$ such that v is the argument (corresponding to the free variables) and v' is a fixed point of the function represented by the closure. This fixed point can be written $\{\text{REC:RESUME},\{C';v\}\}$ and the purpose of the RESUME instruction is to ensure that condition **B** is fulfilled. — One may regard this RESUME instruction as being superfluous because whenever v' is RESUME'd the code will have the form RESUME:C and is thus transformed to REC:RESUME:RESUME:C. However, to simplify the proofs in the remainder of this chapter we shall retain the superfluous RESUME instruction.

6.2 The Substitution Property

In the remainder of this chapter we shall formulate and verify the claim that the code generated agrees with the semantics. This is a rather laborious task which we shall approach in stages and where we ignore lists in order to cut down on the complexity. The first stage aims at establishing a substitution property which will ensure that $\mathbf{K}(\mathtt{fix}[t\underline{\rightarrow}t])$ will only be applied to functions that may indeed be regarded as relocatable code sequences with holes in them.

To motivate the need for this stage it is helpful to temporarily ignore the relocation parameter, i.e. to temporarily assume that **RelCode** equals *Code*. Consider now some frontier type $t\underline{\rightarrow}t$ and some $F\in[\![(t\underline{\rightarrow}t)\rightarrow(t\underline{\rightarrow}t)]\!](\mathbf{K})$. We then have

$$\mathbf{K}(\mathtt{fix})(F) = \text{CALLREC}(\bullet,F(\text{CALL }\bullet))$$

where the intention is that F is a code sequence with holes in it. It would then be helpful if

$$F(\mathbf{K}(\mathtt{fix})(F)) = F(\text{CALLREC}(\bullet,F(\text{CALL }\bullet)))$$

and

$$F(\text{CALL }\bullet)[\mathbf{K}(\mathtt{fix})(F)/\bullet] =$$
$$F(\text{CALL }\bullet)[\text{CALLREC}(\bullet,F(\text{CALL }\bullet))/\bullet]$$

were to agree. To see this note that if we execute $(\mathbf{K}(\mathtt{fix})(F),ST)$ for one step we obtain

$$(F(\text{CALL }\bullet)[\mathbf{K}(\texttt{fix})(F)/\bullet],ST)$$

and since $\mathbf{K}(\texttt{fix})(F)$ is to be a 'kind of fixed point' of F it would be helpful if this configuration was equal to

$$(F(\mathbf{K}(\texttt{fix})(F)),ST)$$

so that the effect of CALLREC($\bullet,\cdots$) indeed is to unfold the fixed point one level. However, this need not be the case as is illustrated by setting

$$F(x) = \begin{cases} \text{FST} & \text{if } x \text{ is of the form CALLREC}(\bullet,\cdots) \\ \text{SND} & \text{otherwise} \end{cases}$$

Luckily this is a contrived example. Even though F is a genuine element[1] of $[\![(t\underline{\rightarrow}t)\rightarrow(t\underline{\rightarrow}t)]\!](\mathbf{K})$ it should be *intuitively* clear that F cannot arise during code generation, that is F does not equal $[\![e]\!](\mathbf{K})(\mathbf{env})$ for any expression e. Our task in the remainder of this section is to make this clear in a *formal* setting. To this end, the set FreeLab(C) of free labels in the code sequence C may be defined inductively on the structure of code sequences. The more important clauses are:

$$\begin{aligned}
&\text{FreeLab}(C_1\hat{\ }C_2) = \text{FreeLab}(C_1) \cup \text{FreeLab}(C_2)\\
&\text{FreeLab}(\text{DELAY}(C)) = \text{FreeLab}(C)\\
&\text{FreeLab}(\text{CALL}(d)) = \{d\}\\
&\text{FreeLab}(\text{CALLREC}(d,C)) = \text{FreeLab}(C)\backslash\{d\}
\end{aligned}$$

Recall that in the previous section we wrote a substitution Σ in the form

$$[C_1,\cdots,C_k/l_1,\cdots,l_k]$$

In this section we shall regard a substitution Σ as a partial function from numbers to code sequences subject to certain conditions. The set **Subst** of substitutions is then defined by

$$\mathbf{Subst} = \{\Sigma{:}N\hookrightarrow \mathit{Code} \mid \text{dom}(\Sigma) \text{ is finite } \wedge \\ \forall l{\in}\text{dom}(\Sigma)\text{: FreeLab}(\Sigma(l)) \subseteq \text{dom}(\Sigma)\ \}$$

It may be turned into a partially ordered set by defining $\Sigma_1 \sqsubseteq \Sigma_2$ whenever $\text{dom}(\Sigma_1) \subseteq \text{dom}(\Sigma_2)$ and $\forall l{\in}\text{dom}(\Sigma_1)$: $\Sigma_1(l) = \Sigma_2(l)$. When we write $\Sigma_1 \sqsubseteq \Sigma_2$ in the sequel it will be the tacit assumption that both Σ_1 and Σ_2 are elements of **Subst**. We often identify $\Sigma{\in}\mathbf{Subst}$ with its graph: $\{(d,C)|d{\in}\text{dom}(\Sigma){\wedge}\Sigma(d){=}C\}$.

We now have the apparatus needed to define the 'substitution predicate'

$$\mathit{compS}[\Sigma]_t\text{: } [\![t]\!](\mathbf{K}) \times [\![t]\!](\mathbf{K}) \rightarrow \{\text{true,false}\}$$

[1] We ignore here the omission of ensuring that $F(\bot) = \bot$.

that is indexed by a well-formed type t of compile-time kind and that is parameterized on a substitution $\Sigma\in$**Subst**. The intention with $compS[\Sigma]_t(x_0,x)$ is that $x_0[\Sigma]$ equals x. The formal definition is by induction on the type t:

$$
\begin{array}{l}
compS[\Sigma]_{\mathrm{A_i}}(x_0,x) \equiv x_0 = x \\[1ex]
compS[\Sigma]_{t_1 \times t_2}((x_{01},x_{02}),(x_1,x_2)) \equiv \\
\qquad compS[\Sigma]_{t_1}(x_{01},x_1) \wedge compS[\Sigma]_{t_2}(x_{02},x_2) \\[1ex]
compS[\Sigma]_{t_1 \rightarrow t_2}(F_0,F) \equiv \\
\qquad \forall \Sigma' \sqsupseteq \Sigma\colon \forall (x_0,x)\colon\ compS[\Sigma']_{t_1}(x_0,x) \Rightarrow \\
\qquad\qquad\qquad\qquad compS[\Sigma']_{t_2}(F_0(x_0),F(x)) \\[1ex]
compS[\Sigma]_{t_1 \underline{\rightarrow} t_2}(RC_0,RC) \equiv \\
\qquad \forall d{>}\mathrm{max}(\mathrm{dom}(\Sigma))\colon\ compS'[\Sigma]_{t_1 \underline{\rightarrow} t_2}(RC_0(d),RC(d)) \\
\qquad \text{where } compS'[\Sigma]_{t_1 \underline{\rightarrow} t_2}(C_0,C) \equiv \\
\qquad\qquad (C{=}\bot \Rightarrow C_0{=}\bot) \wedge \\
\qquad\qquad (C{\neq}\bot \Rightarrow C_0{\neq}\bot \wedge C_0[\Sigma]{=}C \\
\qquad\qquad\qquad\qquad \wedge\ \mathrm{FreeLab}(C_0){\subseteq}\mathrm{dom}(\Sigma))
\end{array}
$$

This is an instance of what is sometimes called a Kripke-logical relation. Mostly it is the obvious structural definition with an equality in the case of compile-time base types. For compile-time function space we have made use of an important trick: to consider all $\Sigma' \in$ **Subst** such that $\Sigma' \sqsupseteq \Sigma$. This will be of importance in Lemmas 6.2.1 and 6.2.2 below. For frontier types we express the desired substitution property and only restrain the relocation parameter d to be outside dom(Σ). As $\Sigma\in$**Subst** we have FreeLab($RC(d)$)$\subseteq$dom(Σ) as well.

Lemma 6.2.1 ('Parameter monotonicity') If $\Sigma\in$**Subst** and $\vdash t$:c the above clauses define an admissible predicate $compS[\Sigma]_t$. Furthermore

$$\Sigma_2 \sqsupseteq \Sigma_1 \wedge compS[\Sigma_1]_t(x_0,x) \Rightarrow compS[\Sigma_2]_t(x_0,x) \qquad \square$$

Proof: The proof is by structural induction on the type t and is mostly straightforward. In the case $t = t_1 \rightarrow t_2$ we use the fact that

$$\forall \Sigma' \sqsupseteq \Sigma_1\colon \cdots$$

implies

$$\forall \Sigma' \sqsupseteq \Sigma_2\colon \cdots$$

whenever $\Sigma_2 \sqsupseteq \Sigma_1$. □

We are now able to show that the definition of *compS* pays off in that it allows to solve the problem discussed in the beginning of this section.

Lemma 6.2.2 ('Substitution property') Assume that $compS[\Sigma]_{t\rightarrow t}(F_0,F)$, that the type t is of the form $t = t_1 \underline{\rightarrow} t_2$, that $d > \max(\mathrm{dom}(\Sigma))$ and that

$$F(\lambda d'.\mathrm{CALL}(d))(d{+}1) \neq \bot$$

Then

$$F(\lambda d'.\mathrm{CALL}(d))(d{+}1)\ [\mathrm{CALLREC}(d,F(\lambda d'.\mathrm{CALL}(d))(d{+}1))/d]$$
$$= F(\lambda d'.\mathrm{CALLREC}(d,F(\lambda d'.\mathrm{CALL}(d))(d{+}1)))(d{+}1)$$

and $\mathrm{FreeLab}(\mathrm{CALLREC}(d,F(\lambda d'.\mathrm{CALL}(d))(d{+}1))) \subseteq \mathrm{dom}(\Sigma)$. □

Proof: It is convenient to write

$$C = F(\lambda d'.\mathrm{CALL}(d))(d{+}1)$$
$$C' = \mathrm{CALLREC}(d,C)$$
$$C'' = F(\lambda d'.C')(d{+}1)$$

and similarly for C_0, C_0' and C_0''. We assume that $C{\neq}\bot$ and must show that $C''{\neq}\bot$, that $C[C'/d] = C''$ and that $\mathrm{FreeLab}(C') \subseteq \mathrm{dom}(\Sigma)$. The proof is in two stages that both proceed by extending Σ with a further pair.

Stage 1: Consider

$$\Sigma_1 = \Sigma \cup \{(d,\mathrm{CALL}(d))\}$$

We have $\Sigma_1{\in}$**Subst** because $\Sigma{\in}$**Subst** and $\mathrm{FreeLab}(\mathrm{CALL}(d)) \subseteq \{d\}$ and it follows that $\Sigma_1 \sqsupseteq \Sigma$. It is immediate to verify that

$$compS[\Sigma_1](\lambda d'.\mathrm{CALL}(d),\lambda d'.\mathrm{CALL}(d))$$

so by $compS[\Sigma](F_0,F)$ we have

$$compS[\Sigma_1](F_0(\lambda d'.\mathrm{CALL}(d)),F(\lambda d'.\mathrm{CALL}(d)))$$

Since $d{+}1{>}\max(\mathrm{dom}(\Sigma_1))$ this yields

$$compS[\Sigma_1](\lambda d'.C_0,\lambda d'.C)$$

It follows that $C_0{\neq}\bot$ and that

$$\mathrm{FreeLab}(C) \subseteq \mathrm{dom}(\Sigma_1) \subseteq \mathrm{dom}(\Sigma) \cup \{d\}$$
$$C_0[\Sigma_1] = C_0[\Sigma] = C$$

Stage 2: Consider

$$\Sigma_2 = \Sigma \cup \{(d,C')\}$$

We have $\Sigma_2 \in$**Subst** because $\Sigma \in$**Subst** and

$$\text{FreeLab}(C') = \text{FreeLab}(C)\backslash\{d\} \subseteq \text{dom}(\Sigma)$$

so clearly $\Sigma_2 \sqsupseteq \Sigma$. It is immediate to verify that

$$compS[\Sigma_2](\lambda d'.\text{CALL}(d),\lambda d'.C')$$

so by $compS[\Sigma](F_0,F)$ we have

$$compS[\Sigma_2](F_0(\lambda d'.\text{CALL}(d)),F(\lambda d'.C'))$$

Since $d+1 > \max(\text{dom}(\Sigma_2))$ this yields

$$compS[\Sigma_2](\lambda d'.C_0,\lambda d'.C'')$$

Since $C_0 \neq \bot$ we get $C'' \neq \bot$ and

$$C'' = C_0[\Sigma \cup \{(d,C')\}]$$

Since $\Sigma \in$**Subst** so that $\text{FreeLab}(\Sigma(l)) \subseteq \text{dom}(\Sigma)$ when $l \in \text{dom}(\Sigma)$ we have

$$C'' = (C_0[\Sigma])[C'/d] = C[C'/d]$$

as was to be shown.

Note that this lemma shows $C[C'/d] = C''$ rather than the equality of $C[C'/d]$ and $F(\mathbf{K}(\texttt{fix})(F))(d+1)$, because $\lambda d'.C' = \lambda d'.\mathbf{K}(\texttt{fix})(F)(d)$ which is different from $\mathbf{K}(\texttt{fix})(F)$. □

To show that the premises of Lemma 6.2.2 do hold when we need to use the substitution property we shall show that **K** interprets all operators in an acceptable way and that this then carries over to all expressions of the mixed λ-calculus and combinatory logic.

Lemma 6.2.3 We have $compS[\Sigma](\mathbf{K}(\phi),\mathbf{K}(\phi))$ for all $\Sigma \in$**Subst** and for all operators ϕ of Table 5.1, except those of form $\texttt{f}_i$ or $\texttt{F}_i$ and provided that the type t indexing $\texttt{fix}[t]$ is always composite and does not involve lists. □

Proof: Clearly we cannot make a general claim about the $\texttt{f}_i$ or $\texttt{F}_i$ as we have not specified the effect of **K** on all of these. However, concrete examples may be found among the exercises. Also we cannot make any claims about $\texttt{fix}[t]$ if t is not composite, as then $\mathbf{K}(\texttt{fix}[t])$ has not been defined, or if t involves (compile-time) lists, as then $compS[\Sigma]_t$ has not been defined.

So let ϕ be one of the remaining operators of Table 5.1 and let us temporarily assume that it is not $\texttt{fix}[t]$. From the 'parameter monotonicity' it follows that we may, without loss of generality, concentrate on $\Sigma=\emptyset$. Since the code $\mathbf{K}(\phi)$ does not explicitly mention any CALLREC or CALL it is fairly straightforward to show

$$compS[\emptyset](\mathbf{K}(\phi),\mathbf{K}(\phi))$$

To be more specific, the type of ϕ is of the form $t_k \rightarrow \cdots \rightarrow t_0$ for $k \geq 0$ and frontier types t_i. If $k=0$ the result is indeed obvious. If $k>0$ one may observe that the assumptions about the arguments of $\mathbf{K}(\phi)$ immediately carry over to the result.

Finally consider $\mathtt{fix}[t]$. The proof is by induction on the structure of the type t. The base cases are when t is pure and when t is a frontier type. The inductive step arises when t is a product of composite types.

The case t is pure. It is straightforward to show

if pure(t) and $\Sigma \in \mathbf{Subst}$

then $compS[\Sigma]_t(x_0,x) \Leftrightarrow x_0 = x$

by induction on t. It is then immediate that $compS[\emptyset](\mathbf{K}(\mathtt{fix}[t]),\mathbf{K}(\mathtt{fix}[t]))$ holds.

The case $t = t_1 \underline{\rightarrow} t_2$ is a frontier type. We consider $\Sigma \in \mathbf{Subst}$, assume

$$\forall \Sigma' \sqsupseteq \Sigma\text{: } \forall (RC_0,RC)\text{: } compS[\Sigma'](RC_0,RC) \Rightarrow$$
$$compS[\Sigma'](F_0(RC_0),F(RC))$$

and show

$$compS[\Sigma](\mathbf{K}(\mathtt{fix})(F_0),\mathbf{K}(\mathtt{fix})(F))$$

So let $d>\max(\mathrm{dom}(\Sigma))$. If $F(\lambda d'.\text{CALL}(d))(d+1) = \bot$ we also have

$$F_0(\lambda d'.\text{CALL}(d))(d+1) = \bot$$

and the result is immediate. Otherwise, write

$$C = F(\lambda d'.\text{CALL}(d))(d+1)$$

and similarly for C_0. The proof mimics Stage 1 in the proof of Lemma 6.2.2. So consider

$$\Sigma_1 = \Sigma \cup \{(d,\text{CALL}(d))\}$$

We have $\Sigma_1 \in \mathbf{Subst}$ because $\Sigma \in \mathbf{Subst}$ and $\text{FreeLab}(\text{CALL}(d)) \subseteq \{d\}$ so clearly $\Sigma_1 \sqsupseteq \Sigma$. It is immediate that

$$compS[\Sigma_1](\lambda d'.\text{CALL}(d),\lambda d'.\text{CALL}(d))$$

so that

$$compS[\Sigma_1](F_0(\lambda d'.\text{CALL}(d)),F(\lambda d'.\text{CALL}(d)))$$

Since $d+1>\max(\mathrm{dom}(\Sigma_1))$ this yields

$$compS[\Sigma_1](\lambda d'.C_0,\lambda d'.C)$$

and it follows that

$$\text{FreeLab}(C) \subseteq \text{dom}(\Sigma) \cup \{d\}$$
$$C_0[\Sigma] = C$$

It is then easy to obtain

$$\text{FreeLab}(\text{CALLREC}(d,C)) \subseteq \text{dom}(\Sigma)$$
$$\text{CALLREC}(d,C_0)[\Sigma] = \text{CALLREC}(d,C)$$

and this is the desired result.

The case t is a product of composite types. To exploit the induction hypothesis one has to show that $compS[\Sigma'](F_0,F)$ carries over to the functions supplied as argument to $\mathbf{K}(\texttt{fix}[t_1])$ and $\mathbf{K}(\texttt{fix}[t_2])$. We refer to [72, Lemma 7.13] for an example of a proof along these lines. □

Lemma 6.2.4 ('Structural induction') Let *penv* be a well-formed position environment (in the sense of Section 5.2) such that

$$\rho_{\text{PS}}(penv) \overset{\text{K}}{\vdash} e : t$$

and assume that neither e nor *penv* involves any lists. If $\Sigma \in \mathbf{Subst}$ is such that

$$compS[\Sigma](\mathbf{K}(\phi),\mathbf{K}(\phi))$$

holds for all operators ϕ that occur in e, then

$$compS[\Sigma](\llbracket e\rrbracket(\mathbf{K}),\llbracket e\rrbracket(\mathbf{K}))$$ □

Note that we have dispensed with explicitly indexing *compS* with type information. If we were to do so it would be helpful to define a *2*-level type $\tau_{\text{PS}}(penv)$ such that $\llbracket penv\rrbracket(\mathcal{I}) = \llbracket\tau_{\text{PS}}(penv)\rrbracket(\mathcal{I})$.

Proof: The proof is by structural induction on the expression e.

The case $e ::= \texttt{f}_i[t]$. We consider $\Sigma' \sqsupseteq \Sigma$, assume $compS[\Sigma'](\mathbf{env}_0,\mathbf{env})$ and must show $compS[\Sigma'](\mathbf{K}(\texttt{f}_i),\mathbf{K}(\texttt{f}_i))$. This is straightforward using the premises of the lemma and the 'parameter monotonicity'.

The cases $\texttt{F}_i$, `Fst`, `Snd`, `Apply`, `Id`, `True`, `False` and `Fix` are similar.

The case e ::= **`true`**. We consider $\Sigma' \sqsupseteq \Sigma$, assume $compS[\Sigma'](\mathbf{env}_0,\mathbf{env})$ and must show $compS[\Sigma'](\mathbf{true},\mathbf{true})$. This is straightforward using the definition of *compS*.

The case `false` is similar.

The case $e ::= \texttt{fix}\ e_0$. We consider $\Sigma' \sqsupseteq \Sigma$, assume $compS[\Sigma'](\mathbf{env}_0,\mathbf{env})$ and must show $compS[\Sigma']([\![e]\!](\mathbf{K})(\mathbf{env}_0),[\![e]\!](\mathbf{K})(\mathbf{env}))$. The induction hypothesis and the 'parameter monotonicity' give

$$compS[\Sigma']([\![e_0]\!](\mathbf{K})(\mathbf{env}_0),[\![e_0]\!](\mathbf{K})(\mathbf{env}))$$

and the premises of the lemma give

$$compS[\Sigma](\mathbf{K}(\texttt{fix}),\mathbf{K}(\texttt{fix}))$$

Using the definition of *compS* we then obtain

$$compS[\Sigma'](\mathbf{K}(\texttt{fix})([\![e_0]\!](\mathbf{K})(\mathbf{env}_0)),\mathbf{K}(\texttt{fix})([\![e_0]\!](\mathbf{K})(\mathbf{env})))$$

which is the desired result.

The cases `Tuple`, `Curry`, $\Box$ and `Cond` are mostly similar.

The case $e ::= \langle e_1,e_2\rangle$. We consider $\Sigma' \sqsupseteq \Sigma$, assume $compS[\Sigma'](\mathbf{env}_0,\mathbf{env})$ and must show $compS[\Sigma']([\![e]\!](\mathbf{K})(\mathbf{env}_0),[\![e]\!](\mathbf{K})(\mathbf{env}))$. The induction hypothesis and the 'parameter monotonicity' give

$$compS[\Sigma']([\![e_i]\!](\mathbf{K})(\mathbf{env}_0),[\![e_i]\!](\mathbf{K})(\mathbf{env}))$$

for $i = 1, 2$ and the desired result then follows immediately from the definition of *compS*.

The cases `fst`, `snd` and `if` are mostly similar.

The case $e ::= \lambda x_i[t'].e_0$. We consider $\Sigma' \sqsupseteq \Sigma$, assume $compS[\Sigma'](\mathbf{env}_0,\mathbf{env})$ and must show $compS[\Sigma']([\![e]\!](\mathbf{K})(\mathbf{env}_0),[\![e]\!](\mathbf{K})(\mathbf{env}))$. This amounts to

$$compS[\Sigma'](\lambda\mathbf{v}.[\![e_0]\!](\mathbf{K})((\mathbf{env}_0,\mathbf{v})),\ \lambda\mathbf{v}.[\![e_0]\!](\mathbf{K})((\mathbf{env},\mathbf{v})))$$

so consider $\Sigma'' \sqsupseteq \Sigma'$, assume $compS[\Sigma''](\mathbf{v}_0,\mathbf{v})$ and show

$$compS[\Sigma'']([\![e_0]\!](\mathbf{K})((\mathbf{env}_0,\mathbf{v}_0)),[\![e_0]\!](\mathbf{K})((\mathbf{env},\mathbf{v})))$$

Using the 'parameter monotonicity' and the definition of *compS* we have

$$compS[\Sigma'']((\mathbf{env}_0,\mathbf{v}_0),(\mathbf{env},\mathbf{v}))$$

and the desired result then follows from the induction hypothesis and the 'parameter monotonicity'.

The case $e ::= e_1(e_2)$. We consider $\Sigma' \sqsupseteq \Sigma$, assume $compS[\Sigma'](\mathbf{env}_0,\mathbf{env})$ and must show $compS[\Sigma']([\![e]\!](\mathbf{K})(\mathbf{env}_0),[\![e]\!](\mathbf{K})(\mathbf{env}))$. The induction hypothesis and the 'parameter monotonicity' give

$$compS[\Sigma']([\![e_i]\!](\mathbf{K})(\mathbf{env}_0),[\![e_i]\!](\mathbf{K})(\mathbf{env}))$$

for i = 1, 2 and the desired result is then immediate from the definition of *compS*.

The case $e ::= \mathrm{x_i}$. We consider $\Sigma' \sqsupseteq \Sigma$, assume $compS[\Sigma'](\mathbf{env_0},\mathbf{env})$ and must show $compS[\Sigma'](\pi_{\mathrm{PS}}(\mathrm{x_i},penv)(\mathbf{env_0}),\pi_{\mathrm{PS}}(\mathrm{x_i},penv)(\mathbf{env}))$ where we use π_{PS} of Section 5.2. We may write

$$\begin{aligned} penv &= (\mathrm{x_{i_1}},t_1)\cdots(\mathrm{x_{i_k}},t_k) \\ \mathbf{env_0} &= (\cdots((\mathbf{void},\mathrm{v_{01}}),\cdots,\mathrm{v_{0k}})) \\ \mathbf{env} &= (\cdots((\mathbf{void},\mathrm{v_1}),\cdots,\mathrm{v_k})) \end{aligned}$$

and from the well-formedness assumption we know that we may define an index j by

$$\mathrm{j} = \max\{\mathrm{j} \mid \mathrm{x_{i_j}} = \mathrm{x_i}\}$$

Then $\pi_{\mathrm{PS}}(\mathrm{x_i},penv)(\mathbf{env_0}) = \mathrm{v_{0j}}$ and $\pi_{\mathrm{PS}}(\mathrm{x_i},penv)(\mathbf{env}) = \mathrm{v_j}$ so from the definition of *compS* we obtain

$$compS[\Sigma'](\mathrm{v_{0j}},\mathrm{v_j})$$

which is the desired result. □

In the statements of the previous lemma we have used *compS* in a context where the two 'syntactic arguments' are always identical. This motivates defining

$$compS_t : [\![t]\!](\mathbf{K}) \to \{\text{true,false}\}$$

by

$$compS_t(x) \equiv \forall\Sigma\in\mathbf{Subst}\text{: } compS[\Sigma]_t(x,x)$$

which by the 'parameter monotonicity' is equivalent to

$$compS_t(x) \equiv compS[\emptyset]_t(x,x)$$

Then lemma 6.2.3 asserts $compS(\mathbf{K}(\phi))$ for all 'acceptable' operators ϕ of Table 5.1 and Lemma 6.2.4 uses this to assert $compS([\![e]\!](\mathbf{K}))$ for all 'acceptable' expressions e of the mixed λ-calculus and combinatory logic.

Having introduced $compS_t$ it is then natural to consider whether we could have dispensed with the $compS[\cdots]_t(\cdots,\cdots)$ predicate and instead have given a direct inductive definition of $compS_t(\cdots)$ in such a way that analogues of Lemmas 6.2.2, 6.2.3 and 6.2.4 could still be proved. So far we have been unable to do this and we suspect that no substitution property (that is analogue of Lemma 6.2.2) could be obtained if such an approach is taken. However, it is worth observing the following properties of $compS_t$.

Lemma 6.2.5 For appropriate elements x, x_1, x_2, F and RC we have

$$compS_{\mathrm{A_i}}(x) \Leftrightarrow \text{true}$$
$$compS_{t_1\times t_2}((x_1,x_2)) \Leftrightarrow compS_{t_1}(x_1) \wedge compS_{t_2}(x_2)$$
$$compS_{t_1\to t_2}(F) \wedge compS_{t_1}(x) \Rightarrow compS_{t_2}(F(x))$$
$$compS_{t_1\underline{\to} t_2}(RC) \Leftrightarrow (\forall d\colon RC(d)\neq\perp \Rightarrow \mathrm{FreeLab}(RC(d))=\emptyset)$$

Proof: The first two double implications are straightforward. For the third implication assume that

$$\forall\Sigma\in\mathbf{Subst}\colon\ compS[\Sigma]_{t_1\to t_2}(F,F)$$
$$\forall\Sigma\in\mathbf{Subst}\colon\ compS[\Sigma]_{t_1}(x,x)$$

and consider $\Sigma\in\mathbf{Subst}$. That

$$compS[\Sigma]_{t_2}(F(x),F(x))$$

is then immediate from the assumptions and the definition of $compS[\Sigma]_{t_1\to t_2}$. For the final double implication we calculate

$$\begin{aligned}
compS_{t_1\underline{\to} t_2}(RC) &\Leftrightarrow compS[\emptyset]_{t_1\underline{\to} t_2}(RC,RC)\\
&\Leftrightarrow \forall d\colon compS'[\emptyset]_{t_1\underline{\to} t_2}(RC(d),RC(d))\\
&\Leftrightarrow \forall d\colon (RC(d)\neq\perp \Rightarrow RC(d)\neq\perp \wedge\\
&\qquad\qquad RC(d)[\emptyset]=RC(d) \wedge\\
&\qquad\qquad \mathrm{FreeLab}(RC(d))=\emptyset))\\
&\Leftrightarrow \forall d\colon (RC(d)\neq\perp \Rightarrow \mathrm{FreeLab}(RC(d))=\emptyset)
\end{aligned}$$

where the first step is using the 'parameter monotonicity'. □

6.3 Well-behavedness of the Code

We now begin by clarifying what well-behavedness of the code generated by **K** is supposed to mean, and later in this section we then show that the code is indeed well-behaved. The basic idea is that the code operates in a stack-like fashion in that it transforms the value on top of the stack and leaves the remainder of the stack unchanged. However, as the following example shows there are some pitfalls.

Example 6.3.1 The code sequence

$$C_1 = [\![\texttt{Tuple(Id,Id)}]\!](\mathbf{K})(\mathbf{void})(1)$$
$$= \text{ENTER:DELAY(RESUME):SWITCH:DELAY(RESUME):TUPLE}$$

is well-behaved. To see this let $v{:}ST$ be any non-empty stack and note that

$$(C_1,v{:}ST) \rightarrow^5 (\varepsilon,\ w{:}ST)$$
$$\text{where } w = \langle\{\text{RESUME},v\},\{\text{RESUME},v\}\rangle$$

(and that by determinacy this is the only execution sequence).

The code sequence

$$C_2 = \text{TUPLE}$$

is *not* well-behaved. To see this consider a stack $v_1{:}v_2{:}ST$ and the execution sequence

$$(C_2,v_1{:}v_2{:}ST) \rightarrow (\varepsilon,w{:}ST)$$
$$\text{where } w = \langle v_1,v_2\rangle$$

Here v_2 has been removed from the resulting stack so it is not just the top element that has been transformed. For the same reason neither of the code sequences

$$C_3 = \text{ENTER, nor}$$
$$C_4 = \text{SWITCH}$$

are well-behaved.

However, if the code sequence C in question contains a RESUME instruction it is less clear whether or not C is well-behaved. As an example the execution sequence

$$(\text{RESUME},\{\text{CONST } \mathbf{b}_i,v\}{:}ST) \rightarrow^3 (\varepsilon,\mathbf{b}_i{:}ST)$$

would seem to suggest that RESUME *is* well-behaved whereas the execution sequence

$$(\text{RESUME},\{\text{TUPLE},v_1\}{:}v_2{:}ST) \rightarrow^3 (\varepsilon,\langle v_1,v_2\rangle{:}ST)$$

would seem to suggest that RESUME is *not* well-behaved. The safe solution is of course to decree that RESUME is not well-behaved but this is totally unacceptable given our (frequent) use of RESUME instructions in the code generation **K**. In particular, even the code for `Id` would not be well-behaved. □

To allow a code sequence containing RESUME instructions to be well-behaved we need to consider the element on top of the stack. Our second attempt at well-behavedness might then be as follows: a code sequence is well-behaved if its effect on a stack with a well-behaved top element only is to transform that top element into another well-behaved element; further, an element on the stack is well-behaved provided all code sequences contained in it are indeed well-behaved. This would seem to overcome the pitfalls exposed in Example 6.3.1: the code sequence CONST $\mathbf{b}_i$ is well-behaved and therefore RESUME is well-behaved when

{CONST $\mathbf{b}_i$,v} is on top of the stack; however, the code sequence TUPLE is not well-behaved and therefore RESUME is not well-behaved when {TUPLE,v_1} is on top of the stack.

It remains to ensure the well-definedness of the well-behavedness predicate. To see that there is a problem note that well-behavedness is 'circularly defined' in that it presupposes well-definedness of elements on the stack and this amounts to well-behavedness of the code sequences contained in these elements. The usual method for 'breaking' such circularity is by appeal to structural induction but this does not work here: if the code sequence of interest is RESUME it is still possible (and indeed very likely) that the element on top of the stack will contain much larger code sequences.

Another method that is sometimes applicable is to regard the definition of the predicate as a recursive definition and to use fixed point theory to obtain the solution. This method fails here because the recursive definition violates the monotonicity requirement. Yet another method is to index the predicate with a counter that expresses the maximum length of execution sequences considered and to regard longer execution sequences as 'infinite'. This method works but leads to a rather 'messy' calculation of new values for the counter (see Exercise 6).

The method we shall adopt uses a well-founded relation defined on a 'measure' that depends on the 'type' of the element on top of the stack and whether or not this element is a thunk. In doing so we shall exploit condition **B** of Section 6.1. Having defined the well-behavedness predicate for elements of the stack it is then rather routine to define well-behavedness for code sequences and other entities.

6.3.1 Definition of the well-behavedness predicates

We first consider the formal definition of the well-behavedness predicate $valW_t$ for elements on the stack. The type t is supposed to be a well-formed *2*-level type of run-time kind that indicates the 'type' of the element on top of the stack. This index is, in principle, dispensable at this stage since the machine has no explicit notion of type. However, it is hardly possible to dispense with the type index in the next stage (Section 6.4) and already in this stage it is helpful in reducing the number of cases to be considered in the proofs that follow. Also it is central for our chosen method for well-definedness to work. So we propose the following definition of $valW$:

$valW_{\underline{A}_i}(\mathbf{b}_j) \equiv$ true

for all basic values $\mathbf{b}_j$ of type $\underline{A}_i$

e.g. **true** and **false** are all the basic values of type $\underline{\mathtt{Bool}}$

$valW_{t_1 \underline{\times} t_2}((v_1,v_2)) \equiv valW_{t_1}(v_1) \wedge valW_{t_2}(v_2)$

$valW_{t_1 \underline{\rightarrow} t_2}(\{C;v_0\}) \equiv \forall v_1:$

$$valW_{t_1}(v_1) \Rightarrow valW_{t_2}(\{C,\langle v_0,v_1\rangle\})$$

$$valW_t(\{C,v\}) \equiv \forall\Delta\in\text{ExSeq}(*,C,v)\text{: } postW_t(\Delta) \wedge nothunk(\Delta)$$

where

$$postW_t(\Delta(0..m)) \equiv \exists v\text{: } \Delta(m) = (\varepsilon,[v]) \wedge valW_t(v)$$

$$nothunk(\Delta(0..m)) \equiv \neg\exists C,C',v',ST\text{: } \Delta(m) = (C,\{C',v'\}\text{:}ST)$$

and for later usage

$$preW_t(\Delta(0..m)) \equiv \exists C,v\text{: } \Delta(0) = (C,[v]) \wedge valW_t(v)$$

To motivate this definition note that it mostly proceeds by structural induction on the type subscript and perhaps with a case analysis on the form of the stack-element given as parameter. So it should be clear that for example $valW_{\underline{t\rightarrow}t}((\mathbf{b}_1,\mathbf{b}_2))$ is intended to be false. The clause for thunks is applicable for all run-time types and simply considers the effect of running the code component of the thunk upon the value component.

Intuitively there are four possible 'outcomes' of running a code sequence upon some value:

- the computation may loop forever, or
- the computation may produce a value as result, or
- the computation may end with a 'dynamic' error, e.g. division by 0, or
- the computation may end with a 'static' error, e.g. that the stack is too short.

In this section we only consider finite execution sequences and so disregard the first 'outcome'. Also, we do not need to explicitly consider the third 'outcome' because the semantics in Table 6.2 has been designed so that 'dynamic' errors lead to looping forever. This is clearly demonstrated by the transitions for HD and TL upon empty elements and by the transition for PRIM(o_i) upon a value v such that $\tilde{o}_i(v)$ is not defined. This may be motivated by an analogy with the treatment of errors in the standard semantics where (in the absence of an 'error' element in the domain) one produces $\perp$ as result. Another more pragmatic motivation is that it reduces the number of cases that needs explicit attention in the proofs that follow. This leaves us with the second and fourth 'outcome'. The formulation of $valW_t(\{C,v\})$ explicitly considers the second 'outcome' and formulates the desired condition. This is done for initial and final stacks of length 1 but we shall see shortly that these stacks can always be extended and that the extensions will be left untouched. The absence of any explicit consideration of the fourth 'outcome' then amounts to the (major) claim that no 'static' errors can arise when executing well-behaved code.

Lemma 6.3.2 The clauses for $valW_t$ define a predicate

$$valW_t : Val \rightarrow \{\text{true,false}\}$$

whenever t is a well-formed *2*-level type of run-time kind that does not involve any list types. □

Proof: We begin by introducing a bit of notation. When $v \in Val$ is a value we write v::thunk to express that it is a thunk, that is $\exists C,u\colon\ v=\{C,u\}$, and we write v::nothunk to express that it is not a thunk, that is $\neg(v$::thunk$)$. We then introduce a partial order on pairs of types and values by

$$(t_1,v_1) \preceq (t_2,v_2) \text{ if and only if } (t_1,v_1) = (t_2,v_2) \text{ or } (t_1,v_1) \prec (t_2,v_2)$$

where

$$(t_1,v_1) \prec (t_2,v_2) \text{ if and only if}$$
$$(t_1 \text{ is a proper subtype of } t_2) \text{ or}$$
$$(t_1{=}t_2 \wedge v_1\text{::nothunk} \wedge v_2\text{::thunk})$$

It is straightforward to check that this defines a well-founded order.

We then show that the clauses for $valW_t(v)$ are well-defined using the principle of complete induction (as in Section 3.2). This amounts to investigating each clause for $valW_t(v)$ and verifying that each $valW_{t'}(v')$ on the right hand side has $(t',v') \prec (t,v)$. This is immediate except when v is a thunk. In this case there is an occurrence of $valW_{t'}(v')$ implicit in $postW_t(\Delta)$. It has $t{=}t'$ but also v'::nothunk due to $nothunk(\Delta)$. Hence $(t',v') \prec (t,v)$ and this completes the proof. □

Turning to code sequences the idea is to define a relation *compW* much like *compS* of Section 6.2. Since we will need the substitution property in order to prove the required result for the `fix` operator we shall need to let *compW* include *compS*. There is no need, however, to let *compW* be parameterized on a substitution, nor is there a need to duplicate the 'syntactic' argument. We thus define

$$compW_t\colon [\![t]\!](\mathbf{K}) \rightarrow \{\text{true,false}\}$$

as follows:

$$compW_{\mathrm{A_i}}(x) \equiv \text{true}$$
$$compW_{t_1 \times t_2}((x_1,x_2)) \equiv compW_{t_1}(x_1) \wedge compW_{t_2}(x_2)$$

$$compW_{t_1 \rightarrow t_2}(F) \equiv compS_{t_1 \rightarrow t_2}(F) \wedge compSW_{t_1 \rightarrow t_2}(F)$$
$$\text{where } compSW_{t_1 \rightarrow t_2}(F) \equiv \forall x\colon\ compW_{t_1}(x) \Rightarrow compW_{t_2}(F(x))$$

$$
\begin{aligned}
comp W_{t_1 \underline{\rightarrow} t_2}(RC) \equiv\ & compS_{t_1 \underline{\rightarrow} t_2}(RC) \wedge compSW_{t_1 \underline{\rightarrow} t_2}(RC) \\
& \text{where } compSW_{t_1 \underline{\rightarrow} t_2}(RC) \equiv \forall d\colon compSW'_{t_1 \underline{\rightarrow} t_2}(RC(d)) \\
& \text{where } compSW'_{t_1 \underline{\rightarrow} t_2}(C) \equiv C \neq \perp \Rightarrow \\
& \qquad\qquad (\forall v \in Val\colon valW_{t_1}(v) \Rightarrow valW_{t_2}(\{C,v\}))
\end{aligned}
$$

Fact 6.3.3 The definition of $compSW'_{t_1 \underline{\rightarrow} t_2}(C)$ is equivalent to

$$C \neq \perp \Rightarrow (\forall \Delta \in \text{ExSeq}(*,C)\colon preW_{t_1}(\Delta) \Rightarrow (postW_{t_2}(\Delta) \wedge nothunk(\Delta)))$$

Lemma 6.3.4 The above clauses define an admissible predicate $compW_t$, whenever t is a well-formed *2*-level type of compile-time kind that does not involve any list types. □

Proof: This is a simple structural induction. □

The relationship with *compS* is given by

Lemma 6.3.5 ('Layered predicates') We have

$$compW_t(x) \Rightarrow compS_t(x)$$

for all $x \in [\![t]\!](\mathbf{K})$ and all well-formed *2*-level types t of compile-time kind that do not involve lists. □

Proof: This is a simple structural induction. □

To motivate the name, 'layered predicates', consider the set $\{S, W\}$ partially ordered as depicted in

Then *compS* and *compW* constitute a 'layer of predicates' where the stronger predicate is higher in the partial ordering. Technically this is intimately connected to the 'parameter monotonicity' of Lemma 6.2.1; in particular one notes the explicit inclusion of $compS_{t_1 \rightarrow t_2}$ in the clause for $compW_{t_1 \rightarrow t_2}$ much as $compS[\Sigma']_{t_1 \rightarrow t_2}$ was included in $compS[\Sigma]_{t_1 \rightarrow t_2}$ whenever $\Sigma' \sqsupseteq \Sigma$.

6.3.2 Operations on execution sequences

To assist in the proofs about the well-behavedness and correctness of code we need to establish some notation for decomposing and combining execution sequences. In doing so we shall take care that the notation applies to finite as well as infinite execution sequences.

We begin by considering an execution sequence Δ and defining the prefix $\Delta\propto C$ of Δ that 'protects' the code sequence C. To be more specific consider $\Delta \in \text{ExSeq}(\infty, C_1\hat{\ }C_2)$ and define

$$\text{I}_1 = \{\ i \mid \exists ST, C\text{: } \Delta(i){=}(C\hat{\ }C_2, ST)\}$$

as the set of indices where C_2 is still present,

$$\text{I}_2 = \{\ i \mid \exists ST, C\text{: } \Delta(i){=}(C\hat{\ }C_2, ST) \wedge C{\neq}\varepsilon\}$$

as the set of indices where C_2 is still present and is also 'untouched', and

$$\text{I}_3 = \{\ i{\in}\text{I}_1 \mid \forall j{<}i\text{: } j{\in}\text{I}_2\ \}$$

If I_3 is infinite, Δ is an infinite execution sequence and each $\Delta(i)$ is of the form $(C_i'\hat{\ }C_2, ST_i)$ and we set

$$(\Delta\propto C_2)(i) = (C_i', ST_i) \text{ for all } i \qquad\qquad (\text{if I}_3 \text{ is infinite})$$

If I_3 is finite it must be of the form $\{0,\cdots,m\}$ and for $i{\leq}m$ each $\Delta(i)$ is of the form $(C_i'\hat{\ }C_2, ST_i)$ and we set

$$(\Delta\propto C_2)(i) = (C_i', ST_i) \text{ for all } i{\leq}m \qquad\qquad (\text{if I}_3{=}\{0,\cdots,m\})$$

Fact 6.3.6 If $\Delta \in \text{ExSeq}(\infty, C_1\hat{\ }C_2)$ then $(\Delta\propto C_2) \in \text{ExSeq}(\infty, C_1)$. □

In an analogous way we may define the prefix $\Delta\propto ST$ of Δ that 'protects' the stack ST. For this we shall write length(ST) for the length of the stack ST and we shall write arity(C) for the number of elements that needs to be on the stack for the first instruction to execute according to Table 6.2. As an example, arity(SWITCH)=2. Next let $\Delta \in \text{ExSeq}(\infty, C)$ have $\Delta(0) = (C, ST_1\hat{\ }ST_2)$ and consider defining $(\Delta\propto ST_2)$. We define

$$\text{J}_1 = \{\ i \mid \exists ST, C\text{: } \Delta(i){=}(C, ST\hat{\ }ST_2)\}$$

as the set of indices where ST_2 is still present,

$$\text{J}_2 = \{\ i \mid \exists ST, C\text{: } \Delta(i){=}(C, ST\hat{\ }ST_2) \wedge \text{arity}(C){\leq}\text{length}(ST)\}$$

as the set of indices where ST_2 is still present and is also 'untouched', and

$$\text{J}_3 = \{\ i{\in}\text{J}_1 \mid \forall j{<}i\text{: } j{\in}\text{J}_2\ \}$$

If J_3 is infinite, Δ is an infinite execution sequence and each $\Delta(i)$ is of the form $(C_i, ST_i'\hat{\ }ST_2)$ and we set

$$(\Delta\propto ST_2)(i) = (C_i, ST_i') \text{ for all } i \qquad\qquad (\text{if J}_3 \text{ is infinite})$$

If J_3 is finite it must be of the form $\{0,\cdots,m\}$ and for $i \leq m$ each $\Delta(i)$ is of the form $(C_i, ST_i'\hat{\ }ST_2)$ and we set

$$(\Delta \propto ST_2)(i) = (C_i, ST_i') \text{ for all } i \leq m \qquad\qquad (\text{if } J_3=\{0,\cdots,m\})$$

Fact 6.3.7 If $\Delta \in \text{ExSeq}(\infty, C)$ is such that $\Delta(0) = (C, ST_1\hat{\ }ST_2)$ then $(\Delta \propto ST_2)$ is defined and $(\Delta \propto ST_2) \in \text{ExSeq}(\infty, C)$. □

It is also helpful with notation for combining execution sequences. The basic observation is that if

$$\Delta = (C_0, ST_0) \rightarrow \cdots \rightarrow (C_{\text{m}}, ST_{\text{m}})$$

and $C \in \mathit{Code}$, $ST \in \mathit{Stack}$ then

$$(C_0\hat{\ }C, ST_0\hat{\ }ST) \rightarrow \cdots \rightarrow (C_{\text{m}}\hat{\ }C, ST_{\text{m}}\hat{\ }ST)$$

However, even if Δ is an execution sequence the modified sequence need not be an execution sequence because when $C \neq \varepsilon$ and $C_{\text{m}} = \varepsilon$ it is likely that we can find some (C', ST') such that $(C_{\text{m}}\hat{\ }C, ST_{\text{m}}\hat{\ }ST) \rightarrow (C', ST')$.

To overcome this obstacle consider $\Delta_1 \in \text{ExSeq}(m_1, C_1)$ and $\Delta_2 \in \text{ExSeq}(\infty, C_2)$ and assume that

$$\Delta_1(m_1) = (\varepsilon, ST)$$

$$\Delta_2(0) = (C_2, ST)$$

for some stack ST. Then Δ_1 & Δ_2 is defined as

$$(\Delta_1 \,\&\, \Delta_2)(i) = \begin{cases} (C_i'\hat{\ }C_2, ST_i) & \text{if } \Delta_1(i) = (C_i', ST_i) \text{ and } i < m_1 \\ \Delta_2(i - m_1) & \text{if } m_1 \leq i \end{cases}$$

Fact 6.3.8 Let $\Delta_1 \in \text{ExSeq}(m_1, C_1)$ and $\Delta_2 \in \text{ExSeq}(\infty, C_2)$ be chosen such that $\Delta_1(m_1) = (\varepsilon, ST)$ and $\Delta_2(0) = (C_2, ST)$ for some stack $ST \in \mathit{Stack}$. It then follows that $(\Delta_1 \,\&\, \Delta_2) \in \text{ExSeq}(\infty, C_1\hat{\ }C_2)$. □

6.3.3 Well-behavedness of operators

We now embark on the long series of results that together constitute an analogue of Lemma 6.2.3, namely that *compW* holds for each operator. The general strategy in these proofs is to consider an execution sequence

$$\Delta \in \text{ExSeq}(m, C_1\hat{\ }\cdots\hat{\ }C_{\text{k}})$$

and then decompose it into execution sequences

$$\Delta_{\text{i}} \in \text{ExSeq}(m_{\text{i}}, C_{\text{i}}) \text{ for i} \in \{1,\cdots,\text{k}\}$$

such that

$$\Delta = \Delta_1 \,\&\, \cdots \,\&\, \Delta_k$$

For each $i \in \{1, \cdots, k\}$ the proof strategy will then be

- to apply the induction hypothesis to Δ_i and lift the result to $\Delta_{i+1} \,\&\, \cdots \,\&\, \Delta_k$, or
- to simulate the transition that C_i gives rise to, i.e. write Δ_i out in detail.

It is therefore helpful with a few facts about how decomposition and combination of execution sequences affect the predicates *preW*, *postW* and *nothunk* on execution sequences.

Fact 6.3.9 ('Properties of *preW*') If $\Delta \in \mathrm{ExSeq}(m, C'\hat{}C)$ then

(a) $preW_t(\Delta) \Leftrightarrow preW_t(\Delta \propto C)$

Fact 6.3.10 ('Properties of *postW*') If $\Delta \in \mathrm{ExSeq}(m, C'\hat{}C)$ then

(a) $postW_t(\Delta \propto C) \wedge m' = \#(\Delta \propto C) \Rightarrow preW_t(\Delta(m'..m))$

(b) $\forall m' \leq m\colon postW_t(\Delta) \Leftrightarrow postW_t(\Delta(m'..m))$

Fact 6.3.11 ('Properties of *nothunk*') If $\Delta \in \mathrm{ExSeq}(m, C'\hat{}C)$ then

(a) If $m' = \#(\Delta \propto C)$ then $nothunk(\Delta \propto C) \Leftrightarrow nothunk(\Delta(0..m'))$

(b) $\forall m' \leq m\colon nothunk(\Delta) \Leftrightarrow nothunk(\Delta(m'..m))$

Due to the frequent use of RESUME instructions it is also helpful with the following lemma that characterizes their behaviour.

Lemma 6.3.12 If $\Delta \in \mathrm{ExSeq}(m, \mathrm{RESUME})$ and $preW_t(\Delta)$ then $postW_t(\Delta) \wedge nothunk(\Delta)$. □

Proof: If $\Delta(0) = (\mathrm{RESUME}, [v])$ and v::nothunk we know that Δ amounts to the execution sequence $(\mathrm{RESUME}, [v]) \rightarrow (\varepsilon, [v])$. Hence $postW_t(\Delta)$ follows and $nothunk(\Delta)$ is immediate.

If $\Delta(0) = (\mathrm{RESUME}, [\{C_1, v_1\}])$ we have $\Delta(1) = (C_1\hat{}\mathrm{RESUME}, [v_1])$ so that $\Delta(1..m) \in \mathrm{ExSeq}(m-1, C_1\hat{}\mathrm{RESUME})$. Let now $\Delta_1 \in \mathrm{ExSeq}(m_1, C_1)$ be given by

$$\Delta_1 = \Delta(1..m) \propto \mathrm{RESUME}$$

From $preW_t(\Delta)$ we have $valW_t(\{C_1, v_1\})$ and thus

$$postW_t(\Delta_1) \wedge nothunk(\Delta_1)$$

We then obtain

$$preW_t(\Delta(1+m_1..m)) \wedge nothunk(\Delta(0..1+m_1))$$

by the properties of *postW* and *nothunk*. In other words $\Delta(1+m_1) = (\text{RESUME},[v_2])$ where v_2::nothunk and $valW_t(v_2)$. It follows that $\Delta = \Delta(0..1+m_1+1)$, that $\Delta(1+m_1+1) = (\varepsilon,[v_2])$ and that $valW_t(v_2)$. Hence

$$postW_t(\Delta) \wedge nothunk(\Delta)$$

has been established. □

As our first result about an operator we now consider `Fst`.

Lemma 6.3.13 $compW_{t_1\underline{\times}t_2\underline{\rightarrow}t_1}(\mathbf{K}(\texttt{Fst}))$ holds for all well-formed types $t_1\underline{\times}t_2\underline{\rightarrow}t_1$ that do not involve lists. □

Proof: We must show *compS* as well as *compSW*. The first result is a consequence of Lemma 6.2.3 so we concentrate on showing $compSW(\mathbf{K}(\texttt{Fst}))$. For this we shall rely heavily on Fact 6.3.3. So let $d>0$, write

$$C = \mathbf{K}(\texttt{Fst})(d) = \text{RESUME:FST:RESUME},$$

let $\Delta\in\text{ExSeq}(m,C)$ and assume that $preW_{t_1\underline{\times}t_2}(\Delta)$. We must show $postW_{t_1}(\Delta) \wedge nothunk(\Delta)$.

Stage 1: Let $\Delta_1\in\text{ExSeq}(m_1,\text{RESUME})$ be given by $\Delta_1 = \Delta\propto\text{FST:RESUME}$. The properties of *preW* give $preW_{t_1\underline{\times}t_2}(\Delta_1)$ so by Lemma 6.3.12 and the properties of *postW* and *nothunk* we have $preW_{t_1\underline{\times}t_2}(\Delta(m_1..m)) \wedge nothunk(\Delta(m_1))$.

Stage 2: Let $\Delta_2\in\text{ExSeq}(m_2,\text{FST})$ be given by $\Delta_2 = \Delta(m_1..m)\propto\text{RESUME}$. We know that $\Delta_2(0)$ is of the form $(\text{FST},[v_2])$ where $valW_{t_1\underline{\times}t_2}(v_2)$ and v_2::nothunk. By inspection of the clauses for *valW* we observe that v_2 must be of the form (v_{21},v_{22}). Hence $m_2 = 1$ and $\Delta_2(m_2) = (\varepsilon,[v_{21}])$ and we know that $valW_{t_1}(v_{21})$.

Stage 3: Let $\Delta_3\in\text{ExSeq}(m_3,\text{RESUME})$ be given by $\Delta_3 = \Delta(m_1+m_2..m)$. By Lemma 6.3.12 we have

$$postW_{t_1}(\Delta) \wedge nothunk(\Delta)$$

and the desired result follows. □

Corollary 6.3.14 A similar result holds for `Snd`, `Id`, `True` and `False`. □

Lemma 6.3.15 $compW_{(t\underline{\rightarrow}t_1)\rightarrow(t\underline{\rightarrow}t_2)\rightarrow(t\underline{\rightarrow}t_1\underline{\times}t_2)}(\mathbf{K}(\texttt{Tuple}))$ holds for well-formed *2*-level types t, t_1 and t_2 of run-time kind that do not involve lists. □

Proof: Let us begin by expanding the statement that needs to be proved and then simplify it to something manageable. So using the definition of *compW* for compile-time function space we must prove

$$compS(\mathbf{K}(\mathtt{Tuple}))$$

$$compSW(\mathbf{K}(\mathtt{Tuple}))$$

The first of these follows from Lemma 6.2.3 so we concentrate on the second. For this we assume

$$compW_{(t \underline{\rightarrow} t_1)}(RC_1)$$

and must show

$$compW_{(t \underline{\rightarrow} t_2) \rightarrow (t \underline{\rightarrow} t_1 \underline{\times} t_2)}\ (\mathbf{K}(\mathtt{Tuple})(RC_1))$$

Proceeding as above this amounts to proving

$$compS(\mathbf{K}(\mathtt{Tuple})(RC_1))$$

$$compSW(\mathbf{K}(\mathtt{Tuple})(RC_1))$$

Concerning the first of these the result follows from Lemma 6.2.3, the assumption about RC_1 and the 'layered predicates' (Lemma 6.3.5), and using Lemma 6.2.5. Concentrating on the second result we assume

$$compW_{(t \underline{\rightarrow} t_2)}(RC_2)$$

and must show

$$compW_{(t \underline{\rightarrow} t_1 \underline{\times} t_2)}(\mathbf{K}(\mathtt{Tuple})(RC_1)(RC_2))$$

Using the definition of *compW* for run-time function space we must prove

$$compS(\mathbf{K}(\mathtt{Tuple})(RC_1)(RC_2))$$

$$compSW(\mathbf{K}(\mathtt{Tuple})(RC_1)(RC_2))$$

Concerning the first of these the result follows from Lemma 6.2.3, the assumption about RC_i and the 'layered predicates' (Lemma 6.3.5), and using Lemma 6.2.5. We are thus left with the second result.

In conclusion, to prove the lemma it suffices to assume

$$compSW_{(t \underline{\rightarrow} t_i)}(RC_i) \text{ for i=1,2}$$

and to show

$$compSW_{(t \underline{\rightarrow} t_1 \underline{\times} t_2)}(\mathbf{K}(\mathtt{Tuple})(RC_1)(RC_2))$$

For this we shall rely heavily on Fact 6.3.3. So let $d>0$ and note that the result is trivial unless $RC_1(d)\neq\perp$ and $RC_2(d)\neq\perp$ in which case also $RC(d)\neq\perp$ and

$$RC(d) = \text{ENTER:DELAY}(RC_2(d))\text{:SWITCH:DELAY}(RC_1(d))\text{:TUPLE}$$

Further, $\Delta\in\text{ExSeq}(m,RC(d),v)$ and $preW_t(\Delta)$. It is immediate to verify that $m=5$ and that

$$\Delta(m) = (\varepsilon,[\langle\{RC_1(d),v\},\{RC_2(d),v\}\rangle])$$

Hence $nothunk(\Delta)$ follows and to show $postW_{t_1\underline{\times}t_2}(\Delta)$ it suffices to show

$$valW_{t_i}(\{RC_i(d),v\}) \text{ for i=1,2}$$

and this result is immediate from the assumptions about the RC_i. □

Lemma 6.3.16 $compW_{(t_2\underline{\rightarrow}t_3)\rightarrow(t_1\underline{\rightarrow}t_2)\rightarrow(t_1\underline{\rightarrow}t_3)}(\mathbf{K}(\square))$ holds for all well-formed *2*-level types t_1, t_2 and t_3 of run-time kind that do not involve lists. □

Proof: As in the proof of Lemma 6.3.15 it suffices to consider RC_1 and RC_2 and assume

$$compSW(RC_i) \text{ for i = 1,2}$$

and show

$$compSW(RC)$$

where $RC = \mathbf{K}(\square)(RC_1)(RC_2)$. We shall use Fact 6.3.3 for this. So let $d>0$ and note that the result is trivial unless $RC_1(d)\neq\perp$ and $RC_2(d)\neq\perp$ in which case also $RC(d)\neq\perp$ and then

$$RC(d) = \text{DELAY}(RC_2(d)){:}RC_1(d)$$

Further let $\Delta\in\text{ExSeq}(m,RC(d))$ and $preW_{t_1}(\Delta)$.

It is immediate to verify that $m\geq1$ so that $\Delta(1..m)\in\text{ExSeq}(m-1,\ RC_1(d))$. From the definition of $compSW$ we also have $preW_{t_2}(\Delta(1..m))$. We may now use $compSW(RC_1)$ to obtain

$$postW_{t_3}(\Delta(1..m)) \wedge nothunk(\Delta(1..m))$$

and the desired property follows from the properties of $postW$ and $nothunk$. □

Lemma 6.3.17 $compW(\mathbf{K}(\texttt{Cond}))$ provided that the type of `Cond` does not involve lists. □

Note that we dispense with type subscripts in the statement and proof of this lemma as no confusion is likely to arise.

Proof: Much as in the proof of Lemma 6.3.15 it suffices to consider RC_1, RC_2 and RC_3 and assume

$$compSW(RC_{\mathrm{i}}) \text{ for i=1,2,3}$$

and show

$$compSW(RC)$$

where $RC = \mathbf{K}(\texttt{Cond})(RC_1)(RC_2)(RC_3)$. We shall use Fact 6.3.3 for this. So let $d>0$ and note that the result is trivial unless $RC_1(d)\neq\perp$, $RC_2(d)\neq\perp$ and $RC_3(d)\neq\perp$ in which case also $RC(d)\neq\perp$ and

$$RC(d) = \text{ENTER}:RC_1(d):\text{BRANCH}(RC_2(d),RC_3(d))$$

Further let $\Delta\in\text{ExSeq}(m,RC(d))$ and $preW(\Delta)$.

Stage 1: It is immediate to verify that $m\geq 1$ and that $\Delta(1)$ may be written as

$$\Delta(1) = (RC_1(d):\text{BRANCH}(RC_2(d),RC_3(d)),[v,v])$$

Stage 2: Let $\Delta_2\in\text{ExSeq}(m_2,RC_1(d))$ be given by

$$\Delta_2 = (\Delta(1..m)\propto\text{BRANCH}(RC_2(d),RC_3(d)))\propto[v]$$

It is straightforward to verify (but not merely by using Fact 6.3.9) that $preW(\Delta_2)$. Using $compSW(RC_1)$ we obtain $postW(\Delta_2) \wedge nothunk(\Delta_2)$. Hence

$$\Delta(1+m_2) = (\text{BRANCH}(RC_2(d),RC_3(d)),[w,v])$$

where $valW(v)$, $valW_{\underline{\texttt{Bool}}}(w)$ and w::nothunk.

Stage 3: By inspection of the clauses for $valW$ we observe that w must be either **true** or **false** as it is not a thunk. Thus

$$\Delta(2+m_2) = (RC_{\mathrm{j}}(d),[v])$$

for j$\in\{2,3\}$ depending on the value of $w \in \{\textbf{true},\textbf{false}\}$. Regardless of the value of j we then have $preW(\Delta(2+m_2..m))$.

Stage 4: Let $\Delta_4\in\text{ExSeq}(m_4,RC_{\mathrm{j}}(d))$ be given by $\Delta_4 = \Delta(2+m_2..m)$. Using $compSW(RC_{\mathrm{j}})$ we obtain $postW(\Delta) \wedge nothunk(\Delta)$ from which the desired result follows from the properties of $postW$ and $nothunk$. □

Lemma 6.3.18 $compW(\mathbf{K}(\texttt{Curry}))$ provided that the type of `Curry` does not involve lists. □

Proof: Much as in the proof of Lemma 6.3.15 it suffices to consider RC_1 and assume

$$compSW(RC_1)$$

and show

$$compSW(RC)$$

where $RC = \mathbf{K}(\texttt{Curry})(RC_1)$. We shall use Fact 6.3.3 for this. So let $d>0$ and note that the result is trivial unless $RC_1(d)\neq\perp$ in which case also $RC(d)\neq\perp$ and

$$RC(d) = \text{CURRY}(RC_1(d))$$

Further let $\Delta\in\text{ExSeq}(m,RC(d),v_0)$ and $preW(\Delta)$.

We know that $m = 1$ and that $\Delta(1) = (\varepsilon,[\{RC_1(d);v_0\}])$. Clearly $nothunk(\Delta)$ and to show $postW(\Delta)$ it suffices to show $valW(\{RC_1(d);v_0\})$. To do so let v_1 be given such that $valW(v_1)$ and show $valW(\{RC_1(d), \langle v_0,v_1\rangle\})$. From $preW(\Delta)$ we have $valW(v_0)$ and hence $valW(\langle v_0,v_1\rangle)$ so by $compSW(RC_1)$ we have the required $valW(\{RC_1(d),\langle v_0,v_1\rangle\})$. □

Lemma 6.3.19 $compW_{((t_1\underline{\rightarrow}t_2)\underline{\times}t_1)\underline{\rightarrow}t_2}(\mathbf{K}(\texttt{Apply}))$ holds for all well-formed types $((t_1\underline{\rightarrow}t_2)\underline{\times}t_1)\underline{\rightarrow}t_2$ that do not involve lists. □

Proof: Much as in the proof of Lemma 6.3.13 it suffices to prove

$$compSW(\mathbf{K}(\texttt{Apply}))$$

and we use Fact 6.3.3 for this. So let $d>0$ and write

$$\mathbf{K}(\texttt{Apply})(d) = \text{RESUME}{:}C'$$

where

$$C' = \text{ENTER:SND:SWITCH:FST:RESUME:}C''$$

$$C'' = \text{APPLY:RESUME}$$

Further let $\Delta\in\text{ExSeq}(m,\mathbf{K}(\texttt{Apply})(d))$ and $preW_{(t_1\underline{\rightarrow}t_2)\underline{\times}t_1}(\Delta)$.

Stage 1: Let $\Delta_1\in\text{ExSeq}(m_1,\text{RESUME})$ be given by $\Delta_1 = \Delta\propto C'$. The properties of $preW$ give $preW_{(t_1\underline{\rightarrow}t_2)\underline{\times}t_1}(\Delta_1)$ so by Lemma 6.3.12 we have $nothunk(\Delta_1)$ and $postW_{(t_1\underline{\rightarrow}t_2)\underline{\times}t_1}(\Delta_1)$.

Stage 2: Let v be given by $\Delta(m_1) = (C',[v])$. From $valW_{(t_1\underline{\rightarrow}t_2)\underline{\times}t_1}(v)$ and the fact that v is not a thunk it follows from inspection of the clauses for $valW$ that v is of the form $\langle u,w\rangle$ where $valW_{t_1\underline{\rightarrow}t_2}(u)$ and $valW_{t_1}(w)$. We then have $m\geq m_1+4$ and

$$\Delta(m_1{+}4) = (\text{RESUME}{:}C'',[u,w])$$

Stage 3: Let $\Delta_3 \in \text{ExSeq}(m_3,\text{RESUME},u)$ be given by

$$\Delta_3 = (\Delta(m_1{+}4..) \propto C'') \propto [w]$$

It is straightforward to verify that $preW_{t_1 \underline{\rightarrow} t_2}(\Delta_3)$ (but not merely by using Fact 6.3.9). Using Lemma 6.3.12 we get $nothunk(\Delta_3)$ and $postW_{t_1 \underline{\rightarrow} t_2}(\Delta_3)$.

Stage 4: It follows that

$$\Delta(m_1{+}4{+}m_3) = (C'',[u',w])$$

where u' is not a thunk, $valW_{t_1 \underline{\rightarrow} t_2}(u')$ and $valW_{t_1}(w)$. By inspection of the clauses for $valW$ it follows that u' is of the form $\{\overline{C};\overline{u}\}$. Then $m \geq m_1{+}5{+}m_3$ and

$$\Delta(m_1{+}5{+}m_3) = (\text{RESUME},[\{\overline{C},\langle\overline{u},w\rangle\}])$$

Furthermore, we have $valW_{t_2}(\{\overline{C},\langle\overline{u},w\rangle\})$ from the assumptions about $\{\overline{C};\overline{u}\}$ and w.

Stage 5: Let $\Delta_5 \in \text{ExSeq}(m_5,\text{RESUME})$ be given by

$$\Delta_5 = \Delta(m_1{+}5{+}m_3..m)$$

We have $preW_{t_2}(\Delta_5)$ so by Lemma 6.3.12 we get $nothunk(\Delta_5)$ and $postW_{t_2}(\Delta_5)$. From this $nothunk(\Delta) \wedge postW_{t_2}(\Delta)$ follows using the properties of $postW$ and $nothunk$. □

The proofs for the remaining operators of Table 5.1, that is `Fix` and `fix`, require a new technique. In both cases the difficulty is that we need to show the well-behavedness of code that works by 'unfolding' itself and therefore we need some way of getting an induction going. There are several ways that can be explored and we shall choose one that will also be useful in the next section.

The general idea is to be able to control the number of unfoldings allowed for the REC and CALLREC instructions. The most convenient way in which to do this is to allow indexing these instructions with a counter n that is decreased every time an unfolding takes place and that gives rise to looping if the index is 0. To be more precise we have the following extension of Table 6.2:

$$(\text{REC}_{\text{n+1}}{:}C,\ \{C';v\}{:}ST) \rightarrow (C,\ \{C',\langle v,v'_{\text{n}}\rangle\}{:}ST)$$
$$\text{where } v'_{\text{n}} = \{\text{REC}_{\text{n}}{:}\text{RESUME},\{C';v\}\}$$

$$(\text{REC}_0{:}C,\ \{C';v\}{:}ST) \rightarrow (\text{REC}_0{:}C,\ \{C';v\}{:}ST)$$

$$(\text{CALLREC}_{\text{n+1}}(l,C'){:}C,\ ST) \rightarrow (C'[\text{CALLREC}_{\text{n}}(l,C')/l]^{\frown}C,\ ST)$$

$$(\text{CALLREC}_0(l,C'){:}C,\ ST) \rightarrow (\text{CALLREC}_0(l,C'){:}C,\ ST)$$

The proof then proceeds by first replacing REC by REC_n in **K**(**Fix**) and CALLREC by CALLREC_n in **K**(**fix**). Next an induction on n is performed, and the basis, n=0, is straightforward in both cases. Finally, the results for REC_n and CALLREC_n for all n must be lifted to results for REC and CALLREC.

To facilitate the last step we introduce a 'syntactic' ordering. The key relationship is that

$$\text{REC}_n \preceq \text{REC}_m \text{ if } n \leq m$$

$$\text{REC}_n \preceq \text{REC}$$

$$\text{CALLREC}_n(l,C_n) \preceq \text{CALLREC}_m(l,C_m) \text{ if } n \leq m \text{ and } C_n \preceq C_m$$

$$\text{CALLREC}_n(l,C_n) \preceq \text{CALLREC}(l,C) \text{ if } C_n \preceq C$$

and this is then extended to elements of *Code* and *Val* in the obvious way, for example

$$\{\text{REC}_7\text{:RESUME,8}\} \preceq \{\text{REC}_8\text{:RESUME,8}\}$$

but

$$\{\text{REC}_7\text{:RESUME,8}\} \not\preceq \{\text{REC}_8\text{:RESUME,9}\}$$

This ordering carries over to elements of **RelCode** by setting

$$RC \preceq RC' \text{ if and only if } \forall d\text{: } RC(d) \preceq RC'(d)$$

and to configurations of the machine by setting

$$(C,[u_1,\cdots,u_k]) \preceq (C',[u'_1,\cdots,u'_k])$$
$$\text{if and only if } C \preceq C' \text{ and } u_i \preceq u'_i \text{ for each i}$$

Taking elements of *Code* as an example, the idea is that the least upper bound of a sequence $(C_n)_n$ of instruction sequences with indexed REC and CALLREC instructions will have a least upper bound C which is similar to each C_n but where (some) indices have been removed. We leave the details to the lemmas below.

Lemma 6.3.20 If $((C_n,u_n))_n$ is a chain with least upper bound (C,u) and if ExSeq(*,C,u)$\neq\emptyset$ then there exists n_0 such that ExSeq(*,C_n,u_n)$\neq\emptyset$ when $n \geq n_0$. □

Proof: We shall prove a stronger result and to state it we shall write

$$\text{ExSeq}(*)(C,ST) = \{\ \Delta\in\text{ExSeq}(*) \mid \Delta(0)=(C,ST)\ \}$$

and similarly for ExSeq(∞)(C,ST) and ExSeq(m)(C,ST). We then claim that if $((C_n,ST_n))_n$ is a chain of configurations with least upper bound (C,ST) and if ExSeq(*)(C,ST)$\neq\emptyset$ then there exists n_0 such that ExSeq(*)(C_n,ST_n)$\neq\emptyset$ when $n\geq n_0$.

The proof is by contradiction. Without loss of generality we may assume that m is the minimal value for which it is possible to have

$\Delta \in$ ExSeq(m)(C,ST)

(C,ST) is the least upper bound of a chain $((C_n,ST_n))_n$

ExSeq(*)(C_n,ST_n)$=\emptyset$ for infinitely many n

From an obvious analogue of Fact 6.1.1 we may determine Δ_n by

$\Delta_n \in$ ExSeq(∞)(C_n,ST_n)

Clearly $m>0$ as otherwise $C=\varepsilon$ in which case $C_n=\varepsilon$ and ExSeq(*)(C_n,ST_n)$\neq\emptyset$ holds for all n. Then C must be of the form i:C' and each C_n must be of the form i_n:C'_n where i is the least upper bound of $(i_n)_n$. Since Δ is finite we know that i cannot be of the form REC_0 or $\text{CALLREC}_0(l,C'')$. It follows that there exists n_0 such that i_n cannot be of the form REC_0 or $\text{CALLREC}_0(l,C''_n)$ when $n\geq n_0$. Then the same transition rule of Table 6.2 (augmented with REC_n and CALLREC_n) must be used in the first step of all Δ_n (with $n\geq n_0$) as well as Δ. It follows that also $(\Delta_n(1))_{n\geq n_0}$ is a chain and that $\Delta(1)$ is not only an upper bound but the least upper bound. However, infinitely many $\Delta_n(1..)$ are infinite and this contradicts the minimality of m. □

Lemma 6.3.21 If $(v_n)_n$ is a chain of values with v as their least upper bound and if $\forall$n: $valW_t(v_n)$ then also $valW_t(v)$. □

Proof: We proceed by structural induction on t. In each case we first consider the situation where v is not a thunk and we then finally consider the situation where v is a thunk. Note that $v_n \preceq v$ implies that v_n is a thunk if and only if v is.

The case t::=$\underline{A}_i$ and v::nothunk. We must have $v_n=v$ for all n and from $valW_t(v_n)$ we obtain $valW_t(v)$.

The case t::=$t_1 \underline{\times} t_2$ and v::nothunk. We must have v to be of the form $\langle u,w\rangle$ and each v_n to be of the form $\langle u_n,w_n\rangle$ such that u is the least upper bound of $(u_n)_n$ and w is the least upper bound of $(w_n)_n$. From $\forall$n: $valW_t(v_n)$ we then obtain $\forall$n: $valW_{t_1}(u_n)$ and $\forall$n: $valW_{t_2}(w_n)$. The induction hypothesis then gives $valW_{t_1}(u)$ and $valW_{t_2}(w)$ from which the desired $valW_t(v)$ follows.

The case t::=$t_1 \underline{\rightarrow} t_2$ and v::nothunk. We must have v to be of the form $\{C;u\}$ and each v_n to be of the form $\{C_n;u_n\}$ such that C is the least upper bound of $(C_n)_n$ and u is the least upper bound of $(u_n)_n$. To show $valW_t(v)$ consider w such that $valW_{t_1}(w)$. We then have

$$\forall n:\ valW_{t_2}(\{C_n,\langle u_n,w\rangle\})$$

and from the induction hypothesis we obtain

$$valW_{t_2}(\{C,\langle u,w\rangle\})$$

which is the desired result.

The case v::thunk. We must have v to be of the form $\{C,u\}$ and each v_n to be of the form $\{C_n,u_n\}$ and such that C is the least upper bound of the chain $(C_n)_n$ and u is the least upper bound of the chain $(u_n)_n$. Now $valW_t(v)$ holds vacuously unless there is

$$\Delta \in \text{ExSeq}(m,C,u)$$

in which case we have to show $postW_t(\Delta) \wedge nothunk(\Delta)$.

We now choose n_0 such that $\text{ExSeq}(*,C_n,u_n)\neq\emptyset$ when $n\geq n_0$. This is possible using Lemma 6.3.20. We then determine Δ_n for $n\geq n_0$ by

$$\Delta_n \in \text{ExSeq}(*,C_n,u_n)$$

We shall show by induction on $j\leq m$ that

$$(\Delta_n(j))_{n\geq n_0} \text{ is a chain with least upper bound } \Delta(j)$$

The base case, $j=0$, is immediate from the assumptions. The induction step follows much as in the proof of Lemma 6.3.20: since Δ_{n_0} is finite we cannot encounter any REC_0 or $\text{CALLREC}_0(l,C''_{n_0})$ in going from $\Delta_{n_0}(j)$ to $\Delta_{n_0}(j+1)$ and then we cannot either in going from $\Delta_n(j)$ to $\Delta_n(j+1)$ for $n\geq n_0$. This completes the numerical induction on $j\leq m$.

Since $((\Delta_n(m))_{n\geq n_0}$ is a chain with least upper bound $\Delta(m)$ and since Δ_{n_0} is finite it follows that for $n\geq n_0$ all Δ_n have length m. From $valW_t(v_n)$ we then have

$$postW_t(\Delta_n) \wedge nothunk(\Delta_n)$$

for all $n\geq n_0$. This amounts to

$$postW_t(\Delta_n(m)) \wedge nothunk(\Delta_n(m))$$

and we then have

$$postW_t(\Delta(m)) \wedge nothunk(\Delta(m))$$

because we have already proved the result for non-thunk values of type t. We then obtain the desired result and this completes the proof. □

Lemma 6.3.22 $compW_{(t\underline{\rightarrow}t)\underline{\rightarrow}t}(\mathbf{K}(\texttt{Fix}[t]))$ holds whenever $(t\underline{\rightarrow}t)\underline{\rightarrow}t$ is a well-formed type that does not involve lists. □

Proof: Much as in the proof of Lemma 6.3.13 it suffices to prove

$$compSW_{(t \underline{\rightarrow} t) \underline{\rightarrow} t}(\mathbf{K}(\mathtt{Fix}[t]))$$

Since $\mathbf{K}(\mathtt{Fix}[t]) = \lambda d.$ RESUME:REC:RESUME this amounts to proving

$$compSW'_{(t \underline{\rightarrow} t) \underline{\rightarrow} t}(\text{RESUME:REC:RESUME})$$

and using Lemma 6.3.12 it suffices to prove

$$valW_{t \underline{\rightarrow} t}(\{C;v\}) \Rightarrow valW_t(\{\text{REC:RESUME},\{C;v\}\}) \qquad \text{(P)}$$

For this we begin by proving

$$valW_{t \underline{\rightarrow} t}(\{C;v\}) \Rightarrow valW_t(\{\text{REC}_\text{n}\text{:RESUME},\{C;v\}\}) \qquad (\text{P}_\text{n})$$

by induction on n. The basis case, n=0, is immediate as

$$\text{ExSeq}(*,\text{REC}_0\text{:RESUME},\{C;v\}) = \emptyset$$

For the inductive step we assume (P_n) and prove $(\text{P}_{\text{n}+1})$. So assume that we have $valW_{t \underline{\rightarrow} t}(\{C;v\})$ and consider

$$\Delta \in \text{ExSeq}(m,\text{REC}_{\text{n}+1}\text{:RESUME},\{C;v\})$$

We know that $m \geq 1$ and that

$$\Delta(1..m) \in \text{ExSeq}(m-1,\text{RESUME},\{C,\langle v,v'_\text{n}\rangle\})$$
$$\text{where } v'_\text{n} = \{\text{REC}_\text{n}\text{:RESUME},\{C;v\}\}$$

From the induction hypothesis we have $valW_t(v'_\text{n})$, and $valW_{t \underline{\rightarrow} t}(\{C;v\})$ then gives

$$valW_t(\{C,\langle v,v'_\text{n}\rangle\})$$

Lemma 6.3.12 and the properties of *postW* and *nothunk* then give

$$postW_t(\Delta) \wedge nothunk(\Delta)$$

This establishes $(\text{P}_{\text{n}+1})$ and completes the numerical induction.
Finally, we obtain (P) using Lemma 6.3.21. □

Lemma 6.3.23 $compW_{(t \rightarrow t) \rightarrow t}(\mathbf{K}(\mathtt{fix}[t]))$ holds for all well-formed and composite types t that do not involve lists. □

Proof: The proof is by induction on the structure of the type t. The base cases are when t is pure and when t is a frontier type.

The case t is pure. As in the proof of Lemma 6.2.3 it is straightforward to show

$$\text{if pure}(t) \text{ then } compW_t(x) \equiv \text{true}$$

by structural induction on t. It is then immediate that

$$compW_{(t \rightarrow t) \rightarrow t}(\mathbf{K}(\texttt{fix}[t])).$$

The case $t = t_1 \underline{\rightarrow} t_2$ is a frontier type. We assume that

$$compW_{t \rightarrow t}(F)$$

and must show

$$compW_t(\mathbf{K}(\texttt{fix}[t])(F))$$

since Lemma 6.2.3 ensures $compS(\mathbf{K}(\texttt{fix}[t]))$. It suffices to consider an arbitrary $d{>}0$ and to show

$$compSW'_t(\mathbf{K}(\texttt{fix}[t])(F)(d))$$

because the *compS* part of the result follows from Lemma 6.2.3 and the 'layered predicates' (Lemma 6.3.5); but it is more convenient to imagine showing

$$compW_t(\lambda d'.\mathbf{K}(\texttt{fix}[t])(F)(d)) \qquad \text{(P)}$$

If $F(\lambda d'.\text{CALL } d)(d{+}1) = \bot$ this is immediate so assume that

$$F(\lambda d'.\text{CALL } d)(d{+}1) \neq \bot$$

and write

$$C = F(\lambda d'.\text{CALL } d)(d{+}1)$$

To prove (P) we begin by proving

$$compW_t(\lambda d'.\text{CALLREC}_\text{n}(d,C)) \qquad (\text{P}_\text{n})$$

by numerical induction on n.

In the base case, n=0, we immediately have

$$compSW_t(\lambda d'.\text{CALLREC}_0(d,C))$$

because ExSeq(*,$\text{CALLREC}_0(d,C),v$)=$\emptyset$ for all values v. Furthermore, we have

$$compS_t(\lambda d'.\text{CALLREC}_0(d,C))$$

much as in Section 6.2. To be more precise it suffices by Lemma 6.2.5 to show that

$$\text{FreeLab}(\text{CALLREC}_0(d,C)) = \emptyset$$

Setting $\Sigma = \{(d,\text{CALL } d)\}$ we have

$$compS[\Sigma]_t(\lambda d'.\text{CALL } d,\lambda d'.\text{CALL } d)$$

so that $compS_{t\to t}(F)$ gives

$$compS[\Sigma]_t(F(\lambda d'.\text{CALL } d),\ F(\lambda d'.\text{CALL } d))$$

and it follows that

$$\text{FreeLab}(C) = \text{FreeLab}(F(\lambda d'.\text{CALL } d)(d+1)) \subseteq \{d\}$$

so that $\text{FreeLab}(\text{CALLREC}_0(d,C))=\emptyset$ follows.

For the induction step we assume (P_n) and show (P_{n+1}). It suffices to prove the *compSW* part, which boils down to

$$compSW'_t(\text{CALLREC}_{n+1}(d,C)),$$

as the *compS* part follows as above. For this we note that (P_n) and the assumptions about F give

$$compW_t(F(\lambda d'.\text{CALLREC}_n(d,C)))$$

from which

$$compSW'_t(F(\lambda d'.\text{CALLREC}_n(d,C))(d+1))$$

follows. Using the 'substitution property' (Lemma 6.2.2, or rather, an obvious analogue) we have

$$compSW'_t(C[\text{CALLREC}_n(d,C)/d])$$

We then claim that this establishes

$$compSW'_t(\text{CALLREC}_{n+1}(d,C))$$

To see this note that for all values v, perhaps such that $valW_{t_1}(v)$, we have that

$$\Delta \in \text{ExSeq}(*,\text{CALLREC}_{n+1}(d,C),v)$$

if and only if

$$\Delta(0) = (\text{CALLREC}_{n+1}(d,C),[v]) \text{ and}$$
$$\Delta(1..) \in \text{ExSeq}(*,C[\text{CALLREC}_n(d,C)/d],v)$$

and note that the properties of *nothunk* and *postW* ensure that

$$postW_{t_2}(\Delta) \wedge nothunk(\Delta)$$

holds if and only if

$$postW_{t_2}(\Delta(1..)) \wedge nothunk(\Delta(1..))$$

This ends the proof by numerical induction.

To be able to conclude (P) it suffices to show

$$compSW'_t(\text{CALLREC}(d,C))$$

This amounts to assuming

$$valW_{t_1}(v)$$

and showing

$$valW_{t_2}(\{\text{CALLREC}(d,C),v\})$$

Using (P_n) we already have

$$valW_{t_2}(\{\text{CALLREC}_n(d,C),v\}) \text{ for all n}$$

and the result then follows using Lemma 6.3.21.

The case t is a product of composite types. This case is analogous to the similar case in the proof of Lemma 6.2.3 in that one must show that $compW(F)$ carries over to the functions supplied as argument to $\mathbf{K}(\mathtt{fix}[t_1])$ and $\mathbf{K}(\mathtt{fix}[t_2])$; as in the proof of Lemma 6.2.3 we simply refer to [72, Lemma 7.13] for an example of a proof along these lines. □

Summary of the well-behavedness properties

The lemmas proved above together yield the following analogue of Lemma 6.2.3:

Corollary 6.3.24 We have $compW(\mathbf{K}(\phi))$ for all operators ϕ of Table 5.1 whose type does not involve lists, except those of form $\mathtt{f}_i$ or F_i and provided that the type t indexing $\mathtt{fix}[t]$ is always composite. □

By analogy with Lemma 6.2.4 we have:

Lemma 6.3.25 ('Structural induction') Let *penv* be a well-formed position environment (in the sense of Section 5.2) such that

$$\rho_{\mathrm{PS}}(penv) \overset{\mathrm{K}}{\vdash} e{:}t$$

and assume that neither e nor *penv* involves any lists. If

$$compW(\mathbf{K}(\phi))$$

holds for all operators ϕ that occur in e, then

$$compW([\![e]\!](\mathbf{K}))$$ □

Proof: The proof is by structural induction on e much as in the proof of Lemma 6.2.4. Apart from using Lemma 6.2.4 to establish the *compS* part of the result, the proof of the *compSW* part proceeds along the same lines as in the proof of Lemma 6.2.4. We dispense with the details. □

6.4 Correctness of the Code

We now have the apparatus needed for showing the correctness of the code generated. There are two ingredients to this, depending on whether or not the execution of a piece of code gives rise to termination. So suppose that some value of the abstract machine represents some semantic value. We shall then show that

- **if** the execution of the code upon that value gives rise to a terminating computation that produces some new value,
  then this value represents the result of applying the semantic function to the original semantic value; and

- **if** the execution of the code upon the original value gives rise to a non-terminating computation,
  then the result of applying the semantic function to the original semantic value gives $\perp$.

Given the determinacy of the abstract machine, and of the mixed λ-calculus and combinatory logic, this constitutes the desired correctness property. In the remainder of this section we shall formalise this notion of correctness and then establish the required correctness properties for the operators and expressions of the mixed λ-calculus and combinatory logic. This turns out to be a rather systematic extension of the development for showing well-behavedness.

6.4.1 Definition of the correctness predicates

We shall begin by adapting the *val* and *comp* predicates of the previous section so as to express the correctness. This calls for adding an additional parameter, namely the corresponding semantic value or function. The predicate on values is

$$valC_t\colon \; Val \times \mathbf{S}(t) \rightarrow \{\text{true,false}\}$$

where t is a well-formed *2*-level type of run-time kind. It is then natural to extend the partial ordering on $\{W,S\}$ to one on $\{W,S,C\}$ such that

and with the understanding that there is no *valS* predicate[2]. Also note that even though the type index was, in principle, dispensable in the definition of *valW*

[2] Simply because the substitution property relates to the 'compile-time level' only.

it seems necessary to include it in the definition of *valC* in order to be able to express the domain in which the semantic entity is an element. We now propose the following definition of *valC* (leaving an explanation of the $\mathcal{B}_i$ function until afterwards).

$$valC_{\underline{A}_i}(\mathbf{b}_j,x) \equiv valW_{\underline{A}_i}(\mathbf{b}_j) \wedge \mathcal{B}_i[\![\mathbf{b}_j]\!] = x$$

$$valC_{t_1\underline{\times}t_2}(\langle v_1,v_2\rangle,x) \equiv \exists x_1,x_2\text{: } x = up((x_1,x_2)) \wedge valC_{t_1}(v_1,x_1) \wedge valC_{t_2}(v_2,x_2)$$

$$valC_{t_1\underline{\rightarrow}t_2}(\{C;v_0\},f) \equiv valW_{t_1\underline{\rightarrow}t_2}(\{C;v_0\}) \wedge valWC_{t_1\underline{\rightarrow}t_2}(\{C;v_0\},f)$$

where $valWC_{t_1\underline{\rightarrow}t_2}(\{C;v_0\},f) \equiv (f \neq \perp) \wedge (\ \forall v_1,x\text{: } (valC_{t_1}(v_1,x) \Rightarrow valC_{t_2}(\{C,\langle v_0,v_1\rangle\},dn(f)x)))$

$$valC_t(\{C,v\},x) \equiv valW_t(\{C,v\}) \wedge valWC_t(\{C,v\},x)$$

where $valWC_t(\{C,v\},x) \equiv \forall\Delta\in \text{ExSeq}(\infty,C,v)\text{: } (\ \Delta\in\text{ExSeq}(*) \Rightarrow postC_t(\Delta,x) \wedge nothunk(\Delta)\ ) \wedge (\ \Delta\in\text{ExSeq}(\omega) \Rightarrow x=\perp)$

where *postC*, and by analogy *preC*, is defined from *valC* in much the same way that *postW*, and *preW*, was defined from *valW*.

We need to explain the role of the $\mathcal{B}_i$ functions. Each $\mathcal{B}_i$ function has functionality

$$\mathcal{B}_i : Val \rightarrow \mathbf{S}(\underline{A}_i)$$

and purports to connect a base value $\mathbf{b}_j$ of type $\underline{A}_i$ with the appropriate element in the standard semantics. Thus

$$\mathcal{B}_{\text{bool}}[\![\mathbf{true}]\!] = \mathbf{true}$$

$$\mathcal{B}_{\text{bool}}[\![\mathbf{false}]\!] = \mathbf{false}$$

etc., but we shall leave the details of the remaining $\mathcal{B}_i$ functions unspecified.

By analogy with Lemma 6.3.2 we have:

Lemma 6.4.1 The clauses for $valC_t$ define a predicate

$$valC_t : Val \times \mathbf{S}(t) \rightarrow \{\text{true,false}\}$$

whenever t is a well-formed *2*-level type of run-time kind that does not involve any list types. □

Proof: The proof is by complete induction using the same well-founded order that was used in the proof of Lemma 6.3.2. We therefore dispense with the details. □

The relationship to *valW* is expressed by:

Lemma 6.4.2 ('Layered predicates') For all well-formed *2*-level types t of run-time kind, $v \in Val$ and $x \in \mathbf{S}(t)$ we have

$$valC_t(v,x) \Rightarrow valW_t(v)$$

Proof: The proof is by induction on the shape of the inference tree for $valC_t(v,x)$, that is, by induction on the well-founded order of the previous lemma. If the first, third or fourth clause of *valC* is used, the result is immediate from the *valW* conjunct that is present in the definition of *valC*. If the second clause is used, the result follows from the induction hypothesis. □

Turning to code sequences we define a predicate

$$compC_t\colon [\![t]\!](\mathbf{K}) \times [\![t]\!](\mathbf{S}) \to \{\text{true,false}\}$$

by structural induction on well-formed *2*-level types t of compile-time kind:

$$compC_{A_i}(x,y) \equiv x{=}y$$

$$compC_{t_1 \times t_2}((x_1,x_2),(y_1,y_2)) \equiv compC_{t_1}(x_1,y_1) \wedge compC_{t_2}(x_2,y_2)$$

$$\begin{aligned} compC_{t_1 \to t_2}(F,G) &\equiv compW_{t_1 \to t_2}(F) \wedge compWC_{t_1 \to t_2}(F,G)\\ \text{where } compWC_{t_1 \to t_2}(F,G) &\equiv \forall x,y\colon\\ &\quad compC_{t_1}(x,y) \Rightarrow compC_{t_2}(F(x),G(y)) \end{aligned}$$

$$\begin{aligned} compC_{t_1 \underline{\to} t_2}(RC,g) &\equiv compW_{t_1 \underline{\to} t_2}(RC) \wedge compWC_{t_1 \underline{\to} t_2}(RC,g)\\ \text{where } compWC_{t_1 \underline{\to} t_2}(RC,g) &\equiv \forall d{>}0\colon compWC'_{t_1 \underline{\to} t_2}(RC(d),g)\\ \text{where } compWC'_{t_1 \underline{\to} t_2}(C,g) &\equiv\\ &(C = \bot \Rightarrow g = \bot) \wedge\\ &(C \neq \bot \Rightarrow g \neq \bot \wedge \forall v,y\colon (valC_{t_1}(v,y)\\ &\qquad \Rightarrow valC_{t_2}(\{C,v\},dn(g)y))) \end{aligned}$$

By analogy with Lemma 6.3.4 we have

Lemma 6.4.3 The above clauses define an admissible predicate $compC_t$, whenever t is a well-formed *2*-level type of compile-time kind that does not involve any list types. □

Proof: This is a simple structural induction. □

The relationship to *compW* is expressed by the following analogue of Lemma 6.3.5:

Lemma 6.4.4 ('Layered predicates') If t is a well-formed *2*-level type of compile-time kind, $x \in [\![t]\!](\mathbf{K})$ and $y \in [\![t]\!](\mathbf{S})$ then

$$compC_t(x,y) \Rightarrow compW_t(x)$$

Proof: This is a simple structural induction. □

6.4.2 Correctness of operators

Having defined the predicates we can next confront the task of proving that they hold for the operators. As has already been said this will turn out to be a rather systematic extension of the proofs of the previous section and we therefore only provide some of the more interesting details.

We begin by observing that one may formulate properties of *preC*, *postC* (and *nothunk*) much as those formulated for *preW*, *postW* (and *nothunk*). This amounts to little more than extending *preW* and *postW* with an additional parameter denoting the semantic value. We therefore dispense with the formulation of these facts.

The characterization of RESUME leads to the following analogue of Lemma 6.3.12.

Lemma 6.4.5 If $\Delta \in \text{ExSeq}(\infty, \text{RESUME})$ and $preC_t(\Delta, x)$ then

- $\Delta \in \text{ExSeq}(*) \Rightarrow postC_t(\Delta, x) \wedge nothunk(\Delta)$
- $\Delta \in \text{ExSeq}(\omega) \Rightarrow x = \perp$

Note that this clearly states the intention with RESUME: it will not change the semantics of the entity on top of the stack but will massage it so that it is not a thunk.

Proof: Let $\Delta(0) = (\text{RESUME}, [v])$. If v is not a thunk we know that

$$\Delta = (\text{RESUME}, [v]) \rightarrow (\varepsilon, [v])$$

so $\Delta \in \text{ExSeq}(*)$, $nothunk(\Delta)$ and $postC_t(\Delta, x)$.

If v is a thunk, that is v::thunk, we can write $v = \{C_1, v_1\}$ so that

$$\Delta(1) = (C_1\hat{\ }\text{RESUME}, [v_1])$$

Let now $\Delta_1 \in \text{ExSeq}(\infty, C_1, v_1)$ be determined by

$$\Delta_1 = \Delta(1..) \propto \text{RESUME}$$

From $valC_t(\{C_1, v_1\}, x)$ we have

- $\Delta_1 \in \text{ExSeq}(*) \Rightarrow postC_t(\Delta_1, x) \wedge nothunk(\Delta_1)$
- $\Delta_1 \in \text{ExSeq}(\omega) \Rightarrow x = \perp$

If $\Delta_1 \in \text{ExSeq}(\omega)$ also $\Delta \in \text{ExSeq}(\omega)$ and we have $x = \perp$ as desired. If $\Delta_1 \in \text{ExSeq}(*)$, that is $\Delta_1 \in \text{ExSeq}(m_1)$ for some m_1, we have

$$\Delta(1+m_1) = (\text{RESUME}, [v_2])$$

for some v_2 such that v_2::nothunk and $valC_t(v_2,x)$. Then

$$\Delta(1+m_1+1) = (\varepsilon,[v_2])$$

and we have $\Delta \in$ExSeq(*), $nothunk(\Delta)$ and $postC_t(\Delta,x)$ as desired. □

We now turn to the operators. The proofs will mimic those of Section 6.3 but with two differences. One is that we have to take the semantic entity into account when proving the result. The other is that the proofs proceed by decomposing execution sequences $\Delta \in$ExSeq(∞) rather than $\Delta \in$ExSeq(*); this means that we must take care to properly handle infinite execution sequences.

By analogy with Lemma 6.3.13 we have

Lemma 6.4.6 $compC_{t_1\underline{\times}t_2\underline{\to}t_1}(\mathbf{K}(\texttt{Fst}),\mathbf{S}(\texttt{Fst}))$ holds whenever $t_1\underline{\times}t_2\underline{\to}t_1$ is a well-formed type that does not involve lists. □

Proof: We must show *compW* as well as *compWC*. The first result is a consequence of Lemma 6.3.13 so we may concentrate on showing *compWC*. For this let $d>0$, write

$$C = \mathbf{K}(\texttt{Fst})(d) = \text{RESUME:FST:RESUME}$$

and note that $C \neq \perp$ as well as $\mathbf{S}(\texttt{Fst}) \neq \perp$. Next let v and y be given such that

$$valC_{t_1\underline{\times}t_2}(v,y)$$

and consider showing $valC_{t_1}(\{C,v\},dn(\mathbf{S}(\texttt{Fst}))(y))$. Using the *compW* part of the result, and that $valC(v,y)$ implies $valW(v)$, it actually suffices to prove

$$valWC_{t_1}(\{C,v\},dn(\mathbf{S}(\texttt{Fst}))(y))$$

For this let $\Delta \in$ExSeq(∞,C,v). As in the proof of Lemma 6.3.13 we now proceed in three stages.

Stage 1: Let $\Delta_1 \in$ExSeq(∞,RESUME,v) be given by

$$\Delta_1 = \Delta \propto \text{FST:RESUME}$$

If $\Delta_1 \in$ExSeq(ω) also $\Delta \in$ExSeq(ω) and we have $y=\perp$ using Lemma 6.4.5; it then follows that $dn(\mathbf{S}(\texttt{Fst}))(y) = \perp$. Otherwise, $\Delta_1 \in$ExSeq(*) and there exists m_1 such that $\Delta_1 \in$ExSeq(m_1); using Lemma 6.4.5 we then have

$$postC_{t_1\underline{\times}t_2}(\Delta(m_1),y) \wedge nothunk(\Delta(m_1))$$

Stage 2: We now know that $\Delta(m_1)$ is of the form (FST:RESUME,$[v_2]$) where v_2::nothunk and $valC_{t_1\underline{\times}t_2}(v_2,y)$. By inspection of the clauses for *valC* it follows that

$$v_2 = \langle v_{21}, v_{22} \rangle$$
$$y = up(y_1, y_2)$$

for appropriate v_{21}, $v_{22} \in Val$ and $y_i \in \mathbf{S}(t_i)$. It is then immediate that

$$valC_{t_1}(v_{21}, y_1)$$
$$\Delta(m_1+1) = (\text{RESUME}, v_{21})$$

and $postC_{t_1}(\Delta(m_1+1), dn(\mathbf{S}(\texttt{Fst}))(y))$ follows.

Stage 3: Let $\Delta_3 \in \text{ExSeq}(\infty, \text{RESUME}, v_{21})$ be given by $\Delta_3 = \Delta(m_1+1..)$. One case is when $\Delta_3 \in \text{ExSeq}(\omega)$ and then also $\Delta \in \text{ExSeq}(\omega)$ and we have $dn(\mathbf{S}(\texttt{fst}))(y) = \bot$ as required using Lemma 6.4.5. Otherwise, $\Delta_3 \in \text{ExSeq}(*)$ and Lemma 6.4.5 ensures

$$postC_{t_1}(\Delta, dn(\mathbf{S}(\texttt{fst}))(y)) \wedge nothunk(\Delta)$$

This concludes the proof of $valWC_{t_1}(\{C,v\}, dn(\mathbf{S}(\texttt{Fst}))(y))$. □

Corollary 6.4.7 A similar result holds for `Snd`, `Id`, `True` and `False`. □

Lemma 6.4.8 $compC_{t'}(\mathbf{K}(\texttt{Tuple}), \mathbf{S}(\texttt{Tuple}))$ holds for all well-formed *2*-level types t' that are of the form $(t \underline{\rightarrow} t_1) \rightarrow (t \underline{\rightarrow} t_2) \rightarrow (t \underline{\rightarrow} t_1 \underline{\times} t_2)$ and that do not involve lists. □

Proof: Lemma 6.3.15 proves the *compW* part of the result and proceeding along the lines of the proof of Lemma 6.3.15 it actually suffices to assume that

$$compC_{t \rightarrow t_i}(RC_i, g_i) \text{ for i=1,2}$$

and to show that

$$compWC(RC, g)$$

where

$$RC = \mathbf{K}(\texttt{Tuple})(RC_1)(RC_2)$$
$$g = \mathbf{S}(\texttt{Tuple})(g_1)(g_2)$$

So let $d>0$ and consider $RC(d)$. If $RC(d)=\bot$ there is some i such that $RC_i(d)=\bot$; from $compWC(RC_i, g_i)$ we then have $g_i=\bot$ and it follows that $g=\bot$ which then establishes $compWC'(RC(d), g)$. If $RC(d)\neq\bot$ then also $RC_1(d)\neq\bot$ and $RC_2(d)\neq\bot$ and we have

$$RC(d) = \text{ENTER:DELAY}(RC_2(d))\text{:SWITCH:DELAY}(RC_1(d))\text{:TUPLE}$$

Furthermore, also $g_1\neq\bot$ and $g_2\neq\bot$ so that $g\neq\bot$ and we have

$$g = up(\lambda y.\ up(dn(g_1)(y),\ dn(g_1)(y)))$$

To show $compWC'(RC(d),g)$ we next consider v and y such that

$$valC_t(v,y)$$

and we must show $valC_{t_1\underline{\times}t_2}(\{RC(d),v\},\ dn(g)(y))$. Using Lemma 6.3.15 (and the 'layered predicates', Lemmas 6.4.4 and 6.4.2) this boils down to showing

$$valWC_{t_1\underline{\times}t_2}(\{RC(d),v\},\ dn(g)(y))$$

So let $\Delta\in$ExSeq$(\infty,RC(d),v)$. It is immediate to see that $\Delta\in$ExSeq(5) and that

$$\Delta(5) = (\varepsilon,[\langle\{RC_1(d),v\},\ \{RC_2(d),v\}\rangle])$$

As $nothunk(\Delta)$ is immediate it remains to show

$$valC_{t_1\underline{\times}t_2}(\langle\{RC_1(d),v\},\{RC_2(d),v\}\rangle,\ up(dn(g_1)(y),dn(g_2)(y)))$$

and given the definition of $valC_{t_1\underline{\times}t_2}$ this follows from

$$valC_{t_i}(\{RC_i(d),v\},\ dn(g_i)(y)) \text{ for i=1,2}$$

which is a consequence of $valC_t(v,y)$ and $compC(RC_i,g_i)$ for i=1,2. □

Lemma 6.4.9 $compC_{t'}(\mathbf{K}(\square),\mathbf{S}(\square))$ holds for all well-formed *2*-level types t' that are of the form $(t_2\underline{\rightarrow}t_3) \rightarrow (t_1\underline{\rightarrow}t_2) \rightarrow (t_1\underline{\rightarrow}t_3)$ and that do not involve lists. □

Proof: Lemma 6.3.16 proves the *compW* part of the result and proceeding along the lines of the proof of Lemma 6.3.16 it actually suffices to assume that

$$compC_{t_2\underline{\rightarrow}t_3}(RC_1,g_1)$$
$$compC_{t_1\underline{\rightarrow}t_2}(RC_2,g_2)$$

and to show that

$$compWC_{t_1\underline{\rightarrow}t_3}(RC,g)$$

where $RC = \mathbf{K}(\square)(RC_1)(RC_2)$ and $g = \mathbf{S}(\square)(g_1)(g_2)$. So let $d>0$ and consider $RC(d)$. If $RC(d)=\bot$ also $RC_i(d)=\bot$ for some i so that $g_i=\bot$ and hence $g=\bot$ as desired. Otherwise, $RC(d)\neq\bot$ in which case $RC_1(d)\neq\bot$ and $RC_2(d)\neq\bot$ and we have

$$RC(d) = \text{DELAY}(RC_2(d))\text{:}RC_1(d)$$

Furthermore, also $g_1\neq\bot$ and $g_2\neq\bot$ so that $g\neq\bot$ and we have

$$g = up(\lambda y.\ dn(g_1)(dn(g_2)(y)))$$

To show $compWC'(RC(d),g)$ we next consider v and y such that

$$valC_{t_1}(v,y)$$

and must show $valC(\{RC(d),v\},dn(g)(y))$. Using Lemma 6.3.16 (and the 'layered predicates', Lemmas 6.4.4 and 6.4.2) this boils down to showing

$$valWC_{t_3}(\{RC(d),v\},dn(g)(y))$$

So let $\Delta \in \text{ExSeq}(\infty,RC(d),v)$. We know that

$$\Delta(1) = (RC_1(d),[\{RC_2(d),v\}])$$

so that

$$\Delta(1..) \in \text{ExSeq}(\infty,RC_1(d),\{RC_2(d),v\})$$

From $compC(RC_2,g_2)$ we have

$$valC_{t_2}(\{RC_2(d),v\},\ dn(g_2)(y))$$

and using $compC(RC_1,g_1)$ we then have

- $\Delta(1..)\in\text{ExSeq}(*) \Rightarrow nothunk(\Delta(1..)) \wedge$
  $postC_{t_3}(\Delta(1..),dn(g)(y))$
- $\Delta(1..)\in\text{ExSeq}(\omega) \Rightarrow dn(g)(y)=\perp$

In both cases the desired result, with Δ replacing $\Delta(1..)$, follows immediately. □

Lemma 6.4.10 $compC(\mathbf{K}(\texttt{Cond}),\mathbf{S}(\texttt{Cond}))$ provided that the type of `Cond` does not involve lists. □

Proof: Lemma 6.3.17 proves the *compW* part of the result and proceeding along the lines of the proof of Lemma 6.3.17 it actually suffices to assume that

$$compC_{\underline{t_1 \rightarrow \texttt{Bool}}}(RC_1,g_1)$$
$$compC_{t_1 \underline{\rightarrow} t_2}(RC_2,g_2)$$
$$compC_{t_1 \underline{\rightarrow} t_2}(RC_3,g_3)$$

and to show that

$$compWC_{t_1 \underline{\rightarrow} t_2}(RC,g)$$

where $RC = \mathbf{K}(\texttt{Cond})(RC_1)(RC_2)(RC_3)$ and $g = \mathbf{S}(\texttt{Cond})(g_1)(g_2)(g_3)$. So let $d>0$ and consider $RC(d)$. If $RC(d)=\perp$ also $RC_i(d)=\perp$ for some i so that $g_i=\perp$ and hence $g=\perp$ as desired. Otherwise, $RC(d)\neq\perp$ in which case $RC_i\neq\perp$ for all i, and we have

$$RC(d) = \text{ENTER}{:}RC_1(d){:}\text{BRANCH}(RC_2(d),RC_3(d))$$

Furthermore, also $g_i \neq \perp$ for all i, so that $g \neq \perp$ and we have

$$g = up(\ \lambda y. \begin{cases} dn(g_2)(y) & \text{if } dn(g_1)(y)=\textbf{true} \\ dn(g_3)(y) & \text{if } dn(g_1)(y)=\textbf{false} \\ \perp & \text{if } dn(g_1)(y)=\perp \end{cases}\ )$$

To show $compWC'(RC(d),g)$ we next consider v and y such that

$$valC_{t_1}(v,y)$$

and must show $valC_{t_2}(\{RC(d),v\},dn(g)(y))$. Using Lemma 6.3.17 (and the 'layered predicates', Lemmas 6.4.4 and 6.4.2) this boils down to showing

$$valWC_{t_2}(\{RC(d),v\},dn(g)(y))$$

So let $\Delta \in \text{ExSeq}(\infty,RC(d),v)$ and let us proceed in stages, as in the proof of Lemma 6.3.17.

Stage 1: We know that

$$\Delta(1) = (RC_1(d){:}\text{BRANCH}(RC_2(d),RC_3(d)),[v,v])$$

Stage 2: Let $\Delta_2 \in \text{ExSeq}(\infty,RC_1(d),v)$ be given by

$$\Delta_2 = (\Delta(1..) \propto \text{BRANCH}(RC_2(d),RC_3(d))) \propto [v]$$

We have $preC_{t_1}(\Delta_2,y)$ and now have two cases depending on whether Δ_2 is finite or not. If $\Delta_2 \in \text{ExSeq}(\omega)$ we have $dn(g_1)(y)=\perp$ from $compC(RC_1,g_1)$; it follows that also $\Delta \in \text{ExSeq}(\omega)$ and that $dn(g)(y)=\perp$ as desired in this case. Otherwise, $\Delta_2 \in \text{ExSeq}(*)$ and we have

$$postC_{\underline{\text{Bool}}}(\Delta_2,dn(g_1)(y)) \wedge nothunk(\Delta_2)$$

from $compC(RC_1,g_1)$.

Stage 3: Writing $\Delta_2 \in \text{ExSeq}(m_2)$ we have

$$\Delta(1+m_2) = (\text{BRANCH}(RC_2(d),RC_3(d)),[w,v])$$

for some $w \in Val$ such that w::nothunk and

$$valC_{\underline{\text{Bool}}}(w,dn(g_1)(y))$$

By inspection of the clauses for $valC$ it follows that w is either **true** or **false**. It follows that

$$\Delta(2+m_2) = (RC_j(d),[v])$$
$$dn(g)(y) = dn(g_j)(y)$$

for a value $j \in \{2,3\}$ depending on w.

Stage 4: Let $\Delta_4 \in \text{ExSeq}(\infty, RC_j(d), v)$ be given by

$$\Delta_4 = \Delta(2+m_2..)$$

Again we have two cases depending on whether Δ_4 is finite or not. If $\Delta_4 \in \text{ExSeq}(\omega)$ we have $dn(g_j)(y)=\perp$ from $compC(RC_j, g_j)$; it follows that also $\Delta \in \text{ExSeq}(\omega)$ and that $dn(g)(y)=\perp$ as desired in this case. Otherwise, $\Delta_4 \in \text{ExSeq}(*)$ and we have

$$postC_{t_2}(\Delta_4, dn(g_j)(y)) \wedge nothunk(\Delta_4)$$

from $compC(RC_j, g_j)$. But using the properties of *postC* and *nothunk* this amounts to

$$postC_{t_2}(\Delta, dn(g_j)(y)) \wedge nothunk(\Delta)$$

which is the desired result as also $\Delta \in \text{ExSeq}(*)$. □

Lemma 6.4.11 $compC(\mathbf{K}(\texttt{Curry}), \mathbf{S}(\texttt{Curry}))$ provided that the type of `Curry` does not involve lists. □

Proof: Lemma 6.3.18 proves the *compW* part of the result and proceeding along the lines of the proof of Lemma 6.3.18 it actually suffices to assume that

$$compC_{(t_0 \underline{\times} t_1) \underline{\rightarrow} t_2}(RC_1, g_1)$$

and to show that

$$compWC_{t_0 \underline{\rightarrow} (t_1 \underline{\rightarrow} t_2)}(RC, g)$$

where $RC = \mathbf{K}(\texttt{Curry})(RC_1)$ and $g = \mathbf{S}(\texttt{Curry})(g_1)$. So let $d>0$ and consider $RC(d)$. If $RC(d)=\perp$ also $RC_1(d)=\perp$ so that $g_1=\perp$ and hence $g=\perp$ as desired. Otherwise, $RC(d)\neq\perp$ in which case $RC_1(d)\neq\perp$ and we have

$$RC(d) = \text{CURRY}(RC_1(d))$$

Furthermore, also $g_1\neq\perp$ so that $g\neq\perp$ and we have

$$g = up(\lambda y_0.\ up(\lambda y_1.\ dn(g)(up(y_0, y_1))))$$

To show $compWC'(RC(d), g)$ we next consider v_0 and y_0 such that

$$valC_{t_0}(v_0, y_0)$$

and must show $valC_{t_1 \underline{\rightarrow} t_2}(\{RC(d), v_0\},\ dn(g)(y_0))$. Using Lemma 6.3.18 (and the 'layered predicates', Lemmas 6.4.4 and 6.4.2) this boils down to showing

$$valWC_{t_1 \underline{\rightarrow} t_2}(\{RC(d), v_0\},\ dn(g)(y_0))$$

For this let $\Delta \in \text{ExSeq}(\infty, RC(d), v_0)$. It is immediate that $\Delta \in \text{ExSeq}(1)$ and that

$$\Delta(1) = (\varepsilon, [\{RC_1(d); v_0\}])$$

Then $nothunk(\Delta)$ is immediate and to show $postC(\Delta, dn(g)(y_0))$ we must show

$$valC_{t_1 \underline{\rightarrow} t_2}(\{RC_1(d); v_0\},\ dn(g)(y_0))$$

Using Lemma 6.3.18 (and the 'layered predicates') this boils down to showing

$$valWC_{t_1 \underline{\rightarrow} t_2}(\{RC_1(d); v_0\}, dn(g)(y_0))$$

It is evident that $dn(g)(y_0) \neq \perp$ so consider v_1 and y_1 such that

$$valC_{t_1}(v_1, y_1)$$

and consider showing

$$valC_{t_2}(\{RC_1(d), \langle v_0, v_1\rangle\},\ dn(dn(g)(y_0))(y_1))$$

From $valC_{t_0}(v_0, y_0)$ and $valC_{t_1}(v_1, y_1)$ we have

$$valC_{t_0 \underline{\times} t_1}(\langle v_0, v_1\rangle,\ up(y_0, y_1))$$

and using $compC_{(t_0 \underline{\times} t_1) \underline{\rightarrow} t_2}(RC_1, g_1)$ we obtain

$$valC_{t_2}(\{RC_1(d), \langle v_0, v_1\rangle\},\ dn(g_1)(up(y_0, y_1)))$$

which is the desired result. □

Lemma 6.4.12 $compC_{((t_1 \underline{\rightarrow} t_2) \underline{\times} t_1) \underline{\rightarrow} t_2}(\mathbf{K}(\texttt{Apply}), \mathbf{S}(\texttt{Apply}))$ holds for all well-formed types $((t_1 \underline{\rightarrow} t_2) \underline{\times} t_1) \underline{\rightarrow} t_2$ that do not involve lists. □

Proof: Lemma 6.3.19 proves the *compW* part of the result so it suffices to prove

$$compWC_{((t_1 \underline{\rightarrow} t_2) \underline{\times} t_1) \underline{\rightarrow} t_2}(RC, g)$$

where $RC = \mathbf{K}(\texttt{Apply})$ and $g = \mathbf{S}(\texttt{Apply})$. So let $d > 0$ and note that $RC(d) \neq \perp$ as well as $g \neq \perp$ and that

$$RC(d) = \text{RESUME}{:}C'$$

$$g = up(\lambda y.\ dn(f)(y_1) \text{ where } (f, y_1) = dn(y))$$

where

$$C' = \text{ENTER:SND:SWITCH:FST:RESUME:}C''$$

$$C'' = \text{APPLY:RESUME}$$

To show $compWC'(RC(d), g)$ we next consider v and y such that

$$valC_{(t_1 \underline{\rightarrow} t_2) \underline{\times} t_1}(v,y)$$

and must show $valC_{t_2}(\{RC(d),v\},\ dn(g)(y))$. Using Lemma 6.3.19 (and the 'layered predicates', Lemmas 6.4.4 and 6.4.2) this boils down to showing

$$valWC_{t_2}(\{RC(d),v\},\ dn(g)(y))$$

So let $\Delta \in \text{ExSeq}(\infty, RC(d), v)$. We proceed in stages as in the proof of Lemma 6.3.19.

Stage 1: Let $\Delta_1 \in \text{ExSeq}(\infty, \text{RESUME}, v)$ be given by $\Delta_1 = \Delta \propto C'$. We now have two cases depending on whether Δ_1 is finite or not. If $\Delta_1 \in \text{ExSeq}(\omega)$ we have $y = \bot$ using Lemma 6.4.5; then also $\Delta \in \text{ExSeq}(\omega)$ and $dn(g)(y) = \bot$ which is the desired result in this case. Otherwise, $\Delta_1 \in \text{ExSeq}(*)$ and there exists m_1 such that $\Delta_1 \in \text{ExSeq}(m_1)$; using Lemma 6.4.5 we then have

$$postC_{(t_1 \underline{\rightarrow} t_2) \underline{\times} t_1}(\Delta(m_1),y) \wedge nothunk(\Delta(m_1))$$

Stage 2: Writing $\Delta(m_1) = (C',[v])$ it follows by inspection of the clauses for $valC$ that v must be of the form

$$v = \langle u,w \rangle$$

It then follows from the definition of $valC_{(t_1 \underline{\rightarrow} t_2) \underline{\times} t_1}$ that also y must be of the form

$$y = up(f,y_1)$$

and where

$$valC_{t_1 \underline{\rightarrow} t_2}(u,f)$$
$$valC_{t_1}(w,y_1)$$

Furthermore,

$$\Delta(m_1+4) = (\text{RESUME}:C'',[u,w])$$

Stage 3: Let $\Delta_3 \in \text{ExSeq}(\infty, \text{RESUME}, u)$ be given by

$$\Delta_3 = (\Delta(m_1+4..) \propto C'') \propto [w]$$

If $\Delta_3 \in \text{ExSeq}(\omega)$ we have $f = \bot$ using Lemma 6.4.5; then also $\Delta \in \text{ExSeq}(\omega)$ and $dn(g)(y) = \bot$ which is the desired result in this case. If $\Delta_3 \in \text{ExSeq}(*)$ there is m_3 such that $\Delta_3 \in \text{ExSeq}(m_3)$ and Lemma 6.4.5 gives

$$postC_{t_1 \underline{\rightarrow} t_2}(\Delta_3,f) \wedge nothunk(\Delta_3)$$

Stage 4: It follows that

$$\Delta(m_1+4+m_3) = (C'',[u',w])$$

where

$$valC_{t_1 \underline{\rightarrow} t_2}(u',f)$$

Since u'::nothunk it follows by inspection of the clauses for *valC* that u' is of the form

$$u' = \{\overline{C};\overline{u}\}$$

Then

$$\Delta(m_1+5+m_3) = (\text{RESUME},[\{\overline{C},\langle\overline{u},w\rangle\}])$$

and $valC_{t_2}(\{\overline{C},\langle\overline{u},w\rangle\}, dn(f)(y_1))$ follows from $valC(\{\overline{C};\overline{u}\},f)$ and $valC(w,y_1)$.

Stage 5: Let $\Delta_5 \in \text{ExSeq}(\infty,\text{RESUME})$ be given by

$$\Delta_5 = \Delta(m_1+5+m_3..)$$

If $\Delta_5 \in \text{ExSeq}(\omega)$ we have $dn(f)(y_1)=\bot$ by Lemma 6.4.5; then also $\Delta \in \text{ExSeq}(\omega)$ and $dn(g)(y)=\bot$ which is the desired result in this case. If $\Delta_5 \in \text{ExSeq}(*)$ we have

$$postC_{t_2}(\Delta_5,dn(f)(y_1)) \wedge nothunk(\Delta_5)$$

by Lemma 6.4.5. Using the properties of *postC* and *nothunk* this yields

$$postC_{t_2}(\Delta,dn(g)(y)) \wedge nothunk(\Delta)$$

which is the desired result in this case. □

For the remaining operators, `Fix` and `fix`, we follow the approach of the previous section. This calls for first establishing a lemma about the behaviour of *valC* when taking least upper bounds.

Lemma 6.4.13 Let $(v_n)_n$ be a chain of values with v as their least upper bound and let $(y_n)_n$ be a chain of semantic values with $y = \bigsqcup_n y_n$ as their least upper bound. If $\forall$n: $valC_t(v_n,y_n)$ then also $valC_t(v,y)$. □

Proof: As in the proof of Lemma 6.3.21 we proceed by structural induction on t. In each case we first consider the situation where v is not a thunk and then finally consider the situation where v is a thunk. As in the proof of Lemma 6.3.21 we have that v_n is a thunk if and only if v is.

The case t::=$\underline{A_i}$ and v::nothunk. As in the proof of Lemma 6.3.21 we must have $v_n=v$ for all n. It then follows that also $y_n=y$ for all n and the desired result is immediate.

The case t::=$t_1\underline{\times}t_2$ and v::nothunk. We must have v to be of the form $\langle u,w\rangle$ and each v_n to be of the form $\langle u_n,w_n\rangle$ such that u is the least upper bound of $(u_n)_n$ and w is the least upper bound of $(w_n)_n$. In a similar way we must have y to be of the form $up(x,z)$ and each y_n to be of the form $up(x_n,z_n)$ such that $x = \bigsqcup_n x_n$ and $z = \bigsqcup_n z_n$. From $\forall$n: $valC_t(v_n,y_n)$ we obtain

$$\forall \mathrm{n}: valC_{t_1}(u_\mathrm{n},x_\mathrm{n})$$

$$\forall \mathrm{n}: valC_{t_2}(w_\mathrm{n},z_\mathrm{n})$$

and using the induction hypothesis we obtain

$$valC_{t_1}(u,x) \wedge valC_{t_2}(w,z)$$

from which the desired result follows.

The case $t::=t_1\underline{\rightarrow}t_2$ and v::nothunk. We must have v to be of the form $\{C;u\}$ and each v_n to be of the form $\{C_\mathrm{n};u_\mathrm{n}\}$ such that C is the least upper bound of $(C_\mathrm{n})_\mathrm{n}$ and u is the least upper bound of $(u_\mathrm{n})_\mathrm{n}$. From $valC_t(v_\mathrm{n},y_\mathrm{n})$ it follows that $y_\mathrm{n}\neq\perp$ from which $y\neq\perp$ is immediate. Concerning $valC_t(v,y)$ we note that the *valW* part follows from Lemma 6.3.21 (and the 'layered predicates', Lemma 6.4.2). To prove (what remains of) the *valWC* part, consider w and z such that

$$valC_{t_1}(w,z)$$

We then have

$$\forall \mathrm{n}: valC_{t_2}(\{C_\mathrm{n},\langle u_\mathrm{n},w\rangle\},dn(y_\mathrm{n})(z))$$

from which

$$valC_{t_2}(\{C,\langle u,w\rangle\},dn(y)(z))$$

follows using the induction hypothesis. This establishes the desired result in this case.

The case v::thunk. We must have v to be of the form $\{C,u\}$ and each v_n to be of the form $\{C_\mathrm{n},u_\mathrm{n}\}$ and such that C is the least upper bound of the chain $(C_\mathrm{n})_\mathrm{n}$ and u is the least upper bound of the chain $(u_\mathrm{n})_\mathrm{n}$. Concerning $valC_t(v,y)$ note that the *valW* part follows from Lemma 6.3.21 (and the 'layered predicates', Lemma 6.4.2). To show $valWC_t(\{C,u\},y)$ we consider

$$\Delta \in \mathrm{ExSeq}(\infty,C,u)$$

and have two cases depending on whether Δ is finite or not.

If $\Delta\in\mathrm{ExSeq}(*)$ we proceed as in the proof of Lemma 6.3.21. Using Lemma 6.3.20 there exists a natural number n_0 such that

$$\Delta_\mathrm{n} \in \mathrm{ExSeq}(*,C_\mathrm{n},u_\mathrm{n}) \text{ for } \mathrm{n}\geq\mathrm{n}_0$$

uniquely determines execution sequences Δ_n. As in the proof of Lemma 6.3.21 we have a natural number m such that

$$\Delta \in \mathrm{ExSeq}(m)$$

$$\Delta_\mathrm{n} \in \mathrm{ExSeq}(m,C_\mathrm{n},u_\mathrm{n}) \text{ for } \mathrm{n}\geq\mathrm{n}_0$$

and such that

$$(\Delta_n(m))_{n\geq n_0} \text{ is a chain with least upper bound } \Delta(m)$$

Using $valC_t(\{C_n,u_n\},y_n)$ we now have

$$postC_t(\Delta_n,y_n) \wedge nothunk(\Delta_n) \text{ for } n\geq n_0$$

from which

$$postC_t(\Delta,y) \wedge nothunk(\Delta)$$

follows using the induction hypothesis (for the same type t but for non-thunk values). This establishes the result in this case.

If $\Delta\in\text{ExSeq}(\omega)$ it is easy to adapt the proof of Lemma 6.3.20 to show also that all

$$\Delta_n \in \text{ExSeq}(\infty,C_n,u_n)$$

have $\Delta_n\in\text{ExSeq}(\omega)$. Using $valC_t(\{C_n,u_n\},y_n)$ it follows that $y_n=\perp$ for all n and hence $y=\perp$ as is the desired result in this case. □

Lemma 6.4.14 $compC_{(t\underline{\rightarrow}t)\underline{\rightarrow}t}$ $(\mathbf{K}(\texttt{Fix}[t]),\mathbf{S}(\texttt{Fix}[t]))$ holds for all well-formed types $(t\underline{\rightarrow}t)\underline{\rightarrow}t$ that do not involve lists. □

Proof: Much as in the proof of Lemma 6.3.22 it suffices to prove

$$compWC_{(t\underline{\rightarrow}t)\underline{\rightarrow}t}(\mathbf{K}(\texttt{Fix}[t]),\mathbf{S}(\texttt{Fix}[t]))$$

as the *compW* part of the result follows from Lemma 6.3.22. For this let $d>0$ and show

$$compWC'_{(t\underline{\rightarrow}t)\underline{\rightarrow}t}(\text{RESUME:REC:RESUME},\ up(\lambda f.\text{FIX}(dn(f))))$$

Using Lemma 6.4.5 it suffices to prove

$$valC_{t\underline{\rightarrow}t}(\{C;v\},up(f)) \Rightarrow valC_t(\{\text{REC:RESUME},\{C;v\}\},\text{FIX}(f)) \qquad \text{(P)}$$

For this we begin by proving

$$valC_{t\underline{\rightarrow}t}(\{C;v\},up(f)) \Rightarrow valC_t(\{\text{REC}_n\text{:RESUME},\{C;v\}\},f^n(\perp)) \qquad (\text{P}_n)$$

by induction on n. The basis case, n=0, is immediate as

$$\text{ExSeq}(*,\text{REC}_0\text{:RESUME},\{C;v\}) = \emptyset$$

$$f^0(\perp) = \perp$$

For the inductive step we assume (P_n) and prove (P_{n+1}). So assume that C, v and f are such that $valC_{t\underline{\rightarrow}t}(\{C;v\},up(f))$ and consider

$$\Delta \in \text{ExSeq}(\infty,\text{REC}_{n+1}\text{:RESUME},\{C;v\})$$

We have

$$\Delta(1..) \in \text{ExSeq}(\infty,\text{RESUME},\{C,\langle v,v'_n\rangle\})$$
$$\text{where } v'_n = \{\text{REC}_n\text{:RESUME},\{C;v\}\}$$

From the induction hypothesis we have

$$valC_t(v'_n,f^n(\bot))$$

and $valC_{t\underline{\rightarrow}t}(\{C;v\},up(f))$ then gives

$$valC_t(\{C,\langle v,v'_n\rangle\},f^{n+1}(\bot))$$

Lemma 6.4.5 then gives

$$postC_t(\Delta,f^{n+1}(\bot)) \wedge nothunk(\Delta)$$

if $\Delta(1..)\in\text{ExSeq}(*)$ and

$$f^{n+1}(\bot) = \bot$$

if $\Delta(1..)\in\text{ExSeq}(\omega)$. This establishes (P_{n+1}) and completes the numerical induction.

Finally, we obtain (P) using Lemma 6.4.13. □

Lemma 6.4.15 $compC_{(t\rightarrow t)\rightarrow t}(\mathbf{K}(\mathtt{fix}[t]),\mathbf{S}(\mathtt{fix}[t]))$ holds for all well-formed and composite types t that do not involve lists. □

Proof: The proof is by induction on the structure of the type t. The base cases are when t is pure and when t is a frontier type.

The case t is pure. As in the proof of Lemma 6.3.23 it is straightforward to show

$$\text{if pure}(t) \text{ then } compC_t(x,y) \equiv x{=}y$$

by structural induction on t. It is then immediate that

$$compC_{(t\rightarrow t)\rightarrow t}(\mathbf{K}(\mathtt{fix}[t]),\mathbf{S}(\mathtt{fix}[t])).$$

The case $t = t_1\underline{\rightarrow}t_2$ is a frontier type. We assume that

$$compC_{t\rightarrow t}(F,G)$$

and must show

$$compC_t(\mathbf{K}(\mathtt{fix}[t])(F),\mathbf{S}(\mathtt{fix}[t])(G))$$

since Lemma 6.3.23 ensures $compW_t(\mathbf{K}(\mathtt{fix}[t]))$. It suffices to consider an arbitrary $d>0$ and to show

$$compWC'_t(\mathbf{K}(\mathtt{fix}[t])(F)(d),\mathbf{S}(\mathtt{fix}[t])(G))$$

because the $compW$ part of the result follows from Lemma 6.3.23 (and the 'layered predicates', Lemma 6.4.4); but it is more convenient to imagine showing

$$compC_t(\lambda d'.\mathbf{K}(\mathtt{fix}[t])(F)(d),\mathbf{S}(\mathtt{fix}[t])(G)) \qquad \text{(P)}$$

We have two cases depending on whether

$$F(\lambda d'.\text{CALL } d)(d+1)$$

equals $\perp$ or not.

The first subcase: Consider the situation where

$$F(\lambda d'.\text{CALL } d)(d+1) = \perp \qquad (1)$$

To proceed we should like to deduce that

$$F(\lambda d'.\text{CALLREC}(d,\text{CALL } d))(d+1) = \perp \qquad (2)$$

This does not follow immediately from the 'substitution property' (Lemma 6.2.2) but may be proved by amending the proof of Lemma 6.2.2. To do so let

$$\Sigma = \{(d,\text{CALLREC}(d,\text{CALL } d))\}$$

and note that $\Sigma \in$ **Subst**. Clearly

$$compS[\Sigma](\lambda d'.\text{CALL } d,\lambda d'.\text{CALLREC}(d,\text{CALL } d))$$

and from $compS[\emptyset](F,F)$ we have

$$compS[\Sigma](F(\lambda d'.\text{CALL } d),\ F(\lambda d'.\text{CALLREC}(d,\text{CALL } d)))$$

Since (1) holds it then follows that (2) holds. — We next claim that

$$compC_t(\lambda d'.\text{CALLREC}(d,\text{CALL } d),up(\perp)) \qquad (3)$$

holds. To prove this it suffices to consider v and y such that

$$valC_{t_1}(v,y)$$

and to show

$$valC_{t_2}(\{\text{CALLREC}(d,\text{CALL } d),v\},\ \perp(y))$$

But this is immediate since any

$$\Delta \in \mathrm{ExSeq}(\infty, \textsc{callrec}(d, \textsc{call}\ d), v)$$

will be infinite and indeed $\bot(y)=\bot$. — Using (3) and $compC_{t\to t}(F,G)$ we then have

$$compC_t(F(\lambda d'.\textsc{callrec}(d, \textsc{call}\ d)),\ G(up(\bot)))$$

From (2) it follows that

$$G(up(\bot)) = \bot$$

so that

$$\mathbf{S}(\mathtt{fix}[t])(G) = \bot$$

As also $\mathbf{K}(\mathtt{fix}[t])(F)(d) = \bot$ this establishes (P) in this case.

The second subcase: Consider the situation where

$$F(\lambda d'.\textsc{call}\ d)(d+1) \neq \bot$$

so that

$$\mathbf{K}(\mathtt{fix}[t])(d) = \textsc{callrec}(d,C)$$
$$\text{where } C = F(\lambda d'.\textsc{call}\ d)(d+1)$$

To establish (P) we begin by proving

$$compC_t(\lambda d'.\textsc{callrec}_{\mathrm{n}}(d,C),\ G^{\mathrm{n}}(up(\bot))) \qquad (\mathrm{P_n})$$

by numerical induction on n.

In the base case, n=0, we immediately have

$$compW_t(\lambda d'.\textsc{callrec}_0(d,C))$$

using the proof of Lemma 6.3.23 and

$$compWC_t(\lambda d'.\textsc{callrec}_0(d,C),\ up(\bot))$$

follows because any

$$\Delta \in \mathrm{ExSeq}(\infty, \textsc{callrec}_0(d,C), v)$$

is infinite and $dn(up(\bot))(y) = \bot(y) = \bot$ regardless of the values v and y.

For the induction step we assume $(\mathrm{P_n})$ and show $(\mathrm{P_{n+1}})$. It suffices to prove the *compWC* part, which boils down to

$$compWC'_t(\textsc{callrec}_{\mathrm{n+1}}(d,C),\ G^{\mathrm{n+1}}(up(\bot)))$$

as the *compW* part follows from the proof of Lemma 6.3.23. For this we note that ($\mathrm{P_n}$) and $compC_{t\to t}(F,G)$ give

$$compC_t(F(\lambda d'.\textsc{callrec}_\mathrm{n}(d,C)),\ G^{\mathrm{n}+1}(up(\bot)))$$

from which

$$compWC'_t(F(\lambda d'.\textsc{callrec}_\mathrm{n}(d,C))(d+1),\ G^{\mathrm{n}+1}(up(\bot)))$$

follows. Using the 'substitution property' (Lemma 6.2.2, or rather, an obvious analogue) we have

$$compWC'_t(C[\textsc{callrec}_\mathrm{n}(d,C)/d],\ G^{\mathrm{n}+1}(up(\bot)))$$

We then claim that this establishes

$$compWC'_t(\textsc{callrec}_{\mathrm{n}+1}(d,C),\ G^{\mathrm{n}+1}(up(\bot)))$$

To see this note that for all values v, perhaps such that $valC_{t_1}(v,y)$ for some y, we have that

$$\Delta \in \mathrm{ExSeq}(\infty,\textsc{callrec}_{\mathrm{n}+1}(d,C),v)$$

if and only if

$$\Delta(0) = (\textsc{callrec}_{\mathrm{n}+1}(d,C),[v]) \text{ and}$$

$$\Delta(1..) \in \mathrm{ExSeq}(\infty,C[\textsc{callrec}_\mathrm{n}(d,C)/d],v)$$

This ends the proof by numerical induction.

To be able to conclude (P) it suffices to show

$$compWC'_t(\textsc{callrec}(d,C),\ \mathbf{S}(\mathtt{fix}[t])(G))$$

This amounts to assuming

$$valC_{t_1}(v,y)$$

and showing

$$valC_{t_2}(\{\textsc{callrec}(d,C),v\},\ dn(\mathbf{S}(\mathtt{fix}[t])(G))(y))$$

Using ($\mathrm{P_n}$) we already have

$$valC_{t_2}(\{\textsc{callrec}_\mathrm{n}(d,C),v\},\ dn(G^\mathrm{n}(up(\bot)))(y)) \text{ for all n}$$

and the result then follows using Lemma 6.4.13.

The case t is a product of composite types. This case is analogous to the similar case in the proof of Lemma 6.2.3 in that one must show that $compC(F,G)$ carries over to the functions supplied as argument to $\mathbf{K}(\mathtt{fix}[t_1])$ and $\mathbf{K}(\mathtt{fix}[t_2])$; as in the proof of Lemma 6.2.3 we simply refer to [72, Lemma 7.13] for an example of a proof along these lines. □

Summary of the correctness properties

The lemmas proved above together yield the following analogue of Lemma 6.2.3 and Corollary 6.3.24:

Corollary 6.4.16 We have $compC(\mathbf{K}(\phi),\mathbf{S}(\phi))$ for all operators ϕ of Table 5.1 whose type does not involve lists, except those of form $\mathtt{f}_i$ or $\mathtt{F}_i$ and provided that the type t indexing $\mathtt{fix}[t]$ is always composite. □

By analogy with Lemmas 6.2.4 and 6.3.25 we have:

Lemma 6.4.17 ('Structural induction') Let *penv* be a well-formed position environment (in the sense of Section 5.2) such that

$$\rho_{\mathrm{PS}}(penv) \overset{\mathrm{K}}{\vdash} e{:}t$$

and assume that neither e nor *penv* involves any lists. If

$$compC(\mathbf{K}(\phi),\mathbf{S}(\phi))$$

holds for all operators ϕ that occur in e, then

$$compC([\![e]\!](\mathbf{K}),[\![e]\!](\mathbf{S}))$$ □

Proof: The proof is analogous to that of Lemma 6.3.25 and is omitted. □

Corollary 6.4.18 Suppose that $\emptyset \overset{\mathrm{K}}{\vdash} e{:}t_1\underline{\rightarrow}t_2$, that $compC(\mathbf{K}(\phi),\mathbf{S}(\phi))$ holds for all operators ϕ that occur in e, and that $valC_{t_1}(v,y)$. Then the execution of $[\![e]\!](\mathbf{K})(\mathbf{void})(1)$ on the stack $[v]$ will either

- loop, in which case $dn([\![e]\!](\mathbf{S})(\mathbf{void}))(y) = \bot$, or
- produce a stack $[w]$ such that $valC_{t_2}(w,dn([\![e]\!](\mathbf{S})(\mathbf{void}))(y))$. □

This corollary immediately carries over to apply also to *programs* of the mixed λ-calculus and combinatory logic; as no difficulties are incurred we dispense with the formal statement.

Bibliographical Notes

The present proof is mostly inspired by [72] where a similar proof is conducted for a metalanguage called $\mathbf{TML}_{sc}$ and for an abstract machine. However, there are a number of differences. In $\mathbf{TML}_{sc}$ there are no run-time functions allowed, and the standard semantics is eager rather than lazy; on the other hand $\mathbf{TML}_{sc}$ allows recursive types and sums at compile-time and run-time. Overall this means that the complexity of $\mathbf{TML}_{sc}$ is slightly smaller than that of *the mixed λ-calculus and combinatory logic.* Concerning the abstract machines the one used here has to support more features, in particular thunks, and so is more expressive; on the other hand it uses structured code which considerably eases the proof effort. In summary we believe that the proof carried out here considers a more complex correctness problem. More importantly, we believe that the techniques of [72] have been further refined, not least the use of 'layered predicates' and 'parameter monotonicity', so that the proof should be more readable.

The proof carried out in this chapter, as well as that of [72], relates to many proof efforts conducted by others. In a sense [52], which is based on [97], is closest in spirit to our approach but it considers the G-machine and graph reduction rather than an abstract machine like ours. A standard reference is [55] and a more recent approach is [88]; the latter does not consider the translation (or compilation) between two syntactically different notations and we believe that this considerably simplifies the burden of proof. Approaches based on an algebraic perspective include [26], [60] and [100]. An often cited operational approach is [87] that relates the reduction rules of the λ-calculus to the SECD-machine.

We should like to offer the conjecture that the proof techniques used in this chapter would seem to carry over to a nondeterministic machine: the choice of a particular Δ∈ExSeq essentially means that we regard nondeterminism as a choice between a number of deterministic futures. Thus in any one of these we have no difficulty in talking about what will happen in the next configuration. — Such a conjecture can hardly be proved in general. Suffice it to say that the present proof technique was originally conceived during a proof of compiler correctness for a nondeterministic and imperative language; it was only abandoned in that setting because it was felt that parallelism did not easily lend itself to this proof technique.

A brief appraisal of the material in Section 6.1 may be found in [69].

Exercises

1. Consider the expression

   `fix(λf[Int→(Int list)].Cons(Id[Int],f))`

   Determine the semantics under the interpretation **K**. Simulate the code on the abstract machine to illustrate that it does not loop although the standard semantics specifies the meaning to be a function returning an infinite list.

2. The code generated in Example 6.1.5 is obviously rather inefficient. However it can be simplified by applying a few *peephole optimizations.* As an example it is always safe to replace the code fragment DELAY(C):RESUME with C^RESUME. Suggest a couple of such optimizations and apply them to

the code generated in Example 6.1.5. How does the resulting code compare with that of Example 6.1.6?

3. Extend the definition of *compS* to allow compile-time lists.

4. Using the result of Exercise 3, extend the proof of Lemmas 6.2.1, (6.2.2), 6.2.3 and 6.2.4 so as to allow compile-time lists.

5. Give an inductive definition of the ordering $\preceq$ on values, code sequences and configurations.

6. (*) Extend the definition of *valW* and *compW* so as to allow lists. To ensure well-definedness of *valW* one idea is to introduce a natural number $n \geq 0$ as a counter on the length of execution sequences considered when making the statements about well-definedness. Well-definedness will then be ensured by judicious modification of the counter n. For code sequences, well-behavedness now means n-well-behavedness for all $n \geq 0$. A code sequence C is n-well-behaved if its effect in $m \leq n_0 < n$ steps on a stack with a n_0-well-behaved top element only is to transform that top element into a $(n_0 - m)$-well-behaved element. Note that by now the circularity would seem to be broken: n-well-behavedness is now defined in terms of n'-well-definedness for $n' < n$. In a similar way the counter should be used to define n-well-behavedness of elements on the stack.

7. Supply the missing details in the proof of Lemma 6.3.20 for showing that $(\Delta_n(1))_{n \geq n_0}$ is a chain with $\Delta(1)$ as its least upper bound.

8. Let $\mathbf{K}(\mathtt{Zero}) = \lambda d.\text{CONST } \mathbf{0}$ and show $compW(\mathbf{K}(\mathtt{Zero}))$.

9. Let $\mathbf{K}(\mathtt{+})$ be defined as in Example 6.1.2 and show $compW(\mathbf{K}(\mathtt{+}))$. (Hint: note the similarities between $\mathbf{K}(\mathtt{+})$ and $\mathbf{K}(\mathtt{Apply})$).

10. Carry out the details needed (in the proof of Lemma 6.4.13) for adapting the proof of Lemma 6.3.20 to show that all Δ_n are infinite if Δ is infinite.

11. Extend Exercise 8 to show $compC(\mathbf{K}(\mathtt{Zero}),\mathbf{S}(\mathtt{Zero}))$.

12. Extend Exercise 9 to show $compC(\mathbf{K}(\mathtt{+}),\mathbf{S}(\mathtt{+}))$.

Chapter 7

Abstract Interpretation

The rationale behind the development of parameterized semantics in Chapter 5 is that it facilitates a multitude of interpretations of the mixed λ-calculus and combinatory logic. We saw examples of 'standard semantics' in Chapter 5 and a code generation example in Chapter 6 and in this chapter we shall give examples of static program analyses. We shall follow the approach of abstract interpretation but will only cover a rather small part of the concepts, techniques and tools that have been developed. The Bibliographical Notes will contain pointers to some of those that are not covered; in particular the notions of *liveness* (as opposed to safety), *inducing* (a best analysis) and *expected forms* (for certain operators).

We cover a basic strictness analysis in Section 7.1. It builds on Wadler's four-point domain for lists of base types but generalizes the formulation to lists of arbitrary types. In Section 7.2 we then illustrate the precision obtained by Wadler's notion of case analysis. We then review the *tensor product* which has been put forward as a way of modelling so-called relational program analyses (as opposed to the independent attribute program analyses). Finally we show that there is a rather intimate connection between these two ideas.

7.1 Strictness Analysis

Strictness of a function means that $\perp$ is mapped to $\perp$. In practical terms this means that if a function is strict it is safe to evaluate the argument to the function before beginning to evaluate the body of the function. Since this method usually leads to a more efficient implementation there has been a great deal of interest in strictness analysis for the implementation of lazy functional languages[1].

Our approach to strictness analysis is via abstract interpretation. The key idea is to 'simulate' the execution of the program (or function) by using abstract values rather than the concrete values of the standard semantics. For a strictness

[1] It is not of interest for eager functional languages because here all functions are strict.

$$
\begin{array}{lcl}
\mathbf{A}(\underline{\mathtt{A_i}}) & = & \mathbf{2} \\
\mathbf{A}(t_1 \underline{\times} t_2) & = & (\mathbf{A}(t_1) \times \mathbf{A}(t_2))_\perp \\
\mathbf{A}(t_1 \underline{\rightarrow} t_2) & = & (\mathbf{A}(t_1) \rightarrow \mathbf{A}(t_2))_\perp \\
\mathbf{A}(t\ \underline{\mathtt{list}}) & = & (\mathcal{O}(\mathbf{A}(t))_\perp)_\perp
\end{array}
$$

Table 7.1: Type part of **A**

analysis to be useful in practice it must terminate on all programs, including those that may diverge in the standard semantics. A sufficient condition for achieving this is that there are only a finite number of abstract values pertaining to any one type. Furthermore, a strictness analysis will only be useful if its results are *safe* (or *correct*) with respect to the standard semantics. We shall formalise this notion later in this section but the key idea is that one must not be able to reach false conclusions from the results of the analysis. For well-known computability reasons this means that in general one cannot hope for a strictness analysis that is *optimal*, that is one that is safe and misses no instances of strictness.

In the absence of perfect information we shall allow the strictness analysis to miss instances of strictness. It is therefore convenient to say that a function is *definitely strict* if the strictness analysis detects this and *not definitely strict* otherwise. So safety of a strictness analysis amounts to saying that a definitely strict function is also strict (with respect to the standard semantics **S**); optimality would then additionally claim that a *not definitely strict* function is also not strict but we shall not be able to obtain this for the analyses developed here. A *trivially safe* strictness analysis would say that all functions are *not definitely strict.*

7.1.1 Types

We shall follow the approach of Chapter 5 and specify the strictness analysis as an interpretation **A**. The type part of this is given in Table 7.1 and will be explained and motivated in the sequel. For the base types, $\underline{\mathtt{A_i}}$, we use the two-point domain

$\mathbf{2}$ =

with elements 0 and 1 and the partial ordering $0 \sqsubseteq 1$. The intention is that 0 means that the corresponding value in the standard semantics is definitely $\perp$ whereas 1 means that it can be any value (possibly also $\perp$).

The interpretation of the type constructors $\underline{\times}$ and $\underline{\rightarrow}$ essentially are as in the standard semantics. Concerning $\mathbf{A}(t_1 \underline{\times} t_2)$ it is natural that a property of a pair of concrete values is a pair of properties, hence the use of $\mathbf{A}(t_1) \times \mathbf{A}(t_2)$. But an element of $\mathbf{S}(t_1 \underline{\times} t_2)$ is not just a pair of values but may also be the new $\bot$-element introduced by the use of lifting for $\mathbf{S}(t_1 \underline{\times} t_2)$. It is feasible to let the property $(\bot,\bot)$ of $\mathbf{A}(t_1)\times\mathbf{A}(t_2)$ describe $\bot$ as well as $up(\bot,\bot)$ of $\mathbf{S}(t_1 \underline{\times} t_2)$ but some lack of precision results: if it is known from the strictness analysis that some function call results in $(\bot,\bot)$ of $\mathbf{A}(t_1)\times\mathbf{A}(t_2)$ we would not be able to determine whether the function is really strict (as when it results $\bot$ of $\mathbf{S}(t_1 \underline{\times} t_2)$) or not (as when it results $up(\bot,\bot)$ of $\mathbf{S}(t_1 \underline{\times} t_2)$). Hence to obtain a useful analysis we use $(\mathbf{A}(t_1)\times\mathbf{A}(t_2))_\bot$ for $\mathbf{A}(t_1 \underline{\times} t_2)$ so that the strictness analysis has the possibility of saying that the result of a function call is $\bot$ rather than $up(\bot,\bot)$. Similar remarks apply to the definition of $\mathbf{A}(t_1 \underline{\rightarrow} t_2)$.

Example 7.1.1 The expression part of the interpretation **A** will be defined in a subsequent subsection but a few examples may be helpful now in order to appreciate Table 7.1. The function `Id`[$\underline{\texttt{Int}}$] is a strict function (under the standard semantics **S**) and it is thus natural to model **A**(`Id`[$\underline{\texttt{Int}}$]) as

$$up(\lambda a.a)$$

This records that **S**(`Id`[$\underline{\texttt{Int}}$]) is a genuine function, i.e. of the form $up(\cdots)$, and that the strictness property of its result equals that of its argument. Consider next the function `Zero`[$t \underline{\rightarrow} \underline{\texttt{Int}}$] that is intended to ignore its argument and always return the number **0**. Since this is not a strict function it is natural to model **A**(`Zero`[$t \underline{\rightarrow} \underline{\texttt{Int}}$]) as

$$up(\lambda a.1)$$

Again this records that **S**(`Zero`[$t \underline{\rightarrow} \underline{\texttt{Int}}$]) is a genuine function and that the strictness property of its result is always 1, irrespective of the strictness property of its argument.

For functions involving composite types strictness is a more complex concept. As an example the function `Fst`[$\underline{\texttt{Int}} \underline{\times} \underline{\texttt{Int}}$] will return $\bot$ (in the standard semantics **S**) if its argument is $\bot$ or is of the form $up(\bot,v)$ for some concrete value v. By using $(\mathbf{2}\times\mathbf{2})_\bot$ as the domain of strictness properties it is therefore natural to model **A**(`Fst`[$\underline{\texttt{Int}} \underline{\times} \underline{\texttt{Int}}$]) as

$$up(\lambda a.a_1 \text{ where } (a_1,a_2)=dn(a))$$

Consider next the function `+`[$\underline{\texttt{Int}} \underline{\times} \underline{\texttt{Int}} \underline{\rightarrow} \underline{\texttt{Int}}$] that is intended to add a pair of integers. It needs both components of the pair and it is therefore natural to model **A**(`+`[$\underline{\texttt{Int}} \underline{\times} \underline{\texttt{Int}} \underline{\rightarrow} \underline{\texttt{Int}}$]) as

$$up(\lambda a.a_1 \sqcap a_2 \text{ where } (a_1,a_2)=dn(a))$$

where $\sqcap$ denotes the binary greatest lower bound operator. (Its existence is guaranteed by Lemma 7.1.6 below.) □

There are many possibilities for how to interpret lists. We cannot directly copy the definition for **S** and use $\mathbf{A}(t)^\infty$ for $\mathbf{A}(t\ \underline{\mathtt{list}})$ as this would not allow describing lists of different lengths. This could be amended by adding a new greatest element, but a disadvantage is that the domain for lists then is infinite. Another approach is to interpret lists as $\mathbf{A}(t)^{\mathrm{n}}\times\mathbf{2}$ for some value of n, possibly n=0. Here we have 'perfect' information for the first n elements of the list but for the remainder of the list we only know whether it is definitely $\perp$ or not. This gives a finite domain but it turns out not to be overly useful in practice.

The approach we shall pursue is to generalize Wadler's construction of a four-point domain for lists of base types, i.e. lists of type $\underline{\mathtt{A_i}}\ \underline{\mathtt{list}}$. We shall exploit the fact that all $\mathbf{A}(t)$ will turn out to be finite complete lattices and we note in passing that continuity is then equivalent to monotonicity[2]. To appreciate the general definition it may be helpful first to explain Wadler's construction. It sets

$$\mathbf{A}(\underline{\mathtt{A_i}}\ \underline{\mathtt{list}}) = (\mathbf{A}(\underline{\mathtt{A_i}})_\perp)_\perp$$

and since $\mathbf{A}(\underline{\mathtt{A_i}}) = \mathbf{2}$ this may be depicted as follows

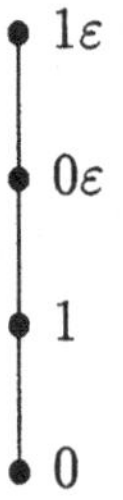

For readability we write 0 for $\perp$, 1 for $up(\perp)$, 0ε for $up(up(0))$ and 1ε for $up(up(1))$. The intention with these strictness properties are as follows:

0	describes the $\perp$-list, i.e. $[\partial$,
1	additionally describes all infinite lists, i.e. $[v_1,v_2,\cdots]$, and all partial lists, i.e. $[v_1,v_2,\cdots\partial$,
0ε	additionally describes all finite lists that have a $\perp$-element, i.e. $[v_1,\cdots,\perp,\cdots,v_k]$,
1ε	additionally describes all finite lists.

Many studies have shown that this domain is useful in practice and many efforts have been vested in finding a generalization to general lists that is equally useful.

To prepare for our generalization we need some terminology. Given a partially ordered set D and a subset $Y\subseteq D$ we define the right-closure of Y, or upwards closure of Y, as

[2]In categorical terms all of Chapter 7 takes place within the category of finite complete lattices and monotonic maps.

$$\text{RC}(Y) = \{ d \in D \mid \exists y \in Y \colon y \sqsubseteq d \}$$

In the literature this is sometimes written $\uparrow Y$. A subset $Y \subseteq D$ is Scott-open, or open in the Scott-topology[3], if and only if

- Y is right-closed, and
- for all chains $(d_n)_n$: if $\bigsqcup_n d_n \in Y$ then $d_n \in Y$ for some n.

Given our restriction to finite domains the second condition is trivial and Scott-open just means right-closed throughout this section. It is immediate that $\text{RC}(Y)$ is the least right-closed set that contains Y. We now define

$$\mathcal{O}(D) = (\{ Y \subseteq D \mid Y = \text{RC}(Y) \wedge Y \neq \emptyset \}, \supseteq)$$

as the partially ordered set of non-empty right-closed sets.

Lemma 7.1.2 If D is a finite complete lattice then $\mathcal{O}(D)$ is a finite complete lattice with least element D, greatest element $\{\top_D\}$ where $\top_D$ is the greatest element of D, and least upper bounds and greatest lower bounds given by $\bigcap$ and $\bigcup$, respectively. □

Proof: It is immediate that $\mathcal{O}(D)$ is a finite partially ordered set and that the least and greatest elements are as stated. (For the greatest element we need that D is a complete lattice rather than just a domain.) For the greatest lower bound $\sqcap\mathcal{Y}$ of a non-empty collection $\mathcal{Y}$ of right-closed sets it suffices to note that $\bigcup\mathcal{Y}$ is right-closed and non-empty (since $\mathcal{Y}$ is) and hence $\sqcap\mathcal{Y} = \bigcup\mathcal{Y}$. For the least upper bound $\bigsqcup\mathcal{Y}$ of a non-empty collection $\mathcal{Y}$ of right-closed sets it suffices to note that $\bigcap\mathcal{Y}$ is right-closed and non-empty since all $Y \in \mathcal{Y}$ have $\top \in Y$ (and $\mathcal{Y} \neq \emptyset$). □

Example 7.1.3 $\mathcal{O}(\mathbf{2})$ has elements $\{0,1\}$ and $\{1\}$ with $\{0,1\} \supseteq \{1\}$. Hence $\mathcal{O}(\mathbf{2})$ is isomorphic to $\mathbf{2}$ with $\{0,1\}$ corresponding to 0 and $\{1\}$ corresponding to 1. It follows that the definition of $\mathbf{A}(t\ \underline{\texttt{list}})$ given in Table 7.1 agrees with the above definition of $\mathbf{A}(\underline{\mathtt{A}}_i\ \underline{\texttt{list}})$ when $t = \underline{\mathtt{A}}_i$. □

The general definition of $\mathbf{A}(t\ \underline{\texttt{list}})$ given in Table 7.1 amounts to $(\mathcal{O}(\mathbf{A}(t))_\perp)_\perp$. For readability we shall write

0	for $\perp$,
1	for $up(\perp)$,
$Y\varepsilon$	for $up(up(Y))$

much as we did for $\mathbf{A}(\underline{\mathtt{A}}_i\ \underline{\texttt{list}})$ above; furthermore, we shall write $y\varepsilon$ for $\text{RC}(\{y\})\varepsilon$. It is straightforward to describe the intended meaning of 0, 1 and $\top\varepsilon$ whereas a little machinery is required for $Y\varepsilon$ when $Y \neq \text{RC}(\{\top\})$. So

[3] We shall not go into any topological considerations here.

0	describes the $\perp$-list, i.e. $[\partial$,
1	additionally describes all infinite lists and all partial lists,
$\top\varepsilon$	describes all lists.

Next consider $Y\varepsilon\in\mathbf{A}(t\ \underline{\texttt{list}})$ where $Y\neq\mathrm{RC}(\{\top\})$. We may write

$$Y = \{a_1,\cdots,a_k\}$$

and we know that k>0. Then

$Y\varepsilon$ describes all infinite lists and all partial lists and some finite lists; a finite list $[v_1,\cdots,v_n]$ is described if there are k values $j_1,\cdots,j_k$ such that the property a_i describes the element v_{j_i}.

Example 7.1.4 For a more complex example concerning lists consider $\mathbf{A}(t\ \underline{\texttt{list}})$ with $t=\underline{\texttt{Int}}\times\underline{\texttt{Int}}$. Here

$\mathbf{A}(t) =$

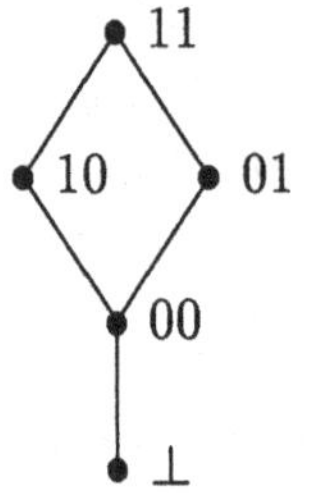

so that

$\mathbf{A}(t\ \underline{\texttt{list}}) =$

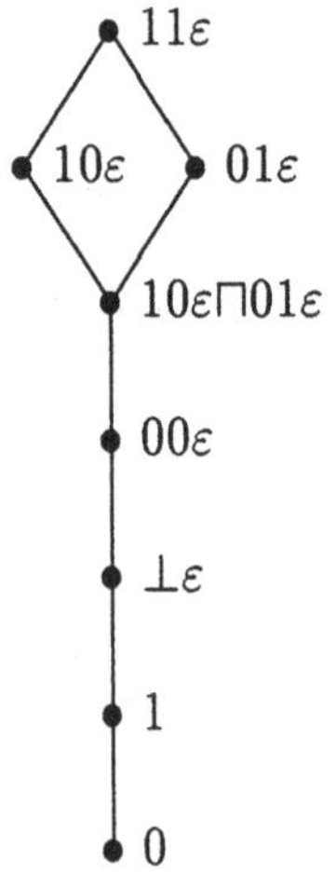

The element $10\varepsilon\sqcap01\varepsilon$ really is $\mathrm{RC}(\{10,01\})\varepsilon = \{10,01,11\}\varepsilon$ but as this equals the greatest lower bound of 10ε and 01ε we shall write it as $10\varepsilon\sqcap01\varepsilon$.

The concrete lists described by these properties may be exemplified as follows:

0	describes $[\partial$,
1	additionally describes $[up(27,27)\partial$,
$\bot\varepsilon$	additionally describes $[\bot]$,
00ε	additionally describes $[up(\bot,\bot)]$,
$01\varepsilon\sqcap 10\varepsilon$	additionally describes $[up(\bot,27),up(27,\bot)]$,
01ε	additionally describes $[up(\bot,27)]$,
10ε	additionally describes (wrt. $01\varepsilon\sqcap 10\varepsilon$) $[up(27,\bot)]$,
11ε	additionally describes $[up(27,27)]$.

This will all be formalised in the next subsection when the safety predicates are formally defined. □

Example 7.1.5 Turning to operations on lists of integers we recall the strictness properties 0, 1, 0ε and 1ε and consider the following functions:

$$\texttt{hd} = \texttt{Hd}[\underline{\texttt{Int}}]$$

$$\begin{aligned}\texttt{length} = \texttt{fix}(\lambda\texttt{f}[&\underline{\texttt{Int}}\ \underline{\texttt{list}} \underline{\rightarrow} \underline{\texttt{Int}}].\\ &\texttt{Cond}(\texttt{Isnil}[\underline{\texttt{Int}}],\ \texttt{Zero}[\underline{\texttt{Int}}\ \underline{\texttt{list}} \underline{\rightarrow} \underline{\texttt{Int}}],\\ &\texttt{+}[\underline{\texttt{Int}\times\texttt{Int}\rightarrow\texttt{Int}}]\square\texttt{Tuple}(\texttt{One}[\underline{\texttt{Int}}\ \underline{\texttt{list}} \underline{\rightarrow} \underline{\texttt{Int}}],\ \texttt{f}\square\texttt{Tl}[\underline{\texttt{Int}}])))\end{aligned}$$

$$\begin{aligned}\texttt{sum} = \texttt{fix}(\lambda\texttt{f}[&\underline{\texttt{Int}}\ \underline{\texttt{list}} \underline{\rightarrow} \underline{\texttt{Int}}].\\ &\texttt{Cond}(\texttt{Isnil}[\underline{\texttt{Int}}],\ \texttt{Zero}[\underline{\texttt{Int}}\ \underline{\texttt{list}} \underline{\rightarrow} \underline{\texttt{Int}}],\\ &\texttt{+}[\underline{\texttt{Int}\times\texttt{Int}\rightarrow\texttt{Int}}]\square\texttt{Tuple}(\texttt{Hd}[\underline{\texttt{Int}}],\ \texttt{f}\square\texttt{Tl}[\underline{\texttt{Int}}])))\end{aligned}$$

The function `hd` computes the head of a list and terminates (under the standard semantics **S**) on all lists except $[\partial$ and $[\,]$. The function `length` computes the length and terminates on all finite lists. Finally the function `sum` computes the sum of the integers and terminates on all finite lists that do not contain a $\bot$-element. We can thus summarize the *optimal* analysis functions *hd*, *length* and *sum* by

	0	1	0ε	1ε
hd	0	1	1	1
length	0	0	1	1
sum	0	0	0	1

As we shall see in the remainder of this chapter it costs considerable effort in order to obtain an analysis producing this result. □

We complete this subsection by noting that each $\mathbf{A}(t)$ is a finite complete lattice as promised.

Lemma 7.1.6 For each well-formed type t of run-time kind Table 7.1 defines a finite complete lattice $\mathbf{A}(t)$. □

$$
\begin{aligned}
& val_{\underline{\mathbf{A}}_i}(v,a) \equiv (a{=}0 \Rightarrow v{=}\bot) \\
& val_{t_1 \underline{\times} t_2}(v,a) \equiv (a{=}\bot \Rightarrow v{=}\bot) \wedge \\
& \qquad\qquad\qquad val_{t_1}(v_1,a_1) \wedge val_{t_2}(v_2,a_2) \\
& \qquad\qquad\qquad \text{where } (v_1,v_2) = dn(v) \\
& \qquad\qquad\qquad \text{and } (a_1,a_2) = dn(a) \\
& val_{t_1 \underline{\rightarrow} t_2}(f,h) \equiv (h{=}\bot \Rightarrow f{=}\bot) \wedge \\
& \qquad\qquad\qquad \forall v{\in}\mathbf{S}(t_1)\colon \forall a{\in}\mathbf{A}(t_1)\colon \\
& \qquad\qquad\qquad\qquad val_{t_1}(v,a) \Rightarrow val_{t_2}(dn(f)(v),dn(h)(a)) \\
& val_{t\ \underline{\mathtt{list}}}(vl,al) \equiv (al{=}0 \Rightarrow vl{=}\bot) \wedge \\
& \qquad\qquad\qquad (al{=}1 \Rightarrow \forall \mathrm{i}{\in}\mathrm{dom}(vl)\colon vl(\mathrm{i}){\neq}\star) \wedge \\
& \qquad\qquad\qquad (al{\notin}\{0,1,\top\varepsilon\} \wedge (\exists \mathrm{i}{\in}\mathrm{dom}(vl)\colon vl(\mathrm{i}){=}\star) \\
& \qquad\qquad\qquad \Rightarrow \exists \jmath{:}dn(dn(al)){\rightarrow}\mathrm{dom}^*(vl)\colon \\
& \qquad\qquad\qquad\qquad \forall a{\in}dn(dn(al))\colon val_t(vl(\jmath(a)),a))
\end{aligned}
$$

Table 7.2: Safety predicate for types of kind r

Proof: This is a straightforward structural induction. Clearly **2** is a finite complete lattice and it follows from Chapter 5 that product, function space and lifting preserve the property. From Lemma 7.1.2 it follows that $\mathcal{O}$ also does. □

7.1.2 The safety property

So far we have only given informal explanations of the intended meaning of the strictness properties in $\mathbf{A}(t)$. Since the definition of the expression part of the interpretation presupposes a clear understanding of these meanings we shall begin by defining two safety predicates: val_t for well-formed types of run-time kind and $comp_t$ for well-formed types of compile-time kind. The predicate val_t has functionality

$$val_t : \mathbf{S}(t) \times \mathbf{A}(t) \rightarrow \{\text{true,false}\}$$

and is defined by structural induction on t in Table 7.2.

The predicate $comp_t$ has functionality

$$comp_t : [\![t]\!](\mathbf{S}) \times [\![t]\!](\mathbf{A}) \rightarrow \{\text{true,false}\}$$

and is defined from val_t using techniques similar to, but somewhat simpler than, those used in Chapter 6; hence it is called a *logical relation* rather than a Kripke-logical relation. The definition is by structural induction on the well-formed compile-time type t, and is given by

$$comp_{\mathsf{A_i}}(v,a) \equiv (v = a)$$

$$\begin{aligned} comp_{t_1 \times t_2}(v,a) \equiv\ & comp_{t_1}(v_1,a_1) \wedge comp_{t_2}(v_2,a_2) \\ & \text{where } (v_1,v_2) = v \\ & \text{and } (a_1,a_2) = a \end{aligned}$$

$$\begin{aligned} comp_{t_1 \to t_2}(f,h) \equiv\ & \forall v \in [\![t_1]\!](\mathbf{S}) \colon \forall a \in [\![t_1]\!](\mathbf{A}) \colon \\ & comp_{t_1}(v,a) \Rightarrow comp_{t_2}(f(v),h(a)) \end{aligned}$$

$$\begin{aligned} comp_{t\ \mathtt{list}}(vl,al) \equiv\ & \mathrm{dom}(vl) = \mathrm{dom}(al) \wedge \\ & \mathrm{dom}^*(vl) = \mathrm{dom}^*(al) \wedge \\ & (\forall \mathrm{i} \in \mathrm{dom}^*(vl) \colon comp_t(vl(\mathrm{i}),al(\mathrm{i}))) \end{aligned}$$

$$comp_{t_1 \underline{\to} t_2}(v,a) \equiv val_{t_1 \underline{\to} t_2}(v,a)$$

Example 7.1.7 Consider the expression `length` and its strictness property *length* as described in Example 7.1.5. One can prove that

$$comp_{\underline{\mathtt{Int\ list\ \to\ Int}}}([\![\mathtt{length}]\!](\mathbf{S})(\mathbf{void}), up(length))$$

and we shall see how this can be used to infer certain strictness properties of `length` without actually calculating $[\![\mathtt{length}]\!](\mathbf{S})(\mathbf{void})$ on any arguments.

As an example consider the list vl=[1,2,...,27∂. It is easy to verify that

$$val_{\underline{\mathtt{Int\ list}}}(vl,1)$$

and from the definition of $val_{\underline{\mathtt{Int\ list\ \to\ Int}}}$ we then get that

$$val_{\underline{\mathtt{Int}}}(dn([\![\mathtt{length}]\!](\mathbf{S})(\mathbf{void}))(vl),\ length\ 1)$$

Since *length* 1 = 0 this amounts to

$$val_{\underline{\mathtt{Int}}}(dn([\![\mathtt{length}]\!](\mathbf{S})(\mathbf{void}))(vl),\ 0)$$

Inspection of the definition of $val_{\underline{\mathtt{Int}}}$ then guarantees that

$$dn([\![\mathtt{length}]\!](\mathbf{S})(\mathbf{void}))(vl) = \bot$$

showing that $[\![\mathtt{length}]\!](\mathbf{S})(\mathbf{void})$ cannot terminate on the list vl.

For another example consider the same list as above but now use the weaker assumption that

$$val_{\underline{\mathtt{Int\ list}}}(vl,0\varepsilon)$$

Then we obtain

$$val_{\underline{\mathtt{Int}}}(dn([\![\mathtt{length}]\!](\mathbf{S})(\mathbf{void}))(vl),\ 1)$$

but this does not suffice for guaranteeing that $[\![\mathtt{length}]\!](\mathbf{S})(\mathbf{void})$ cannot terminate on the list vl. This should not be surprising because the list vl'=[⊥] is also described by 0ε, that is $val_t(vl',0\varepsilon)$, and $[\![\mathtt{length}]\!](\mathbf{S})(\mathbf{void})$ does indeed terminate on vl'. □

The safety predicates val_t and $comp_t$ enjoy a number of properties that are indicative of what one would expect to hold for an arbitrary analysis.

Lemma 7.1.8 For each well-formed type t of kind $\mathbf{r}$ the clauses of Table 7.2 define an admissible predicate

$$val_t : \mathbf{S}(t) \times \mathbf{A}(t) \rightarrow \{\text{true,false}\}$$

that enjoys the following properties:

$$\forall a \in \mathbf{A}(t):\ val_t(\bot_{\mathbf{S}(t)},a)$$
$$\forall v \in \mathbf{S}(t):\ val_t(v,\top_{\mathbf{A}(t)})$$
$$\forall v \in \mathbf{S}(t):\ \forall a_1,a_2 \in \mathbf{A}(t):\ val_t(v,a_1) \wedge a_1 \sqsubseteq a_2 \Rightarrow val_t(v,a_2)$$
$$\forall v \in \mathbf{S}(t):\ \forall a_1,a_2 \in \mathbf{A}(t):\ val_t(v,a_1) \wedge val_t(v,a_2) \Rightarrow val_t(v,a_1 \sqcap a_2)$$
$$\forall v_1,v_2 \in \mathbf{S}(t):\ \forall a \in \mathbf{A}(t):\ v_1 \sqsubseteq v_2 \wedge val_t(v_2,a) \Rightarrow val_t(v_1,a)$$ □

One way to motivate this result is to imagine that

$$val_t(v,a) \equiv \beta_t(v) \sqsubseteq a$$

where $\beta_t : \mathbf{S}(t) \rightarrow \mathbf{A}(t)$ is a *strict* and *continuous* function.

Proof: The lemma may be proved by structural induction on the type t. The case $t=\underline{\mathrm{A}}_i$ is straightforward. The cases $t=t_1\underline{\times}t_2$ and $t=t_1\underline{\rightarrow}t_2$ are rather straightforward consequences of the induction hypothesis. We therefore restrict our attention to the case $t=t'\underline{\texttt{list}}$. Here we have 7 proof obligations: 5 are explicitly listed and 2 are buried in the admissibility statement (namely, that the predicate holds on $(\bot,\bot)$ and that the predicate holds on the least upper bound of a chain when it holds on all elements of the chain). We shall approach these in order of increasing difficulty.

(i) That $val_{t'\underline{\texttt{list}}}([\partial,0)$ holds follows by simple inspection of the definition of $val_{t'\underline{\texttt{list}}}$.

(ii) That $val_{t'\underline{\texttt{list}}}(vl,\top\varepsilon)$ holds for all $vl \in \mathbf{S}(t'\underline{\texttt{list}})$ follows by simple inspection of the definition of $val_{t'\underline{\texttt{list}}}$.

(iii) That $val_{t'\underline{\texttt{list}}}([\partial,al)$ holds for all $al \in \mathbf{A}(t'\underline{\texttt{list}})$ is immediate for al=0, and follows for al=1 or $al=Y\varepsilon$ (for some Y) because $[\partial$ is not finite, i.e. $\neg\exists \mathrm{i} \in \mathrm{dom}([\partial)$: $[\partial(\mathrm{i})=\star$.

(iv) That $vl_1 \sqsubseteq vl_2$ and $val_{t'\underline{\texttt{list}}}(vl_2,al)$ imply $val_{t'\underline{\texttt{list}}}(vl_1,al)$ may be shown by cases on al. If al=0 it is immediate as then $vl_1=vl_2$. If al=1 we have that vl_2 is infinite or partial; it follows that vl_1 also is and hence $val_{t'\underline{\texttt{list}}}(vl_1,al)$. Consider next the case where $al=Y\varepsilon$ for some Y. If vl_1 is not finite, or if $Y=\{\top\}$, the result is immediate so assume that vl_1 is finite and that $Y\neq\{\top\}$. Since vl_1 is finite also vl_2 is and $\mathrm{dom}^*(vl_1) = \mathrm{dom}^*(vl_2)$. From $Y\neq\{\top\}$ and $val_{t'\underline{\texttt{list}}}(vl_2,Y\varepsilon)$ we then have a mapping $\jmath: Y \rightarrow \mathrm{dom}^*(vl_2)$ such that

$$\forall a \in Y\colon val_{t'}(vl_2(\jmath(a)),a)$$

From the induction hypothesis it follows that

$$\forall a \in Y\colon val_{t'}(vl_1(\jmath(a)),a)$$

and this establishes the result.

(v) That $val_{t'\underline{\mathtt{list}}}(vl,al_1)$ and $al_1 \sqsubseteq al_2$ imply $val_{t'\underline{\mathtt{list}}}(vl,al_2)$ may be shown by cases on vl. If $vl=[\partial$ the result follows from a previous result. If vl is not $[\partial$ but is infinite or partial we have $al_1 \sqsupseteq 1$ and hence $al_2 \sqsupseteq 1$; the result is then straightforward. Finally suppose that vl is finite. Then al_1 is of the form $Y_1\varepsilon$ and al_2 is of the form $Y_2\varepsilon$. We may assume that $Y_2 \neq \{\top\}$, and hence $Y_1 \neq \{\top\}$, as otherwise the result is straightforward. From $val_{t'\underline{\mathtt{list}}}(vl,al_1)$ we then have a mapping $\jmath_1\colon Y_1 \rightarrow \mathrm{dom}^*(vl)$ such that

$$\forall a \in Y_1\colon val_{t'}(vl(\jmath_1(a)),a)$$

From $al_1 \sqsubseteq al_2$ we have $Y_1 \supseteq Y_2$. Defining $\jmath_2$ as the restriction of $\jmath_1$ to Y_2 we then have a mapping $\jmath_2\colon Y_2 \rightarrow \mathrm{dom}^*(vl)$ such that

$$\forall a \in Y_2\colon val_{t'}(vl(\jmath_2(a)),a)$$

and this establishes the desired result.

(vi) That $val_{t'\underline{\mathtt{list}}}(vl,al_1)$ and $val_{t'\underline{\mathtt{list}}}(vl,al_2)$ imply $val_{t'\underline{\mathtt{list}}}(vl,\ al_1 \sqcap al_2)$ may be shown by cases on $al_1 \sqcap al_2$. If $al_1 \sqcap al_2=0$ then $al_\mathrm{i}=0$ for some i and the result is immediate. If $al_1 \sqcap al_2=1$ then $al_\mathrm{i}=1$ for some i and the result is immediate. If $al_1 \sqcap al_2=Y\varepsilon$ for some Y we can find Y_1 and Y_2 such that $al_1=Y_1\varepsilon$, $al_2=Y_2\varepsilon$, and $Y=Y_1 \cup Y_2$. If one of Y_1 or Y_2 is $\{\top\}$ then $Y=Y_\mathrm{i}$ for some i and the result is immediate; so assume that $Y_1 \neq \{\top\}$ and that $Y_2 \neq \{\top\}$. If vl is infinite or partial the result is immediate; so assume that vl is finite. We then have mappings

$$\jmath_\mathrm{i}\colon Y_\mathrm{i} \rightarrow \mathrm{dom}^*(vl) \qquad (\text{for } \mathrm{i}=1,2)$$

such that $val_{t'}(vl(\jmath_\mathrm{i}(a)),a)$ holds for all $a \in Y_\mathrm{i}$ (for i=1,2). We may then define

$$\jmath\colon Y \rightarrow \mathrm{dom}^*(vl)$$

by

$$\jmath(a) = \begin{cases} \jmath_1(a) & \text{if } a \in Y_1 \\ \jmath_2(a) & \text{otherwise} \end{cases}$$

and clearly $val_{t'}(vl(\jmath(a)),a)$ holds for all $a \in Y$.

(vii) Finally we must show that $\forall$n: $val_{t'\underline{\mathtt{list}}}(vl_\mathrm{n},al_\mathrm{n})$ implies $val_{t'\underline{\mathtt{list}}}(\bigsqcup_\mathrm{n} vl_\mathrm{n},\ \bigsqcup_\mathrm{n} al_\mathrm{n})$ where $(vl_\mathrm{n})_\mathrm{n}$ and $(al_\mathrm{n})_\mathrm{n}$ are chains. By Lemma 7.1.6 it follows that $\{al_\mathrm{n} | \mathrm{n} \geq 0\}$ is finite. Hence there exists n′ such that $\bigsqcup_\mathrm{n} al_\mathrm{n} = al_{\mathrm{n}'}$. Using a previous result, i.e. *(v)*, we may set $al=al_{\mathrm{n}'}$, assume that

$\forall$n: $val_{t'\underline{\texttt{list}}}(vl_{\text{n}},al)$

and it then suffices to show that $val_{t'\underline{\texttt{list}}}(\bigsqcup_{\text{n}} vl_{\text{n}},al)$. We proceed by cases on al. If al=0 we have $vl_{\text{n}}=\bot$ for all n hence $\bigsqcup_{\text{n}} vl_{\text{n}} = \bot$ as desired. If al=1 all vl_{n} are infinite or partial and it follows that $\bigsqcup_{\text{n}} vl_{\text{n}}$ also is. If $al=\top\varepsilon$ the result is immediate. So assume that $al=Y\varepsilon$ and that $Y\neq\{\top\}$. If $\bigsqcup_{\text{n}} vl_{\text{n}}$ is infinite or partial there is nothing to prove and the result is immediate. If $\bigsqcup_{\text{n}} vl_{\text{n}}$ is finite there is n″ such that vl_{n} is finite (and of the same length as $\bigsqcup_{\text{n}} vl_{\text{n}}$) whenever n≥n″. For each n≥n″ we therefore have a mapping $\jmath_{\text{n}} : Y \to \text{dom}^*(\bigsqcup_{\text{n}} vl_{\text{n}})$ such that

$\forall a\in Y$: $val_{t'}(vl_{\text{n}}(\jmath_{\text{n}}(a)),a)$

There are only finitely many candidates for mappings from Y to dom*($\bigsqcup_{\text{n}} vl_{\text{n}}$) as both Y and dom*($\bigsqcup_{\text{n}} vl_{\text{n}}$) are finite. Hence there exists a mapping

$\jmath : Y \to \text{dom}^*(\bigsqcup_{\text{n}} vl_{\text{n}})$

such that $\jmath=\jmath_{\text{n}}$ for infinitely many n≥n″. We now claim that

$\forall a\in Y$: $val_{t'}(vl_{\text{n}}(\jmath(a)),a)$ (for all n≥n″)

This is immediate if $\jmath_{\text{n}}=\jmath$; if this is not the case we know that there exists n‴≥n such that $\jmath_{\text{n}'''}=\jmath$. We then have

$\forall a\in Y$: $val_{t'}(vl_{\text{n}'''}(\jmath(a)),a)$

and using the induction hypothesis and $vl_{\text{n}}\sqsubseteq vl_{\text{n}'''}$ we also obtain

$\forall a\in Y$: $val_{t'}(vl_{\text{n}}(\jmath(a)),a)$

From the induction hypothesis it then follows that

$\forall a\in Y$: $val_{t'}((\bigsqcup_{\text{n}} vl_{\text{n}})(\jmath(a)),a)$

and this establishes the desired result. □

Lemma 7.1.9 For each well-formed type t of kind c the clauses for $comp_t$ define an admissible predicate

$comp_t : [\![t]\!](\mathbf{S}) \times [\![t]\!](\mathbf{A}) \to \{\text{true,false}\}$ □

Proof: This is a rather straightforward structural induction and we omit the details. □

The safety predicate val_t also enjoys another property that only holds because we were careful to use lifting when interpreting $\underline{\times}$ and $\underline{\to}$. In the case where $val_t(v,a)$ amounts to $\beta_t(v)\sqsubseteq a$ this result says that β_t is $\bot$-reflecting: $\beta_t(v)=\bot$ implies $v=\bot$.

$$\mathbf{A}(\mathtt{Tuple}[t_0 \underline{\rightarrow} t_1 \underline{\times} t_2]) = \lambda h_1.\lambda h_2.$$
$$\begin{cases} up(\lambda a.up(dn(h_1)(a),dn(h_2)(a))) \\ \qquad \text{if } h_1 \neq \bot \text{ and } h_2 \neq \bot \\ \bot \qquad \text{otherwise} \end{cases}$$

$$\mathbf{A}(\mathtt{Fst}[t_1 \underline{\times} t_2]) = up(\lambda a.\ a_1 \text{ where } (a_1,a_2) = dn(a))$$

$$\mathbf{A}(\mathtt{Snd}[t_1 \underline{\times} t_2]) = up(\lambda a.\ a_2 \text{ where } (a_1,a_2) = dn(a))$$

$$\mathbf{A}(\mathtt{Cons}[t_0 \underline{\rightarrow} (t_1\ \underline{\mathtt{list}})]) = \lambda h_1.\lambda h_2.$$
$$\begin{cases} up(\lambda a. \begin{cases} 1 & \text{if } dn(h_2)(a) \sqsubseteq 1 \\ Y\varepsilon \sqcap (dn(h_1)(a))\varepsilon & \text{if } dn(h_2)(a) = Y\varepsilon \end{cases}) \\ \qquad \text{if } h_1 \neq \bot \text{ and } h_2 \neq \bot \\ \bot \qquad \text{otherwise} \end{cases}$$

$$\mathbf{A}(\mathtt{Nil}[t_0 \underline{\rightarrow} (t_1\ \underline{\mathtt{list}})]) = up(\lambda a.\ \top\varepsilon)$$

$$\mathbf{A}(\mathtt{Hd}[t]) = up(\lambda a. \begin{cases} \bot & \text{if } a=0 \\ \top & \text{if } a \sqsupseteq 1 \end{cases})$$

$$\mathbf{A}(\mathtt{Tl}[t]) = up(\lambda a. \begin{cases} 0 & \text{if } a=0 \\ 1 & \text{if } a=1 \\ \top\epsilon & \text{if } a=Y\varepsilon \end{cases})$$

$$\mathbf{A}(\mathtt{Isnil}[t]) = up(\lambda a. \begin{cases} 0 & \text{if } a=0 \\ 1 & \text{if } a \sqsupseteq 1 \end{cases})$$

Table 7.3: Expression part of **A** (part 1)

Lemma 7.1.10 For each well-formed type t of kind $\mathtt{r}$ the predicate val_t enjoys the property

$$\forall v \in \mathbf{S}(t):\ val_t(v, \bot_{\mathbf{A}(t)}) \Rightarrow v = \bot_{\mathbf{S}(t)}$$ □

Proof: This is a rather straightforward structural induction and we omit the details. □

A special instance of this result was already used in Example 7.1.7. It is a key result for the analysis **A** to be useful for optimizations based on strictness analysis.

7.1.3 Expressions

The expression part of the interpretation **A** is specified in Tables 7.3, 7.4 and 7.5. The overall shape of these definitions have much in common with the definition of the interpretation **S** in Chapter 5; major differences arise for run-time lists due

$$\mathbf{A}(\mathtt{f}_{\mathrm{i}}[t]) = \mathbf{f}_{\mathrm{i}}^{t}$$

where $\mathbf{f}_{\mathrm{i}}^{t}$ are unspecified elements in $[\![t]\!](\mathbf{A})$

$$\mathbf{A}(\mathtt{F}_{\mathrm{i}}[t_0 \underline{\rightarrow} t_1]) = \mathbf{F}_{\mathrm{i}}^{t_0 \underline{\rightarrow} t_1}$$

where $\mathbf{F}_{\mathrm{i}}^{t_0 \underline{\rightarrow} t_1}$ are unspecified elements in $[\![t_0 \underline{\rightarrow} t_1]\!](\mathbf{A})$

$$\mathbf{A}(\Box[(t_1 \underline{\rightarrow} t_2)\times(t_0 \underline{\rightarrow} t_1)]) = \lambda h_1.\lambda h_2.$$
$$\begin{cases} up(\lambda a.dn(h_1)(dn(h_2)(a))) & \\ \qquad \text{if } h_1 \neq \bot \text{ and } h_2 \neq \bot & \\ \bot \qquad \text{otherwise} & \end{cases}$$

$$\mathbf{A}(\mathtt{Id}[t]) = up(\lambda a.a)$$

$$\mathbf{A}(\mathtt{True}[t]) = up(\lambda a.\ 1)$$

$$\mathbf{A}(\mathtt{False}[t]) = up(\lambda a.\ 1)$$

$$\mathbf{A}(\mathtt{Cond}[t_0 \underline{\rightarrow} t_1]) = \lambda h_1.\lambda h_2.\lambda h_3.$$
$$\begin{cases} up(\lambda a. \begin{cases} \bot & \text{if } dn(h_1)(a)=0 \\ dn(h_2)(a) \sqcup dn(h_3)(a) & \text{if } dn(h_1)(a)=1 \end{cases}) & \\ \qquad \text{if } h_1 \neq \bot,\ h_2 \neq \bot,\ h_3 \neq \bot & \\ \bot \qquad \text{otherwise} & \end{cases}$$

Table 7.4: Expression part of **A** (part 2)

to the very different nature of $\mathbf{S}(t\ \underline{\mathtt{list}})$ and $\mathbf{A}(t\ \underline{\mathtt{list}})$. The clause for Nil should be obvious as only $\top\varepsilon$ can describe the empty list. Concerning Hd it should be clear that 0 is mapped to $\bot \in \mathbf{A}(t)$ because $\mathbf{S}(\mathtt{Hd})$ applied to $[\partial$ yields $\bot$; all other strictness properties are mapped to $\top$ because they can describe a list $[v\partial$ where v may be any value whatsoever. For Tl we have to map $Y\varepsilon$ to $\top\varepsilon$ because the tail of a list described by $Y\varepsilon$ could be the empty list and this is only described by $\top\varepsilon$. For Isnil we map 0 to 0 and all other strictness properties to 1 because $\mathbf{S}(\mathtt{Isnil})$ will give $\bot$ on $[\partial$ and **false** on any infinite list. For Cons we have two cases depending on whether $dn(h_2)(a)$ is of the form $Y\varepsilon$ or not. If not the resulting list must be partial or infinite and we use the strictness property 1 for this. If it is of the form $Y\varepsilon$ we use the strictness property $Y'\varepsilon$ where

$$Y'\varepsilon = Y\varepsilon \sqcap (dn(h_1)(a))\varepsilon$$

or equivalently

$$Y' = Y \cup \mathrm{RC}(\{dn(h_1)(a)\})$$

This records the fact that the resulting list must also have a component (the first actually) that is described by $dn(h_1)(a)$.

$$\mathbf{A}(\texttt{fix}[t]) = \text{FIX where FIX}(H) = \bigsqcup_{\text{n}} H^{\text{n}}(\bot)$$
$$\text{if } t \text{ is pure}$$
$$\mathbf{A}(\texttt{fix}[t_1 \underline{\rightarrow} t_2]) = \lambda H.\ \bigsqcup_{\text{n}\geq 1} H^{\text{n}}(up(\bot))$$
$$\mathbf{A}(\texttt{fix}[t_1 \times t_2]) = \lambda H.(H_1, H_2(H_1)) \text{ where}$$
$$H_1 = \mathbf{A}(\texttt{fix}[t_1])(\lambda a_1.w_1 \text{ where } (w_1,w_2) = H((a_1, H_2(a_1)))),$$
$$H_2 = \lambda a_1.\mathbf{A}(\texttt{fix}[t_2])(\lambda a_2.w_2 \text{ where } (w_1,w_2) = H((a_1,a_2)))$$
$$\text{and } t_1 \times t_2 \text{ is composite but not pure}$$
$$\mathbf{A}(\texttt{Curry}[t_0 \underline{\rightarrow} (t_1 \underline{\rightarrow} t_2)]) = \lambda h.\ \begin{cases} up(\lambda a_1.\ up(\lambda a_2.\ dn(h)(a) \text{ where } a = up(a_1,a_2))) \\ \quad \text{if } h \neq \bot \\ \bot \quad \text{otherwise} \end{cases}$$
$$\mathbf{A}(\texttt{Apply}[t_0 \underline{\rightarrow} t_1]) = up(\lambda a.\ dn(h)(a') \text{ where } (h,a') = dn(a))$$
$$\mathbf{A}(\texttt{Fix}[t]) = up(\lambda h.\ \text{FIX}(dn(h)))$$

Table 7.5: Expression part of **A** (part 3)

The clause for `Cond` in Table 7.4 is also different from the one for **S**(`Cond`) and the reason is again that **S**(<u>`Bool`</u>) and **A**(<u>`Bool`</u>) are rather different. If the test of the conditional results 0 we know that the result of the conditional in the standard semantics will be $\bot_{\mathbf{S}(t_1)}$ and so we use the strictness property $\bot_{\mathbf{A}(t_1)}$. If the test of the conditional results 1 we know that the result of the conditional in the standard semantics could either be that of the 'then' branch or that of the 'else' branch; consequently we use a strictness property that is the least upper bound of the strictness properties for the 'then' and 'else' branches. — Finally, the interpretation of the (compile-time) fixed point is as in the standard semantics.

Example 7.1.11 Consider the function `length` of Example 7.1.5 and let us perform the strictness analysis **A**. For this it is helpful to write

$$\text{FIX}' = \lambda H.\ \bigsqcup_{\text{n}\geq 1} H^{\text{n}}(up(\bot))$$
$$strict(H) = \lambda h.\ \begin{cases} H\ h & \text{if } h \neq \bot \\ \bot & \text{otherwise} \end{cases}$$

Using the definitions of Example 7.1.1 we then have

$$[\![\texttt{length}]\!](\mathbf{A})(\mathbf{void}) = \text{FIX}'(strict(\lambda h.up(\lambda a.$$
$$\text{case } dn(\mathbf{A}(\texttt{Isnil}))(a) \text{ of}$$
$$0\text{: } 0$$
$$1\text{: } 1 \sqcup (1 \sqcap dn(h)(dn(\mathbf{A}(\texttt{Tl}))(a))))))$$

= FIX′(*strict*(λh.*up*(λa.
case a of
0: 0
1: 1
0ε: 1
1ε: 1)))
= *up*(λa.case a of
0: 0
1: 1
0ε: 1
1ε: 1)

The reason for this result is that the `Isnil`-test will give 1 except on the argument 0. Comparing the result with the optimal behaviour, *up*(*length*), expressed in Example 7.1.5 we note that we have not been able to capture the optimal behaviour on the element 1. — A similar phenomenon would arise for `sum` whereas `hd` is so simple that we have optimal behaviour simply because **A**(`Hd`) was defined to be optimal. □

7.1.4 Proof of safety

To have faith in the strictness analysis we must show that it is safe with respect to the standard semantics. As in Chapter 6 this will amount to a result stating

$$comp_t([\![e]\!](\mathbf{S}),[\![e]\!](\mathbf{A}))$$

for appropriate expressions e and types t. We shall begin by establishing a similar result for each operator of Table 5.1.

Lemma 7.1.12 $comp_t(\mathbf{S}(\texttt{Tuple}[t_0\underline{\rightarrow}t_1\underline{\times}t_2]),\ \mathbf{A}(\texttt{Tuple}[t_0\underline{\rightarrow}t_1\underline{\times}t_2]))$ holds for all well-formed types $t = (t_0\underline{\rightarrow}t_1) \rightarrow (t_0\underline{\rightarrow}t_2) \rightarrow (t_0\underline{\rightarrow}t_1\underline{\times}t_2)$. □

Proof: We may assume that

$$val_{t_0\underline{\rightarrow}t_1}(f_1,h_1)$$

$$val_{t_0\underline{\rightarrow}t_2}(f_2,h_2)$$

and must show

$$val_{t_0\underline{\rightarrow}t_1\underline{\times}t_2}(f,h)$$

where

$$f = \mathbf{S}(\texttt{Tuple}[t_0\underline{\rightarrow}t_1\underline{\times}t_2])(f_1)(f_2)$$

$$h = \mathbf{A}(\texttt{Tuple}[t_0\underline{\rightarrow}t_1\underline{\times}t_2])(h_1)(h_2)$$

If $h{=}\bot$ we know that $h_i{=}\bot$ for some i, hence $f_i{=}\bot$ and $f{=}\bot$ as required; if $f{=}\bot$ the result is immediate from Lemma 7.1.8. So we may assume that $h{\neq}\bot$ and $f{\neq}\bot$. Next consider v and a such that

$$val_{t_0}(v,a)$$

and show

$$val_{t_1\underline{\times}t_2}(dn(f)(v),dn(h)(a))$$

which amounts to

$$val_{t_1\underline{\times}t_2}(up((dn(f_1)(v),dn(f_2)(v))),\ up((dn(h_1)(a),dn(h_2)(a))))$$

Since $val_{t_i}(dn(f_i)(v),dn(h_i)(a))$ follows from the assumptions this easily establishes the result. □

Lemma 7.1.13 $comp_{t_1\underline{\times}t_2\underline{\rightarrow}t_1}(\mathbf{S}(\texttt{Fst}[t_1\underline{\times}t_2]),\ \mathbf{A}(\texttt{Fst}[t_1\underline{\times}t_2]))$ holds for all well-formed types $t_1\underline{\times}t_2\underline{\rightarrow}t_1$. □

Proof: Assume that

$$val_{t_1\underline{\times}t_2}(v,a)$$

In particular, this means that

$$val_{t_1}(v_1,a_1)$$

where $(v_1,v_2) = dn(v)$ and $(a_1,a_2) = dn(a)$. It follows that

$$val_{t_1}(dn(\mathbf{S}(\texttt{Fst}[t_1\underline{\times}t_2]))(v),\ dn(\mathbf{A}(\texttt{Fst}[t_1\underline{\times}t_2]))(a))$$

and this establishes the result. □

Corollary 7.1.14 $comp_{t_1\underline{\times}t_2\underline{\rightarrow}t_2}(\mathbf{S}(\texttt{Snd}[t_1\underline{\times}t_2]),\ \mathbf{A}(\texttt{Snd}[t_1\underline{\times}t_2]))$ holds for all well-formed types $t_1\underline{\times}t_2\underline{\rightarrow}t_2$. □

Lemma 7.1.15 $comp_t(\mathbf{S}(\texttt{Cons}[t_0\underline{\rightarrow}t_1\ \underline{\mathbf{list}}]),\ \mathbf{A}(\texttt{Cons}[t_0\underline{\rightarrow}t_1\ \underline{\mathbf{list}}]))$ holds for all well-formed types $t = (t_0\underline{\rightarrow}t_1) \rightarrow (t_0\underline{\rightarrow}t_1\ \underline{\mathbf{list}}) \rightarrow (t_0\underline{\rightarrow}t_1\ \underline{\mathbf{list}})$. □

Proof: We may assume that

$$val_{t_0\underline{\rightarrow}t_1}(f_1,h_1)$$

$$val_{t_0\underline{\rightarrow}t_1\underline{\mathbf{list}}}(f_2,h_2)$$

and must show

$$val_{t_0\underline{\rightarrow}t_1\underline{\mathbf{list}}}(f,h)$$

where

$$f = \mathbf{S}(\mathtt{Cons}[t_0 \underline{\to} t_1\ \underline{\mathtt{list}}])(f_1)(f_2)$$
$$h = \mathbf{A}(\mathtt{Cons}[t_0 \underline{\to} t_1\ \underline{\mathtt{list}}])(h_1)(h_2)$$

If $h{=}\bot$ we know that $h_i{=}\bot$ for some i, hence $f_i{=}\bot$ and $f{=}\bot$ as required; if $f{=}\bot$ the result is immediate from Lemma 7.1.8. So we may assume that $h{\neq}\bot$ and $f{\neq}\bot$. Next consider v and a such that

$$val_{t_0}(v,a)$$

and show

$$val_{t_1\underline{\mathtt{list}}}(dn(f)(v),dn(h)(a))$$

where we may use that our assumptions ensure that

$$val_{t_1}(dn(f_1)(v),dn(h_1)(a))$$
$$val_{t_1\underline{\mathtt{list}}}(dn(f_2)(v),dn(h_2)(a))$$

We now have two cases:

The case $dn(h_2)(a){\sqsubseteq}1$. In this case $dn(f_2)(v)$ must be a partial (possibly $[\partial)$ or infinite lists and so is

$$dn(f)(v) = \text{CONS}_{\text{PS}}(dn(f_1)(v),dn(f_2)(v))$$

It follows that

$$val_{t_1\underline{\mathtt{list}}}(dn(f)(v),1)$$

and since $dn(h)(a){=}1$ this establishes the result.

The case $dn(h_2)(a){=}Y\varepsilon$ for some Y. We have

$$dn(h)(a) = Y\varepsilon \sqcap (dn(h_1)(a))\varepsilon = (Y{\cup}\mathrm{RC}(\{dn(h_1)(a)\}))\varepsilon$$

If $dn(f_2)(v)$ is partial or infinite so is $dn(f)(v)$ and as above the result is immediate. So assume that $dn(f_2)(v)$ is finite. From

$$val_{t_1\underline{\mathtt{list}}}(dn(f_2)(v),Y\varepsilon)$$

we then obtain a mapping

$$\jmath_2 : (Y\backslash\{\top\}){\to}\mathrm{dom}^*(dn(f_2)(v))$$

such that

$$\forall a'{\in}(Y\backslash\{\top\})\text{: } val_{t_1}(dn(f_2)(v)(\jmath_2(a')),a')$$

Note that this holds regardless of whether $Y\varepsilon=\top\varepsilon$ or not. Now define

$$\jmath : Y\cup\mathrm{RC}(\{dn(h_1)(a)\})\rightarrow\mathrm{dom}^*(dn(f)(v))$$

by

$$\jmath(a') = \begin{cases} 1+\jmath_2(a') & \text{if } a'\in Y\backslash\{\top\} \\ 1 & \text{otherwise} \end{cases}$$

We then claim that

$$\forall a'\in Y\cup\mathrm{RC}(\{dn(h_1)(a)\}):\ val_{t_1}(dn(f)(v)(\jmath(a')),a')$$

The proof is by inspection of $a'\in Y\cup\mathrm{RC}(\{dn(h_1)(a)\})$ and using Lemma 7.1.8. □

Lemma 7.1.16 $comp_{t_0\underline{\rightarrow}t_1\underline{\mathtt{list}}}(\mathbf{S}(\mathtt{Nil}[t_0\underline{\rightarrow}(t_1\underline{\mathtt{list}})]), \mathbf{A}(\mathtt{Nil}[t_0\underline{\rightarrow}(t_1\underline{\mathtt{list}})]))$ holds for all well-formed types $t_0\underline{\rightarrow}(t_1\ \underline{\mathtt{list}})$. □

Proof: It suffices to prove that

$$val_{t_1\underline{\mathtt{list}}}(\mathrm{NIL}_{\mathrm{PS}},\top\varepsilon)$$

and this is immediate. □

Lemma 7.1.17 $comp_{(t\ \underline{\mathtt{list}})\underline{\rightarrow}t}(\mathbf{S}(\mathtt{Hd}[t]),\mathbf{A}(\mathtt{Hd}[t]))$ holds for all well-formed types $(t\ \underline{\mathtt{list}})\underline{\rightarrow}t$. □

Proof: We may assume that

$$val_{t\ \underline{\mathtt{list}}}(v,a)$$

and then have to show that

$$val_t(dn(\mathbf{S}(\mathtt{Hd}[t]))(v),\ dn(\mathbf{A}(\mathtt{Hd}[t]))(a))$$

Using Lemma 7.1.8 this is immediate when $dn(\mathbf{A}(\mathtt{Hd}[t]))(a)=\top$ so assume that $dn(\mathbf{A}(\mathtt{Hd}[t]))(a)=\bot$. Then $a=0$ so that $v=[\partial$ and $dn(\mathbf{S}(\mathtt{Hd}[t]))(v)=\bot$ and the result is then immediate using Lemma 7.1.8. □

Lemma 7.1.18 $comp_{(t\ \underline{\mathtt{list}})\underline{\rightarrow}(t\ \underline{\mathtt{list}})}(\mathbf{S}(\mathtt{Tl}[t]),\mathbf{A}(\mathtt{Tl}[t]))$ holds for all well-formed types $(t\ \underline{\mathtt{list}})\underline{\rightarrow}(t\ \underline{\mathtt{list}})$. □

Proof: We may assume that

$$val_{t\ \underline{\mathtt{list}}}(v,a)$$

and then have to show that

$$val_{t\ \underline{\mathtt{list}}}(\mathrm{TL}_{\mathrm{PS}}(v),dn(\mathbf{A}(\mathtt{Tl}[t]))(a))$$

This is immediate when $dn(\mathbf{A}(\texttt{Tl}[t]))(a)=\top\varepsilon$. The cases where $dn(\mathbf{A}(\texttt{Tl}[t]))(a)$ is 0 or 1 amounts to the cases where a is 0 or 1. If a=0 we have $v=[\partial$ so that $\text{TL}_{\text{PS}}(v)=[\partial$ and $val_{t\ \underline{\texttt{list}}}(\text{TL}_{\text{PS}}(v),0)$ is then immediate. If a=1 we have that v is partial or infinite and so is $\text{TL}_{\text{PS}}(v)$ and $val_{t\ \underline{\texttt{list}}}(\text{TL}_{\text{PS}}(v),1)$ is then immediate. □

Lemma 7.1.19 $comp_{(t\ \underline{\texttt{list}})\underline{\rightarrow}\underline{\texttt{Bool}}}$ $(\mathbf{S}(\texttt{Isnil}[t]),\mathbf{A}(\texttt{Isnil}[t]))$ holds for all well-formed types $(t\ \underline{\texttt{list}})\underline{\rightarrow}\underline{\texttt{Bool}}$. □

Proof: We may assume that

$$val_{t\ \underline{\texttt{list}}}(v,a)$$

and then have to show that

$$val_{\underline{\texttt{Bool}}}(\text{ISNIL}_{\text{PS}}(v),\ dn(\mathbf{A}(\texttt{Isnil}[t]))(a))$$

This is immediate when $dn(\mathbf{A}(\texttt{Isnil}[t]))(a)$ equals 1 so consider the case where it equals 0. Then a=0 so that $v=[\partial$ and $\text{ISNIL}_{\text{PS}}(v)=\perp$ and the result follows. □

Lemma 7.1.20 $comp_t(\mathbf{S}(\square[(t_1\underline{\rightarrow}t_2)\times(t_0\underline{\rightarrow}t_1)]),\ \mathbf{A}(\square[(t_1\underline{\rightarrow}t_2)\times(t_0\underline{\rightarrow}t_1)]))$ holds for all well-formed types $t=(t_1\underline{\rightarrow}t_2)\rightarrow(t_0\underline{\rightarrow}t_1)\rightarrow(t_0\underline{\rightarrow}t_2)$. □

Proof: We may assume that

$$val_{t_1\underline{\rightarrow}t_2}(f_1,h_1)$$
$$val_{t_0\underline{\rightarrow}t_1}(f_2,h_2)$$

and must show

$$val_{t_0\underline{\rightarrow}t_2}(f,h)$$

where

$$f = \mathbf{S}(\square[(t_1\underline{\rightarrow}t_2)\times(t_0\underline{\rightarrow}t_1)])(f_1)(f_2)$$
$$h = \mathbf{A}(\square[(t_1\underline{\rightarrow}t_2)\times(t_0\underline{\rightarrow}t_1)])(h_1)(h_2)$$

If $h=\perp$ we know that $h_i=\perp$ for some i, hence $f_i=\perp$ and $f=\perp$ as required; if $f=\perp$ the result is immediate from Lemma 7.1.8. So we may assume that $h\neq\perp$ and $f\neq\perp$. Next consider v and a such that

$$val_{t_0}(v,a)$$

From $val_{t_0\underline{\rightarrow}t_1}(f_2,h_2)$ we then get

$$val_{t_1}(dn(f_2)(v),dn(h_2)(a))$$

and from $val_{t_1\underline{\rightarrow}t_2}(f_1,h_1)$ we then get

$$val_{t_2}(dn(f_1)(dn(f_2)(v)),\ dn(h_1)(dn(h_2)(a)))$$

and this establishes the result. □

Lemma 7.1.21 $comp_{\underline{t \to} t}(\mathbf{S}(\texttt{Id}[t]),\mathbf{A}(\texttt{Id}[t]))$ holds for all well-formed $t\underline{\to}t$. □

Proof: Straightforward. □

Lemma 7.1.22 $comp_{\underline{t \to \texttt{Bool}}}(\mathbf{S}(\texttt{True}[t]),\mathbf{A}(\texttt{True}[t]))$ holds for all well-formed types $\underline{t \to \texttt{Bool}}$. □

Proof: Straightforward. □

Corollary 7.1.23 $comp_{\underline{t \to \texttt{Bool}}}(\mathbf{S}(\texttt{False}[t]),\mathbf{A}(\texttt{False}[t]))$ holds for all well-formed types $\underline{t \to \texttt{Bool}}$. □

Lemma 7.1.24 $comp_t(\mathbf{S}(\texttt{Cond}[t_0\underline{\to}t_1]),\ \mathbf{A}(\texttt{Cond}[t_0\underline{\to}t_1]))$ holds for all well-formed types $t = (\underline{t_0 \to \texttt{Bool}}) \to (t_0\underline{\to}t_1) \to (t_0\underline{\to}t_1) \to (t_0\underline{\to}t_1)$. □

Proof: We may assume that

$$val_{\underline{t_0 \to \texttt{Bool}}}(f_1,h_1)$$
$$val_{t_0\underline{\to}t_1}(f_2,h_2)$$
$$val_{t_0\underline{\to}t_1}(f_3,h_3)$$

and must show

$$val_{t_0\underline{\to}t_1}(f,h)$$

where

$$f = \mathbf{S}(\texttt{Cond}[t_0\underline{\to}t_1])(f_1)(f_2)(f_3)$$
$$h = \mathbf{A}(\texttt{Cond}[t_0\underline{\to}t_1])(h_1)(h_2)(h_3)$$

If $h=\bot$ we know that $h_i=\bot$ for some i, hence $f_i=\bot$ and $f=\bot$ as required; if $f=\bot$ the result is immediate from Lemma 7.1.8. So we may assume that $h\neq\bot$ and $f\neq\bot$. Next consider v and a such that

$$val_{t_0}(v,a)$$

From $val_{\underline{t_0 \to \texttt{Bool}}}(f_1,h_1)$ we get

$$val_{\underline{\texttt{Bool}}}(dn(f_1)(v),dn(h_1)(a))$$

If $dn(h_1)(a)=0$ we have $dn(h)(a)=\bot$; furthermore $dn(f_1)(v)=\bot$ so that $dn(f)(v)=\bot$ and hence

$$val_{t_1}(dn(f)(v),dn(h)(a))$$

follows from Lemma 7.1.8. If $dn(h_1)(a)$=1 we have

$$dn(h)(a) = dn(h_2)(a) \sqcup dn(h_3)(a)$$

From $val_{t_0 \underline{\rightarrow} t_1}(f_2,h_2)$, $val_{t_0 \underline{\rightarrow} t_1}(f_3,h_3)$ and Lemma 7.1.8 we then get

$$val_{t_1}(dn(f_2)(v),dn(h)(a))$$
$$val_{t_1}(dn(f_3)(v),dn(h)(a))$$

As $val_{t_1}(\perp,dn(h)(a))$ is immediate from Lemma 7.1.8 we then have

$$val_{t_1}(dn(f)(v),dn(h)(a))$$

regardless of the value of $dn(f_1)(v) \in \{\mathbf{true},\mathbf{false},\perp\}$. □

Lemma 7.1.25 $comp_{(t\rightarrow t)\rightarrow t}(\mathbf{S}(\mathtt{fix}[t]),\mathbf{A}(\mathtt{fix}[t]))$ holds for all well-formed and composite types t. □

Proof: The proof is by induction on the type t.

The case t is pure. As in Chapter 6 it is straightforward to show

$$\text{if pure}(t) \text{ then } comp_t(x,y) \equiv (x{=}y)$$

by structural induction on t. It is then immediate that

$$comp_{(t\rightarrow t)\rightarrow t}(\mathbf{S}(\mathtt{fix}[t]),\mathbf{A}(\mathtt{fix}[t]))$$

The case $t{=}t_1 \underline{\rightarrow} t_2$ is a frontier type. Let F and H be given such that

$$comp_{t\rightarrow t}(F,H)$$

We begin by showing

$$val_t(F^{\mathrm{n}}(up(\perp)),H^{\mathrm{n}}(up(\perp))) \qquad \text{(for all n}\geq 0)$$

by induction on n≥0. The basis step, n=0, follows because

$$val_{t_2}(dn(up(\perp))(v),dn(up(\perp))(a))$$

holds for all $v \in \mathbf{S}(t_1)$ and $a \in \mathbf{A}(t_1)$. For the induction step we simply use the assumptions about F and H.

We know that $(F^{\mathrm{n}}(up(\perp)))_{\mathrm{n}\geq 1}$ and $(H^{\mathrm{n}}(up(\perp)))_{\mathrm{n}\geq 1}$ are chains so by admissibility of val_t (Lemma 7.1.8) we have

$$val_t(\mathbf{S}(\mathtt{fix}[t])(F),\mathbf{A}(\mathtt{fix}[t])(H))$$

which is the desired result.

The case t is a product of composite types. This is analogous to the similar case in the proof of Lemma 6.2.3 in that one must show that $comp(F,H)$ carries over to the functions supplied as argument to $\mathbf{S}(\mathtt{fix}[t_i])$ and $\mathbf{A}(\mathtt{fix}[t_i])$; as in the proof of Lemma 6.2.3 we simply refer to [72, Lemma 7.13] for an example of a proof along these lines. □

Lemma 7.1.26 $comp_t(\mathbf{S}(\mathtt{Curry}[t_0\underline{\rightarrow}(t_1\underline{\rightarrow}t_2)]), \mathbf{A}(\mathtt{Curry}[t_0\underline{\rightarrow}(t_1\underline{\rightarrow}t_2)]))$ holds for all well-formed types $t = (t_0\underline{\times}t_1\underline{\rightarrow}t_2) \rightarrow (t_0\underline{\rightarrow}(t_1\underline{\rightarrow}t_2))$. □

Proof: We may assume that

$$val_{t_0\underline{\times}t_1\underline{\rightarrow}t_2}(f_1,h_1)$$

and must show

$$val_{t_0\underline{\rightarrow}(t_1\underline{\rightarrow}t_2)}(f,h)$$

where

$$f = \mathbf{S}(\mathtt{Curry}[t_0\underline{\rightarrow}(t_1\underline{\rightarrow}t_2)])(f_1)$$
$$h = \mathbf{A}(\mathtt{Curry}[t_0\underline{\rightarrow}(t_1\underline{\rightarrow}t_2)])(h_1)$$

If $h{=}\bot$ we know that $h_1{=}\bot$, hence $f_1{=}\bot$ and $f{=}\bot$ as required; if $f{=}\bot$ the result is immediate from Lemma 7.1.8. So we may assume that $h{\neq}\bot$ and $f{\neq}\bot$. Next consider v_0 and a_0 such that

$$val_{t_0}(v_0,a_0)$$

and show that

$$val_{t_1\underline{\rightarrow}t_2}(dn(f)(v_0),dn(h)(a_0))$$

Since $dn(h)(a_0){\neq}\bot$ it suffices to consider v_1 and a_1 such that

$$val_{t_1}(v_1,a_1)$$

and show that

$$val_{t_2}(dn(dn(f)(v_0))(v_1),dn(dn(h)(a_0))(a_1))$$

But we clearly have

$$val_{t_0\underline{\times}t_1}(up(v_0,v_1),up(a_0,a_1))$$

and since

$$dn(dn(f)(v_0))(v_1) = dn(f_1)(up(v_0,v_1))$$
$$dn(dn(h)(a_0))(a_1) = dn(h_1)(up(a_0,a_1))$$

the result follows from $val_{t_0 \underline{\times} t_1 \underline{\rightarrow} t_2}(f_1,h_1)$. □

Lemma 7.1.27 $comp_t(\mathbf{S}(\texttt{Apply}[t_0 \underline{\rightarrow} t_1]),\mathbf{A}(\texttt{Apply}[t_0 \underline{\rightarrow} t_1]))$ holds for all well-formed types $t = (t_0 \underline{\rightarrow} t_1) \underline{\times} t_0 \underline{\rightarrow} t_1$. □

Proof: Assume that

$$val_{(t_0 \underline{\rightarrow} t_1)\underline{\times} t_0}(v,a)$$

and write $(f,v')=dn(v)$ and $(h,a')=dn(a)$. We then have

$$val_{t_0 \underline{\rightarrow} t_1}(f,h)$$
$$val_{t_0}(v',a')$$

so that

$$val_{t_1}(dn(f)(v'),dn(h)(a'))$$

follows. This establishes the desired result. □

Lemma 7.1.28 $comp_{(t \underline{\rightarrow} t)\underline{\rightarrow} t}(\mathbf{S}(\texttt{Fix}[t]),\mathbf{A}(\texttt{Fix}[t]))$ holds for all well-formed types $(t \underline{\rightarrow} t)\underline{\rightarrow} t$. □

Proof: Assume that

$$val_{t \underline{\rightarrow} t}(f,h)$$

We next claim that

$$val_t((dn(f))^{\mathrm{n}}(\bot),(dn(h))^{\mathrm{n}}(\bot)) \qquad \text{(for all n}\geq 0)$$

The proof is by induction on n: the basis step is immediate because val_t is admissible and the induction step follows from $val_{t \underline{\rightarrow} t}(f,h)$. Using admissibility of val_t once more we have

$$val_t(\mathrm{FIX}(dn(f)),\mathrm{FIX}(dn(h)))$$

and this establishes the desired result. □

Summary of the safety properties

The lemmas proved above may be summarized as follows:

Corollary 7.1.29 We have $comp(\mathbf{S}(\phi),\mathbf{A}(\phi))$ for all operators ϕ of Table 5.1, except those of form $\mathtt{f}_i$ or $\mathtt{F}_i$ and provided that the type t indexing $\mathtt{fix}[t]$ is always composite. □

By analogy with the results of Chapter 6 we have:

Lemma 7.1.30 ('Structural induction') Let *penv* be a well-formed position environment (in the sense of Section 5.2) such that

$$\rho_{\text{PS}}(penv) \overset{\text{K}}{\vdash} e : t$$

If

$$comp(\mathbf{S}(\phi),\mathbf{A}(\phi))$$

holds for all operators ϕ that occur in e, then

$$comp([\![e]\!](\mathbf{S}),[\![e]\!](\mathbf{A}))$$ □

Note that we have dispensed with explicitly indexing *comp* with type information. If we were to do so it would be helpful to define a *2*-level type $\tau_{\text{PS}}(penv)$ as discussed in Section 6.2.

Proof: The proof is by structural induction on the expression e much as in the proof of Lemma 6.2.4. We dispense with the details. □

Corollary 7.1.31 Suppose that $\emptyset \overset{\text{K}}{\vdash} e : t_1 \underline{\rightarrow} t_2$ and that $comp(\mathbf{S}(\phi),\mathbf{A}(\phi))$ holds for all operators ϕ that occur in e. Then

$$dn([\![e]\!](\mathbf{S})(\mathbf{void})) \text{ is strict}$$

provided that

$$dn([\![e]\!](\mathbf{A})(\mathbf{void})) \text{ is (definitely) strict.}$$ □

Proof: From Lemma 7.1.30 we have

$$val_{t_1 \underline{\rightarrow} t_2}([\![e]\!](\mathbf{S})(\mathbf{void}),\ [\![e]\!](\mathbf{A})(\mathbf{void}))$$

and

$$val_{t_1}(\bot_{\mathbf{S}(t_1)},\ \bot_{\mathbf{A}(t_1)})$$

is immediate. We then have

$$val_{t_2}(dn([\![e]\!](\mathbf{S})(\mathbf{void}))(\bot_{\mathbf{S}(t_1)}),\ dn([\![e]\!](\mathbf{A})(\mathbf{void}))(\bot_{\mathbf{A}(t_1)}))$$

and by assumption

$$dn(\llbracket e \rrbracket(\mathbf{A})(\mathbf{void}))(\bot_{\mathbf{A}(t_1)}) = \bot_{\mathbf{A}(t_2)}$$

From Lemma 7.1.10 we then have

$$dn(\llbracket e \rrbracket(\mathbf{S})(\mathbf{void}))(\bot_{\mathbf{S}(t_1)}) = \bot_{\mathbf{S}(t_2)}$$

as required. □

This corollary immediately carries over to programs of the mixed λ-calculus and combinatory logic; as no difficulties are incurred we dispense with the formal statement.

7.2 Improved Strictness Analysis

The behaviour of a strictness analysis on lists is often important when assessing its quality and the archetypical functions on lists are the `hd`, `length` and `sum` functions of Example 7.1.5. In our approach, which is based on suitably interpreting the operators of the mixed λ-calculus and combinatory logic, it is straightforward to obtain the optimal analysis of `hd` since it is equivalent to the operator `Hd` and we are not constrained in the analysis prescribed for operators. Concerning `length` and `sum` the compositional approach does present some complications and in Example 7.1.11 we concluded that the analysis **A** did not obtain optimal results for these functions.

In this section we shall investigate two approaches that may rectify this for the functions `length` and `sum` although in general they cannot be optimal for all functions for reasons of computability. One method was already considered by Wadler (for lists of base types) and the other method exploits the tensor product; as we shall see they obtain much the same effect although one is more 'global' in approach and the other is more 'local'. Throughout this section we shall adhere to the simplifying assumptions of Section 7.1: all domains of strictness properties of a given type are finite and hence continuity means no more than monotonicity.

7.2.1 The `Case` construct

In the original formulation of his strictness analysis for lists of base types, Wadler made use of a `Case` construct. It replaces our use of `Isnil`, `Hd` and `Tl` and ensures that the result of a test (using `Isnil`) is not separated from the result of a decomposition (using `Hd` and `Tl`). As was already illustrated in Exercise 4.9 the idea is that

$$\texttt{Case}(e_1,e_2) \qquad (\star)$$

is 'equivalent' to

$$\texttt{Cond(Isnil,}e_1\texttt{,}e_2\Box\texttt{Tuple(Hd,Tl))} \qquad (\star\star)$$

By incorporating **Case** as a new operator we will be able to specify the strictness properties of **Case** freely so that the analysis of ($\star$) is much more precise than the analysis of ($\star\star$).

To appreciate the analysis of **Case** it may be helpful to explain its standard semantics using the 'equivalence' between ($\star$) and ($\star\star$). This leads to:

$$\mathbf{S}(\texttt{Case}[t_0\ \underline{\texttt{list}} \underline{\rightarrow}\ t_1])(f_1)(f_2) = \bot$$
$$\text{if } f_1{=}\bot \text{ or } f_2{=}\bot$$

$$\mathbf{S}(\texttt{Case}[t_0\ \underline{\texttt{list}} \underline{\rightarrow}\ t_1])(f_1)(f_2) = up(\lambda v. \begin{cases} dn(f_1)(v) & \text{if } v{=}[\,] \\ dn(f_2)(up(v',v'')) & \text{if } v{=}\text{CONS}_{\text{PS}}(v',v'') \\ \bot_{\mathbf{S}(t_1)} & \text{if } v{=}[\partial \end{cases})$$
$$\text{if } f_1{\neq}\bot \text{ and } f_2{\neq}\bot$$

For the analysis we then propose the following definition to be motivated below:

$$\mathbf{A}(\texttt{Case}[t_0\ \underline{\texttt{list}} \underline{\rightarrow}\ t_1])(h_1)(h_2) = \bot$$
$$\text{if } h_1{=}\bot \text{ or } h_2{=}\bot$$

$$\mathbf{A}(\texttt{Case}[t_0\ \underline{\texttt{list}} \underline{\rightarrow}\ t_1])(h_1)(h_2) = up(\lambda a. \begin{cases} \bot_{\mathbf{A}(t_1)} & \text{if } a{=}0 \\ dn(h_2)(up(\top_{\mathbf{A}(t_0)},1)) & \text{if } a{=}1 \\ \bigsqcup\{dn(h_2)(up(\sqcap Y', (Y\ominus Y')\varepsilon)) \mid Y'{\subseteq}Y\} & \text{if } a{=}Y\varepsilon \neq \top\varepsilon \\ dn(h_2)(up(\top_{\mathbf{A}(t_0)},\top\varepsilon)) \sqcup dn(h_1)(\top\varepsilon) & \text{if } a{=}\top\varepsilon \end{cases})$$
$$\text{if } h_1{\neq}\bot \text{ and } h_2{\neq}\bot$$

where we use the notation

$$Y\ominus Y' = \text{RC}(\text{Y}\backslash\text{RC}(Y')) \cup \{\top\}$$

To motivate the definition of $\mathbf{A}$(**Case**) we shall give an *informal* proof of the safety of $\mathbf{A}$(**Case**) with respect to $\mathbf{S}$(**Case**).

Lemma 7.2.1 $comp_t(\mathbf{S}(\texttt{Case}[t_0\ \underline{\texttt{list}} \underline{\rightarrow}\ t_1]), \mathbf{A}(\texttt{Case}[t_0\ \underline{\texttt{list}} \underline{\rightarrow}\ t_1]))$ holds whenever $t = (t_0\ \underline{\texttt{list}} \underline{\rightarrow}\ t_1) \rightarrow (t_0\underline{\times}(t_0\ \underline{\texttt{list}}) \underline{\rightarrow}\ t_1) \rightarrow (t_0\ \underline{\texttt{list}} \underline{\rightarrow}\ t_1)$ is a well-formed type. □

Proof: For the non-trivial part of the proof we assume that

$$val_{t_0\underline{\texttt{list}}\underline{\rightarrow}t_1}(f_1,h_1)$$

$$val_{(t_0\underline{\times}(t_0\underline{\texttt{list}}))\underline{\rightarrow}t_1}(f_2,h_2)$$

$$val_{t_0\underline{\texttt{list}}}(v,a)$$

and that none of f_1, f_2, h_1 or h_2 equals $\bot$. The definition of $\mathbf{A}(\texttt{Case})(h_1)(h_2)$ applied to a then amounts to a case analysis upon the strictness property a.

If a=0 we know that the list v is $[\partial$ so that $\mathbf{S}(\texttt{Case})(f_1)(f_2)$ applied to v gives $\bot_{\mathbf{S}(t_1)}$. It is therefore correct to use the strictness property $\bot_{\mathbf{A}(t_1)}$.

If a=1 we know that the list v is infinite or partial. Hence any element v' of $\mathbf{S}(t_0)$ may be the head of v (unless v is $[\partial)$ and the tail v'' of v will still be infinite or partial. Hence $\top_{\mathbf{A}(t_0)}$ correctly describes v' and 1 correctly describes v'' so that

$$dn(h_2)(up(\top_{\mathbf{A}(t_0)},1))$$

correctly describes $dn(f_2)(up(v',v''))$ as well as $\bot_{\mathbf{S}(t_1)}$ (in case v is $[\partial)$.

If $a=\top\varepsilon$ we know nothing about the list v; it may be the empty list [ ], its head v' may be any element of $\mathbf{S}(t_0)$ and its tail v'' may be any list of $\mathbf{S}(t_0\ \underline{\texttt{list}})$. Thus

$$dn(h_1)(\top\varepsilon)$$

correctly describes $dn(f_1)([\,])$ and

$$dn(h_2)(up(\top,\top\varepsilon))$$

correctly describes $dn(f_2)(up(v',v''))$ as well as $\bot_{\mathbf{S}(t_1)}$. By using the least upper bound we obtain a strictness property that correctly describes both possibilities.

Finally consider the case where $a=Y\varepsilon$ and $Y\varepsilon \neq \top\varepsilon$; we then know that the list v cannot be [ ]. It therefore might be natural to use the strictness property

$$dn(h_2)(up(\top,\top\varepsilon))$$

since indeed the head v' of the list v may be any element of $\mathbf{S}(t_0)$. However, the snag is that the tail v'' cannot necessarily be any list of $\mathbf{S}(t_0\ \underline{\texttt{list}})$ because there are certain constraints from Y that may still have to be satisfied. Thus while $dn(h_2)(up(\top,\top\varepsilon))$ would not be incorrect we shall be able to do better.

Consider the situation where v is a finite list; since v is not $[\partial$ it will be of the form $v=\text{CONS}_{\text{PS}}(v',v'')$. We then have a mapping

$$\jmath:\ Y \rightarrow \text{dom}^*(v)$$

such that $val_{t_0}(v(\jmath(a)),a)$ holds for all $a\in Y$. We now have a number of possibilities concerning

$$Y' = \{a\in Y|\jmath(a)=1\}$$

For each of these we shall argue that

$$\forall a\in Y':\ val_{t_0}(v',a)$$
$$val_{t_0\underline{\texttt{list}}}(v'',(Y\ominus Y')\varepsilon)$$

The first of these is immediate and gives

$$val_{t_0}(v',\sqcap Y')$$

using Lemma 7.1.8 where we set $\sqcap\emptyset=\top$. The second of these is immediate if $Y\ominus Y' = \{\top\}$; so assume that $Y\ominus Y'\neq\{\top\}$ and note that RC(Y') then is a proper subset of Y. For each $a\in Y\backslash \mathrm{RC}(Y')$ we have $a\notin Y'$ and hence $\jmath(a)\neq 1$. Thus

$$\jmath'(a) = \jmath(a)-1$$

defines a mapping

$$\jmath' : (Y\backslash \mathrm{RC}(Y')) \rightarrow \mathrm{dom}^*(v'')$$

such that $val_{t_0}(v''(\jmath'(a)),a)$ holds for all $a\in Y\backslash \mathrm{RC}(Y')$. This mapping may be extended (in at least one way) to a mapping

$$\jmath'' : Y\ominus Y' \rightarrow \mathrm{dom}^*(v'')$$

such that $val_{t_0}(v''(\jmath''(a)),a)$ holds for all $a\in Y\ominus Y'$.

Returning to each choice of $Y'\subseteq Y$ we now have a contribution

$$dn(h_2)(up(\sqcap Y',(Y\ominus Y')\varepsilon))$$

and by taking the least upper bound of all of these we correctly describe all possibilities. □

In the definition of **A**(Case[ ]) we may assume that Y' is non-empty as $\sqcap\emptyset=\sqcap\{\top\}$ and $Y\ominus\emptyset=Y\ominus\{\top\}$, and therefore no contributions will be missed. Furthermore one may assume that Y' is right-closed as $\sqcap Y'=\sqcap\mathrm{RC}(Y')$ and $Y\ominus Y'=Y\ominus\mathrm{RC}(Y')$, and therefore no contributions will be missed. In summary we only need to consider those $Y'\in\mathcal{O}(\mathbf{A}(t_0))$ such that $Y'\subseteq Y$.

Example 7.2.2 In the case of lists of base types the above definition of **A**(Case) amounts to the following:

$$\mathbf{A}(\mathtt{Case}[\underline{\mathtt{A_i}}\ \underline{\mathtt{list}} \underline{\rightarrow} t_1])(h_1)(h_2) = \bot$$
$$\text{if } h_1=\bot \text{ or } h_2=\bot$$

$$\mathbf{A}(\mathtt{Case}[\underline{\mathtt{A_i}}\ \underline{\mathtt{list}} \underline{\rightarrow} t_1])(h_1)(h_2) = up(\lambda a.\left\{\begin{array}{ll} 0 & \text{if } a=0 \\ dn(h_2)(up(1,1)) & \text{if } a=1 \\ dn(h_2)(up(1,0\varepsilon)) \sqcup dn(h_2)(up(0,1\varepsilon)) & \text{if } a=0\varepsilon \\ dn(h_2)(up(1,1\varepsilon)) \sqcup dn(h_1)(1\varepsilon) & \text{if } a=1\varepsilon \end{array}\right.)$$
$$\text{if } h_1\neq\bot \text{ and } h_2\neq\bot$$

We shall motivate the definition in the case where $a=0\varepsilon$. Here we use that $a=0\varepsilon$ really stands for $a=Y\varepsilon$ with $Y=\{0,1\}$. The subsets Y' of Y are $\emptyset$, $\{0\}$, $\{1\}$ and $\{0,1\}$ but we only need to consider $\{1\}$ and $\{0,1\}$. Since

$$\sqcap\{0,1\} = 0 \text{ and } \{0,1\}\ominus\{0,1\} = \{1\}$$

and

$$\sqcap\{1\} = 1 \text{ and } \{0,1\}\ominus\{1\} = \{0,1\}$$

this gives the contribution

$$dn(h_2)(up(1,0\varepsilon)) \sqcup dn(h_2)(up(0,1\varepsilon))$$

as stated. — This shows that our general definition of **A**(`Case`) specializes to Wadler's notion of case analysis for lists of base types. □

Example 7.2.3 Using `Case` we may now consider the following definitions of `length` and `sum`:

$$\begin{aligned}\texttt{length}_1 = \texttt{fix}(&\lambda\texttt{f}[\underline{\texttt{Int}}\ \underline{\texttt{list}} \underline{\rightarrow} \underline{\texttt{Int}}].\\ &\texttt{Case}(\texttt{Zero}[\underline{\texttt{Int}}\ \underline{\texttt{list}} \underline{\rightarrow} \underline{\texttt{Int}}],\\ &\texttt{+}[\underline{\texttt{Int}}\underline{\times}\underline{\texttt{Int}}\underline{\rightarrow}\underline{\texttt{Int}}]\Box\texttt{Tuple}(\texttt{One}[(\underline{\texttt{Int}} \underline{\times} \underline{\texttt{Int}}\ \underline{\texttt{list}}) \underline{\rightarrow} \underline{\texttt{Int}}],\\ &\qquad\texttt{f}\Box\texttt{Snd}[\underline{\texttt{Int}}\underline{\times}(\underline{\texttt{Int}}\ \underline{\texttt{list}})]))))\end{aligned}$$

$$\begin{aligned}\texttt{sum}_1 = \texttt{fix}(&\lambda\texttt{f}[\underline{\texttt{Int}}\ \underline{\texttt{list}} \underline{\rightarrow} \underline{\texttt{Int}}].\\ &\texttt{Case}(\texttt{Zero}[\underline{\texttt{Int}}\ \underline{\texttt{list}} \underline{\rightarrow} \underline{\texttt{Int}}],\\ &\texttt{+}[\underline{\texttt{Int}}\underline{\times}\underline{\texttt{Int}}\underline{\rightarrow}\underline{\texttt{Int}}]\Box\texttt{Tuple}(\texttt{Fst}[\underline{\texttt{Int}}\underline{\times}(\underline{\texttt{Int}}\ \underline{\texttt{list}})],\\ &\qquad\texttt{f}\Box\texttt{Snd}[\underline{\texttt{Int}}\underline{\times}(\underline{\texttt{Int}}\ \underline{\texttt{list}})]))))\end{aligned}$$

As we have already said there is no need to redefine `hd` and thus no need to analyse it once again. Using the notation FIX′ and *strict* of Example 7.1.11 we may then perform the following analysis of `length`:

$$\begin{aligned}[\![\texttt{length}_1]\!](\mathbf{A})(\mathbf{void}) &= \mathrm{FIX}'(strict(\lambda h.up(\lambda a.\\ &\quad \text{case } a \text{ of}\\ &\quad 0\text{: } 0\\ &\quad 1\text{: } 1 \sqcap dn(h)(1)\\ &\quad 0\varepsilon\text{: } (1 \sqcap dn(h)(0\varepsilon)) \sqcup (1 \sqcap dn(h)(1\varepsilon))\\ &\quad 1\varepsilon\text{: } (1 \sqcap dn(h)(1\varepsilon)) \sqcup 1)))\\ &= \mathrm{FIX}'(strict(\lambda h.up(\lambda a.\\ &\quad \text{case } a \text{ of}\\ &\quad 0\text{: } 0\\ &\quad 1\text{: } dn(h)(1)\\ &\quad 0\varepsilon\text{: } dn(h)(1\varepsilon)\\ &\quad 1\varepsilon\text{: } 1)))\\ &= up(\lambda a.\text{case } a \text{ of}\\ &\quad 0\text{: } 0\\ &\quad 1\text{: } 0\\ &\quad 0\varepsilon\text{: } 1\\ &\quad 1\varepsilon\text{: } 1)\end{aligned}$$

Thus $dn([\![\texttt{length}_1]\!](\mathbf{A})(\mathbf{void}))$ equals the optimal result of Example 7.1.5. Turning to `sum` we may perform the following analysis:

$$
\begin{aligned}
[\![\texttt{sum}_1]\!](\mathbf{A})(\mathbf{void}) &= \mathrm{FIX}'(\mathit{strict}(\lambda h.\mathit{up}(\lambda a. \\
&\quad \text{case } a \text{ of} \\
&\quad 0\text{: } 0 \\
&\quad 1\text{: } 1 \sqcap dn(h)(1) \\
&\quad 0\varepsilon\text{: } (1 \sqcap dn(h)(0\varepsilon)) \sqcup (0 \sqcap dn(h)(1\varepsilon)) \\
&\quad 1\varepsilon\text{: } (1 \sqcap dn(h)(1\varepsilon)) \sqcup 1))) \\
&= \mathrm{FIX}'(\mathit{strict}(\lambda h.\mathit{up}(\lambda a. \\
&\quad \text{case } a \text{ of} \\
&\quad 0\text{: } 0 \\
&\quad 1\text{: } dn(h)(1) \\
&\quad 0\varepsilon\text{: } dn(h)(0\varepsilon) \\
&\quad 1\varepsilon\text{: } 1))) \\
&= \mathit{up}(\lambda a.\text{case } a \text{ of} \\
&\quad 0\text{: } 0 \\
&\quad 1\text{: } 0 \\
&\quad 0\varepsilon\text{: } 0 \\
&\quad 1\varepsilon\text{: } 1)
\end{aligned}
$$

Thus also $dn([\![\texttt{sum}_1]\!](\mathbf{A})(\mathbf{void}))$ equals the optimal result of Example 7.1.5. □

7.2.2 Tensor products

The use of the `Case` construct allowed us to consider various combinations of the head and tail of a list and we saw in Example 7.2.3 that this sufficed for an optimal analysis of (slightly modified versions of) the `length` and `sum` functions. We shall now see that the same effect can be obtained in a different way through the use of tensor products.

As a first step we shall improve the precision of the tests made in the strictness analysis. To this end we define a new analysis $\mathbf{A}'$ that has

$\mathbf{A}'(\underline{\texttt{Bool}}) =$

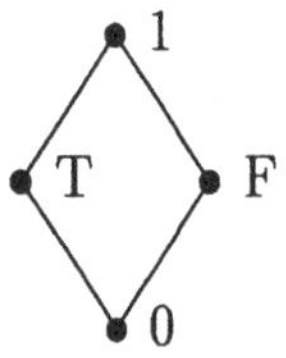

It is now necessary to reconsider the interpretation of the constructs `Isnil`, `True`, `False` and `Cond` that relate to the type $\underline{\texttt{Bool}}$. The motivation for the choice of $\mathbf{A}'(\underline{\texttt{Bool}})$ is that it enables us to define

$$\mathbf{A}'(\texttt{Isnil}[t]) = up(\lambda a. \begin{cases} 0 & \text{if } a{=}0 \\ \text{F} & \text{if } a{\neq}0 \wedge a{\neq}\top\varepsilon \\ 1 & \text{if } a{=}\top\varepsilon \end{cases})$$

so that we may consider interesting lists that are definitely not NIL_{PS}. The interpretation of **True**, **False** and **Cond** is then rather straightforward:

$$\mathbf{A}'(\texttt{True}[t]) = up(\lambda a.\ \text{T})$$

$$\mathbf{A}'(\texttt{False}[t]) = up(\lambda a.\ \text{F})$$

$$\mathbf{A}'(\texttt{Cond}[t_0 \underline{\rightarrow} t_1])(h_1)(h_2)(h_3) = \bot$$

$$\text{if } h_1{=}\bot \text{ or } h_2{=}\bot \text{ or } h_3{=}\bot$$

$$\mathbf{A}'(\texttt{Cond}[t_0 \underline{\rightarrow} t_1])(h_1)(h_2)(h_3) =$$

$$\begin{cases} \bot & \text{if } dn(h_1)(a){=}0 \\ dn(h_2)(a) & \text{if } dn(h_1)(a){=}\text{T} \\ dn(h_3)(a) & \text{if } dn(h_1)(a){=}\text{F} \\ dn(h_2)(a) \sqcup dn(h_3)(a) & \text{if } dn(h_1)(a){=}1 \end{cases}$$

$$\text{if } h_1{\neq}\bot,\ h_2{\neq}\bot \text{ and } h_3{\neq}\bot$$

Example 7.2.4 Assume for the moment that $\mathbf{A}'$ agrees with $\mathbf{A}$ except as specified above. Using the abbreviations FIX′ and *strict* of Example 7.1.11 we may then perform the following analysis of the `length` function:

$$\begin{aligned}
[\![\texttt{length}]\!](\mathbf{A}')(\textbf{void}) = {} & \text{FIX}'(strict(\lambda h.up(\lambda a. \\
& \text{case } dn(\mathbf{A}'(\texttt{Isnil}))(a) \text{ of} \\
& 0\text{: } 0 \\
& \text{T: } 1 \\
& \text{F: } 1 \sqcap dn(h)(dn(\mathbf{A}'(\texttt{Tl}))(a)) \\
& 1\text{: } 1 \sqcup (1 \sqcap dn(h)(dn(\mathbf{A}'(\texttt{Tl}))(a))))))) \\
= {} & \text{FIX}'(strict(\lambda h.up(\lambda a. \\
& \text{case } dn(\mathbf{A}'(\texttt{Isnil}))(a) \text{ of} \\
& 0\text{: } 0 \\
& \text{T: } 1 \\
& \text{F: } dn(h)(dn(\mathbf{A}'(\texttt{Tl}))(a)) \\
& 1\text{: } 1\ ))) \\
= {} & \text{FIX}'(strict(\lambda h.up(\lambda a. \\
& \text{case } a \text{ of} \\
& 0\text{: } 0 \\
& 1\text{: } dn(h)(dn(\mathbf{A}'(\texttt{Tl}))(1)) \\
& 0\varepsilon\text{: } dn(h)(dn(\mathbf{A}'(\texttt{Tl}))(0\varepsilon)) \\
& 1\varepsilon\text{: } 1)))
\end{aligned}$$

$$\begin{aligned}
&= \text{FIX}'(\mathit{strict}(\lambda h.\mathit{up}(\lambda a.\\
&\quad \text{case } a \text{ of}\\
&\quad 0\text{: } 0\\
&\quad 1\text{: } \mathit{dn}(h)(1)\\
&\quad 0\varepsilon\text{: } \mathit{dn}(h)(1\varepsilon)\\
&\quad 1\varepsilon\text{: } 1)))\\
&= \mathit{up}(\lambda a.\text{case } a \text{ of}\\
&\quad 0\text{: } 0\\
&\quad 1\text{: } 0\\
&\quad 0\varepsilon\text{: } 1\\
&\quad 1\varepsilon\text{: } 1)
\end{aligned}$$

We note that the change from **A** to **A**$'$ suffices for obtaining the optimal analysis for `length`. — Turning to `sum` we may perform the following analysis:

$$\begin{aligned}
[\![\texttt{sum}]\!](\mathbf{A}')(\mathbf{void}) &= \text{FIX}'(\mathit{strict}(\lambda h.\mathit{up}(\lambda a.\\
&\quad \text{case } \mathit{dn}(\mathbf{A}'(\texttt{Isnil}))(a) \text{ of}\\
&\quad 0\text{: } 0\\
&\quad \text{T: } 1\\
&\quad \text{F: } \mathit{dn}(\mathbf{A}'(\texttt{Hd}))(a) \sqcap \mathit{dn}(h)(\mathit{dn}(\mathbf{A}'(\texttt{Tl}))(a))\\
&\quad 1\text{: } 1\ )))\\
&= \text{FIX}'(\mathit{strict}(\lambda h.\mathit{up}(\lambda a.\\
&\quad \text{case } a \text{ of}\\
&\quad 0\text{: } 0\\
&\quad 1\text{: } 1 \sqcap \mathit{dn}(h)(1)\\
&\quad 0\varepsilon\text{: } 1 \sqcap \mathit{dn}(h)(1\varepsilon)\\
&\quad 1\varepsilon\text{: } 1)))\\
&= \mathit{up}(\lambda a.\text{case } a \text{ of}\\
&\quad 0\text{: } 0\\
&\quad 1\text{: } 0\\
&\quad 0\varepsilon\text{: } 1\\
&\quad 1\varepsilon\text{: } 1)
\end{aligned}$$

We note that $[\![\texttt{sum}]\!](\mathbf{A}')(\mathbf{void})$ is slightly better than $[\![\texttt{sum}]\!](\mathbf{A})(\mathbf{void})$ but still not optimal (compared to *sum* of Example 7.1.5). □

The analysis **A**$'$ is not yet as powerful as the analysis **A** when the latter is augmented with a `Case` construct and the former is not. The crux of the problem arises when decomposing the strictness property 0ε; here the head can be 1 and the tail 0ε or the head can be 0 and the tail 1ε. However,

$$\mathit{up}(1{,}0\varepsilon) \sqcup \mathit{up}(0{,}1\varepsilon) = \mathit{up}(1{,}1\varepsilon)$$

and so our decomposition degrades to the (obviously correct) observation that the head can be anything and the tail can be anything. Our solution will be to interpret $\mathbf{A}'(t_1\underline{\times}t_2)$ as lifted *tensor product* rather than lifted cartesian product. This will enable us to achieve

$$up(cross(1,0\varepsilon)) \sqcup up(cross(0,1\varepsilon)) \neq up(cross(1,1\varepsilon))$$

for a suitable function *cross*.

To conduct this development we need a few auxiliary notions. A function $f{:}L{\rightarrow}M$ is (binary) *additive* if $f(l_1{\sqcup}l_2) = f(l_1){\sqcup}f(l_2)$ holds for all l_1 and l_2 in L. A function $f{:}L{\times}L'{\rightarrow}M$ is *separately* (binary) *additive* if

$$f(l_1{\sqcup}l_2,l') = f(l_1,l'){\sqcup}f(l_2,l')$$
$$f(l,l'_1 \sqcup l'_2) = f(l,l'_1){\sqcup}f(l,l'_2)$$

for all choices of l_1, l_2, l, l'_1, l'_2 and l'. It is easy to show that if $f{:}L{\times}L'{\rightarrow}M$ is additive then it is also separately additive but the converse does not hold. The tensor product may then be regarded as a way of turning separately additive functions into additive ones. To be more precise consider finite complete lattices L and L'. A pair $(L{\otimes}L',cross)$ is a tensor product of L and L' (with respect to additivity and among the finite complete lattices) provided that

- $L{\otimes}L'$ is a finite complete lattice,

- *cross*: $L{\times}L'{\rightarrow}L{\otimes}L'$ is a continuous (i.e. monotonic) function that is separately additive,

- for all finite complete lattices M and for all continuous (i.e. monotonic) functions $f{:}L{\times}L'{\rightarrow}M$ that are separately additive the following universal property holds: there exists precisely one continuous (i.e. monotonic) function $f^{\otimes} : L{\otimes}L'{\rightarrow}M$ that is additive and satisfies the equation $f^{\otimes}{\circ}cross{=}f$.

This may all be illustrated by the following commuting diagram:

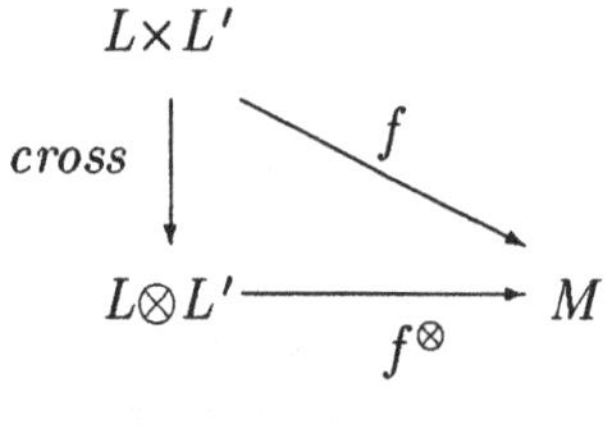

We now have a 'definition' of a tensor product of finite complete lattices L and M; however, we have not guaranteed that a tensor product does exist nor that it is unique if it does. Actually the tensor product exists in quite a general setting (see the Bibliographical Notes) and is unique 'up to isomorphism' (see Exercise 7).

Our next task will be to give a concrete construction of a tensor product of finite complete lattices L and L'. We shall arrange for the elements of $L\otimes L'$ to be certain subsets Y of $L\times L'$. We shall say that a set Y is *left-closed* when $Y = \mathrm{LC}(Y)$ and where

$$\mathrm{LC}(Y) = \{d \mid \exists y \in Y\colon d \sqsubseteq y\}$$

denotes the left-closure (or lower-closure) of Y. We shall say that a set Y is *closed in both components* when $Y = \mathrm{CC}_1(Y)$ and $Y = \mathrm{CC}_2(Y)$ and where

$$\mathrm{CC}_1(Y) = \{(l_1 \sqcup l_2, l') \mid (l_1,l'),(l_2,l') \in Y\}$$
$$\mathrm{CC}_2(Y) = \{(l, l'_1 \sqcup l'_2) \mid (l,l'_1),(l,l'_2) \in Y\}$$

denote the closure in the first and second components, respectively.

Lemma 7.2.5 For each subset $Y \subseteq L\times L'$ the set

$$\mathrm{TC}(Y) = \bigcap \{Y' \subseteq L\times L' \mid Y \subseteq Y' \wedge Y' = \mathrm{LC}(Y') \wedge Y' = \mathrm{CC}_1(Y') \wedge Y' = \mathrm{CC}_2(Y')\}$$

is the least left-closed set that contains Y and is closed in both components. □

Proof: The intersection is not taken over an empty set since $L\times L'$ is a candidate for Y'. Hence $\mathrm{TC}(Y)$ is defined and it is immediate that $Y \subseteq \mathrm{TC}(Y)$. To see that $\mathrm{TC}(Y)$ is left-closed consider $y \in \mathrm{TC}(Y)$ and $d \sqsubseteq y$; then $d \in Y'$ whenever Y' is one of the subsets over which the intersection is taken and hence $d \in \mathrm{TC}(Y)$. In a similar way it can be shown that $\mathrm{TC}(Y)$ is closed in both components. □

We now construct a tensor product by the following data:

$$L\otimes L' = (\{Y \subseteq L\times L' \mid Y \neq \emptyset \wedge Y = \mathrm{LC}(Y) = \mathrm{CC}_1(Y) = \mathrm{CC}_2(Y)\}, \subseteq)$$
$$cross = \lambda(l,l').\ \mathrm{LC}(\{(l,l')\})$$
$$f^{\otimes} = \lambda Y.\ \bigsqcup\{f(l,l') \mid (l,l') \in Y\}$$

Proposition 7.2.6 The above data constructs a tensor product (with respect to additivity and among the finite complete lattices). □

Proof: Since L and L' are finite complete lattices it is immediate that $L\otimes L'$ is a finite partial order. Its least element is $\{(\bot,\bot)\}$ and its greatest element is $L\times L'$. If $\mathcal{Y} \subseteq L\otimes L'$ is a non-empty set of elements the formula

$$\sqcap \mathcal{Y} = \bigcap \mathcal{Y}$$

defines a non-empty set, since all $Y \in \mathcal{Y}$ have $(\perp,\perp) \in Y$, and it is left-closed, because each $Y \in \mathcal{Y}$ is, and closed in both components, because each $Y \in \mathcal{Y}$ is. Hence $\sqcap\mathcal{Y}$ is the greatest lower bound of the non-empty collection $\mathcal{Y}$. It follows that $L \otimes L'$ is a complete lattice. The formula for least upper bounds is

$$\bigsqcup\mathcal{Y} = \mathrm{TC}(\bigcup\mathcal{Y})$$

where in general one cannot dispense with TC.

That *cross*: $L \times L' \rightarrow L \otimes L'$ is a function follows because $\mathrm{LC}(\{(l,l')\})$ is not only left-closed but also closed in each component. Clearly *cross* is monotonic and since $L \times L'$ is finite it follows that it is also continuous. For separate additivity we calculate

$$\begin{aligned} cross(l_1 \sqcup l_2, l') &= \mathrm{LC}(\{(l_1 \sqcup l_2, l')\}) \\ &= \mathrm{TC}(\{(l_1 \sqcup l_2, l')\}) \\ &= \mathrm{TC}(\{(l_1,l'),(l_2,l')\}) \\ &= \mathrm{TC}(\mathrm{LC}(\{(l_1,l')\}) \cup \mathrm{LC}(\{(l_2,l')\})) \\ &= \mathrm{TC}(cross(l_1,l') \cup cross(l_2,l')) \\ &= cross(l_1,l') \sqcup cross(l_2,l') \end{aligned}$$

and similarly for the other component.

Given a function $f{:}L \times L' \rightarrow M$ that is continuous (i.e. monotonic) and separately additive we may define a function

$$f^{\otimes}\colon\ L \otimes L' \rightarrow M$$

by the formula displayed. It is clearly monotonic and by finiteness of $L \otimes L'$ also continuous. Next we calculate

$$\begin{aligned} f^{\otimes}(cross(l,l')) &= \bigsqcup\{f(l_1,l_1') \mid (l_1,l_1') \sqsubseteq (l,l')\} \\ &= f(l,l') \end{aligned}$$

showing that $f^{\otimes} \circ cross = f$. For additivity we observe that

$$f^{\otimes}(Y_1 \cup Y_2) = f^{\otimes}(Y_1) \cup f^{\otimes}(Y_2)$$

and since $Y_1 \sqcup Y_2 = \mathrm{TC}(Y_1 \cup Y_2)$ it suffices to show that

$$f^{\otimes}(Y) = f^{\otimes}(\mathrm{TC}(Y)) \qquad \text{(for all } Y \subseteq L \times L'\text{)}$$

Since $\mathrm{TC}(Y)$ and Y will always be finite we may prove the result by numerical induction on the number of elements of $\mathrm{TC}(Y) \setminus Y$; we shall denote this number by $|\mathrm{TC}(Y) \setminus Y|$. The basis step is immediate because $|\mathrm{TC}(Y) \setminus Y| = 0$ amounts to $Y = \mathrm{TC}(Y)$. For the inductive step we know that Y is not left-closed or not closed in both components. If Y is not left-closed we have $d \sqsubseteq y \in Y$ such that $d \notin Y$; by setting $Y' = Y \cup \{d\}$ we have $\mathrm{TC}(Y) = \mathrm{TC}(Y')$ and

$$f^{\otimes}(Y) = f^{\otimes}(Y) \sqcup f(d) = f^{\otimes}(Y')$$

If Y is left-closed but not closed in the first component we have $(l_1,l') \in Y$ and $(l_2,l') \in Y$ such that $(l_1 \sqcup l_2,l') \notin Y$; by setting $Y' = Y \cup \{(l_1 \sqcup l_2,l')\}$ we have $\mathrm{TC}(Y) = \mathrm{TC}(Y')$ and

$$\begin{aligned} f^{\otimes}(Y) &= f^{\otimes}(Y) \sqcup f(l_1,l') \sqcup f(l_2,l') \\ &= f^{\otimes}(Y) \sqcup f(l_1 \sqcup l_2,l') \\ &= f^{\otimes}(Y') \end{aligned}$$

We proceed in a similar way if Y is not closed in the second component (but is left-closed and closed in the first component). In all cases we obtain a set Y' such that $f^{\otimes}(Y) = f^{\otimes}(Y')$, $\mathrm{TC}(Y) = \mathrm{TC}(Y')$ and $|\mathrm{TC}(Y') \backslash Y'| < |\mathrm{TC}(Y) \backslash Y|$. It follows that

$$f^{\otimes}(Y) = f^{\otimes}(Y') = f^{\otimes}(\mathrm{TC}(Y')) = f^{\otimes}(\mathrm{TC}(Y))$$

where the second equality holds because of the induction hypothesis.

Finally we must show the uniqueness of $f^{\otimes}$. So let $f' : L \otimes L' \to M$ be a continuous and additive function such that $f' \circ cross = f$. Let $Y \in L \otimes L'$ be an arbitrary element of $L \otimes L'$; we can then find $(l_1,l'_1), \cdots,(l_n,l'_n)$ such that

$$Y = \{(l_1,l'_1), \cdots,(l_n,l'_n)\}$$

It follows that

$$Y = \bigcup_{i=1}^{n} \{(l_i,l'_i)\} = \bigcup_{i=1}^{n} cross(l_i,l'_i) = \bigsqcup_{i=1}^{n} cross(l_i,l'_i)$$

so that

$$f'(Y) = \bigsqcup_{i=1}^{n} f'(cross(l_i,l'_i)) = \bigsqcup_{i=1}^{n} f(l_i,l'_i) = f^{\otimes}(Y)$$

This shows that $f' = f^{\otimes}$ and hence $f^{\otimes}$ is unique. □

We can now return to the definition of the interpretation $\mathbf{A}'$. We have already hinted at the interpretation of $\mathbf{A}'(t_1 \underline{\times} t_2)$ where we use

$$\mathbf{A}'(t_1 \underline{\times} t_2) = (\mathbf{A}'(t_1) \otimes \mathbf{A}'(t_2))_{\perp}$$

We now have to consider the operators `Tuple`, `Fst` and `Snd` associated with run-time products:

$$\mathbf{A}'(\texttt{Tuple}[t_0 \underline{\to} t_1 \underline{\times} t_2]) = \lambda h_1.\lambda h_2.$$
$$\begin{cases} up(\lambda a.up(cross(dn(h_1)(a),\ dn(h_2)(a)))) \\ \qquad \text{if } h_1 \neq \perp \text{ and } h_2 \neq \perp \\ \perp \qquad \text{otherwise} \end{cases}$$

$$\mathbf{A}'(\texttt{Fst}[t_1 \underline{\times} t_2]) = up(\lambda a.\ \bigsqcup\{l \mid (l,l') \in dn(a)\})$$

$$\mathbf{A}'(\texttt{Snd}[t_1 \underline{\times} t_2]) = up(\lambda a.\ \bigsqcup\{l' \mid (l,l') \in dn(a)\})$$

Example 7.2.7 In Example 7.1.1 we considered the strictness analysis of the function +[Int×Int→Int] but now the interpretation of run-time products has changed. It is therefore natural to model **A**′(+[Int×Int→Int]) as

$$up(\lambda a.\ \bigsqcup\{l \sqcap l' | (l,l') \in dn(a)\})$$

In this way **A**′(+[Int×Int→Int]) will give 1 when applied to $up(cross(1,1))$ but will give 0 when applied to $up(cross(0,1))$ or $up(cross(0,1) \sqcup cross(1,0))$. □

The analysis of Fst and Snd does not exploit the additional precision of the tensor product and this can hardly be expected otherwise. Concerning the analysis of + we now exploit the additional precision of the tensor product and one may therefore hope that **A**′ will be better than **A**. However, the weak point is that Tuple is the only operator that constructs an element of the tensor product and that this element is of the form $cross(\cdots,\cdots)$. This can be rectified by letting the interpretation of Tuple consider the atoms or the irreducible elements of the argument a (or $dn(a)$). References to approaches following these ideas may be found in the Bibliographical Notes. Here we shall take a shortcut and introduce special operators for exploiting the tensor product. One is

Split[t]

that is supposed to be 'equivalent' to

Tuple(Hd[t],Tl[t])

and the other is

Prod(e_1,e_2)

that is supposed to be 'equivalent' to

Tuple(e_1□Fst[t],e_2□Snd[t])

for a suitable type t. In the standard semantics we thus have

$$\mathbf{S}(\texttt{Split}[t]) = up(\lambda v.\ up(\text{HD}_{\text{PS}}(v),\text{TL}_{\text{PS}}(v)))$$

$$\mathbf{S}(\texttt{Prod}) = \lambda f_1.\lambda f_2. \begin{cases} up(\lambda v.up(dn(f_1)(v_1),dn(f_2)(v_2)) \\ \qquad \text{where } (v_1,v_2)=dn(v)) \\ \qquad \text{if } f_1 \neq \bot \text{ and } f_2 \neq \bot \\ \bot \qquad \text{otherwise} \end{cases}$$

For the analysis we then have

$$\mathbf{A}'(\texttt{Split}[t]) = up(\lambda a.up(\begin{cases} cross(\perp,0) & \text{if } a{=}0 \\ cross(\top,1) & \text{if } a{=}1 \\ \bigsqcup\{cross(\sqcap Y', (Y \ominus Y')\varepsilon) \mid Y' \subseteq Y\} & \text{if } a{=}Y\varepsilon \neq \top\varepsilon \\ cross(\top,\top\varepsilon) & \text{if } a{=}\top\varepsilon \end{cases}))$$

$$\mathbf{A}'(\texttt{Prod}) = \lambda h_1.\lambda h_2. \begin{cases} up(\lambda a.up(\bigsqcup\{cross(dn(h_1)(l),\ dn(h_2)(l')) \mid (l,l') \in dn(a)\})) \\ \quad \text{if } h_1 \neq \perp \text{ and } h_2 \neq \perp \\ \perp \quad \text{otherwise} \end{cases}$$

The definition of $\mathbf{A}'$(`Split`) has many similarities to the definition of $\mathbf{A}$(`Case`). Finally for types and operators not considered so far we shall assume that $\mathbf{A}'$ behaves as $\mathbf{A}$.

Example 7.2.8 In the case of lists of base types the above definition of $\mathbf{A}'$(`Split`) amounts to the following:

$$\mathbf{A}'(\texttt{Split}[t]) = up(\lambda a.up(\begin{cases} cross(0,0) & \text{if } a{=}0 \\ cross(1,1) & \text{if } a{=}1 \\ cross(0,1\varepsilon)\bigsqcup cross(1,0\varepsilon) & \text{if } a{=}0\varepsilon \\ cross(1,1\varepsilon) & \text{if } a{=}1\varepsilon \end{cases}))$$

Naturally this has many similarities to the simplification of $\mathbf{A}$(`Case`) obtained in Example 7.2.2. □

Example 7.2.9 Using `Split` and `Prod` we may now consider the following definitions of `length` and `sum`:

$$\texttt{length}_2 = \texttt{fix}(\lambda \texttt{f}[\underline{\texttt{Int}}\ \underline{\texttt{list}} \underline{\rightarrow} \underline{\texttt{Int}}].\ \texttt{Cond}(\texttt{Isnil}[\underline{\texttt{Int}}],\ \texttt{Zero}[\underline{\texttt{Int}}\ \underline{\texttt{list}} \underline{\rightarrow} \underline{\texttt{Int}}],\ \texttt{+}[\underline{\texttt{Int}}\underline{\times}\underline{\texttt{Int}}\underline{\rightarrow}\underline{\texttt{Int}}] \,\square\, \texttt{Prod}(\texttt{One}[\underline{\texttt{Int}} \underline{\rightarrow} \underline{\texttt{Int}}],\ \texttt{f}) \,\square\, \texttt{Split}[\underline{\texttt{Int}}]))$$

$$\texttt{sum}_2 = \texttt{fix}(\lambda \texttt{f}[\underline{\texttt{Int}}\ \underline{\texttt{list}} \underline{\rightarrow} \underline{\texttt{Int}}].\ \texttt{Cond}(\texttt{Isnil}[\underline{\texttt{Int}}],\ \texttt{Zero}[\underline{\texttt{Int}}\ \underline{\texttt{list}} \underline{\rightarrow} \underline{\texttt{Int}}],\ \texttt{+}[\underline{\texttt{Int}}\underline{\times}\underline{\texttt{Int}}\underline{\rightarrow}\underline{\texttt{Int}}] \,\square\, \texttt{Prod}(\texttt{Id}[\underline{\texttt{Int}}],\ \texttt{f}) \,\square\, \texttt{Split}[\underline{\texttt{Int}}]))$$

Again there is no need to redefine `hd` and thus no need to analyse it once again. Using the notation FIX′ and *strict* of Example 7.1.11 we may then perform the following analysis of `length`:

$[\![\texttt{length}_2]\!](\mathbf{A}')(\textbf{void})$

$= \text{FIX}'(strict(\lambda h.up(\lambda a.$
case $dn(\mathbf{A}'(\texttt{Isnil}))(a)$ of
0: 0

$$\begin{array}{l}
\quad \text{T: } 1 \\
\quad \text{F: } \bigsqcup\{1 \sqcap dn(h)(l') \mid (l,l') \in dn(dn(\mathbf{A}'(\mathtt{Split}))(a))\} \\
\quad 1\text{: } 1 \sqcup (\bigsqcup\{1 \sqcap dn(h)(l') \mid (l,l') \in dn(dn(\mathbf{A}'(\mathtt{Split}))(a))\})))) \\
= \text{FIX}'(\mathit{strict}(\lambda h.up(\lambda a. \\
\quad \text{case } a \text{ of} \\
\quad 0\text{: } 0 \\
\quad 1\text{: } \bigsqcup\{1 \sqcap dn(h)(l') \mid (l,l') \in \mathit{cross}(1,1)\} \\
\quad 0\varepsilon\text{: } \bigsqcup\{1 \sqcap dn(h)(l') \mid (l,l') \in \mathit{cross}(0,1\varepsilon) \sqcup \mathit{cross}(1,0\varepsilon)\} \\
\quad 1\varepsilon\text{: } 1\ ))) \\
= \text{FIX}'(\mathit{strict}(\lambda h.up(\lambda a. \\
\quad \text{case } a \text{ of} \\
\quad 0\text{: } 0 \\
\quad 1\text{: } dn(h)(1) \\
\quad 0\varepsilon\text{: } dn(h)(1\varepsilon) \\
\quad 1\varepsilon\text{: } 1\ ))) \\
= up(\lambda a.\text{case } a \text{ of} \\
\quad 0\text{: } 0 \\
\quad 1\text{: } 0 \\
\quad 0\varepsilon\text{: } 1 \\
\quad 1\varepsilon\text{: } 1)
\end{array}$$

Thus $dn([\![\mathtt{length}_2]\!](\mathbf{A}')(\mathbf{void}))$ equals the optimal result of Example 7.1.5; this should come as no surprise as we also obtained the optimal result in Example 7.2.4. Turning to `sum` we may perform the following analysis:

$$\begin{array}{l}
[\![\mathtt{sum}_2]\!](\mathbf{A}')(\mathbf{void}) \\
\quad = \text{FIX}'(\mathit{strict}(\lambda h.up(\lambda a. \\
\quad\quad \text{case } dn(\mathbf{A}'(\mathtt{Isnil}))(a) \text{ of} \\
\quad\quad 0\text{: } 0 \\
\quad\quad \text{T: } 1 \\
\quad\quad \text{F: } \bigsqcup\{l \sqcap dn(h)(l') \mid (l,l') \in dn(dn(\mathbf{A}'(\mathtt{Split}))(a))\} \\
\quad\quad 1\text{: } 1 \sqcup (\bigsqcup\{l \sqcap dn(h)(l') \mid (l,l') \in dn(dn(\mathbf{A}'(\mathtt{Split}))(a))\})))) \\
\quad = \text{FIX}'(\mathit{strict}(\lambda h.up(\lambda a. \\
\quad\quad \text{case } a \text{ of} \\
\quad\quad 0\text{: } 0 \\
\quad\quad 1\text{: } \bigsqcup\{l \sqcap dn(h)(l') \mid (l,l') \in \mathit{cross}(1,1)\} \\
\quad\quad 0\varepsilon\text{: } \bigsqcup\{l \sqcap dn(h)(l') \mid (l,l') \in \mathit{cross}(0,1\varepsilon) \sqcup \mathit{cross}(1,0\varepsilon)\} \\
\quad\quad 1\varepsilon\text{: } 1\ ))) \\
\quad = \text{FIX}'(\mathit{strict}(\lambda h.up(\lambda a. \\
\quad\quad \text{case } a \text{ of} \\
\quad\quad 0\text{: } 0
\end{array}$$

$$
\begin{aligned}
&1\text{: } 1\sqcap dn(h)(1)\\
&0\varepsilon\text{: } (0\sqcap dn(h)(1\varepsilon)) \sqcup (1\sqcap dn(h)(0\varepsilon))\\
&1\varepsilon\text{: } 1\ )))\\
= \ &up(\lambda a.\text{case } a \text{ of}\\
&0\text{: } 0\\
&1\text{: } 0\\
&0\varepsilon\text{: } 0\\
&1\varepsilon\text{: } 1)
\end{aligned}
$$

Thus also $dn([\![\mathbf{sum}_2]\!](\mathbf{A}')(\mathbf{void}))$ equals the optimal result of Example 7.1.5. This is in contrast to what happened in Example 7.2.4 and is due to our use of tensor product. □

Judging from Examples 7.2.3 and 7.2.9 we can obtain the optimal results for the `hd`, `length` and `sum` functions using either `Case`-analysis or the tensor product (with a few additional operators that could be dispensed with at the price of a more complex theory). One should take care, however, to note that there is a certain 'duality' in the sets considered. For run-time lists we are using right-closed sets whereas for tensor products we are using left-closed sets (that are additionally closed in each component). The use of left-closed sets is rather natural for abstract interpretation as is evidenced by the central role the lower powerdomain plays in many formulations of abstract interpretation. The use of right-closed sets for lists seems to be necessary to capture the essence of Wadler's insight: the ability to describe long finite lists that may have arbitrary elements except that one of these has to be undefined, that is $\perp$. In the terminology of [2] one might say that the Wadler-like analysis of lists necessitates a formulation of liveness aspects in addition to the safety aspects.

It remains to demonstrate the correctness of the analysis $\mathbf{A}'$. For this we shall follow the approach of Section 7.1 (and Subsection 7.2.1) but we have to change the correctness predicates to reflect the differences between the type parts of $\mathbf{A}$ and $\mathbf{A}'$. So we set

$$
\begin{aligned}
val'_{\underline{\mathtt{Bool}}}(v,a) \equiv\ & (v{=}\mathbf{true} \Rightarrow a \sqsupseteq T) \wedge\\
& (v{=}\mathbf{false} \Rightarrow a \sqsupseteq F)\\
val'_{t_1 \underline{\times} t_2}(v,a) \equiv\ & (a{=}\perp\ \Rightarrow v{=}\perp) \wedge\\
& (\exists (a_1,a_2){\in} dn(a)\text{: } val_{t_1}(v_1,a_1) \wedge val_{t_2}(v_2,a_2)\\
& \text{where } (v_1,v_2) = dn(v))
\end{aligned}
$$

and assume that the remaining clauses for val' are as for val. The latter clause clearly demonstrates the intention with the tensor product: an abstract property is a set of pairs of properties and for a given value only one of these pairs needs to be applicable.

Just as we defined the predicate *comp* from *val* we may define the predicate *comp'* from *val'*. We thus obtain an admissible predicate

$$val'_t : \mathbf{S}(t) \times \mathbf{A}'(t) \rightarrow \{\text{true,false}\}$$

for all well-formed types t of run-time kind, and an admissible predicate

$$comp'_t : [\![t]\!](\mathbf{S}) \times [\![t]\!](\mathbf{A}') \rightarrow \{\text{true,false}\}$$

for all well-formed types t of compile-time kind. Our main 'local correctness result' then is the following analogue of Corollary 7.1.29:

Lemma 7.2.10 We have $comp'(\mathbf{S}(\phi),\mathbf{A}'(\phi))$ for every operator ϕ that is either `Prod` or `Split` or is one of the operators of Table 5.1, except those of form $\mathtt{f}_i$ or $\mathtt{F}_i$ and provided that the type t indexing $\mathtt{fix}[t]$ is always composite. □

Proof: Given Corollary 7.1.29 it is only necessary to consider the operators `Cond`, `True`, `False`, `Tuple`, `Fst`, `Snd`, `Prod` and `Split`. The proof is rather straightforward and we dispense with the details. □

It hardly comes as a surprise that we also have the following analogue of Lemma 7.1.30:

Lemma 7.2.11 ('Structural induction') Let *penv* be a well-formed position environment (in the sense of Section 5.2) such that

$$\rho_{\mathrm{PS}}(penv) \overset{\mathsf{K}}{\vdash} e{:}t$$

If

$$comp'(\mathbf{S}(\phi),\mathbf{A}'(\phi))$$

holds for all operators ϕ that occur in e, then

$$comp'([\![e]\!](\mathbf{S}),[\![e]\!](\mathbf{A}'))$$ □

Proof: The proof is by structural induction on the expression e much as in the proof of Lemma 6.2.4. We dispense with the details. □

We also have an analogue of Corollary 7.1.31 and as in Section 7.1 this also carries over to programs of the mixed λ-calculus and combinatory logic; this then ends the demonstration of the correctness of $\mathbf{A}'$.

Bibliographical Notes

There is a wealth of literature on program analysis whether in the form of data flow analysis (as surveyed in [54]) or abstract interpretation (as surveyed in [4]). Strictness analysis, in the form of abstract interpretation, was originally conceived by Mycroft [62] and a useful extension to lists was first given by Wadler [104]. Since then many authors have tried to extend strictness analysis to larger fragments of functional languages (which is 'easy') in a way which maintains the naturality of Wadler's approach (which is 'hard'); we believe the twist used here to be new but some other references are [29, 105, 14].

On the subject of abstract interpretation we have been rather modest in our treatment of techniques. We have only considered the *safety* aspects and [2] is a good reference on the dual notion of *liveness* aspects. Also we have only dealt with safety rather than techniques for *inducing* the best safe analysis and how the study of *expected forms* may make this more applicable in practice; we refer to [78] and [71] for references on this. Another topic not dealt with is the distinction between first order and second order analyses and the relation to partial equivalence relations which is again related to projection analysis [105]. There is a discussion of the relationship between abstract interpretation and projection analysis in [14] but it is not entirely satisfactory.

For functional languages one often formulates abstract interpretation in 'BHA-style' [15]. Our work is closer to the 'TML-style' [66, 70, 71, 45, 78] whose notation is inspired by the 'Cousot-style' [20] (after the 'inventors' of abstract interpretation). As a guide to the literature we shall briefly compare some of the salient features of the different styles, but we do not have the space to explain the concepts fully. One issue is that of notation:

BHA-style	TML-style	Cousot-style
Abs	α (or *abs*)	α
Conc	γ (or *con*)	γ
abs	β	

Here α is the *abstraction map*; it maps a set of values in the standard semantics to the single property that best describes all of them. (For strictness analysis of the integers it would for example map a set $\{\mathbf{3},\mathbf{27},\cdots\}$ of values to the strictness property 1 whereas the set $\{\bot\}$ would be mapped to the strictness property 0.) Next γ is the *concretization map*; it maps a property from the analysis to the set of values in the standard semantics that are described by that property. (For strictness analysis of the integers it would map 1 to $\{\cdots,\mathbf{-1},\mathbf{0},\mathbf{1},\cdots,\bot\}$ and 0 to $\{\bot\}$.) Finally β is the *representation map* (called abstraction map in [15]); it maps a single value in the standard semantics to the property that best describes it. It should thus come as no surprise that $\alpha(Y) = \bigsqcup\{\beta(y)|y\in Y\}$.

Another issue is how to define maps α_t, β_t and γ_t in a structural way over types t. Here the 'TML-style' allows much greater freedom than the other approaches. One example is the ability to use the tensor product in one analysis and the cartesian product in another. Another example is the ability to consider more complex type constructors like recursive types. Finally the study of expected forms is important for implementations of the analyses.

A third issue is the weakest set of assumptions that can be used to obtain some kind of theory. (Clearly the stronger the assumptions the more interesting the theory.) Here the 'Cousot-style' focuses on the concretization map γ *without* requiring (α,γ) to form an adjunction (also known as a Galois-connection). In the 'BHA-style' and the (later versions of the) 'TML-style' focus is placed on a predicate like *val*. This predicate is quite often of the form $val(v,a) \equiv \beta(v) \leq a$; in the 'BHA-style' the partial order $\leq$ always equals $\sqsubseteq$ whereas in the 'TML-style' this is only so for run-time types. In fact analogues of the properties listed in Lemmas 7.1.8 and 7.1.10 may also be found in (extensions of) the 'BHA-style' (see [2]).

The first use of tensor products for abstract interpretation is contained in [66] which also contains formulations for `Tuple` where the irreducible elements are used for case analysis. A similar development but using atoms is contained in [68]. A general study of tensor products of continuous lattices is contained in [8].

A brief appraisal of the material of this chapter may be found in [84].

Exercises

1. Depict the complete lattice $\mathbf{A}((\underline{\mathtt{Int}}\ \underline{\mathtt{list}})\underline{\mathtt{list}})$ and describe the meaning of its six elements.

2. Write $bot_t = \perp_{\mathbf{A}(t)}$ and $top_t = \top_{\mathbf{A}(t)}$. Give an inductive definition of bot_t and top_t that is consistent with this.

3. Prove that $comp_{\underline{t \rightarrow \mathtt{Int}}}(\mathbf{S}(\mathtt{Zero}),\mathbf{A}(\mathtt{Zero}))$ where

   $$\mathbf{S}(\mathtt{Zero}) = up(\lambda v.\ \mathbf{0})$$

   and $\mathbf{A}(\mathtt{Zero})$ is as in Example 7.1.1.

4. Prove that $comp_{\underline{\mathtt{Int} \times \mathtt{Int} \rightarrow \mathtt{Int}}}(\mathbf{S}(+),\mathbf{A}(+))$ where

   $$\mathbf{S}(+) = up(\lambda v.\ v_1{+}v_2 \text{ where } (v_1,v_2){=}dn(v))$$

   (taking $\perp{+}v{=}\perp{=}v{+}\perp$) and $\mathbf{A}(+)$ is as in Example 7.1.1.

5. (*) Define the type part of an interpretation $\mathbf{A}_{\mathrm{III}}$ that more closely mirrors the semantics $\mathbf{S}_{\mathrm{III}}$ of Chapter 5. Extend the interpretation with its expression part and formulate the safety predicate. Prove the safety of a few operators.

6. Let M_1 and M_2 be partially ordered sets. An *isomorphism* θ from M_1 to M_2 is an injective and surjective function $\theta{:}M_1{\rightarrow}M_2$ such that

   $$\forall m,m'{\in}M_1{:}\ m{\sqsubseteq}m' \Leftrightarrow \theta(m){\sqsubseteq}\theta(m')$$

   Show that an isomorphism is a continuous function and that its inverse is also an isomorphism.

7. Let $(M_1, cross_1)$ and $(M_2, cross_2)$ be tensor products of L and L'. Show that there exists an isomorphism θ (as in Exercise 6) from M_1 to M_2 such that $\theta \circ cross_1 = cross_2$. (Hint: consider $cross_1^{\otimes 2}$ and $cross_2^{\otimes 1}$ where $f^{\otimes i}$ denotes $f^{\otimes}$ with respect to $(M_i, cross_i)$.)

8. The lower powerdomain $\mathbf{P}_L(D)$ of a Scott-domain D may be defined as

$$\mathbf{P}_L(D) = (\{Y \subseteq B_D \mid Y \neq \emptyset \wedge Y = LC(Y)\}, \subseteq)$$

Show that

- $\mathbf{P}_L(D)$ is a complete lattice, and
- $\mathbf{P}_L(D)$ is a Scott-domain, and

that $\lambda d.LC(\{d\}) \cap B_D$ is a continuous function from D to $\mathbf{P}_L(D)$.

9. Show that $(\mathbf{P}_L(D \times D'), \lambda(Y, Y').\{(y, y') \mid y \in Y \wedge y' \in Y'\})$ is a tensor product of $\mathbf{P}_L(D)$ and $\mathbf{P}_L(D')$ and determine the formula for $f^{\otimes}$. (Hint: you may assume that D and D' are finite so that $B_D = D$ and $B_{D'} = D'$, but the result holds in general.)

10. (*) Define a function

$$\beta_t : \mathbf{S}(t) \to \mathbf{A}(t)$$

by induction over well-formed run-time types t such that

$$val_t(v, a) \equiv \beta_t(v) \sqsubseteq a$$

where val_t is the correctness predicate of Table 7.2. Show that β_t is strict and continuous (and that it maps compact elements to compact elements).

Chapter 8

Conclusion

In the previous chapters we have focused on the theoretical development of the *language* of the mixed λ-calculus and combinatory logic (Chapters 2, 3 and 4) and on the different *standard* and *non-standard semantics* of the language (Chapters 5, 6 and 7). There are two immediate application areas for this work, one is in the efficient implementation of functional languages and the other is in denotational semantics.

8.1 Optimized Code Generation

Much work in the community of functional languages has been devoted to the development of efficient implementations. This is well documented in [86] which contains a number of techniques that may be used to improve the overall performance of a 'naive' implementation. However, the theoretical soundness of all these techniques has not been established (although [52] goes part of the way). We believe that the main reason for this is that it is not well-understood how to *structure* correctness proofs even for naive code generation schemes. So although we have a firm handle on how to prove the safety of large classes of program analyses it is less clear how to *formally* prove the correctness of exploiting the analyses to generate 'optimized' code.

Before addressing the question on how to improve the code generation of Chapter 6 let us briefly review the techniques we have used. The code generation is specified as an interpretation **K** (in the sense of Chapter 5) and its correctness is expressed by means of Kripke-logical relations. Turning to the strictness analysis of Chapter 7 we take a similar approach: the analysis is specified as an interpretation **A** and its safety is expressed using logical relations. The idea is now to specify the optimizing code generation schemes as interpretations and the goal will be to adapt the technique of (Kripke-)logical relations to express the correctness.

$$\mathbf{O}(\texttt{Tuple}[t_0 \underline{\rightarrow} t_1 \underline{\times} t_2]) = \lambda(RC_1, h_1).\lambda(RC_2, h_2).$$
$$(\mathbf{K}(\texttt{Tuple}[\,])\ RC_1\ RC_2,\ \mathbf{A}(\texttt{Tuple}[\,])\ h_1\ h_2)$$
$$\mathbf{O}(\texttt{Fst}[t_1 \underline{\times} t_2]) = (\mathbf{K}(\texttt{Fst}[\,]), \mathbf{A}(\texttt{Fst}[\,]))$$
$$\mathbf{O}(\texttt{Snd}[t_1 \underline{\times} t_2]) = (\mathbf{K}(\texttt{Snd}[\,]), \mathbf{A}(\texttt{Snd}[\,]))$$
$$\mathbf{O}(\texttt{Cons}[t_0 \underline{\rightarrow} t_1 \underline{\texttt{list}}]) = \lambda(RC_1, h_1).\lambda(RC_2, h_2).$$
$$(\mathbf{K}(\texttt{Cons}[\,])\ RC_1\ RC_2,\ \mathbf{A}(\texttt{Cons}[\,])\ h_1\ h_2)$$
$$\mathbf{O}(\texttt{Nil}[t_0 \underline{\rightarrow} t_1 \underline{\texttt{list}}]) = (\mathbf{K}(\texttt{Nil}[\,]), \mathbf{A}(\texttt{Nil}[\,]))$$
$$\mathbf{O}(\texttt{Hd}[t]) = (\mathbf{K}(\texttt{Hd}[\,]), \mathbf{A}(\texttt{Hd}[\,]))$$
$$\mathbf{O}(\texttt{Tl}[t]) = (\mathbf{K}(\texttt{Tl}[\,]), \mathbf{A}(\texttt{Tl}[\,]))$$
$$\mathbf{O}(\texttt{Isnil}[t]) = (\mathbf{K}(\texttt{Isnil}[\,]), \mathbf{A}(\texttt{Isnil}[\,]))$$

Table 8.1: The optimizing interpretation **O** (part 1)

8.1.1 Using local strictness information

The code generated by **K** can be improved if we have information about strictness. To see this consider the code generated for $e_1 \,\square\, e_2$:

$$[\![e_1 \,\square\, e_2]\!](\mathbf{K}) = \lambda\mathbf{env}.\lambda d.$$
$$\text{DELAY}([\![e_2]\!](\mathbf{K})(\mathbf{env})(d)):([\![e_1]\!](\mathbf{K})(\mathbf{env})(d))$$

Here the computations of e_2 are postponed using the DELAY instruction because the result produced by e_2 need not be required by e_1. However, if we do know that e_1 is strict then we also know that the value of e_2 will be needed and then we can dispense with the DELAY instruction and thus improve the code. To obtain such optimizations we shall specify an interpretation **O** that, essentially, performs **K** and **A** 'in parallel'. This means that the strictness information will always be available so that it may be used to generate better code for operators like $\square$.

The type part of **O** has

$$\mathbf{O}(t_1 \underline{\rightarrow} t_2) = \mathbf{K}(t_1 \underline{\rightarrow} t_2) \times \mathbf{A}(t_1 \underline{\rightarrow} t_2)$$

and the expression part is given in Tables 8.1, 8.2 and 8.3. The interpretation of most of the operators is fairly straightforward because they do not make any use of the strictness information. The interpretation of $\square$ in Table 8.2 consults the strictness properties of its first argument to see if the DELAY instruction for the code can be omitted. In the definition of $\mathbf{O}(\texttt{fix}[t_1 \underline{\rightarrow} t_2])$ given in Table 8.3 we use that the strictness information is independent of the code generated so in the definition of the functional H_2 we simply supply H with an 'arbitrary' first argument, in this case $\lambda d.[\,]$. Having obtained the strictness information for the fixed point we may use it when we define the functional H_1.

$$
\begin{array}{l}
\mathbf{O}(\mathtt{f}_{\mathrm{i}}[t]) = \mathbf{f}_{\mathrm{i}}^{t} \\
\qquad \text{where } \mathbf{f}_{\mathrm{i}}^{t} \text{ are appropriate elements of } [\![t]\!](\mathbf{O}) \\
\mathbf{O}(\mathtt{F}_{\mathrm{i}}[t_0 \underline{\rightarrow} t_1]) = (\mathbf{K}(\mathtt{F}_{\mathrm{i}}[\,]),\ \mathbf{A}(\mathtt{F}_{\mathrm{i}}[\,])) \\
\mathbf{O}(\Box[(t_1 \underline{\rightarrow} t_2) \times (t_0 \underline{\rightarrow} t_1)]) = \lambda(RC_1,\ h_1).\lambda(RC_2,\ h_2). \\
\qquad (RC,\ \mathbf{A}(\Box[\,])\ h_1\ h_2) \text{ where} \\
\qquad RC = \lambda d. \begin{cases}
(RC_2(d)){:}(RC_1(d)) & \\
\qquad \text{if } dn(h_1) \perp = \perp, & \\
\qquad RC_1(d) \neq \perp \text{ and } RC_2(d) \neq \perp & \\
\textsc{delay}(RC_2(d)){:}(RC_1(d)) & \\
\qquad \text{if } dn(h_1) \perp \neq \perp, & \\
\qquad RC_1(d) \neq \perp \text{ and } RC_2(d) \neq \perp & \\
\perp \qquad \text{otherwise} &
\end{cases} \\
\mathbf{O}(\mathtt{Id}[t]) = (\mathbf{K}(\mathtt{Id}[\,]),\ \mathbf{A}(\mathtt{Id}[\,])) \\
\mathbf{O}(\mathtt{True}[t]) = (\mathbf{K}(\mathtt{True}[\,]),\ \mathbf{A}(\mathtt{True}[\,])) \\
\mathbf{O}(\mathtt{False}[t]) = (\mathbf{K}(\mathtt{False}[\,]),\ \mathbf{A}(\mathtt{False}[\,])) \\
\mathbf{O}(\mathtt{Cond}[t_0 \underline{\rightarrow} t_1]) = \lambda(RC_1,h_1).\lambda(RC_2,h_2).\lambda(RC_3,h_3). \\
\qquad (\mathbf{K}(\mathtt{Cond}[\,])\ RC_1\ RC_2\ RC_3,\ \mathbf{A}(\mathtt{Cond}[\,])\ h_1\ h_2\ h_3)
\end{array}
$$

Table 8.2: The optimizing interpretation **O** (part 2)

Example 8.1.1 Consider the `sum` expression of Example 7.1.5:

$$\mathtt{fix}\ (\lambda \mathtt{f}[\,].\mathtt{Cond}(\mathtt{Isnil}[\,],\ \mathtt{Zero}[\,],\ \mathtt{+}[\,] \Box \mathtt{Tuple}(\mathtt{Hd}[\,],\ \mathtt{f} \Box \mathtt{Tl}[\,])))$$

where we have omitted the type information. From Example 6.1.6 we have that $[\![\mathtt{sum}]\!](\mathbf{K})(\mathbf{void})(d)$ equals

$$
\begin{array}{l}
\textsc{callrec}(d,\ \textsc{enter:resume:isnil:} \\
\qquad\qquad \textsc{branch}(\textsc{const}\ \mathbf{0}, \\
\qquad\qquad\qquad \underline{\textsc{delay}}(\textsc{enter:} \\
\qquad\qquad\qquad\qquad \textsc{delay}(\underline{\textsc{delay}}(\textsc{resume:tl:resume}): \\
\qquad\qquad\qquad\qquad\qquad \textsc{call}\ d): \\
\qquad\qquad\qquad\qquad \textsc{switch:} \\
\qquad\qquad\qquad\qquad \textsc{delay}(\textsc{resume:hd:resume}): \\
\qquad\qquad\qquad\qquad \textsc{tuple}): \\
\qquad\qquad\qquad \textsc{resume:enter:snd:resume:} \\
\qquad\qquad\qquad \textsc{switch:fst:resume:tuple:prim}\ +))
\end{array}
$$

The interpretation **O** will give

$$\mathbf{O}(\texttt{fix}[t]) = \text{FIX where FIX } H = \bigsqcup_n H^n(\bot)$$
$$\text{if } t \text{ is pure}$$
$$\mathbf{O}(\texttt{fix}[t_1 \underline{\rightarrow} t_2]) = \lambda H.(\mathbf{K}(\texttt{fix}[\,])\ H_1,\ \mathbf{A}(\texttt{fix}[\,])\ H_2) \text{ where}$$
$$H_1\ RC = RC' \text{ where } (RC', h') = H(RC, \mathbf{A}(\texttt{fix}[\,])\ H_2)$$
$$H_2\ h = h' \text{ where } (RC', h') = H(\lambda d.[\,], h)$$
$$\mathbf{O}(\texttt{fix}[t_1 \times t_2]) = \lambda H.(H_1, H_2(H_1)) \text{ where}$$
$$H_1 = \mathbf{O}(\texttt{fix}[t_1])(\lambda \mathbf{v}_1.\mathbf{w}_1 \text{ where } (\mathbf{w}_1,\mathbf{w}_2) = H((\mathbf{v}_1, H_2(\mathbf{v}_1))))$$
$$H_2 = \lambda \mathbf{v}_1.\mathbf{O}(\texttt{fix}[t_2])(\lambda \mathbf{v}_2.\mathbf{w}_2 \text{ where } (\mathbf{w}_1,\mathbf{w}_2) = H((\mathbf{v}_1,\mathbf{v}_2)))$$
$$\text{and } t_1 \times t_2 \text{ is composite but not pure}$$
$$\mathbf{O}(\texttt{Curry}[t_0 \underline{\rightarrow} (t_1 \underline{\rightarrow} t_2)]) = \lambda(RC,h).$$
$$(\mathbf{K}(\texttt{Curry}[\,])\ RC,\ \mathbf{A}(\texttt{Curry}[\,])\ h)$$
$$\mathbf{O}(\texttt{Apply}[t_0 \underline{\rightarrow} t_1]) = (\mathbf{K}(\texttt{Apply}[\,]), \mathbf{A}(\texttt{Apply}[\,]))$$
$$\mathbf{O}(\texttt{Fix}[t_0 \underline{\rightarrow} t_1]) = (\mathbf{K}(\texttt{Fix}[\,]), \mathbf{A}(\texttt{Fix}[\,]))$$

Table 8.3: The optimizing interpretation **O** (part 3)

$$[\![\texttt{sum}]\!](\mathbf{O})(\textbf{void}) = (RC, [\![\texttt{sum}]\!](\mathbf{A})(\textbf{void}))$$

where $RC(d)$ is as above but *without* the underlined DELAY instructions. To see this note that the outermost DELAY instruction is dispensed with because **+** is strict and the innermost one is dispensed with because **f** itself is strict – the definition of **O**(**fix**[ ]) for frontier types ensures that this information can be used for the recursive call. □

Correctness issues

The correctness of **O** can be proved using Kripke-logical relations. Here we shall briefly outline one such approach; the details of a similar approach may be found in [50] (for a subset of the language without lists). Basically, the proof is in three stages:

Stage 1: It is shown that the code component of **O** satisfies the substitution and well-formedness properties of Chapter 6. The properties are expressed by predicates

$$compS_t\colon\ [\![t]\!](\mathbf{O}) \rightarrow \{\text{true, false}\}$$
$$compW_t\colon\ [\![t]\!](\mathbf{O}) \rightarrow \{\text{true, false}\}$$

The definitions and subsequent proofs are rather trivial modifications of those found in Chapter 6.

Stage 2: It is shown that the strictness component of **O** is safe (in the sense of Chapter 7) with respect to the standard semantics **S**. This result is crucial for the definition of $\mathbf{O}(\mathtt{fix}[t_1 \underline{\rightarrow} t_2])$ in Table 8.3. The property is expressed formally by a predicate

$$compA_t \colon [\![t]\!](\mathbf{S}) \times [\![t]\!](\mathbf{O}) \rightarrow \{\text{true, false}\}$$

The interesting clause in the definition of this predicate is

$$compA_{t_1 \underline{\rightarrow} t_2}(g,(RC,h)) \equiv comp_{t_1 \underline{\rightarrow} t_2}(g,h)$$

The proof of the property is a straightforward modification of the proof in Chapter 7. If desired it may be augmented to show that the strictness component of **O** actually 'equals' **A**.

Stage 3: Finally, the correctness of **O** is expressed by the predicate

$$compC_t \colon [\![t]\!](\mathbf{O}) \times [\![t]\!](\mathbf{S}) \rightarrow \{\text{true, false}\}$$

The interesting clause in the definition is

$$\begin{aligned} compC_{t_1 \underline{\rightarrow} t_2}((RC,h),g) \equiv\ & compW_{t_1 \underline{\rightarrow} t_2}(RC,h) \wedge \\ & compA_{t_1 \underline{\rightarrow} t_2}(g,(RC,h)) \wedge \\ & compWC_{t_1 \underline{\rightarrow} t_2}(RC,g) \end{aligned}$$

where $compWC_{t_1 \underline{\rightarrow} t_2}(RC,g)$ is defined much as in Section 6.4. The proofs follow those of Section 6.4 and only the cases of □ and `fix` are non-trivial. We refer to [50] for the details.

We conclude the discussion of the correctness of **O** by observing that the notion of layered predicates has been extended to include the safety property of the strictness analysis. The 'layer' may therefore be depicted as follows:

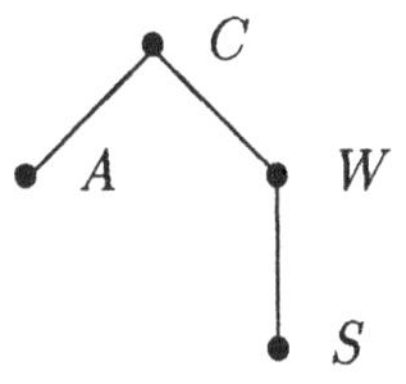

8.1.2 Using right context information

Example 8.1.1 shows that the interpretation **O** gives rise to better code because fewer computations are delayed. However, local strictness information does not suffice for dispensing with all the DELAY instructions we could hope for. Also it does not allow us to remove any of the seemingly unnecessary RESUME instructions. To get such improvements we need information about the *context* of the expressions. We shall distinguish between two kinds of contexts:

- *right context information* is concerned with the remaining computations, i.e. how the result of the current expression is used, and
- *left context information* is concerned with the computations that already have been performed, i.e. how the argument supplied to the current expression has been produced.

We shall now sketch how the interpretation **O** can be extended to take right context information into account so as to generate even fewer DELAY-instructions. The aim will be to show that the concept of parameterized semantics does indeed allow us to specify a wide range of optimizing code generation schemes.

Strictness continuations

In the code generated for `Tuple`(e_1, e_2) we have so far postponed the computations of e_1 and e_2 because we do not know whether or not their results are needed in the remainder of the computation. However, sometimes we do know that the result is needed; an example is the **sum** program where we have `+[ ]` □ `Tuple(···,···)` and where we know that `+` is strict in both components of its argument. When this is the case it will be safe to dispense with the DELAY instructions.

To perform this optimization we need information about the future use of results of subexpressions. This information can be provided by a *strictness continuation* which, basically, is a function that tells whether the remainder of the computation is definitely strict or not. Formally, a strictness continuation κ (for a type $t_1 \underline{\rightarrow} t_2$) is a function in the domain

$$\mathbf{A}(t_2) \rightarrow \mathbf{2}$$

The interpretation $\mathbf{O}_r$ will be an extension of **O** with strictness continuations as right context information. The type part of $\mathbf{O}_r$ is

$$\mathbf{O}_r(t_1 \underline{\rightarrow} t_2) = ((\mathbf{A}(t_2) \rightarrow \mathbf{2}) \rightarrow \mathbf{K}(t_1 \underline{\rightarrow} t_2)) \times \mathbf{A}(t_1 \underline{\rightarrow} t_2)$$

Most of the operators either ignore the strictness continuation or pass it on to their arguments. A couple of examples are

$$\mathbf{O}_r(\texttt{Hd[ ]}) = (\lambda\kappa.\mathbf{K}(\texttt{Hd[ ]}),\ \mathbf{A}(\texttt{Hd[ ]}))$$

$$\mathbf{O}_r(\Box[\ ]) = \lambda(f_1,h_1).\lambda(f_2,h_2).\ (f,\ \mathbf{A}(\Box[\ ])\ h_1\ h_2)\ \text{where}$$

$$f = \lambda\kappa.\lambda d.\begin{cases} (f_2(\kappa \circ dn(h_1))(d)):(f_1(\kappa)(d)) \\ \qquad \text{if } (\kappa \circ dn(h_1))\perp = 0, \\ \qquad f_1(\kappa)(d) \neq \perp \text{ and } f_2(\kappa \circ dn(h_1))(d) \neq \perp \\ \text{DELAY}(f_2(\kappa \circ dn(h_1))(d)):(f_1(\kappa)(d)) \\ \qquad \text{if } (\kappa \circ dn(h_1))\perp \neq 0, \\ \qquad f_1(\kappa)(d) \neq \perp \text{ and } f_2(\kappa \circ dn(h_1))(d) \neq \perp \\ \perp \qquad \text{otherwise} \end{cases}$$

Note that here the strictness continuation κ for the complete construct is supplied unchanged to the first parameter (f_1) whereas it is updated to ($\kappa\mathrm{o}dn(h_1)$) before it is supplied to the second parameter (f_2). Also note that the strictness continuations are computed in a 'backward manner'.

The real benefit of the strictness continuation is apparent for the `Tuple` operator where we have

$$\mathbf{O}_r(\texttt{Tuple}[t_0\underline{\rightarrow}t_1\underline{\times}t_2]) = \lambda(f_1,h_1).\lambda(f_2,h_2).\ (f,\ \mathbf{A}(\texttt{Tuple}[\,])\ h_1\ h_2)$$

$$\text{where } f = \lambda\kappa.\lambda d.\text{ENTER}:$$

$$\begin{cases} f_2(\lambda a.\kappa(up(\top,a)))(d) & \text{if } \kappa(up(\top,\bot)) = 0 \\ \text{DELAY}(f_2(\lambda a.\kappa(up(\top,a)))(d)) & \text{otherwise} \end{cases}$$

$$\text{SWITCH}:$$

$$\begin{cases} f_1(\lambda a.\kappa(up(a,\top)))(d) & \text{if } \kappa(up(\bot,\top)) = 0 \\ \text{DELAY}(f_1(\lambda a.\kappa(up(a,\top)))(d)) & \text{otherwise} \end{cases}$$

$$\text{TUPLE}$$

There are at least three different ways to handle the fixed point operator `fix` in the case of frontier types:

- to *ignore* the strictness continuation in all calls — this is often called *intra*procedural analysis and corresponds to using the most conservative strictness continuation $\lambda a.1$,
- to *specialize* the code generation to the actual strictness continuation for each (recursive or initial) call — this means that we may have several versions of the code for the same fixed point, and
- to *collect* and *approximate* the strictness continuation for all calls — this is often called *inter*procedural analysis and corresponds to the effect obtained when the program is annotated as in a sticky analysis.

Only the first two approaches can easily be specified in the framework of parameterized semantics as developed in Chapter 5. In the first case we simply have

$$\mathbf{O}_r(\texttt{fix}[t_1\underline{\rightarrow}t_2]) = \lambda H.\ (f,\ \mathbf{A}(\texttt{fix}[\,])\ H_2) \text{ where}$$

$$f = \lambda\kappa.\ \mathbf{K}(\texttt{fix}[\,])\ H_1$$

$$H_1\ RC = f'\ (\lambda a.1) \text{ where } (f',h') = H(\lambda\kappa'.RC,\ \mathbf{A}(\texttt{fix}[\,])\ H_2)$$

$$H_2\ h = h' \text{ where } (f',h') = H(\lambda\kappa.\lambda d.[\,],\ h)$$

Unfortunately, the effect of using this definition is that no optimizations take place inside the body of the fixed point. So alternatively we may use the second approach. The idea now is to introduce a table mapping strictness continuations to labels. Initially no labels have been generated so

$$\mathbf{O}_{\mathrm{r}}(\mathtt{fix}[\,]) = \lambda H.\ (spec\ (\lambda\kappa.\bot),\ \mathbf{A}(\mathtt{fix}[\,])\ H_2)$$

where H_2 is as above and *spec* generates the appropriate code:

$$spec\ tab = \lambda\kappa_0.\lambda d_0.\ \text{CALLREC}(d_0,\ f\ \kappa_0\ d_0)$$

where

$$\begin{aligned}(f,h) = H(\lambda\kappa.\lambda d.&\text{if } tab[\kappa_0\mapsto d_0]\ \kappa \neq \bot\\ &\text{then CALL } (tab[\kappa_0\mapsto d_0]\ \kappa)\\ &\text{else CALLREC}(d,\ spec\ (tab[\kappa_0\mapsto d_0][\kappa\mapsto d])\ \kappa\ (d+1)),\\ \mathbf{A}(\mathtt{fix}[\,])\ H_2)&\end{aligned}$$

Example 8.1.2 Consider the expression `sum`. Applying the interpretation $\mathbf{O}_{\mathrm{r}}$ sketched above together with the initial strictness continuation $\lambda a.a$ we get the code

$$\begin{array}{l}\text{CALLREC}(d,\ \text{ENTER:RESUME:ISNIL:}\\ \quad\quad \text{BRANCH(CONST } \mathbf{0},\\ \quad\quad\quad\quad \text{ENTER:}\\ \quad\quad\quad\quad \text{RESUME:TL:RESUME:CALL } d\text{:}\\ \quad\quad\quad\quad \text{SWITCH:}\\ \quad\quad\quad\quad \text{RESUME:HD:RESUME:}\\ \quad\quad\quad\quad \text{TUPLE:}\\ \quad\quad\quad\quad \underline{\text{RESUME:ENTER:SND:RESUME:}}\\ \quad\quad\quad\quad \underline{\text{SWITCH:FST:RESUME:TUPLE:}}\text{PRIM } +))\end{array}$$

so that no DELAY instructions are generated. Note that the optimization has rendered the underlined instructions unnecessary but that this is not exploited by the code generation. □

The idea of using strictness continuations as an additional parameter to the coding interpretation was introduced in [82]. The interpretation is specified in some detail in [50] which also contains a correctness proof for a first-order subset of the language without lists. The proof follows the same lines as the previous proof but is much more complicated because the strictness continuations are passed around as parameters.

Evaluation transformers

Strictness continuations are closely related to the evaluators of Burn [13]. Consider for example an expression e of type $\underline{\mathtt{Int}}\ \underline{\mathtt{list}} \underline{\rightarrow} \underline{\mathtt{Int}}$ and assume that the strictness continuation for the result of e is $\lambda a.a$. Then the domain of strictness continuations for the argument of e contains five elements as indicated below:

	0	1	0ε	1ε
κ_0	1	1	1	1
κ_1	0	1	1	1
κ_2	0	0	1	1
κ_3	0	0	0	1
κ_4	0	0	0	0

For the `sum` expression the strictness continuation will be κ_3, for the `length` expression κ_2 and for the `hd` expression κ_1. The strictness information may be used to determine the degree to which it is safe to evaluate the argument of the expression. This is quite analogous to what is expressed by the evaluators of [13]; and indeed κ_i corresponds to ξ_i for $0 \leq i \leq 3$.

There is no analogue of κ_4 in [13]. This should not be surprising because κ_4 says that the use of the result can never terminate even though the evaluation of the list itself does. This would only be feasible if the strictness continuation for the result was $\lambda a.0$ rather than $\lambda a.a$, and it would seem that [13] only considers the situation where the result will indeed be used.

8.1.3 Using left context information

The code generated by **K** makes no assumptions about the argument on top of the stack. Consequently the code generated contains a lot of RESUME instructions that ensure that the argument is evaluated to the degree required. As an example, +[ ] requires that its argument is fully evaluated so the instruction PRIM + must be preceded by a sequence of instructions that ensure that this definitely will be the case. However, if we do know that the argument is fully evaluated (as in the case of the `sum` expression of Example 8.1.2) then there is no need to generate the sequence of instructions preceding PRIM +. (In terms of Example 8.1.2 one could thus dispense with the underlined instructions.)

The idea is now to keep track of the degree to which the arguments have been evaluated and thereby avoid generating some of the RESUME instructions. This is a typical example of left context information as it is concerned with the computations that have taken place in the past. Below we shall sketch how the interpretations considered so far may be extended to take this information into account.

Evaluation degrees

We shall be interested in properties expressing the degree to which values have been evaluated. So for each run-time type t we shall define an appropriate domain $\mathbf{E}(t)$:

$$\mathbf{E}(\underline{\mathtt{A}}_i) = \mathbf{2}$$

$$\mathbf{E}(t_1 \underline{\times}\ t_2) = (\mathbf{E}(t_1) \times \mathbf{E}(t_2))_\perp$$
$$\mathbf{E}(t_1 \underline{\rightarrow}\ t_2) = (\mathbf{E}(t_1) \rightarrow \mathbf{E}(t_2))_\perp$$
$$\mathbf{E}(t\ \underline{\texttt{list}}) = (\mathcal{O}(\mathbf{E}(t))_\perp)_\perp$$

where $\mathcal{O}(D)$ is the domain of non-empty right closed subsets of D as in Chapter 7.

The rationale for using the two-point domain for the base types is that a base value either is fully evaluated or is a thunk:

1: the value is definitely fully evaluated,

0: the value may not be fully evaluated.

The interpretation of the type constructors mimics that of the strictness analysis of Chapter 7. For products we use lifted cartesian products as this allows us to distinguish between:

$up(\epsilon_1,\epsilon_2)$: the value is definitely a pair with the components evaluated to degree ϵ_1 and ϵ_2, respectively,

$\perp$: the value need not be evaluated to a pair.

For lists we have:

$Y\varepsilon$: the spine of the list is fully evaluated and for each element of the list there is an abstract value in Y describing its evaluation degree,

1: the list is evaluated to head normal form, so it is either [] or it has the form $\cdots : \cdots$, i.e. CONS$_{\text{PS}}(\cdots,\cdots)$,

0: the value need not be evaluated to head normal form.

The execution of the DELAY instruction will always result in a value that is a thunk; this means that the bottom element of $\mathbf{E}(t)$ precisely describes its evaluation degree. On the other hand the execution of the RESUME instruction will always result in a value that is evaluated to some extent. We shall write ω_t (or just ω) for the (unique!) value of $\mathbf{E}(t)$ just above $\perp$; we thus know that RESUME always will return a value that is at least evaluated as specified by ω_t.

Let us first see how the interpretation $\mathbf{K}$ can be modified to take evaluation degrees into account. The type part of the interpretation $\mathbf{K}_\text{l}$ will have

$$\mathbf{K}_\text{l}(t_1 \underline{\rightarrow}\ t_2) = (\mathbf{E}(t_1) \rightarrow \mathbf{K}(t_1 \underline{\rightarrow}\ t_2)) \times (\mathbf{E}(t_1) \rightarrow \mathbf{E}(t_2))$$

The intention is that if $(f,g) \in \mathbf{K}_\text{l}(t_1 \underline{\rightarrow}\ t_2)$ and the evaluation degree of the element on top of the stack is ϵ then $f(\epsilon)$ describes the (relocatable) code generated and $g(\epsilon)$ describes the evaluation degree of the element on top of the stack when the execution of the code has terminated. Note that $g(\epsilon) \neq \perp$ always holds.

The interpretation of the operators is mostly straightforward. Some of the interesting clauses are:

$$\mathbf{K}_l(\texttt{Tuple[ ]}) = \lambda(f_1,g_1).\lambda(f_2,g_2).$$
$$(\lambda\epsilon.\mathbf{K}(\texttt{Tuple[ ]})(f_1\ \epsilon)(f_2\ \epsilon),\ \lambda\epsilon.up(\bot,\bot))$$

$$\mathbf{K}_l(\texttt{Fst[ ]}) = (f,\ \lambda\epsilon.(\omega \sqcup \epsilon_1 \text{ where } (\epsilon_1,\epsilon_2) = dn(\epsilon))) \text{ where}$$

$$f = \lambda\epsilon.\lambda d. \begin{cases} \text{RESUME:FST:RESUME} & \text{if } \epsilon = \bot \\ \text{FST:RESUME} & \text{if } \epsilon = up(\bot,\epsilon_2) \\ \text{FST} & \text{otherwise} \end{cases}$$

$$\mathbf{K}_l(\texttt{+[ ]}) = (f,\ \lambda\epsilon.1) \text{ where}$$

$$f = \lambda\epsilon.\lambda d. \begin{cases} \text{RESUME:ENTER:SND:RESUME:SWITCH:} & \\ \quad\text{FST:RESUME:TUPLE:PRIM} + & \text{if } \epsilon = \bot \\ \text{ENTER:SND:RESUME:SWITCH:FST:} & \\ \quad\text{RESUME:TUPLE:PRIM} + & \text{if } \epsilon = up(0,0) \\ \text{ENTER:SND:RESUME:SWITCH:FST:} & \\ \quad\text{TUPLE:PRIM} + & \text{if } \epsilon = up(1,0) \\ \text{ENTER:SND:SWITCH:FST:RESUME:} & \\ \quad\text{TUPLE:PRIM} + & \text{if } \epsilon = up(0,1) \\ \text{PRIM} + & \text{if } \epsilon = up(1,1) \end{cases}$$

$$\mathbf{K}_l(\Box[\ ]) = \lambda(f_1,g_1).\lambda(f_2,g_2).\ (\lambda\epsilon.\mathbf{K}(\Box[\ ])(f_1\ \bot)(f_2\ \epsilon),\ \lambda\epsilon.(g_1\ \bot)))$$

Note that in the last definition f_1 is applied to the evaluation degree $\bot$ because its argument always will be a thunk.

The fixed point `fix` for frontier types can be handled in different ways: one is to ignore the information about evaluation degrees as in

$$\mathbf{K}_l(\texttt{fix[ ]}) = \lambda H.(\lambda\epsilon.\mathbf{K}(\texttt{fix[ ]})H',\ \lambda\epsilon.\omega) \text{ where}$$
$$H'\ RC = f'\ \bot \text{ where } (f',g') = H(\lambda\epsilon.RC,\ \lambda\epsilon.\omega)$$

Another possibility is to generate specialized code for each evaluation degree. This will involve introducing a table associating labels with evaluation degrees much as we earlier introduced a table associating labels with strictness continuations. Also one can imagine a sticky variant of the analysis of evaluation degrees but as in the previous subsection it is not clear how to formulate this as an interpretation.

Example 8.1.3 The effect of using $\mathbf{K}_l$ rather than $\mathbf{K}$ is minimal as it only allows us to remove rather few RESUME instructions. As an example consider the `sum` expression and assume that the evaluation degree of the argument is 0ε meaning that the spine of the list is evaluated but that the elements need not be evaluated. If we specialize the code generated to the actual evaluation degree we get

CALLREC(d,ENTER:ISNIL:

```
BRANCH(CONST 0,
       DELAY(ENTER:
             DELAY(DELAY(TL):CALLREC(d+1,···)):
             SWITCH:
             DELAY(HD:RESUME):
             TUPLE):
       RESUME:ENTER:SND:RESUME:SWITCH:
       FST:RESUME:TUPLE:PRIM +))
```

where CALLREC(d+1,$\cdots$) is the usual code generated for `sum` using **K** (see Example 8.1.1) but allocated from label d+1. Thus only at the outermost level can we make use of the fact that the argument is partly evaluated; when the recursive call is encountered the argument will definitely be a thunk because of the DELAY instruction and we consequently have to use the 'less optimal' code. □

Combining left and right contexts

The effect of using evaluation degrees as left context is vastly improved when combined with strictness information. The reason is that when we dispense with some of the DELAY instructions also more RESUME instructions will be unnecessary. The interpretation $\mathbf{O}_{\mathrm{rl}}$ sketched below will combine left and right context information. The type part of $\mathbf{O}_{\mathrm{rl}}$ is

$$\begin{array}{rcl}\mathbf{O}_{\mathrm{rl}}(t_1 \underline{\rightarrow} t_2) & = & (\mathbf{E}(t_1) \times (\mathbf{A}(t_2) \rightarrow \mathbf{2}) \rightarrow \mathbf{K}(t_1 \underline{\rightarrow} t_2)) \\ & \times & (\mathbf{E}(t_1) \times (\mathbf{A}(t_2) \rightarrow \mathbf{2}) \rightarrow \mathbf{E}(t_2)) \\ & \times & \mathbf{A}(t_1 \underline{\rightarrow} t_2)\end{array}$$

Compared with $\mathbf{K}_{\mathrm{l}}$ we note that we need the evaluation degree of the argument as well as the strictness continuation in order to determine the evaluation degree of the result. The reason is that the code generated will depend upon both these kinds of information.

The expression part of $\mathbf{O}_{\mathrm{rl}}$ combines the information of $\mathbf{O}_{\mathrm{r}}$ and $\mathbf{K}_{\mathrm{l}}$. As an example consider the definition of $\mathbf{O}_{\mathrm{rl}}(\Box[\,])$:

$$\mathbf{O}_{\mathrm{rl}}(\Box[\,]) = \lambda(f_1,g_1,h_1).\lambda(f_2,g_2,h_2).\ (f,\ g,\ \mathbf{A}(\Box[\,])\ h_1\ h_2)$$

where f and g are defined below. First we have

$$f = \lambda(\epsilon,\kappa).\lambda d.\begin{cases} (f_2(\epsilon,\kappa\circ dn(h_1))(d)):(f_1(g_2(\epsilon,\kappa\circ dn(h_1)),\kappa)(d)) \\ \qquad \text{if } (\kappa\circ dn(h_1))\ \bot = \bot, \\ \qquad f_1(g_2(\epsilon,\kappa\circ dn(h_1)),\kappa)(d) \neq \bot \text{ and} \\ \qquad f_2(\epsilon,\kappa\circ dn(h_1))(d) \neq \bot \\ \mathrm{DELAY}(f_2(\epsilon,\kappa\circ dn(h_1))(d)):(f_1(\bot,\kappa)(d)) \\ \qquad \text{if } (\kappa\circ dn(h_1))\ \bot \neq \bot, \\ \qquad f_1(\bot,\kappa)(d) \neq \bot \text{ and } f_2(\epsilon,\kappa\circ dn(h_1))(d) \neq \bot \\ \bot \qquad \text{otherwise} \end{cases}$$

Note that the strictness continuation is updated as in $\mathbf{O}_r(\Box[\,])$. In the case where a DELAY instruction is generated we supply f_1 with the evaluation degree $\bot$ exactly as in $\mathbf{K}_l$ but if no DELAY instruction is generated we use g_2 to get more precise information. Turning to the definition of g we have

$$g = \lambda(\epsilon,\kappa).\begin{cases} g_1(g_2(\epsilon,\kappa o\,dn(h_1)),\kappa) & \text{if } (\kappa o\,dn(h_1))\,\bot = \bot, \\ g_1(\bot,\kappa) & \text{otherwise} \end{cases}$$

Note that g_1 is supplied with the parameter $g_2(\epsilon,\kappa o\,dn(h_1))$ when the DELAY instruction is not generated.

The combination of evaluation degrees and strictness continuations may also be used in the definition of the interpretation of the Tuple operator:

$$\mathbf{O}_{rl}(\text{Tuple}[\,]) = \lambda(f_1,g_1,h_1).\lambda(f_2,g_2,h_2).\ (f,\ g,\ \mathbf{A}(\text{Tuple}[\,])\ h_1\ h_2)$$

where

$f = \lambda(\epsilon,\kappa).\lambda d.\text{ENTER}:$

$$\begin{cases} f_2(\epsilon,\lambda a.\kappa(up(\top,a)))(d) & \text{if } \kappa(up(\top,\bot)) = 0 \\ \text{DELAY}(f_2(\epsilon,\lambda a.\kappa(up(\top,a)))(d)) & \text{otherwise} \end{cases}$$

$\quad$ SWITCH:

$$\begin{cases} f_1(\epsilon,\lambda a.\kappa(up(a,\top)))(d) & \text{if } \kappa(up(\bot,\top)) = 0 \\ \text{DELAY}(f_1(\epsilon,\lambda a.\kappa(up(a,\top)))(d)) & \text{otherwise} \end{cases}$$

$\quad$ TUPLE

Thus the strictness continuation is used to dispense with the DELAY instructions for the two components and the information about evaluation degrees will ensure that this is recorded in the evaluation degree of the result so that the subsequent computations can make use of it. The function g is defined by

$$g = \lambda(\epsilon,\kappa).up(\text{if } \kappa(up(\bot,\top)) = 0 \text{ then } g_1(\epsilon,\lambda a.\kappa(up(a,\top))) \text{ else } \bot,$$
$$\text{if } \kappa(up(\top,\bot)) = 0 \text{ then } g_2(\epsilon,\lambda a.\kappa(up(\top,a))) \text{ else } \bot)$$

Concerning the fixed point operator fix we have the same options for frontier types as in the previous subsections. However, we shall not go further into this here.

Example 8.1.4 Assume that the evaluation degree of the argument of sum is 0. If the initial strictness continuation is $\lambda a.a$ we then get the code

$$\text{CALLREC}(d,\text{ENTER}:\underline{\text{RESUME}}:\text{ISNIL}:$$
$$\text{BRANCH}(\text{CONST }\mathbf{0},$$
$$\text{ENTER}:$$
$$\underline{\text{RESUME}}:\text{TL}:\underline{\text{RESUME}}:\text{CALL } d:$$

SWITCH:
RESUME:HD:RESUME:
TUPLE:
PRIM +))

Compared with Example 8.1.2 we see that the superfluous DELAY and RESUME instructions are no longer generated.

If the evaluation degree of the argument of `sum` is known to be 0ε, that is the spine of the list has been evaluated but not necessarily the elements, then $\mathbf{O}_{\mathrm{rl}}$ allows us to dispense with even more RESUME instructions, namely those that are underlined in the above code. □

8.1.4 Pre-evaluation of arguments

In the optimizing interpretations seen so far we have used local strictness information and strictness continuations to avoid generating superfluous DELAY instructions. However, knowing that an expression e is definitely strict in its argument (in a given context) also means that it is safe to evaluate its argument *before* evaluating e itself. So if C is the code for e then it will be safe to emit the code sequence RESUME:C. Such optimizations are regarded as very valuable in [86] and in our setting they are particularly interesting for operations like `fix`, `Cond` and `Tuple` where we may risk evaluating the argument more than once.

The optimizations of `fix` and `Cond` may be performed on the basis of *local strictness information.* First consider the following modification of the interpretation of `fix` given in Table 8.3:

$$\mathbf{O}'(\mathtt{fix}[t_1 \underline{\rightarrow} t_2]) = \lambda H.(RC,\ \mathbf{A}(\mathtt{fix}[\,])\ H_2)$$

$$\text{where } RC = \lambda d.\begin{cases} \text{RESUME:}(\mathbf{K}(\mathtt{fix}[\,])\ H_1\ d) & \text{if } dn(\mathbf{A}(\mathtt{fix}[\,])H_2)\bot{=}\bot \\ \mathbf{K}(\mathtt{fix}[\,])\ H_1\ d & \text{otherwise} \end{cases}$$

and H_1 and H_2 are as in Table 8.3. Here we simply use that if the overall expression is strict then it is safe to evaluate its argument before the expression itself.

Next consider how to modify the interpretation of `Cond`:

$$\mathbf{O}'(\mathtt{Cond}[\,]) = \lambda(RC_1,h_1).\lambda(RC_2,h_2).\lambda(RC_3,h_3).$$
$$(RC,\ \mathbf{A}(\mathtt{Cond}[\,])\ h_1\ h_2\ h_3) \text{ where}$$

$$RC = \lambda d.\begin{cases} \text{RESUME:}(\mathbf{K}(\mathtt{Cond}[\,])\ RC_1\ RC_2\ RC_3\ d) \\ \qquad \text{if } (dn(h_1)\bot{=}\bot) \vee (dn(h_2)\bot{=}\bot \wedge dn(h_3)\bot{=}\bot) \\ \qquad \text{and } RC_1(d) \neq \bot,\ RC_2(d) \neq \bot,\ RC_3(d) \neq \bot \\ \mathbf{K}(\mathtt{Cond}[\,])\ RC_1\ RC_2\ RC_3\ d \\ \qquad \text{otherwise} \end{cases}$$

It is safe to make this modification because the conditional is strict in its argument if the test is strict in its argument or both branches are strict in their argument (see Table 7.4).

The optimization of `Tuple` requires that we have information about *strictness continuations* as it is now crucial that at least one of the components of the pair will be needed in the future computations. So we can modify $\mathbf{O}_\mathrm{r}$ to have

$$\mathbf{O}'_\mathrm{r}(\texttt{Tuple}[\;]) = \lambda(f_1,h_1).\lambda(f_2,h_2).\ (f,\ \mathbf{A}(\texttt{Tuple}[\;])\ h_1\ h_2)\ \text{where}$$

$$f = \lambda\kappa.\lambda d.\begin{cases} \text{RESUME}:(RC(d)) & \\ \qquad \text{if } (\kappa(up(\top,\bot))=0) \vee (\kappa(up(\bot,\top))=0) & \\ \qquad \text{and } RC(d) \neq \bot & \\ RC(d) \quad \text{otherwise} & \end{cases}$$

$$(RC,h) = \mathbf{O}_\mathrm{r}(\texttt{Tuple}[\;])\ (f_1,h_1)\ (f_2,h_2)$$

Combining pre-evaluation and evaluation degrees

So far the effect of the pre-evaluating RESUME instructions has been 'lost' because the subsequent code has not taken advantage of them. To overcome this deficiency we must record the effect of the pre-evaluating RESUME instructions and this is exactly what evaluation degrees do for us. As an example consider the following modification of $\mathbf{O}(\square[\;])$:

$$\mathbf{O}'_\mathrm{l}(\square[\;]) = \lambda(f_1,g_1,h_1).\lambda(f_2,g_2,h_2).\ (f,\ g,\ \mathbf{A}(\square[\;])\ h_1\ h_2)\ \text{where}$$

$$f = \lambda\epsilon.\lambda d.\begin{cases} \text{RESUME}:(f_2\ \omega\ d):(f_1\ (g_2\ \omega)\ d) \\ \qquad \text{if } dn(h_1)(dn(h_2)\bot) = \bot,\ \epsilon = \bot, \\ \qquad f_1\ (g_2\ \omega)\ d \neq \bot \text{ and } f_2\ \omega\ d \neq \bot \\ (f_2\ \epsilon\ d):(f_1\ (g_2\ \epsilon)\ d) \\ \qquad \text{if } (dn(h_1)(dn(h_2)\bot) \neq \bot \vee \epsilon \neq \bot), \\ \qquad dn(h_1)\ \bot = \bot,\ f_1\ (g_2\ \epsilon)\ d \neq \bot \text{ and } f_2\ \epsilon\ d \neq \bot \\ \text{DELAY}(f_2\ \epsilon\ d):(f_1\ \bot\ d) \\ \qquad \text{if } dn(h_1)\ \bot \neq \bot, \\ \qquad f_1\ \bot\ d \neq \bot \text{ and } f_2\ \epsilon\ d \neq \bot \\ \bot \qquad \text{otherwise} \end{cases}$$

$$g = \lambda\epsilon.\begin{cases} g_1(g_2(\omega)) & \text{if } (dn(h_1)(dn(h_2)\bot) = \bot \wedge \epsilon = \bot) \\ g_1(g_2(\epsilon)) & \text{if } (dn(h_1)(dn(h_2)\bot) \neq \bot \vee \epsilon \neq \bot) \\ & \text{and } dn(h_1)\ \bot = \bot \\ g_1(\bot) & \text{if } dn(h_1)\ \bot \neq \bot \end{cases}$$

We leave the details to Exercises 3, 4 and 5 and simply illustrate their intended effect in the following example.

Example 8.1.5 Consider the sum expression once again and assume that the evaluation degree of the argument is 0 and that the initial strictness continuation is $\lambda a.a$. The interpretation $\mathbf{O}_{\mathrm{rl}}$ extended to do pre-evaluation of the argument will then give rise to the code

```
RESUME:CALLREC(d,ENTER:ISNIL:
                  BRANCH(CONST 0,
                         ENTER:
                         TL:RESUME:CALL d:
                         SWITCH:
                         HD:RESUME:
                         TUPLE:
                         PRIM +))
```

Here the list is evaluated to head normal form just before each recursive call. □

8.2 Denotational Semantics

Much effort has been devoted to the construction of compiler-generating tools based on semantic formalisms, not least denotational semantics [6, 18, 46, 51, 85, 89, 95, 106]. None of these approaches have succeeded in generating compilers that have been shown to be *correct* and that additionally generate code of reasonable run-time *efficiency* compared with hand-crafted compilers. Naturally, this calls for research directed at understanding and automating those 'ingredients' in the construction of hand-crafted compilers that give them better performance than those generated by systems.

We believe that the techniques developed in this book present a step forward in this direction. Usually, the metalanguage of denotational semantics is a typed λ-calculus, more precisely an extension of the language of Chapter 2 with sum-types and general recursive types (see e.g. [91, 96]) and fortunately most of the techniques developed in this book extend to larger languages (see e.g. [75, 72, 78]). In this section we shall illustrate how the techniques can be applied to a denotational specification of a toy programming language.

One of the important characteristics of hand-crafted compilers is that they distinguish between those computations that are performed by the compiler and those that are performed by the code generated [5]. Efficiency is then obtained by ensuring that as many computations as possible are performed once and for all, that is by the compiler. To this end a number of techniques may be usable:

- errors may be detected at compile-time by type checking or type inference,
- the association of identifiers with values is a two-stage mapping: an environment maps identifiers to storage locations and a state maps storage locations

to values; computations involving the environment may then be performed at compile-time,

- the layout of run-time storage is known at compile-time and may be exploited during code generation, and
- various data flow analyses may be performed to improve the quality of the code generated.

The material presented in the previous chapters shows how such techniques can be applied directly to a functional language. In this section we show how they can be carried over to the semantic specification of an imperative language **Imp**.

8.2.1 The language Imp

We shall consider an extension of a simple while-language with the following features:

- a block construct allows declarations of variables and parameterless recursive procedures,
- variables are declared by var- and const-declarations and only the former can have their values updated by subsequent assignments, and
- it is possible to read an input file and to write an output file.

Formally, the abstract syntax of **Imp** is given by the syntactic categories:

$x, p \in$ `Ide` identifiers

$n \in$ `Num` numerals

$a \in$ `Aexp` arithmetic expressions

$a ::= x \mid n \mid a_1 + a_2 \mid \cdots$

$b \in$ `Bexp` boolean expressions

$b ::= a_1 = a_2 \mid \cdots$

$S \in$ `Stm` statements

$S ::= x := a \mid S_1 \,;\, S_2 \mid \textsf{if } b \textsf{ then } S_1 \textsf{ else } S_2 \mid$
$\quad \textsf{while } b \textsf{ do } S \mid \textsf{read } x \mid \textsf{write } a \mid \textsf{begin } D\ S \textsf{ end} \mid$
$\quad \textsf{call } p$

$D \in$ `Dec` declarations

$D ::= \textsf{var } x;\ D \mid \textsf{const } x = n;\ D \mid \textsf{proc } p \textsf{ is } S;\ D \mid \varepsilon$

$P \in$ `Prog` programs

$P ::= \textsf{program } S$

Semantic domains

Turning to the semantics we shall need an *environment* mapping identifiers to their denotable values. For **Imp** there are three kinds of denotable values:

- *locations* used for identifiers introduced by var-declarations,
- *natural numbers* used for identifiers introduced by const-declarations, and
- *store transformations* used for identifiers introduced by proc-declarations.

The *store* contains a mapping from locations to storable values and for **Imp** the only storable values are the natural numbers. Also the store records the current value of the input and output files.

We shall express these semantic domains as types in the language of Chapter 2. First we shall need three base types:

`Int`	for natural numbers
`Bool`	for truth values
`Loc`	for locations

We then introduce the following *shorthands* for types:

$$
\begin{aligned}
\texttt{In} &= \texttt{Int list} \\
\texttt{Out} &= \texttt{Int list} \\
\texttt{Store} &= (\texttt{Loc}\rightarrow\texttt{Int}) \times (\texttt{In} \times \texttt{Out}) \\
\texttt{Env} &= (\texttt{Ide}\times\texttt{Loc})\ \texttt{list} \times \\
&\quad ((\texttt{Ide}\times\texttt{Int})\ \texttt{list} \times (\texttt{Ide}\times(\texttt{Store}\rightarrow\texttt{Store}))\ \texttt{list})
\end{aligned}
$$

We shall use the meta-variables σ and ρ to range over `State` and `Env`, respectively, when specifying the semantic clauses. Usually the environment is a single mapping from identifiers to denotable values, e.g. `(Ide×(Loc+Int+(Store→Store)))list`, but the language of Chapter 2 does not include the sum-type and in order to keep within the type system of Chapter 2 we therefore use the above definition of `Env`. However, we want to stress that the development to be performed below is equally feasible using the alternative definition.

Semantic functions

Corresponding to the syntactic categories we have the following semantic functions:

$$
\begin{aligned}
\mathcal{A}[\![x]\!] &= \lambda\rho.\texttt{if isvar}(\langle\rho,x\rangle)\\
&\qquad \texttt{then } \lambda\sigma.(\texttt{fst }\sigma)(\texttt{lookup}_{\mathrm{Env}}(\texttt{fst }\rho)(x))\\
&\qquad \texttt{else } \lambda\sigma.\texttt{lookup}_{\mathrm{Env}}(\texttt{fst }(\texttt{snd }\rho))(x)\\
\mathcal{A}[\![n]\!] &= \lambda\rho.\lambda\sigma.\mathcal{N}[\![n]\!]\\
\mathcal{A}[\![a_1 + a_2]\!] &= \lambda\rho.\lambda\sigma.\texttt{+}(\langle\mathcal{A}[\![a_1]\!](\rho)(\sigma),\mathcal{A}[\![a_2]\!](\rho)(\sigma)\rangle)\\
&\vdots\\
\mathcal{B}[\![a_1 = a_2]\!] &= \lambda\rho.\lambda\sigma.\texttt{=}(\langle\mathcal{A}[\![a_1]\!](\rho)(\sigma),\mathcal{A}[\![a_2]\!](\rho)(\sigma)\rangle)\\
&\vdots
\end{aligned}
$$

Table 8.4: Semantics of **Imp**-expressions

$$
\begin{aligned}
\mathcal{N}&: \texttt{Num} \to \texttt{Int}\\
\mathcal{A}&: \texttt{Aexp} \to \texttt{Env} \to \texttt{Store} \to \texttt{Int}\\
\mathcal{B}&: \texttt{Bexp} \to \texttt{Env} \to \texttt{Store} \to \texttt{Bool}\\
\mathcal{S}&: \texttt{Stm} \to \texttt{Env} \to \texttt{Store} \to \texttt{Store}\\
\mathcal{D}&: \texttt{Dec} \to \texttt{Env} \to \texttt{Env}\\
\mathcal{P}&: \texttt{Prog} \to \texttt{In} \to \texttt{Out}
\end{aligned}
$$

Here we have assumed that the syntactic categories `Num`, `Aexp`, $\cdots$ are encoded as base types in the metalanguage. The semantic clauses are given in Tables 8.4, 8.5 and 8.6. We use the following primitive functions:

$\texttt{=}[\texttt{Ide}\times\texttt{Ide}\to\texttt{Bool}]$

$\texttt{=}[\texttt{Int}\times\texttt{Int}\to\texttt{Bool}]$

$\texttt{+}[\texttt{Int}\times\texttt{Int}\to\texttt{Int}]$

$\texttt{isvar}[\texttt{Env}\times\texttt{Ide}\to\texttt{Bool}]$

$\texttt{new}[\texttt{Env}\to\texttt{Loc}]$

$\texttt{init-Env}[\texttt{Env}]$

$\texttt{init-Store}[\texttt{In}\to\texttt{Store}]$

The intended meaning of `=` and `+` should be evident. The function `isvar` takes an environment ρ and an identifier x as parameters and tests whether or not x is recorded in the first component of ρ, that is whether or not it has been introduced by a `var`-declaration. The function `new` takes an environment ρ as a parameter and returns a location that is unused in ρ. The constant `init-Env` produces an initial environment and the function `init-Store` produces an initial store when supplied with the input file.

$$
\begin{aligned}
\mathcal{S}[\![x{:=}a]\!] &= \lambda\rho.\lambda\sigma.\langle \texttt{update}_{\text{Store}}(\texttt{fst}\ \sigma)(\texttt{lookup}_{\text{Env}}(\texttt{fst}\ \rho)(x))\\
&\qquad\qquad (\mathcal{A}[\![a]\!](\rho)(\sigma)),\\
&\qquad \texttt{snd}\ \sigma\rangle\\
\mathcal{S}[\![S_1\ ;\ S_2]\!] &= \lambda\rho.\lambda\sigma.\mathcal{S}[\![S_2]\!](\rho)(\mathcal{S}[\![S_1]\!](\rho)(\sigma))\\
\mathcal{S}[\![\textsf{if}\ b\ \textsf{then}\ S_1\ \textsf{else}\ S_2]\!] &= \lambda\rho.\texttt{test}(\mathcal{B}[\![b]\!](\rho))(\mathcal{S}[\![S_1]\!](\rho))\\
&\qquad (\mathcal{S}[\![S_2]\!](\rho))\\
\mathcal{S}[\![\textsf{while}\ b\ \textsf{do}\ S]\!] &= \lambda\rho.\texttt{fix}(\lambda\texttt{f}.\texttt{test}(\mathcal{B}[\![b]\!](\rho))(\lambda\sigma.\texttt{f}(\mathcal{S}[\![S]\!](\rho)(\sigma)))\\
&\qquad (\lambda\sigma.\sigma))\\
\mathcal{S}[\![\textsf{read}\ x]\!] &= \lambda\rho.\lambda\sigma.\langle \texttt{update}_{\text{Store}}(\texttt{fst}\ \sigma)(\texttt{lookup}_{\text{Env}}(\texttt{fst}\ \rho)(x))\\
&\qquad\qquad (\texttt{hd}\ (\texttt{fst}\ (\texttt{snd}\ \sigma))),\\
&\qquad \langle \texttt{tl}\ (\texttt{fst}\ (\texttt{snd}\ \sigma)),\ \texttt{snd}\ (\texttt{snd}\ \sigma)\rangle\rangle\\
\mathcal{S}[\![\textsf{write}\ a]\!] &= \lambda\rho.\lambda\sigma.\langle \texttt{fst}\ \sigma,\ \langle \texttt{fst}\ (\texttt{snd}\ \sigma),\\
&\qquad\qquad \mathcal{A}[\![a]\!](\rho)(\sigma){:}(\texttt{snd}\ (\texttt{snd}\ \sigma))\rangle\rangle\\
\mathcal{S}[\![\textsf{begin}\ D\ S\ \textsf{end}]\!] &= \lambda\rho.\mathcal{S}[\![S]\!](\mathcal{D}[\![D]\!](\rho))\\
\mathcal{S}[\![\textsf{call}\ p]\!] &= \lambda\rho.\texttt{lookup}_{\text{Env}}(\texttt{snd}\ (\texttt{snd}\ \rho))(p)
\end{aligned}
$$

Table 8.5: Semantics of **Imp**-statements

We also use some auxiliary functions. Two functions operate on the environment:

$$
\begin{aligned}
\texttt{lookup}_{\text{Env}} &= \lambda\texttt{tab}.\lambda\texttt{x}.\texttt{if}\ {=}(\langle\texttt{x},\ \texttt{fst}\ (\texttt{hd}\ \texttt{tab})\rangle)\ \texttt{then}\ \texttt{snd}\ (\texttt{hd}\ \texttt{tab})\\
&\qquad \texttt{else}\ \texttt{lookup}(\texttt{tl}\ \texttt{tab})(\texttt{x})\\
\texttt{update}_{\text{Env}} &= \lambda\texttt{tab}.\lambda\texttt{x}.\lambda\texttt{y}.\langle\texttt{x},\texttt{y}\rangle{:}\texttt{tab}
\end{aligned}
$$

One function operates on the store:

$$\texttt{update}_{\text{Store}} = \lambda\texttt{tab}.\lambda\texttt{x}.\lambda\texttt{y}.\lambda\texttt{x}'.\ \texttt{if}\ {=}(\langle\texttt{x},\texttt{x}'\rangle)\ \texttt{then}\ \texttt{y}\ \texttt{else}\ \texttt{tab}(\texttt{x}')$$

Finally, we use the function

$$\texttt{test} = \lambda\texttt{p}.\lambda\texttt{f}_1.\lambda\texttt{f}_2.\lambda\sigma.\ \texttt{if}\ \texttt{p}(\sigma)\ \texttt{then}\ \texttt{f}_1(\sigma)\ \texttt{else}\ \texttt{f}_2(\sigma)$$

in the clauses for conditional and iteration.

8.2.2 Transformations on the semantic specification

We shall now outline how the development of the earlier chapters may be applied to the semantic specification of the language **Imp**.

$$\mathcal{D}[\![\mathsf{var}\ x;\ D]\!] = \lambda\rho.\mathcal{D}[\![D]\!](\langle \mathtt{update_{Env}}(\mathtt{fst}\ \rho)(x)(\mathtt{new}(\rho)),\ \mathtt{snd}\ \rho\rangle)$$

$$\mathcal{D}[\![\mathsf{const}\ x{=}n;\ D]\!] = \lambda\rho.\mathcal{D}[\![D]\!](\langle \mathtt{fst}\ \rho,\ \langle \mathtt{update_{Env}}(\mathtt{fst}\ (\mathtt{snd}\ \rho))(x)(\mathcal{N}[\![n]\!]),\ \mathtt{snd}\ (\mathtt{snd}\ \rho)\rangle\rangle)$$

$$\mathcal{D}[\![\mathsf{proc}\ p\ \mathsf{is}\ S;\ D]\!] = \lambda\rho.\mathcal{D}[\![D]\!](\langle \mathtt{fst}\ \rho,\ \langle \mathtt{fst}\ (\mathtt{snd}\ \rho),\ \mathtt{update_{Env}}(\mathtt{snd}\ (\mathtt{snd}\ \rho))(p)(\mathtt{fix}(\lambda \mathtt{f}.\mathcal{S}[\![S]\!](\langle \mathtt{fst}\ \rho,\ \langle \mathtt{fst}\ (\mathtt{snd}\ \rho),\ \mathtt{update_{Env}}(\mathtt{snd}\ (\mathtt{snd}\ \rho))(p)(\mathtt{f})\rangle\rangle))\ )\rangle\rangle)$$

$$\mathcal{D}[\![\varepsilon]\!] = \lambda\rho.\rho$$

$$\mathcal{P}[\![\mathsf{program}\ S]\!] = \lambda\iota.\mathtt{snd}(\mathtt{snd}(\mathcal{S}[\![S]\!](\mathtt{init\text{-}Env})(\mathtt{init\text{-}Store}(\iota))))$$

Table 8.6: Semantics of **Imp**-declarations and programs

Introducing types

The semantic clauses of Tables 8.4, 8.5 and 8.6 are specified in the *untyped* λ-calculus of Chapter 2. An analogue of the type inference algorithm of Chapter 2 can be used to transform the clauses into the *typed* λ-calculus. However, in order for this to succeed we have to duplicate the definitions of the functions $\mathtt{lookup_{Env}}$ and $\mathtt{update_{Env}}$ (see Exercise 2 of Chapter 2) so that we get the following versions:

$$\mathtt{lookup_{Env1}}:\ (\mathtt{Ide}{\times}\mathtt{Loc})\mathtt{list}{\to}\mathtt{Ide}{\to}\mathtt{Loc}$$

$$\mathtt{lookup_{Env2}}:\ (\mathtt{Ide}{\times}\mathtt{Int})\mathtt{list}{\to}\mathtt{Ide}{\to}\mathtt{Int}$$

$$\mathtt{lookup_{Env3}}:\ (\mathtt{Ide}{\times}(\mathtt{Store}{\to}\mathtt{Store}))\mathtt{list}{\to}\mathtt{Ide}{\to}(\mathtt{Store}{\to}\mathtt{Store})$$

$$\mathtt{update_{Env1}}:\ (\mathtt{Ide}{\times}\mathtt{Loc})\mathtt{list}{\to}\mathtt{Ide}{\to}\mathtt{Loc}{\to}(\mathtt{Ide}{\times}\mathtt{Loc})\mathtt{list}$$

$$\mathtt{update_{Env2}}:\ (\mathtt{Ide}{\times}\mathtt{Int})\mathtt{list}{\to}\mathtt{Ide}{\to}\mathtt{Int}{\to}(\mathtt{Ide}{\times}\mathtt{Int})\mathtt{list}$$

$$\mathtt{update_{Env3}}:\ (\mathtt{Ide}{\times}(\mathtt{Store}{\to}\mathtt{Store}))\mathtt{list}{\to}\mathtt{Ide}{\to}(\mathtt{Store}{\to}\mathtt{Store}){\to}(\mathtt{Ide}{\times}(\mathtt{Store}{\to}\mathtt{Store}))\mathtt{list}$$

Having done this it is fairly straightforward (but tedious) to annotate the semantic clauses of Tables 8.4, 8.5 and 8.6 with their type information. A couple of examples are given below:

$$\mathcal{S}[\![x{:=}a]\!] = \lambda\rho[\mathtt{Env}].\lambda\sigma[\mathtt{Store}].\langle \mathtt{update_{Store}}(\mathtt{fst}\ \sigma)(\mathtt{lookup_{Env1}}(\mathtt{fst}\ \rho)(x))$$

$$
\begin{aligned}
&\qquad\qquad\qquad\qquad\quad (\mathcal{A}[\![a]\!](\rho)(\sigma)),\\
&\qquad\qquad\quad \texttt{snd}\ \sigma\rangle\\
\mathcal{S}[\![\text{while } b \text{ do } S]\!] &= \lambda\rho[\texttt{Env}].\texttt{fix}(\lambda\texttt{f}[\texttt{Store}\to\texttt{Store}].\\
&\qquad\qquad \texttt{test}(\mathcal{B}[\![b]\!](\rho))\\
&\qquad\qquad\quad (\lambda\sigma[\texttt{Store}].\texttt{f}(\mathcal{S}[\![S]\!](\rho)(\sigma)))\\
&\qquad\qquad\quad (\lambda\sigma[\texttt{Store}].\sigma))\\
\mathcal{D}[\![\text{var } x;\ D]\!] &= \lambda\rho[\texttt{Env}].\mathcal{D}[\![D]\!](\langle\texttt{update}_{\text{Env1}}(\texttt{fst}\ \rho)(x)\\
&\qquad\qquad\qquad\qquad (\texttt{new}[\texttt{Env}\to\texttt{Loc}](\rho)),\\
&\qquad\qquad \texttt{snd}\ \rho\rangle)
\end{aligned}
$$

$$
\begin{aligned}
&\mathcal{D}[\![\text{proc } p \text{ is } S;\ D]\!] =\\
&\quad \lambda\rho[\texttt{Env}].\mathcal{D}[\![D]\!](\langle\texttt{fst}\ \rho,\ \langle\texttt{fst}\ (\texttt{snd}\ \rho),\\
&\qquad\quad \texttt{update}_{\text{Env3}}(\texttt{snd}\ (\texttt{snd}\ \rho))(p)\\
&\qquad\qquad (\texttt{fix}(\lambda\texttt{f}[\texttt{Store}\to\texttt{Store}].\\
&\qquad\qquad\quad \mathcal{S}[\![S]\!](\langle\texttt{fst}\ \rho,\ \langle\texttt{fst}\ (\texttt{snd}\ \rho),\\
&\qquad\qquad\qquad \texttt{update}_{\text{Env3}}(\texttt{snd}\ (\texttt{snd}\ \rho))\\
&\qquad\qquad\qquad\qquad (p)(\texttt{f})\rangle\rangle))\ \rangle\rangle\rangle)
\end{aligned}
$$

The metalanguage of semantic specifications

So far we have been a bit vague about the relationship between the semantic specifications and the languages of Chapters 2 and 3 (and 4). An illustration of this is our earlier phrase that "an analogue of the type inference algorithm of Chapter 2 can be used to transform the clauses into the typed λ-calculus". It should be clear that the right hand sides of the semantic clauses are expressions of the languages studied in Chapters 2, 3 (and 4) provided that we allow $\mathcal{A}[\![a_1]\!]$ etc. as additional primitives. The proper perspective is then that the syntactic category of semantic specifications is built on top on the syntactic categories of expressions and types in much the same way as we have seen that the syntactic category of programs is. We claim that this is rather straightforward and that the adaption of the various algorithms for type inference etc. will not present a major obstacle.

To make this claim credible — without going into the details — let us consider how we dealt with programs. In all of Chapters 2, 3 and 4 we

- translated the program into an 'equivalent' expression,
- performed the transformation on the expression, and

- extracted a program out of the transformed expression.

A similar approach is feasible for semantic specifications provided we have sufficient operations available on the primitive types that represent the syntactic categories. As we take the syntactic categories to be base types we simply assume enough primitive operations.

As a simple example consider the semantic specification of $\mathcal{B}$ of Table 8.4. It may be 'coded' as

$$\begin{aligned}
\mathcal{B} = \texttt{fix}(&\lambda\mathcal{B}'[\texttt{Bexp}\rightarrow\texttt{Env}\rightarrow\texttt{Store}\rightarrow\texttt{Bool}].\lambda b[\texttt{Bexp}].\\
&\texttt{if is-equality}(b)\\
&\texttt{then } \lambda\rho.\lambda\sigma.\texttt{=}(\langle\mathcal{A}(\texttt{fst-arg}(b))(\rho)(\sigma),\ \mathcal{A}(\texttt{snd-arg}(b))(\rho)(\sigma)\rangle)\\
&\texttt{else } \cdots)
\end{aligned}$$

However, we shall not go further into this here.

Introducing binding times

In a hand-crafted compiler for **Imp** we would expect that all operations concerning the environment are performed at compile-time whereas those involving the store are postponed until run-time. We shall now see that the distinction between environment and store can be obtained from the semantic specification above by applying the binding time analysis of Chapter 3.

The starting point for the binding time analysis is the semantic function $\mathcal{P}$ for programs. It is natural to annotate its functionality in the following way:

$$\mathcal{P}\text{: } \texttt{Prog} \rightarrow \underline{\texttt{In}} \rightarrow \texttt{Out}$$

This indicates that the input of an **Imp** program will not be known until run-time. Thus the minimal annotation of the type of $\mathcal{P}$ becomes $\texttt{Prog} \rightarrow \underline{\texttt{In}}\ \underline{\rightarrow}\ \underline{\texttt{Out}}$. With $\texttt{In}$ and $\texttt{Out}$ as run-time types we then, intuitively, get the following annotations:

$$\begin{aligned}
\underline{\texttt{In}} &= \underline{\texttt{Int}}\ \underline{\texttt{list}}\\
\underline{\texttt{Out}} &= \underline{\texttt{Int}}\ \underline{\texttt{list}}\\
\underline{\texttt{Store}} &= (\underline{\texttt{Loc}\rightarrow\texttt{Int}})\ \underline{\times}\ (\underline{\texttt{In}}\ \underline{\times}\ \underline{\texttt{Out}})\\
\texttt{Env} &= (\texttt{Ide}\times\texttt{Loc})\texttt{list} \times\\
&\quad\ ((\texttt{Ide}\times\texttt{Int})\texttt{list} \times (\texttt{Ide}\times(\underline{\texttt{Store}\rightarrow\texttt{Store}}))\texttt{list})
\end{aligned}$$

Here we have used the convention that the abbreviation for a fully underlined type is also underlined itself. With these annotations we then get the following annotations of the functionalities of the semantic functions:

$$\mathcal{N}: \quad \texttt{Num} \to \texttt{Int}$$

$$\mathcal{A}: \quad \texttt{Aexp} \to \texttt{Env} \to (\underline{\texttt{Store}} \underline{\to} \underline{\texttt{Int}})$$

$$\mathcal{B}: \quad \texttt{Bexp} \to \texttt{Env} \to (\underline{\texttt{Store}} \underline{\to} \underline{\texttt{Bool}})$$

$$\mathcal{S}: \quad \texttt{Stm} \to \texttt{Env} \to (\underline{\texttt{Store}} \underline{\to} \underline{\texttt{Store}})$$

$$\mathcal{D}: \quad \texttt{Dec} \to \texttt{Env} \to \texttt{Env}$$

$$\mathcal{P}: \quad \texttt{Prog} \to (\underline{\texttt{In}} \underline{\to} \underline{\texttt{Out}})$$

These annotations indicate that all computations involving the environment can be performed at compile-time whereas those involving the store are postponed until run-time.

Transformations that enhance the binding time annotations

In the above annotations we have pretended that the binding time analysis algorithm for types is immediately applicable to the functionalities of the semantic specifications. However, as was discussed above we must 'encode' the semantic specifications in the expressions studied in Chapters 2, 3 and 4. When we do this it turns out that the behaviour of the right hand sides of the clauses do influence the functionalities of the semantic specifications. We shall discuss two incarnations of this problem below.

The base type Loc is used in the definition of Env whereas $\underline{\texttt{Loc}}$ is used in the definition of $\underline{\texttt{Store}}$. When annotating the clause for $x{:=}a$ we determine the location of x from the environment and use it to update the store. Consequently the binding time analysis of Chapter 3 will insist on Loc being of run-time kind in the definition of the environment Env, and we no longer have the desired separation between environment and store. Looking for a solution we note that Loc refers to compile-time locations and $\underline{\texttt{Loc}}$ to run-time locations and in hand-crafted compilers these notions are distinct: often a run-time location is an address on the run-time stack whereas a compile-time location may be a pair of nesting depth and offset [5]. So rather than equating the two kinds of locations we shall need a function access that transforms compile-time locations into run-time locations: we shall say that it is a function that encodes the *access path*. The detailed definition of this function depends on the machine for which we generate code. Since the store will be an abstraction of the machine state we shall assume that access is a primitive function of the type indicated below:

$$\texttt{access}[\texttt{Loc}\to(\underline{\texttt{Store}}\underline{\to}\underline{\texttt{Loc}})]$$

The semantic clauses can now be modified to use this function whenever we need to pass from a compile-time location to a run-time location. An example is

$$\mathcal{S}[\![x{:=}a]\!] = \lambda\rho[\;].\underline{\lambda}\sigma[\;].\underline{(}\texttt{update}_{\texttt{Store}}\underline{(\texttt{fst}}\ \sigma\underline{)}$$

$$\underline{(}\texttt{access}[\,](\texttt{lookup}_{\text{Env1}}(\texttt{fst}\ \rho)(x))\underline{(\sigma))}$$
$$\underline{(}\mathcal{A}[\![a]\!](\rho)\underline{(\sigma))},$$
$$\underline{\texttt{snd}}\ \sigma\underline{\rangle}$$

Note that the binding time annotation reflects that first x is looked up in the environment at compile-time, then the resulting location is transformed to a run-time location using access, and finally this location is used at run-time to update the store.

Next consider the base type Int which is used as a compile-time type in the definition of Env and as a run-time type in the definition of Store. In the clause for x the binding time analysis of Chapter 3 will force the two kinds of integers to be run-time entities. Thus once again the desired separation between environment and store fails. Looking for a solution we note that a hand-crafted compiler often distinguishes between compile-time and run-time data [5]. In particular the *layout of run-time data* may depend upon the machine we are generating code for: one machine may use 32 bits to represent an integer on the run-time stack whereas another machine may use 64 bits. So rather than forcing the two base types of integers to be the same we shall introduce a primitive function alloc that transforms compile-time integers to run-time integers. As the space allocation procedure depends on the machine at hand we shall let the function take the store as an additional parameter:

$$\texttt{alloc}[\texttt{Int}\rightarrow(\underline{\texttt{Store}\rightarrow\texttt{Int}})]$$

The semantic clauses can now be rewritten to use this function whenever we want to transform a compile-time integer into a run-time integer. Two examples are:

$$\mathcal{A}[\![x]\!] = \lambda\rho[\,].\texttt{if isvar}[\,](\langle\rho,x\rangle)$$
$$\texttt{then}\ \underline{\lambda}\sigma[\,].(\underline{\texttt{fst}}\ \sigma)\underline{(}\texttt{access}[\,](\texttt{lookup}_{\text{Env1}}(\texttt{fst}\ \rho)(x))\underline{(\sigma))}$$
$$\texttt{else}\ \underline{\lambda}\sigma[\,].\texttt{alloc}[\,](\texttt{lookup}_{\text{Env2}}(\texttt{fst}\ (\texttt{snd}\ \rho))(x))\underline{(\sigma)}$$
$$\mathcal{A}[\![n]\!] = \lambda\rho[\,].\underline{\lambda}\sigma[\,].\texttt{alloc}[\,](\mathcal{N}[\![n]\!])\underline{(\sigma)}$$

It turns out that these transformations suffice for keeping the environment and store separate so that the binding time analysis of Chapter 3 no longer forces all operations on the environment to take place at run-time. As is discussed in [72] such transformations are the rule rather than the exception: it is well-known that the generation of good compilers (that is, some that produce efficient code) from denotational specifications is no easy task and that some semantic specifications are more amenable than others. This may be formalised by defining various classes of semantic specifications depending on aspects of their binding time annotation. As was illustrated above one can then use insights from traditional compiler technology to transform from one class into a more amenable class (e.g.

the encoding of the access path using access). We regard this as a major virtue of our approach to compiler construction from semantic specifications:

> *traditional compiler writing insights are used to improve the binding time annotations.*

This is in contrast to using a new 'magic' technique, like partial evaluation. As illustrated in [81] the necessary transformations may often be indicated by *disagreement points* showing where the binding time annotations 'fail'.

Introducing combinators

The final stage, in order to be able to apply the notions of parameterized semantics of Chapter 5, is to transform the *2*-level λ-expressions into expressions of the mixed λ-calculus and combinatory logic. Again the overall approach follows the development outlined above. We shall not go into details but merely present a few 'idealized' equations:

$$\begin{aligned}
\mathcal{S}[\![x{:=}a]\!] &= \lambda\rho[\,].\texttt{Tuple}(\texttt{Update}_{\text{Store}} \,\Box \\
&\qquad\qquad \texttt{Tuple}(\texttt{Fst}[\,], \\
&\qquad\qquad\qquad \texttt{Tuple}(\texttt{access}[\,](\texttt{lookup}_{\text{Env1}}(\texttt{fst}\ \rho)(x)), \\
&\qquad\qquad\qquad\qquad \mathcal{A}[\![a]\!](\rho))), \\
&\qquad\qquad \texttt{Snd}[\,]) \\
\mathcal{A}[\![x]\!] &= \lambda\rho[\,].\texttt{if isvar}[\,](\langle\rho,x\rangle) \\
&\qquad \texttt{then Apply}[\,] \,\Box\, \texttt{Tuple}(\texttt{Fst}[\,], \\
&\qquad\qquad\qquad \texttt{access}[\,](\texttt{lookup}_{\text{Env1}}(\texttt{fst}\ \rho)(x))) \\
&\qquad \texttt{else alloc}[\,](\texttt{lookup}_{\text{Env2}}(\texttt{fst}\ (\texttt{snd}\ \rho))(x)) \\
\mathcal{A}[\![n]\!] &= \lambda\rho[\,].\texttt{alloc}[\,](\mathcal{N}[\![n]\!])
\end{aligned}$$

As should be evident these equations are much shorter than what would have been obtained directly from the algorithm of Chapter 4. To obtain the above results we have performed a few simplifications like changing the functionality of $\texttt{Update}_{\text{Store}}$ to become less curried.

8.2.3 Towards a compiler

We have now shown how to apply

- type inference (Chapter 2),
- binding time analysis (Chapter 3), and

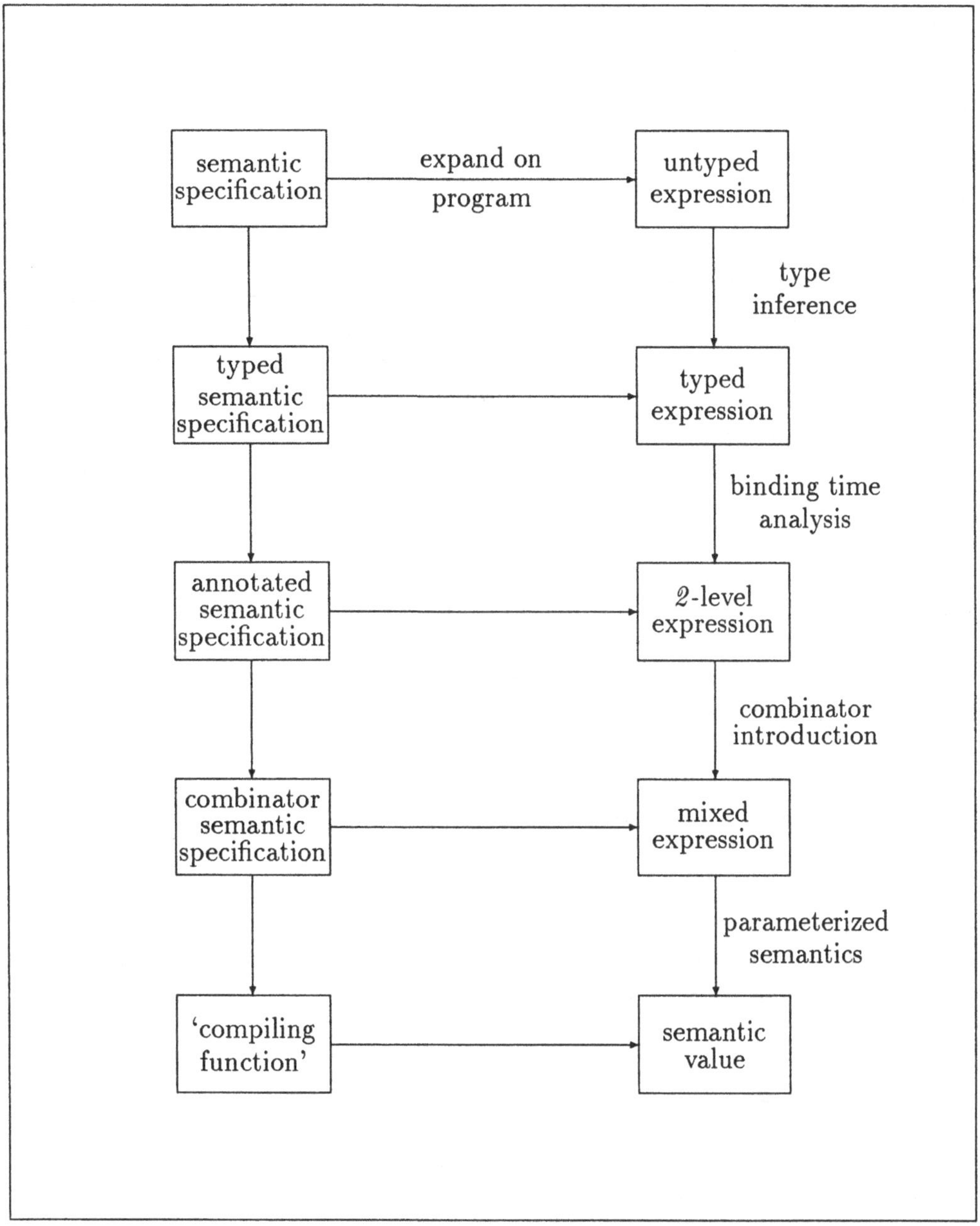

Figure 8.1: Compiler generation

- combinator introduction (Chapter 4)

to the semantic specification of a toy programming language. This line of development may be continued with

- parameterized semantics for code generation or abstract interpretation (Chapters 5, 6, 7 and 8).

Rather than going into the (rather trivial) details of the remaining step we shall present a general picture of the approach that we have taken and of some other approaches that we could have taken. On the left hand side of Figure 8.1 we have semantic specifications of the kind studied in Subsection 8.2.2 and on the right hand side we have expressions of the languages of Chapters 2, 3 and 4 as well as semantic values as given by the parameterized semantics of Chapters 5, 6, 7 and 8. Each vertical arrow represents some 'transformation' on the semantic specification or expression in question. Each horizontal arrow represents the possibility of expanding the semantic specification on some given program.

The naive approach we could have taken in Section 8.2 is to follow the topmost and rightmost route. Then all results of the previous chapters would be directly applicable. However, this represents a rather indirect way of constructing a compiler (assuming that our ultimate parameterized semantics is indeed a code generation like $\mathbf{K}$, $\mathbf{O}$, $\mathbf{O}_{\mathrm{rl}}$ or similar). To come closer to practical concerns one would want to take the leftmost and bottommost route. We illustrated the first three transformations in the previous subsection; the fourth transformation has little content to it — it merely avoids formulating the mixed term by directly interpreting the combinators — and the fifth transformation is quite standard. Thus the 'compiling function' will be a function that directly maps programs to code. It is not quite a compiler because it is an 'abstract function' and not written in any machine language; however, it may serve as a quite useful specification of a compiler.

A natural question to ask is whether the two approaches agree. We do not wish to formally claim that all the small diagrams commute — indeed they probably do not — but surely they give, or should give, 'comparable results' in a vague and intuitive sense that we shall leave unspecified.

8.3 Research Directions

The previous sections have sketched how the techniques of the present book can be applied in the implementation of functional languages and semantic specifications. The following three issues are of fundamental importance when assessing the merits of this development:

- *correctness:* the extent to which the implementation is faithful to the semantics,
- *automation:* the extent to which the implementation is produced without human interaction, and

- *efficiency:* the extent to which the implementation is comparable in efficiency (e.g. time or space) to those obtained by other means.

Below we briefly summarize our main achievements and the areas where further research is still needed.

Correctness

One of the aims of the work reported in this book has been to ensure that the development is provably correct. As a consequence we have occasionally traded efficiency for ease of proving correctness. One example is the simple-minded code generation scheme presented in Chapter 6; it could be improved, e.g. by keeping track of the evaluation degree of the argument as in Section 8.1, but this will render the correctness considerations much more complicated.

We believe that the main problem is to *structure* the correctness proofs in a proper way so that as few aspects as possible have to be dealt with at the same time. In the case of generating optimized code this means that the code generation should be specified in a number of stages where each stage is a refinement of some of the previous ones (much as in Section 8.1). The correctness proof of each stage can then rely on the correctness results of the previous stages. The use of *Kripke-logical relations* seems to provide a convenient basis for this. However, more work is needed to get a better understanding of this issue.

Automation

Another aim of our work has been to develop *algorithms* to perform the various analyses and transformations. As an example, we have presented algorithms for type analysis, binding time analysis and combinator introduction. Also the concept of parameterized semantics is easily implementable so that the complete development can be implemented without too much trouble.

However, in a number of cases we shall hardly be satisfied with the results obtained in this way. As illustrated in Chapters 3 and 4 and in Section 8.2 much more satisfactory results may be obtained if we rewrite the original λ-expressions slightly and if we perform some simple transformations on the intermediate results. At the current stage it is not clear which transformations we should like to perform and in what order and this is an important area for further research.

Efficiency

Many of our considerations have been motivated by the desire to obtain efficient implementations of programming languages. One key ingredient in this is the explicit distinction between *binding times* so that one can avoid having all 'compile-time computations' deferred until run-time. The other key ingredient is the ability to perform program analyses.

Traditionally, data flow analysis has been used to enable *program transformations* at the level of source programs as well as target programs. In this book we have only been concerned with the latter but [79] illustrates how program analyses can be used to validate some well-known program transformations like constant folding. The code optimizations obtained in Section 8.1 largely depend on strictness analysis and more work is needed to exploit other kinds of analyses. Furthermore, it would be interesting to repeat the development for sequential and parallel versions of graph-reduction machines.

Bibliographical Notes

The material of Section 8.1 is heavily based on [82] and some further details may be found in [50]. The observation that strictness and strictness as right context are important for avoiding DELAY instructions was already made in [82] as was the observation that evaluation degrees as left context is important for avoiding RESUME instructions. The observation of the relationship between strictness as right context and Burn's notion of evaluation transformers is new as is the study of pre-evaluation in this framework. Combining all of the ideas into one interpretation still presents some problems, in particular for fixed points and the higher-order constructs and for the associated correctness proofs.

The material of Section 8.2 presents the underlying philosophy behind many of our early papers on the subject matter of this book. The distinction between binding times as a tool in the implementation of programming languages is by no means new (see e.g. [5]) but it is not usually made an explicit notion in semantics. One exception is [99] where there is a distinction between static expression procedures and (dynamic) expression procedures; as discussed in [72] this corresponds quite naturally to our distinction between compile-time functions and run-time functions.

Our treatment of Denotational Semantics is largely based on Section 6 of [72]. It contains a rather detailed study of how to apply a number of heuristics from compiler construction (and semantics) in order to transform a traditional denotational semantics for the language SMALL of [33] into a subset of the mixed λ-calculus and combinatory logic that is amenable to our code generation scheme. This includes

- ensuring that fixed points have composite types, e.g. by transforming a continuation style semantics into direct style,
- ensuring that the desired binding time distinction between environments and stores is maintained, e.g. by using the notion of activation records to encode the access path.

Unlike the treatment in Chapter 6, the results of [72] do not allow run-time function types and so are mainly applicable to PASCAL-like languages.

Exercises

1. Consider the clause for $\mathbf{O}_{\mathrm{r}}(\texttt{Tuple})$ and investigate whether or not some of the occurrences of $\top$ could be replaced by $dn(h_1)(\top)$ or $dn(h_2)(\top)$.

2. Consider the clause for $\mathbf{O}_{\mathrm{r}}(\Box)$ as given in Section 8.1.2. Show that

   $$(strict(\kappa) \circ dn(h_1)) \perp = 0$$

   is equivalent to

   $$(\kappa \circ dn(h_1)) \perp = 0 \vee dn(h_1) \perp = \perp$$

   Discuss the consequences of replacing

   $$(\kappa \circ dn(h_1)) \perp = 0$$

   by

   $$(strict(\kappa) \circ dn(h_1)) \perp = 0$$

   Do you favour this replacement? Discuss whether or not the replacement has any consequences for the continuations supplied to f_2 and f_1.

3. Try to formulate an interpretation $\mathbf{O}_{\mathrm{l}}$ that uses local strictness properties as well as evaluation degrees. Are there any constructs in the language that cannot be handled?

4. Try to extend the interpretation $\mathbf{O}_{\mathrm{l}}$ of Exercise 3 to an interpretation $\mathbf{O}'_{\mathrm{l}}$ that performs pre-evaluation of arguments. Are there any constructs in the language that cannot be handled?

5. Try to use the insights of Exercise 4 to define the interpretation $\mathbf{O}'_{\mathrm{rl}}$ that is like $\mathbf{O}_{\mathrm{rl}}$ but performs pre-evaluation of arguments. Verify that the code generated for sum is as stated in Example 8.1.5. Are there any constructs in the language that cannot be handled?

6. Consider a variant of the language **Imp** where the identifiers introduced by var-declarations are initialised as indicated by

   $$D ::= \mathsf{var}\ x{:=}a;\ D \mid \cdots$$

   Repeat the development of Section 8.2 and make sure that the computations involving the environment still may be performed at compile-time.

Bibliography

[1] S.Abramsky: Strictness Analysis and Polymorphic Invariance, *Programs as Data Objects*, Springer Lecture Notes in Computer Science **217** (1986) 1–23.

[2] S.Abramsky: Abstract Interpretation, Logical Relations and Kan Extensions, *Journal of Logic and Computation* **1** *1* (1990) 5–40.

[3] S.Abramsky: The lazy lambda calculus, *Research Topics in Functional Programming*, D.Turner (ed.), Addison-Wesley (1990) 65–116.

[4] S.Abramsky, C.Hankin: *Abstract Interpretation of Declarative Languages*, Ellis Horwood (1987).

[5] A.V.Aho, R.Sethi, J.D.Ullman: *Compilers – Principles, Techniques and Tools*, Addison-Wesley (1986).

[6] A.W.Appel: Semantics-directed code generation, *Proc. of the 12th ACM Conference on Principles of Programming Languages*, ACM Press (1985) 315–324.

[7] J.Backus: Can Programming be Liberated from the von Neumann Style? A Functional Style and its Algebra of Programs, *Communications of the ACM* **21** (1978) 613–641.

[8] H.-J.Bandelt: The tensorproduct of continuous lattices, *Mathematische Zeitschrift* **172** (1980) 89–96.

[9] H.Bekić: Definable operations in general algebras, and the theory of automata and flowcharts, Springer Lecture Notes in Computer Science **177** (1984) 30–55.

[10] F.Bellegarde: Rewriting Systems on FP Expressions to Reduce the Number of Sequences Yielded, *Science of Computer Programming* **6** (1986) 11–34.

[11] R.S.Bird, P.L.Wadler: *Introduction to Functional Programming*, Prentice-Hall International (1988).

[12] B.Bjerner, S.Holmström: A compositional approach to time analysis of first order lazy functional programs, *Proc. Functional Programming Languages and Computer Architectures*, ACM Press (1989) 157–165.

[13] G.L.Burn: Evaluation transformers — a model for the parallel evaluation of functional languages (extended abstract), *Proc. Functional Programming Languages and Computer Architecture*, Springer Lecture Notes in Computer Science **274** (1987) 446–470.

[14] G.L.Burn: A Relationship Between Abstract Interpretation and Projection Analysis (Extended Abstract), *Proc. ACM Symp. on Principles of Programming Languages*, ACM Press (1990).

[15] G.L.Burn, C.Hankin, S.Abramsky: Strictness analysis for higher-order functions, *Science of Computer Programming* **7** (1986) 249–278.

[16] R.M.Burstall, J.Darlington: A Transformation System for Developing Recursive Programs, *Journal of the ACM* **24** (1977) 44-67.

[17] L.Cardelli: The functional abstract machine, *Bell Labs. Technical Report TR-107* (1983).

[18] H.Christiansen, N.D.Jones: Control flow treatment in a simple semantics-directed compiler generator, in: *Formal Description of Programming Concepts II*, D.Bjørner (ed.), North-Holland (1982) 73–97.

[19] G.Cousineau, P.-L.Curien, M.Mauny: The Categorical Abstract Machine, *Science of Computer Programming* **8** (1987) 173–202.

[20] P.Cousot, R.Cousot: Systematic design of program analysis frameworks, *Proc. 6th ACM Symp. on Principles of Programming Languages*, ACM Press (1979).

[21] P.-L.Curien: *Categorical Combinators, Sequential Algorithms and Functional Programming*, Pitman (1986).

[22] L.Damas, R.Milner: Principal type-schemes for functional programs, *Proc. ACM Symp. on Principles of Programming Languages*, ACM Press (1982) 207–212.

[23] L.Damas: Type Assignment in Programming Languages, *Ph.D.-thesis CST-33-85, University of Edinburgh, Scotland* (1985).

[24] J.Darlington, H.Pull: A program development methodology based on a unified approach to execution and transformation, *Partial Evaluation and Mixed Computation*, D.Bjørner, A.P.Ershov and N.D.Jones (eds.), North-Holland (1988) 117–131.

[25] J.Despeyroux: Proof of translation in natural semantics, *Symposium on Logic in Computer Science* (1986).

[26] P.Dybjer: Using domain algebras to prove the correctness of a compiler, *Proc. STACS 1985*, Springer Lecture Notes in Computer Science **182** (1985) 98–108.

[27] A.P.Ershov: Mixed Computation: Potential Applications and Problems for Study, *Theoretical Computer Science* **18** (1982) 41–67.

[28] M.S.Feather: A System for Assisting Program Transformation, *ACM Transactions on Programming Languages and Systems* **4** (1982) 1–20.

[29] A.B.Ferguson, R.J.M.Hughes: An Iterative Powerdomain Construction, *Functional Programming, Glasgow 1989*, K.Davis and J.Hughes (eds.), Springer (1989) 41–55.

[30] A.J.Field, P.G.Harrison: *Functional Programming*, Addison-Wesley (1988).

[31] J.H.Gallier: *Logic for Computer Science*, Harper & Row (1986).

[32] C.K.Gomard, N.D.Jones: A partial evaluator for the untyped λ-calculus, *Journal of Functional Programming* **1** (1991) 21–69.

[33] M.J.C.Gordon: *The Denotational Description of Programming Languages*, Springer (1979).

[34] P.R.Halmos: *Naive Set Theory*, Springer (1974).

[35] P.G.Harrison: Linearisation: An Optimisation for Nonlinear Functional Programs, *Science of Computer Programming* **10** (1988) 281–318.

[36] F.Henglein: Efficient Type Inference for Higher-Order Binding Time Analysis, *Functional Programming Languages and Computer Archictecture*, Springer Lecture Notes in Computer Science **523** (1991) 448–472.

[37] J.R.Hindley: The principal type-scheme of an object in combinatory logic, *Trans. American Math. Soc.* **146** (1969) 29–60.

[38] P.Hudak, J.Young: A Collecting Interpretation of Expressions (without Powerdomains), *Proc. 15th ACM Symp. on Principles of Programming Languages*, ACM Press (1988) 107–118.

[39] P.Hudak et al.: Report on the Programming Language Haskell — A Non-Strict, Purely Functional Language, Version 1.1, *Yale University* (1991).

[40] G.Huet: Cartesian Closed Categories and Lambda-Calculus, Springer Lecture Notes in Computer Science **242** (1986) 123–135.

[41] J.Hughes: Supercombinators: a new Implementation Method for Applicative Languages, *Proc. of 1982 ACM Conf. on LISP and Functional Programming*, ACM Press (1982) 1–10.

[42] J.Hughes: Strictness detection in non-flat domains, *Proc. Programs as Data Objects*, Springer Lecture Notes in Computer Science **217** (1986) 112–135.

[43] J.Hughes: Backwards Analysis of Functional Programs, *Partial Evaluation and Mixed Computation*, D.Bjørner, A.P.Ershov and N.D.Jones (eds.), North-Holland (1988) 187–208.

[44] S.Hunt, D.Sands: Binding Time Analysis: A New PERspective, *Proc. ACM Symposium on Partial Evaluation and Semantics-Based Program Manipulation*, ACM Press (1991) 154–165.

[45] N.D.Jones, F.Nielson: Abstract Interpretation: a Semantics-Based Tool for Program Analysis, invited paper (in preparation) for *The Handbook of Logic in Computer Science*, Oxford University Press.

[46] N.D.Jones, D.A.Schmidt: Compiler Generation from Denotational Semantics, in: *Semantics Directed Compiler Generation*, Springer Lecture Notes in Computer Science **94** (1980) 70–93.

[47] N.D.Jones, P.Sestoft, H.Søndergaard: An experiment in Partial Evaluation: The Generation of a Compiler Generator, *Proc. of Rewriting Techniques and Applications*, Springer Lecture Notes in Computer Science **202** (1985) 124–140.

[48] U.Jørring, W.L.Scherlis: Compilers and Staging Transformations, *Proc. 13th ACM Symp. on Principles of Programming Languages*, ACM Press (1986) 86–96.

[49] J.Lambek, P.J.Scott: *Introduction to Higher Order Categorical Logic*, Cambridge Studies in Advanced Mathematics **7** (1986).

[50] T.Lange: Correctness of Code Generations based on a Functional Programming Language, *M.Sc.-thesis, Aarhus University, Denmark* (to appear).

[51] P.Lee, U.Pleban: On the use of LISP in implementing denotational semantics, in: *Proc. of the 1986 ACM Conference on LISP and Functional Programming*, ACM Press (1986) 233–248.

[52] D.Lester: Combinator Graph Reduction: A Congruence and its Applications, *Ph.D.-thesis PRG-73, Oxford University, England* (1989).

[53] D.MacQueen, G.Plotkin, R.Sethi: An ideal model for recursive polymorphic types, *Proc. ACM Symp. on Principles of Programming Languages*, ACM Press (1984) 165–174.

[54] T.J.Marlowe, B.G.Ryder: Properties of data flow frameworks: A Unified Model, *Acta Informatica* **28** (1990), 121–163.

[55] R.Milne, C.Strachey: *A Theory of Programming Language Semantics*, Chapman and Hall (1976).

[56] R.Milner, M.Tofte, R.Harper: *The Definition of Standard ML*, MIT Press (1990).

[57] R.Milner: A Theory of Type Polymorphism in Programming, *Journal of Computer Systems* **17** (1978) 348–375.

[58] T.Mogensen: Binding Time Analysis for Higher Order Polymorphically Typed Languages, *TAPSOFT 1989*, Springer Lecture Notes in Computer Science **352** (1989).

[59] M.Montenyohl, M.Wand: Correct flow analysis in continuation semantics, *Proc. 15th ACM Symposium on Principles of Programming Languages*, ACM Press (1988) 204–218.

[60] F.L.Morris: Advice on structuring compilers and proving them correct, *Proc. ACM Conference on Principles of Programming Languages*, ACM Press (1973) 144–152.

[61] P.D.Mosses, D.A.Watt: The use of action semantics, in *Proc. IFIP TC2 Working Conference on Formal Description of Programming Concepts III*, North-Holland (1987).

[62] A.Mycroft: Abstract Interpretation and Optimizing Transformations for Applicative Programs, *Ph.D.-thesis CTS-15-81, University of Edinburgh, Scotland* (1981).

[63] A.Mycroft: The theory and practice of transforming call-by-need into call-by-value, *Proc. 4th International Symposium on Programming*, Springer Lecture Notes in Computer Science **83** (1980).

[64] A.Mycroft: A Study on Abstract Interpretation and 'Validating Microcode Algebraically', in: *Abstract Interpretation of Declarative Languages*, S.Abramsky and C.Hankin (eds.), Ellis Horwood (1987), 199–218.

[65] A.Mycroft, F.Nielson: Strong abstract interpretation using powerdomains, *Proc. ICALP 1983*, Springer Lecture Notes in Computer Science **154** (1983) 536–547.

[66] F.Nielson: Abstract Interpretation using Domain Theory, *Ph.D.-thesis CST-31-84, University of Edinburgh, Scotland* (1984).

[67] F.Nielson: Program Transformations in a Denotational Setting, *ACM Transactions on Programming Languages and Systems* **7** (1985) 359–379.

[68] F.Nielson: Tensor Products Generalize the Relational Data Flow Analysis Method, *Proc. of the 4'th Hungarian Computer Science Conference* (1985) 211–225.

[69] H.R.Nielson, F.Nielson: Semantics Directed Compiling for Functional Languages, *Proc. 1986 ACM Conference on LISP and Functional Programming*, ACM Press (1986) 249–257.

[70] F.Nielson: Towards a Denotational Theory of Abstract Interpretation, *Abstract Interpretation of Declarative Languages*, S.Abramsky and C.Hankin (eds.), Ellis Horwood (1987) 219–245.

[71] F.Nielson: Strictness Analysis and Denotational Abstract Interpretation, *Information and Computation* **76** *1* (1988) 29–92. — Also see *ACM Conference on Principles of Programming Languages*, ACM Press (1987) 120–131.

[72] F.Nielson, H.R.Nielson: Two-Level Semantics and Code Generation, *Theoretical Computer Science* **56** (1988) 59–133.

[73] F.Nielson: A Formal Type System for Comparing Partial Evaluators, *Partial Evaluation and Mixed Computation (Ebberup 1987)*, D.Bjørner, A.P.Ershov and N.D.Jones (eds.), North-Holland (1988) 349–384.

[74] H.R.Nielson, F.Nielson: Automatic Binding Time Analysis for a Typed λ-calculus (Extended Abstract), *Proc. 15th ACM Symp. on Principles of Programming Languages*, ACM Press (1988) 98–106. — The full version is [75].

[75] H.R.Nielson, F.Nielson: Automatic Binding Time Analysis for a Typed λ-calculus, *Science of Computer Programming* **10** (1988) 139–176. — Also see [74].

[76] F.Nielson, H.R.Nielson: 2-level λ-lifting, *Proc. ESOP 1988*, Springer Lecture Notes in Computer Science **300** (1988) 328–343.

[77] F.Nielson, H.R.Nielson: The TML-approach to Compiler-Compilers, *ID-TR 1988-47, Department of Computer Science, Technical University of Denmark* (1988).

[78] F.Nielson: Two-Level Semantics and Abstract Interpretation, *Theoretical Computer Science — Fundamental Studies* **69** *2* (1989) 117–242.

[79] H.R.Nielson, F.Nielson: Transformations on higher-order functions, *Proc. Functional Programming Languages and Computer Architecture*, ACM Press (1989) 129–143.

[80] H.R.Nielson, F.Nielson: Functional Completeness of the Mixed λ-Calculus and Combinatory Logic, *Theoretical Computer Science* **70** (1990) 99–126.

[81] H.R.Nielson, F.Nielson: Eureka definitions for free!, *Proc. European Symposium On Programming 1990*, Springer Lecture Notes in Computer Science **432** (1990) 291–305.

[82] H.R.Nielson, F.Nielson: Context Information for Lazy Code Generation, *Proc. LISP and Functional Programming 1990*, ACM Press (1990) 251–263.

[83] H.R.Nielson, F.Nielson: *Semantics with Applications — A Formal Introduction*, Wiley (1992).

[84] F.Nielson, H.R.Nielson: The Tensor Product in Wadler's Analysis of Lists, *Proc. European Symposium on Programming 1992*, Springer Lecture Notes in Computer Science (to appear).

[85] L.Paulson: Compiler generation from denotational semantics, in: *Methods and Tools for Compiler Construction*, B. Lorho (ed.), Cambridge University Press (1984) 219–250.

[86] S.Peyton Jones: *The Implementation of Functional Programming Languages*, Prentice-Hall (1987).

[87] G.D.Plotkin: Call-by-name, call-by-value and the λ-calculus, *Theoretical Computer Science* **1** (1975) 125–159.

[88] G.D.Plotkin: LCF considered as a programming language, *Theoretical Computer Science* **5** (1977) 223–255.

[89] M.R.Raskovsky: Denotational semantics as a specification of code generators, in: *Proc. of the SIGPLAN 1982 Symposium on Compiler Construction*, ACM Press (1982) 230–244.

[90] J.A.Robinson: A Machine-Oriented Logic based on the Resolution Principle, *Journal of the ACM* **12** (1965) 23–41.

[91] D.A.Schmidt: *Denotational Semantics — A Methodology for Language Development*, Allyn & Bacon (1986).

[92] D.A.Schmidt: Static Properties of Partial Evaluation, *Partial Evaluation and Mixed Computation*, D.Bjørner, A.P.Ershov and N.D.Jones (eds.), North-Holland (1988) 465–483.

[93] D.S.Scott: Data types as lattices, *SIAM J. Comput.* **5** (1976) 522–587.

[94] D.S.Scott: Domains for denotational semantics, *Proc. ICALP 1982*, Springer Lecture Notes in Computer Science **140** (1982) 577–613.

[95] R.Sethi: Control flow aspects of semantics directed compiling, *ACM TOPLAS* **5** *4* (1983) 554–595.

[96] J.E.Stoy: *Denotational Semantics — The Scott-Strachey Approach to Programming Language Theory*, MIT Press (1977).

[97] J.E.Stoy: The Congruence of two Programming Language Definitions, *Theoretical Computer Science* **13** (1981) 151–174.

[98] M.B.Smyth, G.D.Plotkin: The category-theoretic solution of recursive domain equations, *SIAM J. Comput.* **11** (1982) 761–783.

[99] R.D.Tennent: *Principles of Programming Languages*, Prentice-Hall (1981).

[100] J.W.Thatcher, E.G.Wagner, J.B.Wright: More on advice on structuring compilers and proving them correct, *Theoretical Computer Science* **15** (1981) 223–249.

[101] D.Turner: A New Implementation Technique for Applicative Languages, *Software, Practice and Experience* **9** (1979) 31–49.

[102] D.A.Turner: Miranda: A Non-strict Functional Language with Polymorphic Types, *Proc. Functional Programming Languages and Computer Architectures*, Springer Lecture Notes in Computer Science **201** (1985) 1–16.

[103] D.A.Turner: Miranda release 2, on-line manual (1989).

[104] P.Wadler: Strictness analysis on non-flat domains (by abstract interpretation over finite domains), *Abstract Interpretation of Declarative Languages*, S.Abramsky and C.Hankin (eds.), Ellis Horwood (1987) 266–275.

[105] P.Wadler, R.J.M.Hughes: Projections for Strictness Analysis, *Proc. Functional Programming Languages and Computer Architecture*, Springer Lecture Notes in Computer Science **274** (1987), 385–407.

[106] M.Wand: Deriving target code as a representation of continuation semantics, *ACM TOPLAS* **4** *3* (1982) 496–517.

[107] Å.Wikström: *Functional Programming Using Standard ML*, Prentice-Hall International (1987).

Summary of Transformation Functions

ε_{TA},π_{TA} remove type information from expressions or programs.

$\mathcal{E}^{C}_{\text{TA}}$,$\mathcal{P}^{C}_{\text{TA}}$ insert type information into untyped expressions or programs.

ε'_{TA} removes type annotation from variables.

$\mathcal{A}_{\text{TA}}$ collects the polytypes of free variables.

τ_{BTA},ε_{BTA},π_{BTA} remove binding time annotations from types, expressions or programs. The function τ_{BTA} may also be used on type environments and sets of assumptions.

τ^{b}_{BTA},$\varepsilon^{b}_{\text{BTA}}$,$\pi^{b}_{\text{BTA}}$ insert trivial binding time annotations into types (c or r), expressions (c or r) or programs (c or r).

$\mathcal{T}_{\text{BTA}}$,$\mathcal{E}^{C}_{\text{BTA}}$,$\mathcal{P}^{C}_{\text{BTA}}$ insert sensible binding time annotations into types, expressions or programs. The function $\mathcal{T}_{\text{BTA}}$ may be used to enforce agreement with a constraint set C and is then called $\mathcal{T}^{ts}_{\text{BTA}}$.

$\varepsilon'_{\text{BTA}}$ removes type and binding time annotations from variables.

$\overline{\varepsilon}^{tenv}_{\text{BTA}}$ annotates variables with type and binding time annotations.

$\mathcal{A}_{\text{BTA}}$ collects the type and binding time annotations of free variables.

$\varepsilon^{tenv}_{\text{CI}}$,$\pi_{\text{CI}}$ expand combinators in expressions or programs.

$\mathcal{E}^{penv}_{\text{CI}}$,$\mathcal{P}_{\text{CI}}$ introduce combinators for the run-time constructs in expressions or programs.

UD takes care of rules [up] and [down] in the *2*-level λ-calculus.

δ,$\delta\bullet$ take care of shortening of position environments in order to simulate rule [up].

ω,$\omega\bullet$ take care of enlargement of position environments in order to simulate rule [down].

Index

Printed in the United States
By Bookmasters